SUPREME COURT POLITICS:

THE INSTITUTION AND ITS PROCEDURES

By

Susan Low Bloch
Professor of Law
Georgetown University School of Law

Thomas G. Krattenmaker
Dean and Professor of Law
Marshall–Wythe School of Law
College of William and Mary

ST. PAUL, MINN.
WEST PUBLISHING CO.
1994

Library of Congress Cataloging-in-Publication Data

Bloch, Susan L.
    Supreme Court politics : the institution and its procedure / by
Susan L. Bloch, Thomas G. Krattenmaker.
        p.   cm.
    Includes index.
    ISBN 0–314–03492–7
    1. United States. Supreme Court. 2. United States. Supreme
Court—Officials and employees—Selection and appointment.
3. Judicial process—United States. 4. Judicial review—United
States. I. Krattenmaker, Thomas G., 1943–   . II. Title.
KF8742.B58   1994
347.73'26—dc20
[347.30735]   94–9272
                                                                 CIP

ISBN 0–314–03492–7

Thanks to Rich, Rebecca, and Michael

S.L.B.

————————

Thanks to Bevra, Ken, and John

T.G.K.

*

Tributes

Three people planted the seeds of this book in the 1960s. Professor Glendon A. Schubert published *Constitutional Politics* in 1960. Subtitled "The Political Behavior of Supreme Court Justices and the Constitutional Policies That They Make," this book introduced wider audiences to the view that the political and institutional dimensions of the Supreme Court could be studied systematically and that such study could enhance one's appreciation of the quality of U.S. constitutional law. Professor J. Roland Pennock's seminar in Public Law and Jurisprudence at Swarthmore College and Professor Louis Henkin's seminar on The Supreme Court at Columbia Law School made this study come alive and raised many of the questions explored in this book.

Most of our work has consisted of a lot of research, seeking materials that might shed light on the politics of the Supreme Court. For magnificent help in conducting this research, we are indebted to hundreds of Georgetown University Law Center students [1] who have taken our seminar and found ever better materials for subsequent students to study. Most especially, we have been blessed in the past few years with a succession of energetic, dedicated, and talented research assistants who are virtually co-authors of this book. Each deserves a personal paragraph of thanks, but we have to settle for thanking them collectively. Thanks, then, to Mark Adams, Sharon Albright, Patrick Brown, Matthew McCabe, Katherine Miller, and Marc Sorini.

Our colleagues at Georgetown, as well as at several schools throughout the country, for many years have helped us locate materials and track down issues. In this regard, it would be unfair not to single out Professor Vicki Jackson of Georgetown, who has provided aid and comfort at every step of this journey. In addition, Professor Steve Wermiel, of Georgia State helpfully reviewed the entire manuscript and suggested many valuable additions. We are also very grateful for the continuous support and encouragement from Georgetown Dean Judith C. Areen and Georgetown University Law Center Writer's Grants that greatly facilitated our work.

Our families have helped us keep this project going, by pretending to be interested in reading the final product and by making space available, in countless ways, for the time necessary to get it done. Bless you, to Rich, Rebecca, and Michael Bloch and to Bevra, Ken, and John Krattenmaker.

---

[1] At the time we wrote this book, Thomas G. Krattenmaker was Professor of Law at Georgetown University Law Center.

The debt we owe to all the people mentioned above is incalculable. In the final analysis, however, what really drove us to organize and create this book was the inspiration we received from Justice John M. Harlan and Justice Thurgood Marshall, the finest public servants we have ever known and the best bosses we have ever had. If readers find things of value in this book, as we hope they will, please let that discovery be another testament to the memories of these great justices.

A Note on Editing

We did not want the materials selected for this book to appear as thirty second sound-bites, so we have tried to let our authors have their say. But we have been ruthless in trying to hold everyone to central points and we have cut out most of the citations.

Consequently, the reader should know that the original versions of the writings excerpted below are often quite different, at least in form, from the way they are presented here. Footnotes have been dropped without indicating their demise and, where large chunks of text have been edited out (rather than a word or two inside a sentence), these omissions are not generally indicated.

Our overriding intent, however, has been to reproduce faithfully the facts, arguments, and conclusions presented. If you think we have erred in this regard, please let us know.

Lots of people helped us put these pages together. Everyone who works in the Office of Administration at Georgetown University Law Center made a substantial contribution to this effort. Particularly heroic assistance, for which we are deeply grateful, came from Charles Barnes, Mary Ann DeRosa, Lenard Gavin, Toni Patterson, and Vicki White. In addition, one of our own students, Antonio Anaya, provided invaluable proofreading assistance.

*

Acknowledgments

We would like to thank the following for their permission to reprint their writings:

Henry J. Abraham, Justices and Presidents: A Political History of Appointments to the Supreme Court, Third Edition. Copyright © 1974, 1985, 1992 by Henry J. Abraham. Reprinted by permission of Oxford University Press, Inc.

Susan Behuniak–Long, Friendly Fire: Amici Curiae & Webster v. Reproductive Health Services. This article was originally published at 74 Judicature 261 (1991). Copyright © 1991 by Susan Behuniak–Long. Reprinted with the permission of Susan Behuniak–Long.

Robert H. Bork, The Senate's Power Grab, N.Y. Times, June 23, 1993 at A23. Copyright © 1993 by The New York Times Company. Reprinted by permission.

William J. Brennan, Jr., The National Court of Appeals: Another Dissent. This article was originally published at 40 U.Chi.L.Rev. 473 (1973). Copyright © 1973 by the University of Chicago Law Review. Reprinted by permission of the University of Chicago Law Review.

William J. Brennan, Jr., In Defense of Dissents. This article was originally published at 37 Hastings L.J. 427 (1986). Copyright © 1986 by University of California, Hastings College of Law. Reprinted by permission of Hastings Scholarly Publications and William J. Brennan, Jr.

Lincoln Caplan, The Tenth Justice. Copyright © 1987 by Alfred A. Knopf, Inc. Reprinted by permission of Alfred A. Knopf, Inc.

Stephen Carter, The Confirmation Mess. This article was originally published at 101 Harv. L.Rev. 1185 (1988). Copyright © 1988 by Harvard Law Review Association. Reprinted by permission of the Harvard Law Review Association.

Stephen Carter, The Confirmation Mess, Revisited. This article was originally published at 84 Nw.U.L.Rev. 962 (1990). Copyright © 1990 by Stephen Carter. Reprinted with the permission of Stephen Carter.

Lloyd Cutler, Why Not Executive Sessions?, The Washington Post, October 17, 1991 at A23. Copyright © 1991 by The Washington Post. Reprinted by permission.

Sue Davis, Power on the Court: Chief Justice Rehnquist's Opinion Assignments. This article was originally published at 74 Judicature 66 (1990). Copyright © 1990 by Judicature. Reprinted with the permission of Sue Davis.

Bruce J. Ennis, Effective Amicus Briefs. This article was originally published at 33 Cath.U.L.Rev. 603 (1984). Copyright © 1984 by Catholic University Law Review. Reprinted by permission of Catholic University Law Review.

Lee Epstein, A Better Way to Appoint Justices, The Christian Science Monitor, Mar. 17, 1992 at 19. Copyright © 1992 by Lee Epstein and The Christian Science Monitor. Reprinted by permission of Lee Epstein and The Christian Science Monitor.

Samuel Estreicher & John Sexton, Improving the Process: Case Selection by the Supreme Court. This article was originally published at 70 Judicature 41 (1986). Reprinted with the permission of Samuel Estreicher and John Sexton.

Paul Freund, Appointment of Justices: Some Historical Perspectives. This article was originally published at 101 Harv.L.Rev. 1146 (1988). Copyright © 1988 by the Harvard Law Review Association. Reprinted by permission of Harvard Law Review Association.

James A. Gazell, The National Court of Appeals Controversy: An Emerging Negative Consensus. This article was originally published at 6 N.Ill.U.L.Rev. 1 (1986). Copyright © 1986 by the Board of Regents for Northern Illinois University. Reprinted by permission of Northern Illinois University Law Review.

Ruth Bader Ginsburg, Speaking in a Judicial Voice, Madison Lecture, N.Y.U. School of Law, March 9, 1993. Reprinted with the permission of Ruth Bader Ginsburg.

Stephanie B. Goldberg, "What's the Alternative?" A Roundtable on the Confirmation Process, ABA Journal (January 1992). Copyright © 1992 by the ABA Journal. Reprinted by permission of the ABA Journal.

Thomas Halper, Senate Rejection of Supreme Court Nominees. This article was originally published at 22 Drake L.Rev. 102 (September 1972). Copyright © 1972 by Drake University. Reprinted by permission of Drake Law Review.

Thomas Halper, Supreme Court Appointments: Criteria and Consequences. This article was originally published at 21 New York Law Forum 563 (1976). Reprinted by permission of New York Law School Law Review.

Arthur D. Hellman, Case Selection in the Burger Court: A Preliminary Inquiry. This article was originally published at 60 Notre Dame L.Rev. 947 (1985). Copyright © 1985 by Arthur D. Hellman. Reprinted by permission of Arthur D. Hellman.

Arthur D. Hellman, Preserving the Essential Role of the Supreme Court: A Comment on Justice Rehnquist's Proposal. This article was originally published at 14 Fla.St.U.L.Rev. 15 (1986). Copyright © 1986 by Arthur D. Hellman. Reprinted with the permission of Arthur D. Hellman.

Herblock Cartoons, "Historical figures." Originally published in Herblock: A Cartoonist's Life (Lisa Drew–Books–Macmillan, 1993). Reprinted by permission of Herblock Cartoons.

Alpheus Thomas Mason, The Chief Justice of the United States: Primus Inter Pares. This article was originally published at 17 J.Pub.L. 20 (1968). Copyright © 1968 by Emory Law Journal. Reprinted by permission of Emory Law Journal.

Tony Mauro, A Cautious Vote for Cameras in High Court, Legal Times, August 2, 1993 at 10. Copyright © 1993 by the Legal Times. Reprinted by permission of the Legal Times.

Michael W. McConnell, The Rule of Law and the Role of the Solicitor General. This article was originally published at 21 Loy.L.A.L.Rev. 1105 (1988). Copyright © 1988 by the Loyola of Los Angeles Law Review. Reprinted with the permission of the Loyola of Los Angeles Law Review and Michael W. McConnell.

Memorandum Opinion for the Attorney General, Role of the Solicitor General. This article was originally published at 21 Loy.L.A.L.Rev. 1089 (1988). Copyright © 1988 by the Loyola of Los Angeles Law Review. Reprinted with the permission of the Loyola of Los Angeles Law Review. All rights reserved.

Henry P. Monaghan, The Confirmation Process: Law or Politics? This article was originally published at 101 Harv.L.Rev. 1202 (1988). Copyright © 1988 by the Harvard Law Review Association. Reprinted by permission of Henry P. Monaghan and the Harvard Law Review Association.

Thomas R. Morris, States Before the U.S. Supreme Court: State Attorneys General as Amicus Curiae. This article was originally published at 70 Judicature 298 (1987). Copyright © 1987 by Thomas R. Morris and the American Judicature Society. Reprinted with permission of "Judicature, the Journal of the American Judicature Society" and Thomas R. Morris, President and Professor of Political Science, Emory & Henry College, Emory, Virginia.

Alan B. Morrison & D. Scott Stenhouse, The Chief Justice of the United States: More than Just the Highest Ranking Justice. This article was originally published at 1 Const. Comm. 57 (1984). Copyright © 1984 by University of Minnesota Law School and Constitutional Commentary. Reprinted by permission of the publisher and the authors.

Robert F. Nagel, Advice, Consent and Influence. This article was originally published at 84 Nw.L.Rev. 858 (1990). Copyright © 1990 by Northwestern University, School of Law. Reprinted by permission of Northwestern University Law Review.

David M. O'Brien, Storm Center: The Supreme Court in American Politics, Third Edition. Copyright © 1986, 1990, 1993 by David M. O'Brien. Reprinted with permission of David M. O'Brien and W. W. Norton & Company, Inc.

Todd Piccus, Demystifying the Least Understood Branch: Opening the Supreme Court to Broadcast Media. This article was originally published at 71 Texas Law Review 1053 (1993). Copyright © 1993 by the Texas Law Review Association. Reprinted by permission.

D. Marie Provine, Deciding What to Decide: How the Supreme Court Sets Its Agenda. This article was originally published at 64 Judicature 320 (1981). Copyright © 1981 by the American Judicature Society. Reprinted with permission of Doris Marie Provine, Professor of Political Science, Syracuse University, and "Judicature, the Journal of the American Judicature Society."

William H. Rehnquist, The Changing Role of the Supreme Court. This article was originally published at 14 Fla.St.U.L.Rev. 9 (1986). Copyright © 1986 by Florida State University Law Review. Reprinted by permission of Florida State University Law Review.

William H. Rehnquist, The Supreme Court: How It Was, How It Is. Copyright © 1987 by William H. Rehnquist. Reprinted with the permission of William Morrow & Company, Inc.

Rebecca M. Salokar, The Solicitor General: The Politics of Law. Copyright © 1992 by Temple University. Reprinted by permission of Temple University Press.

Glendon A. Schubert, Constitutional Politics: The Political Behavior of Supreme Court Justices and the Constitutional Policies That They Make. Copyright © 1960 by Holt, Rinehart and Winston, Inc. and renewed 1988 by Glendon A. Schubert. Reprinted by permission of Holt, Rinehart and Winston, Inc.

Bernard Schwartz, The Ascent of Pragmatism: The Burger Court in Action. Copyright © 1990 by Bernard Schwartz. Reprinted by permission of Addison-Wesley Publishing Company.

Elliot E. Slotnick, Media Coverage of Supreme Court Decision-Making: Problems and Prospects. This article was originally published at 75 Judicature 128 (1991). Copyright © 1991 by Elliot E. Slotnick. Reprinted with permission of "Judicature, the Journal of the American Judicature Society" and Elliot E. Slotnick.

David A. Strauss and Cass R. Sunstein, The Senate, the Constitution and the Confirmation Process. This article was originally published at 101 Yale L.J. 1941 (1992). Reprinted by permission of The Yale Law Journal Company and Fred B. Rothman & Company.

Stuart Taylor, Jr., Ruing Fixed Opinions, N.Y. Times, February 22, 1988 at A16. Copyright © 1988 by The New York Times Company. Reprinted by permission of The New York Times.

Nina Totenberg, The Confirmation Process and the Public: To Know or Not to Know. This article was originally published at 101 Harv.L.Rev. 1213 (1988). Copyright © 1988 by Harvard Law Review Association. Reprinted by permission of Nina Totenberg and Harvard Law Review Association.

Laurence H. Tribe, God Save This Honorable Court. Copyright © 1985 by Laurence H. Tribe. Reprinted by permission of Random House, Inc.

Twentieth Century Fund, Judicial Roulette: Report of the Twentieth Century Fund Task Force on Judicial Selection. Copyright © 1988 by the

Twentieth Century Fund, New York. Reprinted by permission of Twentieth Century Fund.

G. Edward White, Earl Warren: A Public Life. Copyright © 1982 by Oxford University Press, Inc. Reprinted by permission.

Alexandra K. Wigdor, The Personal Papers of Supreme Court Justices. Copyright © 1986 by Alexandra K. Wigdor. Reprinted with the permission of Alexandra K. Wigdor.

Richard G. Wilkins, An Officer and An Advocate: The Role of the Solicitor General. This article was originally published at 21 Loy.L.A.L.Rev. 1167 (1988). Copyright © 1988 by the Loyola of Los Angeles Law Review. Reprinted with the permission of Loyola of Los Angeles Law Review and Richard G. Wilkins.

Bob Woodward & Scott Armstrong, The Brethren. Copyright © 1979 by Bob Woodward & Scott Armstrong. Excerpts reprinted with permission of Simon & Schuster, Inc.

*

Summary of Contents

*

Table of Contents

SUPREME COURT POLITICS:

THE INSTITUTION AND ITS PROCEDURES

*

INTRODUCTION

A. SCOPE AND PURPOSES OF THE BOOK

Two generations ago, then-professors Frankfurter and Landis, in their classic treatise, *The Business of the Supreme Court,* wrote that "the history of the Supreme Court, as of the Common Law, derives meaning to no small degree from the cumulative details which define the scope of its business, and the forms and methods of performing it—the Court's procedure, in the comprehensive meaning of the term." [1] We take our cue from this observation. Like Frankfurter and Landis, we believe that the Supreme Court's substantive output, as any other organization's, is influenced by the structure of the institution, its personnel and its procedures.

As lawyers, scholars, students, or citizens, we care principally about the end results of the Supreme Court's processes—the three or four volumes of decisions the Court hands down each year. These decisions constitute, in a very practical sense, our constitutional law. But if we are to comprehend that law fully, we should know something about the institution that generates it. For those who wonder where all this constitutional law comes from, and how it gets made, this book provides some answers.

The Constitution itself has very little to say about the Supreme Court of the United States (as it is officially designated). Article III mandates that there shall be one Supreme Court, grants the justices life tenure and protection against diminution in salary, and defines the Court's jurisdiction.[2] Article II distributes power over the process of appointing justices,[3] and Article I implies that one of the justices should serve as Chief Justice.[4]

The Framers left the other institutional details of the Court and its processes to be worked out over time. Thus, it was left to Congress, the President, the Court, or the habits of history to answer such questions as: What kinds of people get appointed to the Court? What kinds of cases will the Court adjudicate? How do these cases get onto the Court's docket? How might the process of case selection influence the kinds of cases chosen for plenary review? How do the justices, individually and collectively, reach their decisions and draft their opinions? What roles

---

1. Felix Frankfurter & James Landis, *The Business of the Supreme Court* vi (1928).

2. U.S. Const. art. III, §§ 1, 2.

3. U.S. Const. art. II, § 2.

4. U.S. Const. art. I, § 3.

1

are played by people or institutions closely connected to the Court, such as the justices' law clerks, the Solicitor General, amici curiae (literally translated as "friends of the court"), and other advocates? To what extent should the Court conduct its business in public, to what extent behind closed doors?

The readings collected in this book are intended to provide some answers to these questions, to explain how constitutional law is made. Our goal has been to collect the best research published on these topics, together with critical analytical commentary by thoughtful, experienced students of the Court. Readers can then inquire more deeply into how and to what extent the Supreme Court's institutional structure and procedures influence the Court's opinions, both the results the opinions reach and the quality and durability of their reasoning. We can also ask whether alterations in the institution might change the law the Court announces.

We believe that the materials in this book can illuminate and deepen everyone's study of constitutional law. The Court's adjudications—its holding, doctrines, results, law—should remain the principal focus of a study of U.S. Constitutional law. But immersing oneself in the process by which that law is forged should be part of that study as well.[5]

B. DIFFERENT MODELS OF JUDICIAL REVIEW [6]

Another way to understand what motivates this book is to recall that the American way of producing judge-made constitutional law is just that, the American way. Many other countries do it differently. This suggests that, to some people at least, the institution and its processes do make a difference.

We assume that most of our readers probably have at least a passing familiarity with the American (or "decentralized" or "diffuse") system of judicial review. In this system, all courts—state and federal—exercise the power to test laws against the United States Constitution. They do so, however, only as an aspect of adjudicating concrete cases that arise in the course of exercising their jurisdiction. Thus, judges in the United States who have authority to issue constitutional interpretations also construe and apply statutes and unwritten law (common law) in the cases they consider; they offer constitutional interpretations only as appropriate means of resolving a lawsuit whose nonconstitutional dimensions are also within their compass. Such a decentralized model of constitutional interpretation is also employed in Canada, Australia, and Japan.

By contrast, most Western European countries follow a different model. In the European system, a specialized, centralized "Constitu-

---

5. It's been said that those who like sausage should not study the method by which sausage is made. Fortunately, watching constitutional law being made rarely makes one feel worse about the end product and is usually fun to do!

6. For most of the ideas in this section, we are indebted to our colleague, Professor Vicki Jackson. Specific illustrations of other countries' practices are drawn from Mauro Cappelletti, *The Judicial Process in Comparative Perspective* (1989).

tional Court" is the only tribunal empowered to render binding judicial interpretations of the national constitution. Other courts, often controlled by a "Supreme Court," decide cases involving statutory interpretation or administrative law issues. Frequently, the Constitutional Court is empowered to rule on the constitutionality of proposed or recently adopted legislation before any concrete controversy arises under the statute. Austria, France, Germany, Italy, and some eastern European nations employ such centralized, specialized "Constitutional Courts."

Consider how the American and European models generate different issues concerning the make-up and processes of courts. Regarding judicial appointments, the American model requires respected people possessing general legal skills; the European model, by contrast, seems to place a comparatively higher premium on respected people with astute political skills for its Constitutional Court. As another example, the methods and purposes of case selection differ in the two systems. The United States Supreme Court has to superintend federal statutory, administrative and common law as well as constitutional law. Under the European model, the Constitutional Court has only constitutional law responsibilities. Further, Constitutional Courts are frequently empowered to hear complaints brought directly to them by persons claiming a violation of a basic constitutional right. Under the American model, inquiries into citizens' complaints usually are handled initially by ordinary trial courts. Appellate courts come into the picture only as reviewers of trial court decisions.

Reflection on the essential differences between the centralized European and decentralized American models of judicial review suggests a critical point. It must be true that the function judicial constitutional interpretation is designed to serve within a governmental system will influence the structure and processes of the courts that wield such power. Thus, the United States Supreme Court's institutional design and behavior can be evaluated, in part, by asking whether these processes help the Court perform the role we assign to it. We should also expect, from considering these differing systems of judicial review, that the choice of particular methods of choosing judges, selecting cases, and adjudicating disputes will have some effect on the nature, scope and content of the law the courts make. Therefore, understanding how the Court operates should deepen our understanding of the law it pronounces.

C. ORGANIZATION

Chapter One provides a more detailed, concrete demonstration of the arguments just advanced. There we present a heavily edited version of the Court's decision in *Planned Parenthood of Southeastern Pennsylvania v. Casey,* ___ U.S. ___, 112 S.Ct. 2791, 120 L.Ed.2d 674 (1992), a recent, controversial, closely divided set of opinions concerning the constitutional right of abortion. We follow *Casey* with two distinct sets of questions. The first set concerns the doctrinal aspects of *Casey,* asking the kinds of questions one ordinarily expects to ask or answer in a general constitutional law course. The second set of questions addresses the Supreme Court as a political institution. These questions reveal how understanding the Court as a governmental organization might lead to different, but no less illuminating or important, questions about *Casey*.

The book then proceeds to consider the processes and standards for the appointment of justices (Chapter Two), the methods and criteria for case selection or agenda setting (Chapter Three), the manner in which the justices agree on and produce formal opinions (Chapter Four), the roles played by various key participants in the institution—such as the Solicitor General, amici curiae, and the law clerks (Chapter Five), and some persistent proposals for reform of the institution and its processes (Chapter Six).

Chapter One

THE COURT IN ACTION: THE ABORTION CONTROVERSY

On January 22, 1973, the Supreme Court handed down its decision in *Roe v. Wade,* 410 U.S. 113, 93 S.Ct. 705, 35 L.Ed.2d 147, announcing for the first time that the Constitution protects a woman's fundamental right to choose an abortion. *Roe* was an enormously controversial opinion that has continued to generate virulent debates through the present time. The decision has affected how virtually everyone—including the public, the Justices, the President, the Solicitor General, and amicus curiae—views the Court and the Constitution. The abortion controversy has also affected public perceptions of the manner in which people outside the Court should play their roles, stimulating debate over such issues as whom the President should appoint to the Court and how much control the White House should exercise over the Solicitor General. For those reasons we have chosen to begin our studies by examining the Court's most recent decision in this controversial area, *Planned Parenthood of Southeastern Pennsylvania v. Casey,* ___ U.S. ___, 112 S.Ct. 2791, 120 L.Ed.2d 674 (1992).

In this section, we provide an edited version of *Casey,* the Court's latest pronouncement on both the continuing vigor (or lack thereof) and the reach of *Roe v. Wade.* We follow the *Casey* opinion with two sets of questions. The first set poses the kinds of inquiries one might expect to pursue in a conventional course on constitutional law. These questions focus on the justices' reasoning—so that the reader may try to define the holding of *Casey,* to discern the doctrine regarding abortion rights on which that holding rests, and to identify the various values the justices use in defining and resolving the issues *Casey* presents.

The second set of questions leads the reader through *Casey* as it might appear to one concentrating not on formal legal doctrine but on the Supreme Court as a policy-making institution and the processes it employs to make decisions. For example, we ask about the parties' strategy in seeking Supreme Court review and about the role the presidential nomination and the senatorial confirmation process played in shaping *Casey*'s outcome. If *Roe* had not been decided as it was, would Judge Robert Bork have been confirmed? If *Roe* had been decided as it was and Bork, instead of Kennedy, had been confirmed, what would have been the likely outcome in *Casey*? Do the answers to these questions tell us something about *Roe,* the appointment process, both, or neither? Exploring these and the other questions we raise after *Casey* dramatically illustrates the significance that the institution and its processes can have on the substance of constitutional law.

PLANNED PARENTHOOD OF SOUTHEASTERN PENNSYLVANIA v. CASEY

__ U.S. __, 112 S.Ct. 2791, 120 L.Ed.2d 674 (1992).

JUSTICE O'CONNOR, JUSTICE KENNEDY, and JUSTICE SOUTER announced the judgment of the Court and delivered the opinion of the Court with respect to Parts I, II, III, V–A, V–C, and VI, an opinion with respect to Part V–E, in which JUSTICE STEVENS joins, and an opinion with respect to Parts IV, V–B, and V–D.

I

Liberty finds no refuge in a jurisprudence of doubt. Yet 19 years after our holding that the Constitution protects a woman's right to terminate her pregnancy in its early stages, Roe v. Wade, 410 U.S. 113 (1973), that definition of liberty is still questioned. Joining the respondents as amicus curiae, the United States, as it has done in five other cases in the last decade, again asks us to overrule *Roe*.

At issue in these cases are five provisions of the Pennsylvania Abortion Control Act of 1982 as amended in 1988 and 1989. The Act requires that a woman seeking an abortion give her informed consent prior to the abortion procedure, and specifies that she be provided with certain information at least 24 hours before the abortion is performed. § 3205. For a minor to obtain an abortion, the Act requires the informed consent of one of her parents, but provides for a judicial bypass option if the minor does not wish to or cannot obtain a parent's consent. § 3206. Another provision of the Act requires that, unless certain exceptions apply, a married woman seeking an abortion must sign a statement indicating that she has notified her husband of her intended abortion. § 3209. The Act exempts compliance with these three requirements in the event of a "medical emergency," which is defined in § 3203 of the Act. In addition to the above provisions regulating the performance of abortions, the Act imposes certain reporting requirements on facilities that provide abortion services. §§ 3207(b), 3214(a), 3214(f).

Before any of these provisions took effect, the petitioners, who are five abortion clinics and one physician representing himself as well as a class of physicians who provide abortion services, brought this suit seeking declaratory and injunctive relief. Each provision was challenged as unconstitutional on its face. The District Court entered a preliminary injunction against the enforcement of the regulations, and, after a

3–day bench trial, held all the provisions at issue here unconstitutional, entering a permanent injunction against Pennsylvania's enforcement of them. 744 F.Supp. 1323 (E.D.Pa.1990). The Court of Appeals for the Third Circuit affirmed in part and reversed in part, upholding all of the regulations except for the husband notification requirement. 947 F.2d 682 (1991). We granted certiorari.

The Court of Appeals found it necessary to follow an elaborate course of reasoning even to identify the first premise to use to determine whether the statute enacted by Pennsylvania meets constitutional standards. And at oral argument in this Court, the attorney for the parties challenging the statute took the position that none of the enactments can be upheld without overruling Roe v. Wade. We disagree with that analysis; but we acknowledge that our decisions after *Roe* cast doubt upon the meaning and reach of its holding. [W]e find it imperative to review once more the principles that define the rights of the woman and the legitimate authority of the State respecting the termination of pregnancies by abortion procedures.

After considering the fundamental constitutional questions resolved by *Roe*, principles of institutional integrity, and the rule of stare decisis, we are led to conclude this: the essential holding of Roe v. Wade should be retained and once again reaffirmed.

It must be stated at the outset and with clarity that *Roe*'s essential holding, the holding we reaffirm, has three parts. First is a recognition of the right of the woman to choose to have an abortion before viability and to obtain it without undue interference from the State. Before viability, the State's interests are not strong enough to support a prohibition of abortion or the imposition of a substantial obstacle to the woman's effective right to elect the procedure. Second is a confirmation of the State's power to restrict abortions after fetal viability, if the law contains exceptions for pregnancies which endanger a woman's life or health. And third is the principle that the State has legitimate interests from the outset of the pregnancy in protecting the health of the woman and the life of the fetus that may become a child. These principles do not contradict one another; and we adhere to each.

II

Constitutional protection of the woman's decision to terminate her pregnancy derives from the Due Process Clause of the Fourteenth Amendment. It declares that no State shall "deprive any person of life, liberty, or property, without due process of law." The controlling word in the case before us is "liberty." It is tempting, as a means of curbing the discretion of federal judges, to suppose that liberty encompasses no more than those rights already guaranteed to the individual against federal interference by the express provisions of the first eight amendments to the Constitution. But of course this Court has never accepted that view.

It is a promise of the Constitution that there is a realm of personal liberty which the government may not enter. We have vindicated this principle before. Marriage is mentioned nowhere in the Bill of Rights and interracial marriage was illegal in most States in the 19th century, but the Court was no doubt correct in finding it to be an aspect of liberty protected against state interference by the substantive component of the Due Process Clause in Loving v. Virginia, 388 U.S. 1, 12 (1967).

Neither the Bill of Rights nor the specific practices of States at the time of the adoption of the Fourteenth Amendment marks the outer limits of the substantive sphere of liberty which the Fourteenth Amendment protects. See U.S. Const., Amend. 9.

The inescapable fact is that adjudication of substantive due process claims may call upon the Court in interpreting the Constitution to exercise that same capacity which by tradition courts always have exercised: reasoned judgment. Its boundaries are not susceptible of expression as a simple rule. That does not mean we are free to invalidate state policy choices with which we disagree; yet neither does it permit us to shrink from the duties of our office. As Justice Harlan observed: "Due process has not been reduced to any formula; its content cannot be determined by reference to any code. The best that can be said is that through the course of this Court's decisions it has represented the balance which our Nation, built upon postulates of respect for the liberty of the individual, has struck between that liberty and the demands of organized society. If the supplying of content to this Constitutional concept has of necessity been a rational process, it certainly has not been one where judges have felt free to roam where unguided speculation might take them. The balance of which I speak is the balance struck by this country, having regard to what history teaches are the traditions from which it developed as well as the traditions from which it broke. That tradition is a living thing. A decision of this Court which radically departs from it could not long survive, while a decision which builds on what has survived is likely to be sound. No formula could serve as a substitute, in this area, for judgment and restraint." Poe v. Ullman, 367 U.S., at 542 (HARLAN, J., dissenting from dismissal on jurisdictional grounds).

Men and women of good conscience can disagree, and we suppose some always shall disagree, about the profound moral and spiritual implications of terminating a pregnancy, even in its earliest stage. Some of us as individuals find abortion offensive to our most basic principles of morality, but that cannot control our decision. Our obligation is to define the liberty of all, not to mandate our own moral code. The underlying constitutional issue is whether the State can resolve these philosophic questions in such a definitive way that a woman lacks all choice in the matter, except perhaps in those rare circumstances in which the pregnancy is itself a danger to her own life or health, or is the result of rape or incest.

Our law affords constitutional protection to personal decisions relating to marriage, procreation, contraception, family relationships, child rearing, and education. These matters, involving the most intimate and personal choices a person may make in a lifetime, choices central to personal dignity and autonomy, are central to the liberty protected by the Fourteenth Amendment. At the heart of liberty is the right to define one's own concept of existence, of meaning, of the universe, and of the mystery of human life. Beliefs about these matters could not define the attributes of personhood were they formed under compulsion of the State.

These considerations begin our analysis of the woman's interest in terminating her pregnancy but cannot end it, for this reason: though the abortion decision may originate within the zone of conscience and belief, it is more than a philosophic exercise. Abortion is a unique act. It is an act fraught with consequences for others: for the woman who must live with the implications of her decision; for the persons who perform and assist in the procedure; for the spouse, family, and society which must confront the knowledge that these procedures exist, procedures some deem nothing short of an act of violence against innocent human life; and, depending on one's beliefs, for the life or potential life that is aborted. Though abortion is conduct, it does not follow that the State is entitled to proscribe it in all instances. That is because the liberty of the woman is at stake in a sense unique to the human condition and so unique to the law. The mother who carries a child to full term is subject to anxieties, to physical constraints, to pain that only she must bear. That these sacrifices have from the beginning of the human race been endured by woman with a pride that ennobles her in the eyes of others and gives to the infant a bond of love cannot alone be grounds for the State to insist she make the sacrifice. Her suffering is too intimate and personal for the State to insist, without more, upon its own vision of the woman's role, however dominant that vision has been in the course of our history and our culture. The destiny of the woman must be shaped to a large extent on her own conception of her spiritual imperatives and her place in society.

While we appreciate the weight of the arguments made on behalf of the State in the case before us, arguments which in their ultimate formulation conclude that *Roe* should be overruled, the reservations any of us may have in reaffirming the central holding of *Roe* are outweighed by the explication of individual liberty we have given combined with the force of stare decisis. We turn now to that doctrine.

III

A

[W]hen this Court reexamines a prior holding, its judgment is customarily informed by a series of prudential and pragmatic considerations designed to test the consistency of overruling a prior decision with the ideal of the rule of law, and to gauge the respective costs of reaffirming and overruling a prior case. Thus, for example, we may ask whether the rule has proved to be intolerable simply in defying practical workability; whether the rule is subject to a kind of reliance that would lend a special hardship to the consequences of overruling and add inequity to the cost of repudiation; whether related principles of law have so far developed as to have left the old rule no more than a remnant of abandoned doctrine; or whether facts have so changed or come to be seen so differently, as to have robbed the old rule of significant application or justification.

1

Although *Roe* has engendered opposition, it has in no sense proven "unworkable," representing as it does a simple limitation beyond which a state law is unenforceable. While *Roe* has, of course, required judicial assessment of state laws affecting the exercise of the choice guaranteed against government infringement, and although the need for such review will remain as a consequence of today's decision, the required determinations fall within judicial competence.

2

Abortion is customarily chosen as an unplanned response to the consequence of unplanned activity or to the failure of conventional birth control, and except on the assumption that no intercourse would have occurred but for *Roe*'s holding, such behavior may appear to justify no reliance claim. Even if reliance could be claimed on that unrealistic assumption, the argument might run, any reliance interest would be de minimis. This argument would be premised on the hypothesis that reproductive planning could take virtually immediate account of any sudden restoration of state authority to ban abortions.

To eliminate the issue of reliance that easily, however, one would need to limit cognizable reliance to specific instances of sexual activity. But to do this would be simply to refuse to face the fact that for two decades of economic and social developments, people have organized intimate relationships and made choices that define their views of themselves and their places in society, in reliance on the availability of abortion in the event that contraception should fail. The ability of women to participate equally in the economic and social life of the Nation has been facilitated by their ability to control their reproductive lives. The Constitution serves human values, and while the effect of reliance on *Roe* cannot be exactly measured, neither can the certain cost of overruling *Roe* for people who have ordered their thinking and living around that case be dismissed.

3

No evolution of legal principle has left *Roe*'s doctrinal footings weaker than they were in 1973. No development of constitutional law since the case was decided has implicitly or explicitly left *Roe* behind as a mere survivor of obsolete constitutional thinking.

It will be recognized, of course, that *Roe* stands at an intersection of two lines of decisions, but in whichever doctrinal category one reads the case, the result for present purposes will be the same. The *Roe* Court itself placed its holding in the succession of cases most prominently exemplified by Griswold v. Connecticut. When it is so seen, *Roe* is clearly in no jeopardy, since subsequent constitutional developments have neither disturbed, nor do they threaten to diminish, the scope of recognized protection accorded to the liberty relating to intimate relationships, the family, and decisions about whether or not to beget or bear a child.

Roe, however, may be seen not only as an exemplar of *Griswold* liberty but as a rule (whether or not mistaken) of personal autonomy and bodily integrity, with doctrinal affinity to cases recognizing limits on governmental power to mandate medical treatment or to bar its rejection. If so, our cases since *Roe* accord with *Roe*'s view that a State's interest in the protection of life falls short of justifying any plenary override of individual liberty claims. Cruzan v. Director, Missouri Dept. of Health, 497 U.S. 261, 278 (1990).

Finally, one could classify *Roe* as sui generis. If the case is so viewed, then there clearly has been no erosion of its central determination. The original holding resting on the concurrence of seven Members of the Court in 1973 was expressly affirmed by a majority of six in 1983, see Akron v. Akron Center for Reproductive Health, Inc., 462 U.S. 416 (1983) (*Akron I*), and by a majority of five in 1986, see Thornburgh v. American College of Obstetricians and Gynecologists, 476 U.S. 747 (1986). More recently, in Webster v. Reproductive Health Services, 492 U.S. 490 (1989), although two of the present authors questioned the trimester framework in a way consistent with our judgment today, see id., at 518 (REHNQUIST, C.J., joined by WHITE, and KENNEDY, JJ.); id., at 529 (O'CONNOR, J., concurring in part and concurring in judgment), a majority of the Court either decided to reaffirm or declined to address the constitutional validity of the central holding of *Roe*.

Nor will courts building upon *Roe* be likely to hand down erroneous decisions as a consequence. Even on the assumption that the central holding of *Roe* was in error, that error would go only to the strength of the state interest in fetal protection, not to the recognition afforded by the Constitution to the woman's liberty.

The soundness of this prong of the *Roe* analysis is apparent from a consideration of the alternative. If indeed the woman's interest in deciding whether to bear and beget a child had not been recognized as in *Roe*, the State might as readily restrict a woman's right to choose to carry a pregnancy to term as to terminate it, to further asserted state interests in population control, or eugenics, for example. Yet *Roe* has been sensibly relied upon to counter any such suggestions. E.g., Arnold v. Board of Education of Escambia County, Ala., 880 F.2d 305, 311 (CA11 1989) (relying upon *Roe* and concluding that government officials violate the Constitution by coercing a minor to have an abortion); Avery v. County of Burke, 660 F.2d 111, 115 (CA4 1981) (county agency inducing teenage girl to undergo unwanted sterilization on the basis of misrepresentation that she had sickle cell trait).

4

We have seen how time has overtaken some of *Roe*'s factual assumptions: advances in maternal health care allow for abortions safe to the mother later in pregnancy than was true in 1973 and advances in neonatal care have advanced viability to a point somewhat earlier. But these facts go only to the scheme of time limits on the realization of competing interests, and the divergences from the factual premises of 1973 have no bearing on the validity of *Roe*'s central holding, that viability marks the earliest point at which the State's interest in fetal life is constitutionally adequate to justify a legislative ban on nontherapeutic abortions.

5

Within the bounds of normal stare decisis analysis, then, and subject to the considerations on which it customarily turns, the stronger argument is for affirming *Roe*'s central holding, with whatever degree of personal reluctance any of us may have, not for overruling it.

B

In a less significant case, stare decisis analysis could, and would, stop at the point we have reached. But the sustained and widespread debate *Roe* has provoked calls for some comparison between that case and others of comparable dimension that have responded to national controversies and taken on the impress of the controversies addressed. Only two such decisional lines from the past century present themselves for examination, and in each instance the result reached by the Court accorded with the principles we apply today.

The first example is that line of cases identified with Lochner v. New York, 198 U.S. 45 (1905), which imposed substantive limitations on legislation limiting economic autonomy in favor of health and welfare regulation, adopting, in Justice Holmes' view, the theory of laissez-faire. The Lochner decisions were exemplified by Adkins v. Children's Hospital of D.C., 261 U.S. 525 (1923), in which this Court held it to be an infringement of constitutionally protected liberty of contract to require the employers of adult women to satisfy minimum wage standards. Fourteen years later, West Coast Hotel Co. v. Parrish, 300 U.S. 379 (1937), signalled the demise of Lochner by overruling Adkins. In the meantime, the Depression had come and, with it, the lesson that seemed unmistakable to most people by 1937, that the interpretation of contractual freedom protected in Adkins rested on fundamentally false factual assumptions about the capacity of a relatively unregulated market to satisfy minimal levels of human welfare.

The second comparison that 20th century history invites is with the cases employing the separate-but-equal rule for applying the Fourteenth Amendment's equal protection guarantee. They began with Plessy v. Ferguson, 163 U.S. 537 (1896), holding that legislatively mandated racial segregation in public transportation works no denial of equal protection, rejecting the argument that racial separation enforced by the legal machinery of American society treats the black race as inferior. But this understanding of the facts and the rule it was stated to justify were repudiated in Brown v. Board of Education, 347 U.S. 483 (1954). The Court in *Brown* observ[ed] that whatever may have been the understanding in *Plessy*'s time of the power of segregation to stigmatize those who were segregated with a "badge of inferiority," it was clear by 1954 that legally sanctioned segregation had just such an effect. Society's understanding of the facts upon which a constitutional ruling was sought in 1954 was thus fundamentally different from the basis claimed for the decision in 1896. *West Coast Hotel* and *Brown* each rested on facts, or an understanding of facts, changed from those which furnished the claimed justifications for the earlier constitutional resolutions. Each case was comprehensible as the Court's response to facts that the country could understand, or had come to understand already, but which the Court of an earlier day, as its own declarations disclosed, had not been able to perceive. As the decisions were thus comprehensible they were also defensible, not merely as the victories of one doctrinal school over another by dint of numbers (victories though they were), but as applications of constitutional principle to facts as they had not been seen by the Court before.

Because the case before us presents no such occasion it could be seen as no such response. Because neither the factual underpinnings of *Roe*'s central holding nor our understanding of it has changed (and because no other indication of weakened precedent has been shown) the Court could not pretend to be reexamining the prior law with any justification beyond a present doctrinal disposition to come out differently from the Court of 1973. To overrule prior law for no other reason than that would run counter to the view repeated in our cases, that a decision to overrule should rest on some special reason over and above the belief that a prior case was wrongly decided.

C

[O]verruling *Roe*'s central holding would not only reach an unjustifiable result under principles of stare decisis, but would seriously weaken the Court's capacity to exercise the judicial power and to function as the Supreme Court of a Nation dedicated to the rule of law.

As Americans of each succeeding generation are rightly told, the Court cannot buy support for its decisions by spending money and, except to a minor degree, it cannot independently coerce obedience to its decrees. The Court's power lies, rather, in its legitimacy, a product of substance and perception that shows itself in the people's acceptance of the Judiciary as fit to determine what the Nation's law means and to declare what it demands.

The Court must take care to speak and act in ways that allow people to accept its decisions on the terms the Court claims for them, as grounded truly in principle, not as compromises with social and political pressures having, as such, no bearing on the principled choices that the Court is obliged to make. Thus, the Court's legitimacy depends on making legally principled decisions under circumstances in which their principled character is sufficiently plausible to be accepted by the Nation.

The need for principled action to be perceived as such is implicated to some degree whenever this, or any other appellate court, overrules a prior case. This is not to say, of course, that this Court cannot give a perfectly satisfactory explanation in most cases.

In two circumstances, however, the Court would almost certainly fail to receive the benefit of the doubt in overruling prior cases. There is, first, a point beyond which frequent overruling would overtax the country's belief in the Court's good faith. If that limit should be exceeded, disturbance of prior rulings would be taken as evidence that justifiable reexamination of principle had given way to drives for particular results in the short term. The legitimacy of the Court would fade with the frequency of its vacillation.

That first circumstance can be described as hypothetical; the second is to the point here and now. Where, in the performance of its judicial duties, the Court decides a case in such a way as to resolve the sort of intensely divisive controversy reflected in *Roe* and those rare, comparable cases, its decision has a dimension that the resolution of the normal case does not carry. It is the dimension present whenever the Court's interpretation of the Constitution calls the contending sides of a national controversy to end their national division by accepting a common mandate rooted in the Constitution.

The Court is not asked to do this very often, having thus addressed the Nation only twice in our lifetime, in the decisions of *Brown* and *Roe*. But when the Court does act in this way, its decision requires an equally rare precedential force to counter the inevitable efforts to overturn it and to thwart its implementation. [T]o overrule under fire in the absence of the most compelling reason to reexamine a watershed decision would subvert the Court's legitimacy beyond any serious question.

Some cost will be paid by anyone who approves or implements a constitutional decision where it is unpopular, or who refuses to work to undermine the decision or to force its reversal. The price may be criticism or ostracism, or it may be violence. An extra price will be paid by those who themselves disapprove of the decision's results when viewed outside of constitutional terms, but who nevertheless struggle to accept it, because they respect the rule of law. To all those who will be so tested by following, the Court implicitly undertakes to remain steadfast, lest in the end a price be paid for nothing. The promise of constancy, once given, binds its maker for as long as the power to stand by the decision survives and the understanding of the issue has not changed so fundamentally as to render the commitment obsolete.

Like the character of an individual, the legitimacy of the Court must be earned over time. So, indeed, must be the character of a Nation of people who aspire to live according to the rule of law. Their belief in themselves as such a people is not readily separable from their understanding of the Court invested with the authority to decide their constitutional cases and speak before all others for their constitutional ideals. If the Court's legitimacy should be undermined, then, so would the country be in its very ability to see itself through its constitutional ideals. The Court's duty in the present case is clear. In 1973, it confronted the already-divisive issue of governmental power to limit personal choice to undergo abortion, for which it provided a new resolution based on the due process guaranteed by the Fourteenth Amendment. Whether or not a new social consensus is developing on that issue, its divisiveness is no less today than in 1973, and pressure to overrule the decision, like pressure to retain it, has grown only more intense. A decision to overrule *Roe*'s essential holding under the existing circumstances would address error, if error there was, at the cost of both profound and unnecessary damage to the Court's legitimacy, and to the Nation's commitment to the rule of law. It is therefore imperative to adhere to the essence of *Roe*'s original decision, and we do so today.

IV

The woman's liberty is not so unlimited, however, that from the outset the State cannot show its concern for the life of the unborn, and at a later point in fetal development the State's interest in life has sufficient force so that the right of the woman to terminate the pregnancy can be restricted.

That brings us, of course, to the point where much criticism has been directed at *Roe,* a criticism that always inheres when the Court draws a specific rule from what in the Constitution is but a general standard. We conclude, however, that the urgent claims of the woman to retain the ultimate control over her destiny and her body, claims implicit in the meaning of liberty, require us to perform that function. Liberty must not be extinguished for want of a line that is clear. And it falls to us to give some real substance to the woman's liberty to determine whether to carry her pregnancy to full term.

We conclude the line should be drawn at viability, so that before that time the woman has a right to choose to terminate her pregnancy. We adhere to this principle for two reasons. First, as we have said, is the doctrine of stare decisis.

The second reason is that the concept of viability, as we noted in *Roe,* is the time at which there is a realistic possibility of maintaining and nourishing a life outside the womb, so that the independent existence of the second life can in reason and all fairness be the object of state protection that now overrides the rights of the woman. [T]here is no line other than viability which is more workable. The viability line also has, as a practical matter, an element of fairness. In some broad sense it might be said that a woman who fails to act before viability has consented to the State's intervention on behalf of the developing child. The woman's right to terminate her pregnancy before viability is the most central principle of Roe v. Wade. It is a rule of law and a component of liberty we cannot renounce.

On the other side of the equation is the interest of the State in the protection of potential life. The weight to be given this state interest, not the strength of the woman's interest, was the difficult question faced in *Roe.*

Roe v. Wade speaks with clarity in establishing not only the woman's liberty but also the State's "important and legitimate interest in potential life." That portion of the decision in *Roe* has been given too little acknowledgement and implementation by the Court in its subsequent cases. Those cases decided that any regulation touching upon the abortion decision must survive strict scrutiny, to be sustained only if drawn in narrow terms to further a compelling state interest. Not all of the cases decided under that formulation can be reconciled with the holding in *Roe* itself that the State has legitimate interests in the health of the woman and in protecting the potential life within her. In resolving this tension, we choose to rely upon *Roe,* as against the later cases.

Roe established a trimester framework to govern abortion regulations. Under this elaborate but rigid construct, almost no regulation at all is permitted during the first trimester of pregnancy; regulations designed to protect the woman's health, but not to further the State's interest in potential life, are permitted during the second trimester; and during the third trimester, when the fetus is viable, prohibitions are permitted provided the life or health of the mother is not at stake. Most of our cases since *Roe* have involved the application of rules derived from the trimester framework.

The trimester framework no doubt was erected to ensure that the woman's right to choose not become so subordinate to the State's interest in promoting fetal life that her choice exists in theory but not in fact. We do not agree, however, that the trimester approach is necessary to accomplish this objective. Though the woman has a right to choose to terminate or continue her pregnancy before viability, it does not at all follow that the State is prohibited from taking steps to ensure that this choice is thoughtful and informed.

We reject the trimester framework, which we do not consider to be part of the essential holding of *Roe.* A logical reading of the central holding in *Roe* itself, and a necessary reconciliation of the liberty of the woman and the interest of the State in promoting prenatal life, require, in our view, that we abandon the trimester framework as a rigid prohibition on all previability regulation aimed at the protection of fetal life. The trimester framework suffers from these basic flaws: in its formulation it misconceives the nature of the pregnant woman's interest; and in practice it undervalues the State's interest in potential life, as recognized in *Roe.* As our jurisprudence relating to all liberties save perhaps abortion has recognized, not every law which makes a right more difficult to exercise is, ipso facto, an infringement of that right. An example clarifies the point. We have held that not every ballot access limitation amounts to an infringement of the right to vote.

Rather, the States are granted substantial flexibility in establishing the framework within which voters choose the candidates for whom they wish to vote. Anderson v. Celebrezze, 460 U.S. 780, 788 (1983); Norman v. Reed, 112 S.Ct. 698, 711 (1992).

The abortion right is similar. Numerous forms of state regulation might have the incidental effect of increasing the cost or decreasing the availability of medical care, whether for abortion or any other medical procedure. The fact that a law which serves a valid purpose, one not designed to strike at the right itself, has the incidental effect of making it more difficult or more expensive to procure an abortion cannot be enough to invalidate it. Only where state regulation imposes an undue burden on a woman's ability to make this decision does the power of the State reach into the heart of the liberty protected by the Due Process Clause.

[D]espite the protestations contained in the original *Roe* opinion to the effect that the Court was not recognizing an absolute right, the Court's experience applying the trimester framework has led to the striking down of some abortion regulations which in no real sense deprived women of the ultimate decision. Those decisions went too far because the right recognized by *Roe* is a right "to be free from unwarranted governmental intrusion into matters so fundamentally affecting a person as the decision whether to bear or beget a child." Eisenstadt v. Baird, 405 U.S., at 453. Not all governmental intrusion is of necessity unwarranted; and that brings us to the other basic flaw in the trimester framework: even in *Roe*'s terms, in practice it undervalues the State's interest in the potential life within the woman.

The very notion that the State has a substantial interest in potential life leads to the conclusion that not all regulations must be deemed unwarranted. Not all burdens on the right to decide whether to terminate a pregnancy will be undue.

⌈A finding of an undue burden is a shorthand for the conclusion that a state regulation has the purpose or effect of placing a substantial obstacle in the path of a woman seeking an abortion of a nonviable fetus.⌋ A statute with this purpose is invalid because the means chosen by the State to further the interest in potential life must be calculated to inform the woman's free choice, not hinder it. And a statute which, while furthering the interest in potential life or some other valid state interest, has the effect of placing a substantial obstacle in the path of a woman's choice cannot be considered a permissible means of serving its legitimate ends.

What is at stake is the woman's right to make the ultimate decision, not a right to be insulated from all others in doing so. Regulations which do no more than create a structural mechanism by which the State, or the parent or guardian of a minor, may express profound respect for the life of the unborn are permitted, if they are not a substantial obstacle to the woman's exercise of the right to choose.

Regulations designed to foster the health of a woman seeking an abortion are valid if they do not constitute an undue burden.

We give this summary:

(a) To protect the central right recognized by Roe v. Wade while at the same time accommodating the State's profound interest in potential life, we will employ the undue burden analysis as explained in this opinion. An undue burden exists, and therefore a provision of law is invalid, if its purpose or effect is to place a substantial obstacle in the path of a woman seeking an abortion before the fetus attains viability.

(b) We reject the rigid trimester framework of Roe v. Wade. To promote the State's profound interest in potential life, throughout pregnancy the State may take measures to ensure that the woman's choice is informed, and measures designed to advance this interest will not be invalidated as long as their purpose is to persuade the woman to choose childbirth over abortion. These measures must not be an undue burden on the right.

(c) As with any medical procedure, the State may enact regulations to further the health or safety of a woman seeking an abortion. Unnecessary health regulations that have the purpose or effect of presenting a substantial obstacle to a woman seeking an abortion impose an undue burden on the right.

(d) Our adoption of the undue burden analysis does not disturb the central holding of Roe v. Wade, and we reaffirm that holding. Regardless of whether exceptions are made for particular circumstances, a State may not prohibit any woman from making the ultimate decision to terminate her pregnancy before viability.

(e) We also reaffirm *Roe*'s holding that "subsequent to viability, the State in promoting its interest in the potentiality of human life may, if it chooses, regulate, and even proscribe, abortion except where it is necessary, in appropriate medical judgment, for the preservation of the life or health of the mother." Roe v. Wade, 410 U.S., at 164–165.

These principles control our assessment of the Pennsylvania statute, and we now turn to the issue of the validity of its challenged provisions.

V

The Court of Appeals applied what it believed to be the undue burden standard and upheld each of the provisions except for the husband notification requirement. We agree generally with this conclusion.

A

Because it is central to the operation of various other requirements, we begin with the statute's definition of medical emergency. Under the statute, a medical emergency is "that condition which, on the basis of the physician's good faith clinical judgment, so complicates the medical condition of a pregnant woman as to necessitate the immediate abortion of her pregnancy to avert her death or for which a delay will create serious risk of substantial and irreversible impairment of a major bodily function."

[T]he Court of Appeals stated: "we read the medical emergency exception as intended by the Pennsylvania legislature to assure that compliance with its abortion regulations would not in any way pose a significant threat to the life or health of a woman." We conclude that, as construed by the Court of Appeals, the medical emergency definition imposes no undue burden on a woman's abortion right.

B

We next consider the informed consent requirement. 18 Pa.Cons. Stat.Ann. § 3205. Except in a medical emergency, the statute requires that at least 24 hours before performing an abortion a physician inform the woman of the nature of the procedure, the health risks of the abortion and of childbirth, and the "probable gestational age of the unborn child." The physician or a qualified nonphysician must inform the woman of the availability of printed materials published by the State describing the fetus and providing information about medical assistance for childbirth, information about child support from the father, and a list of agencies which provide adoption and other services as alternatives to abortion. An abortion may not be performed unless the woman certifies in writing that she has been informed of the availability of these printed materials and has been provided them if she chooses to view them.

Our prior decisions establish that as with any medical procedure, the State may require a woman to give her written informed consent to an abortion. Petitioners challenge the statute's definition of informed consent because it includes the provision of specific information by the doctor and the mandatory 24–hour waiting period. The conclusions reached by a majority of the Justices in the separate opinions filed today and the undue burden standard adopted in this opinion require us to overrule in part some of the Court's past decisions, decisions driven by the trimester framework's prohibition of all previability regulations designed to further the State's interest in fetal life.

In Akron I, 462 U.S. 416 (1983), we invalidated an ordinance which required that a woman seeking an abortion be provided by her physician with specific information "designed to influence the woman's informed choice between abortion or childbirth." As we later described the *Akron I* holding in Thornburgh v. American College of Obstetricians and Gynecologists, 476 U.S., at 762, there were two purported flaws in the Akron ordinance: the information was designed to dissuade the woman from having an abortion and the ordinance imposed "a rigid requirement that a specific body of information be given in all cases, irrespective of the particular needs of the patient * * *."

To the extent *Akron I* and *Thornburgh* find a constitutional violation when the government requires, as it does here, the giving of truthful, nonmisleading information about the nature of the procedure, the attendant health risks and those of childbirth, and the "probable gestational age" of the fetus, those cases go too far, are inconsistent with

Roe's acknowledgment of an important interest in potential life, and are overruled. It cannot be questioned that psychological well-being is a facet of health. Nor can it be doubted that most women considering an abortion would deem the impact on the fetus relevant, if not dispositive, to the decision. In attempting to ensure that a woman apprehend the full consequences of her decision, the State furthers the legitimate purpose of reducing the risk that a woman may elect an abortion, only to discover later, with devastating psychological consequences, that her decision was not fully informed.

We also see no reason why the State may not require doctors to inform a woman seeking an abortion of the availability of materials relating to the consequences to the fetus, even when those consequences have no direct relation to her health. An example illustrates the point. We would think it constitutional for the State to require that in order for there to be informed consent to a kidney transplant operation the recipient must be supplied with information about risks to the donor as well as risks to himself or herself. A requirement that the physician make available information similar to that mandated by the statute here was described in *Thornburgh* as "an outright attempt to wedge the Commonwealth's message discouraging abortion into the privacy of the informed-consent dialogue between the woman and her physician." 476 U.S., at 762. We conclude, however, that informed choice need not be defined in such narrow terms that all considerations of the effect on the fetus are made irrelevant. This requirement cannot be considered a substantial obstacle to obtaining an abortion, and, it follows, there is no undue burden. The Pennsylvania statute also requires us to reconsider the holding in *Akron I* that the State may not require that a physician, as opposed to a qualified assistant, provide information relevant to a woman's informed consent. 462 U.S., at 448. Since there is no evidence on this record that requiring a doctor to give the information as provided by the statute would amount in practical terms to a substantial obstacle to a woman seeking an abortion, we conclude that it is not an undue burden. Our analysis of Pennsylvania's 24–hour waiting period between the provision of the information deemed necessary to informed consent and the performance of an abortion under the undue burden standard requires us to reconsider the premise behind the decision in *Akron I* invalidating a parallel requirement. We consider that conclusion to be wrong. The idea that important decisions will be more informed and deliberate if they follow some period of reflection does not strike us as unreasonable, particularly where the statute directs that important information become part of the background of the decision.

Whether the mandatory 24–hour waiting period is nonetheless invalid because in practice it is a substantial obstacle to a woman's choice to terminate her pregnancy is a closer question. The findings of fact by the District Court indicate that because of the distances many women must travel to reach an abortion provider, the practical effect will often be a delay of much more than a day because the waiting period requires that a woman seeking an abortion make at least two visits to the doctor. The

District Court also found that in many instances this will increase the exposure of women seeking abortions to "the harassment and hostility of anti-abortion protestors demonstrating outside a clinic." 744 F.Supp., at 1351. As a result, the District Court found that for those women who have the fewest financial resources, those who must travel long distances, and those who have difficulty explaining their whereabouts to husbands, employers, or others, the 24-hour waiting period will be "particularly burdensome." Id., at 1352.

These findings are troubling in some respects, but they do not demonstrate that the waiting period constitutes an undue burden. In light of the construction given the statute's definition of medical emergency by the Court of Appeals, and the District Court's findings, we cannot say that the waiting period imposes a real health risk.

We also disagree with the District Court's conclusion that the "particularly burdensome" effects of the waiting period on some women require its invalidation. A particular burden is not of necessity a substantial obstacle. Whether a burden falls on a particular group is a distinct inquiry from whether it is a substantial obstacle even as to the women in that group. And the District Court did not conclude that the waiting period is such an obstacle even for the women who are most burdened by it. Hence, on the record before us, and in the context of this facial challenge, we are not convinced that the 24-hour waiting period constitutes an undue burden.

C

Section 3209 of Pennsylvania's abortion law provides, except in cases of medical emergency, that no physician shall perform an abortion on a married woman without receiving a signed statement from the woman that she has notified her spouse that she is about to undergo an abortion. The woman has the option of providing an alternative signed statement certifying that her husband is not the man who impregnated her; that her husband could not be located; that the pregnancy is the result of spousal sexual assault which she has reported; or that the woman believes that notifying her husband will cause him or someone else to inflict bodily injury upon her. A physician who performs an abortion on a married woman without receiving the appropriate signed statement will have his or her license revoked, and is liable to the husband for damages.

The District Court heard the testimony of numerous expert witnesses, and made detailed findings of fact regarding the effect of this statute. These included:

"273. The vast majority of women consult their husbands prior to deciding to terminate their pregnancy * * *.

* * *

"279. The 'bodily injury' exception could not be invoked by a married woman whose husband, if notified, would, in her reasonable belief, threaten to (a) publicize her intent to have an abortion to family, friends or acquaintances; (b) retaliate against her in future child custody or divorce proceedings; (c) inflict psychological intimidation or emotional harm upon her, her children or other persons; (d) inflict bodily harm on other persons such as children, family members or other loved ones; or (e) use his control over finances to deprive her of necessary monies for herself or her children * * *.

* * *

"281. Studies reveal that family violence occurs in two million families in the United States. This figure, however, is a conservative one that substantially understates (because battering is usually not reported until it reaches life-threatening proportions) the actual number of families affected by domestic violence. In fact, researchers estimate that one of every two women will be battered at some time in their life * * *.

"282. A wife may not elect to notify her husband of her intention to have an abortion for a variety of reasons, including the husband's illness, concern about her own health, the imminent failure of the marriage, or the husband's absolute opposition to the abortion * * *.

"283. The required filing of the spousal consent form would require plaintiff-clinics to change their counseling procedures and force women to reveal their most intimate decision-making on pain of criminal sanctions. The confidentiality of these revelations could not be guaranteed, since the woman's records are not immune from subpoena * * *.

"284. Women of all class levels, educational backgrounds, and racial, ethnic and religious groups are battered * * *.

"285. Wife-battering or abuse can take on many physical and psychological forms. The nature and scope of the battering can cover a broad range of actions and be gruesome and torturous * * *.

"286. Married women, victims of battering, have been killed in Pennsylvania and throughout the United States * * *.

"287. Battering can often involve a substantial amount of sexual abuse, including marital rape and sexual mutilation * * *.

"288. In a domestic abuse situation, it is common for the battering husband to also abuse the children in an attempt to coerce the wife * * *.

"289. Mere notification of pregnancy is frequently a flashpoint for battering and violence within the family. The number of battering incidents is high during the pregnancy and often the worst abuse can be associated with pregnancy * * *. The battering husband may deny parentage and use the pregnancy as an excuse for abuse * * *.

"290. Secrecy typically shrouds abusive families. Family members are instructed not to tell anyone, especially police or doctors, about the abuse and violence. Battering husbands often threaten their wives or her children with further abuse if she tells an outsider of the violence and tells her that nobody will believe her. A battered woman, therefore, is highly unlikely to disclose the violence against her for fear of retaliation by the abuser * * *.

* * *

"294. A woman in a shelter or a safe house unknown to her husband is not 'reasonably likely' to have bodily harm inflicted upon her by her batterer, however her attempt to notify her husband pursuant to section 3209 could accidentally disclose her whereabouts to her husband. Her fear of future ramifications would be realistic under the circumstances.

"295. Marital rape is rarely discussed with others or reported to law enforcement authorities, and of those reported only few are prosecuted * * *.

"296. It is common for battered women to have sexual intercourse with their husbands to avoid being battered. While this type of coercive sexual activity would be spousal sexual assault as defined by the Act, many women may not consider it to be so and others would fear disbelief * * *.

"297. The marital rape exception to section 3209 cannot be claimed by women who are victims of coercive sexual behavior other than penetration. The 90–day reporting requirement of the spousal sexual assault statute, 18 Pa.Cons.Stat.Ann. § 3218(c), further narrows the class of sexually abused wives who can claim the exception, since many of these women may be psychologically unable to discuss or report the rape for several years after the incident * * *.

"298. Because of the nature of the battering relationship, battered women are unlikely to avail themselves of the exceptions to section 3209 of the Act, regardless of whether the section applies to them." 744 F.Supp., at 1360–1362.

These findings are supported by studies of domestic violence. [The Court then summarized the findings of several studies of spousal abuse.]

The limited research that has been conducted with respect to notifying one's husband about an abortion, although involving samples too small to be representative, also supports the District Court's findings of fact. The vast majority of women notify their male partners of their decision to obtain an abortion. In many cases in which married women do not notify their husbands, the pregnancy is the result of an extramarital affair. Where the husband is the father, the primary reason women do not notify their husbands is that the husband and wife are experiencing marital difficulties, often accompanied by incidents of violence.

This information and the District Court's findings reinforce what common sense would suggest. In well-functioning marriages, spouses discuss important intimate decisions such as whether to bear a child. But there are millions of women in this country who are the victims of regular physical and psychological abuse at the hands of their husbands. Should these women become pregnant, they may have very good reasons for not wishing to inform their husbands of their decision to obtain an abortion.

The spousal notification requirement is thus likely to prevent a significant number of women from obtaining an abortion. It does not merely make abortions a little more difficult or expensive to obtain; for many women, it will impose a substantial obstacle. We must not blind ourselves to the fact that the significant number of women who fear for their safety and the safety of their children are likely to be deterred from procuring an abortion as surely as if the Commonwealth had outlawed abortion in all cases. The unfortunate yet persisting conditions we document above will mean that in a large fraction of the cases in which § 3209 is relevant, it will operate as a substantial obstacle to a woman's choice to undergo an abortion. It is an undue burden, and therefore invalid.

In keeping with our rejection of the common-law understanding of a woman's role within the family, the Court held in *Danforth* that the Constitution does not permit a State to require a married woman to obtain her husband's consent before undergoing an abortion. 428 U.S., at 69. The principles that guided the Court in *Danforth* should be our guides today. For the great many women who are victims of abuse inflicted by their husbands, or whose children are the victims of such abuse, a spousal notice requirement enables the husband to wield an effective veto over his wife's decision. Whether the prospect of notification itself deters such women from seeking abortions, or whether the husband, through physical force or psychological pressure or economic coercion, prevents his wife from obtaining an abortion until it is too late, the notice requirement will often be tantamount to the veto found unconstitutional in *Danforth*. The women most affected by this law—those who most reasonably fear the consequences of notifying their husbands that they are pregnant—are in the gravest danger.

The husband's interest in the life of the child his wife is carrying does not permit the State to empower him with this troubling degree of authority over his wife. The contrary view leads to consequences reminiscent of the common law. A husband has no enforceable right to require a wife to advise him before she exercises her personal choices. A State may not give to a man the kind of dominion over his wife that parents exercise over their children.

Section 3209 embodies a view of marriage consonant with the common-law status of married women but repugnant to our present understanding of marriage and of the nature of the rights secured by the Constitution. Women do not lose their constitutionally protected liberty when they marry. The Constitution protects all individuals, male or female, married or unmarried, from the abuse of governmental power, even where that power is employed for the supposed benefit of a member of the individual's family. These considerations confirm our conclusion that § 3209 is invalid.

D

We next consider the parental consent provision. Except in a medical emergency, an unemancipated young woman under 18 may not obtain an abortion unless she and one of her parents (or guardian) provides informed consent as defined above. If neither a parent nor a guardian provides consent, a court may authorize the performance of an abortion upon a determination that the young woman is mature and capable of giving informed consent and has in fact given her informed consent, or that an abortion would be in her best interests.

We have been over most of this ground before. Our cases establish, and we reaffirm today, that a State may require a minor seeking an abortion to obtain the consent of a parent or guardian, provided that there is an adequate judicial bypass procedure. Under these precedents, in our view, the one-parent consent requirement and judicial bypass procedure are constitutional.

E

Under the recordkeeping and reporting requirements of the statute, every facility which performs abortions is required to file a report stating its name and address as well as the name and address of any related entity, such as a controlling or subsidiary organization. In the case of state-funded institutions, the information becomes public.

For each abortion performed, a report must be filed identifying: the physician (and the second physician where required); the facility; the referring physician or agency; the woman's age; the number of prior pregnancies and prior abortions she has had; gestational age; the type of abortion procedure; the date of the abortion; whether there were any pre-existing medical conditions which would complicate pregnancy; medical complications with the abortion; where applicable, the basis for the determination that the abortion was medically necessary; the weight of the aborted fetus; and whether the woman was married, and if so, whether notice was provided or the basis for the failure to give notice. Every abortion facility must also file quarterly reports showing the number of abortions performed broken down by trimester. See 18 Pa.Cons.Stat. §§ 3207, 3214 (1990). In all events, the identity of each woman who has had an abortion remains confidential.

We think that all the provisions at issue here except that relating to spousal notice are constitutional. Although they do not relate to the State's interest in informing the woman's choice, they do relate to health. The collection of information with respect to actual patients is a vital element of medical research, and so it cannot be said that the requirements serve no purpose other than to make abortions more difficult. Nor do we find that the requirements impose a substantial obstacle to a woman's choice. At most they might increase the cost of some abortions by a slight amount. While at some point increased cost could become a substantial obstacle, there is no such showing on the record before us.

VI

Our Constitution is a covenant running from the first generation of Americans to us and then to future generations. It is a coherent succession. Each generation must learn anew that the Constitution's written terms embody ideas and aspirations that must survive more ages than one. We accept our responsibility not to retreat from interpreting the full meaning of the covenant in light of all of our precedents. We invoke it once again to define the freedom guaranteed by the Constitution's own promise, the promise of liberty.

JUSTICE BLACKMUN, concurring in part, concurring in the judgment in part, and dissenting in part.

I join parts I, II, III, V–A, V–C, and VI of the joint opinion of JUSTICES O'CONNOR, KENNEDY, and SOUTER, ante.

Three years ago, in Webster v. Reproductive Health Serv., 492 U.S. 490 (1989), four Members of this Court appeared poised to "cast into darkness the hopes and visions of every woman in this country" who had come to believe that the Constitution guaranteed her the right to reproductive choice. But now, just when so many expected the darkness to fall, the flame has grown bright.

I do not underestimate the significance of today's joint opinion. Yet I remain steadfast in my belief that the right to reproductive choice is entitled to the full protection afforded by this Court before *Webster*. And I fear for the darkness as four Justices anxiously await the single vote necessary to extinguish the light.

I

Make no mistake, the joint opinion of Justices O'Connor, Kennedy, and Souter is an act of personal courage and constitutional principle. In contrast to previous decisions in which Justices O'Connor and Kennedy postponed reconsideration of Roe v. Wade, 410 U.S. 113 (1973), the authors of the joint opinion today join Justice Stevens and me in concluding that "the essential holding of *Roe* should be retained and once again reaffirmed." In brief, five Members of this Court today recognize that "the Constitution protects a woman's right to terminate her pregnancy in its early stages." What has happened today should serve as a model for future Justices and a warning to all who have tried to turn this Court into yet another political branch.

[W]hile I believe that the joint opinion errs in failing to invalidate the other regulations, I am pleased that the joint opinion has not ruled out the possibility that these regulations may be shown to impose an unconstitutional burden. The joint opinion makes clear that its specific holdings are based on the insufficiency of the record before it. I am confident that in the future evidence will be produced to show that "in a large fraction of the cases in which [these regulations are] relevant, [they] will operate as a substantial obstacle to a woman's choice to undergo an abortion." Ante.

II

Today, no less than yesterday, the Constitution and decisions of this Court require that a State's abortion restrictions be subjected to the strictest of judicial scrutiny. Under this standard, the Pennsylvania statute's provisions requiring content-based counseling, a 24–hour delay, informed parental consent, and reporting of abortion-related information must be invalidated.

A

State restrictions on abortion violate a woman's right of privacy in two ways. First, compelled continuation of a pregnancy infringes upon a woman's right to bodily integrity by imposing substantial physical intrusions and significant risks of physical harm. During pregnancy, women experience dramatic physical changes and a wide range of health consequences. Labor and delivery pose additional health risks and physical demands. In short, restrictive abortion laws force women to endure physical invasions far more substantial than those this Court has held to violate the constitutional principle of bodily integrity in other contexts.

Further, when the State restricts a woman's right to terminate her pregnancy, it deprives a woman of the right to make her own decision about reproduction and family planning—critical life choices that this Court long has deemed central to the right to privacy. The decision to terminate or continue a pregnancy has no less an impact on a woman's life than decisions about contraception or marriage. Because motherhood has a dramatic impact on a woman's educational prospects, employment opportunities, and self-determination, restrictive abortion laws deprive her of basic control over her life.

A State's restrictions on a woman's right to terminate her pregnancy also implicate constitutional guarantees of gender equality. By restricting the right to terminate pregnancies, the State conscripts women's bodies into its service, forcing women to continue their pregnancies, suffer the pains of childbirth, and in most instances, provide years of maternal care. The State does not compensate women for their services; instead, it assumes that they owe this duty as a matter of course. This assumption—that women can simply be forced to accept the "natural" status and incidents of motherhood—appears to rest upon a conception of women's role that has triggered the protection of the Equal Protection Clause. See, e.g., Mississippi Univ. for Women v. Hogan, 458 U.S. 718, 724–726 (1982); Craig v. Boren, 429 U.S. 190, 198–199 (1976).

B

Roe identified two relevant State interests: "an interest in preserving and protecting the health of the pregnant woman" and an interest in "protecting the potentiality of human life." 410 U.S., at 162. With respect to the State's interest in the health of the mother, "the compelling point * * * is at approximately the end of the first trimester," because it is at that point that the mortality rate in abortion approaches that in childbirth. Roe, 410 U.S., at 163. With respect to the State's interest in potential life, "the 'compelling' point is at viability," because it is at that point that the fetus "presumably has the capability of meaningful life outside the mother's womb." Ibid. In order to fulfill the requirement of narrow tailoring, "the State is obligated to make a reasonable effort to limit the effect of its regulations to the period in the trimester during which its health interest will be furthered." Akron, 462 U.S., at 434.

In my view, application of this analytical framework is no less warranted than when it was approved by seven Members of this Court in Roe. Strict scrutiny of state limitations on reproductive choice still offers the most secure protection of the woman's right to make her own reproductive decisions, free from state coercion. No majority of this Court has ever agreed upon an alternative approach. The factual premises of the trimester framework have not been undermined and the Roe framework is far more administrable, and far less manipulable, than the "undue burden" standard adopted by the joint opinion.

The [most telling] criticism of the trimester framework is that it fails to find the State's interest in potential human life compelling throughout pregnancy. No member of this Court—nor for that matter, the Solicitor General, Tr. of Oral Arg. 42—has ever questioned our holding in Roe that an abortion is not "the termination of life entitled to Fourteenth Amendment protection." 410 U.S., at 159. Accordingly, a State's interest in protecting fetal life is not grounded in the Constitution. Nor, consistent with our Establishment Clause, can it be a theological or sectarian interest. It is, instead, a legitimate interest grounded in humanitarian or pragmatic concerns.

But legitimate interests are not enough. To overcome the burden of strict scrutiny, the interests must be compelling. The question then is how best to accommodate the State's interest in potential human life with the constitutional liberties of pregnant women. Again, I stand by the views I expressed in Webster: "The viability line reflects the biological facts and truths of fetal development; it marks that threshold moment prior to which a fetus cannot survive separate from the woman and cannot reasonably and objectively be regarded as a subject of rights or interests distinct from, or paramount to, those of the pregnant woman. At the same time, the viability standard takes account of the undeniable fact that as the fetus evolves into its postnatal form, and as it loses its dependence on the uterine environment, the State's interest in the fetus' potential human life, and in fostering a regard for human life in general, becomes compelling. As a practical matter, it establishes an easily applicable standard for regulating abortion while providing a pregnant woman ample time to exercise her fundamental right with her responsible physician to terminate her pregnancy." 492 U.S., at 553–554.

In sum, Roe's requirement of strict scrutiny as implemented through a trimester framework should not be disturbed.

C

Application of the strict scrutiny standard results in the invalidation of all the challenged provisions. Indeed, as this Court has invalidated virtually identical provisions in prior cases, stare decisis requires that we again strike them down.

III

At long last, The Chief Justice admits it. Gone are the contentions that the issue need not be (or has not been) considered. There, on the first page, for all to see, is what was expected: "We believe that *Roe* was wrongfully decided, and that it can and should be overruled consistently with our traditional approach to stare decisis in constitutional cases."

The Chief Justice's criticism of *Roe* follows from his stunted conception of individual liberty. While recognizing that the Due Process Clause protects more than simple physical liberty, he then goes on to construe this Court's personal-liberty cases as establishing only a laundry list of particular rights, rather than a principled account of how these particular rights are grounded in a more general right of privacy. This constricted view is reinforced by The Chief Justice's exclusive reliance on tradition as a source of fundamental rights. Given The Chief Justice's exclusive reliance on tradition, people using contraceptives seem the next likely candidate for his list of outcasts.

Even more shocking than The Chief Justice's cramped notion of individual liberty is his complete omission of any discussion of the effects that compelled childbirth and motherhood have on women's lives. The Chief Justice's view of the State's compelling interest in maternal health has less to do with health than it does with compelling women to be maternal.

Under his standard, States can ban abortion if that ban is rationally related to a legitimate state interest—a standard which the United States calls "deferential, but not toothless." Yet when pressed at oral argument to describe the teeth, the best protection that the Solicitor General could offer to women was that a prohibition, enforced by criminal penalties, with no exception for the life of the mother, "could raise very serious questions." Tr. of Oral Arg. 49.

But, we are reassured, there is always the protection of the democratic process. While there is much to be praised about our democracy, our country since its founding has recognized that there are certain fundamental liberties that are not to be left to the whims of an election. A woman's right to reproductive choice is one of those fundamental liberties. Accordingly, that liberty need not seek refuge at the ballot box.

IV

In one sense, the Court's approach is worlds apart from that of The Chief Justice and Justice Scalia. And yet, in another sense, the distance between the two approaches is short—the distance is but a single vote.

I am 83 years old. I cannot remain on this Court forever, and when I do step down, the confirmation process for my successor well may focus on the issue before us today. That, I regret, may be exactly where the choice between the two worlds will be made.

JUSTICE STEVENS, concurring in part and dissenting in part.

I

The Court is unquestionably correct in concluding that the doctrine of stare decisis has controlling significance in a case of this kind, notwithstanding an individual justice's concerns about the merits. The central holding of Roe v. Wade, 410 U.S. 113 (1973), has been a "part of our law" for almost two decades. It was a natural sequel to the protection of individual liberty established in Griswold v. Connecticut, 381 U.S. 479 (1965).

II

My disagreement with the joint opinion begins with its understanding of the trimester framework established in *Roe.* Contrary to the suggestion of the joint opinion, it is not a "contradiction" to recognize that the State may have a legitimate interest in potential human life and, at the same time, to conclude that that interest does not justify the regulation of abortion before viability (although other interests, such as maternal health, may). The fact that the State's interest is legitimate does not tell us when, if ever, that interest outweighs the pregnant woman's interest in personal liberty. It is appropriate, therefore, to consider more carefully the nature of the interests at stake.

Weighing the State's interest in potential life and the woman's liberty interest, I agree with the joint opinion that the State may " 'expres[s] a preference for normal childbirth,' " that the State may take steps to ensure that a woman's choice "is thoughtful and informed," and that "States are free to enact laws to provide a reasonable framework for a woman to make a decision that has such profound and lasting meaning." Serious questions arise, however, when a State attempts to "persuade the woman to choose childbirth over abortion." Ante. Decisional autonomy must limit the State's power to inject into a woman's most personal deliberations its own views of what is best. The State may promote its preferences by funding childbirth, by creating and maintaining alternatives to abortion, and by espousing the virtues of family; but it must respect the individual's freedom to make such judgments.

Under these principles, §§ 3205(a)(2)(i)–(iii) of the Pennsylvania statute are unconstitutional. Those sections require a physician or counselor to provide the woman with a range of materials clearly designed to persuade her to choose not to undergo the abortion. While the State is free, pursuant to § 3208 of the Pennsylvania law, to produce and disseminate such material, the State may not inject such information into the woman's deliberations just as she is weighing such an important choice.

Under this same analysis, §§ 3205(a)(1)(i) and (iii) of the Pennsylvania statute are constitutional. Those sections, which require the physician to inform a woman of the nature and risks of the abortion procedure and the medical risks of carrying to term, are neutral requirements comparable to those imposed in other medical procedures. Those sections indicate no effort by the State to influence the woman's choice in any way. If anything, such requirements enhance, rather than skew, the woman's decisionmaking.

III

The 24–hour waiting period required by §§ 3205(a)(1)–(2) of the Pennsylvania statute raises even more serious concerns.

[T]here is no evidence that the mandated delay benefits women or that it is necessary to enable the physician to convey any relevant information to the patient. The mandatory delay thus appears to rest on outmoded and unacceptable assumptions about the decisionmaking capacity of women. A woman who has, in the privacy of her thoughts and conscience, weighed the options and made her decision cannot be forced to reconsider all, simply because the State believes she has come to the wrong conclusion. The joint opinion's reliance on the indirect effects of the regulation of constitutionally protected activity is misplaced; what matters is not only the effect of a regulation but also the reason for the regulation.

Part of the constitutional liberty to choose is the equal dignity to which each of us is entitled. A woman who decides to terminate her pregnancy is entitled to the same respect as a woman who decides to carry the fetus to term. The mandatory waiting period denies women that equal respect.

IV

In my opinion, a correct application of the "undue burden" standard leads to the same conclusion concerning the constitutionality of these requirements. A state-imposed burden on the exercise of a constitutional right is measured both by its effects and by its character: A burden may be "undue" either because the burden is too severe or because it lacks a legitimate, rational justification.

The 24–hour delay requirement fails both parts of this test. The findings of the District Court establish the severity of the burden that the 24–hour delay imposes on many pregnant women. Yet even in those cases in which the delay is not especially onerous, it is, in my opinion, "undue" because there is no evidence that such a delay serves a useful and legitimate purpose.

The counseling provisions are similarly infirm. Whenever government commands private citizens to speak or to listen, careful review of the justification for that command is particularly appropriate. The statute requires that this information be given to all women seeking abortions, including those for whom such information is clearly useless, such as those who are married, those who have undergone the procedure in the past and are fully aware of the options, and those who are fully convinced that abortion is their only reasonable option. Nor can the information required by the statute be justified as relevant to any "philosophic" or "social" argument either favoring or disfavoring the abortion decision in a particular case. In light of all of these facts, I conclude that the information requirements in § 3205(a)(1)(ii) and §§ 3205(a)(2)(i)–(iii) do not serve a useful purpose and thus constitute an unnecessary—and therefore undue—burden on the woman's constitutional liberty to decide to terminate her pregnancy.

CHIEF JUSTICE REHNQUIST, with whom JUSTICE WHITE, JUSTICE SCALIA, and JUSTICE THOMAS join, concurring in the judgment in part and dissenting in part.

The joint opinion, following its newly-minted variation on stare decisis, retains the outer shell of Roe v. Wade, 410 U.S. 113 (1973), but beats a wholesale retreat from the substance of that case. We believe that *Roe* was wrongly decided, and that it can and should be overruled consistently with our traditional approach to stare decisis in constitutional cases. We would uphold the challenged provisions of the Pennsylvania statute in their entirety.

I

[P]etitioners insist that we reaffirm our decision in Roe v. Wade, supra, in which we held unconstitutional a Texas statute making it a crime to procure an abortion except to save the life of the mother.[1] We agree with the Court of Appeals that our decision in *Roe* is not directly implicated by the Pennsylvania statute, which does not prohibit, but simply regulates, abortion. But, as the Court of Appeals found, the state of our post–*Roe* decisional law dealing with the regulation of abortion is confusing and uncertain, indicating that a reexamination of that line of cases is in order.

In Roe v. Wade, the Court recognized a "guarantee of personal privacy" which "is broad enough to encompass a woman's decision whether or not to terminate her pregnancy." 410 U.S., at 152–153. We are now of the view that, in terming this right fundamental, the Court in *Roe* read the earlier opinions upon which it based its decision much too broadly. Unlike marriage, procreation and contraception, abortion "involves the purposeful termination of potential life." Harris v. McRae, 448 U.S. 297, 325 (1980). One cannot ignore the fact that a woman is not isolated in her pregnancy, and that the decision to abort necessarily involves the destruction of a fetus.

---

1. Two years after *Roe,* the West German constitutional court, by contrast, struck down a law liberalizing access to abortion on the grounds that life developing within the womb is constitutionally protected. Judgment of February 25, 1975, 39 Bverfge 1 (translated in Jonas & Gorby, West German Abortion Decision: A Contrast to Roe v. Wade, 9 J. Marshall J. Prac. & Proc. 605 (1976)). In 1988, the Canadian Supreme Court followed reasoning similar to that of *Roe* in striking down a law which restricted abortion. Morgentaler v. Queen, 1 S.C.R. 30, 44 D.L.R. 4th 385 (1988).

Nor do the historical traditions of the American people support the view that the right to terminate one's pregnancy is "fundamental." The common law which we inherited from England made abortion after "quickening" an offense. At the time of the adoption of the Fourteenth Amendment, statutory prohibitions or restrictions on abortion were commonplace. By the turn of the century virtually every State had a law prohibiting or restricting abortion on its books.

We think, therefore, that the Court was mistaken in *Roe* when it classified a woman's decision to terminate her pregnancy as a "fundamental right" that could be abridged only in a manner which withstood "strict scrutiny." In so concluding, we repeat the observation made in Bowers v. Hardwick, 478 U.S. 186 (1986): "Nor are we inclined to take a more expansive view of our authority to discover new fundamental rights imbedded in the Due Process Clause. The Court is most vulnerable and comes nearest to illegitimacy when it deals with judge-made constitutional law having little or no cognizable roots in the language or design of the Constitution."

II

In our view, authentic principles of stare decisis do not require that any portion of the reasoning in *Roe* be kept intact. Erroneous decisions in constitutional cases are uniquely durable, because correction through legislative action, save for constitutional amendment, is impossible. It is therefore our duty to reconsider constitutional interpretations that "depart from a proper understanding" of the Constitution. Garcia v. San Antonio Metropolitan Transit Authority, 469 U.S., at 557.

The joint opinion discusses several stare decisis factors which, it asserts, point toward retaining a portion of *Roe*. Two of these factors are that the main "factual underpinning" of *Roe* has remained the same, and that its doctrinal foundation is no weaker now than it was in 1973. Of course, what might be called the basic facts which gave rise to *Roe* have remained the same—women become pregnant, there is a point somewhere, depending on medical technology, where a fetus becomes viable, and women give birth to children. But this is only to say that the same facts which gave rise to *Roe* will continue to give rise to similar cases. It is not a reason, in and of itself, why those cases must be decided in the same incorrect manner as was the first case to deal with the question.

[A]ny traditional notion of reliance is not applicable here. The joint opinion thus turns to what can only be described as an unconventional— and unconvincing—notion of reliance, a view based on the surmise that the availability of abortion since *Roe* has led to "two decades of economic and social developments" that would be undercut if the error of *Roe* were recognized. Surely it is dubious to suggest that women have reached their "places in society" in reliance upon *Roe*, rather than as a result of their determination to obtain higher education and compete with men in the job market, and of society's increasing recognition of their ability to fill positions that were previously thought to be reserved only for men.

In the end, having failed to put forth any evidence to prove any true reliance, the joint opinion's argument is based solely on generalized assertions about the national psyche, on a belief that the people of this country have grown accustomed to the *Roe* decision over the last 19 years and have "ordered their thinking and living around" it. As an initial matter, one might inquire how the joint opinion can view the "central holding" of *Roe* as so deeply rooted in our constitutional culture, when it so casually uproots and disposes of that same decision's trimester framework. Furthermore, at various points in the past, the same could have been said about this Court's erroneous decisions that the Constitution allowed "separate but equal" treatment of minorities, see Plessy v. Ferguson, 163 U.S. 537 (1896), or that "liberty" under the Due Process Clause protected "freedom of contract." See Adkins v. Children's Hospital of D.C., 261 U.S. 525 (1923); Lochner v. New York, 198 U.S. 45 (1905).

Apparently realizing that conventional stare decisis principles do not support its position, the joint opinion advances a belief that retaining a portion of *Roe* is necessary to protect the "legitimacy" of this Court.

[T]he joint opinion goes on to state that when the Court "resolves the sort of intensely divisive controversy reflected in *Roe* and those rare, comparable cases," its decision is exempt from reconsideration under established principles of stare decisis in constitutional cases.

The joint opinion picks out and discusses two prior Court rulings that it believes are of the "intensely divisive" variety, and concludes that they are of comparable dimension to *Roe* (Lochner v. New York, supra, and Plessy v. Ferguson, supra). It appears to us very odd indeed that the joint opinion chooses as benchmarks two cases in which the Court chose not to adhere to erroneous constitutional precedent, but instead enhanced its stature by acknowledging and correcting its error, apparently in violation of the joint opinion's "legitimacy" principle. See West Coast Hotel Co. v. Parrish, supra; Brown v. Board of Education, supra. One might also wonder how it is that the joint opinion puts these, and not others, in the "intensely divisive" category, and how it assumes that these are the only two lines of cases of comparable dimension to *Roe*. There is no reason to think that either *Plessy* or *Lochner* produced the sort of public protest when they were decided that *Roe* did.

Taking the joint opinion on its own terms, we doubt that its distinction between *Roe*, on the one hand, and *Plessy* and *Lochner*, on the other, withstands analysis. The joint opinion acknowledges that the Court improved its stature by overruling *Plessy* in *Brown* on a deeply divisive issue. And our decision in *West Coast Hotel*, which overruled Adkins v. Children's Hospital, supra, and *Lochner*, was rendered at a time when Congress was considering President Franklin Roosevelt's proposal to "reorganize" this Court and enable him to name six additional Justices in the event that any member of the Court over the age of

70 did not elect to retire. It is difficult to imagine a situation in which the Court would face more intense opposition to a prior ruling than it did at that time, and, under the general principle proclaimed in the joint opinion, the Court seemingly should have responded to this opposition by stubbornly refusing to reexamine the *Lochner* rationale, lest it lose legitimacy by appearing to "overrule under fire."

There is also a suggestion in the joint opinion that the propriety of overruling a "divisive" decision depends in part on whether "most people" would now agree that it should be overruled. The Judicial Branch derives its legitimacy, not from following public opinion, but from deciding by its best lights whether legislative enactments of the popular branches of Government comport with the Constitution.

The decision in *Roe* has engendered large demonstrations, including repeated marches on this Court and on Congress, both in opposition to and in support of that opinion. A decision either way on *Roe* can therefore be perceived as favoring one group or the other. But this perceived dilemma arises only if one assumes, as the joint opinion does, that the Court should make its decisions with a view toward speculative public perceptions. If one assumes instead, as the Court surely did in both *Brown* and *West Coast Hotel,* that the Court's legitimacy is enhanced by faithful interpretation of the Constitution irrespective of public opposition, such self-engendered difficulties may be put to one side.

The end result of the joint opinion's paeans of praise for legitimacy is the enunciation of a brand new standard for evaluating state regulation of a woman's right to abortion—the "undue burden" standard. As indicated above, Roe v. Wade adopted a "fundamental right" standard under which state regulations could survive only if they met the requirement of "strict scrutiny." While we disagree with that standard, it at least had a recognized basis in constitutional law at the time *Roe* was decided. The same cannot be said for the "undue burden" standard, which is created largely out of whole cloth by the authors of the joint opinion. It is a standard which even today does not command the support of a majority of this Court. And it will not, we believe, result in the sort of "simple limitation," easily applied, which the joint opinion anticipates. In sum, it is a standard which is not built to last.

Because the undue burden standard is plucked from nowhere, the question of what is a "substantial obstacle" to abortion will undoubtedly engender a variety of conflicting views. For example, in the very matter before us now, the authors of the joint opinion would uphold Pennsylvania's 24–hour waiting period, concluding that a "particular burden" on some women is not a substantial obstacle. But the authors would at the same time strike down Pennsylvania's spousal notice provision, after finding that in a "large fraction" of cases the provision will be a substantial obstacle. And, while the authors conclude that the informed consent provisions do not constitute an "undue burden," JUSTICE STEVENS would hold that they do.

The sum of the joint opinion's labors in the name of stare decisis and "legitimacy" is this: Roe v. Wade stands as a sort of judicial Potemkin Village, which may be pointed out to passers by as a monument to the importance of adhering to precedent. But behind the facade, an entirely new method of analysis, without any roots in constitutional law, is imported to decide the constitutionality of state laws regulating abortion. Neither stare decisis nor "legitimacy" are truly served by such an effort.

We have stated above our belief that the Constitution does not subject state abortion regulations to heightened scrutiny. A woman's interest in having an abortion is a form of liberty protected by the Due Process Clause, but States may regulate abortion procedures in ways rationally related to a legitimate state interest. Williamson v. Lee Optical of Okla., Inc., 348 U.S. 483, 491 (1955); cf. Stanley v. Illinois, 405 U.S. 645, 651–653 (1972). With this rule in mind, we examine each of the challenged provisions.

III

A

Section 3205(a)(1) requires a physician to disclose certain information about the abortion procedure and its risks and alternatives. This requirement is certainly no large burden, as the Court of Appeals found that "the record shows that the clinics, without exception, insist on providing this information to women before an abortion is performed." 947 F.2d, at 703. We are of the view that this information "clearly is related to maternal health and to the State's legitimate purpose in requiring informed consent." Akron v. Akron Center for Reproductive Health, 462 U.S., at 446.

Section 3205(a)(2) compels the disclosure, by a physician or a counselor, of information concerning the availability of paternal child support and state-funded alternatives if the woman decides to proceed with her pregnancy. Here again, the Court of Appeals observed that "the record indicates that most clinics already require that a counselor consult in person with the woman about alternatives to abortion before the abortion is performed." Id., at 704–705. We conclude that this required presentation of "balanced information" is rationally related to the State's legitimate interest in ensuring that the woman's consent is truly informed, and in addition furthers the State's interest in preserving unborn life. That the information might create some uncertainty and persuade some women to forgo abortions does not lead to the conclusion that the Constitution forbids the provision of such information. Indeed, it only demonstrates that this information might very well make a difference, and that it is therefore relevant to a woman's informed choice.

Petitioners are correct that [the 24 hour mandatory waiting period] will result in delays for some women that might not otherwise exist, therefore placing a burden on their liberty. But the provision in no way prohibits abortions, and the informed consent and waiting period requirements do not apply in the case of a medical emergency. See 18 Pa.Cons.Stat. §§ 3205(a), (b) (1990). We are of the view that, in providing time for reflection and reconsideration, the waiting period helps ensure that a woman's decision to abort is a well-considered one, and reasonably furthers the State's legitimate interest in maternal health and in the unborn life of the fetus.

B

In addition to providing her own informed consent, before an unemancipated woman under the age of 18 may obtain an abortion she must either furnish the consent of one of her parents, or must opt for the judicial procedure that allows her to bypass the consent requirement. Under the judicial bypass option, a minor can obtain an abortion if a state court finds that she is capable of giving her informed consent and has indeed given such consent, or determines that an abortion is in her best interests.

This provision is entirely consistent with this Court's previous decisions involving parental consent requirements.

C

Section 3209 of the Act contains the spousal notification provision. Such a law requiring only notice to the husband "does not give any third party the legal right to make the [woman's] decision for her, or to prevent her from obtaining an abortion should she choose to have one performed." Hodgson v. Minnesota, supra, 497 U.S. at 496 (Kennedy, J., concurring in judgment in part and dissenting in part). The District Court found that the notification provision created a risk that some women who would otherwise have an abortion will be prevented from having one. For example, petitioners argue, many notified husbands will prevent abortions through physical force, psychological coercion, and other types of threats. But Pennsylvania has incorporated exceptions in the notice provision in an attempt to deal with these problems. For instance, a woman need not notify her husband if the pregnancy is the result of a reported sexual assault, or if she has reason to believe that she would suffer bodily injury as a result of the notification. 18 Pa.Cons.Stat. § 3209(b) (1990). Furthermore, because this is a facial challenge to the Act, it is not enough for petitioners to show that, in some "worst-case" circumstances, the notice provision will operate as a grant of veto power to husbands. Ohio v. Akron Center for Reproductive Health, 497 U.S., at 514. Because they are making a facial challenge to the provision, they must "show that no set of circumstances exists under which the [provision] would be valid." Ibid. This they have failed to do.

The question before us is therefore whether the spousal notification requirement rationally furthers any legitimate state interests. We conclude that it does. First, a husband's interests in procreation within marriage and in the potential life of his unborn child are certainly substantial ones. The State itself has legitimate interests both in protecting these interests of the father and in protecting the potential life of the fetus, and the spousal notification requirement is reasonably related to advancing those state interests. By providing that a husband will usually know of his spouse's intent to have an abortion, the provision makes it more likely that the husband will participate in deciding the fate of his unborn child, a possibility that might otherwise have been denied him. This participation might in some cases result in a decision to proceed with the pregnancy. The State also has a legitimate interest in promoting "the integrity of the marital relationship." 18 Pa.Cons.Stat. § 3209(a) (1990). In our view, the spousal notice requirement is a rational attempt by the State to improve truthful communication between spouses and encourage collaborative decision-making, and thereby fosters marital integrity. In our view, it is unrealistic to assume that every husband-wife relationship is either (1) so perfect that this type of truthful and important communication will take place as a matter of course, or (2) so imperfect that, upon notice, the husband will react selfishly, violently, or contrary to the best interests of his wife.

D

The Act also imposes various reporting requirements. The reports do not include the identity of the women on whom abortions are performed, but they do contain a variety of information about the abortions. The District Court found that these reports are kept completely confidential. [T]hese reporting requirements rationally further the State's legitimate interests in advancing the state of medical knowledge concerning maternal health and prenatal life, in gathering statistical information with respect to patients, and in ensuring compliance with other provisions of the Act.

JUSTICE SCALIA, with whom THE CHIEF JUSTICE, JUSTICE WHITE, and JUSTICE THOMAS join, concurring in the judgment in part and dissenting in part.

My views on this matter are [that the] permissibility of abortion, and the limitations upon it, are to be resolved like most important questions in our democracy: by citizens trying to persuade one another and then voting. A State's choice between two positions on which reasonable people can disagree is constitutional even when (as is often the case) it intrudes upon a "liberty" in the absolute sense. Laws against bigamy, for example—which entire societies of reasonable people disagree with—intrude upon men and women's liberty to marry and live with one another. But bigamy happens not to be a liberty specially "protected" by the Constitution.

That is, quite simply, the issue in this case: not whether the power of a woman to abort her unborn child is a "liberty" in the absolute sense; or even whether it is a liberty of great importance to many women. Of course it is both. The issue is whether it is a liberty protected by the Constitution of the United States. I am sure it is not. I reach that conclusion not because of anything so exalted as my views concerning the "concept of existence, of meaning, of the universe, and of the mystery of human life." Rather, I reach it for the same reason I reach the conclusion that bigamy is not constitutionally protected—because of two simple facts: (1) the Constitution says absolutely nothing about it, and (2) the longstanding traditions of American society have permitted it to be legally proscribed.[2]

The Court's statement that it is "tempting" to acknowledge the authoritativeness of tradition in order to "curb the discretion of federal judges," ante, at 5, is of course rhetoric rather than reality; no government official is "tempted" to place restraints upon his own freedom of action, which is why Lord Acton did not say "Power tends to purify." The Court's temptation is in the quite opposite and more natural direction—towards systematically eliminating checks upon its own power; and it succumbs.

Beyond that brief summary of the essence of my position, I will not swell the United States Reports with repetition of what I have said before; and applying the rational basis test, I would uphold the Pennsylvania statute in its entirety. I must, however, respond to a few of the more outrageous arguments in today's opinion, which it is beyond human nature to leave unanswered. I shall discuss each of them under a quotation from the Court's opinion to which they pertain.

> "The inescapable fact is that adjudication of substantive due process claims may call upon the Court in interpreting the Constitution to exercise that same capacity which by tradition courts always have exercised: reasoned judgment."

Assuming that the question before us is to be resolved at such a level of philosophical abstraction, in such isolation from the traditions of American society, as by simply applying "reasoned judgment," I do not see how that could possibly have produced the answer the Court arrived at in Roe v. Wade, 410 U.S. 113 (1973). Today's opinion describes the methodology of *Roe,* quite accurately, as weighing against the woman's interest the State's " 'important and legitimate interest in protecting the potentiality of human life.' " But "reasoned judgment" does not begin by begging the question, as *Roe* and subsequent cases unquestionably did by assuming that what the State is protecting is the mere "potentiality of human life." The whole argument of abortion opponents is that what the Court calls the fetus and what others call the unborn child is a human life. Thus, whatever answer *Roe* came up with after conducting its "balancing" is bound to be wrong, unless it is correct that the human fetus is in some critical sense merely potentially human. There is of course no way to determine that as a legal matter; it is in fact a value judgment. Some societies have considered newborn children not yet human, or the incompetent elderly no longer so.

The emptiness of the "reasoned judgment" that produced *Roe* is displayed in plain view by the fact that, after more than 19 years of

2. The Court's contention that the only way to protect childbirth is to protect abortion shows the utter bankruptcy of constitutional analysis deprived of tradition as a validating factor. It drives one to say that the only way to protect the right to eat is to acknowledge the constitutional right to starve oneself to death.

effort by some of the brightest (and most determined) legal minds in the country, after more than 10 cases upholding abortion rights in this Court, and after dozens upon dozens of amicus briefs submitted in this and other cases, the best the Court can do to explain how it is that the word "liberty" must be thought to include the right to destroy human fetuses is to rattle off a collection of adjectives that simply decorate a value judgment and conceal a political choice. Those adjectives might be applied, for example, to homosexual sodomy, polygamy, adult incest, and suicide, all of which are equally "intimate" and "deeply personal" decisions involving "personal autonomy and bodily integrity," and all of which can constitutionally be proscribed because it is our unquestionable constitutional tradition that they are proscribable. It is not reasoned judgment that supports the Court's decision; only personal predilection.

"Liberty finds no refuge in a jurisprudence of doubt."

One might have feared to encounter this august and sonorous phrase in an opinion defending the real Roe v. Wade, rather than the revised version fabricated today by the authors of the joint opinion. The shortcomings of *Roe* did not include lack of clarity: Virtually all regulation of abortion before the third trimester was invalid. But to come across this phrase in the joint opinion—which calls upon federal district judges to apply an "undue burden" standard as doubtful in application as it is unprincipled in origin—is really more than one should have to bear.

The joint opinion explains that a state regulation imposes an "undue burden" if it "has the purpose or effect of placing a substantial obstacle in the path of a woman seeking an abortion of a nonviable fetus." An obstacle is "substantial," we are told, if it is "calculated, [not] to inform the woman's free choice, [but to] hinder it." This latter statement cannot possibly mean what it says. Any regulation of abortion that is intended to advance what the joint opinion concedes is the State's "substantial" interest in protecting unborn life will be "calculated [to] hinder" a decision to have an abortion. It thus seems more accurate to say that the joint opinion would uphold abortion regulations only if they do not unduly hinder the woman's decision. That, of course, brings us right back to square one: Defining an "undue burden" as an "undue hindrance" (or a "substantial obstacle") hardly "clarifies" the test. Consciously or not, the joint opinion's verbal shell game will conceal raw judicial policy choices concerning what is "appropriate" abortion legislation.

I agree, indeed I have forcefully urged, that a law of general applicability which places only an incidental burden on a fundamental right does not infringe that right, see R.A.V. v. St. Paul, 112 S.Ct. 2538 (1992); Employment Division, Dept. of Human Resources of Ore. v. Smith, 494 U.S. 872, 878–882 (1990), but that principle does not establish the quite different (and quite dangerous) proposition that a law which directly regulates a fundamental right will not be found to violate the Constitution unless it imposes an "undue burden." It is that, of course, which is at issue here: Pennsylvania has consciously and directly regulated conduct that our cases have held is constitutionally protected. The appropriate analogy, therefore, is that of a state law requiring purchasers of religious books to endure a 24–hour waiting period, or to pay a nominal additional tax of 1 cent. The joint opinion cannot possibly be correct in suggesting that we would uphold such legislation on the ground that it does not impose a "substantial obstacle" to the exercise of First Amendment rights. The "undue burden" standard is not at all the generally applicable principle the joint opinion pretends it to be; rather, it is a unique concept created specially for this case, to preserve some judicial foothold in this ill-gotten territory. In claiming otherwise, the three Justices show their willingness to place all constitutional rights at risk in an effort to preserve what they deem the "central holding in *Roe*."

To the extent I can discern any meaningful content in the "undue burden" standard as applied in the joint opinion, it appears to be that a State may not regulate abortion in such a way as to reduce significantly its incidence. The joint opinion repeatedly emphasizes that an important factor in the "undue burden" analysis is whether the regulation "prevents a significant number of women from obtaining an abortion"; whether a "significant number of women * * * are likely to be deterred from procuring an abortion"; and whether the regulation often "deters" women from seeking abortions. We are not told, however, what forms of "deterrence" are impermissible or what degree of success in deterrence is too much to be tolerated. Thus, despite flowery rhetoric about the State's "substantial" and "profound" interest in "potential human life," and criticism of *Roe* for undervaluing that interest, the joint opinion permits the State to pursue that interest only so long as it is not too successful. Reason finds no refuge in this jurisprudence of confusion.

> "While we appreciate the weight of the arguments * * * that Roe should be overruled, the reservations any of us may have in reaffirming the central holding of *Roe* are outweighed by the explication of individual liberty we have given combined with the force of stare decisis."

The Court's reliance upon stare decisis can best be described as contrived. It insists upon the necessity of adhering not to all of *Roe*, but only to what it calls the "central holding." It seems to me that stare decisis ought to be applied even to the doctrine of stare decisis, and I confess never to have heard of this new, keep-what-you-want-and-throw-away-the-rest version. I wonder whether, as applied to Marbury v. Madison, 1 Cranch 137 (1803), for example, the new version of stare decisis would be satisfied if we allowed courts to review the constitutionality of only those statutes that (like the one in *Marbury*) pertain to the jurisdiction of the courts.

I am certainly not in a good position to dispute that the Court has saved the "central holding" of *Roe,* since to do that effectively I would have to know what the Court has saved, which in turn would require me to understand (as I do not) what the "undue burden" test means. I must confess, however, that I have always thought, and I think a lot of other people have always thought, that the arbitrary trimester framework, which the Court today discards, was quite as central to *Roe* as the arbitrary viability test, which the Court today retains. It seems particularly ungrateful to carve the trimester framework out of the core of *Roe,* since its very rigidity (in sharp contrast to the utter indeterminability of the "undue burden" test) is probably the only reason the Court is able to say, in urging stare decisis, that *Roe* "has in no sense proven 'unworkable.'" I suppose the Court is entitled to call a "central holding" whatever it wants to call a "central holding"—which is, come to think of it, perhaps one of the difficulties with this modified version of stare decisis. I thought I might note, however, that the following portions of *Roe* have not been saved:

● Under *Roe,* requiring that a woman seeking an abortion be provided truthful information about abortion before giving informed written consent is unconstitutional, if the information is designed to influence her choice, Thornburgh, 476 U.S., at 759–765; Akron I, 462 U.S., at 442–445. Under the joint opinion's "undue burden" regime (as applied today, at least) such a requirement is constitutional.

● Under *Roe,* requiring that information be provided by a doctor, rather than by nonphysician counselors, is unconstitutional, Akron I, supra, at 446–449. Under the "undue burden" regime (as applied today, at least) it is not.

● Under *Roe,* requiring a 24–hour waiting period between the time the woman gives her informed consent and the time of the abortion is unconstitutional, Akron I, supra, at 449–451. Under the "undue burden" regime (as applied today, at least) it is not.

● Under *Roe,* requiring detailed reports that include demographic data about each woman who seeks an abortion and various information about each abortion is unconstitutional, Thornburgh, supra, at 765–768. Under the "undue burden" regime (as applied today, at least) it generally is not.

> "Where, in the performance of its judicial duties, the Court decides a case in such a way as to resolve the sort of intensely divisive controversy reflected in *Roe* * * *, its decision has a dimension that the resolution of the normal case does not carry. It is the dimension present whenever the Court's interpretation of the Constitution calls the contending sides of a national controversy to end their national division by accepting a common mandate rooted in the Constitution."

The Court's description of the place of *Roe* in the social history of the United States is unrecognizable. Not only did *Roe* not, as the Court suggests, resolve the deeply divisive issue of abortion; it did more than anything else to nourish it, by elevating it to the national level where it is infinitely more difficult to resolve.

Roe's mandate for abortion-on-demand destroyed the compromises of the past, rendered compromise impossible for the future, and required the entire issue to be resolved uniformly, at the national level. [T]o portray *Roe* as the statesmanlike "settlement" of a divisive issue, a jurisprudential Peace of Westphalia that is worth preserving, is nothing less than Orwellian. *Roe* fanned into life an issue that has inflamed our national politics in general, and has obscured with its smoke the selection of Justices to this Court in particular, ever since. And by keeping us in the abortion-umpiring business, it is the perpetuation of that disruption, rather than of any *pax Roeana,* that the Court's new majority decrees.

"To overrule under fire * * * would subvert the Court's legitimacy * * *.

"To all those who will be * * * tested by following, the Court implicitly undertakes to remain steadfast * * *. The promise of constancy, once given, binds its maker for as long as the power to stand by the decision survives and * * * the commitment [is not] obsolete * * *.

"[The American people's] belief in themselves as * * * a people [who aspire to live according to the rule of law] is not readily separable from their understanding of the Court invested with the authority to decide their constitutional cases and speak before all others for their constitutional ideals. If the Court's legitimacy should be undermined, then, so would the country be in its very ability to see itself through its constitutional ideals."

The Imperial Judiciary lives. It is instructive to compare this Nietzschean vision of us unelected, life-tenured judges—leading a Volk who will be "tested by following," and whose very "belief in themselves" is mystically bound up in their "understanding" of a Court that "speaks before all others for their constitutional ideals"—with the somewhat more modest role envisioned for these lawyers by the Founders. "The judiciary * * * has * * * no direction either of the strength or of the wealth of the society, and can take no active resolution whatever. It may truly be said to have neither FORCE nor WILL but merely judgment * * *." The Federalist No. 78, 393–394 (G. Wills ed. 1982). Or, again, to compare this ecstasy of a Supreme Court in which there is, especially on controversial matters, no shadow of change or hint of alteration ("There is a limit to the amount of error that can plausibly be imputed to prior courts,"), with the more democratic views of a more humble man: "The candid citizen must confess that if the policy of the Government upon vital questions affecting the whole people is to be irrevocably fixed by decisions of the Supreme Court, * * * the people will have ceased to be their own rulers, having to that extent practically resigned their Government into the hands of that eminent tribunal." A. Lincoln, First Inaugural Address (Mar. 4, 1861).

It is particularly difficult, in the circumstances of the present decision, to sit still for the Court's lengthy lecture upon the virtues of "constancy," of "remaining steadfast," of adhering to "principle." Among the five Justices who purportedly adhere to *Roe,* at most three agree upon the principle that constitutes adherence (the joint opinion's "undue burden" standard)—and that principle is inconsistent with *Roe.* To make matters worse, two of the three, in order thus to remain steadfast, had to abandon previously stated positions. It is beyond me how the Court expects these accommodations to be accepted "as grounded truly in principle, not as compromises with social and political pressures having, as such, no bearing on the principled choices that the Court is obliged to make."

[T]he notion that the Court must adhere to a decision for as long as the decision faces "great opposition" and the Court is "under fire" acquires a character of almost czarist arrogance. We are offended by these marchers who descend upon us, every year on the anniversary of *Roe,* to protest our saying that the Constitution requires what our society has never thought the Constitution requires. These people who refuse to be "tested by following" must be taught a lesson. We have no Cossacks, but at least we can stubbornly refuse to abandon an erroneous opinion that we might otherwise change—to show how little they intimidate us.

[T]he American people love democracy and the American people are not fools. As long as this Court thought (and the people thought) that we Justices were doing essentially lawyers' work up here—reading text and discerning our society's traditional understanding of that text—the public pretty much left us alone. Texts and traditions are facts to study, not convictions to demonstrate about. But if in reality our process of constitutional adjudication consists primarily of making value judgments, then a free and intelligent people's attitude towards us can be expected to be (ought to be) quite different. The people know that their value judgments are quite as good as those taught in any law school— maybe better. If, indeed, the "liberties" protected by the Constitution are, as the Court says, undefined and unbounded, then the people should demonstrate, to protest that we do not implement their values instead of ours. Not only that, but confirmation hearings for new Justices should deteriorate into question-and-answer sessions in which Senators go through a list of their constituents' most favored and most disfavored alleged constitutional rights, and seek the nominee's commitment to support or oppose them. Value judgments, after all, should be voted on, not dictated; and if our Constitution has somehow accidently committed them to the Supreme Court, at least we can have a sort of plebiscite each time a new nominee to that body is put forward.

There is a poignant aspect to today's opinion. Its length, and what might be called its epic tone, suggest that its authors believe they are bringing to an end a troublesome era in the history of our Nation and of our Court. "It is the dimension" of authority, they say, to "call the contending sides of national controversy to end their national division by accepting a common mandate rooted in the Constitution."

There comes vividly to mind a portrait by Emanuel Leutze that hangs in the Harvard Law School: Roger Brooke Taney, painted in 1859, the 82d year of his life, the 24th of his Chief Justiceship, the second after his opinion in *Dred Scott*. He is all in black, sitting in a shadowed red armchair, left hand resting upon a pad of paper in his lap, right hand hanging limply, almost lifelessly, beside the inner arm of the chair. He sits facing the viewer, and staring straight out. There seems to be on his face, and in his deep-set eyes, an expression of profound sadness and disillusionment. Perhaps he always looked that way, even when dwelling upon the happiest of thoughts. But those of us who know how the lustre of his great Chief Justiceship came to be eclipsed by *Dred Scott* cannot help believing that he had that case—its already apparent consequences for the Court, and its soon-to-be-played-out consequences for the Nation—burning on his mind. I expect that two years earlier he, too, had thought himself "calling the contending sides of national controversy to end their national division by accepting a common mandate rooted in the Constitution."

We should get out of this area, where we have no right to be, and where we do neither ourselves nor the country any good by remaining.

Notes and Questions

A. Looking at *Casey* as a doctrinal exposition of constitutional law, we might ask questions such as:

1. Precisely how (if at all) has *Casey* changed the law? For example, consider, after *Casey*, whether and to what extent the practical power of the state to prevent or discourage abortion has changed with respect to (a) a wealthy, educated, adult woman in her first month of pregnancy who has firmly determined to have an abortion; (b) a destitute, educated, adult woman in her first month of pregnancy who firmly desires to have an abortion but has no funds to pay for one; (c) a median income, poorly educated adult woman in her first month of pregnancy who is unsure whether to have an abortion or to continue the pregnancy to birth.

2. Although the *Casey* joint opinion (i.e., the opinion signed by Justices O'Connor, Kennedy, and Souter) says it is rejecting the *Roe* trimester approach, viability generally occurs at the outset of the third trimester and the *Casey* joint opinion appears to continue *Roe's* treatment of post-viability/third trimester abortions. Consequently, the doctrinal changes effected by *Casey* appear to be (a) to collapse the first two trimesters into one pre-viability period and (b) to apply to all pre-viability abortions an "undue burden" standard. What new facts or new theories or new insights required these justices, assertedly highly attuned to the value of stare decisis, to make these changes?

3. What is an "undue burden"? Why was the husband notification, but not the 24 hour waiting period, an undue burden? Did opponents of the law simply fail to present sufficient evidence of the costs a 24 hour waiting period imposes? Or is the point that, for these purposes, burdens are not

measured by economic costs but by physical risks? If Pennsylvania levied a $75 tax on each abortion would that be an undue burden?[1]

4. The joint opinion seems to rest, in some large measure, upon the conclusions that the state has a legitimate interest in potential life and that this interest was undervalued in *Roe*. Yet the joint opinion also seems to conclude (or assume) that this state interest becomes more potent (or more legitimate) as the pregnancy progresses. Therefore, for example, post-viability abortions may be much more closely regulated for the sole reason that the state's countervailing interest is much higher. Why does the state's interest in potential life become stronger when the life is capable of existence outside the womb? Why isn't the state's interest in potential life at its highest when the life can be sustained only if it remains in the womb?

5. The opinions of the five justices in the majority seek to describe with greater care and precision the basis for *Roe's* conclusion that a woman's decision whether or not to seek an abortion is a constitutionally protected right. Would these opinions equally well explain why bigamy or homosexual acts, between consenting adults, are constitutionally protected? Would the dissenting justices' views on the derivation of constitutional rights permit them to conclude that the Constitution protects the use of contraceptives or migration from state to state?

6. We don't know of a single case where the Supreme Court said, "The existing interpretation of this aspect of the Constitution is wrong, but, the principle of stare decisis nevertheless compels us to adhere to it." Consequently, the joint opinion's discussion of stare decisis, and its role in defining the Court's legitimacy, is difficult to evaluate. Does the joint opinion (which, in the name of stare decisis, overrules *Roe's* trimester framework and several interpretations of *Roe* written by the same justices who sat on the *Roe* Court) mean to establish a new principle of precedent: that the precedent which stare decisis protects is the subsequently discovered "central holding" of the case rather than the precise results the opinion reaches, the rules of law it announces, or the reasoning process it employs?

B. Looking at *Casey* as the product of an institution, with its own bureaucracy and procedures, we might ask questions such as:

1. Should *Casey* be understood principally as the outcome, not of intellectual or legal debates over the meaning of "liberty" and "due process," but of fierce contests between a Republican presidency and a majority Democratic Senate over control of the Supreme Court? Isn't *Casey* the most visible result of the Senate's rejection of President Reagan's nomination of Judge Robert Bork? Did the dynamics of the confirmation process lead nominee Judge David Souter to agree, implicitly, that he would not seek a complete uprooting of *Roe*? Will the *Casey* opinion reduce the heat the abortion issue generates in subsequent confirmation hearings because future

---

1. In thinking about what constitutes an "undue burden," it may be helpful to remember that, if the justices who composed the *Casey* Court were asked whether the constitutional law of abortion rights should include an undue burden test, they would vote, 6–3, that it should not. That is, the undue burden standard is part of the law only in the sense that, so long as Justices Blackmun and Stevens sit (or are replaced by people with their views), if three other members of the Court can be convinced that an abortion regulation is an undue burden the regulation will be invalidated.

nominees will be able to say that *Casey* has now settled the status of abortion under the Constitution? Alternatively, is Justice Scalia correct that the Court's adherence to *Roe* legitimizes turning confirmation hearings into plebiscites on value judgments?

2. Petitioners filed their certiorari petition far in advance of its due date. What could they seek to gain by this strategy? Respondents filed their response to the petition for certiorari in less than their allotted time, thus further increasing the chance that the Court would hear and decide *Casey* before the 1992 elections. Why would they choose to do this? Can the Court appropriately consider the potential impact on an upcoming election in deciding whether to grant cert and when to schedule the case for argument? Do you think the result in *Casey* had an impact on the 1992 election? When all the *Casey* dust has settled, the result is an opinion that, just like the Court of Appeals opinion, applies an "undue burden" test and upholds all but one of the contested laws. Why, then, did the Court grant cert in the first place? If the *Casey* dissenters voted to grant cert, does that appear, in retrospect, to be a strategic miscalculation?

3. Footnote 11 of Justice Blackmun's opinion (omitted above) changed from its original form in U.S. Law Week, which publishes Supreme Court opinions immediately after they are announced. In Law Week, he referred to Chief Justice Rehnquist's opinion as a "plurality opinion." 60 Law Week 4825 n. 11 (6–30–92) ("Obviously, I do not share the plurality's views of homosexuality as sexual deviance.") By the time Blackmun's opinion was published in the Supreme Court Reporter, he referred to that opinion as "Chief Justice Rehnquist's." ___ U.S. at ___ n. 11; 112 S.Ct. at 2853 n. 11 (July 15, 1992 advance sheets) ("Obviously, I do not share The Chief Justice's views of homosexuality as sexual deviance.") What do these facts suggest about the likely evolution of the decision making process in this case? More generally, given what we know about the process of assigning, writing, and circulating opinions, to what extent do you suppose the joint opinion's discussions of *Roe*'s "central holding," the value of stare decisis, and the bases of the Court's legitimacy were the product of prolonged and careful discussions among all members of the Court?

4. Note the references in the joint opinion (at the outset of Part I) and in Justice Blackmun's opinion (in Part III) to the participation by the Solicitor General. What would explain the Solicitor General's appearance, both in filing a brief and in participating in oral argument, in such a case? Does this participation appear to have helped or hindered the Administration's cause? Note that the plurality opinion indicates that the Solicitor General had asked the Court, on five occasions, to overrule *Roe*. Does this suggest the Court was annoyed with the SG? That the SG's participation was counter-productive?

5. Given what we now know about the various justices' attitudes about the issues posed by *Casey,* what do you think would have been the elements of a truly effective amicus curiae brief (a) in support of the Pennsylvania statutes, (b) in opposition to those statutes? Would such a brief be concerned principally with arguing law or with presenting facts? In whose name(s) would it be submitted?

6. The joint opinion dwells at some length on the Court's legitimacy in the eyes of the public. To what extent does the Court, rightly or wrongly, gain public support because of the procedures it employs? Consider, for example, the role of oral argument, of expressing results through legal opinions, of conducting most of the Court's business in secret, of managing its own docket.

7. How do you think the *Casey* opinion(s) will affect legislators considering abortion laws? What effect is *Casey* likely to have on the chance that Congress will pass a Freedom of Choice Act?

Chapter Two

APPOINTING SUPREME
COURT JUSTICES

Supreme Court justices set their own agenda and do their own work. Consequently, the principal factor that affects the kind and quality of the Supreme Court's work is the character and ability of the justices themselves. This is an institution where the identity of its personnel clearly matters.

Article II, Section 2 of the United States Constitution provides that the President "shall nominate, and by and with the Advice and Consent of the Senate, shall appoint * * * Judges of the Supreme Court." [1] In addition to these constitutionally prescribed actors, the American Bar Association has also become involved in the process. Since 1956, the Standing Committee on the Judiciary of the ABA has taken upon itself the task of investigating and evaluating Supreme Court nominees put forth by the President.

From the first Supreme Court appointment by President Washington until the most recent appointments, the process of selecting Supreme Court justices has been the subject of intense discussion and debate. The materials that follow seek to reflect the main themes of these debates, particularly as they have occurred in the past decade. We divide the readings into four sections. Section A provides facts and data about the nomination and confirmation processes, establishing an historical overview of appointments to the Court. Section B contains passionate, and conflicting, analyses of the central questions of policy and theory that surround the appointment process: what standards should Presidents employ in nominating justices and what standards should the Senate use in acting on those nominations? Section C presents a series of recent case studies—the nominations of Judges Bork, Souter, Thomas,

---

1. U.S. Const. art. II, § 2.

and Ginsburg—through which the historical, policy, and theoretical issues can be examined concretely.[2] Finally, Section D reports several recent proposals to reform the appointment process.

Our experience has been that these rather lengthy materials can be read in either of two ways. Reading only Sections A, B, and D—while skipping, or reading only selected parts of, Section C which contains the four case studies—should suffice for the reader principally interested in a readably concise overview of the history of the nomination and confirmation processes, competing views about the respective roles that the Senate and the President should play, and suggestions for reforming the process. The four case studies in Section C will be of interest to those who wish to pursue these issues in greater depth, to apply our theoretical questions to real problems, or to study and think about the specific questions that dominated Senate consideration of the Bork, Souter, Thomas, and Ginsburg hearings.

---

2. It is our experience that analysis and discussion of the facts and issues raised in Sections A and B are best undertaken in the context of deliberating (or debating) the case studies set out in Section C.

HISTORICAL FIGURES

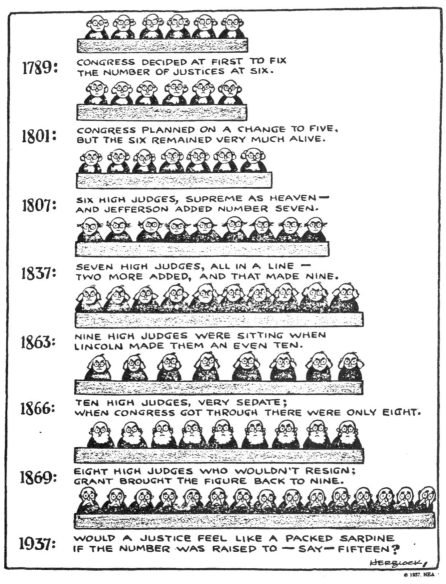

1789: CONGRESS DECIDED AT FIRST TO FIX THE NUMBER OF JUSTICES AT SIX.

1801: CONGRESS PLANNED ON A CHANGE TO FIVE, BUT THE SIX REMAINED VERY MUCH ALIVE.

1807: SIX HIGH JUDGES, SUPREME AS HEAVEN — AND JEFFERSON ADDED NUMBER SEVEN.

1837: SEVEN HIGH JUDGES, ALL IN A LINE — TWO MORE ADDED, AND THAT MADE NINE.

1863: NINE HIGH JUDGES WERE SITTING WHEN LINCOLN MADE THEM AN EVEN TEN.

1866: TEN HIGH JUDGES, VERY SEDATE; WHEN CONGRESS GOT THROUGH THERE WERE ONLY EIGHT.

1869: EIGHT HIGH JUDGES WHO WOULDN'T RESIGN; GRANT BROUGHT THE FIGURE BACK TO NINE.

1937: WOULD A JUSTICE FEEL LIKE A PACKED SARDINE IF THE NUMBER WAS RAISED TO — SAY — FIFTEEN?

HERBLOCK

© 1937, NEA

From *Herblock*: *A Cartoonist's Life* (Lisa Drew Books—MacMillan, 1993.) Reprinted by permission of Herblock Cartoons.

A. WHO GETS NOMINATED AND CONFIRMED?

We begin with an excerpt from an article by Professors Strauss and Sunstein that describes the history of the constitutional convention's adoption of the appointment process as we now know it. Thereafter, Professor Freund's article neatly summarizes the significant events in the history of presidential nominations and congressional confirmations for Supreme Court justices. He describes both landmark confirmation battles and noteworthy changes in the public process over the past two centuries. A short excerpt by Professor Abraham describes the role of the American Bar Association in the process.

Following these are two articles by Professor Halper that probe more deeply and systematically into what history tells us usually occurs in the nomination and confirmation processes. In "Supreme Court Appointments: Criteria and Consequences," Halper looks at the empirical data in order both to explode some myths about what factors tend to underlie presidential choices of Supreme Court nominees and to explain some factors that surely, if not overtly, have affected presidential choices. Similarly, in "Senate Rejection of Supreme Court Nominees," Halper not only provides basic data on the frequency of Senate rejections but argues strongly that we have wrongly focussed on the rejected nominees' backgrounds and qualifications in seeking explanations for those rejections that occur. Both articles were written before the flurry of nominations and confirmation controversies during the Reagan and Bush administrations. Halper's analysis appears, nevertheless, to explain very well what was occurring during this period and so gives us more confidence in his conclusions.[3]

While these materials serve principally as background for subsequent analysis, they also raise several questions on their own. Why has each nominee to the Court been a lawyer? Prior political involvement and previous judicial experience are frequently traits of successful nominees; do these facts reflect important qualifications for the job or do they serve as surrogates for other values (such as predictability or centrism) that Presidents and Senators usually seek? A substantial majority of Supreme Court justices has been drawn from a very narrow segment of American society. Does or should this affect our judgment about the Court's proper roles and its ability to perform them?

DAVID STRAUSS [†] AND CASS SUNSTEIN, [††] THE SENATE, THE CONSTITUTION AND THE CONFIRMATION PROCESS [*]
101 Yale L.J. 1491, 1494–1502 (1992)

* * *

I. THE CONSTITUTION

The Constitution fully contemplates an independent role for the Senate in the selection of Supreme Court Justices. Article II, Section 2 provides that the President "shall nominate, and by and with the Advice

---

3. H. Abraham, *Justices and Presidents* 39–70 (3d ed. 1992) covers the issues Halper raises, but in a more personalized and anecdotal fashion. For details on the people involved in controversial nominations and on those justices who do and do not exhibit characteristics usually associated with Supreme Court nominees, this book is an excellent source.

† Professor of Law, University of Chicago Law School. Strauss served as Special Counsel to the United States Senate Committee on the Judiciary in connection with the nomination of Justice David H. Souter to the Supreme Court. * * *

†† Karl N. Llewellyn Professor of Jurisprudence, University of Chicago, Law School and Department of Political Science.

* Reprinted by permission of The Yale Law Journal Company and Fred B. Rothman & Company from *The Yale Law Journal*, Vol. 101, pp. 1491–1524.

and Consent of the Senate, shall appoint * * * Judges of the supreme Court." These words assign two distinct roles to the Senate—an advisory role before the nomination has occurred and a reviewing function after the fact. The consent requirement, if the Senate takes it seriously, places pressure on the President to give weight to senatorial advice as well. At the same time, the advisory function makes consent more likely. The clause thus envisions a genuinely consultative relationship between the Senate and the President. It assumes a deliberative process, jointly conducted, concerning the composition of the Court.

History supports this view of the text. The most explicit and elaborate contemporaneous exposition was given by George Mason in 1792. Mason wrote:

> I am decidedly of opinion, that the Words of the Constitution * * * give the Senate the Power of interfering in every part of the Subject, except the Right of nominating * * *. The Word *"Advice"* here clearly relates in the Judgment of the Senate on the Expediency or Inexpediency of the Measure, or Appointment; and the Word *"Consent"* to their Approbation or Disapprobation of the Person nominated; otherwise the word *Advice* has no Meaning at all—and it is a well known Rule of Construction, that no Clause or Expression shall be deemed superfluous, or nugatory, which is capable of a fair and rational Meaning. The Nomination, of Course, brings the Subject fully under the Consideration of the Senate; who have then a Right to decide upon its Propriety or Impropriety. The peculiar Character or Predicament of the Senate in the Constitution of the General Government, is a strong Confirmation of this Construction.

As the records of the Constitutional Convention demonstrate, the Constitution's drafters widely shared Mason's view. The Convention had four basic options of where to vest the appointment power: it could have placed the power (1) in the President alone, (2) in Congress alone, (3) in the President with congressional advice and consent, or (4) in Congress with Presidential advice and consent. Some version of each of these options received serious consideration.

The ultimate decision to vest the appointment power in the President stemmed from a belief that he was uniquely capable of providing the requisite "responsibility." A single person would be distinctly accountable for his acts. At the same time, however, the Framers greatly feared a Presidential monopoly of the process. They worried that such a monopoly might lead to a lack of qualified and "diffused" appointees, and to patronage and corruption. The Framers also feared insufficient attentiveness to the interests of different groups affected by the Court.

An important feature of the debates was the Framers' effort to design the appointments process in a way that would protect the interests of the small states. In thinking about the appointment of Supreme Court Justices, the Framers thus focused on the likelihood that nominees would be attentive to the various interests affected by the

Court. Conflicts between large and small states, a principal political question of the founding period, present a much less important issue today. But there are now other conflicting interests that are profoundly affected by the composition of the Supreme Court. The Framers contemplated a senatorial role precisely to protect such interests, and to assure a degree of political oversight of the likely votes of Supreme Court nominees. The central importance of this political concern to the selection process, as that process was originally designed, strongly argues against a Presidential monopoly today.

The compromise that finally emerged—the system of advice and consent—was designed to counteract all of these various fears. Throughout the Convention, representatives of the smaller states were especially skeptical of a large Presidential role and insistent on the need for the safeguards that the Senate could provide. Representatives of the larger states, concerned with congressional partiality and lack of responsibility, sought to constrain the Senate. The requirement of senatorial advice and consent simultaneously responded to both sets of concerns.

A. The Early Agreement on Congressional Appointment

It is important to understand that during almost all of the Convention, the Framers agreed that the Senate alone or the legislature as a whole would appoint the judges. The current institutional arrangement emerged in the last days of the process. On June 5, 1787, the standing provision required "that the national Judiciary be [chosen] by the National Legislature." James Wilson spoke against this provision and in favor of Presidential appointment. He claimed that "intrigue, partiality, and concealment" would result from legislative appointment, and that the President was uniquely "responsible." John Rutledge responded that he "was by no means disposed to grant so great a power to any single person. The people will think we are leaning too much towards Monarchy."

James Madison agreed with Wilson's concerns about legislative "intrigue and partiality," but he "was not satisfied with referring the appointment to the Executive." Instead, he proposed to place the power of appointment in the Senate, "as numerous eno' to be confided in—as not so numerous as to be governed by the motives of the other branch; and as being sufficiently stable and independent to follow their deliberative judgments." Thus, on June 5, by a vote of nine to two, the Convention accepted the vesting of the appointment power in the Senate.

On June 13, Charles Cotesworth Pinckney and Roger Sherman tried to restore the original provision for appointment of the Supreme Court by the entire Congress. Madison renewed his argument and the motion was withdrawn.

The issue reemerged on July 18. Nathaniel Ghorum claimed that even the Senate was "too numerous, and too little personally responsible, to ensure a good choice." He suggested, for the first time, that the President should appoint the Justices, with the advice and consent of the

Senate—following the model set by Massachusetts. Wilson responded that the President should be able to make appointments on his own, but that the Ghorum proposals were an acceptable second best. Alexander Martin and Sherman endorsed appointments by the Senate, arguing that the Senate would have greater information and—a point of special relevance here—that "the Judges ought to be diffused," something that "would be more likely to be attended to by the 2d. branch, than by the Executive." Edmund Randolph echoed this view.

In the end, Wilson's proposal that the President alone make appointments was rejected by a vote of six to two. At that point, Ghorum moved, as an alternative, that the President should nominate and appoint judges with the advice and consent of the Senate. On this the vote was evenly divided, four to four.

Madison then proposed Presidential nomination with an opportunity for Senate rejection, by a two-thirds vote, within a specified number of days. Changing his earlier position, Madison urged that the executive would be more likely "to select fit characters," and that "in case of any flagrant partiality or error, in the nomination, it might be fairly presumed that ⅔ of the 2d. branch would join in putting a negative on it." Pinckney spoke against this proposal, as did George Mason, who argued: "[A]ppointment by the Executive [is] a dangerous prerogative. It might even give him an influence over the Judiciary department itself."

The motion was defeated by six to three. By the same vote, the earlier Madison proposal, in which the Senate would appoint the Justices, was accepted.

The issue next arose on August 23. Robert Morris argued against the appointment of officers by the Senate, considering "the body as too numerous for the purpose; as subject to cabal; and as devoid of responsibility." But it was not until September 4 that the provision appeared in its current form. Morris made the only recorded pronouncements on the new arrangement and seemed to speak for the entire, now unanimous assembly. Morris said, "[A]s the President was to nominate, there would be responsibility, and as the Senate was to concur, there would be security." Great weight should be given to the remarks made by Morris because of their timing. The Convention accepted the provision with this understanding.

B. The Meaning of the Shift to Presidential Appointment With Advice and Consent by the Senate

This picture leaves something of a puzzle. For almost all of the Convention, the appointment power was vested in the Senate. At the last moment, it was shifted to the President, with the advice and consent of the Senate. What accounts for the shift?

We speculate that two developments played an important role. First, on July 16, 1787, the Convention approved the Great Compromise, allowing equal representation for the states within the Senate despite their differences in population. This additional security for the small states may have provided those states with a degree of reassurance that made a Presidential initiative in the appointments process significantly less threatening. That reassurance, going to the structure of the document, may have made it less necessary to insist on limiting the President's role in appointments.

Second, the assessment of Presidential powers appears to have changed in a major way when the Founders devised the Electoral College, thereby allowing a degree of representation of states qua states in the selection of the President. As we have seen, much of the resistance to Presidential power came from the small states, which feared that the President would be inattentive to their interests. Once it was decided that the President would be selected through the new, protective route, the small states had a new degree of security against the obvious risks, from their point of view, of pure majoritarianism. They therefore would have found it less threatening to vest the power of appointment in the President in the first instance. The Framers could accomplish the central goal of ensuring "responsibility" without undue risk to state interests.

But there is no evidence of a general agreement that the President should have plenary power over the appointments process. On the contrary, the ultimate design mandated a role for the Senate in the form of the advice and consent function. In this way, it carried forward the major themes of the debates. With respect to the need for a Presidential role, the new system ensured "responsibility" and guarded against the risk of partiality in the Senate. With respect to resistance to absolute Presidential prerogative, the principal concerns included (1) a fear of "monarchy" in the form of exclusive Presidential appointment; (2) a concern for "deliberative judgments"; (3) a belief that "the Judges ought to be diffused," that is, diverse in terms of their basic commitments and alliances; (4) a fear of executive "influence over the Judiciary department itself"; and (5) a desire for the "security" that a senatorial role would provide.

As Mason's comments suggest, the Senate's role was to be a major one, allowing the Senate to be as intrusive as it chose. Even Hamilton, perhaps the strongest defender of Presidential power, emphasized that the President "was bound to submit the propriety of his choice to the discussion and determination of a different and independent body." Of course, the President retained the power to continue to offer nominees of his selection, even after an initial rejection. He could continue to name people at his discretion. Crucially, however, the Senate was granted the authority to continue to refuse to confirm. It also received the authority to "advise."

These simultaneous powers would bring about a healthy form of checks and balances, permitting each branch to counter the other. That system was part and parcel of general deliberation about Supreme Court membership. The Convention debates afford no basis for the view that the Senate's role was designed to be meager. On the contrary, they suggest a fully shared authority over the composition of the Court. That shared authority was to include all matters that the Senate deemed relevant, including the nominee's point of view.

As we have noted, this argument derives particular force from the centrality of the question of states' interests to the debate over the appointments process. The split between the large and small states was among the most important political issues of the period. Some delegates were fearful that all judicial nominees would come from large states. More generally, state rivalry, dominating the debates over the appointments clause, was the functional equivalent of the most sharply disputed of current legal and political debates. There can be no question that the "advice and consent" role was intended to provide, in Morris' terms, "security." And there can be no question that a central aspect of "security" was the power to refuse to confirm nominees insensitive to the interests of a majority of the states. In this sense, political commitments were understood to be a properly central ingredient in senatorial deliberations.

C. The Early Practice

The practice of the Senate in the early days of the republic and thereafter attests to the same conclusion. George Washington's nomination of John Rutledge, then Chief Justice of South Carolina, as Chief Justice of the United States is the most revealing case in point. Rutledge's challenge to the Jay Treaty, negotiated by Washington with Great Britain, played a pivotal role in the confirmation process. The Jay Treaty was challenged by the Republicans as a concession to Britain but approved by the Federalists as a way of keeping the peace. Rutledge attacked the treaty in a prominent speech in Charleston. The Federalists sought to block the Rutledge appointment on straightforwardly political grounds. Hamilton, a leader of the support for the Jay Treaty, led the opposition to Rutledge. The Senate ultimately rejected Rutledge for political reasons, by a vote of fourteen to ten.

Nor was the Rutledge rejection unique. In 1811, the Senate rejected Madison's appointment of Alexander Wolcott, partly on the basis of political considerations. In 1826, President Adams' appointment of Robert Trimble was nearly rejected on political grounds. The 1828 nomination of John Crittenden, a Whig, was ultimately prevented through postponement, and squarely on ideological grounds. Similar episodes occurred in the first half of the nineteenth century. In fact, during the nineteenth century, the Senate blocked one of every four nominees for the Court, frequently on political grounds.

The Senate has at times insisted on the "advice" segment of its constitutional mandate. In 1869, President Grant nominated Edwin Stanton after receiving a petition to that effect signed by a majority of the Senate and the House. In 1932, the Chair of the Judiciary Committee, George W. Norris, insisted on the appointment of a liberal Justice to replace Oliver Wendell Holmes. Greatly influenced by a meeting with Senator William Borah, President Hoover eventually appointed Benjamin Cardozo to the Court. The Senator persuaded President Hoover to move Cardozo, then at the bottom of the President's list of preferred nominees, to the top.

D. The Constitutional Structure

We have established that the constitutional text and history support an independent role for the Senate in the confirmation process. In the particular context of judicial appointments, there is an additional and highly compelling concern, one that stems from constitutional structure. It may be granted that the Senate ought generally to be deferential to Presidential nominations involving the operation of the executive branch. For the most part, executive branch nominees must work closely with or under the President. The President is entitled to insist that those nominees are people with whom he is comfortable, both personally and in terms of basic commitments and values.

The case is quite different, however, when the President is appointing members of a third branch. The judiciary is supposed to be independent of the President, not allied with him. It hardly needs emphasis that the judiciary is not intended to work under the President. This point is of special importance in light of the fact that many of the Court's decisions resolve conflicts between Congress and the President. A Presidential monopoly on the appointment of Supreme Court Justices thus threatens to unsettle the constitutional plan of checks and balances.

Constitutional text, history, and structure strongly suggest that the Senate is entitled to assume a far more substantial role than it has in the recent past. There are analogies to proposed legislation and treaties, and to the Presidential veto. No one thinks that the Senate must accept whatever bill or treaty the President suggests simply because it is a "competent" proposal; it would be odd indeed to claim that the President must sign every bill before looking closely at the merits. Under the Constitution, the role of the Senate in the confirmation process should be approached similarly.

* * *

PAUL A. FREUND,* APPOINTMENT OF JUSTICES: SOME HISTORICAL PERSPECTIVES **
101 Harv.L.Rev. 1146, 1146–1162 (1988)

The recent proceedings on three successive nominations to the Supreme Court raise anew recurring questions about the role and process of senatorial advice and consent. The questions, which are intertwined, relate to the standards and criteria to be applied and to the means whereby the Senate should inform itself in order to fulfill its role. This brief essay will address the two issues in order. The recent episodes will emerge as a convergence of two twentieth-century currents:

* Carl M. Loeb University Professor Emeritus, Harvard Law School.

toward a broader conception of a nominee's essential qualifications, and toward a wider participation, within and without the Senate, in the process of judging those qualifications. Though focus on the nominee's character remains paramount, the other dominant factors have shifted from sectional and party affiliations to social and judicial philosophy, and the normal procedure has changed from secret Senate hearings and debates to an intensive public inquiry into those broadened criteria.
* * *

I.

* * *

To appreciate the appointing process in its first century one must keep in mind both the nature of the Court's business in that period and the corresponding nature of the political system. Whereas the Framers contemplated "one Supreme Court" and a governmental structure safe-guarded against partisan factions, events very early overcame these assumptions. The bulk of the Justices' business consisted of individual circuit duties, and the rise of organized parties produced intense demands, in Congress and in the press, for partisan loyalty. The identification of a seat with a particular circuit led to a controlling influence of the senators from that region in the confirmation process. Thus parochialism combined with partisanship to shape appointments to the Court.

The system, however flawed, did produce, however fortuitously, some outstanding Justices. The appointment of Joseph Story is illustrative. On the death in 1810 of Justice William Cushing of Massachusetts, President Madison looked to New England for a successor. Two of his nominees, Levi Lincoln and John Quincy Adams, both of Massachusetts, declined after being confirmed. Alexander Wolcott, of Connecticut, was rejected, although Madison's party controlled the Senate, because the New England Federalists were offended by Wolcott's strict enforcement, as United States Attorney, of the highly unpopular Embargo and Non–Intercourse Acts, and because even Madison's party was unenthusiastic about the nomination. Story, the fourth nominee, aged thirty-two, nominally of Madison's Democratic–Republic party in Massachusetts, was nominated and confirmed despite Thomas Jefferson's warning, abundantly vindicated during a long and powerful tenure, that he was at heart a Federalist, a "pseudo-Republican." * * *

Factional divisions of another kind, this time intraparty divisions, bedeviled President Tyler's repeated attempts in 1843 and 1844 to fill two vacancies on the Court, those left by the deaths of Justices Smith Thompson of New York and Henry Baldwin of Pennsylvania. To fill the Thompson vacancy Tyler looked to New York and, in December 1843, nominated John C. Spencer, a scholarly lawyer who had served as Secretary of War and then as Secretary of the Treasury. It was a time when a charismatic party leader could wield great power; unfortunately for Spencer he encountered both the opposition of the New York Whigs and the enmity of Henry Clay, who clearly dominated the party against a politically weak President. After the Senate's rejection of Spencer, Tyler nominated Chancellor Reuben Walworth of New York, who also ran afoul of the state political machine, and whose nomination was withdrawn after the Senate postponed action on it. A third effort succeeded. Following the defeat of the Whigs in the election of 1844, Tyler submitted the name of his third choice, Samuel Nelson, chief justice of the New York Supreme Court, who was promptly confirmed.

Meanwhile the Baldwin vacancy had arisen, and Tyler looked to Pennsylvania. His weakness within his own Whig party proved insurmountable. Two successive nominations failed: that of Edward King, a judge in Philadelphia, was tabled until the election and then withdrawn; on that of John M. Read of Philadelphia, a former United States Attorney, no action was taken. Not until twenty-eight months after Baldwin's death, and after a new election, was the vacancy filled, when President Polk's nomination of Robert M. Grier of the Pittsburgh area was speedily confirmed.

In the absence of open hearings and debates in the Senate on nominations, appraisals of nominees were furnished by a politically polarized press and by intimate correspondence among influential figures in legal and political circles. The range and worth of the latter can be epitomized by two assessments of John Read. Richard Peters, the former Reporter of the Supreme Court and a faithful Whig, wrote to Justice McLean that Read was "as suited for a Judge as I am for an admiral." James Buchanan, welcoming the ascendancy of the Democrats, wrote that there were few, if any, lawyers in Philadelphia superior to Read, and that "[h]e holds a ready and powerful political pen and is a gentleman of the strictest honour and integrity."

The appointment of a Chief Justice, though less constrained by local politics, could nevertheless conform to what Justice Frankfurter called "that odd lottery by which men get picked for the Supreme Court." In the case of President Grant's multiple efforts to fill the vacancy caused by the death in 1873 of Chief Justice Salmon P. Chase, parochialism was replaced by ineptitude. After Roscoe Conkling of New York, seemingly intent on still higher office, declined the nomination, Grant nominated his Attorney General, George H. Williams of Oregon. The nomination drew fire from several sides on the basis of incompetence and lack of character. Williams was linked to the abrupt removal of a United States Attorney in Oregon who was investigating political frauds in that state. The final stroke was the discovery that Williams had purchased with public funds a landaulet, complete with a footman, and two horses for the use of himself and his wife (herself a focus of disapproval in Washington)—perquisites not enjoyed by senators. Facing rejection, the nominee asked that his name be withdrawn.

Grant's next choice was an eccentric one. He nominated Caleb Cushing of Massachusetts, seventy-four years old, an able lawyer with a history of shifting political allegiances. It appears that the nomination was based on a strange sense of protocol. In England, Sir Roundell

Palmer, chief British counsel in the *Alabama* claims arbitration at Geneva, had recently been created Lord Chancellor Selborne. Symmetry suggested that Cushing, who was the senior American counsel at Geneva, be similarly honored, if only for a short tenure. The Judiciary Committee reported the nomination favorably, though without enthusiasm. A revelation from the Civil War files of the War Department, however, brought the appointment to a sudden halt. In 1861 Cushing had written a letter, in a friendly vein, to President Jefferson Davis of the Confederacy, recommending a former clerk in the Attorney General's office for a suitable position, citing the young man's allegiance to the Confederate cause. Grant was appalled when the letter was shown to him and promptly recalled the nomination, removing an injunction of secrecy applicable to the letter.

The fixation on international symmetry, however, was not removed. Morrison R. Waite, a practicing lawyer in Cleveland, had been the third in rank of our counsel at Geneva, serving with Cushing and William M. Evarts, and he became Grant's third nominee for the center seat on the Court. Although Waite was little known outside Ohio, the Senate, with a sense of relief, readily confirmed him. Judge Ebenezer Rockwood Hoar remarked that Waite was the luckiest individual known to the law, an innocent third party without notice. As it turned out, the lucky ones were the Court and the country.

The circuit-riding duties of the Justices, which had been ameliorated, were finally eliminated by the Circuit Court of Appeals Act of 1891. That legislation did not abruptly end the tendency to make an appointment from the state or circuit of the retiring judge. The most pronounced example of this practice was the so-called New England seat on the Court, a succession broken only in 1932 with the justly acclaimed appointment by President Hoover of Chief Judge Benjamin N. Cardozo of New York to succeed Justice Holmes.   * * *

From 1894 to 1930 there were no further rejections, but the focus of concern in the Senate underwent a marked shift, coincident with the Court's increased activity in judging the merits of social and economic legislation under the due process clauses of the fifth, and especially the fourteenth, amendments. The turning point was President Wilson's nomination, in late January, 1916, of Louis D. Brandeis of Boston. He was one of the very few nominees to the Court who had held no public office, but he was a nationally-known public figure because of his challenges to such established practices and institutions as bankers' control of big business, interlocking corporate directorships, the New Haven railroad management, abuses in industrial life insurance, and inefficient corporate consolidations. In courts, in print, and in legislative hearings, he had championed savings bank life insurance, cooperatives, minimum-wage and maximum-hour laws, collective bargaining, and the responsibility of labor unions. He regarded himself as a conservative, in the sense of Macaulay's dictum that to reform is to preserve, but he was perceived in the upper reaches of Boston's financial and business community as a dangerous radical.

The opposition couched its attack in terms of questionable character and lack of judicial temperament, and occasionally anti-Semitism became overt, but essentially the campaign against the nominee rested on the repugnance of his social and economic views. Writing in *The New Republic,* Walter Lippmann put it concisely: Brandeis was deemed untrustworthy only by "the powerful but limited community which dominated the business and social life of Boston. He was untrustworthy because he was troublesome." Lippmann was responding to a petition opposing the nomination circulated by President A. Lawrence Lowell of Harvard, signed by fifty-five prominent Bostonians. Notably missing among the signatures was that of President Emeritus Charles W. Eliot, Boston's (and perhaps the nation's) first citizen, who wrote a deeply-felt, appreciative letter highly praising the nomination. On a lower level, of the eleven Harvard Law School professors, nine signed an endorsement, with one dissenting and one not voting. Labor unions signified their support. Opposed was the president of the American Bar Association, Elihu Root, joined by six of the sixteen living ex-presidents of the association, including William Howard Taft.

Four agitated months elapsed between the nomination and ultimate confirmation. Both sides mounted organized campaigns. During this period Brandeis himself made no public statement, but he was energetic in fortifying his lieutenants with suggestions and detailed documentation for their use. His law partner, Edward F. McClennen, took up residence in Washington, where he kept in touch with Attorney General Thomas Gregory, and was assisted at a distance, and through occasional conferences, by George W. Anderson, United States Attorney in Boston, Professor Felix Frankfurter, Norman Hapgood, editor of *Harper's Weekly,* and others. Briefs and counterbriefs, petitions, memoranda, and letters poured forth from both sides to the Judiciary Committee, the President, and the weekly and daily press. The hearings before a subcommittee, which were open to the public at the behest of Attorney General Gregory, produced two thousand printed pages.

The outcome was anticlimactic. The full committee voted favorably on strict party lines, ten to eight, and the Senate confirmed on June 1, 1916, by a vote of forty-seven to twenty-two, with only one Democrat breaking ranks. The successful outcome owed much to President Wilson, whose resolute support rested on close personal association with Brandeis, an unofficial adviser in the early years of the administration. "I can never live up to my Brandeis appointment," the President later remarked to Hapgood. Anticlimactic though the final result may have been, the whole episode was indeed a watershed; in the nature of the nominee, in the underlying conflict of forces, in the organized campaigning, and in the breadth of participation at the confirmation stage, it foreshadowed the shape of future appointment battles.

Economic interests, close to the surface in the controversy over Brandeis, emerged undisguised when President Hoover nominated Charles Evans Hughes to succeed Chief Justice Taft in 1930. This time roles were reversed. The opposition was led by Progressives and some

Democrats, who, viewing the nominee's representation of utilities and other major corporations, perceived him as a menacing reactionary. The critics identified the arguments advanced on behalf of private clients as the judicial philosophy of the counsel, giving too little weight to Hughes' record as an Associate Justice from 1910 to 1916. To paraphrase Professor Zechariah Chafee, it is better to judge a nominee by the books in his library at home than by a list of clients in his office. At least it proved so in the case of Hughes. Confirmed by a vote of fifty-two to twenty-six, on the Court he found occasion to reject many of the controverted positions he had taken at the bar.

* * *

One vacant seat remained to be filled by President Hoover, owing to the death of Justice Edward T. Sanford of Tennessee. Within a few weeks of Hughes' confirmation the President submitted the name of Judge John J. Parker of North Carolina, a member of the Fourth Circuit Court of Appeals. In the Senate, the Progressives and liberal Democrats, sensing the strength they had displayed in the contest over Hughes, determined to wage an intensive attack on what they perceived to be the Republicans' "southern strategy."

The aftershock of the Hughes debates proved to be more severe than those earlier tremors. Although the immediate reaction to the nomination among labor spokesmen and blacks in North Carolina was favorable, national leaders of those groups soon mounted an assault. The principal witnesses in the opposition were William Green, president of the American Federation of Labor, and Walter White, acting executive secretary of the National Association for the Advancement of Colored People. Labor opposed Parker because of an opinion he wrote upholding a "yellow dog" contract as the basis for enjoining a strike for union recognition; the latter group found offensive a political speech by Parker in his unsuccessful gubernatorial bid in 1920—a speech in which, to rebut charges that he was a Negro sympathizer, he asserted that Negroes did not want the suffrage and Republicans did not want them to vote. After extensive debate the Senate rejected the nomination, forty-one to thirty-nine, with the opposition composed of an odd coalition of Progressives, liberal Democrats, and southern Democrats representing states with a substantial black voting population. The vacancy thus left was filled by the nomination of Owen J. Roberts of Philadelphia and his unanimous immediate approval by the Senate. In one of the ironies of history, Judge Parker later showed himself to be more supportive of New Deal measures than was Justice Roberts. In response to a remark suggesting this comparison, Justice Black observed that "John Parker was a better judge after the hearing than before it."

A third vacancy in the Hoover administration arose with the retirement of Justice Holmes in January 1932, but the process of filling it was substantially less political than that for the first two vacancies. Despite his misgivings about placing a third New Yorker on the Court (to join Hughes and Stone), the President was persuaded to nominate Judge

Cardozo, who was unanimously approved. It was probably the most popular act of the administration (though this may be faint praise), and it suggests that one of the most politically advantageous decisions that a weakened President can take is to appoint to the Supreme Court a universally respected jurist.

The next significant confirmation battles occurred in the 1960's. President Johnson's attempt in the summer of 1968 to elevate Justice Fortas to the Chief Justiceship failed through a combination of circumstances, political and personal. The President's own power was ebbing as an election approached; there was a growing sentiment that the course of the Court under Chief Justice Warren should be altered; there was uneasiness about Fortas' advisory relationship with the President, which included support of his military policy in Vietnam; and there was disquiet about the Justice's acceptance of funds furnished by former clients. Finally, some members of the Senate were offended when, after the conclusion of four days of questioning by the Judiciary Committee, Fortas declined an invitation to testify further about outside activities. Although the committee approved the nomination by a vote of eleven to six, senators mounted a filibuster and a motion for cloture failed to gain the necessary two-thirds vote; Fortas eventually requested withdrawal of the nomination. Shortly thereafter he resigned as Associate Justice.

A backlash from the Fortas episode appeared to be responsible for the rejection of Judge Clement Haynsworth, Jr., of the Fourth Circuit Court of Appeals, President Nixon's nominee in 1969 to succeed Justice Fortas. The Judiciary Committee hearings revealed that Haynsworth had ruled on cases involving corporations in which he had a minor shareholder's interest. Although the conflict of interest might otherwise have seemed inconsequential, and although the American Bar Association committee endorsed Haynsworth, the situation aroused a sauce-for-the-goose sentiment, and the nomination was defeated, fifty-five to forty-five.

President Nixon's second nominee, Judge G. Harrold Carswell of the Fifth Circuit Court of Appeals, drew a torrent of opposition. Although he also received approval from the American Bar Association committee, Carswell met with vehement and widespread disapproval, not least in the academic community, because of the nominee's apparent racial bias and, more generally, his want of professional stature. The nomination was defeated fifty-one to forty-five.

The vacancy on the Supreme Court was finally filled by the appointment of Judge Harry Blackmun of the Eighth Circuit Court of Appeals, whose nomination was promptly and unanimously approved by the Judiciary Committee and the Senate. Any geographic imperative was clearly laid to rest as Justice Blackmun joined his fellow Minnesotan, Chief Justice Burger, on the Court. Any inference that a conservative Southerner could not be confirmed was subsequently negated in 1971 by President Nixon's acclaimed appointment of Lewis F. Powell, Jr., of Virginia, whose enlightened position on civil rights had been quietly effective, and who was warmly and unanimously approved by the Judiciary Committee and confirmed by the Senate with only one negative vote.

As a cautionary note in appraising the appointment process, it should be pointed out that significant issues may be unforeseen. While, for example, issues of economic due process and federal-state powers dominated the confirmation debates on Hughes, his replacement of Taft in fact ushered in a period of marked invigoration of the guarantees of civil liberties and civil rights, providing a foundation for future advances in these areas. Moreover, even if the issues remain constant, a nominee's subsequent views may on occasion turn an appointment into a presidential disappointment, as when Justice Holmes failed to support President Theodore Roosevelt's antitrust program, when Justice Stone, formerly President Coolidge's Attorney General, became an ally of Justices Holmes and Brandeis, or when Justice Clark joined in overturning President Truman's takeover of the steel mills during the Korean War. Contingency, which has had a conspicuous role in the process of appointment, is not eliminated once an appointment is made.

II.

The history of unsuccessful nominations has suggested that, although politics in the partisan sense has never ceased to be a factor, it has been increasingly outweighed by politics in the larger, Aristotelian sense—a perception that an individual's identity is conditioned by his or her associations, inclinations, and sympathies, concomitant with a heightened awareness of the Supreme Court's role in the social, economic, and political life of the nation. This broadened conception of the appropriate standards for appointment to the Supreme Court has been accompanied, as was said at the outset, by more openness and wider participation in the appointment process itself. Every schoolchild knows that the Senate met in closed session through the years 1789–93. What is less familiar is the fact that thereafter, when the Senate met to act upon nominations of all types, it normally sat in closed executive session until 1929, and that the practice of calling on a nominee for the Supreme Court to appear before the Judiciary Committee did not begin until 1939.

Until 1929 the practice was to consider all nominations in closed executive session unless the Senate, by a two-thirds vote taken in closed session, ordered the debate to be open. Objections to closed sessions were repeatedly raised by Senators, but to no avail, save that in isolated instances, as in the nomination of Brandeis in 1916 and that of Stone in 1925, the shield of secrecy was removed by a vote of the requisite majority.

* * *

A separate and troublesome question arises over calling the nominee before the Judiciary Committee or a subcommittee. It was not until the nomination of Felix Frankfurter in 1939 that the practice began of questioning a nominee to the Court.[54] The bitterly contested nominations of Brandeis, Hughes, and Parker were all debated and resolved without an appearance by the nominee. Brandeis, to be sure, did meet with two doubtful Senators at an informal dinner in Washington at the home of Norman Hapgood. Judge Parker replied to charges against him by letters and telegrams after an adverse report by the Judiciary Committee, but the Committee had rejected a motion to permit him to make an appearance.

Professor Frankfurter was urged by Steve Early, presidential assistant at the White House, to appear before the Committee, and a few days before the hearings he received a telegram from Senator Neely of West Virginia, chairman of the subcommittee, inviting him to "be present, at your pleasure, either in person or by counsel." Frankfurter told Early that his teaching duties had priority, and replied to Neely that he had "no wish to make any statement in support of my own nomination," adding that he had asked Dean Acheson "to put himself at the disposal of your Committee." When these responses were made public, Frankfurter received a telegram from his sagacious old friend C.C. Burlingham of the New York bar, advising with characteristic pungency that the declination should rest on the availability of the nominee's public record and that the reference to law school duties was "feeble." Acheson did attend the first day of hearings to "hold a watching brief." That day produced a series of adverse witnesses close to the outer edge of reality. When the hearings resumed two days later Frankfurter himself was present, accompanied by Acheson. He read the following opening statement:

> I am very glad to accede to this committee's desire to have me appear before it. I, of course, do not wish to testify in support of my own nomination. Except only in one instance, involving a charge against a nominee concerning his official act as Attorney General, the entire history of this committee and of the Court does not disclose that a nominee to the Supreme Court has appeared and testified before the Judiciary Committee. While I believe that a nominee's record should be thoroughly scrutinized by this committee, I hope you will not think it presumptuous on my part to suggest that neither such examination nor the best interests of the Supreme Court will be helped by the personal participation of the nominee himself. I should think it improper for a nominee no less than for a member of the Court to express his personal views on controversial political issues affecting the Court. My attitude and outlook on relevant matters have been fully expressed over a period of years

54. There was one exception to the old practice. In 1925, the Committee allowed Harlan F. Stone to appear in order to explain his conduct as Attorney General in declining to dismiss an indictment, believed to have been politically inspired, brought by his predecessor against Senator Burton Wheeler of Montana. The questioning was limited to that issue, and Stone evidently emerged with his position strengthened. In a letter to a friend he wrote, "I did not foresee that they would deliver themselves into my hands quite so completely." A. Mason, Harlan Fiske Stone: Pillar of the Law 197 (1956).

and are easily accessible. I should think it not only bad taste but inconsistent with the duties of the office for which I have been nominated for me to attempt to supplement my past record by present declarations.

That is all I have to say.

Questioning followed, some of it manifestly hostile, revolving around charges, most of which had been aired by witnesses on the first day, that sought to link Frankfurter to the Communist Party through the Sacco–Vanzetti case, his friendship with Professor Harold Laski, the British Labor Party publicist, and especially his membership on a national committee of the American Civil Liberties Union. * * * Pressed continually to state his own views on Communism, Frankfurter gave a ringing statement of his profound attachment to the principles of the American Constitution, which were antithetical to the tenets of Communism as he understood them. This passionate expression met with prolonged applause from the spectators. The nomination was unanimously approved by the Committee and the Senate. Subsequently Frankfurter recalled the experience: "I thought that it would be just a little room where we'd sit around. I found that this was Madison Square Garden." He then added, * * * "In fact, I took charge. It was the only thing to do."

* * *

Ten years after Frankfurter's precedent-breaking appearance, his misgivings were echoed by Judge Sherman Minton of the Seventh Circuit Court of Appeals, nominated to the Court by President Truman in 1949, who respectfully declined the Judiciary Committee's invitation to appear for questioning. His letter referred to Frankfurter's statement, spoke of "serious questions of propriety," and pointed to his public record as a senator and judge. His prior service as a senator from Indiana brought into play senatorial courtesy, which may have averted a more disruptive conflict over his position. As it was, several Republicans, unhappy over President Truman's fourth appointment of a Democrat to the Court, voiced strong criticism of Minton's stand and of the too-relaxed questioning of previous nominees. Minton's nomination, acceptable to the two Republican members from his state, was endorsed by a nine-to-two vote of the Judiciary Committee; a motion to recommit lost, forty-five to twenty-one. Finally the nomination was confirmed by the Senate, forty-eight to sixteen.

Thus there was a sea-change in the practice of the Senate in less than twenty years after the nomination of Judge Parker in 1930. Parker desired to testify and was refused; Minton was asked to testify and only reluctantly was his refusal accepted. Subsequently, the questioning of nominees, with varying degrees of intensity and relevance, has been treated as traditional. * * *

ROLE OF THE ABA IN THE APPOINTMENT PROCESS

The Standing Committee on the Judiciary of the ABA, established in 1945, has come to play a potentially significant role in the judicial selection process. The fifteen member committee, with representatives from each of the circuits including the federal circuit and a chairperson, is asked to evaluate judicial nominees and report its rating. The committee's role in the appointment of lower court judges is greater than at the Supreme Court level, but as the following excerpt from *Justices and Presidents* indicates, beginning in 1956 the committee began to get involved in the evaluation of Supreme Court nominees and has found that it can play a significant role. In reading this excerpt, ask whether the role played by the ABA is appropriate. Should the ABA be more assertive? Less assertive?

HENRY J. ABRAHAM,* JUSTICES AND PRESIDENTS: A POLITICAL HISTORY OF APPOINTMENTS TO THE SUPREME COURT
35–37 (1992)

[T]he committee's services were [first] enlisted to evaluate Supreme Court nominees when President Eisenhower nominated William J. Brennan, Jr., to the Court in 1956, [but] only *after* the nominee's identity had been made public and transmitted to the Senate Judiciary Committee for action. [T]he ABA Committee [used] only the rankings of "qualified" or "unqualified." This procedure was followed in each of the Supreme Court nominations after Brennan's, until Blackmun was appointed in the spring of 1970, hence embracing the following: Whittaker, Stewart, Byron R. White, Goldberg, Fortas, Thurgood Marshall, Fortas again (the aborted promotion), Thornberry (not acted on by the Senate because its refusal to promote Fortas resulted in Warren's withdrawal of his resignation, thus negating the vacancy), Burger, Haynsworth, and Carswell (the last two rejected). The committee stuck to the classification of "qualified" in all but a few instances: thus, in 1963 it ranked Goldberg "highly acceptable" but considered it inappropriate to express "an opinion to the degree of qualification." Yet it did express just such an opinion in the case of Judge Haynsworth in 1969—first and unanimously "highly qualified," then on reconsideration "highly qualified," but only by an 8:4 vote. In the Carswell case the committee returned to its "qualified" designation (although more than a few observers wondered how he merited that).

In response to a storm of criticism following its actions in endorsing Haynsworth and Carswell (the former twice), the committee's chairman, Lawrence E. Walsh, a Nixon ally—and the president's number-two representative at the Paris Peace Talks on the Vietnam War for some months—announced an impending change in the committee's Supreme Court nomination classification system. Beginning with the selection of Judge Blackmun early in 1970, the committee adopted a new top

* Excerpts from Henry J. Abraham, *Justices and Presidents: A Political History of Appointments to the Supreme Court,* Third Edition, by Henry J. Abraham. Copyright 1974, 1985, 1992 by Henry J. Abraham. Reprinted by permission of Oxford University Press, Inc.

classification of "high standards of integrity, judicial temperament, and professional competence" and substituted categories of "not opposed" and "not qualified" for the erstwhile dichotomy of "qualified" and "unqualified." It signified a tacit admission that under the latter system almost anyone could have been rated as "qualified." Evidently pleased with the committee's new classification and its endorsement of Blackmun with the new top category, Attorney General Mitchell yielded to the importunities of Chairman Walsh: on July 23, 1970, Mitchell wrote him that henceforth the Nixon administration would allow the ABA Committee to screen potential nominees for the Supreme Court *in advance* of their submittal to the Senate Judiciary Committee. Considerable approbation in otherwise critical circles followed the announcement, for it also had become evident that its investigation of Blackmun, in sharp contrast to the sketchy report the committee had rendered to the Senate in just six days in the Carswell case, had been rigorous: it had interviewed some two hundred presumably knowledgeable individuals, including upward of one hundred judges and lawyers, and had reviewed all of Judge Blackmun's court opinions in an effort to determine the candidate's qualifications in terms of "integrity * * * judicial temperament and professional competence."

Yet the era of good tone was destined to be short lived. When Justices Hugo L. Black and John Marshall Harlan II announced their resignations in September 1971, the administration moved rapidly to submit possible nominees to the ABA Committee, starting with Richard H. Poff, Republican congressman from Virginia. The ABA Committee, after interviewing almost four hundred individuals, awarded Congressman Poff the ABA's highest recommendation. After Poff withdrew, there came the much-publicized * * * candidacy of "The Six," whose names reached the press and public even before the Walsh Committee went to work on them. The attorney general in submitting the names of "The Six" urged speed—the Court had already begun its October 1971 term with but seven sitting members—and requested concentration on the administration's two top choices, Judge Lillie and Mr. Friday. Apparently, little or no work was done on the other four candidates, giving rise to later suspicions that they were decoys.

The ABA Committee, now working almost constantly, interviewed another four hundred people in connection with each of the two nominees. The results were distressing. Whatever qualifications Judge Lillie and Lawyer Friday possessed, they were at best marginal in terms of what is required for service on the Supreme Court of the United States. The committee responded with a unanimous vote for "not qualified" for Judge Lillie and a 6:6 tie (6 votes "not qualified," 6 votes "not opposed") for Mr. Friday. The fat was in the fire. When the ABA's actions, complete with votes, reached the news media only an hour or so after the attorney general had received them, the administration barely attempted to conceal its anger. Just who was responsible for the leak is difficult to establish, but this observer, for one, is satisfied that it did not come from the ABA Committee itself: either it was from personnel in the Justice Department or from members or staff of the Senate Judiciary Committee. There is some evidence that it came from both sources, with the initial divulgence made by the Justice Department. Within a matter of days Attorney General Mitchell addressed a sizzling letter to ABA President Leon Jaworski and Chairman Walsh of the committee informing them that at least the incumbent administration would no longer apply to the committee for its advice on nominees to the Supreme Court and that it would return to the practice of sending nominees directly to the Senate.

> The events of the past week have made it clear that our concern for confidentiality of communications between Justice and the Committee was well founded, and I can only conclude that there is no practical way to avoid unauthorized disclosure of the names submitted and the advice of your committee with respect thereto despite the best efforts of the committee * * *. Like you, I had hoped that the new procedure would be useful and productive. However, under the circumstances, I have concluded that the only fair and proper course is to resume the long-standing practice of submitting the Attorney General's recommendations directly to the President.

[Thereafter the pattern has been to submit only announced nominees to the committee and not to seek prenomination advice].

THOMAS HALPER,* SUPREME COURT APPOINTMENTS: CRITERIA AND CONSEQUENCES **
21 N.Y.L.Forum 563, 563–584 (1976)

* * *

[W]hile the Constitution provides that the President "shall nominate, and with the Advice and Consent of the Senate, shall appoint * * * Judges of the Supreme Court * * *," nowhere does it indicate what qualifications these critically important appointees should possess. No criteria are even hinted at. The President, as a consequence, is left free to make "his own decisions, and often he has his own ideas on the subject, either as to specific candidates or as to the qualifications he wants." As outsiders, of course, we can never be sure that we know the standards he applies. Moreover, traditionally, the selection process is carried out in secret and the emerging appointment described in ritual platitudes. Later on, historians may provide anecdotes and gossip, and satisfactorily explain specific choices, but what is needed is an overall view, drawing on data concerning all the Justices. * * *

The basis of this study is that the obvious selection criteria—good character, legal competence and congenial political philosophy—are of

* Assistant Professor of Political Science at Baruch College. A.B., 1963 St. Lawrence University, M.A., 1967, Ph.D., 1970 Vanderbilt University.

** Excerpts from Thomas Halper, *Supreme Court Appointments: Criteria and Consequences,* reprinted by permission of New York Law School Law Review.

only moderate help to Presidents. Recognizing the importance of the appointments and their own limited knowledge of constitutional law and the individual candidates, it will be argued, Presidents either consciously or unconsciously tend to fall back on a different set of standards: party loyalty, political experience and position in the upper social strata. In this way, they hope to reduce the uncertainty of the consequences of their actions by recourse to familiar, comfortable and hopefully predictable attributes.

For purposes of this study, the history of the Court has been divided into four segments, following roughly the schema of Robert McCloskey's standard in *The American Supreme Court.* Era I, 1789 through 1836, takes the Court from its birth through the Jackson administration, and is loosely congruent with the Age of Marshall. Era II, 1837 through 1868, includes the years preceding, during, and just after the Civil War through the Andrew Johnson administration. For the most part, it coincides with the Age of Taney. Era III, 1869 through 1932, is the longest period, encompassing Reconstruction, the Republican national hegemony, and what might be called the Age of Business Enterprise. Finally, Era IV, 1933 to date, includes the New Deal and Democratic national dominance and, with some exaggeration, could be termed the Age of Liberalism.

I.   The Limits of the Obvious

Soon after assuming office, President Washington wrote to Edmund Randolph that "the selection of the fittest characters to expound the laws and dispense justice has been an invariable subject of my anxious concern."   * * *

* * *

[But,] the whole notion of "good character," upon reflection, is hard to pin down. Even when we operationalize it in an apparently noncontroversial way, we may discover the results so displeasing that we find ourselves developing reservations about the concept itself. At the very minimum, for example, good character would seem to exclude racism. Thus, the argument might proceed, a former slaveowner, an ex-member of the Ku Klux Klan, and an advocate of wartime detention camps for Japanese–Americans would clearly be disqualified. Yet their exclusion would have robbed the Court not of notorious bigots, but of ardent champions of the rights of racial minorities: John Marshall Harlan, Hugo Black, and Earl Warren. On the other hand, the authors of the Court's most infamous racial decisions probably would have slipped through the net. Justice Taney freed his own slaves decades before he wrote *Scott v. Sanford,* and Justice Brown's generally moderate views were conventional and far less passionate than his bold stand in *Plessy v. Ferguson* might indicate. Even incontrovertible and flagrant departures from acts inconsistent with good character, in short, do not necessarily foreclose the issue for all time; nor do past acts of good character guarantee its continuance. As a potent abstract criterion for judicial selection, good character loses much of its salience when translated into real life terms.

What, then, of legal competence? From the beginning, it, like good character, has been assumed to be essential. * * *

But * * * competence, like good character, may be hard to define in a useful fashion. Does competence, for example, suggest that an appointee has demonstrated a clear mastery of the process of judicial reasoning? Perhaps. But this is a question easier posed than answered, for the process itself is most often analogical, in which the problem confronting the Justice is: "When will it be just to treat different cases as though they were the same?" Reasonable men will differ in their answers, for the analogy is "not so much a mode of attempting a proof, as a mode of attempting to dispense with the serious labor of proving." More properly a form of argument than of logic, the analogy ensures that the judicial decision will depend upon that judgment lurking beneath the intellectual underbrush that Holmes termed "the inarticulate major premise." Since there are no hard and fast rules as to what constitutes a valid analogy, examining the work of a prospective nominee rarely offers unambiguous and fatally damaging evidence as to his legal or rational competence.

Another method of estimating competence—clear, objective, and easy to apply—is to identify it with judicial experience. We know, of course, that they are really not the same things, and yet a significant amount of the latter might seem a reasonable guarantee of a modicum of the former. Arguing against "on the job" training for Supreme Court Justices, moreover, appears plausible, and so, has long had considerable public appeal. * * * Yet the common sense of this approach is refuted by history; for as one distinguished Justice, who himself lacked such training, observed, "the correlation between prior judicial experience and fitness for the functions of the Supreme Court is zero." Requiring significant judicial experience would have excluded many of the most illustrious of Justices, such as Marshall, Story, Taney, Curtis, Miller, Bradley, Hughes, Brandeis, Stone, Black, Frankfurter, Jackson, and Warren. It would not, however, have prevented the naming of such indifferent performers as Samuel Chase, Catron, Davis, Brown, Day, Sanford, and Vinson. The problem with placing undue emphasis upon judicial experience, in the words of one scholar, is that it ignores the plain fact that major questions with which the Supreme Court deals require a political judgment more than technical proficiency in private law.

* * *

The third obvious standard is sharing the President's political philosophy. In the final analysis, it might be argued, Presidents are not moralists concerned with the appointee's soul or legal academicians grading his judicial opinions. They are politicians concerned with public policy. Themselves incontestably political, Presidents tend to perceive the Court primarily in political terms, and are far more interested in the political, economic, and social consequences of its actions than with their legal rationales.   Theodore Roosevelt, therefore, was assuredly not alone when, in writing to his friend, Senator Henry Cabot Lodge, he declared:

> I should hold myself as guilty of an irreparable wrong to the nation if I should put [on the Court] any man who was not absolutely sane and sound on the great national policies for which we stand in public life.

Yet how are Presidents to determine whether a man is "sane and sound"?   The dilemma, as Lincoln put it, is that "we cannot ask a man what he will do, and if we should and he should answer us, we should despise him for it."   Gauging the candidate's soundness is difficult enough even when the President knows the appointee.   President Wilson mistook his Attorney General's antitrust zeal for liberalism, and named to the Court James C. McReynolds, the most reactionary Justice of the twentieth century.   Even Roosevelt himself erred in predicting Holmes's soundness on trust-busting.   When the President, as is most commonly the case, does not know the candidate, gauging his soundness is that much harder;   he must rely upon the opinions of third parties, among whom the most vocal ordinarily are the candidate's backers, who share the common salesmen's maladies of distortion and omission.   Additionally, there is always the possibility that the appointee may change or that the Court may reveal facets of him that had heretofore been hidden.   Warren became more liberal than President Eisenhower had expected;   Black disclosed a greater intellect than President Roosevelt had assessed.   Further, changing times may alter the policy consequences of a given judicial philosophy.   Frankfurter's self-restraint, that had earlier served liberal causes by curbing a conservative Court, came later to serve conservative causes by curbing a liberal Court.   Thus, even trying to insist that appointees share the President's political values is an approach fraught with danger.

Presidents, of course, are politically sophisticated.   They want good character, legal competence, and a "proper" political philosophy from their Supreme Court appointees, but they recognize that the surface simplicity of these criteria is misleading.   It is not that they are without worth, but merely that by themselves they are insufficient.   And so Presidents supplement the obvious, openly acknowledged criteria with other standards, the importance of which is rarely admitted.

II. Hedging the Bets

Since Presidents tend to be more interested in their appointees' political views than in their character or competence, the supplemental criteria for the most part fall in this area.   Thus, while it may be difficult to discover or predict an appointee's soundness as to his political philosophy, it is at least possible to demand that he be sound in partisan terms.   Presidents are free to make their choices only from members of their own party, and, as Table 1 indicates, to a very striking degree this is exactly what they have done.

Table 1

PARTIES OF JUSTICES AND
APPOINTING PRESIDENTS

Presidents	Justices			
	Federalists	Democrats	Whigs	Republican
Federalists	100%	0%	0%	0%
Democrats	0	95	0	5
Whigs	0	50	50	0
Republicans	0	18	0	82

Ninety percent of the appointees shared their Presidents' party affiliation. * * *

A selection prerequisite even more common than party loyalty is political experience. Frankfurter has supplied its rationale:

> Not annointed priests, but men with proved grasp of affairs, who have developed resilience and spaciousness of mind through seasoned and diversified experience in a work-a-day world, usually in public life, are the judges who have wrought abidingly on the Supreme Court.

But it is not merely that Presidents fear unworkable decisions from cloistered minds. In addition, there is the belief that a political record aids in predicting the individual's future behavior, and that a substantial immersion in politics will ensure that he is acquainted with the customs and rules that help to govern political life and prevent him from seeking to change things radically or quickly.

With the sole exception of George Shiras, every Justice has been politically active before his appointment, nearly all of them in some formal governmental capacity. The Justice Department has been an especially fertile source for appointees; of the last twenty-five successful nominations, seven had held high Justice Department positions immediately prior to their selection, and an eighth had worked for the Department as a youth. The Senate has supplied six Justices in this century, but the last chosen directly from that body was in 1945. Given recent difficulties in getting nominations confirmed and the practice of the Senate's routinely approving nominees from its own ranks, however, the Senate may well become a major supplier of Justices once again. So widespread is the presumption of a political background that nearly two-thirds of the Justices came from families that had been deeply political. Most often, in fact, the Justices' fathers themselves had been officeholders at the federal, state, or local level, or at least had engaged in political management. In any case, it is probably safe to say that, from the President's vantage, political experience constitutes the most significant factor of personal data utilized in the selection process.

The third supplemental selection criterion is requiring that the appointee occupy a high position in the nation's socio-economic strata.

For such a person, ordinarily self-interest, often confused with the public good, would operate to ensure that the Court not attempt to alter society in any fundamental fashion. No conspiracy, either among the Justices or between them and the Executive, is suggested; persons sharing the same general perspectives and goals will act in mutually agreeable ways without the need of cabals. In fact, it may be that the insistence upon the appointee's coming from a highly-favored stratum was for a long time so taken for granted that Presidents rarely bothered to examine it.

Although the data are not always clear and unambiguous, it appears that approximately two-thirds of the Justices came from high strata homes, in which their fathers were bankers, doctors, lawyers, prosperous merchants or manufacturers, or wealthy farmers or land speculators. About one-fifth were born into middle strata homes, where the fathers were middle class farmers, clergymen, professors, and so forth. The remainder, it appears, came from low-strata homes headed, for example, by small farmers, laborers, or mechanics. By Era IV, however, these proportions had changed significantly. Since 1933, appointees have come from high, middle, and low strata backgrounds in about equal measures.

Given the quality of these data, it may be helpful to supplement them with other indices of strata position. One of these is education. For many years it was assumed that a classical education at an elite college or university or at least at a fine private school was a virtual necessity to the development of the proper judicial intellect and sensibility. * * *

In both legal and non-legal education [of the justices], high quality institutions, tutors, and apprenticeships predominate. * * * Yet * * * there are unmistakable signs that the stress on elite education is waning. Thus, in Eras I and II, only eight and twenty-one percent of the Justices, respectively, attended average quality colleges and schools; in Eras III and IV, the percentages were thirty-six and forty-four, respectively. Similarly, in Eras I and II, none of the Justices attended an average quality law school and only one was self-taught; in Eras III and IV, however, twenty-five and twenty-eight percent, respectively, attended average quality law schools or were self-taught. Oddly enough, this decline in the proportion of appointees from high quality colleges and law schools seems to be accelerating at the very time that growth in enrollment and financial assistance have made these institutions far more accessible to members of the middle and lower strata than ever before. This anomaly to some extent undercuts the conclusion that the reduced percentage of elite graduates reflects a concomitant broadening of the strata represented in the Court.

* * *

A second indicator of social strata is the Justice's ethnic background. Table 4 suggests a pattern similar to that occurring with respect to education.

Bloch Sup.Ct.Politics--3

Table 4 [53]

JUSTICES' ETHNIC BACKGROUNDS

	High Status	Low Status
Era I (1789–1836)	96%	4%
Era II (1837–1868)	100	0
Era III (1869–1932)	91	9
Era IV (1933–)	84	16
Total	92	8

The dominance of Justices from Western and Northern European ethnic backgrounds was, until Era IV, almost complete. During this period, when low status ethnic groups nearly doubled their highest previous representation, the first black Justice was appointed, an act of enormous symbolic value. Clearly, then, there has been a movement toward broadening the Court's ethnic and social strata base.

It would be easy to exaggerate the extent of these changes. Thus far, despite the millions of immigrants from Southern and Eastern Europe, only three appointees from the two regions have been selected. Nor has a single appointee of Latin American or Asian heritage been chosen. Upper strata ethnic groups, despite recent trends, remain quite overwhelming.

A third indicator of social strata is the Justice's religion. Table 5 reveals several significant changes that have taken place over the years:

Table 5

JUSTICES' RELIGIONS

	High Status Protestants	Low Status Protestants	Roman Catholics	Jews
Era I (1789–1836)	81%	15%	4%	0%
Era II (1837–1868)	50	50	0	0
Era III (1869–1932)	45	40	10	5
Era IV (1933–)	50	31	8	12
Total	56	33	7	5

In Era I, the dominance of high status Protestants was nearly total.[55] Not until President John Quincy Adams appointed Robert Trimble in 1826, was one outside this rubric named to the Court and

53. High status ethnic groups include the English, the Welsh, the Scots–Irish, the French, the Dutch, the Scandinavian, the German, and the Austrian. Low status ethnic groups include the Irish, the Spanish, the Bohemian, the Russian, and the African.

55. High status Protestants include Episcopalians, Presbyterians, Unitarians, Congregationalists, Quakers, and Dutch Reformed; low-status Protestants include Baptists, Methodists, Lutherans, Disciples of Christ, and those identified simply as Protestants. This generally follows the schema employed by H.W. Schneider, Religion in 20th Century America 228 (1952).

Justice Trimble was the twentieth appointee. Such a pattern could not withstand both the rapid population growth of low status Protestants, and a whole series of social forces—industrialization, urbanization and immigration—that disrupted the high status Protestants' political and economic control over the nation. Thus, in Era II, the Court's appointees were split evenly between high and low status Protestants. In later eras, Catholics and Jews were to become potent political forces as well, and gain seats in the Court. This development, however, seems to have taken place solely at the expense of low status Protestants. For while high status Protestants lost but five percentage points from Era II to Era III and have since gained them back, low status Protestants dropped ten and nine points, respectively. These figures approximate the gains of Catholics and Jews. The religious division over the past three eras could not be plainer if half the Court were openly allocated to high status Protestants and the other half to all other religions. * * *

Partly, this may reflect the tradition of high status Protestants entering politics and the law. Partly, it may reflect the effect of high status Protestants' overrepresentation in the White House, for such Presidents have appointed seventy-seven percent of all Justices, and fifty-six percent of their appointees were high status Protestants. Yet the importance of high status Protestants choosing similar Justices can be overstated; low status Protestant and Catholic Presidents were also biased in favor of high status Protestants, making half of their selections from that group.

As for non-Protestant Justices, a tradition has grown, according to which one seat each is to be reserved for a Catholic and a Jew. Moreover, it seems fair to predict that a similar practice will emerge regarding blacks and women. Catholic and Jewish representation, however, is only a custom, and departures have occurred. Thus, continuous Catholic representation since 1894 was broken for seven years following Justice Murphy's death in 1949, and continuous Jewish representation since 1916 was broken by President Nixon's failure to name a Jew to replace Justice Fortas who left the Court in disgrace in 1969. By the same token, these religions have each had two representatives simultaneously, and, with the growth of the Catholic population and the rise to national prominence of numerous Catholic politicians, this religion may be assigned two seats in a few years or perhaps even graduate to the "unassigned" level with the Protestants. Jews, on the other hand, will do well merely to regain and retain their single seat.

In examining such indicators of social strata position as education, ethnicity and religion, one is struck by the central theme that shows through each variation: virtual complete high strata dominance prevails at the outset, only to be reduced as lower strata gain ever larger representation. Yet, despite this trend, today, nearly two centuries after Washington's first appointments, high strata groups account for a disproportionate share of the Court's membership.

III. SOME CONCLUSIONS

Despite all the pious talk about character, competence, and philosophy, it is obvious that ostensibly common sense criteria are of only limited value to a President trying to decide whom he shall place on the Supreme Court. * * *

Not surprisingly, therefore, Presidents rely not only upon these openly acknowledged and clearly defensible standards, but also upon other considerations they are less willing to admit. The strongest of these is political. * * * [T]here can be no real question that the political consideration is uppermost in a President's mind. The task of the Justices is too important not to require from them the kind of political sophistication that can come only from experience; predicting their Court behavior is too difficult not to require that at the very least they be party regulars.

Another consideration—less potent than political experience and party loyalty but still significant—is the appointee's position in the social strata. * * * From the outset, advantaged persons, *i.e.* white males with high status ethnic background and religious affiliation from prosperous and respected homes, have had a vastly disproportionate representation on the Court. * * *

Upper strata representation, to be sure, has not been perfectly constant over time, and in fact in recent years one can discern a marked reduction in its importance. * * * Nevertheless, whatever the explanation and despite the reduction, members of the upper strata are still much more likely to be appointed to the Court than their numbers in society might suggest.

This would not matter much if the Court were the apolitical institution it pretends to be, and its Justices were "mere legal automatons, with no more give and take in their minds than you will find in a terrier watching a rathole." [65] But judicial reasoning—analogical, often dealing with constitutional or statutory phrases of amoeboid flexibility—is profoundly political, especially at the level of the Supreme Court which rarely bothers itself with simple, straightforward cases. * * * Justices often, perhaps not even always noticing it themselves, will have recourse to their own values, beliefs, and opinions. One need not be a Marxist to perceive how these can be influenced by one's placement in stratified society. The upper strata bias of its membership, therefore, has almost certainly affected the Court's decisions. Thus, it is probably no coincidence that, historically, the Court has consistently sided with upper strata interests: with corporations at the expense of states seeking to regulate them; with slaveowners at the expense of slaves; with management at the expense of labor; and with whites at the expense of blacks. This trend has continued until recent years. Not without cause did a frustrated New Deal Attorney General complain, "Never in its entire

65. Mencken, *The Library: The Great*   (1932).
Holmes Mystery, 26 Am. Mercury 123, 125

history can the Supreme Court be said to have for a single hour been representative of anything except the relatively conservative forces of the day." It would be simplistic and false, of course, to interpret the Court's actions as mechanically predetermined consequences of the Justices' own social positions. However, it would be equally misleading to forget that Justices are human, too, and cannot replace the habits and beliefs of a lifetime with the ease with which they change from business suit to judicial robe. * * *

Unavoidably, one is led to ask whether there might not be a better way to appoint Justices. * * * The chief obstacle [to reform] is that reform itself is ordinarily construed to mean nonpolitical, and inasmuch as the Justice's task is profoundly political, it is simply unrealistic to expect that these considerations could ever be banished from one's appointment. It is occasionally suggested that a "neutral" actor, like the organized bar, be given greater influence, but in fact there are no truly neutral actors, and the American Bar Association's experiences with the Brandeis and Carswell nominations offer small comfort to advocates of this position. In any case, given the primacy of politics and public opinion in a democracy, and the already marked insulation of the Court from normal political pressures, efforts directed toward de-politicizing the appointment process would probably be unwise. Only a Mr. Dooley could seriously argue that the Court is *too* responsive to political factors and ought to be made even less accountable than it is now. Moreover, it is not at all obvious that the current system, with all its flaws, is working badly. In terms of competence, intellect, and integrity, it seems difficult to maintain that the Court has been more poorly served by its selection process than have the Presidency and Congress by theirs. A 1970 survey of sixty-five law school deans and professors of law, history, and political science found only eight Justices to be "failures," and five of these served only rather brief tenures. The implication would appear to be that we ought to be quite cautious about tinkering with the appointing system in any serious way. * * *

THOMAS HALPER,* SENATE REJECTION
OF SUPREME COURT NOMINEES **
22 Drake L.Rev. 102, 102–112 (1972)

The President proposes, as the saying goes, and the Senate disposes. The President, that is, "shall nominate, and by and with the Advice and Consent of the Senate, shall appoint * * * Judges of the Supreme Court." Ordinarily, in recent times, the Senate, like a symphony hall audience, has dutifully (if generally unenthusiastically) registered its approval. Thus, from 1894 until 1968, there was but one exception to the rule of Senate acquiescence, the rejection of John J. Parker in 1930.

* Assistant Professor in Political Science, Coe College. A.B. 1963, St. Lawrence University; M.A. 1967, Ph.D. 1970, Vanderbilt University—Ed.

** Excerpts from Thomas Halper, *Senate Rejection of Supreme Court Nominees,* reprinted by permission of Drake Law Review.

Other than Parker, the Senate approved, often with little deliberation, forty-five appointees during this seventy-four year span. In 1968, however, much to the surprise of most journalistic observers who had predicted a continuation of the pattern, the Senate failed to confirm Abe Fortas as Chief Justice, thereby also blocking the nomination of Homer Thornberry as Associate Justice. Then in 1969, it rejected the nomination of Clement Haynsworth as Associate Justice. And in 1970, it turned down G. Harrold Carswell, who had been selected to fill the same vacancy. Most recently, in 1971 it posed a serious challenge to William Rehnquist before his ultimate confirmation. Earlier assumptions of senatorial complacency have been left in a shambles.

By examining the history of the Court, we can see that senatorial rejection is by no means a new phenomenon. Up to 1894, at least one nominee was turned down, not voted on, or withdrawn in virtually every decade; and, in fact, in one three year period from 1844 to 1846, five nominations were rejected. Overall, twenty-five such nominations have suffered this fate, a proportion far higher than for any other federal office. * * *

Eleven nominees were voted down by the Senate, thirteen were withdrawn or were not voted on, and one was not formally named due to an earlier rejection having eliminated a vacancy. Since 103 nominees have been accepted, nearly one fifth of all presidential selections have been rejected. How is this to be explained?

I. UNQUALIFIED NOMINEES

The most obvious explanation for the rejections is simply that the nominees were not qualified. Certainly, this has been the most commonly heard response from the Senators themselves. Nor should this be surprising, for as one Washington journalist has wryly observed, "The notion seems widespread that the Senate ought to approve a Supreme Court nominee unless the man is proved either a blackguard or a legal incompetent so cretinous that mention of a tort puts him in mind of Viennese pastry."

* * * This cry of "unqualified"—the most politic and common of explanations—is also, however, upon closer examination among the least persuasive of arguments.

One reason for this is that useful qualifications are quite difficult to prescribe. * * * [E]xamining the written work of a nominee rarely offers unambiguous and fatally damaging evidence as to his legal and rational limitations. A Senator's reaction to a nominee's work, as a consequence, is likely to be governed less by its logic than by the assumptions it embodies and the goals it furthers. Value considerations, in other words, are apt to be decisive: Does this nominee sufficiently appreciate the importance of law as an instrument of stability? or of change? Is he sufficiently solicitous of the rights of private property? or of the propertyless? Is he sufficiently protective of the rights of those accused of crime? or of society? The question, of course, is: What is "sufficient" and the answer is: It depends. It depends upon who you are, what you have, and what you want. And inasmuch as values can be neither verified nor falsified, value arguments quickly come to resemble childhood disputes over the alleged superiority of chocolate ice cream to vanilla. Thus, although specific Senators may oppose a nominee for reason of disagreement with his values (or "philosophy"), it is no easy matter to speak of useful value qualifications. For the only values that nearly every Senator would demand—like belief in the rule of law or willingness to uphold the Constitution—are so widely found among prospective nominees that they would probably exclude no one.

* * *

All of this suggests that, while the Senate votes on the nominee, his qualifications are not apt to be decisive in determining his rejection. In fact, the most distinguished of historians of the Court could find only four instances in which charges of lack of qualifications played a decisive part in rejection,[32] and since his study, the number has grown by but one.[33] In trying to account for rejected nominees, then, it is not enough to examine their qualifications. We must look elsewhere, too, and in doing so, investigate two other possibilities—that the Senate's rejections tend to reflect its hostility toward the President or toward the Court itself.

II. THE SENATE AND THE PRESIDENT

To a considerable extent, senatorial-presidential conflict is endemic to the American constitutional system, due to formal constitutional checks and balances, extraconstitutional developments, differing electoral constituencies, clashing personal and party values and ambitions, and so on. Sometimes, this conflict focuses on a presidential nominee to the Court, who becomes a pawn in the struggle and may be rejected. Why does this conflict erupt at some times but not at others? Several explanations may be offered.

First, the "jackal theory": a substantial portion of the Senate is always potentially hostile to the President, but will oppose him on a matter as important as a Supreme Court nomination only if he appears especially weak politically. The Senate, in this view, is like a jackal whose readiness to strike is conditioned on its enemy's inability to retaliate.

Since the President's strength is related to his electoral performance and declines toward the end of his administration when the number of rewards and punishments at his disposal shrinks drastically, this working schema was created to facilitate analysis: Presidents who will be reelected are considered strongest. This includes the first terms of all two-term Presidents and the first three terms of Franklin Roosevelt. That these Presidents have been elected once and will be elected again is a

---

32. C. Warren, The Supreme Court in United States History 758 (1928). Henry Abraham, perhaps the leading contemporary constitutional historian, names only two rejected nominees whom he believes were truly unqualified. H. Abraham, The Judicial Process 84–85 (2d ed. 1968).

33. Judge G. Harrold Carswell.

testament to their popularity with the electorate and effectiveness with the Congress. Presidents who will be elected only once are considered next strongest. This includes all one-term Presidents and all Vice–Presidents who became President and were elected once through their own efforts. That they have been elected once and could be elected again but were not suggests that they were less strong than those who were. Presidents who cannot be re-elected were considered the next strongest. This includes the second terms of all two-term Presidents except Franklin Roosevelt. An informal two-term tradition made binding by the twenty-second amendment prevented these Presidents from running again, and this inhibition weakened them significantly. Finally, Presidents who ascended to the office from the vice-presidency and were not elected on their own are considered the weakest. That they were never elected probably indicates a lower level of popularity with the electorate and of effectiveness with Congress. Presidents assassinated during their first terms and President Nixon are excluded from this schema, since their full electoral stories were not or have not been played out to their conclusions. If there is any worth to the jackal theory, we would expect the percentage of nominees turned down—the "rejection rate"—to increase as the President's strength decreases. Table 2 expresses the findings.

Table 2

REJECTION RATES FOR PRESIDENTS OF VARIOUS STRENGTHS

	Presidents who will be re-elected	Presidents who will be elected only once	Presidents who cannot be re-elected	Presidents who were never elected
Appointments Confirmed	39	35	14	4
Appointments Rejected	3	8	5	6
Rejection Rate	7.3%	18.6%	26.3%	60%

Clearly, the data support the jackal theory, for there is a strong relationship between presidential weakness and rejection of appointees. This leads us to expect an even higher rejection rate in a President's last year in office, when he is most vulnerable as a "lame duck." Not only are the rewards and punishments at his command at their lowest point, but also the desire of his senatorial opponents to have his successor make appointments is at its zenith. Our expectation is confirmed. Eight out of fifteen lame duck nominations have been rejected, a rejection rate of 53.3%. Vice–Presidents who ascended to the presidency and were not re-elected fared especially poorly, losing all four of their lame duck nominations.

Second, the "image theory": a substantial portion of the Senate is always potentially hostile to the President, but will oppose him on a matter as important as a Supreme Court nomination only if he has an obviously unpopular image with the electorate. His unpopularity increases the incentives for opposition by making defeat of the nominee more likely and the chances of the President or his party losing the next presidential election greater. The ineffectiveness dramatized by a senatorial defeat would be especially embarrassing and damaging to a President already burdened with an unfavorable public image. His unpopularity also reduces the costs and risks of opposition, for the likelihood that he will be defeated on the nomination and that his party will be defeated in the next presidential election seriously restricts the sanctions he can bring to bear against recalcitrant Senators. This has the effect of influencing marginal Senators who do not feel strongly about the nominee and would support him under other circumstances. That the Court is "our most important symbol of government" and that much of its importance lies in its symbolic role reinforces the tendency on the part of the Senate to take advantage of the President's falling public image.

If there were validity in this "image theory," we would expect Presidents suffering from poor public images to have rejection rates significantly higher than Presidents not suffering from such images. Table 3 indicates the rejection rate for unpopular Presidents.

Table 3

APPOINTMENT RECORD OF UNPOPULAR PRESIDENTS

President	Years of Unpopularity	Appointments Confirmed	Appointments Rejected
J. Adams	1798–1801	3	0
J.Q. Adams	1825–1829	1	1
Van Buren	1837–1841	3	0
Tyler	1841–1845	1	4
Fillmore	1850–1853	0	0
Pierce	1856–1857	0	1
Buchanan	1860–1861	3	0
Lincoln	1861–1862	0	0
A. Johnson	1865–1869	0	1
Grant	1875–1877	2	0
Cleveland	1893–1897	3	3
Hoover	1930–1933	1	1
Truman	1946–1947 and 1951–1953	0	0
L. Johnson	1968–1969	0	2
		17	13

The rejection rate for unpopular Presidents is 43.3%, well over twice the level of that of other Presidents, 18.3%. The image theory thus receives very substantial support.

One question that arises at this point is whether the jackal and image theories are mutually reinforcing. The answer is an unambiguous "yes." For 18.6% of the appointees of all Presidents elected only once were rejected, as against 31.3% of those of unpopular Presidents elected only once; 26.3% of the appointees of all Presidents in the second of two terms were rejected, as against 60% of those of unpopular Presidents in their second terms; and 60% of the appointees of all Presidents not elected were rejected, as against 75% of those of unpopular Presidents not elected. By the same token, while 53.3% of the appointees of lame duck Presidents were rejected, 75% of those of unpopular lame ducks were turned down.

* * * To a sizeable degree, in short, Senate rejection of Supreme Court nominees seems to reflect the chamber's relationship with the President.

III. THE SENATE AND THE COURT

The Supreme Court, as the "least dangerous branch," has been embroiled in fewer major conflicts with Congress than has the President. What is more likely than such a clash is that an overly adventurous Court has raised hackles among the general public, and become unpopular with large portions of it. In these circumstances, some Senators may be more willing to oppose an appointee than would otherwise be the case. The appointee is not likely to repudiate the decisions of his colleagues-to-be, and thus voting on whether to approve him may seem to some Senators similar to voting on whether to approve the Court itself.

Moreover, judicial unpopularity is inevitably accompanied by an erosion of the Court's appearance as sacrosanct and nonpolitical. This image, however, is one of its chief lines of defense against its foes. Thus, the erosion leaves opposition to the Court easier, less costly, and more effective—and this opposition may, of course, take the form of opposition to specific nominations. * * *

If there were substance to this theory, we would expect the rejection rate to rise during periods of the Court's unpopularity. The data distributed themselves in this fashion:

Table 4

APPOINTMENT RECORD OF UNPOPULAR COURTS

Years of Unpopularity	Appointments Confirmed	Appointments Rejected
1857–1869	5	4
1933–1937	0	0
1957–1958	2	0
1967–1972	6	4
	13	8

The rejection rate during periods of unpopular Courts is 38.1%, nearly triple the 13.5% rate prevailing at other times. An unpopular Court, then, plainly permits or encourages greater opposition to nominees. A caveat is due, however, for the number of appointments made during such periods is small because the Court has not ordinarily been very unpopular. The exceptions—the years from *Dred Scott* through *Ex parte McCardle* and from Franklin Roosevelt's election to *West Coast Hotel v. Parrish,* the Court-curbing battle of the Eisenhower years, and the contemporary disenchantment—have produced only twenty-one nominations. Yet though the number of nominees is small, there are signs that the Court's unpopularity interacts with presidential unpopularity and weakness, making confirmation in these relatively few cases truly difficult. Thus, the rejection rate for those seven instances when Court and presidential unpopularity both are present is 57.1%, and for the three instances when Court unpopularity and a lame duck President coexist is 100%. And Presidents unlucky enough to be elected but once and during a time of Court unpopularity have seen two-thirds of their nominees rejected. Presidents in the first of two terms and non-elected Presidents have not fared well, either, though they have been involved in only five cases and one case, respectively.

An unpopular Court, then, seems to promote rejection—especially if the Court's unpopularity coincides with presidential weakness or unpopularity—but it has occurred too infrequently to be counted as a truly major causal factor.

B. WHAT STANDARDS SHOULD THE PRESIDENT AND THE SENATE APPLY?

This section explores what the roles of the President and the Senate should be. The articles herein basically agree that the Senate's participation is and will continue to be actively political, but they each offer somewhat different formulations for what that role should look like.

In reading the articles, think about the following questions.

First, what should the responsibility of the Senate be? Should it simply try to assure that the nominee is honest and competent or should it try to ascertain and evaluate the nominee's legal philosophy? What is entailed in pursuing any of these questions? How can the Senate determine "honesty," "competence," or "legal philosophy?" A particular question that affects every confirmation hearing is whether the Senate should seek to ascertain the nominee's views on certain issues. Since Presidents obviously choose their nominees, at least in part, on the basis of predictions as to how they will vote and since the Court does make policy, it might seem logical and proper for Senators to satisfy themselves about the nominee's views. On the other hand, if each Senator casts his or her vote on the basis of a nominee's reaction to an issue that the Senator selects, every nominee is likely to be rejected. Further, one might ask whether today's hot issue is likely to be a major question for the Court ten years in the future. More fundamentally, it has been argued that subjecting a nominee's views to a plebiscite is inconsistent with the belief that independent judicial review should restrain legislative power. Are there sensible answers to this dilemma concerning the Senate's role in judging the soundness of a nominee's philosophy?

Second, should the Senators consider whom the nominee is replacing and how the nominee is likely to affect the balance on the Court? Should the role of the Senate vary with the different types of appointments it confirms? Note that Article II, Section 2 of the Constitution prescribes the appointment process for Justices of the Supreme Court, as well as for Ambassadors and Cabinet officials. The language used for all these cases is the same: The President "shall nominate, and by and with the advice and consent of the Senate, shall appoint * * *." Should the role of the Senate be the same in all these cases? Or should there be more deference to the President in the case of Cabinet officials and less with respect to Supreme Court justices? The same section also requires that the President obtain "the advice and consent of the Senate" to make treaties. Is the Senate's role in the treaty process different from its role in the appointment process? Even though the relevant text is the same?

Third, consider whether the Senate should have more of a role in advising the President at the nomination stage and if so, what that role might be and how it might be implemented. Does the Constitution contemplate such a role? Does it permit Congress to mandate such a role or only authorize the President to voluntarily seek such advice?

Fourth, consider whether special factors should apply during extended periods of divided government (when the President and Senate are controlled by different political parties.) Should there be a conscious effort to try to make the Court "balanced," assuming one can agree on what "balance" means and can predict how to achieve it?

Our experience has been that, although these questions are both critical and interesting, they are difficult to analyze in the abstract. Therefore, we recommend that they be considered more concretely against the factual backgrounds laid out in the case studies in the following section.

STEPHEN CARTER,* THE CONFIRMATION MESS **
101 Harv.L.Rev. 1185, 1185–1201 (1988)

Constitutional theory is widely regarded by scholars as one of the great disasters in contemporary legal thought. None of the popular theories is seen as finally workable, all are contingent and internally chaotic, and the courts that must do the serious work of interpreting the Constitution show no serious interest in any of them. The ever-messier business of nominating and confirming Justices to serve on the Supreme Court is, in its way, contributing to the chaos. * * * The Senate, unable

---

* Professor of Law, Yale University.

to agree on the precise role that it should play in the selection process, now finds itself trapped between the notion that it should act to enforce a set of professional standards, reviewing nominees only to ensure that they possess proper qualifications, and the idea that it should inquire deeply into the substantive judicial philosophy of each nominee, to keep from the Court those whose constitutional visions are too extreme for the American people to stomach. Neither of these roles is a useful one for the Senate to play—the one because it trivializes the process, the other because it trivializes the Constitution. There is higher ground, however, and this is a small story about how the Senate might get there.

I. THE PAPER RECORD

It has become something of a commonplace in the wake of the Bork debacle to assert that Robert Bork was, on paper, perhaps the best qualified candidate in many decades to be nominated to serve on the Supreme Court. The implication is that there exists a set of ideal objective criteria by which nominees should be judged. The criteria most bandied about (and not merely in the Bork battle) involve professional accomplishment: cases briefed and argued, law review articles authored, judicial or other public service, and so on. The list is perhaps not very different from what a top law firm or leading law school would look for in its next hire. The effect is to objectify a process that the Constitution seems to treat as political. In this idealized vision, appointment to the Court becomes not the outcome of a political struggle between President and Senate, but almost a reward for the lawyer who has compiled the most resume points when the time comes to stop and add up the scores.

Intellectual capacity is hardly irrelevant to qualification for service on the Supreme Court. The vision of appointment as a reward, however, does more than establish a baseline; it treats a Justiceship like a merit promotion, and it implies that "professional qualifications" are more important than anything else. * * *

It is plainly quite useful to a senator to be able to explain a vote against a nominee for the Supreme Court—or, for that matter, against a nominee for any federal court—on the ground that, whatever one may think of the individual's politics or policies, the nominee was not qualified. * * *

Indeed, it is perfectly sensible for the Senate to review a candidate's professional experience to determine whether she meets some baseline standard of legal and intellectual competence. Serious difficulties arise, however, from treating the candidate's paper qualifications as sufficient in and of themselves to justify appointment. The obvious problem is that the model of the confirmation process as essentially a resume review is profoundly ahistorical. Those who designed the process plainly contemplated the Senate's role as a significant check on presidential discretion.[6] The less obvious problem is that even if the resume review

---

6. *See, e.g.,* The Federalist No. 76, at 457 (A. Hamilton) (C. Rossiter ed. 1961)   (suggesting that the Senate's role in confirmation "would be an excellent check upon a

model is appealing, the traditional credentials—prior judicial experience stands out as an exception—seem to bear little relation to the work of a judge. Why are excellence in legal scholarship or significant experience in litigation important parts of the ideal resume?

* * * A scholar may produce outstanding scholarship and show evidence of a fine mind. Yet the nominee who refuses to abandon positions taken as a scholar is arguably too closed-minded to serve as a judge; the scholar who abandons those positions at will is left open to the charge of sacrificing principle for expediency.

Especially in the field of constitutional theory, moreover, many legal scholars are accustomed to dealing with problems at a relatively high level of generality, often adducing principles from arcane philosophies and even from the air rather than from the needs of particular cases. Possibly such individuals are ideal Justices—perhaps they will do equal justice to all persons because they are not accustomed to thinking about parties as persons. But they may also be disastrous as Justices, precisely because their habits of mind may not press them to think hard enough about the practical problems that arise from the application of abstract principles to concrete cases.

Another claim, and one that partly answers the concern over a lack of familiarity with the problems of deciding real cases, is that the ideal nominee should have litigated real cases before real judges. But experience in twisting law to fit facts and facts to fit preferred results is an obvious qualification only for judging of a particular kind—the kind in which the answer is more important than the route one takes to find it. A skill at crafting an argument for a result is not the same as a skill at finding the result the law requires. If the second skill is more desirable in judges than the first, it may be more important to find lawyers who have done good work advising clients on the legality of planned conduct than lawyers who have built their reputations by solving their clients' problems in the courts. * * *

II. THE PAPER TRAIL

* * *

There is a sense in which the ultimate amenability of the Court to politics is something to be celebrated, for the nomination process is often the only effective device by which the people can signal their approval of the work of the Court or try to force a shift in course. "Here the people rule," President Ford announced after the resignation of his predecessor, and no doubt opponents of a defeated Supreme Court nomination are tempted to make the same proclamation. After all, if maintenance of the constitutional system requires a polity that believes that it governs itself, it is useful that the system should provide an occasional reminder of who ultimately is in charge. It ought to come as no surprise,

spirit of favoritism in the President" and make it less likely that "disposition of of-   fices would be governed by * * * his private inclinations and interests"). * * *

consequently, that politicians so readily embrace the current academic fashion that invites the Senate to assess something called "judicial philosophy" in deciding whether to consent to a nomination.

But "judicial philosophy," especially as the term is used by proponents of quizzing judicial nominees about their own, is not easy to distinguish from the prediction of results in concrete cases. * * * Trying to define it in a way that accurately captures what the advocates of substantive scrutiny mean by it, but that does not threaten judicial independence, is harder still.

Most Americans, after all, know the Court principally by the results that it reaches. In public debate, aside from a handful of such political buzzwords as "intent of the Framers" and "judicial activism," judicial philosophy in the sense that is of interest to constitutional theorists does not exist. * * *

Never mind that theorists might question, for example, whether the right to reproductive privacy has a *constitutional* basis; those who think the right a good thing are satisfied that it has a *judicial* basis, that is, that the Supreme Court includes at least five Justices who want to protect it. When the people and their representatives talk of "protecting our basic rights," or even "maintaining the essential balance," it is hard to imagine that they mean much more than "making sure we still have the votes." The constitutional rights defined by the Court's decisions take on an independent virtue, quite distinct from any theory of constitutional interpretation, and it is those rights, not a theory, that the political rhetoric about judicial philosophy is meant to protect.

This is surely the message behind the purported discovery of a series of smoking guns in the intellectual baggage that Judge Bork brought to his confirmation hearings. Critics insisted that Judge Bork's constitutional theory was outside the mainstream of contemporary jurisprudence, but unless the mainstream is defined very narrowly, this charge is surely incorrect as a factual matter. One of the gravest weaknesses of the liberal constitutional theory that currently dominates the academy is its inability to point to much in the Constitution's text or history to explain the supposed wrongheadedness of the conservative assault on the work of the modern Court. Judge Bork was pilloried, for example, for his dogged reliance on the original understanding as a tool for interpretation. Whatever the degree of controversy among legal scholars on originalism as a method, however, it is just that—a controversy. Originalism plainly has its supporters, including Justices of the Supreme Court of the United States, who do not blink at originalism as a strategy when it serves their interests.

The more sophisticated version of the assault suggested that Judge Bork's theory as applied would lead to results out of step with what the American people would prefer. But this claim, too, is an argument over concrete cases, for the American people, whatever their reverence for the Constitution itself, however strong their affection for particular rights, cannot fairly be said to share a constitutional theory. * * *

* * * Members of the Senate are practical politicians, not noted for voting to reject Supreme Court nominees if the vote will cause trouble back home. This in turn suggests that the fundamental charge against Judge Bork—that the results that a Justice Bork might reach would not match the results that the American people would prefer—was true. Certainly his views as understood by the American people seemed out of step with their own. Yet even assuming an identity between the views he was perceived to have and the views he had in fact, what is the message in his rejection on this ground? The message must surely be that when the people and their senators and their President talk about "judicial philosophy," they have in mind not adherence to a particular theory, but "people who will reach the results we like," and that both the President and the Senate (and through them, perhaps, the people) see the appointment process as an opportunity to pack the Court with Justices who will vote the right way.

If this is so, then anyone who cares about the integrity of constitutional theory and the independence of the courts should be troubled. At bottom, all the ringing phrases about permitting the ascension only of Justices whose constitutional views are congruent with those of the people—even assuming that the senators know what the people are thinking—contradict first principles of judicial review. Beginning constitutional law students are taught that the Supreme Court serves as a countermajoritarian brake. The institution of judicial review exists precisely to thwart, not to further, the self-interested programs of temporary majorities.

Thus a worrisome paradox emerges. On the one hand, the courts exist at least in part to limit majority sway. On the other, the courts are to be peopled with judges selected at least in part because their constitutional judgments are consistent with those of the majority. Even for a critic who disdains theory and revels in concrete results, this process of judicial selection can be attractive only if one knows (and agrees with) the predilections of a majority of the senators—or of * * * [their constituents.] For the scholar who believes in the possibility of constitutional theory, the collapse of the nomination and confirmation process into a battle over concrete results carries the potential for disaster.

Constitutional theory is concerned principally with the Constitution as a document and the Supreme Court as an institution. For a constitutional theorist who cares about more than results, a decision is only as legitimate as the judicial process that it reflects. Constitutional theorists therefore take seriously the analysis that the majority in a given case presents in defense of its work. To the theorist, what matters is the legitimacy of the reasoning offered by the Justices to connect the Constitution to the end result. If there is no connection—if the decision seems to represent no more than a personal predilection or perhaps a guess—then a serious theorist must conclude that the Court is not doing its job. If the Justices are appointed because their personal predilections suggest an affection for particular results that the senators also like, the theorist must conclude that the Senate is trying to prevent the Court from doing its job.

To wrap the armor of countermajoritarian independence around individuals selected on the basis of predictions about how they will vote represents the enshrinement, through life tenure, of the popular political judgments of particular eras about the proper scope of constitutional protections—a peculiar fealty to pay to the notion of a written Constitution. Interpretation of a written Constitution should reflect a dispassionate search for fundamental constitutional principles that transcend even the most deeply felt popular passions of a given political moment. Extending life tenure to the judiciary protects the possibility of that dispassionate search. A confirmation process aimed consciously at preserving or overturning particular precedents might be justifiable were the Justices to serve, for example, eight- or ten- or twelve-year terms. But if Justices are selected not because they are wise but because they are right, it is not easy to see why they *should* serve for life. Constitutional amendments—the locking-in of new binding rules—supposedly require something more than the concurrence of the President and a bare majority of the Senate. To concede the propriety of denying appointment to the Supreme Court on the basis of a prediction of concrete results is to encourage efforts to determine constitutional meaning through a different mechanism, one too easily manipulated by temporary political majorities.

Judicial independence, if the concept is to have any force, is not a cloak that can be thrown around a new Justice at the very last minute—after the administration of the oath. Independence must arrive earlier, and cover all potential nominees, from the moment that a sitting Justice retires or dies. A nominee is not independent when she is quizzed, openly or not, on the degree of her reverence for particular precedents. If the President who must select a nominee or the Senate that must confirm one can in effect elicit campaign promises while the vacancy exists, then they surely would be justified in complaining bitterly should those promises later be broken.

And yet it is easy to understand how a Senate casting about for its proper role in the process might have stumbled down the path toward electing rather than confirming Supreme Court nominees.   * * *

Passing entirely the question of what judicial philosophy *is,* it should be perfectly plain that at any level much more sophisticated than "Will this nominee vote my party's line?" the members of the Senate are not competent to evaluate it. The carefully nuanced scholarly debate over judicial philosophy is certainly beyond the interest, and probably beyond the ken, of most members of the Senate. * * * This is no knock on the senators; it is, if anything, a knock on the notion that something as obscure and subtle as "judicial philosophy" is a sensible measuring stick for use in the essentially political process of selecting judges.

* * * The Senate may lack the institutional capacity to evaluate judicial philosophy in any non trivial theoretical sense, but that should

not limit the senators to assessing the so-called "professional qualifications of the nominee." It simply means that the Senate ought to look elsewhere in seeking to discover what special expertise it might bring to bear on the confirmation process.

III.   THE SOUL OF DEMOCRACY

* * *

The Senate, responsive to public will but also sharing some of the distance of the courts, has the ability to give voice not simply to the passions of the moment, but to the enduring and fundamental values that shape the specialness of the American people. The institutional design of bicameralism makes this balance possible: what the House votes in its haste, the Senate may reconsider at its leisure. * * *

Giving voice to the deepest common values of the American order does not mean masquerading as either a professional standards review board or a law school appointments committee. It means doing what responsible members of the Senate do best: representing their constituents by reaching conclusions based on a relatively disinterested dialogue, which may be a principally internal one, about the policy most congruent with the fundamental aspirations and long-term interests of the American people.

This dialogue has little to do with predicting results in specific cases. A reflective Senate would refuse to speculate about a potential nominee's likely votes, and would eschew any inquiry into judicial philosophy, not merely because the body might be institutionally incapable of evaluating a nominee's philosophy, but also because the long-term interest of the American people requires what, at a deep level, most Americans probably want or believe that they have: an independent judiciary. * * * A reflective Senate would understand the threat to judicial independence that is posed when the appointment process is used, by Senate and President alike, as a means for pursuing the short-term partisan end of validating or overturning particular lines of cases.[19]

* * *

There is * * * no reason for the Senate to set itself the task of keeping off the Court nominees whose views stray too far beyond the discourse of the mainstream, for the senators are then policing for criminals unlikely to appear. If a nominee's ideas fall within the very broad range of judicial views that are not radical in any nontrivial sense—and Robert Bork has as much right to that middle ground as any

---

19. The tough question is what the Senate should do if its members feel bound (under the argument presented here) to ignore the nominee's "judicial philosophy," when they know full well that the President has (illegitimately) taken that very factor into account. One possibility is to ignore the illegitimate factor in any case, on the ground that the President's breach of duty should not lead to the same breach by the Senate. If, however, the Senate cannot comfortably countenance what the President has done, it is better to reject the nominee out of hand, citing the President's illegitimate conduct, than to damage the judiciary further by adding another layer of substantive review.

other nominee in recent decades—the Senate enacts a terrible threat to the independence of the judiciary if a substantive review of the nominee's legal theories brings about a rejection.

The dilemma, then, is this: how can the Senate carry out its responsibility to give voice to the deepest values and aspirations of the American people, while at the same time not compromising the necessary independence of the Justices? The answer may be to undertake what members of the Senate seem mysteriously reluctant to do—to try to get a sense of the whole person, an impression partaking not only of the nominee's public legal arguments, but of her entire moral universe.

The rhetoric of judging insists that judges should put aside their personal beliefs when called upon to decide what the law requires. In constitutional adjudication especially, however, no matter how much judges strive to interpret without regard to their background morality, they cannot hope for a complete separation of judgment from judge. In this sense, constitutional interpretation is like the interpretation of any other text. The words of the Constitution do not, by themselves, determine very much, and all who must strive to interpret and apply the text, no matter how great their intellectual force or legal sophistication, must at some point make leaps of faith not wholly explicable by reference to standard tools for interpretation. There is in every interpretive task a moment when the interpreter's own experience and values become the most important data. That moment cannot be spotted in advance, any more than the pressing issues of ten years hence can be predicted today. But it is certain that the moment will come, and the Senate can help the nation to be ready when it does.

The issue, finally, is not what sort of theory the nominee happens to indulge, but what sort of person the nominee happens to be. There are two senses in which this judgment ought to matter. First, the nominee ought to be a person for whom moral choices occasion deep and sustained reflection. Second, the nominee ought, in the judgment of the Senate, to be an individual whose personal moral decisions seem generally sound. In moments of crisis, we call upon the Court for a statement of law and, more often than most theorists care to admit, we receive instruction in practical morality instead. At such times, what matters most is not what sort of legal philosophers sit on the Court, but what sort of moral philosophers sit there. Even when times are less difficult and the issues less divisive, the background moral vision of the judge and the degree of her moral reflectiveness nevertheless play significant parts in shaping her interpretive conclusions. This background moral vision and the capacity for moral reflection are perhaps the most important aspects of the judicial personality, and it is for these that the Senate, which enjoys the political space to reflect on the fundamental values of the nation, ought to be searching.

Thus the political task in the real world of real interpretive problems is to people the bench not with Justices holding the right constitutional theories but with Justices possessing the right moral instincts. In this sense, it is far less useful to know that a nominee has ruled that private clubs violate no constitutional provisions when they discriminate against nonwhites than to know whether the nominee herself has belonged to a club with such policies, and for how long. A legal theory leading to the conclusion that private clubs are not regulated by the Constitution is a matter of debate, a matter on which one may take instruction, a matter for a later change of mind. But a lifelong habit of associating by choice with those who prefer not to associate with people of the wrong color tells something vitally important about the character and instincts of a would-be constitutional interpreter, something not easily disavowed by so simple an expedient as, for example, resigning from the club.

Legal theories, like legal institutions, are ultimately no better than those who take them in charge. Within the universe of acceptable legal discourse—a universe for which the system will screen quite effectively without aid from the Senate—a morally upright proponent of an unpopular or eccentric theory will likely turn out to be a better Justice than one who propounds an acceptable theory but whose personal morality is cynical or mendacious. * * *

The Senate would not, of course, be able to predict the particular results that the morally upright Justice would reach in concrete cases, and the reflective Senate would not try. There would be no campaign promises. And yet, over the very long run, as new and unexpected issues arise, there should evolve a healthy convergence between the moral direction of the Justice and the fundamental moral vision of the nation the Justice serves. The popular sense should come to be one of a good, trusted, upstanding individual sitting on the bench, so that even when the people dislike her work, they will obey her—not simply because of her legal authority, but because she is someone held in respect. This prospect might in turn reduce today's tension between the ideal of judicial independence and the demand that the courts support particular political programs. And in the worst of times, when fresh and unexpected issues present grim moral choices, the times when the courts might be most desperately needed, the morally superior individual will almost certainly be the morally superior jurist.

There is, of course, a risk to an approach that seeks to evaluate the personal moral judgment of the nominee: the wall between the public and the private domains, a wall that is dear to liberal and libertarian theory, might be breached. "Has this nominee violated marital vows?" the senators might demand. "Has that one voted Republican? Used marijuana? Had an abortion?" None of these queries can be dismissed as entirely irrelevant, unless one wants to suppose a theory of human motivation that rigorously separates the moral premises for actions on the two sides of the wall. Relevance, however, is not the same as propriety, and the question is who will decide what lines of relevant inquiry are nevertheless inappropriate. Perhaps the Senate is too risky a place to lodge the power of decision. And yet, if members of the Senate who must reach a moral judgment on the nominee are not to be trusted to draw a line between what may legitimately be considered and what may not, then it is not easy to see why they ought to be trusted with any other aspect of the confirmation decision. For if there is indeed a line between the two, its very location—like the location of the line that bounds rational discourse—is a question not of abstract theory, but of politics. Senators inclined to vote "No" because the nominee has had an abortion, or because she refuses to say whether she has or not, must make their decisions in light of the practical political consequences. The political consequences of rejecting a nominee because she has had an abortion, in turn, say something important about the kind of moral judgment that the American people are prepared to respect.

That perhaps is too idealized a notion of the relationship between the American people and the Supreme Court. Perhaps results really are all that matter. Presidents often act as though they value only results, the interest groups that campaign for and against each nomination seem bent entirely on prediction, and the Court itself is hardly immune to the criticism that the result in many cases is all that drives its analysis. But even if there is in the end less truth than aspiration in the vision of an independent and reflective Supreme Court, the Senate of the United States, designed to combine a degree of political sensitivity with the distance necessary for reflection and deliberation, should be the last institution of government to surrender the myth.

ROBERT F. NAGEL,* ADVICE, CONSENT, AND INFLUENCE **
84 Nw.U.L.Rev. 858, 858–875 (1990)

Article II, section 2 of the Constitution states that the President "shall nominate, and by and with the Advice and Consent of the Senate, shall appoint * * * Judges of the supreme Court * * *." This provision presents important questions about the appropriate division of responsibilities between the President and the Senate. A correlative matter is the extent of the responsibility of a judicial nominee to provide information during the appointment process.

Although some politicians and a few academics continue to articulate doubts and reservations about energetic, substantive Senate review of judicial nominees, we seem—as a matter of both practice and theory—to be drifting toward a norm of active Senate participation. I shall begin by describing this norm, its intellectual bases, and some of its operational implications. I then raise some doubts about the norm and suggest a slightly different role for the Senate. In general terms, the point I want to develop is that screening the beliefs of nominees may be at odds with the goal of establishing political influence over the Supreme Court.

* Rothgerber Professor of Constitutional Law at the University of Colorado School of Law.

** Reprinted by special permission of Northwestern University School of Law, Volume 84, Issues 3 & 4, Northwestern University Law Review, (1990), pp. 858–875.

Influence may depend not so much on the decision whether to "consent" as on the utilization of the confirmation process as an opportunity to give "advice."

I.

It is somewhat hazardous to generalize about a developing norm of active Senate participation in the judicial selection process. Even very recent history shows considerable variation. Since 1894, only John Parker, Abe Fortas, Clement Haynesworth, G. Harrold Carswell, Robert Bork, and Douglas Ginsburg can fairly be said to have been rejected by the Senate. Indeed, it is common to contrast the vigorous nineteenth-century tradition of Senate review with a relatively mild twentieth-century record. Despite the recent experiences of Bork and Ginsburg, the Senate during the past ten years has approved Rehnquist (as Chief Justice), O'Connor, Scalia, and Kennedy. The thoroughness of the evaluation of these individuals has fluctuated, and at least sometimes questioning was casual. Some senators continue to assert that their proper role is a limited one, while others can be expected to rediscover the attractions of institutional modesty when the political backdrop changes.

Nevertheless, on the whole, we are developing a norm of active Senate participation—a conscientious effort to evaluate not only the nominees' qualifications, but also their beliefs and probable voting patterns on the Court. The most dramatic evidence of such a norm is the Senate's consideration of Robert Bork's nomination. The Senate's inquiry was prolonged and detailed; it led to the rejection of a person who has been plausibly described as one of the "best qualified candidates for the Supreme Court of this or any other era." This action was not—or did not appear to be—based on geographic, ethnic, or other narrow political considerations. Rather, it appeared to be based on disagreement with the nominee's judicial philosophy and with dissatisfaction over the positions he was likely to take if appointed to the Court.

There are a number of reasons to believe that the Bork nomination represents not an aberration, but an especially vivid manifestation of the underlying current norm. A judicial nominee first appeared at a confirmation hearing in 1925. Since 1955, such appearances have become an entrenched practice. Beginning in 1959, with the hearings on Potter Stewart's nomination, senators have considered it proper to use the occasion of the nominee's appearance to inquire about specific cases, judicial philosophy, and attitudes on issues likely to come before the Court. While different nominees have set different limits on how willing they are to answer these questions, generally they do not resist the idea that senators should be interested in such matters. Indeed, intellectually strong nominees like Fortas, Rehnquist, and Bork on occasion have openly praised and welcomed broad inquiries. Ideological review quickly has become the common practice and accepted norm.

The most compelling reason for senators to concern themselves with the ideology and philosophy of nominees is the same reason that Presidents do. Although it is fashionable (and also partially accurate) to characterize the Burger Court's record as vacillating, uninspiring, and moderately conservative, the deeper truth is that in the twenty years since the appointment of Warren Burger as Chief Justice, the extent of the Supreme Court's influence over public policy has grown significantly and inexorably. Beginning roughly in 1971, the Court began to announce a series of doctrines that vastly increased the range of issues subject to judicial supervision. Thus, under the Burger Court, the federal courts used racial classifications and a host of costly devices to achieve integrated results in hundreds of school districts. Judicial management of prison systems in more than two-thirds of the states was established. For the first time, the Court undertook systematic monitoring of public aid to parochial schools. The Burger Court initiated serious review of governmental use of gender classifications. It insisted on judicial supervision of public regulation of abortion. It imposed minimal procedural protections on the decisionmaking procedures of public schools, prison disciplinary boards, university tenure committees, and other public institutions. It labeled as "speech" advertising, exotic dancing, and campaign contributions and extended first amendment protections to prisoners and corporations. It supervised the design of death penalty statutes and made profoundly important determinations about the operation of the executive branch, including the need for confidentiality in Presidential conversations and the impact of legislative vetoes in hundreds of federal statutes. It opened the door for judicial supervision of patronage, jury selection, political gerrymandering, and criminal sentencing. While the Warren Court made judicial power seem dramatic and morally exciting, the Burger Court made judicial power seem routine and inevitable.

Twenty years ago, it might have been possible to believe that the appointment of a few competent, gray-haired Republicans to the Court would remove the federal judiciary from many areas of political controversy. It is now clear that, in one direction or another, the Court will be a pervasive influence on a wide range of issues that can only in a partial and peripheral way be considered legal rather than political. What legal realism established intellectually, the Burger Court established as a matter of brute fact.

During approximately the same period, as the Burger Court was decisively destroying any possibility of believing that the Court's function is nonpolitical, the less important justifications for limited Senate review were also being discredited. Writing in 1970, Charles L. Black, Jr., concluded an important essay on the judicial selection process by stating:

> To me, there is just no reason at all for a Senator's not voting, in regard to confirmation of a Supreme Court nominee, on the basis of a full and unrestricted review, not embarrassed by any presumption, of the nominee's fitness for the office. In a world that knows a man's social philosophy shapes his judicial behavior, that philosophy is a factor in his fitness. If it is a philosophy the Senator thinks will

make a judge whose service on the Bench will hurt the country, then the Senator can do right only by treating this judgment of his, unencumbered by deference to the President's, as a satisfactory basis in itself for a negative vote. I have as yet seen nothing textual, nothing structural, nothing prudential, nothing historical, that tells against this view.

* * * Black's basic constitutional arguments, while stated tentatively, remain persuasive. It is true, as he argued, that the phrase "advice and consent" does not itself suggest a limited role—indeed, the word "advice" connotes free-wheeling consideration of any factor that might be thought relevant to a President's decision. It is also true, as he argued, that Justices are not a part of the executive branch and therefore, that nothing inherent to the President's executive duties requires legislative deference. I have not seen any effort to refute Black's assessment of the framers' intent, an assessment that emphasized early proposals giving sole power of appointment to the Senate and subsequent arguments that seemed to assume a significant role for the Senate.

Potentially, of course, the most far-reaching objection to the Black position is based on formalistic assumptions. To the extent that the task of judges is only to find the law in legal texts—if social philosophy does not and should not "shape judicial behavior"—it can be thought that the Senate's role should be restricted to assessing a nominee's technical skills. Yet, inquiry into opinions about specific cases might be relevant here, too, since the best proof of technical skills might be demonstrated by textual or historical interpretation. In any event, few today would reject Black's position by rejecting his realist assumptions.

A modern version of the formalist argument does exist, although it is a dissenting view. Some commentators, including Stephen Carter, argue that inquiries into philosophy tend to degenerate into inquiries about probable voting patterns—a result Carter considers inconsistent with judicial review because that institution is intended to "thwart, not to further, the self-interested programs of temporary majorities." The nature of the judicial function, then, requires that the Senate aim its review at deeper considerations. What kinds of considerations? Because Carter fully accepts the realist view that "[t]here is in every interpretative task a moment when the interpreter's own experience and values become the most important data," he concludes that the Senate should judge the nominee as a person: would she possess "the right moral instincts"? Thus the modern version of the formalist position leads to a kind of moral technocratic standard; the issue is not whether the nominee is a skilled lawyer, but whether the nominee is a good person.

Carter's position would divert Senate attention from both general and specific legal beliefs to evaluating a candidate's personal qualities. But even a senator accepting Carter's position might reach much the same kinds of conclusions about the scope of a proper inquiry as did Charles Black. Probable votes are, by Carter's own assumptions, one measure of personal moral qualities. And while it may be true that concern about specific decisional outcomes will tend to be associated with narrow self-interest, it is not necessarily true that self-interest is unrelated to the kinds of profound values that Carter and others think judicial review should protect. Indeed, Carter's concept of judicial review is that fundamental, long-term aspirations can be given expression in the accretion of specific decisions that the Court makes. If so, it is hard to see why political interest in specific results, even if self-interested, cannot also be connected to profound, lasting hopes and beliefs.

A related argument is that the Senate should confine its evaluation to the nominee's professional fitness (rather than moral fitness) because narrow professionalism is all the Senate is qualified to judge. As Bruce Fein engagingly writes, "[t]he Senate, simply stated, is ill-suited intellectually, morally, and politically to pass on anything more substantive than a nominee's professional fitness * * *. Because senators tend to be intellectually shallow and result-oriented, their ostensible inquiries into 'judicial philosophy' will almost invariably degenerate into partisan posturing." This is not a basis for a nominee's refusal to answer questions, unless nominees are entitled to censor the information available to the Senate on the basis of their own assessment of the capacities of those who are supposed to be assessing them. If, on the other hand, the argument is addressed to the Senate, it seems safe to say it is unlikely to succeed. And it should not. Democratic self-government requires that elected officials decide issues about which they are not expert. Legislators are obliged to deal with matters, such as nuclear strategy and economic policy, that are at least as esoteric as judicial philosophy. Unless judicial confirmation can be distinguished from all other legislative duties, Fein's argument is in principle an attack on representative government. Moreover, even passing the dubious claim that senators tend to be intellectually more shallow than judicial nominees or the executive branch officials who select them, it still does not follow that the Senate is in fact unqualified to inquire into jurisprudential questions. Philosophy and doctrine are not, after all, self-contained. Legal ideas have consequences—they change lives. Senators are certainly qualified to consider the impact of the law's abstractions.

Other proposals for limiting the Senate's role are relatively modest, and none is especially persuasive. Some are simply prudential. Senator Orrin Hatch, for example, argues that substantive review by the Senate creates a risk of deadlock as each political party retaliates for the last rejection. More generally, some who have studied the often tawdry history of Senate participation in judicial selection conclude that the process can diminish the public's perception of the Court "as an independent institution." In both instances, the concern is ultimately about the effect of Senate review on the functioning of the Court. Such risks are real, but they argue for responsible ideological review rather than for some technocratic standard. Excessive partisanship and diminished respect for the Court are dangers, but another danger is that a functioning and respected Court will, in Black's words, "hurt the country." If the predicted harm is great and seems likely, a senator could sensibly conclude that damage to the Court was the lesser risk. * * *

Felix Frankfurter, while conceding the legitimacy of the Senate's interest in a nominee's beliefs, appeared to think that personal appearance was undignified and unnecessary. Paul Freund still takes something close to this view. While many would concede that personal testimony is often an inefficient and even ineffective way to evaluate a nominee, it is surely impossible to take the position that a nominee's answers and demeanor are inevitably unhelpful or irrelevant.

* * * Separation of powers is still invoked in the form of a distinction between questions about general philosophy and questions about specific cases, especially cases that are likely to come before the Court. This distinction can be couched as an aspect of separation of powers because the articulated concern is to protect the integrity of the Court's decisionmaking process. It is thought that answers about specific cases or issues might bind the nominee in future deliberations or, at the least, appear to be trading a future vote for confirmation. One of the difficulties with this limitation is that its implications for nominees' behavior are so unclear. It can be thought to preclude answers that *bear* on any matter that *might* come before the Court; if so, a nominee could refuse to discuss all issues, opinions, or beliefs relevant to virtually any legal question. It can be construed more narrowly and preclude only the communication of legal opinions (as distinguished from political philosophy, personal views, and so on). More narrowly still, it might apply only to debatable cases or to cases that the nominee actually foresees coming before the Court. Recent nominees have generally thought the limitation consistent with appearing personally and with answering questions about both legal philosophy and at least some specific legal issues. The limitation is difficult to maintain during the course of questioning. In any event, it does not restrict senators' voting on the basis of predictions about a nominee's positions on cases likely to arise. As usually formulated, it only regulates sources of information rather than the types of information that senators are entitled to consider. The limitation is confusing in its implications and more an irritant than an important challenge to the premises behind the norm of active, ideological review.

Even this minimal restriction has been subjected to powerful criticism. Grover Rees, who had some responsibility for judicial selections in the Reagan Justice Department, argues that views on specific cases are a relevant and important basis for understanding a nominee's actual philosophy and temperament, and that questions can be framed to ask for present opinions rather than for commitments. Of course, public cynicism is sufficient to create some danger of an appearance of impropriety, but this is a problem even if nominees resist public expression of opinions about particular cases. After all, the whole point of active Senate review is to decide whether a nominee's "service on the Bench will hurt the country"—a determination which, as a practical matter, requires predicting a nominee's votes on particular cases. Questions about personal background, general philosophy, and judicial approach are patently designed to afford a basis for such predictions. Moreover, the nominee's answers are usually designed to provide vague reassurance about future voting behavior. In this circumstance, avoiding direct discussion of what everyone is interested in seems at best a nicety and at worst a charade. * * *

The perplexing issue is not whether a nominee should refuse to answer questions about cases that might arise; the difficult issue is to identify the outer limits to a proper exchange on this subject. Suppose a nominee is asked, "Will you commit here and now to vote to overturn [or to uphold] *Roe v. Wade?*" Suppose, further, that the inquiring senator adds, "Before you answer, let me emphasize that your response will largely determine for me whether your service on the bench will hurt the country, so unless you tell me you are going to reverse [uphold] *Roe,* I am going to vote against you." Now, assume a nominee answers the question directly: "Senator, read my lips; I will vote to reverse [uphold] *Roe v. Wade* at the first opportunity." This exchange at first seems reprehensible. The nominee has indicated how a case should be decided and has done so in an apparent effort to gain appointment to the Court. However, the exchange only takes realism seriously. To use Professor Black's words again, "in a world that knows that a man's social philosophy shapes his judicial behavior," it is necessary to admit that personal belief can influence a judge's decision and in some circumstances might be determinative. This is to say that any self-aware person could know, without regard to the particulars of a lawsuit, how she is going to vote in at least some cases. It is unimportant that the nominee's answer is made in an effort to gain confirmation, because an honest nominee would want his or her intentions to coincide with the preferences of both the President and the Senate. That is what makes the nomination appropriate to begin with.

Suppose the question is changed to this: "Will you commit here and now not to vote to reverse *Brown v. Board of Education?*" As others have suggested, anyone who could not answer this question probably does not deserve to be a judge. It is not a significant distinction between the question about *Brown* and the question about *Roe* that *Brown* is "settled" law. The content of an answer about *Brown* can communicate predispositions with respect to those desegregation issues likely to be litigated. Anyway, one reason for asking about a settled case is to ensure that it remains settled; the nominee's answer about *Brown* is in a sense more of a commitment than the answer about *Roe,* because the former is a commitment not even to hear a case. Both answers would be relevant to the Senate's inquiry because both cases are exceedingly important. Nominees can provide firm answers, not because the legal problems in either case are easy, but because both cases turn on basic issues of legal philosophy and personal morality. The Senate's job in the nomination process is to get such commitments, and the nominees' responsibility is to give the best present opinions that they can.

This does not mean that a nominee should make specific commitments with respect to any case or with respect to long "laundry lists" of potential cases. But this proviso does not rest on the need to protect the judicial process. The problem is not that "commitments" are being made. If it is a president's or a senator's task to use the nomination process to shape a Court that will not harm the country, a nominee's detailed set of commitments would seem better than a few commitments on major issues like desegregation or abortion. But the longer the list of cases on which the nominee is willing to take positions, the less plausible is the claim that the particulars of the facts or the argumentation should make no difference. Thus, willingness to make commitments on many cases (and hence on close cases) would not exactly be improper; it might, however, indicate reckless disregard for specifics. The problem is not separation of powers; the problem is an unjudicious nominee. * * *

In sum, the major modern limitation on the Senate's role—the rule that nominees should not answer questions about how they will vote on specific issues that might come before the Court—is a weak constraint. While it can be used as an excuse for avoiding controversial issues, as a conscientious position it should not prevent answers on a few major issues about which a nominee can properly have inflexible views; nor should it prevent answers on any number of minor issues if the nominee's response is framed carefully to maintain the distinction between opinions of a nominee and decisions of a Justice.

We are developing a norm of substantive, ideological Senate review of nominees to the Supreme Court because, as Charles Black saw almost twenty years ago, there is one very strong reason for active review—that is, the broad impact that the Court's performance has on public policy—and no strong reasons against it. * * * It is now the conventional wisdom to view the appointment process as an appropriate occasion for the political culture to communicate its views on legal issues to the federal judiciary and thereby to shape the development of the law. For so many to agree that politics should influence law, perhaps, is not surprising today. But given the realistic assumptions underlying the conventional wisdom, it is surprising that so much emphasis is placed on controlling the identity of the specific individuals appointed to the bench.

II.

The logic of the conventional wisdom seems straightforward. If it is a proper responsibility of politicians to influence the development of the law, then politicians should carefully screen individual nominees to maximize the chances that preferred values will be reflected in the Court's opinions. The assumption is that trying to predict judicial behavior will at least be more effective than the alternatives, which are usually assumed to amount only to some form of non-ideological review (or "rubber-stamping"). This is the innocent logic of purposeful behavior: why not at least try?

One answer is that in the area of judicial selection, as in so many other areas, intentional behavior can backfire. Full Senate review will, for example, tend to legitimate the Supreme Court's decisions because the Justices, by definition, will have satisfied the Senate not only as to their general qualifications and character, but also as to their political values, judicial philosophy, and even their probable voting behavior. To the extent that senators are publicly identified with Justices, it might be more difficult for senators to engage in public criticism of later judicial decisions, to vote for either substantive or jurisdictional bills that cut against the Court's positions, or to consider the drastic remedy of impeachment. If the evident goal of the Senate's advice and consent function is to pick Justices who will make good decisions, bad judicial performance reflects poorly on senatorial skill and judgment. Moreover, to the extent that the Senate has taken public responsibility for the views of the Justices, political accountability is spread and thereby obscured. If the public disapproves of the work of the Rehnquist Court, it will not be sufficient to hold the President responsible at the polls; to the extent that the Senate's role is to shape the Court's performance, it will also be necessary to replace key senators, a more complex and unlikely eventuality. In short, the methods for achieving political influence over the shape of public law include post-appointment controls; it is at least possible that "rubber-stamping" nominees may be more compatible with some of these than is active screening during the appointment process.

Such risks become more serious to the extent that Senate review creates only an appearance of selectivity and control. * * * There are a number of reasons to expect more illusion than reality in the screening process. It is commonplace to note that even Presidents are frequently surprised by the behavior of their appointees. This seems inevitable. The role, viewpoint, associations, and institutional perspective of a Justice are drastically different than for any other job. There is probably no way even for a nominee to be sure how he or she will react to those unique circumstances. Presidents at least have the opportunity to search and select actively; the Senate, no matter how ambitious its announced objectives, can only reject. No one really knows how Robert Bork would have voted as a Justice, and it is certainly impossible to know how different Justice Kennedy will turn out to be than Bork might have been. In addition, even if thorough ideological screening could be successful, as Henry Monaghan has noted, there are natural limits to public interest and senatorial energy. Although conscientious review can be expected to be consistently honored as a matter of rhetoric and form, thorough screening has been and is likely to be episodic, so that actual influence over the Court's performance will be limited even under the most optimistic assumptions.

Nevertheless, as recent history demonstrates, the norm of ideological screening can be expected to produce an occasional event like the Bork hearings—hearings which represent the most effort and intellectual seriousness that can reasonably be expected. Bork had an unusually full record of intellectual writing and of public service, so that senators had a tempting amount of material from which to make predictions and judgments. The public could be interested in the process because it was plausible to believe that Bork might have significant impact on the Court's decisions and because some of his expressed views and public behavior had been controversial. And political efforts expended on the Bork hearings held the promise of a real payoff; that is, since Bork was closely identified with an Administration that was politically injured and at the end of its term, the classic conditions for rejection existed.

If the Bork hearings represent a high water mark for the modern norm, what do they tell us about the effectiveness of ideological screening for achieving political influence over the Court? An answer to this question depends on assumptions about the sorts of political considerations that should influence the development of public law. There is far less consensus about this than there is about the more general proposition that politics should shape law through the appointment process. It is usually thought that senators should give effect to high-toned reflections on law and public policy. Thus, Bruce Ackerman describes the Bork hearings "as a part of this ongoing project in self-government" under a Constitution which "provid[es] us with institutions and a language by which we may discriminate between the passing show of normal politics and the deeper movements in popular opinions which * * * ultimately *earn* a democratic place in the constitutional law * * *." Stephen Carter criticizes the Bork hearings for emphasizing "whether a Bork appointment would further or hinder the articulated interests * * * of women, or of nonwhites, or of * * * Congress * * *." He suggests that the hearings should have focused instead on "the fundamental aspirations and long-term interests of the American people." Ronald Dworkin's description is different from Carter's, but his prescription is also high-minded. He says the hearings were "an extended seminar on the Constitution" and humbly urges that they represent a rejection of "crude historicism" and an acceptance of "a jurisprudence * * * of principle." And Laurence Tribe writes that the ideal is a "concerted, collective effort by the upper house of Congress to articulate a vision of the Constitution's future, and to scrutinize potential Justices in that vision's light * * *."

It is only to be expected that if the Senate is to understand its function as creating something so august as constitutional law, we should gravitate to the most familiar and reassuring model for guiding the Senate's deliberations. And that model, obviously, is judging. Thus, one paradoxical consequence of self-conscious commitment to political law-creation is the suppression of the political character of senatorial politics. Senators should act, we are told, like meta-Justices: since senators, by choosing the Justices who will develop the law, create the law indirectly, they should themselves make overarching determinations about the role of historicism in interpretation, the enduring values of the American people, and so on. In short, we are willing to tolerate political influence over the law during the process of appointment, but only if politicians adopt the perspective and the vocabulary of judges.

This gravitational pull of the legal culture was amply illustrated during the Bork hearings. Senators were praised in the press for their learned questions on textualism, judicial restraint, the place of stare decisis in constitutional law, and other matters of legal philosophy. There were elaborate debates about arcane legal doctrines, including the proper standard of review in gender discrimination cases—senators talking about tiers of scrutiny!—subtle variations in the clear and present danger test, and the inter-relationship between fifth amendment due process and fourteenth amendment equal protection. Senators' brows were furrowed about penumbras and the ninth amendment, about the containability of the category "political speech," and about the objectivity of the reasonable relationship test as compared to that of the rationality test.

The effects of legalizing political discourse are, given the realist assumptions that underlie the norm of active ideological review, mostly unfortunate. Because the focus is on legal philosophy and legal doctrine, nominees have a natural advantage if their views on these subjects are difficult to ascertain. The issue before the Senate is whether there is some reason for rejection—that is, whether a nominee has committed or will commit some intellectual offense. Thus, nominees who are forthcoming during the hearings or have established records on legal issues will be at risk more than those whose legal opinions are obscure, nonexistent, or withheld. One effect, then, of trying to predict judicial behavior is to favor nominees who are relatively unpredictable. The consequences are graphically illustrated by the meandering, and often astonishing, performance of the Burger Court.

It is true, on the other hand, that although the Senate cannot be sure what direction it is giving the Court, ideological review does tend to keep those with expressed and unacceptable views off the bench. While this is negative influence over the development of the law, it is influence. However, the legalization of political discourse that accompanies ideological review means that the legal establishment is likely to control the exercise of this negative influence. Someone has to advise the senators on how to participate in judge-like conversations and on how to evaluate the nominees' answers. Who better than the elites of the practicing bar and the academy? Is Bork outside the mainstream of legal thought? Better ask those who make up the mainstream. Hence, not only the general values but even specific pet theories of a few eminent professors—theories about the unenumerated rights of the ninth amendment or the breadth of the principle at stake in *Griswold*—can momentarily masquerade as deep political consensus. This professorial influence accounts for what seems in retrospect to be the dream-like quality to much of Bork's interrogation. Did senators really insist that constitutional text and framers' intent cannot serve as guides to interpretation and that a judge's fidelity to such materials would be inconsistent with a two-hundred year "tradition"?[41] Did members of Congress actually

---

41. *See, e.g., Bork Hearings* at 259 (Senator Specter arguing that *Brown v. Board* of *Education* was "at very sharp variance with what the Framers had intended"), 578

welcome judicial readiness to negate legislative decisions and to invite such actions on the basis of the Justices' feelings about the "needs of the Nation" or the fact of an individual's existence? [42] And did politicians repeatedly take positions that could be characterized as supporting judicial solicitude for such politically controversial causes as homosexuality, obscenity, and subversive speech? [43] All these lines of questioning did occur, and in the argumentative, intellectualized atmosphere of the hearings they did not seem to create political embarrassment for senators. But they do not exactly have those qualities of stolid common sense and moderation that we like to think characterize the general public's instincts. The questions certainly reflect views that are fashionable in academic circles. It is a sad irony that purposeful effort to democratize the Court should result in enhanced power for groups that already have disproportionate influence over the shape of the law.

Legalized discourse, of course, did not entirely replace normal politics during the Bork hearings. Although some of the tactics were rough and unfair, we must look to some of these unjudicious moments to see how political screening can be constructive. Two of the most troubling but also most useful parts of the hearings were the exchanges on *Griswold v. Connecticut* and *Shelly v. Kraemer,* cases that are routinely demolished in first-year law school classrooms. Bork's doubts about the reasoning in these decisions did not put him outside the mainstream; intellectually, those doubts and arguments put him near the heart of the law's commitment to clarity, consistency, and principle. Nevertheless, Bork came away the loser on both subjects. Why did arguments, which seem strong in the nation's law school classrooms and in its legal journals, seem weak in the arena of politics?

The reason, obviously, is that what counts in political life is different from what counts in the legal culture. In politics, ideas and justifications matter less and they matter differently; consequently, interest in nuance and abstraction seems suspicious rather than admirable. The position on *Griswold* that seemed powerful had little to do with theories of interpretation or the ninth amendment. What was compelling was

(Specter arguing that the Court has a "consistent tradition" of protecting values rooted in conscience of the people rather than in specific language), 682 (Specter claiming a popular "consensus by the tradition of our Court" that judges should rule even though they had no law), and 683 (Specter arguing that "law does not depend on an understanding of original intent" and that original intent may be impossible to identify).

42. *See, e.g., id.* at 262 (Senator Specter's approval of *Bolling v. Sharpe* based on Justices' "feelings" about "the needs of the nation.") and 296 (Senator Biden arguing that right to privacy arises because humans exist).

43. Regarding homosexuality, see *id.* at 88 (Senator Biden asking whether any legislative body can regulate sexual behavior of "a married couple, or anyone else"). *See also id.* at 124–25 (Bork linking right to privacy with protection of homosexual conduct and use of cocaine and asking Senator Kennedy, "Privacy to do what, Senator?"). As to obscenity, see *id.* at 256 (Senator Specter apparently criticizing Bork for having written that the first amendment does not reach pornography or obscenity). As to subversion, see *id.* at 412 (Senator Specter defending Holmes's statement that if proletarian dictatorship is "destined to be accepted by the dominant forces of the community * * * they should be given their chance and have their way.").

that people have come to expect some judicial protection of their sexual privacy and that they want such protection. The position on *Shelley* that seemed powerful had little to do with the legal mainstream's views on state action. What was compelling was that racially exclusionary covenants are no longer usual or expected, and that the interest of minority groups in integrated housing has gained wide acceptance and legitimacy. It seemed quirky, if not sinister, for a nominee to dwell on explanations in arenas where widespread perceptions of normalcy, intense desires, and strongly-felt interests are what count.

By exposing legal thinking to broader political values and forms of discourse, the Bork hearings provided a useful testing ground. While not a plebiscite or anything close to one, the tone and content of the hearings sent important messages about the acceptability of decisional outcomes and justificatory norms to the executive branch, to sitting judges, and to would-be judges. This sort of influence depends not on selection, but on communication. It is "advice." The desire to give advice is one reason senators want to confront nominees personally.
* * *

Unfortunately, the legalization of discourse during the Bork hearings crowded out much of the politics, giving nonlegal standards only occasional and implicit force. Consider how little information was developed, in all those days of witnesses and questioning, on the actual effects of the Supreme Court's doctrines and decisions. A few representatives of law enforcement organizations spoke about crime and dangers to police officers, and black politicians emphasized the importance of the changes that the Warren Court achieved in the South, and economist Thomas Sowell offered an opinion about the effects of affirmative action. On the other hand, an overwhelming proportion of the witnesses were law professors who spoke of philosophy and doctrine, and these subjects also dominated the senators' statements and questions.

There was virtually no interest in whether the performance of the Court in the last ten or twenty years has been good for the country or in how that performance might be improved. What have the federal courts done to public schooling? Have they in fact reduced discipline and sapped local involvement? How much racial integration has been achieved, and should numerical balance be given more or less priority in the years ahead? Have the Court's separation of powers decisions on matters such as the legislative veto turned out to be, as many at first feared, harmful to maintaining accountability over administrative agencies? Have the privacy decisions strengthened or undermined family life? How serious an impediment has the exclusionary rule been to effective law enforcement? Has extension of free speech protections in areas like campaign finance regulation and defamation been healthy or destructive for our system of free debate? * * * Such questions could not have been answered definitively; it would not have been possible even to begin to deal with all of them. But time would better have been spent on these kinds of questions than on the bottomless jurisprudential

and doctrinal issues to which the senators devoted most of their resources. * * *

If the legal culture is properly concerned with ideas, the political
culture is properly concerned with the consequences of ideas—with the
everyday effects of abstractions on perception, aspiration, and self-
interest. The Senate's pre-occupation with the decision whether to
consent to Bork's nomination left little room for the development of the
sort of information and overt pressure that could have amounted to
important advice about whether and in what respects the Supreme Court
should be changing direction.

CONCLUSION

The Bork hearings were the most that can be hoped for from the
modern norm of active Senate review. This norm is based on the
assumption that politics should help shape the law. To the extent that
the hearings required a judicial nominee to listen to and speak the
language of politics, they provided limited but significant political influence over the Court. Unfortunately, this language was often excluded or
submerged. The Bork hearings, therefore, certainly raise a serious
doubt about whether, especially on more ordinary occasions, purposeful,
self-conscious efforts to predict and control outcomes are consistent with
the assumption that politics can bring something important to bear on
public law through appointment decisions. The hearings were at their
best when they created a political forum—a place where the answers
that dominate in the legal culture were not fully satisfactory and where
legal discourse seemed limited and sounded tinny. They were at their
worst when senators tried to be judges, which they did as a natural
result of their efforts to exert indirect control over doctrines and outcomes. Achieving appropriate democratic influence over the Supreme
Court requires more concern with past performance and less with
prediction, more self-assurance about politics and less pre-occupation
with law.

STEPHEN CARTER,* THE CONFIRMATION MESS, REVISITED **

84 Nw.U.L.Rev. 962, 962–975 (1990)

I. ASKING THE QUESTIONS

For an institution that sits atop what is supposed to be the least
dangerous branch of the federal government, the Supreme Court of the
United States excites a remarkable degree of cautious and envious
affection. We love it, we hate it, we cherish it, we fear it—but, most
importantly, when one of its members steps aside and leaves a vacancy,
we all feel as though we own it. It is *our* Court, and, in the rhetoric of
the moment of nomination and confirmation, it ought to articulate *our*
values. Choosing a new Justice nowadays is a bit like hiring a new

* Professor of Law, Yale University.   Reprinted with the permission of Stephen
** Copyright (c) 1990 by Stephen Carter.   Carter.

servant—one wants to see prior experience, excellent references, a judicious temperament, and an instinct for knowing the master's will.

* * *

I am firmly on record as believing, and I continue to believe, that when senators ask questions intended to elicit information that will permit them to predict the votes that a nominee will cast if confirmed, they are engaging in an activity that represents a profound threat to judicial independence. Approving nominees who will vote the "right way" means enshrining the politically expedient judgments of a given era as fundamental constitutional law. That cannot be what life tenure was designed to achieve, and if it is, then life tenure is a despotic horror that we ought to sweep away.

That said, I hasten to add that I only believe that asking the questions is constitutionally improper. I do not consider the questions unconstitutional. On the contrary, if one conceives unconstitutionality as a prediction of what a court is likely to do in fact (a conception that presumably would have appealed to Holmes), then I am quite clear that questions intended to make prediction easier are *not* unconstitutional. I would not want the courts involved at all. I am quite confident that the senators are entitled under the Constitution to cast votes for or against a nominee on any basis they choose—be it judicial philosophy, political party, race, religion, or color of hair—and that no court ought to give relief in a suit claiming wrongful denial of confirmation. * * *

Casting votes on any grounds they please, including disagreement with judicial philosophy or prediction of particular votes, is, I emphasize, what I believe the Constitution *permits* the senators to do. That is not the same as saying that I think exercising this particular prerogative is a good idea. Actually, I think that making a decision on the basis of a predicted vote is contrary to the spirit of separation of powers in general, and of an independent judiciary in particular.

I have used the term "constitutional impropriety" to capture the idea that there are things that courts should not (or mistakenly do not) forbid, even though they are contrary to the spirit of the Constitution, and even contrary to its structure. Under this model, a Senate decision to reject a nominee because, for example, she was a black woman would be constitutionally improper. But it would not be unconstitutional. Similarly, a Senate decision to approve a nominee because she promised to uphold a controversial bit of legislation would be constitutionally improper, but it would not be unconstitutional.

In fact, even though a nominee can and should decline to express a view on pending cases, it is certainly constitutionally permissible (although still, I believe, improper) for a senator to refuse to vote to confirm on the basis of that very refusal to speak. For example, Senator McClellan, who as a member of the Senate Judiciary Committee voted against the confirmation of Thurgood Marshall as an Associate Justice (McClellan did not vote on the Senate floor), was one of several senators who hoped to obtain the nominee's commitment to overturn *Miranda v. Arizona,*[15] the decision requiring police officers to inform suspects of their rights before beginning any custodial interrogation. Marshall, as Solicitor General, had argued for the result that the senators now favored, but at his confirmation hearings he refused to say whether he would, if the case arose again, vote in accordance with his brief. The following colloquy ensued:

SENATOR McCELELLAN * * *. Do you subscribe to the philosophy expressed in the majority of the *Miranda* opinion * * *?

JUDGE MARSHALL. I would say again, I respectfully state to you, Senator, that this is certainly a case that is on its way to the Supreme Court right now.

SENATOR McCLELLAN. But it is already ruled on. This is the ruling of the Court.

JUDGE MARSHALL. But there are other cases. The *Miranda* case is not the end. The case itself says in three or four places in the opinion that they do not know what Congress intends to do, they do not know—

SENATOR McCLELLAN. I am not talking about legislation. I am asking you now about the Constitution. Do you think that the Constitution requires that evidence be excluded?

JUDGE MARSHALL. I cannot comment on what is coming up to the Court.

SENATOR McCLELLAN. But this has already been there.

JUDGE MARSHALL. But there are hundreds of other ones on the way that are variations on this.

SENATOR McCLELLAN. Of course there are, but this is specific and has been done.

JUDGE MARSHALL. Well, Senator, I respectfully say that it would be improper for me to tell you and the committee or anybody else how I intend to vote.

SENATOR McCLELLAN. It is not improper, may I say, for me to weigh your reluctance to answer.

JUDGE MARSHALL. It certainly is not.

SENATOR McCLELLAN. Very well.

JUDGE MARSHALL. It certainly is not. You have a perfect right to try to find out—

SENATOR McCLELLAN. I will try to pursue one or two further questions. Do you subscribe to the philosophy that the fifth amendment right to assistance of counsel requires that counsel be present before police can interrogate the accused?

JUDGE MARSHALL. That is part of the *Miranda* rule.

15. 384 U.S. 436 (1966).

SENATOR McCLELLAN. Yes.

JUDGE MARSHALL. And, as I say, I can't comment, because it is coming back up.

SENATOR McCLELLAN. I have to wonder, from your refusal to answer, if you mean the negative.

JUDGE MARSHALL. Well, that is up to you sir. But I have never been dishonest in my life.

SENATOR McCLELLAN. I did not say that. But you lead me to wonder why I cannot get the answer.

Marshall's position, of course, was quite simple. It would be wrong, he insisted, to make the promises that McClellan and others demanded. By refusing to make the promises, he in effect denied the senators the information that they needed in order to predict his votes. And whether McClellan and others chose to penalize him for it or not, Marshall was right to remain silent.

II. GETTING THE ANSWERS

[Some aspects of the] battle over the Bork nomination * * * mirrored the controversy over Thurgood Marshall's nomination almost exactly twenty years earlier. Marshall, like Bork, came to his hearing with a magnificent resume: successful litigator (twenty-nine victories in thirty-four Supreme Court arguments), judge on the Court of Appeals for the Second Circuit (in those days unquestionably the nation's second most important court), and Solicitor General of the United States. At that time of his nomination, Marshall was already one of the great figures of twentieth-century American law. His hearings should have been a bit like a coronation. Instead, there was an air of *lese majeste* about the thing, as senators nitpicked through his record. * * *

The parallels between Marshall and Bork begin with the way that the two nominations were characterized. Opponents of Bork said that he was a narrow ideologue rather than a principled conservative. Change "conservative" to "liberal" and the same proposition can be found in criticism of Marshall. Marshall's nomination was opposed, like Bork's, because it would upset the rough left-right balance on the Court. Critics of Bork complained that the moderate swing vote of Lewis Powell would be replaced by the vote of a right-wing ideologue. Critics of Marshall complained that the moderate swing vote of Tom Clark would be replaced by the vote of a left-wing ideologue.

Like Bork's critics, who focused much on the "swing-vote" argument on *Roe v. Wade,* Marshall's critics had a particular case in mind when they spoke of the Court's alignment. They worried that Marshall might have turned around the 5–4 vote in *Walker v. City of Birmingham,* the case that held that court orders cannot be challenged by disobedience and, more important for the political moment, sustained the contempt citation and jail sentence of Martin Luther King, Jr., for parading in Birmingham without a permit and in defiance of an injunction. Had

Marshall been on the Court when *Walker* was decided, so the worried opponents insisted, Dr. King might have gotten away with his defiance.

And there was much more. Marshall's critics, like Bork's, took him to task for blaspheming any number of icons—only they were icons that faced to the right rather than to the left. Bork was attacked for his disrespect of Supreme Court precedent, and, sometimes, for disrespecting constitutional theories—for example, the theory that the ninth amendment provides judicially enforceable rights—that the Supreme Court has never embraced. Marshall was criticized for urging the Supreme Court to overturn venerable precedents and for disrespecting other constitutional theories—for example, the view that the fourteenth amendment permits separate-but-equal segregation—that the Supreme Court had recently rejected.

Both candidates, moreover, were accused of lacking judicial temperament, of being too much the advocate, and of being too committed to their particular models of justice to engage in the dispassion (that word again) that their opponents suggested was the proper approach to the judicial process. Bork, it was said, was too much the abstract philosopher, ungenerous toward individuals, and ever the pleader for such special interests as free enterprise. Marshall, according to the critics, was disqualified because his lifetime of struggling for racial justice had warped his vision, as evidenced, for example, by the many speeches he had given strongly espousing his civil rights ideals. Bork had given addresses questioning whether the due process clause protected unenumerated fundamental rights. Marshall had given briefings questioning the constitutional authority of law enforcement officials to plant listening devices without court orders. Bork was attacked for denying that the Constitution is a living document. Marshall was attacked for endorsing the same proposition. On and on similar questions went, the painstaking dissection of every public comment by the nominee, the cross-examination about every nuance, all in the purported service of enabling the Senate to discover the nominee's judicial philosophy—that is, all in the service of helping the senators figure out which way the nominee, if confirmed, would vote.

* * *

Bork's opponents made much of the identities and arguments of the interest groups that opposed him, giving prominent mention in the Committee Report to the objections of forty percent of full-time faculty members of accredited law schools and a variety of bar groups. Marshall's opponents gave similar prominence to a report of nearly three-quarters of the chief justices of the state supreme courts, charging that the Warren Court's work (which Marshall was expected to carry on) generally disregarded principles of federalism and the rights of states.

Of course, Marshall was subjected to other lines of questioning, some of them far more offensive than what Bork had to face.

* * *

But the fact that the attacks on Marshall were worse does not mean that the attacks on Bork were justified or fair. * * * Sadly, if the Bork mess has made one thing clear, it is that the outrage about inappropriate tactics turns out to be a matter of whose ox is being gored.

* * *

IV. INTEREST GROUPS AND JUDICIAL MEDIOCRITY

Even a would-be Justice whose nomination has successfully been cast in the political mode can be confirmed. But sometimes the confirmation will be rocky. Eleven senators voted against the nomination of Thurgood Marshall. The Marshall confirmation battle came in the late middle age of the civil rights movement, after Selma and Birmingham and the Audobon Ballroom but before Memphis, and the heat of the matter is evidenced by the fact that some twenty senators considered it the better part of valor not to show up to vote.

It would not be accurate, I think, to say that interest groups were responsible for the votes against Marshall, any more than they deserve the credit or, if one prefers, the blame for the defeat of Bork. What the interest groups can do, and perhaps will do for the foreseeable future, is raise the costs to future nominees by spreading on the public record arguments and allegations and conclusions that will make the nominees seem to be among the least savory of characters. Perhaps in the long run, interest group activity of this kind (combined with the ridiculous salaries, which any number of forces in the society are conspiring to keep depressed) will simply make highly qualified individuals shun judicial service. After all, who will want to go through (and put families through) what it too often takes to become a judge—to say nothing of a Justice?

Well, one might respond, there is always somebody. And that's true. Perhaps Ralph Nader is right, and the benches will be filled with the advocates for the oppressed (*i.e.*, the members of the legal staffs of the interest groups), to whom salaries that judges earn might be quite attractive. Many of these people would, of course, be outstanding candidates for judicial office. What Nader overlooks—and what I fear the interest groups that line up in opposition to various nominees often overlook as well—is that none of this will screen out the truly ambitious, who might be beyond shame, or might simply learn from Bork's experience and try to be more cautious about expressing their views much earlier in their careers.

What a judiciary we will have then! Ignoring Plato's advice, we will ultimately fill the federal bench with those who want most to be there rather than those perhaps we most need. No doubt there are any number of earnest, hard working, morally reflective lawyers of good will and good nature who would be very fine judges, but who will look the whole thing over and say, "No thanks." And if we treat them as Marshall and Bork were treated, and underpay them into the bargain, we will have few arguments available to overcome their understandable reluctance.

How sad to discourage public service at a time when a growing ethic of selfishness makes it hard enough to convince so many of our best that the Government (capital G) is anything other than a burden on well-educated and well-paid Baby Boomers, or, at best, a supplier of resume points. In the long run, driving away people we ought to be drawing in can only lead us to a judicial branch full of mediocrities—a prospect likely to please virtually no one.

DAVID STRAUSS [†] AND CASS SUNSTEIN,[††] THE SENATE, THE CONSTITUTION AND THE CONFIRMATION PROCESS
101 Yale L.J. 1491, 1491–1524 (1992)*

It is difficult to find anyone who is satisfied with the way Supreme Court Justices are appointed today. Many of the criticisms are prompted by partisanship, of course. But there is a substantial element of truth in the complaints made by partisans on both sides. And those who are not partisan, but who simply want a healthy process that conforms to the constitutional design and is likely to produce the best appointments, have perhaps the most to criticize.

In this Essay, we suggest that a return to the confirmation process contemplated by the text and structure of the Constitution—a process in which the Senate plays a more independent role than it does today—would help eliminate aspects of the system that both sides, Administration supporters as well as Administration critics, find objectionable. It would also produce a better Court along two dimensions: a Court with Justices of greater distinction, and a Court that reflects a more appropriate diversity of views.

Although often overstated, the criticisms of the current process are telling. Supporters of the Administration object that members of the Senate, and private groups generally critical of the Administration, expend enormous energy not in disinterested inquiry but in trying to "catch" the nominee: to find some statement in her record that reveals a belief so extreme as to be "out of the mainstream." The hearings themselves consist of trying to get the nominee to betray views that will be unacceptable to the public at large, or, failing that, to make inconsistent statements that can be used as evidence of an unprincipled "confirmation conversion." As a result, the Administration's supporters insist, many potential candidates with distinguished records are effectively

† Professor of Law, University of Chicago Law School. Strauss served as Special Counsel to the United States Senate Committee on the Judiciary in connection with the nomination of Justice David H. Souter to the Supreme Court. * * *

†† Karl N. Llewellyn Professor of Jurisprudence, University of Chicago, Law School and Department of Political Science.

* Reprinted by permission of The Yale Law Journal Company and Fred B. Rothman & Company from *The Yale Law Journal,* Vol. 101, pp. 1491–1524.

disqualified from the Court because their opponents can unfairly attack them with isolated statements they have made in the past. The result is an unduly political and sensationalistic spectacle that degrades the Court, the Senate, and the nominee.

The Administration's opponents reply that the real problem is that, for the Administration, filling vacancies on the Supreme Court has become a public relations offensive: one that consists of managing images and hiding the ball, while at the same time pushing the Court in a consistent and (to them) unhealthy direction. The President, his opponents say, chooses "stealth" nominees whom he has reason to believe are deeply conservative, but whose views the Senate will not be able to uncover. The White House then carefully prepares the nominees for the confirmation hearings, to the point where there is now practically a script: the nominee is open-minded, has "no agenda," enthusiastically accepts both *Brown v. Board of Education* and *Griswold v. Connecticut,* is humbled by the difficulty of being a Justice, and admires Justice Harlan.

The nominees commit themselves to liberal-sounding principles of privacy and racial and gender justice; but the commitments are at such a high level of platitudinous abstraction that they reveal nothing about the nominees' views on controversial issues. And if anything potentially embarrassing surfaces from the nominees' records, the Administration's opponents say, the nominees try to distance themselves from it or to shift attention to other, more attractive aspects of their backgrounds. The consequence is a confirmation process that amounts to a media event unedifying for the public, undignified for the country, and unlikely to produce outstanding Justices or an outstanding Court.

Both of these accounts are exaggerated, but neither, unhappily, is very far from the mark. Indeed, the criticisms, though coming from sharply different sources, tend to converge. From the standpoint of the original constitutional plan, the current practice is indeed inadequate. Under the constitutional plan, the confirmation process should involve informed and tempered deliberation within the Senate, the White House, and the public at large about the best way to achieve a distinguished Supreme Court. At the very least, the President and the Senate should attempt to obtain Justices of outstanding character, of high intellectual caliber, and with qualities that will contribute something new or of particular value to the existing Court. Many members of the Senate and the Administration have tried hard to carry out this task. But it is—to understate the matter—improbable that existing procedures are well suited to its fulfillment.

The unfortunate current situation has many causes, but one that is most immediately apparent is the prolonged division of the federal government between the two political parties. Nominees selected by Republican Presidents have filled the last eleven vacancies on the Supreme Court (and sixteen of the last twenty). But eight of the eleven appointments were made while the Senate was solidly controlled by

Democratic majorities. Nothing remotely similar has happened before in our history. Despite this unprecedented situation, Republican Presidents have made ideological appointments with little senatorial opposition, even though the Senate was usually controlled by another party. Any effort to evaluate the current situation must come to terms with this striking fact.

One possible response to divided government, and to the troubled Supreme Court confirmation process it has produced, is for the Senate to be more deferential to the Administration's preferences. The Senate might confine itself to a role similar to that traditionally played by the American Bar Association and other advisory groups: to inquire into whether the nominee meets certain standards of character and professional distinction. Under this approach, the Senate could not appropriately consider a nominee's basic commitments or views on controversial issues, unless those views were so extreme as to call into question the nominee's character or competence.

Confining the Senate to this deferential role would certainly eliminate some of the current complaints about the antagonistic nature of the confirmation process, and to this extent it would be an advance. But there is not much else to commend it. From the constitutional standpoint, this recommendation seems perverse. The Constitution requires that the Senate give its "Advice and Consent" to nominations; this language contemplates a more active role than simple acquiescence whenever a nominee is not deeply objectionable. Beyond that, nothing in the structure of the Constitution or the nature of Supreme Court appointments suggests that the Senate should be so deferential. The Senate, no less than the President, is elected by the people. Supreme Court Justices, unlike executive branch appointees, are not the President's subordinates. Often the Court must mediate conflicts between the President and the Congress; one party to a conflict should not have the dominant role in choosing the mediator.

In our view there are other ways, more consistent with the constitutional plan, to deal with the defects of the current confirmation process. The first step is essentially the opposite of the proposal for Senate deference. We suggest that the Senate should assert its constitutional prerogatives more forcefully, unabashedly claiming an independent role. Specifically, the Senate should insist that it has both the authority to "advise" the President and the power to withhold its "consent" because it disagrees with the nominee's basic commitments on the kinds of issues that are likely to come before the Court.

When Congress considers the President's legislative initiatives, it is not deferential. No one would suggest that Congress should pass every bill the President proposes unless the bill fails some minimal test, analogous to a minimal test of character and competence. Congress is free to reject proposed legislation for political reasons. This is a most familiar part of the system of checks and balances. There is no reason for nominations to the Supreme Court to command greater deference.

At first glance it might seem that our proposal can only make matters worse. The problem, one might say, is that the confirmation process is already too partisan, too focused on ideology, too much a media spectacle, and too unmindful of the qualities of genuine distinction that Supreme Court Justices should have. We do not disagree with the premise. The current process is too ideological and partisan. But paradoxically, the best first step toward a cure—the best way to obtain distinguished Justices under current conditions—is for the Senate to assert, rather than abdicate, its role as an equal partner in the appointment process. Partisanship in Supreme Court nominations is indeed problematic. But one-sided partisanship—in which only the President, and not the Senate, is allowed to be partisan—is much worse.

The approach we recommend permits us to suggest several palliatives for the problems posed by partisanship in the confirmation process. In particular, we argue for a reduced emphasis on the role of the confirmation hearings and greater use of the Senate's "advice" function and of the pre-nomination record. The current emphasis on the hearings has produced many of the current difficulties. An independent role, combined with revisions in the process, would yield significant improvements.

* * *

II. THE SENATE'S ROLE IN AN ERA OF DIVIDED GOVERNMENT

For much of the twentieth century, the Senate has not made independent judgments of the kind we urge for Supreme Court nominees. Until 1968, only one nominee had been rejected by the Senate in this century. There is some controversy over exactly how independent a role the Senate played in the nineteenth century.

But since 1969, circumstances have changed. Current conditions—conditions that are unique in our history—justify a more active role for the Senate. These circumstances include a large number of consecutive appointments by Presidents of one party during a period of divided government; the danger of intellectual homogeneity on the current Court; overt ideological attacks by the President on the Court and the self-conscious screening of nominees to the Court by the executive branch; the effective exclusion of the Senate from the selection of lower federal court judges; and the increased importance of separation of powers questions. Under these conditions, deference by the Senate is likely to produce neither a Court of high quality nor a Court with the appropriate range of views.

A. Eleven Consecutive Appointments During a Period of Divided Government

The most important circumstance is, of course, prolonged divided government—specifically, the eleven consecutive Republican appointments, all made while the Democrats controlled the House, eight while the Democrats controlled the Senate.

American politics has not, in general, been characterized by the alternation of parties in power. Republicans dominated the national government between the Civil War and the New Deal. Democrats then dominated until 1968, and Republicans have won five of the last six Presidential elections.

Even so, it is nearly unprecedented for one party to fill eleven consecutive vacancies. This is partly the result of the fact that President Carter was the only President in history to serve a full term without making a single appointment. More important, however, most of these appointments have been made while the Democrats thoroughly controlled Congress. In the past, one party has tended to dominate national politics entirely, controlling both elected branches. The last quarter-century of divided government is genuinely unique in our history.

To be sure, the Supreme Court is supposed to be independent of the political controversies of the moment. Its independence is reflected in the constitutional provisions for life tenure and nondiminution of salary. The Court should not track popular opinion; its duty is to interpret the Constitution. But the constitutional plan insulates the Court only to a certain extent. The Constitution makes the Court responsive to popular sentiment as well. The desire for responsiveness is reflected in a selection process in which the President and the Senate play crucial and mutually constraining roles. The Constitution responds to the risk that a Court whose members serve for life may grow too far out of touch with societal convictions. The Constitution ensures that the Court will in a certain sense be attuned to the prevailing interpretive aspirations of the public at large.

When the people over time elect Presidents of different parties, and Presidents of each party contribute to the Court, this function is well served. The Court's membership then has some connection with the political balance in the country. When, as during the Roosevelt and Truman Administrations and during most of the post-Civil War period, the people turn over both Congress and the Presidency to one party, this function is again served, though in a different way. The Court does not reflect a balance between the parties—because there is no such balance in the country. Rather, the Court reflects the dominance of one side of the debate. After 1936, for example, the New Deal "won"; the nation was thoroughly committed to it, and Democrats dominated both branches. The Court, with thirteen consecutive appointees by Democratic Presidents, properly reflected the fact that the nation had made up its mind.

But in the last twenty-five years the nation has not made up its mind. It has elected mostly Republican Presidents, but mostly Democratic Senates. The composition of the Supreme Court played a role in Presidential campaigns, and it is possible that this issue helped settle the elections as well. We know of no evidence that the composition of the Court has ever played a significant role in either Presidential or senatorial elections. Of course, it is theoretically possible that people voted for Republican Presidential candidates because they wanted a certain kind of Supreme Court; but it is also possible that the composition of the Court played a role in senatorial elections. Any relevant mandate is therefore quite muddled.

In any case, the country has not reached closure on the questions of constitutional method or constitutional result that were raised in the Warren Court, the Burger Court, and the Rehnquist Court. On the contrary, the country is deeply divided. In these circumstances, if the Court is to stay in touch with public convictions (in the limited way that the appointment power envisions), it should not reflect only the President's views. It should reflect the Senate's as well.

* * *

C. Screening of Nominees by the Administration, With a View Toward Likely Voting Patterns and Judicial Commitments

If the President, regardless of his statements during a campaign, deliberately sought to make nonpartisan appointments, the Senate would have much less warrant for injecting concerns about likely voting patterns. But with two arguable exceptions—Justices Stevens and Powell—there can be little doubt that recent Republican Presidents have made appointments on the basis of their criticisms of the Court, attempting to fill vacancies with people with certain predictable commitments. We do not suggest that there has necessarily been a "litmus test" on such issues as abortion or affirmative action. But it seems indisputable that these Presidents have generally attempted to choose Justices with predictable views about the role of the Court, and whose positions on the most controversial issues facing the Court were likely to conform to the President's own views.

President Nixon did not attempt to conceal the real bases of his appointments. When he announced the appointments of Chief Justice Burger and Justice Blackmun, for example, he said that one of his reasons for choosing them was to change the Court's direction in criminal procedure cases. Nixon said his appointees shared his conservative judicial philosophy in contrast to the "activist" philosophy of the Warren Court, obviously referring to their basic judicial orientation, especially in such areas as race discrimination and criminal procedure.

In the Reagan and Bush Administrations, the screening of Justices has been institutionalized. (The same is true of federal lower court judges, an important point we consider below.) Officials in the Department of Justice and the White House have played a prominent role in selecting Justices. The public statements of Presidents Reagan and Bush have also generally confirmed that the nominees were chosen because of their conceptions of the appropriate judicial role.

* * *

E. The Increased Importance of Separation of Powers Issues

As one would expect, the era of divided government has given rise to an unusually large number of disputes between the branches. Often the Court must resolve disputes involving the allocation of power between the President and the Congress. The constitutionality of the independent counsel provision of the Ethics in Government Act of 1978, the Gramm–Rudman–Hollings Act, and the Sentencing Commission are recent illustrations. In the future, there is likely to be litigation over the constitutionality of institutional arrangements designed to limit Presidential control of the administrative process.

The problem, however, goes much deeper. Recurring and now sharply debated issues of statutory construction have raised important conflicts between the executive branch and the Congress. Such issues include, most notably, the role of legislative history in statutory interpretation and the degree of deference to be given to administrative interpretations of statutes. In the resolution of such conflicts lies much of the de facto power of the executive branch and the legislature. For example, there would be a large increase in executive power, in some ways at the expense of the Congress, if the Supreme Court were to hold that legislative history is irrelevant and that administrative interpretations prevail in the face of any slight ambiguity in the statutory text.

* * *

Traditionally the Court has functioned as a mediator between the branches. But it cannot perform that function well if one branch sees the appointment process as an opportunity to put sympathetic Justices on the Court, while the other branch simply defers to the nomination of anyone whose views are not demonstrably extreme.

F. The Danger of Intellectual Homogeneity on the Court

Other things being equal, the Court benefits when it is composed of Justices with a range of views. The qualifier is important: we do not mean to suggest that the Court should have a member who believes that *Brown v. Board of Education* should be overruled, or who considers welfare laws unconstitutional. But with respect to a significant number of issues, the Court can perform its task better if there is a diversity of opinions.

* * *

First, because the Supreme Court's jurisdiction is discretionary, the Justices' ability to identify problems in the legal system is in some ways as important as their ability to decide fully briefed cases. Judges with distinctive views notice legal problems that other judges do not see—not through ignorance or malice, but because of differing priorities. Once an issue is brought to general attention, everyone might agree on what the outcome should be. But the issue might not have come to the Court's attention at all were it not for the distinctive concerns of one of the Justices. The certiorari process has often benefitted from intellectual diversity of this kind, and it is important that it continue to do so.

Second, the Court's internal deliberations will suffer if the Court does not consist of Justices with differing views. If they are willing to listen, judges of one general outlook will learn a great deal from those with other basic orientations. Notably, one of the most significant theoretical contributions of the founding period consisted of the insistence, by the Federalists against the Anti–Federalists, that heterogeneity could be a creative and productive force. As Alexander Hamilton wrote in *The Federalist,* "the jarring of parties * * * often promote[s] deliberation." One need not romanticize the real-world consequences of internal deliberation in order to suggest that differences in perspective often improve both the collective reasoning process and the outcomes.

Litigants alone cannot provide the necessary perspective. The quality of advocacy before the Court is uneven, and even the best advocate usually plays only a limited role in comparison with a member of the Court. Divergent views should be presented, and pressed, during internal deliberations, when the Court is formulating results and reasons. In this regard, litigants are inevitably inadequate.

Finally, throughout American history, dissenting opinions have helped Congress and the President—and even future generations—formulate their responses to the Court. A Court that lacks a liberal voice—or a conservative one—would not carry out these educative tasks as well. It is hard for the American public to think about what the Court is doing if cases include no opinions presenting different sides.

There remains the question of what counts as diversity, and of when a "diverse" view is so extreme as to be unacceptable. These questions are hard to answer in the abstract. On the one hand, the current Court is by no means monolithic in the sense that all of its members agree on everything important. In any nine-member body, there will be genuine disagreements. And, as we said, we do not think that the Court is insufficiently diverse because it lacks anyone who believes, for example, that *Brown v. Board of Education* is wrong, or that the Constitution requires revolutionary socialism. On the other hand, the current Court now lacks any member fundamentally committed to the views on constitutional method and constitutional results represented by judges like Hugo Black, William Brennan, William Douglas, Thurgood Marshall, and Earl Warren. These views cannot be characterized as marginal or as having nothing valuable to offer on their behalf. They have substantial support in the state and federal judiciaries, and from the public, Congress, professionals, and academics. Views of this sort provide a valuable perspective to the Court.

For present purposes, however, we do not have to define the boundaries of the acceptable diversity of views. The need for a diversity of views on the Court strongly argues in support of the position we advance: namely, that the Senate should take an independent role in Supreme Court nominations. In a period of divided government, Senate independence will naturally produce a diversity of views on the Court. When the nation has made up its mind about an issue—as the nation did about the New Deal in the late 1940's and as it has today about *Brown*—individuals who are at odds with the national consensus will find no support in either the Senate or the Administration. Where the nation has not made up its mind—as ours has not, for example, about affirmative action, abortion, sexually explicit speech, or the separation of church and state—an independent Senate role will ensure that the Court is not monolithic, and that its deliberations have the quality that will be absent if there is no serious encounter with divergent views.

All of these considerations suggest that, under current circumstances, the Senate should undertake an independent role in evaluating nominees to the Supreme Court. The Senate is entitled to insist that the next nominee be a "liberal" or a "moderate." It should not perceive itself as constrained by the Presidential election to confirm all minimally competent nominees who are not "out of the mainstream." In the words of the Constitution, the Senate is entitled to claim that it will not confirm any President's nominee unless there has been a process involving "advice" as well as "consent."

LAURENCE H. TRIBE,* GOD SAVE THIS HONORABLE COURT
106–110, 132–137 (1985)

PRESERVING THE OVERALL BALANCE: TESTING NOMINEES IN CONTEXT

There is a second lens through which any prospective Supreme Court appointee should be viewed. Even if a particular nominee is qualified and falls within all the limits so far suggested, we must ask how confirmation of the individual Justice would affect the *overall balance* of the Court. This shift in focus may mean that nominees who fall *within* the President's and a given Senator's circles of acceptability, when considered on their own merits, will fall *outside* the tighter circle drawn by a Senator when considering the context of the nominee's appointment. This is the way it has, at times, been—and the way it should be.

On one level, this concern for balance should remind us that the current Supreme Court is overwhelmingly white, male, and Protestant. At various times in its history, the diversity of the Supreme Court was enhanced through such customs as a "New York seat" (from 1806 to 1894), a "New England seat" (1789 to 1932), a "Jewish seat" (1916 to 1970), or a "Catholic seat" (1894 to 1949, and 1956 to the present). Obviously, mere tokenism is not a serious policy to pursue in Supreme Court appointments, and these appointment traditions could never by themselves create the kind of diverse and finely poised Court that the republic needs. But given the long tradition of conscious attention to

---

* From *God Save This Honorable Court* by Laurence H. Tribe. Copyright © 1985 by Laurence H. Tribe. Reprinted by permission of Random House, Inc.

geographic and religious diversity on the Court, the promotion of increased diversity with respect to gender and race is certainly a legitimate value to keep in mind.

On a more probing level, the President, the Senate, and individual Senators should consider what impact a particular appointment would have in the context of the distribution of judicial inclinations that characterizes the Court at the time that appointment is made. One important aim, although too few Presidents have actively pursued it, should be to produce a healthy mix of competing views. To use the standard, if often misleading, labels a Court that includes five "liberal" Justices, two "conservatives," and one "moderate" at its center, could be dangerously imbalanced by another "liberal" appointment, while a bench comprising four "conservatives," three "moderates," and a single "liberal" already tilts too far in the opposite direction and could be righted only by the addition of another "liberal." A Supreme Court with three or four Justices of both the "liberal" and "conservative" persuasions and a pair of vacancies to be filled presents a prime opportunity for the addition of two centrists to provide "swing" votes as checks upon extremes at both ends of the spectrum. The Senate's ideal role is as a ballast—to adjust the drift of the Supreme Court as represented by a given appointment.

Such concern for diversity and balance certainly does not justify a Senate refusal to confirm a nominee to whom the Senators' only objection is that the candidate would not have been *their* first or even second choice. In Supreme Court appointments the Constitution allows only the President his "druthers." Allowing each Senator to confirm solely from the Senator's own "short list" would prescribe paralysis in the Supreme Court appointment process. But if the appointment of a particular nominee would push the Court in a substantive direction that a Senator conscientiously deems undesirable because it would upset the Court's equilibrium or exacerbate what he views as an already excessive conservative *or* liberal bias, then that Senator can and should vote against confirmation. To vote otherwise would be to abdicate a solemn trust.

There is one seeming paradox in the idea of voting against an otherwise qualified nominee solely on the basis of the effect the appointment would have on the Court's overall equilibrium and direction: such a vote makes a nominee's confirmation turn not only on the potential Justice's intrinsic merit and suitability for a seat on the Supreme Court, but also on the specific vacancy being filled, the impact of previous appointments, and the configuration and inclination of those who still serve on the Court at the time of the appointment. For example, when Peter Daniel was nominated by President Martin Van Buren in 1841, the Court already had a pronounced anti-federal bias resulting from Van Buren's previous appointment of John McKinley, and from five Jackson appointments. When considered alone, Daniel, a respected politician and experienced federal judge, was an acceptable candidate; but in 1841 the Supreme Court needed greater breadth of political disposition, not another intensely partisan Jacksonian Democrat. The Court Van Buren and Jackson left behind them was too doctrinaire to contend with the threat to the Union created by the increasing separatism of the Southern states—a separatism fueled by the Court's own promotion of states' rights. So Daniel should have been rejected.

Considering judicial nominations in context can just as easily make a particular candidate even more—rather than less—attractive. The Court from which Justice William O. Douglas retired in 1975 was in some ways in need of a new center of gravity. The Court had been highly progressive on the civil liberties front during the years Earl Warren was Chief Justice, and had also handed down decisions that revolutionized the rights of the accused. With the appointment of Chief Justice Warren Burger and three other Justices by President Nixon, the Court lurched in the opposite direction and retrenched on those recently recognized liberties. President Gerald Ford's nomination of Judge John Paul Stevens to replace Douglas was a nicely balanced act of statesmanship. Stevens was a sound choice on his own merits; he was a respected expert in antitrust law, and in his five years on a federal appellate court he had earned a reputation as an open-minded judge. When evaluated in the context of the Burger Court to which he was nominated, Justice Stevens became an even more suitable choice, for the ideologically divided Court was in need of a moderate jurist who defies traditional categories. While he has usually operated at the Court's center, Justice Stevens often writes separate concurring opinions that reach the same results by routes different from those taken by the majority, and he has been a vigorous voice in dissent from the opinions of the Nixon appointees when he believes that they side too much with government against those accused of crime.

If this contextual approach to appointment appears complex and difficult for a Senator to apply, we must remember that no one promised that the confirmation process would be any easier than other senatorial duties. If the contextual approach seems unfair to the nominee, we must remember that the Senate is not reviewing the qualifications of nominees in order to award them yet more framed certificates to hang on their office walls. A Supreme Court seat is not a merit badge, no matter how meritorious a nominee may be when his or her qualifications are assessed in artificial isolation. What is at stake, after all, is the composition of the highest court in the land and the future of the Constitution—a future that we have seen powerfully shaped by individual Justices. Senators would be gravely remiss in their duty to the nation if they supported appointments that would force the Supreme Court to veer off onto—or, indeed, to remain stuck on—what the Senators themselves perceive as a constitutionally dangerous course simply because they could not bring themselves to think hard about the Constitution, to hurt a nominee's feelings, or to deny the President his fondest wish.

One possible objection to this emphasis on balance is the proposition that the Supreme Court ought to be kept in step with the times; shifts in the national temperament—be they progressive or conservative, libertarian or authoritarian—*ought* to change the kinds of Justices we appoint. But such an argument profoundly misconceives the role of the Supreme Court in our tripartite system of government. The Court should not merely reflect the spirit of the times; that is the proper role of the political branches. If the Court becomes merely a snapshot of the presently predominant social and political philosophies, it is doomed by the regime of life tenure to become an anachronism.

One might think that a well-balanced Supreme Court bench would be a natural product of the appointment system, since the Justices are replaced one at a time, and since the Court is a collage that comprises and collects, at any given moment, the choices of several Presidents. But, as we have seen, the great majority of the Justices who have served on the Court since its creation were appointed in the same year as another Justice. It is far from uncommon for a plurality or even a majority of the members of the Court to be the result of a single President's nominations. Then, too, even Supreme Courts whose composition is the work of several presidential hands can be remarkably uniform in outlook. Since it takes only five Justices to make a majority, Supreme Courts of varied origin have given us decisions that are remarkably monolithic.

In 1905, early in the Supreme Court's period of hostility toward socio-economic legislation directed at correcting market failures, the Court consisted of Justices appointed by no fewer than six different Presidents. Those Chief Executives were a diverse group, ranging from Rutherford B. Hayes to Theodore Roosevelt to Grover Cleveland. Thirty-one years later, the *Lochner* era was still in full swing, with the Court striking down minimum wage laws and New Deal legislation with apparent abandon. Yet the membership of the Court had been completely transformed; it now consisted of Justices appointed by five Presidents as different from one another as Herbert Hoover, Calvin Coolidge, and Woodrow Wilson. In 1965, in the heyday of the Warren Court, the nine Justices owed their nominations to four Presidents, including F.D.R., Dwight Eisenhower, and John Kennedy. The 1973 Court that decided the abortion case, *Roe v. Wade*, was the work of five Presidents—three Democrats and two Republicans. The Supreme Court as of early 1985, hardly a model of diversified balance, nevertheless owes its members' appointments to six Presidents as unlike one another in their political outlooks as John Kennedy, Gerald Ford, and Ronald Reagan.

Thus it is clear that the mechanics of presidential nomination, individual Senate confirmation, and life tenure cannot by themselves assure a balanced Supreme Court. It is the responsibility of the President and the Senate to reassess the diversity of outlook represented on the Court each time a vacancy occurs. The trajectory of the Court's recent decisions should be charted, and the parameters of acceptability discussed in the preceding chapter should be adjusted accordingly, to make certain that the new appointment will not tend to push the Court too far off course, in any direction.

What constitutes a desirable path for the Supreme Court is, of course, open to debate—and should be debated. The fact that the Constitution puts the power of appointment jointly into the hands of both the President and the Senate, for reasons examined more closely in the next chapter, suggests that each political branch ought to act as a balance for the pull asserted by the other.

In discussing judicial appointments in the context of the future direction of the Supreme Court, the shorthand labels "left" and "right," "liberal" and "conservative," are too blunt to be of much value. Although the problem of Supreme Court equilibrium is of enduring significance, to understand its dynamics we must get down to cases. The Supreme Court as composed in early 1985 provides a rich source of material to illustrate this book's perspectives, even though the Courts to which this book's basic lessons might be applied in the 1990s and beyond may well look very different indeed, and may pose problems of context quite unlike those of the present era. For purposes of illustration, though, the present Court will have to do. On too many occasions, as it happens, the present Supreme Court has narrowly skirted perilous cliffs; these examples reinforce the lesson that careless and unexamined appointments could all too easily push the Court over the edge. It is a lesson whose relevance is timeless, even if the present occasion for learning it will pass.

THE VIRTUES OF THE SENATE AS AN EQUAL PARTNER

A brief look at how the Senate came to have a role in the appointment process is illuminating. One of the original drafts of the Constitution envisioned the Congress itself actually electing the Justices. And the Constitutional Convention adopted a draft that had the Senate alone choose the members of the Supreme Court. This scheme in fact remained in the draft until the final days of the Convention, after the idea of appointment by presidential nomination with Senate consent was twice voted down. Finally, the current provision was accepted—as a compromise between those who desired a stronger President and those who envisioned a weaker one.

But as the times have changed, so have the institutions of Presidency and Senate that are involved in the process of appointing Justices. The "original intent" of the Framers of our Constitution should not be, and indeed cannot be, the final authority in constitutional discourse on this issue any more than on others. The reasons for dividing the appointment power between the Senate and the President two hundred years ago are not necessarily identical with the reasons for such a division of power today.

The Framers thought they were creating a Presidency that would be won by a man—women couldn't even *vote* then—elected by a small, elite body, the Electoral College, and a Senate selected by the legislatures of the states. Today the President is elected in a monumental festival of microphones, TV cameras, popular campaigning, and ideological mass movements—hardly the insular body of civil leaders on whom the

Framers relied to put the nation's highest office in safe hands. And ever since the ratification of the Seventeenth Amendment in 1913, Senators have been directly elected by the people rather than selected by the state legislatures; many Senate races in the last decade have taken on the aura and trappings of mini (and sometimes *not* so mini) presidential races. For these reasons, whatever notions the authors of the Constitution held about authority and legitimacy must be reconsidered in light of the significant changes in the way we pick our President and our Senators. The electoral process for both is far more democratic now. And with respect to Supreme Court appointments, this is the common denominator of the Senate's virtues as compared with the President's: the Senate is more diverse, more representative, more accountable.

Unlike the President, who can never be more than one person at a time, the Senate as a body has a hundred different heads. The Senate comprises members from all fifty states, and will usually include members of both genders, many different religious and ethnic backgrounds, and, sometimes, members of different races. Senators are of different ages and come from different occupations and different backgrounds. Although hardly a mirror of our nation's broad cultural and racial diversity, the Senate will always be more varied in geographic and socio-economic characteristics than a single person in the White House could ever be. These virtues of diversity were recognized even in *The Federalist Papers,* where the Senate's role was seen in part as ensuring that the President did not simply pick nominees "coming from the same State to which he belonged."

The need for diversity among the voices that question and confirm Supreme Court Justices is greater today than ever before. Although the nation has grown more homogeneous under the influence of convenient travel and the mass media, critical differences remain. And while at one time some diversity on the Court was maintained through customs like having a "New York seat" or a "Jewish seat," many of these traditions are no longer observed and would in any event be insufficient to create the kind of balanced Supreme Court we desire. The hopes expressed by some that the pioneering service of Justice Thurgood Marshall (the first black Justice) and Justice Sandra Day O'Connor (the first woman on the Court) would result in the establishment of a "minority seat" or a "woman's seat" must be tempered by the recognition that such fragile entitlements can pass away. We cannot rely on the willingness of Presidents to maintain, much less expand, such traditions. Only the active involvement of the Senate, pressing the hopes and dreams of people from all regions, all walks of life, can keep the Court from becoming narrow, isolated, and removed from the many and varied threads that make up the rich tapestry we call America.

The Senate represents diversity in our country in another, possibly more important way. Although the President is both Chief Executive and the leader of his party, the Senate inevitably includes members of both parties, and therefore reflects a more diverse range of political philosophies. It takes only a cursory glance to appreciate the fallacy in suggesting that since the President is elected by a majority of voters, it would be democratic to let him alone choose the Justices. After all, even the fortunate winner of a 60 per cent majority has failed to gain the support of the other 40 per cent of the country. True, our winner-take-all system does not give the substantial minority anything resembling control of the presidency for 40 per cent of the time. Yet there seems no sound reason why the person chosen by just 60 per cent of the voters—what we call a landslide—should be allowed 100 per cent of the time to select Supreme Court Justices, and perhaps a full Court majority, reflecting his views alone.

This is of particular concern in a case where a President with a less stunning victory—such as Abraham Lincoln, who won with but 39 per cent of the popular vote in a four-way election, or Benjamin Harrison, who took office with *fewer* popular votes than his opponent, Grover Cleveland, and won only in the Electoral College—may be in a position to name four or more Justices. But the point remains strong even when the President wins by a landslide, because the size of the avalanche is irrelevant to the question whether the President has a mandate to remake the Supreme Court in his own image. In this century, only the election of F.D.R. in 1936 could honestly be said to have given the President such a mandate, because that was the one campaign in which Supreme Court appointments surfaced as a major issue and in which the victor won by a mandate-sized margin. When the President is elected on such a constitutionally extraneous platform as prosperity, patriotism, and personality, the electorate has not given the President a blank check to redirect the Supreme Court, because the campaign did not draw on that particular account. And, finally, there is the puzzle of the nine Justices nominated by men not elected to the presidency at all—those who have succeeded to that office from the vice presidency.

The character of the Senate, which always includes a minority party, lends itself to representing the full range of relevant views in the appointment process—and properly so. For the people have spoken in electing the Senate as well as the President. And, in their own way, the Senators represent the popular will as much as, or more than, the President does. Indeed, if the "people" have installed a majority of one party in the Senate, and the leader of a different party in the White House, it becomes flatly false to assert that *either* party was chosen to choose our Justices. This is not to say that Justices should be apportioned to political parties in the way that a parliamentary system dispenses coalition seats in a European cabinet. But this *is* to say that seats on the Court should not be viewed as slots in an American cabinet—as policy-making roles rightfully given only to the President's lieutenants because that is "what the people wanted." Unity *within* the executive branch may be essential; unity *between* the two political branches, especially when the issue is the shape and direction of the judiciary, is not.

The Senate represents a more lasting view of the American majority as well. Unlike the President, chosen by one potentially ephemeral snapshot of the electorate on one Tuesday in one November, the Senate is really *three* pictures of public sentiment, superimposed to create a multi-dimensional image of a varied people. Since Senators rotate their terms, with one-third of the hundred being elected in each even-numbered year, and with each serving a six-year term, the Senate reflects the majority of the voters through a longer, moving picture. And, like any moving picture, the Senate may be better able to capture a fuller and truer image of the country than any single snapshot could. Thus, in 1930, with public discontent over economic conservatism on the rise, the progressive and responsive Senate wisely resisted Herbert Hoover's nomination of Judge John Parker and instead confirmed Justice Owen Roberts to the Court, bringing to that tribunal the Justice who "switched" in time to lead the Court to uphold vital New Deal legislation.

Active Senate involvement also tends to ensure that Supreme Court majorities are not allowed to perpetuate themselves by selecting their successors. Although the Constitution, nearing its bicentennial, is to be passed down from generation to generation, its reading and interpretation must to some degree change to reflect the new realities of each new era, and must change by means more continuous and evolutionary than frequent resort to the always difficult amendment process would permit. The Court cannot be the organic institution that it must be in our evolving society if one constitutional philosophy—adopted by one set of Justices—is foisted upon successive generations as the Court becomes a virtually hereditary body.

As we saw with Grant's capitulation to the choice of Justice Grier, and more dramatically in the three decades of Taft's dominance of the selection process, a President is far more likely than the Senate to be susceptible to a Justice's suggestions for the Court. The Senate, if only because its members are more numerous and respond to a far wider range of influences, is much less likely to be herded into selecting a Justice's choice for the Court or the Court's choice for itself. Justices aware of a Senate's active role are also less likely to attempt to exert their influence, for almost any effort to affect the opinions of a body like the Senate is sure to become public in short order. Although fear of public exposure and backlash seems never to have bothered Chief Justice Taft, sensibilities in this media age are more attuned to ethical taints. Senate participation in the selection process thus preserves the dynamic element of constitutional choice by ensuring that a changing majority, and not any fixed one, picks the Justices.

The Twenty-second Amendment's limit on presidential tenure adds yet another element to the equation. Unlike any Senator, a President entering his second term knows as a matter of constitutional mandate that it must be his last. As a "lame duck," such a President faces a situation unique in American politics—a political career that has reached the highest plateau, and now is fixed to end on a given date. The lame-duck President comes to his second term with extensive political debts owed to those who supported his two electoral successes, but with no real stake in a political future. Thus he is free to mortgage our constitutional future to discharge, perhaps in the best of faith, the political debts he has accumulated over the years both to individuals and to constituencies. The Senate, on the other hand, is always filled with members pondering their political tomorrows. They are therefore more accountable. This is what the Senate has recognized when, on six different occasions, it has refused to confirm a Supreme Court nomination made by a lame-duck President after he has lost reelection or has chosen not to run again.

There is one situation in which the Senate must be particularly wary in reviewing appointments—whenever the President nominates a Senator to the Supreme Court. Here the Senate's institutional prerogatives do not so vigorously counteract those of the President. By tradition, the Senate confirms such nominations with almost no investigation and with amazing, rather than deliberate, speed. Even such mediocre selections as President Harry Truman's nominations of his former fellow Senators Harold Burton and Sherman Minton can be slipped through the Senate with the lubrication of "senatorial comity." The case of F.D.R.'s 1937 nomination of Alabama Senator Hugo Black bears reflection as well. Although Black was seen as a controversial radical by many in the Senate, he was confirmed in five short days—he was, after all, a member of The Club One Hundred. Three weeks later, a series of Pulitzer Prize-winning articles revealed that Justice Black had been a dues-paying member of the Ku Klux Klan, and had been given one of its highest awards. A debate gripped the nation, with many major newspapers calling for the new Justice's resignation. But by the time the information came out, the former Senator had been confirmed and sworn in and was on vacation in Europe. Although Hugo Black probably would and should have been confirmed in any event, the country should at least have had the timely knowledge that it lacked about his past—knowledge it was denied by the Senate's hasty action on the nomination of "one of its own."

Nonetheless, the Senate will, and should, remain the ultimate guardian of Supreme Court nominations. The vigil must be well kept, for with the nomination power a President's influence over the country can extend for years, sometimes decades, beyond any popular or political limit. When we select Supreme Court Justices, we create a judicial time capsule: we freeze an image of the Constitution that one person holds today and send it off to be observed by, and to shape, the future. No other national office in American government operates in this time-delay manner. A President's decisions about war and peace, or about the economy, may stay with us for years to come, but at least the Presidents themselves are gone in, at most, eight years. A Supreme Court Justice may serve four times as long. This is not to suggest that Justices should have terms that end when the President's does. This *is* to suggest that we need to heed more voices, and to think more deeply, when such grave decisions are made, projecting power that will affect us—and will shape the ways we live and even the ways we die—for decades to come.

Any suggestion that Supreme Court nominations are the President's to dispense, like the Queen of England's New Year's Day list of knighthoods and titles, ignores how much is at stake when those nominations are made.   The next Justice appointed will in all probability still be sitting on the Supreme Court in the year 2001.   What constitutional vision will he or she impose on America in the twenty-first century?   What votes will that next Justice cast in the coming decades on matters vital to our future?   In which historic 5–4 majorities will that Justice's views prove decisive?   Which other votes will that Justice's views sway?   What landmark opinions, what great dissents, will that Justice write in the continuing dialogue between the Court and the country over the meaning of our Constitution?   The answers to these questions *matter*.   For the Senate must serve as a fierce and tenacious guardian over access to these nine important chairs.   Only a broadly based, aggressively contested, scrupulously considered choice now can ensure that the Supreme Court's constitutional vision will be a bright one.

NINA TOTENBERG,* THE CONFIRMATION PROCESS AND THE PUBLIC: TO KNOW OR NOT TO KNOW **
101 Harv.L.Rev. 1213, 1213–1229 (1988)

In the confirmation process as it has developed in the twentieth century, the public has played the role of the wife with an unfaithful husband.   The wife and the public have one thing in common: they are the last to know.

The President romances his nominee, with a little help from his business associate, the Senate.   The Senate, a guy who doesn't like to make trouble for himself, doesn't ask too many questions.   And by the time the public finds out about the nominee, it's too late to do anything about it.   The nominee has a lifetime seat on the Supreme Court.

The nomination of Judge Robert Bork to the Supreme Court changed all that.   But it is yet unclear whether the Bork confirmation process was aberrational or trend-setting.   Until 1987, the process of confirming a Supreme Court Justice was, for the most part, veiled in ignorance.   Senate investigations were paltry, with most information unearthed not by the Senate, but by the press and other outside sources; the hearings themselves were verbal minuets illuminating almost nothing about the nominee's views.

Until 1981, even the words of the nominee were heard only by those in the hearing room—it wasn't until the confirmation hearings of Sandra Day O'Connor that radio microphones or TV cameras were permitted to record the event.[1]   But simply allowing the public to witness the hearing isn't enough.   Unless something actually happens during the confirma-

---

* Legal Affairs Correspondent, National Public Radio.

** Reprinted by permission of Nina Totenberg and Harvard Law Review Association.

1. Telephone interview with Duke Short, Senate Judiciary Committee staff (Mar. 3, 1988).

tion process, it is little more than a charade. Uncomfortable as it may be for all concerned, confirmation screening means digging, probing, learning about a nominee. The confirmation process is the last chance to affect the least accountable branch of government. It should involve letting the public know the facts and judge for itself. Only when the veil of public ignorance is lifted will the public and the Senate face squarely the question whether a given nominee should be put on the Supreme Court.

To be sure, most senators would rather not spend their time and political capital on an arduous confirmation process. It is a politically risky business. Controversial issues are likely to be stirred up. A confirmation battle can only create new enemies back home. And what does the politician get for his trouble? Nothing concrete. No legislation. No campaign money. Maybe he'll satisfy some of his supporters, but he'll infuriate others. At rock bottom, all a senator gets out of the confirmation process, if it turns controversial, is some personal satisfaction that comes from doing what he thinks is right.

In addition, the confirmation process, if done properly, is an enormous amount of work. Staff members must be pulled off more politically remunerative projects to help. The nominee's writings—often tens of thousands of pages—have to be found, read, digested, and analyzed. His or her background, finances, and every professional move should be looked at. For the senators who sit on the Judiciary Committee, it is a truly staggering piece of work, commensurate with the staggering responsibility of confirming a Supreme Court Justice—and it is a responsibility which, by and large, the Senate Judiciary Committee has abdicated.

Many of the investigations and hearings conducted by the Judiciary Committee have been shockingly thin. Felix Frankfurter, nominated to the Court in 1939, was the first nominee to testify at his confirmation hearing. Before that time, the Senate had relied on little more than secondhand accounts of the nominee's character. Modern Senate investigations show little improvement. Nineteen days after Warren Burger was nominated to be Chief Justice, the Senate confirmed him by a vote of 74–3. The confirmation stories for Justices Harry Blackmun, John Paul Stevens, and others are similar.

William Rehnquist's 1971 confirmation hearings are a prime example of the Senate's failure to fulfill its investigative role. Exhausted by the recent confirmation battles over G. Harrold Carswell and Clement Haynsworth, the Senate sought desperately to avoid strictly scrutinizing the nominee. It was only after Rehnquist had testified before the Judiciary Committee that reporters and civil rights advocates turned up witnesses in Rehnquist's home state of Arizona—witnesses who said the nominee had harassed and intimidated black voters just seven years earlier as part of an effort to discourage blacks from voting in large numbers. Senator James O. Eastland, Chairman of the Judiciary Committee, refused to recall Rehnquist to the witness stand; instead, the

Committee submitted written questions to the nominee, who categorically denied the allegations against him: "In none of these years did I personally engage in challenging the qualifications of any voters." The Judiciary Committee, without calling any witnesses (many of whom had signed affidavits testifying to Rehnquist's activities) and without sending its own investigators to Arizona, finally decided that the charges against Rehnquist were "at the very most a case of mistaken identification."

Back in 1971, the charges made against Rehnquist received relatively little attention from the national press, in large part because neither Rehnquist nor other witnesses were called to testify on the matter. Fifteen years later, however, when Rehnquist was nominated to be Chief Justice, the matter surfaced again. This time, the press and other organizations found a number of important witnesses who had not surfaced before. James Brosnahan, a former assistant U.S. attorney in Arizona, told the Judiciary Committee that he had been called to a predominantly black precinct in 1964 to investigate charges of voter harassment. Brosnahan said he had been accompanied by an FBI agent and that he found William Rehnquist "serving as a challenger in that precinct." Two other leading community members who knew Rehnquist personally—former Democratic state chairman Charles N. Pine and Dr. Sidney Smith, a college professor who worked as a poll watcher—also said that they had seen Rehnquist systematically challenging black voters.

FBI corroboration, however, was unavailable in 1986: twenty-two years after the fact, the FBI had no records identifying which agent, if any, had accompanied Brosnahan to the precinct on the date in question. Local party officials no longer had their records, and some participants in those election monitoring events were dead.

The failure to pursue the allegations in 1971 came back to haunt the 1986 hearings in a most unsettling way, leaving the matter unresolved and unresolvable. If the voter harassment charges were in fact a case of mistaken identity, then William Rehnquist was left unfairly with a cloud over his head, and thirty-three votes against him on the Senate floor. If the harassment charges were true, then the Chief Justice of the United States lied under oath.

The bottom line is that the Judiciary Committee in 1971 did not do its job. Indeed, the Committee seems to pursue information aggressively only when the President makes a nomination that some on the Committee view as overtly offensive. Only then is there some real scrutiny.

For example, when President Lyndon Johnson nominated his long-time friend and advisor Justice Abe Fortas to be Chief Justice, conservatives were outraged. True, they were motivated by political self-interest—they hoped the upcoming election would deliver the White House and the nomination into their hands in a matter of months. But they also discerned that Fortas had remained close to the President in a political sense long after he had been named to the Court and was supposed to be an independent voice ruling on issues that were often of direct concern to the President. In addition, conservatives disliked Fortas' liberal judicial philosophy and made no bones about it during the confirmation hearings. Republican Strom Thurmond railed against the Court's criminal law decisions and tried in vain to get Fortas to discuss them. Referring to a 1957 ruling,[15] Thurmond cried out: *"Mallory*—I want that word to ring in your ears * * *. Mallory, a man who raped a woman, admitted his guilt, and the Supreme Court turned him loose on a technicality." Fortas refused to discuss in any way his view of the Constitution and the criminal law. But the hearings raised enough doubts to block his promotion to Chief Justice. Eventually, he was forced off the Court after press revelations that he had accepted $20,000 from a foundation controlled by the family of an indicted stock manipulator. In the Fortas case the Judiciary Committee, prodded by Republican conservatives, did its job, with the final blow delivered by the press.

The role of the press in the Fortas hearings was not anomalous. All too often, it is the press or some private organization that does the kind of investigation that the Committee should do. The case of G. Harrold Carswell is another fine example. Carswell's nomination followed the defeat of Clement Haynsworth's nomination, when neither the Judiciary Committee nor the Senate had the stomach for another fight. Within days of the nomination, however, those outside Congress began turning up critical information. A local reporter in Jacksonville, Florida, uncovered a 1948 Carswell speech advocating segregation. Then a researcher for the Washington Research Project uncovered documents signed by Carswell changing the segregated Tallahassee municipal golf course into a private club in order to allow it to continue practicing racial discrimination. At the time Carswell signed the documents as one of the incorporators, he was the United States Attorney for the area, and the Supreme Court had just ruled that public recreational facilities could not be segregated. At his confirmation hearing, Carswell first denied being an incorporator; then, when it became clear the Committee had the documents, he admitted it. He insisted there was no racial motive in the $1–a–year lease of the public golf course, built with $35,000 in federal aid, to a private club. He said repeatedly that he had not recently seen the documents, which he had signed in 1956. It wasn't until after the hearing that press reports revealed that, on the eve of his confirmation hearing, Carswell had been shown the documents and had answered questions about them from representatives of the American Bar Association Judicial Screening Committee.

There were Senators who were aggressive about pursuing Carswell—Birch Bayh, Philip Hart, Joseph Tydings, and Edward Kennedy. The Committee as a whole, however, was a reluctant investigator; instead of recalling Carswell, it voted 13–4 to send his nomination to the floor with its stamp of approval. The full Senate too was a reluctant dragonslayer. The vote to defeat the Carswell nomination was a bare

15. Mallory v. United States, 354 U.S.   been appointed to the Court at the time the
449 (1957). Justice Fortas had not yet   case was decided.

51–45. Many in the Senate, quite simply, preferred not to know the facts about Carswell.

Some will say that the kind of aggressive inquiry I am urging here goes too far, that it threatens the independence of the judiciary and a standard of ordinary civility. No one can say that the confirmation process when properly done is a pleasant process. It isn't. But the power being confirmed is awesome, and the effort should be commensurate with the responsibility. Supreme Court Justices are appointed for life. They are the most powerful members of the least accountable branch of government. They will never face the electorate. At the moment, the public does not even have television or radio access to the oral arguments before the Court. Why should the public be asked to accept a pig in a poke? Why shouldn't the public know a great deal about the nominee's background, and at least something about his or her judicial views? The Constitution, in fact, contemplates one branch of government being insulated from passions and politics. But the Founding Fathers did not contemplate an appointment process without political checks and balances.

Yet in modern confirmation hearings, even when real and obvious questions should have been raised, often they were not. In the Rehnquist hearings in 1986, for example, the nominee was never asked with any specificity about his health—even though Rehnquist had been admitted to a Washington hospital in 1981 because of a reaction suffered when he tried to stop taking a drug he had used for some time for back pain. For months prior to his hospitalization, Supreme Court reporters had noticed Rehnquist's peculiar physical behavior on the bench and his slurred speech. When reporters learned in 1981 that he had been admitted to George Washington Hospital, a hospital spokesman said the medication had affected his "mental clarity" and "ability to express himself." At his confirmation hearing for Chief Justice five years later, all indications were that the medication had been improperly prescribed by a doctor, and that Justice Rehnquist was just fine. But in an era when the President's prostate is diagrammed on TV, not one member of the Senate Judiciary Committee dared ask the nominee for Chief Justice of the United States to explain to the American people what had happened to him and to demonstrate that everything was now under control.

Beyond the more personal issues, senators have found it absolutely impossible, until the Bork hearings, to engage the nominees in a meaningful discussion of their views on the great constitutional issues of our time. Although nominees should not be asked to commit themselves on a question that may come before the Court, it hardly seems right that a nominee should be permitted to give an answer that is a fancy version of "trust me."

Judge Antonin Scalia's confirmation hearing less than two years ago was the essence of "trust me." When then Chairman–Strom Thurmond asked Scalia if *Marbury v. Madison* "requires the President and the

Congress to always adhere to the Court's interpretation of the Constitution," Scalia responded, "I do not think I should answer questions regarding any specific Supreme Court opinion, even one as fundamental as *Marbury v. Madison.*" When Senator Edward Kennedy asked Scalia about his views of national security versus individual rights, Scalia responded, "I am seriously interested in both of the principles." When Senator Dennis DeConcini asked Scalia whether he agreed with current Supreme Court rulings that establish different standards for judging sex discrimination and race discrimination, Scalia responded, "I do not think I should be in the position of saying whether I agree or disagree with the Supreme Court law on the subject." And when Senator Biden asked Scalia if he believed in a constitutional right of privacy, Scalia responded, "I don't think I could answer that, Senator, without violating the line I've tried to hold."

Perhaps the most extraordinary exchanges occurred on the subject of the Freedom of Information Act—legislation which Scalia had criticized at length as a bureaucrat, in academic writings, and in judicial opinions. When Senator Patrick Leahy asked Scalia if he had advised President Ford to veto the legislation in 1974, Scalia, who had been an assistant attorney general back then, refused to answer, citing attorney-client privilege. When Senator DeConcini questioned Scalia about his 1982 article ripping apart the purposes of the Freedom of Information Act, Scalia responded, "I guess you can hold it [the article] to me as being my views at the time." When DeConcini followed up by asking if those were still Scalia's views, the nominee responded, "I do not think I should say."

My point here is not to skewer Scalia, but to suggest that the Committee should require some cooperation from a nominee in discussing general judicial philosophy as a condition for confirmation. The Senate should not fly blind—and finally, in the Bork case, it didn't have to.

The Committee's hearings on the nomination of Judge Robert Bork were, in my view, the first time the process worked properly. Leaving aside for the moment the question of outside influences, the Senate, for a change, gave itself enough time, and the senators prepared themselves. They asked probing but, for the most part, respectful and proper questions, and they knew enough to follow up and find out what the nominee really meant in his answers.*

* * *

Aside from the questioning at the hearing itself, we can debate forever whether forces outside the hearing room had any substantial effect on the process. Television certainly had an influence on the process. If Robert Bork had looked like Cary Grant, perhaps the public would have responded less harshly, perhaps not. We will never know for

_____

* Ed. Note: See Bork Hearings, *infra,* Section C.

sure. Television is a reality, however, and like it or not, we will have to live with it, to the tune of Ollie North or Robert Bork.

Certainly the process in Bork's case was also affected by the advertising campaign against him, but my guess is that the effect was minimal. The now famous People for the American Way ad starring Gregory Peck was aired as a paid commercial in only seven cities (and on CNN) a total of eighty-five times at a cost of $165,000. The ad received the most attention when Bork backers attacked it and major broadcast news organizations aired it, along with the attack, as part of the nightly news.

Despite these outside influences, I find it indisputable that the heart of the Bork confirmation process was the nominee's five days of testimony. Perhaps the questioning by one or two senators was hostile to the point of rudeness, but it was Bork's answers, not the questions, that did in the nominee.

There were certain kinds of answers that in my view were particularly harmful. Indeed, even Bork admits that one answer was an error. Ironically, it was in response to a question from one of his supporters. Asked by Senator Alan Simpson why he wanted to sit on the Court, Bork responded that it would be "an intellectual feast." Although he added that he would like to help maintain the country's constitutional structure, there was no specific mention of the answer the public may have expected: to serve justice. Similarly, when asked about his ruling in *American Cyanamid* allowing a manufacturer who used toxic chemicals to give female workers the choice of being sterilized or losing their jobs, Bork responded by noting, accurately, that this was a case of statutory interpretation. But instead of immediately indicating that perhaps the choice in this case was painfully dictated by law and precedent, he said: "I suppose the five women who chose to stay on that job with higher pay and [who] chose sterilization—I suppose that they were glad to have the choice—they apparently were—that the company gave them."

By that afternoon, Betty Riggs, one of the women who had been sterilized, had contacted the Committee. In a telegram she wrote (with help from her lawyer) Riggs said: "I cannot believe that Judge Bork thinks we were glad to have the choice of getting sterilized or getting fired. Only a judge who knows nothing about women who need to work could say that. I was only 26 years old, but I had to work, so I had no choice * * *. This was the most awful thing that happened to me. I still believe it's against the law, whatever Bork says."

Although Judge Bork has, since his defeat, publicly criticized his treatment at the hands of the Senate Judiciary Committee, Republican senators, including his staunch defenders, were careful to praise Chairman Biden for his fairness in conducting the hearings. The nominee was fully briefed about information on which he would be questioned. The Committee abided by the nominee's desires in regard to scheduling and length of questioning each day. Finally, and perhaps most importantly, Bork was never "surprised" with any new revelation.

Thus, some senators found his answers particularly lame when he was questioned about a prior statement regarding precedent. Throughout the hearings, Bork had testified that he had great regard for, and would normally be inclined to follow, legal precedent; indeed, in his opening statement to the Committee, he said that "a judge must have a great respect for precedence [sic]" and "[r]espect for precedent is a part of the great tradition of our law." So it was stunning to the listening audience when Senator Edward Kennedy played a tape recording of remarks Bork had made at Canisius College in Buffalo, New York, less than two years earlier. The hearing room was silent as Robert Bork's voice on tape said: "I don't think that in the field of constitutional law precedent is all that important * * *. I think the importance is what the Framers were driving at, and to go back to that."

Despite having been provided with a transcript of his remarks the day before, Bork's only response to the tape was that his remarks were not "a full and measured response" to questions from students, and that the remarks were not part of his prepared text. To many, however, the tape was real-world evidence that Bork was not leveling with the Committee. The scene played on every major news program that night.

In sum, the Judiciary Committee's performance in the Bork case was generally good—despite some demagoguery on all sides. Yet even in this case, where the Committee amassed an enormous amount of information, it was sometimes either timid or lazy. My guess is that the Committee was somehow afraid of really tackling Bork's role in the Saturday Night Massacre. It was the press, not the Committee, that turned up some new evidence raising questions about Bork's previous statements regarding his role in the firing of Watergate special prosecutor Archibald Cox and its aftermath.

Bork had testified in 1982 at his appellate court confirmation hearing that after he had fired Cox, he had guaranteed the remaining special prosecution staff the right "to go to court to get the White House tapes." But Bork's testimony was contradicted by the very lawyers whom Bork claimed to have assured—and it was the press that first contacted these lawyers and found the contradiction. According to Senate sources, Judiciary Committee Chairman Biden did not want the lawyers who disputed Bork's testimony to testify. But Senator Kennedy insisted, and the testimony, particularly from former deputy special prosecutor Henry Ruth, was viewed as harmful to Bork's credibility.

The Judiciary Committee, having done its job well in the Bork hearings, promptly reverted to its old ways in the aftermath of the Bork nomination. Despite the fact that almost nothing was known about the new nominee, Douglas Ginsburg, Committee Chairman Joseph Biden committed virtually no time or resources to screening the nominee. Having completed one exhausting confirmation battle, Biden and many on his committee simply didn't have the energy or the commitment to do their jobs properly a second time. Biden scheduled confirmation hearings to begin December 7, roughly five weeks after the nomination was announced. By contrast, when the Republicans controlled the Senate and Sandra Day O'Connor was nominated, the Committee took almost nine weeks to study her record before holding hearings. For the nomination of William Rehnquist to be Chief Justice, the Committee took six weeks, for Antonin Scalia seven weeks, and for Robert Bork eleven weeks.

It was soon clear that the Ginsburg nomination would not be without controversy. Within days of the nomination, serious questions were raised in press reports about possible conflicts of interest in the nominee's conduct of his duties as assistant attorney general. Another problem arose upon review of the Senate questionnaire Ginsburg filled out when he was nominated to the court of appeals. The questionnaire showed that he had responded to the critical question about his trial experience with an answer that was, at best, misleading. In answering the question, "How many cases have you tried to verdict or judgment?," he had replied with an unqualified "thirty-four," and only elsewhere in the questionnaire had he indicated that his statistical answers were meant to include all the cases he supervised as head of the antitrust division of the Justice Department. Even with these clouds hovering over Ginsburg's head, there was still no indication that the Judiciary Committee would put off its hearings to allow enough time for thorough investigation.

Again, the Senate seemed deliberately to take a back seat to the press, and the press, sensing that something was wrong, was certainly in hot pursuit. Those of us in the press checking out Ginsburg were turning up new leads almost daily. We were sometimes tripping over each other as we pursued our inquiries. We were also sometimes tripping over members of the American Bar Association screening committee who were covering the same ground. We were not tripping over Senator Biden's investigative staff, nor were we tripping over the FBI. In the Ginsburg case, as in so many instances in the past, it was not the responsible constitutional branches of government that did the job. Rather it was a nongovernment institution, the press, with the Bar Association not far behind.

The final blow for Ginsburg, of course, was the revelation that he had smoked marijuana while a professor at Harvard Law School. Some have questioned whether this information should have been made public. Why not? Although it is fair to note that smoking marijuana was common in Ginsburg's generation, it was also a crime, albeit a misdemeanor. And he was, or so the President and Attorney General Edwin Meese told us, the law-and-order candidate for the Court. A perfectly good argument can be made that pot smoking should not be dispositive, but not that it should be information hidden from the public. After all, if Douglas Ginsburg had been an applicant for a job as an assistant United States Attorney, he would have been rejected under Reagan Administration rules on grounds that he had smoked marijuana after being admitted to the bar.

Once Ginsburg withdrew and President Reagan nominated Anthony Kennedy, Senator Biden again decided to rush the confirmation process. Apparently having learned nothing from the Ginsburg fiasco or the Bork process, he scheduled the Kennedy hearings not only with a minimal five weeks to prepare, but also in the last week of the congressional session.[84] This scheduling virtually guaranteed that the senators would not be fully prepared for the hearings, and that the senators pressed with constant floor votes and other committee conferences in the last days of the legislative session would not be able to sit through the hearings, to follow them, or to pursue intelligent lines of inquiry.

The Kennedy confirmation hearings, although more probing than hearings of the past, were nevertheless reminiscent of the days when senators preferred not to know. The hearings took just three days, and not one committee investigator was even sent to California to look into the judge's background. This is not to suggest that there was anything untoward in Judge Kennedy's history; it is simply to note that there was no investigation other than the FBI's.

During the day and a half of testimony from Kennedy, the nominee was considerably more responsive than pre-Bork nominees. For example, he answered questions about his views on the right to privacy. But most senators were reluctant to ask many of the questions they freely asked Bork. While Bork, for example, was asked repeatedly to explain his rulings on gender discrimination, Kennedy was not. Indeed, at the end of the hearing, Chairman Biden shocked reporters by declaring in an interview that he had "grave reservations" about the nominee's civil rights record. But Biden, in his questioning, had given no hint of such "grave reservations" and in fact had not asked the nominee about many of the cases that Biden said gave rise to his concern.

The most persistent questioning came from Senator Gordon Humphrey of New Hampshire. Although Humphrey did ask some questions that a nominee could not properly answer, there were other times when it seemed, to me at least, that he was understandably frustrated, as, for example, when he asked Kennedy about the death penalty. Capital punishment has been repeatedly upheld by the Supreme Court by lopsided votes, and so it seemed odd that Judge Kennedy refused to answer Humphrey's questions on the subject, on the grounds of propriety. If a nominee is honestly undecided on this issue, that seems to me to be the right answer: "I don't know because I haven't finally resolved the question in my own mind." If, however, a nominee has fixed views

84. *See Dec. 14 Hearings Set on Judge Kennedy, New York Times,* Nov. 21, 1987, at 54, col. 1. In fairness, Biden had been asked by several Democrats not to hold hearings in January. Two Democrats had tough reelection campaigns and wanted to get the confirmation process behind them. A third, Senator Paul Simon, was running for President, and needed to be in Iowa and New Hampshire campaigning, not in Washington carrying out his duties on the Judiciary Committee. But other senators pressed Biden to allow more time. Unfortunately, in this case, as in almost all others, it was not the seriousness of the task that dictated the conduct of the confirmation process, but rather the path of least resistance.

on a subject of settled law, claiming propriety as a reason for not being forthright with the Senate is just a ruse.

The public has a role to play in choosing who will serve on the nation's highest Court. That role cannot be performed without knowledge. The confirmation process should not be some trick or shell game in which the public is left to guess every essential fact about the nominee. For years, the confirmation process has been treated as if public knowledge were somehow dangerous. But we depend on knowledge to run a democracy. Over and over again in our history—most recently in the Iran–Contra hearings—we have learned the dangers of secret government. Government by deliberate ignorance is only marginally better.

Perhaps the system worked well when Supreme Court appointments were not so high-profile, when Presidents picked nominees based on personal knowledge or high reputation, and the Senate went along with few questions. But those days are long gone. Ronald Reagan campaigned on a promise to change the Supreme Court and he changed the selection process into a far more deliberate one, using a fine screen to sift through the potential candidates.

Perhaps the President has the right to do that. After all, using such a system, he is far less likely to be surprised. But what of the public's desires? The Senate is the public's surrogate, the public's check on executive power. The Senate should pay careful attention to the opinions of the people without compromising the independence of its decision or converting the advice and consent function into a majoritarian election procedure. In this, it must and does rely to a great extent on the Senate Judiciary Committee. The first part of the Senate Judiciary Committee's job must be to investigate the nominee thoroughly. Usually, it fails miserably, relying with great consistency on the press and even the Bar Association to do its work. Even the Committee's subpoena power is a tool unused. On a number of occasions in the past, it has failed to use subpoenas to pursue leads turned up by others. Second, and just as important, is the matter of questioning the nominee about his or her views. It is difficult to draw the line between proper and improper questions, and to balance the need for information about a nominee against the need to preserve a judge's independence. But our democracy has always had to balance and to draw lines, and this area should not be an exception. Judicial independence must not be used to shield nominees from revealing their general views—views that they would happily express to others in private conversation. Likewise, senators and their constituencies should not be asked to endorse nominees whose views, if known, would be abhorrent. Senators Kennedy and Biden, for example, have every right to know that Judge Bork does not believe in a broad constitutional right to privacy, and to vote against him because of it. Likewise, Senator Humphrey, who does not believe in such a privacy right, has the right to do the opposite. Senators hopefully will not turn confirmation proceedings into a surrogate system of electing judges. Given the enormous difficulty of defeating Supreme

Court nominees, it is unlikely that it will ever become the norm. Rather, it seems more likely that the Senate will reject only nominees who truly offend it.

The Bork hearings demonstrated that questioning can be conducted in a usually civilized, and often enlightening, way. The public learned a great deal about the nominee, the Court, and the Constitution during those hearings. What became clear eventually is that many of the controversial decisions of the past thirty years—decisions the Reagan administration pledged to reverse—have been accepted by the majority of the American public. Indeed, the public seemed to support most of the Court's decisions in the areas of race and sex discrimination, free speech, privacy, and even abortion. The public, for a change, got a chance to see and evaluate a Supreme Court nominee's views, and decided that it didn't want that nominee making the law of the land. The Senate gave serious consideration to the public's views and, I think, reached the same conclusion on its own.

For many of us who grew up in an era when it was somehow unseemly for a nominee to comment meaningfully on anything, it is difficult to advocate a confirmation process based on disclosure and discourse instead of concealment and camouflage. One must concede that in an open process there is certainly the danger of nominee-bashing of the worst sort. But the direction of the Supreme Court has become a major political, social, and legal issue of our times. The only time a Supreme Court nominee is accountable at all to the public is before he or she is confirmed. The public deserves to find out beforehand about the men and women who, if confirmed, will be the final arbiters of the rules by which the country is governed. And the Senate is entitled to take the public's views into account when deciding whether to consent to the nomination.

C. THE NOMINATION AND CONFIRMATION OF SUPREME COURT JUSTICES—CASE STUDIES OF THE NOMINATIONS OF ROBERT BORK, DAVID SOUTER, CLARENCE THOMAS, AND RUTH BADER GINSBURG

In this section are excerpts from the Senate Judiciary Committee Reports on the recent nominations of Judge Robert Bork, Judge David Souter, Judge Clarence Thomas, and Judge Ruth Bader Ginsburg. In reading them, ask whether the Senators applied the proper standards of evaluation, whether the level of questioning by the Senators was appropriate, whether the answers given or not given were adequate, and whether you would have voted to confirm each of these nominees. Consider in this regard the difference between the responses of these nominees and those of Judge Scalia in 1986. Judge Scalia would not even give his assessment of *Marbury v. Madison:*

> *Marbury v. Madison* is one of the pillars of the Constitution. To the extent that you think a nominee would be so foolish, or so extreme as to kick over one of the pillars of the Constitution, I suppose you should not confirm him. But I do not think I should answer

questions regarding any specific Supreme Court opinion, even one as fundamental as *Marbury v. Madison.*

Nomination of Judge Antonin Scalia: Hearings before the Committee on the Judiciary, United States Senate, 99th Cong. 2nd Sess. 33 (1986). Notwithstanding his refusal to answer such basic questions, Judge Scalia was confirmed unanimously.

1. The Nomination of Robert Bork

As the following report indicates, Judge Bork was not at all reticent; he willingly answered virtually all the Senators' questions. Despite this, or arguably because of this, he was rejected. The Senate Judiciary Committee voted 9–5 to recommend that his nomination be rejected.[1] Judge Bork refused to withdraw his name and President Reagan, sympathetic to Judge Bork's desire to obtain a vote of the full Senate, did not retract the nomination. On October 23, 1987, the Senate voted 58–42 not to confirm Robert Bork, the largest margin of defeat ever for a Supreme Court nominee.[2]

What accounts for this sharp contrast in the treatment of Judges Scalia and Bork? Why was Judge Scalia confirmed unanimously while Judge Bork endured the worst defeat in history, even though conventional wisdom asserts that Judge Scalia was as conservative as Judge Bork? Was it simply that the Republicans had control over the Senate in 1986 but not in 1987? Was the result influenced by the relative difference in standing that President Reagan enjoyed during the two nomination processes? How relevant was it that Scalia was replacing a conservative (Warren Burger), while Bork would have replaced a moderate (Justice Powell)? Can a future nominee, after the hearings for Judge Bork, get confirmed if he or she gives answers similar to those given by Judge Scalia? Or has the confirmation process for Judge Bork permanently changed the process?[3]

NOMINATION OF ROBERT H. BORK TO BE AN ASSOCIATE JUSTICE OF THE UNITED STATES SUPREME COURT

October 13, 1987.—Ordered to be printed.

S.Exec.Rep. No. 100–7, 100th Cong., 1st Sess. (1987).

Mr. Biden, from the Committee on the Judiciary,
submitted the following REPORT together with
ADDITIONAL, MINORITY, AND SUPPLEMENTAL VIEWS

The Committee on the Judiciary, to which was referred the nomination of Judge Robert H. Bork to be an Associate Justice of the United

---

1. Voting to report the nomination with a negative recommendation were Senators Biden, Kennedy, Byrd, Metzenbaum, DeConcini, Leahy, Heflin, Simon, and Spector. Voting against the negative recommendation were Senators Thurmond, Hatch, Simpson, Grassley, and Humphrey.

2. D. Savage, *Turning Right: The Making of the Rehnquist Supreme Court* 146 (1992).

3. Because of the extensive length of the Senate Report, we have found it necessary to edit it heavily. We have, however, included the table of contents so that the reader can both follow our excerpts and know what was edited out.

States Supreme Court, having considered the same reports unfavorably thereon, a quorum being present, by a vote of nine yeas and five nays, with the recommendation that the nomination be rejected.

CONTENTS

Part Three: A Critical Analysis of Judge Bork's Positions on Leading Matters
I.   The Right to Privacy—The Right To Be Let Alone
    A.   Before the Hearings, the Right to Privacy Had Been a Principal Part of Judge Bork's Attack on the Supreme Court
    B.   At the Hearings, Judge Bork Confirmed His Pre–Hearing Views About a Right to Privacy
    C.   Judge Bork's Denial of the Right to Privacy Places the Entire Line of Privacy Decisions at Risk, and Is Likely To Prevent Any Subsequent Development and Extension of It
II. Civil Rights
    A.   Judge Bork Has Opposed Civil Rights Legislation
    B.   Judge Bork Has Criticized the Decision Banning Enforcement of Racially Restrictive Covenants
    C.   Judge Bork Has Rejected the Decision Banning School Segregation in Washington, D.C.
    D.   Judge Bork Has Criticized the Poll Tax Decision
    E.   Judge Bork Has Criticized the One Person, One Vote Decisions
    F.   Judge Bork Has Criticized Decisions Upholding a Ban on Literacy Tests
III. The Equal Protection Clause and Gender Discrimination
    A.   Prior to the Hearings, Judge Bork Did Not Include Women Within the Coverage of the Equal Protection Clause
    B.   Judge Bork's Testimony at the Hearings Was His First Publicly Expressed Approval of Including Women Within the Scope of the Equal Protection Clause
    C.   Judge Bork's "Reasonable Basis" Standard Does Not Provide Women with Adequate Protection and Is Not the Standard Used by Justice Stevens
IV. First Amendment
    A.   Dissident Political Speech
    B.   While Judge Bork's Testimony About First Amendment Protection for Art, Literature and Expressive Speech Was Somewhat Reassuring, It Nonetheless Must Be Read Against the Background of His Prior Statements
V.   Executive Power
    A.   Judge Bork Has a Restricted View of Congress's War Powers
    B.   Judge Bork Has a Narrow View of Congress's Power to Limit Intelligence Activities
    C.   Judge Bork Has Said that the Special Prosecutor Legislation Is Unconstitutional
    D.   Judge Bork Has Opposed the Notion of Congressional Standing to Challenge Presidential Actions
    E.   Judge Bork's Views on Executive Privilege Are Entirely Consistent with and Analogous to His Position on Congressional Standing
VI. Watergate
    A.   Judge Bork's Actions During and After the Saturday Night Massacre Remain Controversial
    B.   Judge Bork's Discharge of Special Prosecutor Archibald Cox Violated an Existing Justice Department Regulation Which Had the Force and Effect of Law
    C.   The Evidence and Testimony on Certain Factual Questions Are Contradictory. But at a Minimum They Establish that Judge

* * *

II. THE NOMINEE

Judge Bork was born on March 1, 1927, in Pittsburgh. He attended the University of Pittsburgh for a short time and then enlisted in the United States Marine Corps in 1945. He served until 1946, when he was honorably discharged. Following military service, he attended the University of Chicago, where he received a Bachelor of Arts degree. During his first year at the University of Chicago Law School, Judge Bork enlisted in the Marine Corps Reserves. He was called back to duty in 1950 and served in active military duty until 1952. He received his law degree from the University of Chicago Law School in 1953. From 1953–1954, he was a research associate with the University of Chicago Law School's Law and Economics Project.

From 1954–1962, the nominee engaged in the private practice of law. He practiced first with the New York firm of Wilkie, Owen, Farr, Gallagher & Watson and then later was an associate and partner at the Chicago firm of Kirkland, Ellis, Hodson, Chaffetz & Masters.

From 1962–1973, the nominee was a member of the faculty of the Yale Law School. * * *

From 1973–1977, Judge Bork served as Solicitor General of the United States. In this capacity, he argued a number of cases before the Supreme Court. Judge Bork briefly served as Acting Attorney General from 1973–1974.

In 1977, Judge Bork returned to the faculty of the Yale Law School. * * *

In 1981, Judge Bork returned to private practice as a partner in Kirkland & Ellis, working out of the Washington office.

From 1982 to the present, Judge Bork has served as a judge on the U.S. Court of Appeals for the District of Columbia Circuit.

* * *

PART TWO: THE CONSTITUTION'S UNENUMERATED RIGHTS

I.   Judge Bork's View of the Constitution Disregards This Country's Tradition of Human Dignity, Liberty and Unenumerated Rights

The Bork hearings opened on the eve of the celebration of the 200th anniversary of our Constitution. The hearings proved to be about that Constitution, not just about a Supreme Court nominee.

The hearings reaffirmed what many understand to be a core principle upon which this nation was founded: Our Constitution recognizes inalienable rights and is not simply a grant of rights by the majority. Chairman Biden's opening statement identified these fundamental principles:

> I believe all Americans are born with certain inalienable rights. As a child of God, I believe my rights are not derived from the Constitution. My rights are not derived from any government. My rights are not derived from any majority. My rights are because I exist. They were given to me and each of my fellow citizens by our Creator, and they represent the essence of human dignity. (Comm. Print Draft, Vol. 1, at 68.)

This image of human dignity has been associated throughout our history with the idea that the Constitution recognizes "unenumerated rights." These are rights beyond those specifically mentioned in the Constitution itself, rights that are affirmed by the grand open-ended phrases of the document: "liberty," "due process," "equal protection of the laws" and others. The sober responsibility of preserving the meaning and content of these rights has fallen to the judiciary, and especially to the Supreme Court.

Against this understanding of the Constitution, and of human dignity, Judge Bork offers an alternative vision—that Americans have no rights against government, except those specifically enumerated in the Constitution. The contrast was stated cogently by Professor Philip Kurland:

> I think it makes all the difference in the world whether you start with the notion that the people have all the liberties except those that are specifically taken away from them, or you start with the notion, as I think Judge Bork now has, that they have no liberties

except those which are granted to them.   (Comm. Print Draft, Vol. 3, at 1391.)

* * *

A. Judge Bork's Judicial Philosophy Does Not Recognize the Concept of Unenumerated Rights and Liberties

1. Judge Bork's Core Theory

Judge Bork has consistently described his constitutional theory as "intentionalist," meaning that he considers it the function of a judge to determine the intentions of the body that wrote the laws and to apply those intentions to the case brought before the court.   Interpreting law is thus a matter of discerning the original intent of those responsible for making it.

Judge Bork reaffirmed this view in his opening statement before the committee:

> The judge's authority derives entirely from the fact that he is applying the law and not his own personal values * * *.   How should a judge go about finding the law?   The only legitimate way is by attempting to discern what those who made the law intended. The intentions of the lawmakers govern, whether the lawmakers are the Congress of the United States enacting a statute or those who ratified our Constitution and its various amendments.   (Comm. Print Draft, Vol. 1, at 78–79.)

* * *

2. Judge Bork's Judicial Philosophy Leads Him to Conclude that the Constitution "Specified Certain Liberties and Allocates All Else to Democratic Processes"

The implications of Judge Bork's theory of original intent are quite clear from his writings, speeches and testimony.   The most dramatic consequence of his theory is the rejection of the concept of unenumerated rights and liberties.   He has consistently held to the view, both before and during the hearings, that the Constitution should not be read as recognizing an individual right unless that right can be specifically found in a particular provision of the document.

In particular, Judge Bork has repeatedly rejected the well-established line of Supreme Court decisions holding that the liberal clauses of the Fifth and Fourteenth Amendments protect against governmental invasion of a person's substantive personal liberty and privacy.   He has said, for example, that:

> [T]he choice of "fundamental values" by the Court cannot be justified.   Where constitutional materials do not clearly specify the value to be preferred, there is no principled way to prefer any claimed human value to any other.   The judge must stick close to the text and the history, and their fair implications, and not con-

struct new rights. ("Neutral Principles and Some First Amendment Problems," 47 *Indiana Law Journal* 1, 8 (1971).)

Judge Bork has also disregarded the text of the Ninth Amendment, which provides that "[t]he enumeration in the Constitution of certain rights, shall not be construed to deny or disparage other retained by the people." In Judge Bork's view, while there are alternative explanations for the Amendment,

> if it ultimately turns out that no plausible interpretation can be given, the only recourse for a judge is to refrain from inventing meanings and ignore the provision, as was the practice until recently. ("Interpretation of the Constitution," 1984 Justice Lester W. Roth Lecture, University of So. California, October 25, 1984, at 16; emphasis added.)

This suggested disregard for the Amendment is consistent with Judge Bork's general recommendation about a judge's role "when his studies leave him unpersuaded that he understands the core of what the Framers intended" with respect to a particular constitutional provision:

> [The judge] must treat [the provision] as nonexistent, since, in terms of expression of the framers' will, it is nonexistent. * * * When the meaning of a provision * * * is unknown, the judge has in effect nothing more than a water blot on the document before him. * * *

According to Judge Bork, "[t]he Constitution specified certain liberties and allocates all else to democratic processes." ("Judicial Review and Democracy," *Society,* Nov./Dec. 1986 at 7; emphasis added.) Thus, under Judge Bork's view, the court interferes with the "democratic process" whenever it recognizes a right that is not specified in the Constitution. As he said in a 1985 speech and reaffirmed at the hearings, the Constitution is essentially a zero-sum system, in which rights for some necessarily come only at the expense of others:

> SENATOR SIMON. One point, at a speech at Berkeley in 1985, you say * * * '[When] a court adds to one person's constitutional rights it subtracts from the rights of others.' Do you believe that is always true?
>
> JUDGE BORK. Yes, Senator. I think it's a matter of plain arithmetic. * * *
>
> SENATOR SIMON. I have long thought it is kind of fundamental in our society, that when you expand the liberty of any of us, you expand the liberty of all of us.
>
> JUDGE BORK. I think, Senator, that is not correct. (Comm. Print Draft, Vol. 1, at 289, 421; emphasis added.)

B. *This Nation Was Conceived with the Recognition of Pre-existing Inalienable Rights that the Constitution Does Not Specifically Enumerate But Nonetheless Acknowledges and Protects*

The founding documents of American constitutionalism—the Declaration of Independence, the Constitution and the Bill of Rights—were accepted not because they exhausted the protection of basic rights but because they expressly protected unenumerated rights as well. * * *

The broad purposes of this plan are clear from the language of the founding documents. As former Congresswoman and Professor Barbara Jordan testified: "The Declaration of Independence preceded the Constitution, and the Declaration of Independence speaks of inalienable rights endowed by our Creator * * *, among them life, liberty, [and the] pursuit of happiness." (Comm. Print Draft, Vol. 1, at 787.) The Fifth Amendment states that no person shall be deprived of liberty." The Ninth Amendment mandates that "[t]he enumeration in the Constitution, of certain rights, shall not be construed to deny or disparage others retained by the people." Finally, the Fourteenth Amendment—with its specific protection of "liberty"—was added with a similar purpose: To restrain the power of the states to infringe the fundamental rights of any person.

The intent to protect inalienable, unenumerated rights is clear from the history of the Bill of Rights. Originally, many opposed a Bill of Rights, fearing that the express protection of certain rights would justify an inference that rights not specifically identified were subject to governmental control.

* * *

Despite [such] fears * * *, a number of states were very much concerned about the absence of a Bill of Rights. These states ratified the Constitution on the understanding that a Bill of Rights, including a general provision that there should be no negative inference from the express protection of certain rights that unenumerated rights are not also protected, would shortly be added to the Constitution. * * *

The Ninth Amendment, of course, expressly rebuts the negative inference feared by many of the Founders.

* * *

In *Richmond Newspapers v. Virginia,* 448 U.S. 555 (1980), the [Supreme] Court stated:

The Constitution's draftsmen * * * were concerned that some important rights might be thought disparaged because not specifically guaranteed.

Madison's efforts, culminating in the Ninth Amendment, served to allay the fears of those who were concerned that expressing certain guarantees could be read as excluding others. (*Id.;* emphasis added.)

Thus, the history surrounding the drafting and ratification of the Bill of Rights indicates that there had to be an express guarantee that unenumerated rights would be fully protected. The Ninth Amendment is at the core of both the Constitution and the ratification debates. The concept of unenumerated rights illustrates the depth of the tradition that the Founders meant to protect by the Ninth Amendment.

C. Judge Bork's Approach to Liberty and Unenumerated Rights Is Outside the Tradition of Supreme Court Jurisprudence

Judge Bork's approach to liberty and unenumerated rights sets him apart from every other Supreme Court Justice. Indeed, not one of the 105 past and present Justices of the Supreme Court has ever taken a view of liberty as narrow as that of Judge Bork. As Professor Tribe testified:

> If [Judge Bork] is confirmed as the 106th Justice, [he] would be the first to read liberty as though it were exhausted by the rights * * * the majority expressly conceded individuals in the Bill of Rights. He would be the first to reject an evolving concept of liberty and to replace it with a fixed set of liberties protected at best from an evolving set of threats. (Tribe statement, Comm. Print Draft, Vol. 2, at 7.)

In particular, Judge Bork's philosophy is outside the mainstream of such great judicial conservatives as Justices Harlan, Frankfurter and Black, as well as such recent conservatives as Justices Stewart, Powell, O'Connor and Chief Justice Burger. Each of these members of the Court accepted and applied some concept of liberty, substantive due process and unenumerated rights.

* * *

1. In the 19th Century, the Supreme Court Recognized the Concept of Unenumerated Rights

From the earliest days of the Republic, "the Supreme Court has consistently and unanimously recognized that in adopting the Constitution, the people of the United States did not place the bulk of their hard-won liberty in the hands of government, save only for those rights specifically mentioned in the Bill of Rights or elsewhere in the document." (Tribe statement, Comm. Print Draft, Vol. 2, at 19; emphasis in original.)

In *Fletcher v. Peck,* 10 U.S. (6 Cranch.) 87, 135, 139 (1810), for example, Chief Justice Marshall barred a state's revocation of a series of land grants by relying, in part, on "general principles which are common to our free institutions." The Chief Justice noted that the "nature of society and government [may limit the] legislative power." Justice Story, in *Terret v. Taylor,* 13 U.S. (9 Cranch.) 43 (1815), struck down a state's attempt to divest a church of its property simply by declaring that the statute violated "principles of natural justice" and the "fundamental laws of every free government," as well as the "spirit and letter" of the Constitution.

The Court was even clearer in its recognition of certain fundamental rights in *Hurtado v. California,* 110 U.S. 516 (1884). It rejected the view that the Fourteenth Amendment—commanding that "[n]o State shall deprive any person of life, liberty, or property, without due process of law"—addressed only the fairness of legal procedures. The Court stated that the concept of limited government underlying the Constitution "guarantee[s] not particular forms of procedure, but the very substance of individual rights to life, liberty and property," protecting "those fundamental principles of liberty and justice which lie at the base of all our civil and political institutions * * *." (*Id.* at 532, 535.)

2. *The Justices of This Century, Including the Leading Conservative Justices, Have Recognized Unenumerated Rights*

a. *Justices Frankfurter and Harlan*

Some witnesses have supported Judge Bork on the ground that his expressions of "judicial restraint" put him in the tradition of Felix Frankfurter and John Marshall Harlan. * * *

Justice Frankfurter summarized his views on the liberty clause of the Fourteenth Amendment in *Rochin v. California,* 342 U.S. 165, 169 (1952):

> These standards of justice are not authoritatively formulated anywhere as though they were specifics. Due process of law is a summarized constitutional guarantee of respect for those personal immunities which, as Mr. Justice Cardozo twice wrote for the Court, are "so rooted in the traditions and conscience of our people as to be ranked as fundamental," *Snyder v. Massachusetts,* 291 U.S. 97, 105 (1934), or are "implicit in the concept of ordered liberty." *Palko v. Connecticut,* 302 U.S. 319, 325 (1937).

In Justice Frankfurter's view, the due process clause "expresses a demand for civilized standards * * * [which] neither contain the peculiarities of the first eight amendments nor are * * * confined to them." *Louisiana ex rel. Francis v. Resweber,* 329 U.S. 459, 468 (1947) (Frankfurter, J., concurring). The clause, he said, possessed "independent potency." *Adamson v. California,* 332 U.S. 46, 66 (1947) (Frankfurter, J., concurring). * * *

* * *

Like Justice Frankfurter, Justice Harlan argued for a conception of the due process clause that was flexible and was independent of, but drawing support from, the Bill of Rights. The clearest and most expansive expositions of Justice Harlan's views on liberty and due process are found in *Poe v. Ullman,* 367 U.S. 497 (1961) (Harlan, J., dissenting), and *Griswold v. Connecticut,* 381 U.S. 479 (1965) (Harlan, J., concurring in the judgment).

In *Poe,* Justice Harlan disagreed with the dismissal on procedural grounds of a challenge to Connecticut's ban on the use of contraceptives. He argued that the law should be struck down as "an intolerable and unjustifiable invasion of privacy in the conduct of the most intimate concerns of an individual's personal life." (367 U.S. at 539.) Justice Harlan then set forth his view of the appropriate constitutional framework:

> Due process has not been reduced to any formula; its content cannot be determined by reference to any code. The best that can

be said is that through the course of this Court's decisions it has represented the balance which our Nation, built upon postulates of respect for the liberty of the individual, has struck between that liberty and the demands of organized society. If the supplying of content to this constitutional concept has of necessity been a rational process, it certainly has not been one where judges have felt free to roam where unguided speculation might take them. The balance of which I speak is the balance struck by this country, having regard to what history teaches are the traditions from which it developed as well as the traditions from which it broke. That tradition is a living thing. A decision of this Court which radically departs from it could not long survive, while a decision which builds on what has survived is likely to be sound. No formula could serve as a substitute, in this area, for judgment and restraint. (367 U.S. at 542 (Harlan, J., dissenting); emphasis added.)

* * *

In *Griswold,* the Court struck down the Connecticut law. Justice Harlan stated that the proper constitutional analysis required an examination of whether the law "infringes the Due Process Clause of the Fourteenth Amendment because the enactment violated basic values 'implicit in the concept of ordered liberty,' *Palko v. Connecticut,* 302 U.S. 319, 325." (*Griswold,* 381 U.S. at 500.)

* * *

b. *Justice Brandeis*

Justice Brandeis expressed his conception of liberty in slightly different, albeit no less eloquent, terms. In a dissent now recognized as expressing the Court's majority view, he said:

> The makers of the Constitution undertook to secure conditions favorable to the pursuit of happiness. They recognized the significance of man's spiritual nature, of his feelings and of his intellect. They knew that only a part of the pain, pleasure and satisfactions of life are to be bound in material things. They sought to protect Americans in their beliefs, their thoughts, their emotions and their sensations. They conferred, as against the Government, the right to be let alone—the most comprehensive of rights and the right most valued by civilized man. (*Olmstead v. United States,* 277 U.S. 438, 478 (1928); emphasis added.)

c. *Justice Black*

While Justice Black's views on "liberty" were far different from those of Justice Frankfurter and Justice Harlan, they were still more expansive than those espoused by Judge Bork.

In *Loving v. Virginia,* 388 U.S. 1 (1967), for example, Justice Black joined the opinion of the Court striking down a state law prohibiting interracial marriage. The Court held not only that the law violated the Equal Protection Clause, but also that it deprived the petitioners of "liberty" within the meaning of the Due Process Clause. The Court said: "The freedom to marry has long been recognized as one of the vital personal rights essential to the orderly pursuit of happiness by free men." (*Id.* at 12.)

In *Bolling v. Sharpe,* 347 U.S. 497 (1954), Justice Black joined the opinion of the Court holding that segregation by law in District of Columbia public schools deprived children of their "liberty" under the Fifth Amendment. The Court reasoned that the term "liberty" cannot be "confined to mere freedom from bodily restraint" but "extends to the full range of conduct which the individual is free to pursue * * *." (*Id.* at 499–500.)

Justice Black also joined the Court's opinion in *Skinner v. Oklahoma,* 316 U.S. 535 (1942), which held that a law permitting the sterilization of habitual criminals violated the Equal Protection Clause of the Fourteenth Amendment. Central to the Court's analysis was the decision to subject the law to strict scrutiny because it affected "one of the basic civil rights of man. Marriage and procreation are fundamental to the very existence of the human race." (*Id.* at 541.)

* * *

II. The Theory of Precedent or "Settled Law" Held by Judge Bork Cannot Transform His Judicial Philosophy Into an Acceptable One for the Supreme Court

A. *While Judge Bork's Theory of Precedent Appears to Lessen the Friction Between His Philosophy of Original Intent and Accepted Supreme Court Decisions, It Leaves Many Uncertainties and Concerns*

Judge Bork has applied his theory of the Constitution to attack a large number of Supreme Court decisions, including many landmark cases. Reconsidering these cases would reopen debate on many significant issues. Perhaps this is why Judge Bork said in response to a question by Senator Thurmond, "anybody with a philosophy of original intent requires a theory of precedent." (Comm. Print Draft, Vol. 1, at 101.) While a theory of precedent appears to lessen the friction between Judge Bork's philosophy and accepted Supreme Court decisions, it creates in the end many uncertainties and concerns of its own.

* * *

Under questioning by Senator Thurmond, * * * Judge Bork said:

What would I look at [before overruling a prior decision]? Well, I think I would look and be absolutely sure that the prior decision was incorrectly decided. That is necessary. And if it is wrongly decided—and you have to give respect to your predecessors' judgment on these matters—the presumption against overruling remains, because it may be that there are private expectations built up on the basis of the prior decision. It may be that governmental and private institutions have grown up around that prior decision. There is a need for stability and continuity in the law. There is a need for predictability in legal doctrine. (Comm. Print Draft, Vol. 1, at 101.)

* * *

Later, in response to a question from Senator Heflin, Judge Bork added countervailing considerations—considerations that argued in favor of overruling a precedent:

Now, of course, against [upholding a precedent] is—if it is wrong, and secondly, whether it is a dynamic force so that it continues to produce wrong and unfortunate decisions. I think that was one of the reasons the court in Erie Railroad against Tompkins overruled Swift against Tyson, a degenerative force, but I think what Brandeis or somebody can maybe call dynamic potential. (Comm. Print Draft, Vol. 1, at 268.)

* * *

Finally, Judge Bork concluded his testimony by emphasizing his respect for precedent:

* * * [W]hen I say [the result in a case is required by] "the law," I regard precedent as an important component of the law. As I have described many times here, there are a number of important precedents that are today so woven into the fabric of our system that to change or alter them would be, in my view, unthinkable. (Comm. Print Draft, Vol. 1, at 721–22.)

* * *

B. *Judge Bork's Combination of Original Intent and Settled Law Creates an Irresolvable Tension Between His Oft–Repeated Desire to Reformulate Constitutional Law and His Willingness to Follow a Decision He Believes To Be Profoundly Wrong*

1. *Judge Bork Has Often Announced His Firm Conviction that Many Supreme Court Decisions Are Flatly Wrong and Ought To Be Overruled*

Judge Bork's embrace of precedent sets up a sharp tension with his often repeated proclamations of the ease with which a judge with his views can overrule erroneous decisions. Judge Bork's record, in fact, strongly suggests a willingness to "reformulate" "broad areas of constitutional law." ("Neutral Principles" at 8.)

In January of this year, for example, Judge Bork claimed:

Certainly at the least, I would think that an originalist judge would have no problem whatever in overruling a non-originalist precedent, because that precedent by the very basis of his judicial philosophy, has no legitimacy. (Remarks to the *First Annual Lawyers Convention of the Federalist Society*, January 31, 1987, at 126.)

* * *

During the hearings, Senator Kennedy played an audio tape of the question and answer period following a 1985 speech in which Judge Bork made perhaps his clearest declaration to that effect:

I don't think that in the field of constitutional law precedent is all that important. I say that for two reasons. One is historical and traditional. The court has never thought constitutional precedent was all that important. The reason being that if you construe a statute incorrectly, the Congress can pass a law and correct it. If you construe the Constitution incorrectly Congress is helpless. Everybody is helpless. If you become convinced that a prior court has misread the Constitution I think it's your duty to go back and correct it. Moreover, you will from time to time get willful courts who take an area of law and create precedents that have nothing to do with the name of the Constitution. And if a new court comes in and says, 'Well, I respect precedent,' what you have is a ratchet effect, with the Constitution getting further and further away from its original meaning, because some judges feel free to make up new constitutional law and other judges in the name of judicial restraint follow precedent. I don't think precedent is all that important. I think the importance is what the Framers were driving at, and to go back to that. (*Canisius College Speech*, October 8, 1985, *quoted in* Comm. Print Draft, Vol. 1, at 523–24, emphasis added.)

Following the playing of this tape, the following exchange took place:

SENATOR KENNEDY. Those statements speak for themselves. Your own words cast strong doubt upon your adherence to precedent that you think is wrong.

JUDGE BORK. Senator, you and I both know that it is possible, in a give and take question and answer period, not to give a full and measured response. You and I both know that when I have given a full and measured response, I have repeatedly said there are some things that are too settled to be overturned.

* * *

C. *Judge Bork's Theory of Settled Law Applies Less to Cases Extending Individual Liberties Than to Cases Making Structural or Institutional Changes in Government, and Thus Would Not Protect Those Individual Rights Cases that Judge Bork Has Criticized*

Judge Bork has said that "the Court's treatment of the Bill of Rights is theoretically the easiest to reform." (*Attorney General's Conference Speech*, Jan. 24–26, 1986, at 9.) Decisions involving the Bill of Rights largely involve the expansion of individual rights. As such, complex social institutions and economic structures do not usually build up around them. They are thus typically different from cases like those expanding the power of Congress to regulate commerce or the power of the U.S. government to issue paper money as legal tender. These latter cases have become, in Judge Bork's words, "the basis for a large array of social and economic institutions, [therefore] overruling them would be disastrous." (Comm. Print Draft, Vol. 1, at 102.) If such institutions have not grown up around Bill of Rights cases, they are to that extent easier to reform. As Professor Grey explained:

> These examples [of the Commerce Clause and the Legal Tender Cases] illustrate the very weak character of the constraints imposed by precedent on the overruling of "erroneous" constitutional precedent. In both cases, the protected precedents expanded governmental power. In both cases, any attempt to overrule them would involve social upheavals of vast dimensions, and would be completely impractical. Decisions defining and protecting individual constitutional rights rarely if ever are so socially entrenched. It is difficult to think of any individual rights decision or line of decisions that, if overruled, would present the intractable practical difficulties posed by the cases Judge Bork has used as examples. Indeed, I have not found any example in his pre-nomination discussions of the doctrine of precedent of any constitutional decision protecting individual rights that he identifies as even presumptively immune from overruling. (Grey Statement, Comm. Print Draft, Vol. 2, at 1108; emphasis added.)

During the committee hearings, Judge Bork for the first time made some specific references to individual rights decisions that were, in his view, "settled." They were *Brandenburg, Shelley v. Kraemer* and *Bolling v. Sharpe,* and some of the freedom of the press cases. Each is, to varying degrees, difficult to square with Judge Bork's announced criteria for refusing to overrule a decision. Even putting that aside, however, there still is a tremendous area—in which the Court has given content to unenumerated rights and liberties—where his prior stated positions are not in the least constrained by his statements before the committee concerning settled law.

D. *Judge Bork's Statements About the Application of Settled Law to Old Conflicts Say Little About His Willingness To Apply the Tradition of Unenumerated Rights to New Conflicts Between Government and the Individual that May Arise*

The Supreme Court's prior decisions, whether settled or not, cannot cover all new situations, under even the broadest reading of those cases. It is in the context of these new cases that Judge Bork's theory of original intent would stand without any of the constraining influence of precedent. Thus, "Judge Bork's record is * * * a source of concern because of what it reveals about how he is likely to approach novel issues of liberty and equality that will emerge in the years ahead, issues where a Justice has a leeway that is not closely channelled by precedent." (Gewirtz statement, Comm. Draft Print, Vol. 2, at 1186.)

* * *

PART THREE: A CRITICAL ANALYSIS
OF JUDGE BORK'S POSITION
ON LEADING MATTERS

I. THE RIGHT TO PRIVACY—THE RIGHT TO BE LET ALONE

* * *

B. *At the Hearings, Judge Bork Confirmed His Pre-
Hearing Views About a Right to Privacy*

At the hearings, Judge Bork repeated in various ways the claim that
although "[t]here is a lot of privacy in the Constitution," (Comm. Print
Draft, Vol. 1, at 217), there is no "generalized" right to privacy of the
kind necessary to support *Griswold* and its progeny. He testified that in
the Constitution there is no "unstructured, undefined right of privacy
[such as the right] that Justice Douglas elaborated [in Griswold]."
(Comm. Print Draft, Vol. 1, at 87.)

* * *

When Senator Hatch queried him about Justice Black's view of the "so-
called privacy right," Judge Bork seemed to endorse the view that the
right "was utterly unpredictable." (Comm. Print Draft, Vol. 1, at 157.)
He described his objection to a "generalized" right to privacy:

Nobody knows what that thing means. But you have to define
it; you have to define it. And the court has not given it definition.
That is my only point. (Comm. Print Draft. Vol. 1, at 218.)

At this juncture, Judge Bork's objection seemed to be that the Court had
not defined the privacy right sufficiently, so that it is "utterly unpredictable."

It became clear, however, that Judge Bork also believes that there is
no constitutional right extending privacy protections beyond those provided by specific amendments.

* * *

First, Judge Bork testified that *Griswold* did not contain a correct
understanding of the liberty and due process clauses of the Fourteenth
Amendment: "Well, if they apply the due process clause that way * * *.
Why not in *Griswold v. Connecticut* and why not in all kinds of cases?
You are off and running with substantive due process which I have long
thought is a pernicious constitutional idea." (Comm. Print Draft, Vol. 1,
at 262.) Second, he testified that the Ninth Amendment provided no
justification for the result in *Griswold*. (Comm. Print Draft. Vol. 1, at
102–03; 224–25; 241.) Third, he said he would have dissented in
Griswold. (Comm. Print Draft. Vol. 1, at 573.) Finally, in response to
Senator Heflin, Judge Bork testified, "I do not have available a constitutional theory which would support a general, defined right [of privacy]."
(Comm. Print Draft, Vol. 1, at 266.)

Thus, Judge Bork has rejected all the offered rationales for a right
to privacy of the sort necessary to support *Griswold* and its progeny, as

well as the entire constitutional tradition of unenumerated rights upon which it rests. It appears that Judge Bork adheres to his earlier view that "the result" in *Griswold* could not be reached by "interpretation" of the Constitution. (*Catholic University Speech* at 4.) At the same time, he left open the possibility that "maybe somebody would offer" him a new argument for the right that he would accept. (Comm. Print Draft, Vol. 1, at 90.)

In the committee's view, it is unlikely that a successful new argument will be proffered. As several witnesses testified, the arguments in support of a right to privacy have in the course of our constitutional history been presented; indeed, they were all summarized or alluded to in the *Griswold* case itself. (*See* Comm. Print Draft, Vol. 3, at 1611–13; Tribe testimony, Comm. Print Draft, Vol. 2, at 45 ("I do not think that constitutional law is a game of hide and seek. The idea that there might be a right hiding there from Judge Bork to be discovered in the next decade * * * is not very plausible").) * * *

As Chairman Biden concluded after two-and-a-half weeks of hearings:

> Will [Judge Bork] be part of the progression of 200 years of history of every generation enhancing the right to privacy and reading more firmly into the Constitution protection for individual privacy? Or will he come down on the side of government intrusion? I am left without any doubt in my mind that he intellectually must come down for government intrusion and against expansion of individual rights. (Comm. Print Draft, Vol. 3, at 1615.)

C. Judge Bork's Denial of the Right to Privacy Places the Entire Line of Privacy Decisions at Risk, and Is Likely to Prevent Any Subsequent Development and Extension of It

During the hearings, Judge Bork expounded on his theory of "settled law"—of accepting past cases even though they were wrong. He offered to the committee new examples of cases with which he still disagreed, but which he would not overrule because they had become, in his view, settled law. (*See* Part Two, Section II, *supra.*) Judge Bork did not include within his examples any of the privacy decisions. Accordingly, Judge Bork left the committee with the clear impression that he feels free to overrule any or all of the privacy decisions. And given his conclusion that the doctrine of substantive due process is "pernicious" (Comm. Print Draft, Vol. 1, at 262), there is a substantial risk of overruling.

The committee recognizes that Judge Bork testified that he would entertain arguments that these cases were the sort that should not be overruled. (*See e.g.,* Comm. Print Draft, Vol. 1, at 268.) At the very least, however, he can be expected to limit them to their narrow facts. To do otherwise would mean that they would continue to operate as a "generative" force in the law, producing new erroneous decisions. (*See* Part Two, Section II, *supra.*) Thus, if he did not overrule these cases, there is a substantial risk that he would certainly leave the right to privacy inapplicable to future cases.

* * *

II. Civil Rights

* * *

B. *Judge Bork Has Criticized the Decision Banning Enforcement of Racially Restrictive Covenants*

In *Shelley v. Kraemer,* 334 U.S. 1 (1948), the Supreme Court unanimously held that the Fourteenth Amendment prohibited enforcement of racially restrictive covenants in residential real property agreements. In his *Indiana Law Journal* article, Judge Bork was harshly critical of the *Shelley* decision, writing that it was "impossible" to justify that decision through application of neutral principles. ("Neutral Principles" at 17.)

During his testimony, Judge Bork repeated his criticism of the *Shelley* decision, but sought to undercut the significance of that criticism by stating:

> Shelley against Kraemer has never been applied again. It has had no generative force. It has not proved to be a precedent. As such, it is not a case to be reconsidered. It did what it did; it adopted a principle which the Court has never adopted again. And while I criticized the case at the time, it is not a case worth reconsidering. (Comm. Print Draft, Vol. 1, at 86.)

In fact, *Shelley* has been applied by the Supreme Court in many later decisions, including *Barrows v. Jackson,* 346 U.S. 249 (1953) (barring award of damages for breach of racially restrictive covenant); *Moose Lodge v. Irvis,* 407 U.S. 163, 171, 179 (1972); and *Palmore v. Sidoti,* 466 U.S. 429, 432 n. 1 (1984).

In light of Judge Bork's harsh criticism of *Shelley,* the committee entertains substantial doubt as to whether and how the nominee would apply that fundamental decision in future cases.

C. *Judge Bork Has Rejected the Decision Banning School Segregation in Washington, D.C.*

In *Bolling v. Sharpe,* 347 U.S. 497 (1954), a companion case to *Brown v. Board of Education,* 347 U.S. 483 (1954), the Supreme Court held that the Due Process Clause of the Fifth Amendment prohibited school segregation in the District of Columbia. In so doing, the Court ruled that the concept of "liberty" enshrined in the Due Process Clause contained a requirement that the federal government ensure that no person is denied the equal protection of the laws.

During his testimony before the Committee, Judge Bork indicated that he thought that *Bolling* was wrongly decided, stating "I think that constitutionally that is a troublesome case * * *," and "I have not thought of a rationale for it." (Comm. Print Draft, Vol. 1, at 262–63.)

(Judge Bork, indicated, however, that he would never "dream of overruling" the decision. *Id.* at 264.)

Judge Bork's view that *Bolling* was wrongly decided leaves open to doubt whether he would *ever* hold that the federal government is prohibited from denying persons the "equal protection of the laws." It would appear from Judge Bork's criticism of *Bolling* that he, Bork, might well hold that there is no constitutional basis on which to challenge discrimination by the federal government.

D.   Judge Bork Has Criticized the Poll Tax Decision

For many years, poll taxes were used to keep poor, largely minority, persons from exercising their fundamental right to vote. In *Harper v. Virginia Board of Elections*, 383 U.S. 663 (1964), the Supreme Court struck down poll taxes, holding that:

> [A] State violates the Equal Protection Clause of the Fourteenth Amendment whenever it makes the affluence of the voter or payment of any fee an electoral standard. Voter qualifications have no relation to wealth nor to paying this or any other tax. (*Id.* at 666; footnote omitted.)

During his 1973 confirmation hearings, Judge Bork testified that "as an equal protection case, [*Harper*] seemed to me wrongly decided." (Solicitor General Hearings at 17.) When asked whether he thought *Harper* had contributed to the welfare of the nation, Judge Bork responded:

> I do not really know about that * * *. As I recall, it was a very small poll tax, it was not discriminatory and I doubt that it had much impact on the welfare of the nation one way or the other. (*Id.*)

* * *

In his testimony before the committee, Judge Bork reiterated his view that the Supreme Court was wrong in the *Harper* case to hold that poll taxes are unconstitutional in the absence of an express showing of racial discrimination. (Comm. Print Draft, Vol. 1 at 128–29; 363, 430–31, 530–31.) Senator Heflin's colloquy with Judge Bork on this issue is informative:

> Senator Heflin. Well, you know, I have looked back on a lot of decisions, but this poll tax * * * gives me concern. You basically * * * say that it was not discriminatory.

> Judge Bork. There was no allegation of discrimination in that case.

> Senator Heflin. There was no allegation? Is that the distinction you made? Because there is no question to me that a poll tax that required three years of history of payment, that the last payment had to be six months in advance, and you had to go to the courthouse to pay it was designed to prevent the poor and blacks from voting. I do not think there is any question that it is.

JUDGE BORK. Senator, I did not discuss the case in those terms, and the Supreme Court did not discuss the case as one in which a poll tax was designed to keep blacks from voting. (Comm. Print Draft, Vol. 1, at 431–32; emphasis added.)

And as Vilma Martinez testified: "Among the problems with Judge Bork's disagreement with *Harper* is the fact that the Supreme Court in its decision expressly recognized that the 'Virginia poll tax was born of a desire to disenfranchise the Negro.' *Harper*, 383 U.S. at 666 n. 3." (Comm. Print Draft. Vol. 3, at 2157; *see generally id.* at 2157–59.)

Ms. Martinez also identified another problem with Judge Bork's criticism of *Harper:*

Even if the poll tax laws struck down in *Harper* and in * * * other cases had not been racially motivated, Judge Bork's criticism of *Harper* as being wrongly decided is worrisome for another reason, *i.e.,* that he believes that financial and property restrictions on the fundamental right to vote are perfectly consistent with his view of the equal protection clause. If so, Judge Bork disagrees with settled equal protection law holding that states may not restrict the fundamental right to vote to owners of real property * * *. (Comm. Print Draft, Vol. 3, at 2159; citations omitted.)

The committee strongly believes that in a democratic society, no person should be denied the fundamental right to vote because he or she is too poor to pay a poll tax. Judge Bork's criticism of the *Harper* decision striking down poll taxes reflects a pronounced lack of sensitivity to how the law affects real persons.

E. Judge Bork Has Criticized the One Person, One Vote Decisions

In a line of cases extending from *Baker v. Carr,* 369 U.S. 186 (1962), and *Reynolds v. Sims,* 377 U.S. 533 (1964), the Supreme Court has held that the Equal Protection Clause of the Fourteenth Amendment requires that state and local legislative districts be apportioned in accordance with the one person, one vote principle. Judge Bork has been extremely critical of the Supreme Court's one man, one vote decisions, writing in 1968 that "on no reputable theory of constitutional adjudication was there an excuse for the doctrine [they] imposed." ("The Supreme Court Needs A New Philosophy," at 166.)

* * *

And in an interview on June 10, 1987, Judge Bork stated:

I think [the] Court stepped beyond its allowable boundaries when it imposed one man, one vote under the Equal Protection Clause. That is not consistent with American political history, American political theory, with anything in the history or the structure or the language of the Constitution. (*Worldnet Interview,* United States Information Agency, June 10, 1987, Tr. at 22–23.)

Before the committee, Judge Bork adhered to these views quite vigorously, stating that "as an original matter, [the one man, one vote

principle] does not come out of anything in the Constitution * * *."
(Comm. Print Draft, Vol. 1, at 136.)

As former Congresswoman Barbara Jordan so eloquently testified,
the Supreme Court's one person, one vote decisions opened up the
political process for millions of Americans whose votes had been diluted
by malapportioned legislatures. Representative Jordan described her
experience as follows:

> I filed for the election to the Texas House of Representatives. I
> ran. I lost. But I got 46,000 votes. I was undaunted. I said I will
> try again because my qualifications are what this community needs.
> So in 1964, I ran again * * *. I lost. But I got 64,000 votes.

> Why could I not win? I will tell you why. The Texas legisla-
> ture was so malapportioned that just a handful of people were
> electing a majority of the legislature. I was trying to play by the
> rules, and the rules were not fair. But something happened. A
> decision was handed down: *Baker v. Carr.* * * *

> Following *Baker v. Carr,* a series of cases were decided. The
> Texas legislature was required, mandated by the Supreme Court to
> reapportion itself. It reapportioned. So in 1966, I ran again. The
> third time. This time, in one of those newly created State senatorial
> districts, I won. (Comm. Print Draft, Vol. 1, at 785–86.)

During his testimony, Judge Bork demonstrated a lack of understanding of the harm created by malapportioned legislatures. He suggested that "if the people of this country accept one man, one vote, that
is fine. They can enact it any time they want to." (Comm. Print Draft,
Vol. 1, at 131.) Once again, former Representative Jordan summarized
the problem in compelling terms:

* * *

> Gentlemen, when I hear that, my eyes glaze over. If that were
> the case, I would right now be running my 11th unsuccessful race
> for the Texas House of Representatives. I cannot abide that.
> (Comm. Print Draft, Vol. 1, at 787; *see also* Martinez statement,
> Comm. Print Draft, Vol. 3, at 2161–62.)

The committee believes that the American people accept the one
person, one vote principle as a fundamental component of constitutional
equality. Judge Bork's persistent failure to accept this fundamental
principle, we believe, demonstrates a deeply rooted hostility to the role of
the courts in protecting individual rights and the integrity of the political
process.

* * * Professor Burke Marshall, who served as Assistant Attorney
General in charge of the Civil Rights Division from 1961–1965, expressed
grave concern about the totality of Judge Bork's views on the Supreme
Court's landmark civil rights cases:

> [I]t is not my purpose to criticize Judge Bork for his views about
> any single one of these decisions. No doubt there is something to

his views in each case, considered separately. No doubt there is indeed some arguably valid ground on which any Supreme Court decision can be described as incompletely or wrongly reasoned. The real concern is with the tenor, the tone and the substance of Judge Bork's discussion of these matters. It seems to show no awareness, no understanding of the enormity and the scope of the system of racial injustice that was implemented by law in this country. And that insensitivity has to do importantly with what is wrong, both historically and in terms of constitutional purpose, with Judge Bork's ungenerous concept of the role of the federal judiciary, and especially the Supreme Court, under the equal protection clause and the other provisions of the Civil War Amendments. It was the judiciary, followed by the executive, and followed again by the Congress, with its action in turn legitimated and fortified by the judiciary, that enabled this nation finally to confront and to resolve under law the terrible burdens of racial oppression * * *. Judge Bork's reaction to racial issues, and his whole concept of the constitutional role of the judiciary, would have stifled rather than supported the accomplishments of the period. (Marshall statement, Comm. Print Draft, Vol. 1, at 842.)

In short, Judge Bork has consistently criticized legislation and Supreme Court decisions advancing civil rights for all Americans.

To be sure, Judge Bork was not the only opponent of the Civil Rights Act of 1964, and some of the decisions he criticized were not unanimous. But Judge Bork's criticism of and opposition to the broad number and variety of civil rights achievements discloses a troubling pattern. In the committee's view, this persistent pattern of criticism of civil rights advances, coupled with a conspicuous failure to suggest alternative methods for achieving these critical objectives, reflects a certain hostility on Judge Bork's part to the role of the courts in ensuring our civil rights. The committee's reaction to Judge Bork's long record of criticism of the country's achievements in the field of civil rights was exemplified by Senator Kennedy's comment to Judge Bork:

With all your ability, I just wish you had devoted a little of your talent to advancing * * * equal rights rather than criticizing so many of the decisions protecting rights and liberties. Lawyers can always make technical points, but [a] justice ought to be fair. (Comm. Print Draft, Vol. 1, at 132.)

In light of Judge Bork's demonstrated hostility to the fundamental role of the courts in protecting civil rights, the committee strongly believes that confirming Judge Bork would create an unacceptable risk that as a Supreme Court Justice, he would reopen debate on the country's proudest achievements in the area of civil rights and return our country to more troubled times.

III. THE EQUAL PROTECTION CLAUSE AND GENDER DISCRIMINATION

The words of the Equal Protection Clause are grand but general: "nor shall any state * * * deny to any person within its jurisdiction the equal protection of the laws." One of the more troubling aspects of Judge Bork's philosophy of equality under the Constitution is his application of the general language of the Clause to discrimination on the basis of gender.

The committee explored two principal questions with Judge Bork on this issue. First, does he believe that the Equal Protection Clause applies to women? Second, by what standard should a court evaluate a challenge to a law that discriminates between men and women? The committee finds that Judge Bork's philosophy—as expressed both before and during the hearings—raises very serious concerns.

A. *Prior to the Hearings, Judge Bork Did Not Include Women Within the Coverage of the Equal Protection Clause*

Prior to the hearings, Judge Bork engaged in a sustained critique of applying the Equal Protection Clause to women. He argued that to extend the Clause to women departs from the original intent of the Fourteenth Amendment, produces unprincipled and subjective decision-making and involves the courts in "enormously sensitive" and "highly political" matters.

In 1971, for example, then-Professor Bork said that "cases of race discrimination aside, it is always a mistake for the court to try to construct substantive individual rights under the * * * equal protection clause" and that "[t]he Supreme Court has no principled way of saying which non-racial inequalities are impermissible." ("Neutral Principles" at 17, 11.)

Judge Bork reiterated that position more than 10 years later, after ascending to the bench:

> We know that, historically, the Fourteenth Amendment was meant to protect former slaves. It has been applied to other racial and ethnic groups and to religious groups. So far, it is possible for a judge to minimize subjectivity. But when we abandon history and a very tight analogy to race, as we have, the possibility of principled judging ceases. (Untitled Speech, *Catholic University,* March 31, 1982 at 18–19.)

In this same speech, Judge Bork insisted that the courts were not competent to decide which legislative attitudes toward women were legitimate judgments, and which were outmoded stereotypes:

> There being no criteria available to the court, the identification of favored minorities will proceed according to current fads in sentimentality * * *. This involves the judge in deciding which motives for legislation are respectable and which are not, a denial of the majority's right to choose its own rationales. (*Id.* at 18, emphasis added.)

One month later, he repeated this objection again, complaining about the "extension of the Equal Protection Clause to groups * * * that were historically not intended to be protected by that clause." ("Federalism and Gentrification," *Yale Federalist Society,* April 24, 1982, at 9.)

As recently as June 10, 1987, less than a month before his nomination, Judge Bork reiterated his view:

> I do think the Equal Protection Clause probably should have been kept to things like race and ethnicity. * * * When the Supreme Court decided that having different drinking ages for young men and women violated the equal protection clause [in *Craig v. Boren*, 429 U.S. 190 (1976)], I thought that was * * * to trivialize the Constitution and to spread it to areas it did not address. (*Worldnet Interview*, June 10, 1987, at 12; emphasis added.)

B. *Judge Bork's Testimony at the Hearings Was His First Publicly Expressed Approval of Including Women Within the Scope of the Equal Protection Clause*

During his testimony, Judge Bork publicly stated for the first time that he now believes that the Equal Protection Clause should be extended beyond race and ethnicity, and should apply to classifications based on gender. According to Judge Bork, "[e]verybody is covered—men, women, everybody." (Comm. Print Draft, Vol. 1, at 230.) Judge Bork explained that all forms of governmental classifications were unconstitutional unless they had a "reasonable basis." (*See, e.g.,* Comm. Print Draft, Vol. 1, at 135, 230, 231, 306, 309.) He also said that he would reach the same results that the Supreme Court had reached in virtually all of its recent sex discrimination cases. (*See e.g.,* Comm. Print Draft, Vol. 1, at 306; 309.) Finally, Judge Bork testified that his standard was the same as that utilized by Justice Stevens.

Judge Bork's rationale for his change in position was that the Equal Protection Clause should be interpreted according to evolving standards and social mores about the role of women:

> As the culture changes and as the position of women in society changes, those distinctions which seemed reasonable now seem outmoded stereotypes and they seem unreasonable and they get struck down. That is the way a reasonable basis test should be applied. (Comm. Print Draft, Vol. 1, at 135.)

C. *Judge Bork's "Reasonable Basis" Standard Does Not Provide Women with Adequate Protection and Is Not the Standard Used by Justice Stevens*

A comparison of Judge Bork's pre-hearing views and his hearing testimony is striking. Putting aside the apparent change in views, his position that the Equal Protection Clause covers women does not go to the heart of the debate over the Court's role in reducing gender discrimination. The central debate concerns the standard of equal protection that should apply in such cases. Importantly, that standard is a presumptive guide to courts to use in evaluating claims of gender-based discrimination. The pertinent question is thus whether Judge Bork's currently expressed position would adequately protect women from such discrimination. For several reasons, the committee believes that it would not.

1. The "Reasonable Basis" Test Has Previously Been Used
to Uphold Discriminatory Legislative Classifications

Prior to the 1970s, the Supreme Court used a "reasonableness" concept to uphold a variety of legislative classifications based on gender. As Professor Sylvia Law testified: "Reasonable basis has been a standard that has upheld state power to draw lines, to discriminate if you will, if any state of facts can reasonably be conceived that would sustain the law." (Comm. Print Draft, Vol. 2, at 938.)

* * *

4. Judge Bork's "Reasonable Basis" Test Cannot Be
Explained in Terms That Are Consistent With His Original Intent
Framework and Is Contrary to His Own Guidelines
for Judicial Decision–Making

The standard articulated by Judge Bork during his testimony seems unmoored from his basic methodology. "[N]othing about * * * [Judge Bork's standard] can be explained in terms of the text of the document [the Constitution] or the 'original intent' of the Framers or ratifiers of the Fourteenth Amendment, from which Judge Bork would derive his warrant as an enforcer of the Constitution." (Tribe statement, Comm. Print Draft, Vol. 2 at 28.) And as Professor Gewirtz asks rhetorically: "How can an 'originalist' who believes that the 14th Amendment was not intended to embody a principle concerning sex equality find a warrant to displace a legislature's use of sex classifications?" (Gewirtz statement, Comm. Print Draft, Vol. 2, at 1195.)

Furthermore, Judge Bork's "reasonable basis" test seems to be at odds with his own decision-making framework, which seeks to minimize a judge's subjective preferences and values. "It is hard to imagine a more vague and unpredictable standard than asking whether there is a 'reasonable basis' for a law." (Gewirtz statement, Comm. Print Draft, Vol. 2. at 1195.) Accordingly, Judge Bork's standard appears to invite precisely the kind of unstructured decision-making that his writings of many years argue against.

* * *

Prior to the hearings, Judge Bork said on several occasions—most recently, less than one month before his nomination—that the Equal Protection Clause of the Fourteenth Amendment should not be applied to women. At the hearings, Judge Bork announced for the first time that he would apply the Clause to women pursuant to a "reasonable basis" standard. The Committee agrees with Senator Specter's statement that there is

> substantial doubt about Judge Bork's application of this fundamental legal principle where he has over the years disagreed with the scope of coverage and has a settled philosophy that constitutional rights do not exist unless specified or are within original intent. (Statement of Senator Specter, October 1, 1987, Cong. Record, S 13318.)

And as Professor Williams, focusing on Judge Bork's standard of review, concluded:

> Judge Bork's view on women's equality under the Constitution makes his nomination for a position on the highest court in the land a matter of deep uneasiness for persons concerned with the equality of the sexes. (Williams testimony, Comm. Print Draft, Vol. 2, at 956.)

IV. First Amendment

In 1971, while a Professor at Yale Law School, Judge Bork wrote his now famous *Indiana Law Journal* article entitled "Neutral Principles and Some First Amendment Problems." In his analysis of the First Amendment, Judge Bork reached the following rather striking conclusion:

> Constitutional protection should be accorded only to speech that is explicitly political. There is no basis for judicial intervention to protect any other forum of expression, be it scientific, literary or that variety of expression we call obscene or pornographic. Moreover, within that category of speech we ordinarily call political, there should be no constitutional obstruction to laws making criminal any speech that advocates forcible overthrow of the government * * * or the violation of any law. ("Neutral Principles" at 20.)

* * *

A. Dissident Political Speech

1. *Prior to the Hearings, Judge Bork Flatly Rejected the Holmes and Brandeis "Clear and Present Danger" Test and the Supreme Court's Formulation of that Test in* Brandenburg v. Ohio

During World War I and the Red Scare period that followed, the Supreme Court began to consider the conditions under which political speech that calls for law-breaking or violence could be prohibited. Although a majority of the Court at that time held that such speech could be suppressed even though there was no immediate threat of law-breaking or violence, (*see Abrams v. United States*, 250 U.S. 616 (1919) and *Gitlow v. New York*, 268 U.S. 652 (1925)), Justices Holmes and Brandeis wrote stirring and historic dissents.

Their dissenting view—that the Constitution allows political speech to be stopped only when there is a "clear and present danger" of violence or law-breaking—began to be adopted by the Supreme Court in the 1950s, and a similar but somewhat more stringent test eventually was accepted by a unanimous Supreme Court in *Brandenburg v. Ohio*, 395 U.S. 444 (1969). The Court held in *Brandenburg* that speech calling for violence or law-breaking could be forbidden only if such speech called for, and would probably produce, "imminent lawless action." This standard, therefore, addresses the nature of the speech itself and the chance that, realistically, it will lead to any harm under the circumstances in which it was uttered. Prior to the hearings, Judge Bork made three separate attacks on the *Brandenburg* decision and its underlying doctrine.

First, in his 1971 *Indiana Law Journal* article, then-Professor Bork removed from the protection of the First Amendment "any speech advocating the violation of law," even if it presents no danger of violence or law-breaking. ("Neutral Principles" at 31.)

Second, in a 1979 speech at the University of Michigan, he repeated that view and called *Brandenburg* a "fundamentally wrong interpretation of the First Amendment." (Michigan Speech at 21.) * * *

Third, in a speech delivered to the Judge Advocate General's School two years after he became a judge, the nominee expressed his continuing displeasure with *Brandenburg,* which he defined as holding that "catatonic sentiments * * * could not be inhibited or punished in any way." ("The Constitution and the Armed Forces," *Judge Advocate's General School,* May 4, 1984, at 5–6.)

* * *

2. During the Hearings, Judge Bork First Said that He Agreed with Brandenburg, and Then that He Still Disagreed with It but Would Accept the Precedent as "Settled Law"

Judge Bork actually took two distinct positions at the hearings on advocacy of law-breaking, both of which were different from his previous position. The first time the issue arose, he stated that "the Supreme Court has come to the *Brandenburg* position—which is okay * * *. That is a good test." (Comm.Print Draft, Vol. 1, at 247.) And in answer to Senator Leahy's question, "At one point, you felt the *Brandenburg* case was a fundamentally wrong interpretation of the First Amendment. Today you feel it is right," Judge Bork answered, "It is right" and "the First Amendment also says that we will take that chance [that violence might occur]." (Comm.Print Draft, Vol. 1, at 249, 252.)

The next day, his answers were different. He told Senator Specter, "[o]n *Brandenburg,* I did not say my mind had changed * * *. I think *Brandenburg* may have gone too—went too far, but I accept *Brandenburg* as a judge and I have no desire to overturn it." (Comm.Print Draft, Vol. 1, at 409.) And immediately after he said: "It's settled law. That's all I've said. I haven't said that these writings [that is, his earlier criticisms of *Brandenburg*] were wrong." (*Id.*) Judge Bork reiterated this view for the remainder of his testimony.

* * *

3. Judge Bork's Changing Positions on Brandenburg Indicate that He Might Not Fully Apply this Vital Precedent

A major concern voiced by several members of the committee (particularly by Senator Specter)—and voiced generally about those issues that Judge Bork accepted as "settled law"—was how he would apply doctrines of which he expressly disapproved in new cases with new facts. The committee finds several reasons for concern.

First, notwithstanding his acceptance at the hearings of the *Brandenburg* decision, Judge Bork was steadfast in his refusal to accept the "clear and present danger" doctrine on which *Brandenburg* was based. * * *

Second, Judge Bork stated that he saw *Cohen v. California,* 403 U.S. 15 (1971), and *Hess v. Indiana,* 414 U.S. 105 (1973), as obscenity cases because vulgar words were included in the political speech at issue in each. (Committee Print Draft, Vol. 1, at 251, 411.) In contrast, no member of the Court in either case (and *Cohen* was a unanimous decision) * thought the vulgarity of the speech was in any way relevant to whether or not it was protected, and both decisions directly applied the rule of *Brandenburg*.

* * *

Thus, there is great concern that in new cases, Judge Bork would find reasons not to apply the rules from decisions he dislikes but says are too "settled" to overturn completely. * * *

Political dissidents who make statements that flirt with the edges of the law rarely make very appealing parties in a lawsuit. It is for precisely that reason that the basic values of our political system are seriously threatened in cases that involve the sometimes incendiary and generally unpopular speech of such dissidents. Our system is built upon the precept that any political speech, short of that which will produce imminent violence, furthers public understanding and national progress—sometimes by showing the virtues of the existing system.

And sometimes dissident speech becomes the precursor of political change and ultimately, a new national consensus. * * *

Justice Oliver Wendell Holmes's classic dissent in *Abrams v. U.S.*—as noted, a position adopted years ago by the Supreme Court—provides the most expressive and stirring statement of the values at stake:

> [W]hen men have realized that time has upset many fighting faiths, they may come to believe * * * that the ultimate good desired is better reached by free trade in ideas—that the best test of truth is the power of the thought to get itself accepted in the competition of the market, and that truth is the only ground upon which their wishes safely can be carried out. That at any rate is the theory of our Constitution. (*Abrams v. United States,* 250 U.S. 616, 630 (1919).)

B. *While Judge Bork's Testimony About First Amendment Protection for Art, Literature and Expressive Speech Was Somewhat Reassuring, It Nonetheless Must Be Read Against the Background of His Prior Statements*

    1. *Prior to the Hearings, Judge Bork's Views Left a Broad Area of First Amendment Expression Unprotected*

---

* [Ed.] Neither *Cohen* nor *Hess* was unanimous.

In his 1971 *Indiana Law Journal* article, then-Professor Bork argued that the First Amendment only protected explicitly political speech. Judges should never intervene, he said, to "protect any other form of expression, be it scientific, literary or that variety of expression we call obscene or pornographic." ("Neutral Principles" at 20.) Judge Bork publicly recanted that view in his 1973 Solicitor General confirmation hearings, and indicated that he believed the First Amendment should have a somewhat broader scope.

In subsequent speeches and interviews, Judge Bork made clear that he no longer believed speech had to be clearly political to be protected by the First Amendment. Instead, he said that speech must be related to and "directly feed" the political process. For example, after identifying political speech as the core of the First Amendment, Judge Bork stated in a 1979 speech:

> But there is no occasion, on this rationale, to throw constitutional protection around forms of expression that do not directly feed the democratic process. It is sometimes said that works of art, or indeed any form of expression, are capable of influencing political attitudes. But in these indirect and relatively remote relationships to the political process, verbal or visual expression does not differ at all from other human activities, such as sports or business, which are also capable of affecting political attitudes, but are not on that account immune from regulation. (*Michigan Speech* at 8–9.)

* * *

Accordingly, under Judge Bork's views prior to the hearings, a broad area of expression traditionally viewed as included within the scope of the First Amendment would be unprotected. A Rubens painting could not be hung in a museum if the city council chose to prohibit it. The same would be true of a ban on performances by the Alvin Ailey Dance Troupe.

2. During the Hearings, Judge Bork Drew Back Substantially from His Prior Remarks

At the hearings, Judge Bork drew back substantially from his 1985 remarks. He explained that "if I was starting over again, I might sit down and draw a line that did not cover some things that are now covered," (Comm.Print Draft, Vol. 1, at 303.) but stated that he would "gladly" accept the Supreme Court's First Amendment decisions protecting non-political expression. Referring to the well-established principle that speech is protected regardless of its lack of relationship to the political process, Judge Bork said: "That is what the law is, and I accept that law." (Comm.Print Draft, Vol. 1, at 402.)

* * *

The committee finds that Judge Bork's testimony was somewhat reassuring on the question of First Amendment protection for non-political speech. While his testimony was welcome, however, it "still

must be read," in Senator Leahy's words, "against the background of
Judge Bork's prior statements on the issue." (Statement on the Confirmation of Judge Robert Bork, Cong.Record, September 30, 1987, S
13128, S 13130.) As Senator Leahy concluded:

> Judge Bork may have long ago abandoned the "bright line"
> distinction between protected political and unprotected non-political
> speech, but his responses to interviewers as recently as this past
> May and June clearly state that the existence of First Amendment
> protection should be affected by where speech falls in relation to a
> "wavering line" between speech that feeds into the "way we govern
> ourselves" and speech that does not, a line that must be drawn on a
> "case by case basis."
>
> When he came before the Judiciary Committee, Judge Bork
> conceded that this line, whether bright or "wavering," is irrelevant
> to the scope of the First Amendment. By his confirmation testimo-
> ny, Judge Bork accepted a consensus that has existed for decades.
> (*Id.* at S 13130.)

* * *

IX.   JUDGE BORK'S ROLE AS SOLICITOR GENERAL AND AS A COURT OF APPEALS JUDGE

* * *

*2. Judge Bork's Role As Solicitor General Is Not Particularly
Relevant*

* * * Judge Bork's role as Solicitor General was substantially less
reflective of his personal or legal viewpoints than his supporters have
characterized it. By his own admission before this committee in 1973,
he viewed his role as that of "the government's appeal lawyer." Even in
submitting amicus briefs when the government was not a party to a suit,
he acknowledged that his position was substantially restricted by the
views of other Justice Department officials and federal agencies.

* * *

B. Court of Appeals Judge

The committee has carefully analyzed Judge Bork's record as an
intermediate judge on the United States Court of Appeals for the District
of Columbia Circuit. Based on this analysis, two conclusions can be
drawn. First, the fact that none of Judge Bork's majority opinions has
ever been reversed tells us little about the nominee's suitability for the
Supreme Court. Second, several of Judge Bork's opinions demonstrate
that he has often taken an activist role and that on occasion he has been
insensitive to the claims of minorities.

*1. The Lack of Reversals Says Little About the Nominee's Suitabili-
ty for the Supreme Court*

It is true that none of Judge Bork's majority opinions has been
reversed by the Supreme Court. More importantly, however, none of
Judge Bork's majority opinions has ever been reviewed by the Supreme

Court. Accordingly, the lack of reversals says little about Judge Bork's suitability for the Supreme Court.

It has been suggested that failure of the Supreme Court to review any of Judge Bork's opinions is itself significant, perhaps implying a judgment by the Supreme Court that his opinions are correct. Such an implication is completely unsupportable. As former Chief Justice Burger testified, "the Court does not explain why it denies review." (Comm. Print Draft, Vol. 2, at 700) In fact, as Professor Judith Resnik said, "[The Supreme] Court has reminded us time and time again that the fact that it does not take a case [for review] has absolutely zero legal weight." (Comm.Print Draft, Vol. 2, at 1247.) Many cases decided by the court of appeals may be in error, but will nevertheless not be changed by the Supreme Court due to the extremely limited capacity of that Court to review cases.

Conceding the fact that the failure of the Court to review a lower court decision means nothing, the final attempt to make something of Judge Bork's appellate record relies upon the number of decisions he has written or participated in that have not been reversed (almost all of them were not reviewed, either). Judge Bork's supporters cite the 110 or so majority decisions he has written and more than 400 decisions he has joined. These statistics are of little utility. In any year, the courts of appeals decide about 31,000 cases, while the Supreme Court receives about 5,000 cases for review and renders opinions in only 150 to 170.

* * *

2. As an Intermediate Court Judge, the Nominee Has Been Constitutionally and Institutionally Bound to Follow Supreme Court Precedent

There is yet another reason why, in the committee's view, the statistical summaries of the nominee's Court of Appeals record do not support his elevation to the Supreme Court. As an intermediate court judge, the nominee has been constitutionally and institutionally bound to respect and apply Supreme Court precedent. Indeed, Judge Bork has explicitly recognized that duty in some of his decisions. (*See Franz v. United States,* 712 F.2d 1428 (D.C.Cir.1983); *Dronenburg v. Zech,* 741 F.2d 1388 (D.C.Cir.1984).) Thus, Judge Bork's lack of reversals says nothing about his potential for activism if confirmed as an Associate Justice on the Supreme Court, where he would be free of such restraints.

* * *

3. Several of Judge Bork's Opinions Show Him to Be a Judicial Activist Who Is Insensitive to the Claims of Minorities and Women

Several of Judge Bork's opinions on the D.C.Circuit show him to be not an apostle of judicial restraint but a marked judicial activist. The Committee believes that a brief recitation of some of these cases illustrate this point, and demonstrate that Judge Bork has often been insensitive to the claims of minority and disadvantaged groups.

a. Vinson v. Taylor

Vinson v. Taylor, 753 F.2d 141, *rehearing denied,* 760 F.2d 1330 (D.C.Cir.1985), *aff'd sub nom. Meritor Savings Bank v. Vinson,* 106 S.Ct. 2399 (1986), is the leading case on sexual harassment in the workplace. It is clear from a careful reading that Chief Justice Rehnquist's opinion for a unanimous Supreme Court took a far more sensitive approach to liability for such harassment than did Judge Bork's dissent from the D.C.Circuit's decision not to rehear the case en banc.

The facts can be briefly summarized. Vinson, a bank teller, claimed that her supervisor insisted that she have sex with him and that she did so because she feared she would be fired if she did not. Vinson claimed that over the next several years, her supervisor made repeated sexual demands, fondled her in front of other employees, exposed himself to her and forcibly raped her on several occasions. The trial court dismissed the claim, saying that their relationship was "voluntary." The D.C.Circuit reversed, holding that if the supervisor made "Vinson's toleration of sexual harassment a condition of her employment," her voluntariness "had no materiality whatsoever."

The D.C.Circuit was asked to rehear the case, and the full court declined. Judge Bork dissented from the denial of the rehearing. Attacking the original decision, Judge Bork argued that "voluntariness" should be a complete defense in a sexual harassment case. He said that "[t]hese rulings seem plainly wrong. By depriving the charged person of any defenses, they mean that sexual dalliance, however voluntarily engaged in, becomes harassment whenever an employee sees fit, after the fact, to so characterize it." (760 F.2d at 1330.)

Writing for a unanimous Supreme Court, then-Justice Rehnquist held that the correct test for sexual harassment was whether the employer created "an intimidating, hostile, or offensive working environment." On behalf of the Court, he concluded that "[t]he correct inquiry is whether [plaintiff] by her conduct indicated that the alleged sexual advances were unwelcome, not whether her actual participation in sexual intercourse was voluntary." (106 S.Ct. 2406.)

The *Vinson* decision is fundamentally important on the question of sexual harassment in the workplace, a problem that is all too common.
* * *

Judge Bork's position on liability for sexual harassment was flatly rejected by the Supreme Court. While some witnesses appearing on Judge Bork's behalf, as well as some members of the committee, have argued that Judge Bork and the Supreme Court adopted essentially the same positions, this claim is inaccurate. The crux of the issue lies in "the difference between what is voluntary and what is welcome." (Comm.Print Draft, Vol. 2., at 969.) And the Committee agrees with Judge Hufstedler's assessment of the sharp difference between these two concepts:

> I will put it this way. A decision by a dissident who wants to leave the Soviet Union who is told, yes, you can leave; of course, your family must stay. You can say that he stayed voluntarily. Did

he stay because he welcomed that choice? That is the problem with respect to the female employee who is put into this sexual harassment situation. And the difference is, Judge Bork treated the issue of voluntariness without recognizing that when the elements of choice are so far reduced, so, you do it, you go to bed with me or you are not going to be promoted, or fired, is my way of saying that is the kind of non-choice you get.

So that that is a very significant difference between the way Judge Bork viewed the situation and the way the Supreme Court did. (Comm.Print Draft, Vol. 2, at 969–70.)

As summarized by Professor Babcock, Judge Bork's position

just fails to recognize the seriousness of sexual harassment as a tremendous burden to women's equality in the workplace. When he talks about voluntariness as a defense, the Supreme Court says it is not voluntariness; it is whether these are unwelcome advances.

This is just a completely different way of looking at it. The Supreme Court does not use words like 'dalliance' when it is talking about sex discrimination. It uses words like allegations of serious criminal offenses * * *. [Judge Bork] was talking about voluntariness. The Supreme Court is talking about whether it is unwelcomed. (Comm.Print Draft, Vol. 2, at 970.)

b.   Oil, Chemical and Atomic Workers International Union v. American Cyanamid Co.

Judge Bork's opinion in *Oil, Chemical and Atomic Workers International Union v. American Cyanamid Company,* 741 F.2d 444 (D.C.Cir. 1984), offers a restrictive interpretation of a key Congressional statute. In a telling way, Judge Bork's approach to the case complements his *Vinson* decision in demonstrating his insensitivity to conditions of workplace coercion. It also minimizes the significance of procreative freedoms in our society.

The case arose out of the decision of the American Cyanamid Company to exclude from its Willow Island, W.Va., plant all women of childbearing age unless a woman offered proof of surgical sterilization. (741 F.2d 444, 445.) The company adopted this policy in order to prevent further exposure of women workers to lead, a toxic substance according to Occupational Safety and Health Act regulations. (29 C.F.R. Part 1910.1025; Occupational Exposure to Lead, 43 Fed.Reg. 52952 *et seq.* (Preamble) and 43 FedReg. 54353 *et seq.* (Attachments to the Preamble for the Final Standard).) The policy was an alternative to compliance with the lead exposure standards.

After five women underwent surgical sterilization to retain their jobs, the Secretary of Labor issued a citation alleging a violation of the "general duty clause" of the Occupational Safety and Health Act. This clause commands that employers "furnish to each of his employees * * * a place of employment * * * free from recognized hazards that are likely to cause death or serious physical harm to his employees." (29 U.S.C.

Section 654(a)(1).) The "general duty" clause furthers OSHA's policy "to assure so far as possible every working man and woman in the nation safe and healthy working conditions * * *." (29 U.S.C. Section 651(b).)

American Cyanamid attempted to comply with the general duty clause by forcing some of its women workers to submit to surgical sterilization or be fired. This policy affected women between the ages of 16 and 50 years. [741 F.2d 444, 446].

In his opinion for the court, Judge Bork upheld the decision of the Occupational Safety and Health Review Commission that the policy was not covered under OSHA, so that the employees had no rights under the Act to prevent implementation of the policy.

Judge Bork's opinion failed to mention that a previous decision of the D.C.Circuit suggested that under OSHA the exclusion of fertile women from the workplace might be actionable. (*See United Steelworkers of America v. Marshall,* 647 F.2d 1189, 1238 n. 74 (D.C.Cir.1980).) In *Marshall,* the court wrote: "We think that fertile women can find statutory protection from such discrimination in the OSH Act's own requirement that OSHA standards ensure that 'no employee will suffer material impairment of health * * *.' " (*Id.*)

In his opinion, Judge Bork implied that the harm from lead exposure was a risk faced only by women workers and developing fetuses. In fact, OSHA found that "[m]ale workers may be rendered infertile or impotent, and both men and women are subject to genetic damage which may affect both the course and outcome of pregnancy." (29 C.F.R. Section 1910.1025 (1978) at 815; *see also* Attachments to Final Standard for Occupational Exposure to Lead, 43 Fed.Reg. 54421, 54424 (1978).) These findings were upheld by the court in *Marshall.* (647 F.2d at 1256–58.)

Judge Bork's opinion also suggests that the company had no alternative but to dismiss women who chose not to be sterilized. (741 F.2d at 450.) And as Judge Bork testified in response to questions from Senator Hatch: "[T]his was a case with no satisfactory solution for anybody. I mean there was nothing to do. There was no satisfactory way to solve it." (Comm.Print Draft, Vol. 1, at 714.)

The record of this case shows, however, that a number of alternatives were proposed by the Union petitioners and the Secretary of Labor in the proceedings below and that the Oil, Chemical and Atomic Workers (OCAW) had asked the court to permit fact-finding on the question of whether there were alternatives to the sterilization policy. In its brief, the union stated:

> OCAW and the Secretary [of Labor] offered in the Commission Proceedings to present evidence to establish that Cyanamid could have provided protection to fetuses without requiring the surgical sterilization of employees, and they sought discovery to refute Cyanamid's opposing contentions. But because the ALJ [administrative

law judge], at Cyanamid's urging, disposed of the case by adopting the threshold position that the sterilization rule wasn't a hazard cognizable under the Act, a factual record was not made on this seriously disputed point. (Comm.Print, Vol. 3, at 1630–31.)

Judge Bork's opinion precluded fact-finding on this central issue— whether there were alternatives to the policy adopted by American Cyanamid.

Judge Bork's opinion and his testimony before the Committee illustrated his failure to appreciate the coercive nature of the "choice" American Cyanamid presented to its women workers. When he testified before this Committee, Judge Bork said the company "offered a choice to the women. Some of them, I guess, did not want to have children." (Comm. Print Draft, Vol. 1, at 448.) Later he said that "I suppose the five women who chose to stay on that job with higher pay and chose sterilization—I suppose that they were glad to have the choice—they apparently were—that the company gave them" (Comm. Print Draft, Vol. 1, at 450.). But the telegram and letter sent to this Committee by Betty Riggs—a woman who submitted to sterilization rather than lose her job—highlighted Judge Bork's insensitivity to the dilemma that confronted these women.

This discussion of "choice" is reminiscent of Judge Bork's use of "voluntary" to describe situations of sexual harassment in the workplace. (*See* Section (a), *supra*, discussing *Vinson*.) In a telegram received by Senators Metzenbaum and Biden, Betty Riggs, a woman who submitted to sterilization rather than lose her job, told the story of her choice:

> I cannot believe that Judge Bork thinks we were glad to have the choice of getting sterilized or getting fired. Only a judge who knows nothing about women who need to work could say that. (Comm. Print Draft, Vol. 1, at 539.)

In her subsequent letter, dated September 28, 1987, Ms. Riggs spoke clearly of economic coercion and humiliation:

> I had surgery because I had to have the job and felt I had no choice. If I lost my job I would have lost my home and I also needed it to help support my parents, my father was totally blind and my mother had emphysema * * *.

> During this time we were harassed, embarrassed, and humiliated by some supervisors and some fellow workers. They referred to us like animals, such as dogs being spayed or neutered. They told us we were branded for life.

* * *

c. *Bartlett v. Bowen*

In *Bartlett v. Bowen, 816 F.2d 695 (D.C.Cir.), reh. denied,* 824 F.2d 1240 (D.C.Cir.1987), Judge Bork adopted in dissent a novel and unprecedented approach to the doctrine of sovereign immunity (pursuant to which a governmental unit can be sued only if it consents). The plaintiff, Josephine Neuman, a member of the Christian Science faith, entered a Christian Science nursing facility and received care until she died. Medicare refused to pay the $286 for the nursing home care. Ms. Neuman's sister, Mary Bartlett, sued on the ground that the refusal to provide benefits violated First Amendment rights of the free exercise of religion. The Medicare Act, permitted "judicial review" of a "final decision" of the Secretary of the Department of Health and Human Services only if the amount in controversy is $1,000 or more. The issue in *Bartlett* was whether that statute barred federal court review of the First Amendment claim.

The majority held that the federal courts could review the constitutional claim. Judge Bork dissented and, in the words of the majority, "relie[d] on an extraordinary and wholly unprecedented application of the notion of sovereign immunity to uphold the Act's preclusion of judicial review." (*Id.* at 703.) The majority said that Judge Bork took "great pains to disparage" a leading Supreme Court decision, which suggested that Congress could not preclude review, as Judge Bork would have it, of constitutional claims. And, continued the majority, Judge Bork "ignore[d] clear precedent" from his own Circuit that followed the Supreme Court decision and made "no mention of the Supreme Court's very recent affirmation of [the decision]—using exactly the same language." (*Id.* at 702–03.)

The majority concluded that Judge Bork's view that Congress may not only legislate, but also may "judge the constitutionality of its own actions," would destroy the "balance implicit in the doctrine of separation of powers." (*Id.* at 707.) * * *

X. JUDGE BORK'S SO-CALLED "CONFIRMATION CONVERSION:" THE WEIGHT THE SENATE MUST GIVE TO NEWLY ANNOUNCED POSITIONS

As Senator Leahy has said, Judge Bork throughout the hearings told the committee many things "that he has never told anyone else before— at least not in public—about his approach to fundamental constitutional issues." (Statement of Senator Leahy, September 30, 1987, S 13128, S 13129.) Much has been made of this so-called "confirmation conversion."

In the committee's view, the issue is not whether Judge Bork was candid in those aspects of his sworn testimony that seem to contradict many of his previously announced positions. In Senator Specter's words, "it is not a matter of questioning his credibility or integrity, or his sincerity in insisting that he will not be disgraced in history by acting contrary to his sworn testimony * * *." (Specter statement, Congressional Record, Oct. 1, 1987, S 13319.) Rather, "the real issue is what weight the Senate should give to these newly expressed views," (Leahy Statement at 6), in light of Judge Bork's "judicial disposition in applying principles of law which he has so long decried." (Specter statement, Cong.Record, S 13319.)

The Committee has concluded that Judge Bork's newly announced positions are not likely fully to outweigh his deeply considered and long-held views. The novelist William Styron cut to the heart of this matter when he said that the Senate must decide whether Judge Bork's new positions reflect "a matter not of passing opinion but of conviction and faith." (Comm.Print Draft, Vol. 2, at 585.) "Measured against this standard, Judge Bork's testimony * * * mitigates some of his previous statements, but does not erase them from the record which the Senate must consider." (Leahy statement, Cong.Record at S 13129.) Underscoring this conclusion is, in Senator Heflin's words, "the absence of writings or prepared speeches which recite a change in his earlier views and the reasons for such change." (Heflin Closing Statement at 4.) In the end, the Committee is concerned that Judge Bork will bring to the "constitutional controversies of the 21st century" the conviction and faith of his long-held judicial philosophy and not that of his newly announced positions.

There were three principal changes in positions that Judge Bork announced for the first time, at least publicly, at the hearings. These related to: (1) the Equal Protection Clause of the Fourteenth Amendment and gender discrimination, (2) dissident political speech under the First Amendment, and (3) First Amendment protection for artistic expression.

* * *

Any discussion of the so-called "confirmation conversion" would not be complete without mention of the principal area in which Judge Bork did not change his views. On the related questions of liberty, unenumerated rights and the right to privacy, Judge Bork's views have not changed in any substantial degree. He still challenges the role of the Supreme Court in defining liberty; he still challenges the legitimacy of *Griswold* and its progeny; and he still maintains that the people of the nation have only those rights that are specified in the text of the Constitution.

The hearing record is, therefore, quite clear. In some areas, Judge Bork has come to rest at a point near the consensus that was reached by the Supreme Court and by most legal scholars almost a quarter-century ago. In other areas, Judge Bork's views have not changed at all, and place him at odds with every Supreme Court Justice, past or present. Once again, Senator Leahy's words reflect the conclusion of the Committee:

> This * * * shows that Judge Bork's views are now different from some of the more isolated positions he previously sought to defend. But it also shows that, at this point in his long career, he still does not demonstrate a passion for vindicating the individual rights of Americans that matches his passion for a rigorous and coherent legal theory of the Constitution. (Leahy statement, Cong.Record at S 13129.)

And in the words of Senator Heflin:

> A life-time position on the Supreme Court is too important a risk to a person who has continued to exhibit—and may still possess—a proclivity for extremism in spite of confirmation protestations. (Heflin closing statement at 6.)

MINORITY VIEWS
Introduction

The hearings on Judge Bork were some of the most far-ranging, probing, and exhaustive ever undertaken by the Committee. The nominee was the most open and forthright to appear before the Committee. The hearings focused on several basic areas: the qualifications of the nominee; the nominee's view of the Constitution; the nominee's view of the role of the judiciary; the nominee's views on specific issues such as civil rights, the right of privacy; First Amendment rights, antitrust issues, and criminal law issues; his view of precedents; and his role in dismissing Watergate special prosecutor Archibald Cox. In each instance, Judge Bork's record and thoughtful responses place him well within the conservative mainstream of American jurisprudence.

As for qualifications, no one seriously questions that Judge Bork is eminently qualified by virtue of his ability, integrity and experience. Therefore, opponents attacked Judge Bork in other areas, such as his view of the judiciary's role in our democracy. However, Judge Bork's belief that judges should merely interpret, and not make, law is clearly the accepted view of most Americans. Additionally, Judge Bork's understanding of Constitutional principles of limited federal power is both intellectually honest and comports with historical and contemporary analysis of this great document.

The major criticisms leveled at Judge Bork are the result of misunderstandings by his critics: First, a misunderstanding of the difference between the role of a professor and that of a judge, and second, a misunderstanding of Judge Bork's position on substantive issues. Despite sloganeering and misrepresentations to the contrary, Judge Bork is well within the judicial mainstream on such issues as individual liberties, civil rights, the First Amendment, criminal law issues, antitrust matters, and the value of precedent.

Along with a vast number of judges and legal scholars, Judge Bork disapproves of a Court-created generalized "right of privacy." What this means is that Judge Bork does not believe that judges are free, at their whims, to create new "rights." His view that Constitutional rights must have a basis in the Constitution is being portrayed by some as extremism, as an unpredictable philosophy. In reality, Judge Bork's comprehensive theory of jurisprudence is firmly based in our judicial history, and is at least as predictable as any other judicial philosophy, and certainly more so than one which strains to "create" new rights.

* * *

A. QUALIFICATIONS

Judge Robert Heron Bork is among the most qualified nominees to the Supreme Court in recent history. Former Chief Justice Warren Burger said Judge Bork is one of the best qualified candidates for the Supreme Court in 50 years. * * *

Even members of the Committee who are opposed to Judge Bork's confirmation acknowledged Judge Bork's fitness for the Supreme Court. For example, the Chairman told Judge Bork that "you are an honorable and decent man. There is nothing in your background that I have seen that in any way indicates that you are not, in terms of character, fit to serve on any court in any position in this country." He also called Judge Bork a "very bright man," who is "principled."

* * *

Those who support this nomination are even stronger in their praise for Judge Bork. Those who testified on his behalf include former President Ford and former Chief Justice Burger. Seven former Attorneys General supported his nomination. * * * In addition, Justice John Paul Stevens took the unusual step of publicly endorsing Judge Bork's elevation to the Supreme Court. * * *

Judge Griffin Bell, former Attorney General during the Carter administration was among a number of prominent Democrats voicing support for Judge Bork, declaring that "if [he] were in the Senate [he] would vote for" Judge Bork. He said, "I like to see a man go to the Court who is going to be his own judge, be his own man, and I think that is the way it is going to turn out." Former White House Counsel Lloyd Cutler testified on behalf of Judge Bork's nomination and gave his view that:

> On the whole, I think he would come much closer as a sitting Justice if he is confirmed to a Justice like Justice Powell and Justice Stevens—and I remind you that that is precisely what Justice Stevens himself said, that "you will find in Judge Bork's opinions a philosophy similar to that you will see in the opinions of Justice Stewart, Justice Powell, and some of the things that I * * * have written."

* * *

Judge Bork, continuing in the long tradition of eminent jurists from John Marshall to Hugo Black to the two most recent appointees to the Supreme Court, believes that judges may override the policy choices made by democratic bodies only if that choice conflicts with a right that can fairly be discerned from the text, history and structure of the Constitution. Where the Constitution is silent—and it is deliberately silent on some of the most fundamental issues—those choices are to be made by the political process. Judges cannot impose their own version of "goodness" on legislatures. If there is no right anywhere in the Constitution which forecloses challenged legislative action, there is no warrant for a judge to overturn the value preferences because it furthers some abstract notion of goodness on which the Constitution is silent.

A judge's personal opinion as to the wisdom of legislation is entitled to no more deference than any other person's; it is the Constitution that defines individual's liberties that cannot be usurped by the majority. That being the case, unless a judge can locate a right in that Constitution, then he has no right, no legitimate basis, for concluding that his personal preferences are superior to all others and may thus be imposed on American society. As Judge Bork has written:

> The question non-interpretivism can never answer is what legitimate authority a judge possesses to rule society when he has no law to apply * * * what entitles a judge to tell an electorate that disagrees that they must be governed by that philosophy? To see how extraordinary the claims of the non-interpretivists are it is useful to reflect that, if a judge wrote a statute and used it to decide a case before him, we would all regard that as an egregious usurpation of power, even though, it being a statute, the legislature could repeal or modify it. If moral philosophy would not justify a judge-written statute, how can it justify a judge-written constitution * * *?

Bork, *Foreword to G. McDowell, The Constitution and Contemporary Constitutional Theory* at VIII (1985). In other words, if courts use extra-constitutional principles to determine cases, if they strike down legislative or executive action based on their personal notions of the public good, they usurp powers not given to them by the Constitution. They transform our representative democracy into a judicial autocracy, and abandon the rule of law based on the consent of the governed for the rule of individuals based on the judge's subjective notions of what is best for society. For this reason, judges who enforce values not firmly grounded in the Constitution share in an activist mode of judicial review that cannot legitimately take place in our Madisonian, constitutional democracy.

To be sure, the Judiciary must be "activist" in that it zealously protects and furthers values that can actually be found in the Constitution and applies those values to conditions that the framers did not foresee. So there is nothing to the charge that faithfulness to the original meaning of the framers would somehow lead to diminution of constitutional values or exclude from constitutional protection such modern developments as electronic surveillance or the broadcast media. Again, Judge Bork himself has made this point quite eloquently when he wrote:

> The important thing, the ultimate consideration, is the constitutional freedom that is given into our keeping. The judge who refuses to see new threats to an established constitutional value, and hence provides a crabbed interpretation that robs the provision of a sole, fair and reasonable meaning fails in his judicial duty. That duty, I repeat, is to ensure that the powers and freedom the framers

specified are made effective in today's circumstances * * *. In a case like this, it is the task of the judge in this generation to discern how the framers' values, defined in the context of the world they knew, apply to the world we know. The world changes in which unchanging values find their application.

Ollman v. Evans, 750 F.2d at 995–96 (Bork, J., concurring).

However, the fact that a judge should give full scope to *constitutional* values in light of new threats to that value, cannot and does not mean that a judge is thereby free to somehow invent and impose *new* values wholly divorced from anything in the Constitution because he believes that these values are more "in tune" with the values shared by contemporary society. In the first place, it borders on the absurd to suggest that nine (or five) unelected, life-tenured judges are better able to discern and implement "consensus" values of a diverse, pluralistic society than are the elected, fixed-term representatives who have adopted the law being invalidated.

Most fundamentally, however, to engage in such judicial activism is to deprive, others of perhaps the most fundamental right secured to them in the Constitution: the right to self-government. Every time a court invents a new right, it correspondingly diminishes the area of democratic choice. While some may applaud this shrinking of democracy, because they are unable to convince others of the wisdom of their policies, this result can only be attained at the expense of democracy and the freedom of the American people.

The current judicial controversy over the constitutionality of the death penalty illustrates this distinction, as well as the wisdom of Judge Bork's judicial philosophy. Some justices believe that convicted murderers have a constitutional "right" not to be subjected to capital punishment. Of course, the source of this "right" is not the Constitution. To the contrary, the Constitution expressly acknowledges the availability of capital punishment in at least four different places. * * *

Consequently, some Justices look *beyond* the Constitution to create such a right, asserting that the death penalty is inconsistent with "evolving standards of decency that mark the progress of a maturing society." *Gregg v. Georgia,* 428 U.S. 153, 227 (1976) (Brennan, J., dissenting). This, of course, is the "enlightened" judicial philosophy to which Judge Bork's opponents insists he must subscribe. The capital punishment controversy perfectly illustrates why such a philosophy is illegitimate in a society dedicated to Government by the people and the accuracy of Judge Bork's observation that "a judge who looks outside the Constitution looks inside himself—and nowhere else." *A Conference on Judicial Reform,* June 14, 1982, at 5.

As with all invented rights, a right to be free of capital punishment is not derived from any evolving moral standard of *society,* but only the judges personal moral code. As with all invented rights, it does not enhance freedom but redistributes it. Inventing rights for murderers denies rights to victims and, more important, the right of society to fix appropriate punishment for violent crime.

Of course, inventing rights can be used to serve "conservative" as well as "liberal" political ends. For example, in the early part of this century, the Supreme Court used the vague language of the due process clause of the 14th Amendment to strike down a host of economic and social legislation, typified by Justice Peckham's conclusion in *Lochner v. New York,* 198 U.S. 45 (1905), that "[t]he general right [of an employer] to make a contract in relation to his business is part of the liberty of the individual protected by [the due process clause] of the 14th Amendment of the Federal Constitution." That case used the due process clause to invalidate a State law limiting the number of hours that a baker could work to 60 hours per week. So important did this precedent become that the period in which the Supreme Court used the due process clause to invalidate progressive social reform legislation became known as the *Lochner* era.

* * *

Judge Bork has indicated that the adoption of any extraconstitutional values through the due process clause is an illegitimate judicial usurpation of legislative authority. See Bork, *The Constitution, Original Intent, and Economic Rights,* 23 San Diego L.Rev. 823 (1986). Judge Bork has therefore clearly indicated that he will apply the Constitution neutrally. He will not put his views ahead of the law by prohibiting States from adopting progressive social reform legislation that interferes with free markets. By the same token, he will will not put the views of certain groups ahead of the law and recast the Constitution to accommodate their agenda. He will apply the Constitution and laws of the United States neutrally, without regard to the results. It is therefore most difficult to discern a *principled* or *consistent* basis for opposing Judge Bork's confirmation as Supreme Court Justice. Accordingly, it must be that Judge Bork's opponents deem fit only those judges who invent rights with which they agree. If the radical agenda consequently becomes a litmus test for confirmation to be a Federal judge, this irretrievably politicizes the judiciary, threatens its basic independence, and makes an end run around the democratic process to produce results that the people do not want and that are deeply rooted only in the conscience of the special interest groups and of a majority of the life-tenured, unelected Justices of the Supreme Court before whom these groups argue.

G. A MAINSTREAM JURIST

Opponents of Judge Bork's nomination say he is an extremist and outside the mainstream of constitutional thought, and that if confirmed he will disrupt the delicate balance of the Supreme Court. These two charges, however, pose an inherent contradiction. If Judge Bork is such an extremist, he will plainly be unable to obtain the four votes necessary to impose his will on the Supreme Court. By the same token, if he can command the votes necessary to craft a majority, that must mean that a majority of the Supreme Court is outside the mainstream.

The latter proposition merits closer examination. Is Justice Scalia, confirmed unanimously just last year by this body, outside the mainstream? Is Justice O'Connor, confirmed unanimously by the Senate in 1981, outside the mainstream? Is Justice White, an appointee of President John F. Kennedy, outside the mainstream? Is Chief Justice Rehnquist, twice confirmed to the Supreme Court by this Senate, outside the mainstream? Are all these distinguished members of the Supreme Court extremists? The answer clearly must be in the negative. Yet it cannot be said that Judge Bork is an extremist who will command the votes of this working majority of the Court without also suggesting that these other four Justices are extremists outside the mainstream. Therefore, unless his vote will fail to "tip the balance" as claimed, Judge Bork too must be within the mainstream.

In fact, this Senate has confirmed men and women of integrity, and it is well known that Judge Bork's judicial philosophy of interpretivism—that is, interpreting, not making, the law—is well within the mainstream of constitutional thought. * * *

* * * For example, in *Bowers v. Hardwick,* 106 S.Ct. 2841, 2846 (1986), when the Court found that there is no constitutional right to engage in homosexual conduct, Justice White, joined by Chief Justice Burger and Justices Powell, Rehnquist, and O'Connor, wrote:

> The Court is most vulnerable and comes nearest to illegitimacy when it deals with judge-made constitutional law having little or no cognizable roots in the language or design of the Constitution * * *. There should be, therefore, great resistance to expand the substantive reach of [the Due Process] Clauses, particularly if it requires redefining the category of rights deemed to be fundamental. Otherwise, the Judiciary necessarily takes to itself further authority to govern the country without express constitutional authority.

* * *

Historically, moreover, numerous other Justices, from widely varying positions on the ideological spectrum, have also shared the position that the original meaning of the constitutional text must guide constitutional interpretation. For example, in recent times, the great conservative Justice John Marshall Harlan expressed his agreement with the philosophy of original intent. In his separate opinion in *Oregon v. Mitchell,* 400 U.S. 112, 203 (1970), he stated:

> When the court disregards the express intent and understanding of the Framers, it has invaded the realm of the political process to which the amending power was committed, and it has violated the constitutional structure which is its highest duty to protect.

The great civil libertarian, Justice Hugo Black took a similar view. In his dissenting opinion in *Griswold v. Connecticut,* 381 U.S. 479, 513 (1965), he clearly articulated his belief that the Federal courts have only the limited task of applying and interpreting the text of the Constitution, rather than enforcing values not found in the Constitution. He stated:

> While I completely subscribe to the holding of *Marbury v. Madison* * * * that our Court has constitutional power to strike down statutes, state or federal, that violate commands of the Federal Constitution, I do not believe that we are granted power by the Due Process Clause or any other constitutional provision to measure constitutionality by our belief that legislation is arbitrary, capricious or unreasonable, or accomplishes no justifiable purpose, or is offensive to our own notion of "civilized standards of conduct." Such an appraisal of the wisdom of legislation is an attribute of the power to make laws, not the power to interpret them.

* * *

Justice Robert Jackson, another Roosevelt appointee to the Supreme Court, also sharply criticized judicial activism, which at the time had been marked by an aggressive use of the due process clause to invalidate social and economic regulations with which the Justices did not agree. As an Assistant Attorney General in 1937, Robert Jackson decried this activist trend of reading extraconstitutional values into the Constitution. He stated:

> Let us squarely face the fact that today we have two Constitutions. One was drawn and adopted by our forefathers as an instrument of statesmanship and as a general guide to the distribution of powers and the organization of government * * *. The second Constitution is the one adopted from year to year by the judges in their decisions * * *. The due process clause has been the chief means by which the judges have written a new Constitution and imposed it upon the American people.

See Cooper and Lund, *Landmarks of Constitutional Interpretation,* 40 Policy Rev. 10 (1987). Thus, Justices Harlan, Black, and Jackson, three of the truly outstanding Justices of our era, have decried the use of values not rooted in the constitutional text to invalidate popular legislation. If Judge Bork is outside the mainstream, so are these giants of 20th Century jurisprudence.

* * *

[T]he interpretivist view of constitutional adjudication adhered to by Judge Bork is not only within the mainstream of constitutional thought, it defines the mainstream.

H. Judge Bork and Justice Scalia

The fact that Judge Bork is firmly situated within the constitutional mainstream is closely related to another, perhaps more interesting question that has already been raised. Last year, 98 Senators voted to confirm Judge Antonin Scalia to be an Associate Justice of the United States Supreme Court, and not one opposed the nomination. As discussed above, Justice Scalia, like Judge Bork plainly believes that the

Constitution is to be interpreted as law, and not as a warrant for the imposition of the judge's moral predilections on society. If anything, Justice Scalia adheres to a more stringent view of the ability of judges to evolve constitutional guarantees to take account of modern circumstances than does Judge Bork. Compare *Ollman v. Evans,* 750 F.2d 970, 993 (D.C.Cir.1984) (Bork, J., concurring), with *id.* 1036 (Scalia, J., dissenting).

Judge Bork and Judge Scalia served together for 4 years on the D.C. Circuit. In 86 cases on which they sat together, they agreed 84 times. That is 98 percent agreement. And the only significant case on which they disagreed was *Ollman,* in which Judge Bork was to Judge Scalia's left. Many of the cases that became most controversial at Judge Bork's hearings, moreover, were cases joined by Judge Scalia on the D.C. Circuit. See, *e.g., Dronenburg v. Zech,* 741 F.2d 1388 (D.C.Cir.1984; *Restaurant Corp. of America v. NLRB,* 801 F.2d 1410 (D.C.Cir.1986); *Vinson v. Taylor,* 760 F.2d 1330 (D.C.Cir.1985) (dissent from denial of rehearing *en banc*); *Oil, Chemical, and Atomic Workers v. American Cyanamid Co.,* 741 F.2d 444 (D.C.Cir.1984). And yet no one has even attempted an explanation of why there is such controversy over Judge Bork when the Senate unanimously confirmed Judge Scalia to the Supreme Court just last year. Judge Bork's record shows that, like Justice Scalia, he has outstanding qualifications to be an Associate Justice of the United States Supreme Court, and should be confirmed for that position.

CIVIL RIGHTS

A. INTRODUCTION

If the social change is mandated by a principle in the Constitution or in a statute, then the Court should go ahead and bring about social change. *Brown v. Board of Education* brought about enormous social change and quite properly.

(Robert H. Bork, Testimony before the Senate Judiciary Committee, Sept. 16, 1987, at 91.)

B. CONSTITUTIONAL PROTECTIONS AGAINST RACIAL AND GENDER DISCRIMINATION

The Committee heard testimony confirming Judge Bork's unwaivering commitment to equal justice under the law throughout his distinguished career. As a private practitioner, professor, Solicitor General and finally as a member of the Court of Appeals for the District of Columbia Circuit, Judge Bork's actions truly do speak louder than the allegation of his critics.

As a young associate in a large Chicago law firm, Judge Bork successfully fought to end the firm's policy of excluding Jewish lawyers. As Solicitor General, he moved quickly to put an end to the exclusion of the first black woman, Deputy Solicitor General Jewel Lafontant, from meetings and policy decisions. He lent the power and prestige of his position to a movement designed to bring more women lawyers into the

Justice Department. This personal commitment to civil rights became more and more evident to the Committee as it examined Judge Bork's positions on both Constitutional and statutory issues.

Judge Bork's dedication to the eradication of racial discrimination has been apparent from his earliest academic writings. Thus, in 1971, Professor Bork wrote of the 14th Amendment:

> it was intended to enforce a core idea of black equality against government discrimination. And the Court, because it must be neutral, cannot pick and choose between competing gratifications and, likewise, cannot write the detailed code the framers omitted, requiring equality in this case but not in another. * * *

(Bork, *Neutral Principles and Some First Amendment Problems,* 47 Ind.L.J. 1, 14–15 (1971).)

As a matter of Constitutional theory, Bork has been a consistent defender of the Supreme Court's decision in *Brown v. Board of Education.* * * *

Notwithstanding Judge Bork's strong record in expanding and enforcing the civil rights statutes, much attention focused on a three-page article he wrote some 25 years ago. In that article, Professor Bork prefaced his remarks on the proposed Civil Rights Act of 1964 by stating, "[o]f the ugliness of racial discrimination there need be no argument." Bork, "Civil Rights—A Challenge," *The New Republic,* August 31, 1963, 21–24 at 22. He went on to question the *principle* of government coercion of private associational decisions. The Congress which passed the Civil Rights Act recognized the validity of Professor Bork's concerns when it exempted certain quasi-private establishments—the so-called Mrs. Murphy's boarding houses—from coverage under the act.

Judge Bork has since publicly disavowed this opposition to the Public Accommodations Act both in the classroom at Yale and before this Committee in 1973. The Committee heard testimony from members of Judge Bork's staff at the Solicitor General's office including that of Ms. Jewell LaFontant, the first black woman to hold the post of Deputy Solicitor General. Ms. LaFontant was unequivocal in confirming Solicitor Bork's personal commitment to vigorous enforcement of the civil rights laws. Moreover, the nominee himself stated before the Committee:

> I think the 1964 Act really did an enormous amount to bring the country together and bring blacks into the mainstream, and I think that is the way I should have judged the statute in the first place instead of on these abstract libertarian principles.

* * *

2. VOTING RIGHTS

* * *

The testimony also confirmed Judge Bork's unwavering commitment to an active judicial role in enforcing electoral fairness under the Constitution. Judge Bork reiterated his support for the principle of judicial oversight of legislative reapportionment announced in the case of *Baker v. Carr,* 369 U.S. 186 (1962), although as he indicated in 1971, he would decide these cases under the guarantee of a republican form of government embodied in Art. IV, § 4 of the Constitution. As Judge Bork wrote in 1968:

> Population shifts and a number of other factors had left a number of legislatures wretchedly apportioned, and political routes to reform were blocked precisely because the aggrieved voters were underrepresented. The Warren Court can hardly be faulted for entering this previously avoided thicket * * *.

Bork, *The Supreme Court Needs a New Philosophy, Fortune,* December, 1968, p. 166.

* * *

Some witnesses and Committee Members expressed concern that Judge Bork would not apply the one-person one-vote rule. Judge Bork explained that such a rigid approach often leads to the division of cities and towns into separate voting districts, and can actually be used to dilute the voting strength of minority groups. Several academic panelists noted that there is growing discontent on the Supreme Court itself concerning the rigid standard. * * *

Judge Bork also indicated that he would apply the Equal Protection Clause to reapportionment cases. As he summarized his position before the Committee:

> Nobody doubts that an apportionment which is discriminatory can be struck down. Nobody doubts that an apportionment which a majority cannot change should be struck down. The only question is whether this rigid formula [one person-one-vote] is good or not.

Some witnesses attempted to disparage Judge Bork's exceptional record on voting rights issues by suggesting that he is in favor of racially-biased poll taxes. This criticism is wholly unfounded. Judge Bork's only testimony on the subject of poll taxes in these hearings concerned the Supreme Court's decision in *Harper v. Virginia Board of Elections,* 383 U.S. 663 (1966). In *Harper,* the Court invalidated Virginia's $1.50 poll tax. Judge Bork testified that "I have no desire to bring poll taxes back into existence. I do not like them myself." At the same time, Judge Bork explained that the Court's reasoning appeared to him to be deficient, views that he had given to this Committee in 1973. * * *

Judge Bork observed that, prior to *Harper,* "[t]he poll tax was familiar in American history and nobody ever thought it was unconstitutional unless it was racially discriminatory." He also pointed out that "Congress had just recently drafted and proposed" and the states "had adopted an anti-poll tax amendment to the Constitution which this

Congress carefully limited to federal elections so as to leave state poll taxes in place if states chose to have them. That seemed to me a little odd, therefore, that the Court would come along and mop up something that Congress [deliberately did not] amend the Constitution to accomplish." Judge Bork's comments seem uncontestable. Under the rationale of the *Harper* decision, the 24th Amendment is a pointless constitutional change.

Judge Bork's analysis of the *Harper* decision in 1973 and again in these hearings does not in any way suggest a weakened support for the voting rights of minorities. Judge Bork testified before the Committee that if the tax had been "applied in a discriminatory fashion, it would have clearly been unconstitutional." But, as Judge Bork pointed out, the *Harper* court simply ignored this issue. Justices Black, Stewart, and Harlan made much the same points in their dissents. *Id.,* at 672 (Black, J., dissenting); *id.,* at 683 n. 5 (Harlan, J., dissenting).

* * *

A number of respected commentators concur with Judge Bork's observation in analysis of *Harper*. Alexander Bickel agreed with Justice Black's dissent that the Court gave " 'no reason' " for its decision, A. Bickel, *The Supreme Court and the Idea of Progress* 59 (1970), and Professor Cox conceded that the opinion seemed "almost perversely to repudiate every conventional guide to legal judgment." A. Cox, *The Warren Court: Constitutional Decision as an Instrument of Reform* 125, 134 (1968). Professor Kurland, who has harshly criticized many Warren Court decisions, called *Harper* "one of the Court's shakiest opinions." P. Kurland, *Politics, the Constitution, and the Warren Court* p. 164 (1970).

* * *

3. EQUAL PAY ACT

Corning Glass v. Brennan, 417 U.S. 188 (1974), is recognized as a landmark Equal Pay Act case. In this case Solicitor General Bork filed an amicus brief arguing that men could not be paid more than women for similar jobs on different shifts. The brief gives full effect to congressional will seeking to thwart reduced payments to women performing the same work as men.

* * *

4. TITLE VI

Title VI of the Civil Rights Act includes a provision banning discrimination based "on the ground of race, color, or national origin," in "any program or activity receiving Federal financial assistance." First a district court, and then an appellate court found that this provision was not violated when a public school system took no affirmative steps to teach English to 1,800 students of Chinese ancestry. The full court voted to deny a rehearing, leaving intact the appellate court's decision that "every student brings to the starting line of his educational career different advantages and disadvantages" and that the act does not impose affirmative teaching obligations on the school system. Despite these rulings below, Solicitor General Bork not only filed an amicus brief urging reversal, but he successfully argued that title VI reached actions with only a discriminatory effort, even absent any discriminatory intent. He thus simultaneously put the Government on record that the title VI prohibition on discrimination applies broadly and can be proven without evidence that the defendant intended to discriminate. In 1973, these were leading and unsettled issues in civil rights law.

* * *

F. Conclusion

In response to the question "where was Judge Bork on civil rights," the answer is in the Supreme Court fighting for the rights of minorities and on the appellate court expanding the protections of the Constitution, title VI, title VII, the Voting Rights Act and the Equal Pay Act.

RIGHT TO PRIVACY

Another area Judge Bork discussed was the Constitution's protection of individual liberty. As Judge Bork's testimony before, and subsequent letters to the Committee indicated, the Constitution protects numerous and important aspects of liberty. For instance, the First Amendment protects freedom of speech, press, and religion; the Fourth Amendment protects "[t]he right of the people to be secure in their persons, houses, papers, and effects, against unreasonable searches and seizures;" and the Sixth and Seventh amendments protect the right to trial by jury. All of these freedoms and more are fundamental. Judge Bork has made it quite plain that, in his view, a judge who fails to give these freedoms their full and fair effect fails in his judicial duty. But Judge Bork has also stated that merely because a judge must be tireless to protect the liberties guaranteed by the Constitution does not mean that judges should make up a right to liberty or personal autonomy not found in the Constitution. Once a judge moves beyond the constitutional text, history, and the structure the Constitution creates, he has only his own sense of what is important or fundamental to guide his decision-making. We believe, as Judge Bork does, that a judge has no greater warrant to depart from the Constitution than does Congress or the President. In other words, judges, even of the Supreme Court, are not above the law.

This means that where the constitutional materials do not specify a value to be protected and have thus left implementation of that value to the democratic process, an unelected judge has no legitimate basis for imposing that value over the contrary preferences of elected representatives. When a court does so, it lessens the area for democratic choice and works a significant shift of power from the legislative to the judicial branch. While the temptation to do so is strong with respect to a law as "nutty" and obnoxious as that at issue in *Griswold v. Connecticut*, 381 U.S. 479 (1965), the invention of rights to correct such a wholly misguided public policy inevitably involves the judiciary in much more difficult policy questions about which reasonable people disagree, such as abortion or homosexual rights.

As Judge Bork has told us, while a legislator obviously can and should make distinctions between such things as the freedom to have an abortion and the freedom to use contraceptives, a court cannot engage in such *ad hoc* policymaking. A court cannot invent rights that apply only in one case and are abandoned tomorrow in a case that cannot fairly be distinguished. The process of inventing such rights is contrary to the basic premises of self-government and inconsistent application denies litigants the fairness and impartiality they are entitled to expect from the judiciary.

* * *

It is difficult to understand why abortion is a constitutionally protected liberty but homosexual sodomy is not. Neither activity is mentioned in the Constitution, both involve activity between consenting adults, and "[p]roscriptions against [both activities] have ancient roots."

Judge Bork said it this way at the hearings:

[L]et me repeat about this created, generalized, and undefined right to privacy in *Griswold*. Aside from the fact that the right was not derived by Justice Douglas in any traditional mode of constitutional analysis, * * * we do not know what it is. We do not know what it covers. It can strike at random. *For example the Supreme Court has not applied the right of privacy consistently and I think it is safe to predict that the Supreme Court will not.* For example, if it really is a right of sexual freedom in private, as some have suggested, then *Bowers v. Hardwick,* which upheld a statute against sodomy as applied to homosexuals, is wrongly decided. Privacy to do what, Senators? You know, privacy to use cocaine in private? Privacy for businessmen to fix prices in a hotel room? We just do not know what it is. (Emphasis added.)

Some have said that the principle may be that individuals have a constitutional right to use their bodies as they wish. Not only is this principle to be found nowhere in the Constitution, but also its application would invalidate laws against prostitution, consensual incest among adults, bestiality, drug use, and suicide, not to mention draft laws and countless safety measures such as laws requiring the use of seat belts and motorcycle helmets. This principle is thus far too general to support a particular decision without sweeping in these other cases. Unless the American people decide that judges should be given far more authority and responsibility for running our society, the Constitution requires that they follow the law.

* * *

But those who now urge reliance on the Ninth Amendment see a different set of natural rights emanating from the Ninth Amendment.

For example, Professor Tribe filed a brief with the Supreme Court in *Bowers v. Hardwick* suggesting that one of the rights "retained by the people" under the Ninth Amendment is the right to engage in homosexual sodomy. Equally plausible are claims that the Ninth Amendment protects drug use, mountain climbing, and consensual incest among adults. Certainly the text of the amendment makes no distinction among any of these "rights." Therefore, unless the Ninth Amendment is to be read to invalidate all laws that limit individual freedoms, judges who invoke the clause selectively will be doing nothing more than imposing their subjective morality on society. The Constitution nowhere authorizes them to do so.

Although Justice Goldberg's concurrence in *Griswold* invoked the Ninth Amendment, Judge Bork has explained that the problems just discussed are probably the reason why the Supreme Court has *never* rested a decision on the Ninth Amendment. For instance, even Justice Douglas, the author of the majority opinion in *Griswold,* stated in a concurring opinion in the companion case to *Roe v. Wade,* that "The Ninth Amendment obviously does not create federally enforceable rights." *Doe v. Bolton,* 410 U.S. 179, 210 (1973) (Douglas, J., concurring). Unless someone can find a way both to read the Ninth Amendment to apply against the States and to discover which additional rights are retained by the people, there is no principled way for a judge to rely on the clause to invalidate State laws.

* * *

THE FIRST AMENDMENT

Judge Bork's testimony fully established that he would vigorously defend first Amendment freedoms. Judge Bork's judicial record plainly demonstrates his powerful solicitude for the freedom of speech and the press. His testimony also answered the concern expressed by some about a theoretical position on the first amendment that he arrived at when he was a law professor in 1971. See Bork, *Neutral Principles and Some First Amendment Problems,* 47 Ind.L.J. 1 (1971). Judge Bork's testimony established that he had long ago publicly abandoned the aspect of his theory that some found most troubling—namely, that the first Amendment protects only "explicitly political" speech though he reaffirmed his view that obscenity is unprotected. With respect to his strong criticism of the Holmes/Brandeis "clear and present danger test" for determining when the government can regulate speech advocating violent overthrow of the government or law violation, Judge Bork emphasized that his principle theoretical objection was with Holmes' rationale and that his objection to the test itself, as refined in *Brandenburg v. Ohio,* 395 U.S. 444 (1969), was one of degree. Judge Bork also indicated that he was sufficiently comfortable with *Brandenburg* that he would accept it as being within a firmly established line of precedent that cannot be disturbed. In sum, Judge Bork affirmed the position that he accepts and would vigorously implement the current corpus of first Amendment doctrine.

JUDICIAL RECORD

As the hearings clearly revealed, Judge Bork's judicial record on the first Amendment demonstrates that, as an Associate Justice of the U.S. Supreme Court, Robert H. Bork would be a consistent and implacable foe of censorship. Judge Bork's opinions indicate that he would afford the press and broadcast media protection from censorship to a degree which sometimes exceeds under prevailing Supreme Court doctrine.
* * *

Judge Bork's concurrence in *Ollman v. Evans,* 750 F.2d 970 (D.C.Cir.1984), is perhaps his most celebrated first Amendment opinion. This libel case is particularly important because it describes not only Judge Bork's first Amendment philosophy, but also his readiness to apply constitutional values to new threats that the Framers could not possibly have foreseen. In *Ollman,* Judge Bork's opinion was issued over a dissent by Judge (later Justice) Scalia, who stated: "It seems to me that the concurrence embarks upon a course of, as it puts it, constitutional 'evolution,' with very little reason and with very uncertain effect upon the species." *Ollman v. Evans,* 750 F.2d 971, 1036 (1984) (Scalia J., dissenting). Thus, Judge Scalia, whom this Committee and the full Senate unanimously approved for Associate Justice one year ago, sharply criticized Judge Bork for taking too *expansive* a view of individual liberties protected by the Bill of Rights. In *Ollman,* Judge Bork stated:

> We know very little of the precise intentions of the framers and ratifiers of the speech and press clauses of the first amendment. But we do know that they gave unto our keeping the value of preserving free expression and, in particular, the preservation of political expression, which is commonly conceded to be at the core of those clauses. Perhaps the framers did not envision the libel action as a major threat to that freedom * * *. But if, over time, the libel action becomes a threat to the central meaning of the first amendment, why should not judges adapt their doctrines?

Id. at 996. Applying the constitutional value found in the first Amendment to modern circumstances, Judge Bork concluded that, while existing Supreme Court decisions had already established some safeguards to protect the press from the chilling effect of libel actions, "in the past few years, a remarkable upsurge in libel actions, accompanied by a startling inflation of damage awards, has threatened to impose a self-censorship on the press which can as effectively inhibit debate and criticism as would overt governmental regulation that the first amendment would most certainly prohibit." *Id.* Accordingly, Judge Bork held that the lawsuit should be dismissed on the first amendment ground that the circumstances surrounding the allegedly defamatory statements showed them to be mere "rhetorical hyperbole" and therefore not actionable. *Id.* at 1010.

* * *

Similarly, while closely adhering to precedent, Judge Bork's opinions have shown that he believes that the Supreme Court has not gone far enough in protecting the broadcast media from government censorship. Prevailing Supreme Court case law has made an explicit distinction between the print media, the editorial content of which cannot be regulated, see *Miami Herald v. Tornillo,* 418 U.S. 241 (1974), and the broadcast media, the editorial decisions of which may be regulated according to such federal policies as the fairness doctrine and the requirement that persons criticized on the air be given a right to reply. (*Red Lion v. FCC,* 395 U.S. 367 (1969).) The distinction drawn by the Supreme Court rests on the so-called "scarcity doctrine," holding that the broadcast media, unlike the printed press, operate over scarce airwaves, and the fact of scarcity permits government regulation of the airwaves as a public trust.

In *Telecommunications Research & Action Center v. FCC,* 801 F.2d 501 (D.C.1986), Judge Bork faced a challenge to the Federal Communication Commission decision holding that teletext, a textual medium broadcast over a previously unused portion of the airwaves, could not be subject to government regulation because it was akin to a print medium. Scrupulously adhering to precedent with which he disagreed, Judge Bork, joined by Judge (later Justice) Scalia, held that because teletex was broadcast over scarce public airwaves, *Red Lion*'s scarcity doctrine necessarily governed. At the same time, however, applying the first amendment to modern, real life circumstances, Judge Bork argued that there was no principled way to distinguish print from broadcast media based on the scarcity of communications resources and, therefore, that *Tornillo* should preclude any government control over the editorial content of broadcasting. Judge Bork has repeated in other cases, as well, the theme that the editorial decisions of broadcasters deserve more protection than currently afforded by prevailing Supreme Court opinions, although he has consistently and rigorously adhered to controlling precedent. See, *e.g., Branch v. FCC,* 824 F.2d 37 (D.C.Cir.1987); *Loveday v. FCC,* 707 F.2d 1443 (1983).

* * *

POLITICAL SPEECH

Judge Bork's testimony fully answered the concern that some members of the committee expressed regarding his earlier, professorial position that the First Amendment applied only to "explicitly political" speech. See Bork, *Neutral Principles,* 47 Ind.L.J. at 27–28. First, he had long since publicly abandoned that strict, theoretical view of the First Amendment in favor of a theory that encompassed a considerably wider variety of communicative expression. (Hearings, 9/16/87 at 95–97, 109–110.) Second, to the extent that any difference remained between his present theoretical posture and prevailing first amendment doctrine, Judge Bork indicated: "There is now a vast corpus of First Amendment decisions, and I accept those decisions as law, and I am not troubled by them." (Hearings, 9/17/87 at 20.)

* * *

Even in 1971, Professor Bork described the theories expressed in his article as "informal," "tentative," and "exploratory," intended to be "ranging shots" and "speculations." At the hearings, Judge Bork indicated that he had long ago abandoned his strict 1971 view on the first amendment. He explained: "I tried to follow a bright line. The bright line, I have become convinced, particularly since sitting on first Amendment cases on the court, the bright line is impossible."

* * * This change in emphasis from a bright line theory apparently had occurred as early as 1973, for in his confirmation hearings to be Solicitor General, Professor Bork took the position that political speech was "the core of the first amendment," and "as you move out from there the first amendment's claims may still exist but certainly by the time * * * they reach the area of pornography, and so forth, the claim of first amendment protection becomes more tenuous." *Nominations of Joseph T. Sneed to Be Deputy Attorney General and Robert H. Bork to Be Solicitor General,* Hearings Before the Committee on the Judiciary, United States Senate, 93rd Congress, 1st Sess. at 12 (1973). The line would be drawn at the point when "the speech no longer has *any relation* to those processes" by which we govern ourselves and becomes "purely a means for self-gratification." (Worldnet Interview at 25) Although this line cannot be identified with "great precision," Judge Bork's theory would clearly put "forms of art * * * which are pornography and things approaching it" in the unprotected category. *Id.* at 25, 26–27. Judge Bork clarified his position that a court must examine all material that the community tries to suppress as obscene and make a judgment whether in fact the material meets the legal definition of obscenity.

* * *

With respect to art, as well, protection is plainly not absent under the academic theory to which Judge Bork has ascribed over the years. It was noted in the hearings, for example, both the enormous relevance that the Bauhaus movement in art had for the political culture in Weimar, Germany and the urgency with which the Nazis suppressed it. Such art would undoubtedly qualify for protection under Robert Bork's professorial view of the free speech guarantee. By contrast, the kind of "art" that his writings and speeches has repeatedly and paradigmatically excluded from first Amendment protection is pornography and obscenity. See, *e.g., Neutral Principles,* 47 Ind.L.J. at 29; *The Individual, the State, and the First Amendment* 15–17 (1979) ("University of Michigan Speech"); Bork, "Judge Bork Replies," 70 *ABA Journal* 132 (Feb.1984); Worldnet Interview at 26–27. In this respect, a question posed about the Joffrey Ballet is useful in pinpointing the real area of theoretical controversy. Whether the Joffrey Ballet would be protected under a pure application of Judge Bork's academic theory is a question of line drawing the difficulty of which he has readily conceded, but the point is that the American people are not going to ban the Joffrey Ballet. Some local communities in this nation may well choose to ban nude dancing, however, and, as Judge Bork stated during his testimony, his view of the first Amendment would let these communities, through the political process, express their views on nude dancing.

* * *

In any case, to the extent that any marginal differences may exist between Judge Bork's academic perspective on the first Amendment and the doctrinal status quo, Judge Bork stated in his confirmation hearings that he views existing first Amendment doctrine as being so deeply embedded in the fabric of our society and our law that he accepts it as settled precedent and feels comfortable giving it a full and fair application. Judge Bork stated:

> I certainly have no desire to go running around trying to upset settled bodies of law which are not, to say the least, pernicious * * *. I would accept that line of First Amendment cases gladly, not grudgingly.

CONCLUSION

As these views indicate, Judge Robert Bork is eminently qualified by ability, integrity, and experience to serve as Associate Justice of the Supreme Court. The failure of the Senate to confirm him will be a failure larger than simply denying one qualified nominee a place on the Court. It will be a disservice to the process by rewarding those who have turned the nominating process into a negative campaign of distortions; it will be a disservice to the judiciary of this country who should not be forced to endure such a politicized process; and most importantly, it will be a disservice to the American people, who not only will be denied the service of this intellect on the Court, but will also see the judiciary have its independence threatened by activist special interest groups.

* * *

2. *The Nomination of David Souter*

On July 20, 1990, Justice Brennan announced his resignation from the Court. With surprising swiftness, President Bush nominated David Souter to be his replacement. Few had heard of him and he quickly became known as the "stealth candidate." After three days of hearings, the Judiciary Committee approved his nomination by a vote of 13–1 [3]. On October 2, 1990, the Senate, voting 90–9, confirmed Souter as the 105th Justice.

In reading the Senate Judiciary Report, consider whether the President was well-advised to select someone so unknown and so inexperi-

---

3. Only Senator Kennedy voted against the motion to report the nomination with a favorable recommendation.

enced in the federal sector. To what extent was this the logical and predictable reaction to the Bork hearings? Is the Court and the public well-served by this development?

After reading the report, look back at the opinion in *Casey* in chapter one and consider to what extent Justice Souter's vote is consistent with his testimony on stare decisis in his hearing. Do you think he felt bound by his statements in the hearing? Should he have been? Some Justices have claimed that recent appointees have consulted the transcripts from their hearing when considering how to vote. Is that appropriate?

NOMINATION OF DAVID H. SOUTER TO BE AN ASSOCIATE JUSTICE OF THE UNITED STATES SUPREME COURT

October 1, 1990.—Ordered to be printed.

S.Exec.Rep. 101–32, 101st Cong., 2d Sess (1990).

Mr. Biden, from the Committee on the Judiciary,
submitted the following
REPORT
together with
ADDITIONAL AND MINORITY VIEWS

The Committee on the Judiciary, to which was referred the nomination of Judge David H. Souter to be an Associate Justice of the United States Supreme Court, having considering the same, reports favorably thereon, a quorum being present, by a vote of 13 yeas and 1 nay, with the recommendation that the nomination be approved.

* * *

III. THE NOMINEE

Judge Souter was born on September 17, 1939, in Melrose, Massachusetts. He received his Bachelor of Arts degree from Harvard College in 1961. Judge Souter was a Rhodes Scholar, and attended Magdalen College, Oxford, between 1961 and 1963. He received his legal education at Harvard Law School, which he attended from 1963 to 1966.

From 1966 to 1968, the nominee engaged in the private practice of law with the Concord, New Hampshire law firm of Orr and Reno.

The nominee served for 10 years in the office of Attorney General for the State of New Hampshire. From 1968 to 1971, he was an Assistant Attorney General. From 1971 to 1976, the nominee was Deputy Attorney General. And from 1976 to 1978, he was Attorney General.

From 1978 to 1983, the nominee served as Associate Justice of the Superior Court of New Hampshire.

From 1983 to 1990, the nominee served as Associate Justice of the Supreme Court of New Hampshire.

In 1990, President Bush appointed Judge Souter to the U.S. Court of Appeals for the First Circuit, a position he held for five months before his nomination to the Supreme Court.

* * *

ADDITIONAL VIEWS OF CHAIRMAN BIDEN

Introduction

* * * No nominee in a quarter-century had come to this committee with less known about his constitutional philosophy than David Souter. And no nomination—at any time since the 1930s—had come before the Senate at a moment of such importance, in terms of setting the future direction of the Supreme Court.

As this critical moment, this committee had an obligation to learn all that it could about Judge Souter's constitutional philosophy. And at this critical moment, I believe that the burden of proof rested on the nominee to demonstrate that he is the person whom the Senate should confirm to sit on the nation's highest court.

In my view, Judge Souter met his burden of proof with respect to some matters, and failed to do so with respect to others. His philosophy was neither proven to be wholly inappropriate, or wholly acceptable, for confirmation.

In several areas, there were reassuring signs. For example, in the area of freedom of speech, Judge Souter indicated his support for Justice Brennan's landmark precedent of *New York Times Co. v. Sullivan,* 376 U.S. 254 (1964); for the Supreme Court's ban on the prior restraint of the press; and for the decision in *Brandenburg v. Ohio,* 395 U.S. 444 (1969), that permits speech that urges civil disobedience.

In the field of Free Exercise of religion, Judge Souter indicated that he had "no reason to raise questions about the appropriateness of the strict scrutiny test" (Transcript, Sept. 14, at 46) for laws that impair religious practices. Thus, Judge Souter suggested that he disagreed with the Supreme Court's recent and restrictive decision in *Employment Division of Oregon v. Smith,* 110 S.Ct. 1595 (1990), that undermines religious freedom in our country. This, again, is a very encouraging point of view.

In the area of stare decisis, Judge Souter detailed a philosophy that shows a proper respect for precedent. And quite hearteningly, Judge Souter particularly emphasized that—before the Supreme Court reverses a prior ruling—it should take into account "whether private citizens * * * have relied upon the precedent in their own planning to such a degree that * * * it would be a great hardship in overruling it now." (Transcript, Sept. 13, at 137.) This distinguishes Judge Souter from other nominees, who said that they would look only to whether governmental structures and social institutions have been built up around a particular decision—Judge Souter's view is, quite obviously, more reassuring than this more limited approach.

And, finally, for this side of the ledger—and most importantly—Judge Souter categorically rejected the archconservative judicial philosophy of "original intent:" the view that the meaning of constitutional provisions should be limited to the specific intentions of their framers.

This doctrine—as Judge Souter himself acknowledged—would undermine many of the most important decisions the Supreme Court has given us through the years: *Brown v. Board of Education,* 347 U.S. 483 (1954); the one person, one vote rulings; and the Court's rulings that outlaw discrimination against women.

Judge Souter said that this "original intent" doctrine is "not * * * the appropriate criterion of constitutional meaning." (Transcript, Sept. 13, at 214.) And, in response to my question, "does the correct interpretation of a constitutional provision * * * change over time?," Judge Souter said, "principles don't change, but our perceptions of the world around us and the need for those principles do." (Transcript, Sept. 17, at 196–97.)

In all of these critical respects, Judge Souter clearly proved to the committee that his judicial philosophy was sound—and even highly commendable. In all of these critical respects, Judge Souter met his burden of proof—and then some.

As these Additional Views indicate, in four other areas, though, Judge Souter left the committee with a more mixed record.

First, there is the area of establishment of religion. Here, Judge Souter criticized the prevailing Supreme Court rule of *Lemon v. Kurtzman,* 403 U.S. 602 (1971)—which is not an exceptional view—but he did so without indicating what guarantees of religious liberty he would impose in its place.

As a result, we were left with a very unclear picture of how Judge Souter approaches this important issue; we have very little idea how "high" he thinks the "wall of separation" between church and state ought to be.

Second, there is the area of race discrimination. Here, too, some things Judge Souter said were quite hopeful: He called the struggle for racial equality the "most tragic" problem confronting the nation, and he suggested that, in his view, at least some types of affirmative action programs are permissible.

Yet aspects of Judge Souter's record as Attorney General of New Hampshire and of his testimony before the committee were troubling. Again, the record is a mixed one.

Third, there is the area of gender discrimination. Judge Souter criticized the Supreme Court's current middle-tier scrutiny for laws that discriminate on the basis of gender, and even implied that the basis for his criticism was that the Court's existing standard fails to provide adequate protection for women's rights.

Yet I found disappointing Judge Souter's failure to indicate clearly whether his standard in this area would, in fact, be more rigorous—or, inappropriately, less rigorous—than current law. The nominee's tone suggested that he was headed in the right direction, but I do not know for sure—and I would feel more comfortable if I did.

Finally, there is the area of privacy and reproductive choice. Here, Judge Souter did say some encouraging things. He agreed that there is a marital right to privacy, and that the right of married couples to make choices about procreation is "at the core" of that fundamental right. (Transcript, Sept. 13, at 116.) He agreed that the Constitution protects unenumerated rights, and more specifically, that there is substantive content in the Due Process Clauses of the Fifth and Fourteenth Amendments, and the Ninth Amendment—important guarantees of the liberties of all Americans.

And perhaps most importantly, he flatly rejected the methodology being advanced by Chief Justice Rehnquist and Justice Scalia for determining when, in the future, privacy rights will be recognized by the Court. Judge Souter said that he "could not accept [their] view" (Transcript, Sept. 14, 160)—and I find that very, very encouraging.

At the opposite end of the spectrum in the privacy area, however, I found most troubling Judge Souter's declaration that the issue of whether unmarried persons have any fundamental right of privacy is "an open question." (Transcript, Sept. 17, at 230.) I firmly believe that this is not an "open question:" Individuals do have a right to privacy, that right is fundamental, and the Supreme Court—in 26 opinions, written by 10 different justices over the past 17 years—has recognized this fundamental right.

Between the privacy issues on which Judge Souter met his burden of proof—and the issue on which Judge Souter failed—is one vital privacy issue that Judge Souter declined to speak to altogether: whether a woman's fundamental right not to be pregnant continues after her birth control fails.

* * * I feel that Judge Souter could have told us far more about his views in this area without compromising his judicial independence, or indicating how he would vote on a request to overrule *Roe v. Wade,* 410 U.S. 113 (1973). Judge Souter's refusal to talk at all about his philosophy in this area frustrated the committee's exercise of its constitutional responsibilities, and I find it another, very troubling aspect of this nomination.

In sum, then, we have before us a nominee that satisfied his burden of proof with respect to some issues, straddled the line on others, failed on some, and left us with a question mark on still other matters. This mixed picture makes his nomination a very, very difficult case. But after weighing the evidence closely, and studying the record intensely, I decided to vote to confirm David Souter as Associate Justice of the Supreme Court.

Taking Judge Souter at his word, I believe that he clearly demonstrated himself not to be a doctrinaire legal conservative. He clearly distinguished himself from a quite broad school of legal conservatism—including some conservative positions now being taken by members of the current Court:

He rejected Justice Scalia's cramped formula for determining when fundamental, unenumerated rights should be acknowledged;

He rejected two shibboleths of the rigid interpretivists by saying that the Due Process Clause does protect substantive liberties—and that the meaning of constitutional provisions cannot be limited to the "original intent" of their framers;

He rejected the Court's recent majority opinion in the *Smith* case, on religious freedom; and

He rejected the conservative view that courts must stay out of the realm of addressing "profound social problems"—indeed, Judge Souter insisted that the court must intervene in these areas when a "vacuum of responsibility" exists. (Transcript, Sept. 14, at 14.)

This repeated rejection of the precepts of modern arch-conservative legal thought—of rigid interpretivism—proved to me what Judge Souter was not: Namely, he is not the sort of man who, if confirmed, would run roughshod over the important precedents handed down by the Supreme Court over the past three decades.

But that alone was not enough. Beyond proving what he is not, Judge Souter also proved to me, affirmatively, that much about his philosophy—about his approach to dealing with the issues of the future—merits my consent to his confirmation.

Weighing most heavily in this respect were Judge Souter's statements that he believes that judges must vindicate rights not explicit in the Constitution; that the Due Process Clause protects unenumerated liberties; that a fundamental right to privacy exists; that he would use a broader, and not a narrow, methodology in deciding when the Court should recognize such rights; and the judges must use the Bill of Rights to protect the rights of minorities.

These statements, of course, give me no clear sense of how Judge Souter is going to rule on any one particular case. That is how it should be: I believe that searches should not be made for case-specific commitments from the nominee. But what these statements—and many others—do indicate is that Judge Souter has an approach on most issues that—though far more conservative than I would hope for the Court—is nonetheless an acceptable one.

I believe that this was true for "most issues." Unfortunately, Judge Souter's refusal to discuss reproductive choice leaves me with no indication at all of where he will come out on this issue—indeed, it leaves me with no indication at all of even how he thinks about this constitutional question.

What Judge Souter did tell the committee, however, was this: "I have not made up my mind and I do not go on the court saying I must go one way or I must go another way." (Transcript, Sept. 14, at 128.) This statement goes a step beyond refusing to tell us his view on reproductive freedom, and tells us—if Judge Souter is to be believed, and I do believe him—that his mind is an open one.

* * * I strongly believe that a woman's right to choose is fundamental, and protected by our Constitution. And I believe that any attempts to read that right out of the Constitution are misdirected, and reflect a mistaken understanding of the true majesty of the Liberty Clause of the Fourteenth Amendment to our Constitution.

I also know, however, that the President of the United States has the diametrically opposed view. The President has pledged to see *Roe* overruled, and believes it to be wrong. He obviously has no intention of submitting, and will never submit, a nominee who adheres to my view on this matter. I know that—we all know that.

It is one thing to reject a nominee who would come to the Court opposed to reproductive freedom; if the President attempted to send up such a nominee—one who shared the President's view on the choice question—he or she would find a serious fight in the Senate. But if this committee were to go a step further, and also reject a nominee who genuinely seems to be open-minded on this question—neither committed to the President's view or the opposing viewpoint—if we make that a litmus test for confirmation—we will have an eight-member Court for a long time to come.

Under the circumstances of sharp diversion between the White House and the Senate, I believe that the best we can hope for is a judge who has an expansive methodology for interpreting privacy rights generally, and a genuinely—and I emphasize genuinely—open-minded view of a woman's privacy right after conception occurs. Judge Souter is not the sort of judge I would nominate if I were president, but I think that he is about the best we can expect in the divided-government situation we now face.

Of course, this does not mean that I can be confident that Judge Souter will vindicate a woman's right to choose—we do not know where he will be on that question. It does mean, in my view, that he is about the best we are going to do on this score from this Administration.

With this realistic lens as my perspective, I supported Judge Souter's confirmation. I do not do so enthusiastically, and * * * I do not do so without reservation.

PART ONE: JUDGE SOUTER'S APPROACH TO INTERPRETING THE CONSTITUTION

Judge Souter has stated that he takes an "interpretivist" approach to the Constitution. In his testimony, for example, he said: "I regard myself as within the broad umbrella of interpretivism." (Transcript, Sept. 17, at 124–25.)

The precise meaning of "interpretivism" is very much a matter of controversy. Interpretivism is generally thought of as an approach to the interpretation of the Constitution that emphasizes the importance of the constitutional text. But self-described interpretivists can take sharply varying views on central constitutional issues. * * *

In an important dissenting opinion he wrote while a Justice on the Supreme Court of New Hampshire, Judge Souter explained his approach to the interpretation of the New Hampshire constitution in the following terms:

> The court's interpretive task is * * * to determine the meaning of the [constitutional] language as it was understood when the framers proposed it and the people ratified it as part of the original constitutional text that took effect in June of 1784. ("In re Estate of Dionne," 518 A.2d 178, 181 (1986).)

At first glance, it appears that this approach calls for a rigid interpretation of the Constitution, under which the Constitution protects only those individual rights that the Framers of its provisions specifically sought to protect. Under that approach, several of the landmark decisions of the last half-century might well be incorrect.

For example, in *Brown v. Board of Education,* 347 U.S. 483 (1954), the Supreme Court ruled that racial segregation in public schools is unlawful. But there is evidence that the people who drafted and adopted the Equal Protection Clause of the Fourteenth Amendment never intended to outlaw segregation.

Similarly, there is no question that those who drafted and adopted the Fourteenth Amendment did not intend to invalidate discrimination against women, which was endemic at the time the amendment was adopted. But in a series of decisions beginning in 1971, the Supreme Court has held that the Equal Protection Clause requires close scrutiny of gender-based classifications. (See, e.q., *Reed v. Reed,* 404 U.S. 71 (1971); *Craig v. Boren,* 429 U.S. 190 (1976).)

When asked about these and other cases, Judge Souter asserted that his approach was consistent with these decisions. He explained that his concern was with the "meaning" of the constitutional provision or the "principle" that the framers of the provision had adopted, rather than the "specific intent" or specific "applications" that the Framers had in mind.

For example, Judge Souter stated:

> My approach to interpretation is not a specific intent approach. The approach has got to take into consideration the text of the provisions in question and * * * the meaning of that text is not to be confined by reference simply to the specific applications that may have been, as it were, in the mind either individually or institutionally of the people who proposed the amendment * * *. [W]hen we look for the original meaning, we are looking for meaning and for

principle. We are not confining ourselves simply to immediately intended application. (Transcript, Sept. 17, at 31.)

In response to my question, Judge Souter distinguished his approach from that which he described as "original intent, or the intentionalist school," and he explicitly repudiated the latter:

> [W]hen I speak of original intent, or the intentionalist school, I am talking particularly about that view that the meaning of the provision or the application of the provision should somehow be confined to those specific instances or problems which were in the minds of those who adopted and ratified the provision, and that the provision should be applied only to those instances or problems. *I do not accept that view.* (Transcript, Sept. 17, at 197–96 (emphasis added).)

* * *

Under the approach Judge Souter described, only constitutional "principles"—the principle of equal protection, the principle of due process—remain the same. The law can develop as each generation applies those principles to its contemporary realities. Judge Souter made this point explicit in response to questioning from me:

> THE CHAIRMAN. Now, Judge, under your approach does the correct interpretation of a constitutional provision * * * change over time?

> JUDGE SOUTER. Principles don't change, but our perceptions of the world around us and the need for those principles do * * *. In 1954 [when *Brown v. Board of Education* was decided,] they saw something which they did not see [when *Plessy v. Ferquson,* 163 U.S. 567, which approved the "separate but equal" doctrine, was decided] in 1896. Now I will say, as I have said before that I think *Plessy* was wrongly decided, but I also understood that there was a perception which the experience of 58 years had allowed the Court in 1954 to make and they saw an application for a principle which was not seen in 1896.

* * *

Accordingly, Judge Souter stated that, under his approach, the practice of closely scrutinizing gender classifications is sound, even though the Framers of the Equal Protection Clause "would not have had the slightest inkling that that clause was going to be applied to gender discrimination." (Transcript, Sept. 17, at 30.) Judge Souter also said that the Fourteenth Amendment establishes the principle of "one person, one vote," even though there is strong evidence that its drafters and adopters did not intend to establish such a principle. (Transcript, Sept, 17, at 54, 198.) And Judge Souter endorsed the historical expansion of Congress's Commerce Clause power, because the Framers "wrote more generally than they probably intended by way of application at the time that they wrote it, but they wrote what they wrote." (Transcript, Sept. 17, at 30.)

* * *

In addition, Judge Souter noted that the "courts must accept their own responsibility for making a just society." (Transcript, Sept. 14, at 13.) He added:

> One of the things that is almost a factor or a law of nature, as well as of constitutional growth, is that if there is, in fact, a profound social problem and the Constitution speaks to that, and if the other branches of Government do not deal with it, ultimately, it does and must land before the bench of the judiciary. (Transcript, Sept. 14, at 13–14.)

Judge Souter's testimony on the role that tradition must play in giving content to the Due Process Clause is also consistent with this view, rather than with a narrow interpretivism that looks only to the understandings of constitutional provisions that were held at the time they were adopted. Judge Souter rejected the view embraced by Justice Scalia in *Michael H. v. Gerald D.,* 109 S.Ct. 2333, 2344 n. 6 (1989), that a liberty interest under the Due Process Clause can be based only on "the most specific level at which a relevant tradition protecting, or denying protection to, the asserted right can be identified." Judge Souter stated: "[W]e cannot, as a matter of definition at the beginning of our inquiry, narrow the acceptable evidence to the most narrow evidence possible * * *." (Transcript, Sept. 14, at 161.)

I am in general agreement with the approach to constitutional interpretation that Judge Souter described in his testimony. Nonetheless, Judge Souter's record on this point gives rise to some reservations, for two reasons.

First, it is not immediately clear that the flexible, adaptable approach that Judge Souter explained in his testimony is the same as the philosophy he stated in his *Dionne* dissent. The *Dionne* approach seems to seek an interpretation that is established at the time the constitutional provision is adopted. * * *

At one point in a colloquy with me, Judge Souter seemed to recognize the potential inconsistency between his general approach and the view he described in *Dionne;* he suggested that *Dionne* was an unusual case because the New Hampshire constitutional provision was relatively specific. (Transcript, Sept. 17, at 204–05.) I note that Judge Souter might also have distinguished his *Dionne* approach on the ground that it was dictated by New Hampshire precedents that would not necessarily apply to the interpretation of the United States Constitution. (See 518 A.2d at 181.) But Judge Souter did not draw this distinction. Instead, his position was that "the ultimate criterion of meaning for me in the *Dionne* case was exactly what I think the ultimate criterion should have been and was for the Supreme Court of the United States in *Brown,*" (Transcript, Sept. 14, at 62.)

In addition, while Judge Souter seemed to depart from the narrow historicism of *Dionne* when he was discussing the Fourteenth Amendment and the Commerce Clause, he used a different approach in connection with the Establishment Clause. Senator Leahy asked Judge Souter about an argument, currently made by some, that the Establishment Clause was originally intended only to prevent literal establishments of religion and to maintain government neutrality among Christian sects.

The approach Judge Souter outlined in his testimony about the Fourteenth Amendment would lead one to think that he would question this interpretation on the ground that the Establishment Clause enacts a broad principle of religious neutrality that cannot be cabined by a showing of specific historical intentions. But Judge Souter did not take that position in response to Senator Leahy's questions. Instead, he suggested that this extraordinarily narrow interpretation, if historically correct, should be considered by the Court, subject only to the claims of stare decisis.

* * *

I have some concern, therefore, that Judge Souter might not be fully committed to the approach to constitutional interpretation that he described in his testimony, and may instead follow the approach suggested by the *Dionne* concurring opinion. That this latter approach would be unacceptable is sufficiently shown by the fact that it would call into question *Brown*, the gender discrimination decisions, the principle of "one person, one vote," and numerous other important advances in constitutional law.

My second reservation concerns Judge Souter's repeated self-description as an "interpretivist." There appears to be a severe tension between "interpretivism" and the approach to constitutional interpretation that Judge Souter described in his testimony.

The core idea of interpretivism is close attention to the text of the Constitution as a source of restraint on judges. Judge Souter's interpretive approach, to be sure, begins with the Constitution's text. But this alone tells us little, because few, if any, judges and scholars do not begin constitutional interpretation with the text. The approach Judge Souter described in moving beyond the Constitution's text is appealing because it extracts from the text, not specific commands, but broad principles and aspirations—the principles of "equal protection" and "due process," for example. These principles are so broad, however, that it is not clear what is left of the "interpretivist" idea to which Judge Souter professes allegiance.

Moreover, Judge Souter explicitly embraced the idea that the Due Process Clause has a substantive content. And * * * Judge Souter unequivocally endorsed the existence of fundamental constitutional rights that are not enumerated in the Constitution.

I find all of this testimony very positive, but wonder how it can be reconciled with Judge Souter's purported adherence to "interpretivism."

In summary, some aspects of Judge Souter's approach to constitutional interpretation remain unclear and appear to be unsettled. Overall, however, I am pleased that Judge Souter explicitly rejected a narrow approach to constitutional interpretation that would confine the meaning of the Constitution's majestic phrases to the specific intentions of those who drafted them; instead, he outlined a coherent judicial philosophy that allows for the orderly growth of the law.

Consequently, I believe that Judge Souter's over-all interpretive philosophy warrants my support for his confirmation.*

* * *

PART EIGHT: JUDGE SOUTER'S VIEWS ON STARE DECISIS

The doctrine of stare decisis—"to stand by things decided"—protects and promotes the stability, efficiency and legitimacy of the legal system. Judge Souter's record on the New Hampshire Supreme Court, as well as his testimony before the committee, suggest that the nominee has a healthy respect for precedent, and that he would exercise caution and prudence when asked to reverse existing doctrine.

A. *While a Member of the New Hampshire Supreme Court,*
Judge Souter Showed Great Deference to Precedent

Judge Souter's opinions on the New Hampshire Supreme Court suggest a strong attachment to the doctrine of stare decisis, at least in the context of statutory interpretation.

For example, in two cases, he joined a majority opinion because he thought the issue was controlled by existing precedent, even though he disagreed with that precedent. * * * Furthermore, in one of those cases, the controlling precedent was a case that reversed a ruling Judge Souter had made as a trial judge; there was little doubt, therefore, that he disagreed with the precedent. * * * In other cases, Judge Souter wrote a concurrence to emphasize that he could reach a result solely on the basis of precedent and did not have to engage in the extended analysis that the majority had used. * * *

It is true, of course, that these are statutory cases. As such, they are not necessarily indicative of how Judge Souter would apply stare decisis in constitutional cases, in which the Supreme Court has historically showed less deference to precedent. Nonetheless, Judge Souter's opinions on the New Hampshire Supreme Court demonstrate a strong respect for precedent in statutory cases, and suggest a deference to precedent generally. They can be read to illustrate that he will not simply disregard that respect when confronted with challenges to prior decisions interpreting the Constitution.

B. *Judge Souter's Testimony Also Evinces*
a Strong Respect for Precedent

Under questioning by Senator Thurmond, Judge Souter articulated his theory of stare decisis and the "series of considerations which courts

---

* [Ed.] Parts Two through Seven are omitted.

should bear in mind in deciding whether a prior precedent should be followed or should not be." (Transcript, September 13, at 135.)

The first question to be addressed, Judge Souter testified, is whether the court concludes that the precedent was correct when originally decided. He stated that if a determination is made that the case was not correctly decided, several factors must then be evaluated.

The first factor listed by Judge Souter was the "degree and the kind of reliance that has been placed upon" the precedent. Elaborating on this "reliance," Judge Souter said:

> We ask in some context[s] *whether private citizens in their lives have relied upon [the precedent] in their own planning to such a degree that, in fact, it would be a great hardship in overruling it now.* (Transcript, Sept. 13, at 137 (emphasis added).)

In response to questioning by Senator Specter about the kinds of cases to which this factor would be relevant, Judge Souter made clear that "I can certainly tell you that the issue of reliance is not an issue which is limited to commercial cases." (Transcript, Sept. 17, at 247.) While Judge Souter did not elaborate on the non-commercial cases to which this factor would apply, it is encouraging that he explicitly rejected limiting this factor to the commercial context.

The second factor identified by Judge Souter is "whether legislatures have relied upon [the precedent], in legislation which assumes the correctness of that precedent." (Transcript, Sept. 13, at 137.)

The third factor he identified is "whether the court in question or other courts have relied upon it, in developing a body of doctrine." Elaborating on this factor, Judge Souter said:

> If a precedent, in fact, is consistent with a line of development which extends from its date to the present time, then the cost of overruling that precedent is, of course, going to be enormously greater and enormously different from what will be the case in instances in which the prior case either has not been followed or the prior case has simply been eroded, chipped away at, as we say, by later determinations. (Transcript, Sept. 13, at 137–38.)

Finally, Judge Souter noted the well-recognized distinction between the application of stare decisis in statutory cases and its application in constitutional cases. He suggested looking to "other means of overruling the precedent"—that is, legislation enacted by Congress—in the context of statutory cases. (Transcript, Sept. 13, at 138.)

These factors constitute a thoughtful and reasoned approach to stare decisis. Importantly, when discussing the question of reliance, Judge Souter emphasized the degree to which private citizens have relied on the case—as opposed to the reliance of governmental and private institutions, which can limit the applicability of this factor to commercial and administrative law decisions. By focusing on the degree of reliance by private citizens and by explicitly extending this factor beyond simply commercial law cases, Judge Souter appears to recognize the precedential value of decisions in the areas of civil rights and civil liberties. While I am concerned about the degree to which he would consider the fact that a prior decision had been "chipped away at," on balance I have concluded that the factors identified by Judge Souter are appropriate.

Judge Souter's approach to stare decisis is important not only because of the factors he listed, but also because of the factors he did not list. Some justices have noted, for example, that because they are oath-bound to the Constitution, they owe little or no deference to prior decisions interpreting the Constitution. Justice Scalia has argued, for example, that it would violate his oath to uphold the Constitution were he to adhere to a prior decision that he considers to be "a plainly unjustified intrusion upon the democratic process in order that the Court might save face." (*South Carolina v. Gathers,* 109 S.Ct. 2207, 2218 (1989) (Scalia, J., dissenting); see also Douglas, *Stare Decisis,* 49 Colum.L.Rev. 735, 736 (1949).) During his testimony on stare decisis, Judge Souter made no reference at all to this argument and in no way suggested that his oath might lessen the need to pay appropriate deference to prior constitutional decisions.

PART NINE: JUDGE SOUTER TESTIFIED THAT HE MADE NO COMMITMENTS TO THE ADMINISTRATION IN CONNECTION WITH HIS NOMINATION OR CONFIRMATION

Judge Souter testified that he made no commitment to the Administration in connection with either his nomination or confirmation.

* * *

This is as it should be. Nominees should not, of course, give any "assurances" to anyone regarding how they would vote on particular cases that may come before the Court. Judge Souter's testimony in this respect has been reassuring, in light of news reports that had raised some concerns in this area.

CONCLUSION

In supporting the confirmation of David Hackett Souter, I am not saying that I am giving this nominee, or any other nominee, the "benefit of the doubt." Nor am I saying that a nominee need only prove himself or herself not to be extremist to win this committee's approval.

The burden of proof is on the nominee—and it is a burden that this nominee, in my view, just barely met. Any future nominee who fails to meet that burden—and again, I emphasize how close this nominee came to that line—will be vigorously opposed by me.

The Administration should be careful not to learn the wrong lesson from the committee's lop-sided vote in Judge Souter's favor. Our approval is not a sign that the Senate intends to be lax about exercising its advice and consent power, or intends to use that power only to screen out extremist nominees. Rather, it is a sign that we take this power seriously, and that we intend to exercise it responsibly—and in doing so,

Judge Souter falls within the sphere of candidates acceptable to this committee.

Other nominees, if more conservative than this one, could well fall outside of that sphere:

> For example, a nominee who criticizes the notion of unenumerated rights, or the right to privacy, would, in my view, be unacceptable.

> A nominee whose view of the Fourteenth Amendment's Equal Protection Clause has led him or her to have a cramped vision of the Court's role in creating a more just society would, in my view, be unacceptable.

> And a nominee whose vision of the First Amendment's guarantees of freedom of speech and religion would constrain those provisions' historic scope would, in my view, be unacceptable.

But Judge Souter is not such a nominee. *His vision of the Constitution is not mine—but it is clearly not that of the Court's hard-line conservatives, either. He is not a man whom I would nominate to the Court—but he is not a man whose nomination I will oppose.*

Thus, with a hopeful heart—and with open eyes—I support the confirmation of Judge David Hackett Souter.

ADDITIONAL VIEWS OF SENATOR HATCH

Judge Souter's excellent educational and legal background and his demonstrated knowledge of the law at the hearing all attest to his competence and ability. I believe he will join the Supreme Court with an independent mind, willing to consider different points of view on the cases which will come before him.

I also believe that he will seek to interpret and apply the law according to its original meaning. I do not believe that he will impose his own policy preferences on the American people in the guise of judging. The role of the judicial branch is to enforce the provisions of the Constitution and the laws we enact in Congress as their meaning was originally intended by their framers. That meaning must then be applied to the facts and circumstances before the judge—facts and circumstances perhaps never contemplated by the framers of the legal provision being applied. But the meaning—the underlying principle of the provision—does not change. * * *

Some urge us to reject Judge Souter because he did not commit himself to uphold *Roe v. Wade.* But what would happen if different senators impose litmus tests on a variety of issues—could any nominee ever be confirmed?

Some people would make a very strong case that religious liberty issues, discrimination issues, federalism issues and other issues are so crucial that we must demand to know in advance how a nominee will rule.

Ben Wattenberg, a Democrat who is a senior fellow at the American Enterprise Institute, says that quotas should be the litmus test. He criticized a 5–4 decision from June permitting racial set-asides in the FCC's award of television and radio licenses. Suppose 20 senators apply that litmus test, and 15 other senators apply a church/state litmus test seeking to reverse the school prayer decisions, and 15 other Senators impose a litmus test on reversing the *Miranda* decision and *Mapp v. Ohio* imposing the exclusionary rule on the states.

How can any nominee be confirmed if we viewed our role this way?

A President may one day send us a nominee supported by proabortion groups. How would they feel if other senators and I took up Ben Wattenberg's cue on imposing a litmus test on reverse discrimination, another group imposed a litmus test on overturning *Miranda* and the exclusionary rule, and a third group of prolife senators, totalling 51 senators, imposed a litmus test on reversing *Roe v. Wade?*

MINORITY VIEWS OF SENATOR EDWARD M. KENNEDY

I oppose the confirmation of Judge David H. Souter to the Supreme Court.

* * *

In the past half century, the Supreme Court has played a central role in the effort to make America a better and fairer land. The Court outlawed school segregation in the 1950's, removed barriers to the right to vote in the 1960's, and established a far-reaching right to privacy, including the right to abortion in the 1970's. In other ways as well, the Supreme Court strengthened the basic rights of minorities and took steps to end the second-class status of women in our society. But in the decade of the 1980's, as a result of a strategy of ideological appointments in the Reagan years, the Court has seemed to pause in carrying out this important role, and in many cases has actually turned back the clock. On many of these issues, the current Court seems to be divided 4–4, so that the Senate's decision on this nomination is likely to tip the balance in one direction or the other.

In considering a Supreme Court nomination, the Senate must make two inquiries. The first is the threshold issue: Does the nominee have the intelligence, integrity, and temperament to meet the responsibilities of a Supreme Court Justice?

But that is only the beginning, not the end, of the inquiry. The Senate also must determine whether the nominee possesses a clear commitment to the fundamental values at the core of our constitutional democracy.

In this second inquiry, the burden of proof rests with the nominee. Our constitutional freedoms are the historic legacy of every American. They are too important, and the past sacrifices made to protect those freedoms have been too great, to be entrusted to judges who lack this clear commitment. If a Senator is left with substantial doubts about a nominee's dedication to these core values, our own constitutional responsibility requires us to oppose the nomination.

This is not to suggest any single-issue litmus test. Nominees should be judged on their overall approach to the Constitution. I have frequently supported nominees whose views on particular constitutional issues are very different from my own. But the Senate should not confirm a Supreme Court nomination unless we are persuaded that the nominee is committed to upholding the essential values at the heart of our constitutional tradition.

Recent developments at the Supreme Court have increased the importance of this inquiry by the Senate. Over the past few years, the Court has retreated from its historic role in protecting civil rights and civil liberties. In case after case, the Court has also adopted narrow and restrictive interpretations of important civil rights laws enacted by Congress. The Senate is entitled to ensure that nominees to the nation's highest court share Congress's view that these laws must be interpreted generously, to eliminate discrimination in all its forms.

Judge Souter has a distinguished intellectual background. He has spent the great majority of his legal career in public service. But aspects of his record on the bench and while serving in the New Hampshire Attorney General's Office have raised troubling questions about the depth of his commitment to the indispensable role of the Supreme Court in protecting individual rights and liberties under the Constitution.

Far from dispelling these concerns, Judge Souter's testimony before this committee reinforced them. In particular, my concerns center on the fundamental constitutional issues of civil rights, the right to privacy, and the power of Congress and the courts to protect these basic rights.

* * *

3. *The Nomination of Clarence Thomas*

On June 27, 1991, Justice Thurgood Marshall, to the surprise of many, announced his retirement. Although he had always promised "to serve out his term," that is, serve his entire life tenure, he explained his unexpected decision in typically colorful language; he decided to retire because, he said: "I am getting old and coming apart."[1] When asked whether he thought President Bush should replace him with an African–American, Marshall observed: " * * * there's no difference between a black snake and a white snake; they'll both bite."[2] Once again, President Bush named his nominee very quickly. On July 1, 1991, four days after Marshall's announcement, Bush nominated Clarence Thomas, an African–American who had been chairman of the Equal Employment Opportunity Commission and a judge on the United States Court of Appeals for the District of Columbia. In naming Thomas, President

---

1. Linda Campbell, *Health May be Fading, But Marshall's Wit Still Sharp,* Chicago Tribune, June 29, 1991, at C1.

2. Bob Dart, *Marshall's Choice for Successor?* The Atlanta Journal and Constitution, June 29, 1991, at A10.

Bush asserted that Thomas' race had not been a factor in the nomination.

The following section has two parts. The first contains excerpts from the Report of the Senate Judiciary Committee. On September 27, 1991, the Committee split evenly, 7–7, in its decision whether or not to report favorably on the nomination.[3] The Committee did, however, vote to report the nomination, without any recommendation, to the full Senate so that it could vote. The accompanying report, excerpted herein, explains why the Committee was divided.

In reading the Report, consider to what extent Thomas' race did matter and whether it should have. Note also how Thomas tried to distance himself from many of the public positions he had taken previously. Compare this with Judge Bork's so-called "confirmation conversion" and ask whether these two men were treated equally with respect to this issue. Consider whether the opposition to Thomas stemmed from the sense that, as he restated his positions, it became less clear precisely what he believed.

On October 6, 1991, one day before the full Senate was scheduled to vote on the Thomas nomination, and nine days after the Judiciary Committee had split 7–7, National Public Radio and Newsday published allegations that Clarence Thomas had sexually harassed Anita Hill ten years earlier. (Anita Hill had worked with Thomas at the Department of Education and then became his assistant when he was named Chairman of the EEOC. At the time of the Thomas' nomination, Hill was a tenured professor of law at the University of Oklahoma.) At first, the Senate planned to proceed with the scheduled vote but, confronted with an overwhelming outcry from women's groups, the Senate unanimously decided to delay the vote for one week and to reopen the hearings to allow Thomas and Hill to testify.[4] (Under Senate procedures, a unanimous vote was required to delay the scheduled vote.) The resulting three days of hearings were riveting, garnering better ratings than the competing championship games in major league baseball.[5] At the end of the special hearing, the Senate voted. On October 15, 1991, by a Senate vote of 52–48, Clarence Thomas was confirmed, earning the dubious dual distinctions of surviving the closest confirmation vote in the twentieth century [6] and receiving more negative votes than any other successful nominee in the Court's history.[7]

The excerpts following the Senate Judiciary Committee Report contain two Senators' views of these unusual proceedings and the

3. Voting against the motion to report the recommendation favorably were Senators Biden, Kennedy, Metzenbaum, Simon, Kohl, Heflin, and Leahy (all Democrats). Voting in favor of the motion were Senators Thurmond, Brown, Hatch, Simpson, Grassley, Spector, and DeConcini (the only Democrat on this side).

4. 137 Cong.Rec. S14,565–66 (daily ed. October 8, 1991).

5. John Carmody, *The TV Column,* The Washington Post, October 15, 1991 at E4.

6. D. Savage, *Turning Right,* Wiley & Sons (1992) at 449.

7. Apple, Jr., *The Thomas Confirmation: Senate Confirms Thomas, 52–48, Ending Week of Bitter Battle,* The New York Times, October 16, 1991, at A1.

process by which each finally decided how to cast his vote. In reading the statements of Senators Byrd and DeConcini, consider the following questions: Is the existing confirmation process an adequate forum to address accusations of personal misconduct such as sexual harassment? Can we revise the process to make it more adequate? Or should such inquiries be irrelevant? Would independent questioners improve the process, so that Senators would not have to play the dual role of inquisitor and juror? Should hearings involving such intimate and provocative accusations be televised or is television coverage distorting?

Did the Senate Judiciary Committee behave properly in initially ignoring the Hill charges because she insisted on strict confidentiality? Should we improve the FBI investigatory procedures? Who bears the burden of proof in such proceedings? Do you think that Clarence Thomas would have been confirmed if Anita Hill's allegations had become public and subject to scrutiny during the initial hearings and not required a separate hearing after many Senators had publicly announced their intention to vote for confirmation? Did that sequence of events influence the decision as to who had the burden of proof? Should it have?

NOMINATION OF CLARENCE THOMAS TO BE AN ASSOCIATE JUSTICE OF THE UNITED STATES SUPREME COURT

October 1 (legislative day, September 19), 1991.—Ordered to be printed
S.Exec.Rep, 102d Cong., 1st Sess. (1991)

Mr. Biden, from the Committee on the Judiciary,
submitted the following
REPORT
together with
ADDITIONAL AND SUPPLEMENTAL VIEWS

The Committee on the Judiciary, to which was referred the nomination of Judge Clarence Thomas to be an Associate Justice of the U.S. Supreme Court, having considered the same, reports the nomination, a quorum being present, without recommendation, by a vote of 13 yeas and 1 nay, having failed to report favorably thereon, by a vote of 7 yeas and 7 nays.

* * *

III. THE NOMINEE

Judge Thomas was born on June 23, 1948, in Savannah, GA. He received his bachelor of arts degree from Holy Cross College in 1971. Judge Thomas pursued his legal education at Yale Law School, receiving his juris doctor in 1974.

From 1974 to 1977, the nominee served as an assistant attorney general for the State of Missouri.

From 1977 to 1979, Judge Thomas worked as an attorney for the Monsanto Co., located in St. Louis, MO.

From 1979 to 1981, the nominee was a legislative assistant for U.S. Senator John C. Danforth, of Missouri.

In 1981, the nominee served for 2 months as a consultant to the Office of Civil Rights, U.S. Department of Education. He then served for 10 months as Assistant Secretary for Civil Rights, U.S. Department of Education.

From 1982 to 1990, the nominee was Chairman of the Equal Employment Opportunity Commission.

In 1990, President Bush appointed Judge Thomas to the United States Court of Appeals, a position he held for 17 months before his nomination to the Supreme Court.

IV. The American Bar Association's Evaluation

A. *The Standing Committee's Assessment*

The American Bar Association uses three ratings for Supreme Court nominees: "Well qualified," "qualified," and "not qualified." Twelve of the fifteen members of the association's standing committee on the Federal judiciary, chaired by Ronald L. Olson, found Judge Thomas to be qualified for appointment to the Supreme Court. Two members of the standing committee found Judge Thomas to be not qualified, and one member abstained from voting. (Letter from Ronald L. Olson to Chairman Biden, September 14, 1991, at 8.)

* * *

* * * The standing committee minority of two concluded that Judge Thomas "does not have the depth or breadth of professional experience sufficient to place him at the top of the legal profession, as is required by the [Standing] Committee's criteria for appointment to the Supreme Court of the United States." (*Id.* at 8.)

* * *

ADDITIONAL VIEWS OF CHAIRMAN BIDEN

The decision to oppose the confirmation of a nominee to the U.S. Supreme Court is a solemn one. And with respect to this nominee, Judge Clarence Thomas, I have no doubt about his character, credentials, competence, or credibility. Instead, the basis for my opposition to the confirmation of Judge Thomas concerns his judicial philosophy—the approach he would use in deciding how to interpret the enabling phrases of our Constitution.

Introduction

In terms of judicial philosophy, Judge Thomas came to the hearings with a record that was troubling in several respects. Over the course of his professional life, he had expressed views that aligned him with the ultraconservatives seeking to fundamentally alter our society. The constitutional philosophy set forth in Judge Thomas' articles and speeches would result in radical, and in my opinion undesirable, changes in the relationship between government and individuals.

First, Judge Thomas seemed to advocate a change in the degree to which society could protect the environment, the workplace, and the public health and safety. Judge Thomas had approved the notion of an activist Court that would greatly increase the constitutional protection given to economic and property rights, striking down laws that regulated businesses and corporations.

Second, Judge Thomas appeared to seek a change in the degree to which government could interfere in the personal lives of individuals. Judge Thomas had praised or associated himself with arguments for greater government control over matters of family and personal life. In particular, Judge Thomas seemed comfortable with permitting government intrusions into that most private realm of decisions concerning procreation and other intimate matters.

Third, Judge Thomas had endorsed an extreme view of separation of powers which, if taken to the conclusion endorsed by its advocates, would radically redefine the balance of power between the branches of the Federal Government. This view holds that much of the current structure of our government impermissibly infringes on the power of the Executive. Having also expressed a strong hostility to Congress, Judge Thomas seemed to advocate a major shift in power away from the legislative branch and toward the executive branch.

In short, Judge Thomas' writings and speeches sketch a judicial philosophy that, if realized, would reverse the balance this country has struck between the rights of individuals, the obligations of businesses and corporations, and the power of government. The question concerning me as the hearings began was whether this was an accurate picture of Judge Thomas' judicial philosophy.

During the hearings, Judge Thomas sought to explain his views. I accept the sincerity of his testimony, and some of his explanations satisfied my concerns. On balance, however, my concerns remain. First of all, I was troubled by Judge Thomas' repeated resistance to discussing his own views when asked about decisions of the Supreme Court. Perhaps the best way to gain insight into a nominee's judicial philosophy is to use the Supreme Court's existing constitutional and statutory decisions to frame the dialogue.

Judge Thomas' reluctance even to comment on already decided cases, apparently for fear of revealing his own views, was pronounced. I discussed this with him in the final hours of his testimony, after hearing yet another of his refusals to discuss a legal principle:

> The CHAIRMAN. * * * Judge, you are going to be * * * a judge who is not bound by stare decisis, [who] has nothing at all that would bind you other than your conscience, and so I am a little * * * edgy when you give an answer and you say, "well, that's the

policy," as if you are still going to be a Circuit Court of Appeals judge * * *.

You are going to take a philosophy to that Court with you, * * * and you are not limited * * * from reaching a conclusion different than that which the Court has reached thus far * * *.

JUDGE THOMAS. Well, I understand that, Mr. Chairman, but what I have attempted to do is to not agree or disagree with existing cases.

The CHAIRMAN. You are doing very well at that.

JUDGE THOMAS. The point that I am making or I have tried to make is that I do not approach these cases with any desire to change them, and I have tried to indicate that, to the extent that individuals feel, well, I am foreclosed from a—

The CHAIRMAN. If you had a desire to change it, would you tell us?

JUDGE THOMAS. I don't think so * * *. (Transcript, Sept. 16, at 172–73.)

Judge Thomas' last comment appears to have been said in jest, but in the end, he had declined comment or provided only vague remarks on the many constitutional issues—great and small, contentious and settled—about which he was asked. Perhaps Judge Thomas was advised that this approach was a sound political strategy designed to ensure confirmation. If that is the case, it is not a strategy I am prepared to accept.

* * *

Judge Thomas may ultimately turn out to be a Justice who will strike a balance between the individual, government, and businesses and corporations in a way that is acceptable. But, based on the record before me, I am not certain he would. Given what is at stake with this nomination—and given where the Court stands now—I cannot take the chance.

PART ONE: JUDGE THOMAS' APPROACH TO INTERPRETING THE CONSTITUTION

While still in the executive branch, Judge Thomas gave a series of speeches and wrote several articles in which he employed the terminology of "natural law," "natural rights," and the "higher law background" of the Constitution, including especially the contents of the Declaration of Independence. These repeated and expansive references strongly suggested that Judge Thomas believed these concepts were crucial tools for understanding the Constitution, and for reaching correct constitutional decisions.

In itself, the use of natural law terminology should not be a source of concern. Basic natural law principles, by whatever name, should and do inform our Constitution. This was the main point of contention between my own understanding of the Constitution—and that of the majority of Americans—as compared to Robert Bork's understanding, which denied any role for the recognition of rights beyond those expressly and specifically stated in the document itself.

In contrast to that view, most Americans, including myself, believe that the "higher law" of the Constitution provides a basis for understanding the broad, liberty-enhancing phrases of the Constitution. It does so because it provides the foundation for a government of limited powers derived from the consent of the people. Within this natural law tradition, rights are viewed as residing initially in each person due to their humanity, not because government bestowed rights on its citizens.
* * *

Down through the years of American constitutional thought, others have viewed the concept of natural law quite differently. Some have used it in ways that today seem inimical, rather than consistent, with our view of liberty. For example, the language of natural law has been invoked as a justification for denying women full access to careers outside the home (See *Bradwell v. Illinois,* 83 U.S. 130 (1873), Bradley, J., concurring.) It has also been used in Supreme Court decisions in the late 1800's and into the 1900's, to limit the legitimate authority of society to regulate commercial behavior, in the name of the natural rights of "liberty of contract." (See *Allgeyer v. Louisiana,* 165 U.S. 578 (1897), *Lochner v. New York,* 198 U.S. 45 (1905).)

And, today, natural law is again being used, for instance, by advocates of radical restrictions on society's authority to regulate for the public welfare, this time in the name of the fifth amendment's prohibition on the taking of private property without just compensation, (see Epstein, R., "Takings" (1986) at 5), as well as by those who urge that the Court return to the earlier "liberty of contract" jurisprudence of the *Lochner* era. (See Macedo, S., "The New Right and the Constitution" (1987).)

* * *

So the question with respect to Judge Thomas is not whether he endorses natural law principles, but which natural law principles does he embrace and what does he mean by his endorsement of them.   * * *

A. *Judge Thomas Had Written Extensively About Natural Law and the Constitution*

Prior to the hearings, Judge Thomas' speeches provided ample reason to suppose that his vision of natural law, whatever its details were, played a significant role in his interpretation of the Constitution. In a speech to the Federalist Society at the University of Virginia School of Law, he said:

> The higher law background of the American Constitution, whether explicitly appealed to or not, provides the only firm basis

for a just, wise, and constitutional decision. (Speech at the University of Virginia, March 5, 1988, at 11.)

* * *

In a set of "Notes on Original Intent," Judge Thomas repeated his understanding of the centrality of natural law and natural rights to judicial decisionmaking. First he quoted a letter from Andrew Hamilton, who had defended American rights against a Tory critic by saying that "the source of all your errors, sophisms, and false reasonings is a total ignorance of the natural rights of mankind." Then, Judge Thomas asserted that this advice "could apply to virtually any judge * * * of * * * today. * * * The natural rights, higher law understanding of our Constitution is the non-partisan basis for limited, decent, and free government." (Notes on Original Intent, undated).

These examples could be multiplied, all in support of the fundamental conclusion that for Judge Thomas, important parts of the Constitution are "inexplicable" or "unintelligible" without an understanding of their higher law origins. * * *

B. Judge Thomas' Testimony on Natural Law Failed to Satisfy Concerns About His Approach to Interpreting the Constitution

At the hearings, however, a different understanding of the role of natural law emerged from Judge Thomas' testimony. When first asked about his use of natural law principles, Judge Thomas said:

> I don't see a role for the use of natural law in constitutional adjudication. My interest in exploring natural law and natural rights was purely in the context of political theory. (Transcript, Sept. 10, at 137.)

Soon thereafter, Judge Thomas explained that his interest in natural law had started with, and been limited to, his interest in understanding the theory by which people like Abraham Lincoln and Frederick Douglass argued for the end of slavery:

> My interest in this area started with the notion, with a simple question: How do you end slavery? By what theory do you end slavery? After you end slavery, by what theory do you protect the right of someone who was a former slave or someone like my grandfather, for example, to enjoy the fruits of his or her labor? At no point did I or do I believe that the approach of natural law or that natural rights has a role in constitutional adjudication. (Transcript, Sept. 10, at 143.)

* * *

Judge Thomas took pains to insist that the rights being enforced by courts are being enforced because they are constitutional rights, not because they are natural rights. As he put it:

[Sometimes, the Framers] reduced to positive law in the Constitution aspects of life principles they believed in; for example, liberty. But when it is in the Constitution, it is not a natural right; it is a constitutional right. And that is the important point. (Transcript, Sept. 11 at 6.)

This disclaimer still leaves an important question unanswered. If the Framers placed a natural right in the Constitution when they used words like "liberty" or "due process" or "privileges and immunities," how are Justices 200 years later to understand what these constitutional guarantees mean? * * *

One answer to this question is that of the specific intent or intentionalist school of interpretation. This school holds that, whatever the motives or principles of the Framers may have been, what has been reduced to positive law is only the specific intentions or specific applications the Framers had in mind when they drafted the words of the Constitution. Under this approach, several landmark decisions of the last half-century might well prove incorrect.

Another answer to this question of interpretation is that subsequent justices should attempt to understand what principle the Framers meant to "reduce to positive law," and to decide cases consistently with the Justices' best understanding of that principle. And there are other possibilities. What answer a Justice gives is one of the most crucial aspects of that judicial philosophy. * * * Regrettably, Judge Thomas never satisfactorily articulated an answer to this question.

* * *

[A]t some points during the hearing, Judge Thomas' position seemed to be first, that judges should not appeal directly to their understanding of natural law, independent of what has been enacted as positive law in the Constitution; and, second, that those enacting our Constitution believed in natural law and placed some natural law concepts in the Constitution, thereby reducing those concepts to positive law. These constitutional rights are enforceable by judges.

Finally, to ascertain the meaning of these phrases, Judge Thomas seemed to be saying, third, that judges must appeal, at least in part, to an understanding of natural law as understood by the Framers, because it was natural law that formed part of the Framers' own understanding of what those words mean.

Yet, when I put this third proposition to Judge Thomas, he resisted it.

The CHAIRMAN. Now, you say that they put some of these natural law principles in the document in words like 'liberty,' you just mentioned. You indicate that once 'liberty' was in the Constitution, it becomes positive law. But now comes the hard question, as you and I both know. A judge has to define what 'liberty' means. Now, how does a judge know what the ambiguous term liberty means in the Constitution? * * * Even though you reject the direct application of natural law in constitutional adjudication, you would use natural law to understand what the Framers had in mind when they interpreted these broad notions. Isn't that correct?

JUDGE THOMAS. Not quite, Senator. Let me make two points there. The Framers' view of the principle of liberty is the important point.

* * *

Whatever natural law is, is separate and apart. The important point is what did the Framers think they were doing. What were their views.

* * *

The second point is this: That is only a part of what we conceive of this notion in our society. The world didn't stop with the Framers. The concept of liberty wasn't self-defining at that point.

* * *

And that is why I think it is important, as I have indicated, that you then look at the rest of the history and tradition of our country.

* * *

In the end, Judge Thomas' answers simply do not tell us very much about the interpretive approach he will employ on the Court.

Insofar as natural law is concerned, I believe that the most fair-minded reading of the totality of Judge Thomas' testimony can decisively support just two conclusions: First, we did not learn precisely what those views are; and second, whatever they are, natural law functions for Judge Thomas as a substantially less significant tool in constitutional adjudication than was to be supposed before the hearings.

* * *

Natural law occupied some of the committee's time at the hearing simply because Judge Thomas himself had invoked the language of natural law so often that the committee believed that this would provide an avenue along which to explore the underlying issues.

Labels aside, however, we learned very little additional information about Judge Thomas' general constitutional methodology. As has already been noted, Judge Thomas believes, as do I, that the Framers understanding of words like "liberty"—

     * * * is only a part of what we conceive of this notion in our society. The world didn't stop with the Framers. The concept of liberty wasn't self-defining at that point. * * * [T]hat is why I think it is important, as I have indicated, that you then look at the rest of the history and tradition of our country. (Transcript, Sept. 12, at 27.)

To say that history and tradition informs the Constitution is, unfortunately, as imprecise a statement as saying that the higher law background informs the Constitution. In both cases, one wants to know how those concepts inform the Constitution before the statement can be evaluated. * * * An extremely narrow view of the application of history and tradition would freeze the Constitution in our past nearly as effectively as the specific intent school of thought would, whereas broader views of the role of history and tradition permit the Constitution to continue to evolve in meaning and application.

We learned very little about how Judge Thomas would apply history and tradition to give meaning to the Constitution. * * *

For him, the answers undoubtedly have still to be worked out. For now, what he had to say on the subject came down to this:

> JUDGE THOMAS. How do we look at history and tradition, how do we determine how our country has advanced and grown, it is a very difficult enterprise. It is an amorphous process at times, but it is an important process. (Transcript, Sept. 12, at 34.)

In sum, Judge Thomas appeared before the committee with a judicial philosophy that was unclear and uneven. * * *

This point should not be misunderstood: it is by no means necessary that a Justice take his or her seat on the Court with a well worked out judicial methodology; some of our most distinguished jurists have developed their constitutional methodology while on the Court.

What is disturbing here is that Judge Thomas came before the committee having made some highly controversial pronouncements on a variety of subjects that pertain to the Court's business—on privacy, on economic and property rights, on the equal protection clause and the civil rights acts, and on the separation of powers. The committee was interested in knowing what approach Judge Thomas would take to these subjects, as well as to the Constitution as a whole. What we discovered was a nominee who still had not worked through the issues. * * *

PART TWO: JUDGE THOMAS' VIEWS ON PRIVACY, REPRODUCTIVE
FREEDOM, AND UNENUMERATED RIGHTS

In supporting the nomination of Justice Souter to the Court last year, I emphasized that a nominee bears the burden of proving that he or she falls within the sphere of candidates acceptable to this committee, and I indicated that a nominee who rejected the notion that our Constitution protects unenumerated rights, including the right to privacy, would, in my view, be unacceptable. This is because the rejection of this notion would mean that such a nominee would put at risk not only those rights the Court has already acknowledged, but also that the nominee lacked an expansive view of our Constitution that would guide us safely into the future.

* * *

Prior to the hearings, Judge Thomas' record on the right of privacy, reproductive freedom, and unenumerated rights generally—while not definitive—was troubling. To the extent he had expressed views, they were hostile to these concepts. While Judge Thomas had [not] addressed the issue of abortion, it was not simply his opinion on a woman's right to choose that troubled me. My concern was his apparently much broader criticism of an unenumerated right of privacy—of the very idea that there is a realm of intimate matters into which the Government may not intrude.

During the hearings, Judge Thomas conceded that the Constitution, and in particular the 14th amendment, protects some sort of privacy right, at least for married couples. But Judge Thomas declined to provide full answers to most of the questions he was asked on this subject.

He declined to describe in detail his overall methodology for approaching privacy claims. He did not reveal a decisive view on whether individuals had a right of privacy protected by the liberty clause of the 14th amendment. Nor did he say whether, in his view, the scope of the right of privacy—for married or single people—extended in any circumstances to decisions about procreation. His reticence to answer these questions, in light of his prior record, is profoundly troubling. He has failed to convince me that he endorses a broad and expanding conception of the Constitution's protection of the right of privacy.

A. Judge Thomas Has Criticized Judicial Recognition of an Unenumerated Right of Privacy

In a series of speeches and articles, Judge Thomas implied his disagreement with those who believe the Constitution grants broad protection to the right of each individual to make intimate decisions without government intrusion. He had criticized the constitutional sources identified by the Court as embodying such protection, namely the 14th and the 9th amendments. * * *

At the hearing, Judge Thomas seemed first to concede that every individual, whether single or married, had a right of privacy with respect to matters of procreation:

> The CHAIRMAN. * * * Now, you said that the privacy right of married couples is fundamental, and as I understand it now, you told me—correct me if I am wrong—that the privacy right of an individual on procreation is fundamental. Is that right?

> JUDGE THOMAS. I think that is consistent with what I said and I think consistent with what the Court held in *Eisenstadt v. Baird* [405 U.S. 438 (1972)]. (Transcript, Sept. 12, at 50.)

Shortly thereafter, however, he spoke only of a marital right to privacy in responding to a question asked by Senator Kennedy:

> JUDGE THOMAS. Senator, * * * I think I have indicated here today and yesterday that there is a privacy interest in the Constitution, in the liberty component of the Due Process Clause, and that

marital privacy is a fundamental right, and marital privacy then can only be impinged on or only be regulated if there is a compelling State interest. * * * (Transcript, Sept. 12, at 82.)

As a result, I asked Judge Thomas again about his belief in an individual's right to privacy:

The CHAIRMAN. Judge, very simply, if you can, yes or no: Do you believe that the Liberty Clause of the Fourteenth Amendment of the Constitution provides a fundamental right to privacy for individuals in the area of procreation, including contraception?

JUDGE THOMAS. Senator, I think I answered earlier yes, based upon the precedent of *Eisenstadt v. Baird.*

The CHAIRMAN. Well, you know, * * * *Eisenstadt v. Baird* was an equal protection case. * * * That is not the question I am asking you. Let me make sure and say it one more time. Do you believe the Liberty Clause of the Fourteenth Amendment of the Constitution provides a fundamental right of privacy for individuals in the area of procreation, including contraception?

JUDGE THOMAS. I think I have answered that, Senator.

The CHAIRMAN. Yes or no?

JUDGE THOMAS. Yes, and—

* * *

I have expressed on what I base that, and I would leave it at that. (Transcript, Sept. 12, at 119–20.)

In an attempt to more clearly understand his views, I submitted to Judge Thomas, after the hearings, a written question on the right of privacy. My letter recited Judge Thomas' testimony on this issue, and asked the following question:

Do you believe that the due process component of the Fourteenth Amendment's liberty clause—independent of the equal protection clause and the case of *Eisenstadt v. Baird*—provides a fundamental right of privacy with respect to procreation and contraception?

Judge Thomas' answer to this question, in its entirely, was as follows:

As I sought to make clear in my testimony, I believe that *Eisenstadt* was correct on both the privacy and equal protection grounds.

* * *

The result of Judge Thomas' reticence to discuss his views is that, even after the hearings, even after my repeated attempts to engage him in a dialogue on this issue, I am left without any clear idea of what Judge Thomas means when he says the 14th amendment protects a right of privacy. What is the scope and nature of that right? Where does it come from?   Who enjoys this right?   These questions remain unanswered.

* * *

B.   Judge Thomas Refused to Discuss His
Views on Reproductive Freedom

* * *

I was disappointed by Judge Thomas' reticence to discuss the issue of reproductive freedom even at the most general level.   Again, I am not referring to the specific question of whether the result in *Roe v. Wade* was correct—a question I did not ask Judge Thomas.   But Judge Thomas would not even discuss, for example, whether a woman has any protected liberty interest at stake in matters of procreation, or whether the Court should apply strict scrutiny in reviewing such an asserted interest.   Answering these questions would not have revealed whether Judge Thomas agreed with *Roe,* because even if Judge Thomas had acknowledged that women have a fundamental right to choose whether to continue a pregnancy, he could still disagree with the result in *Roe.*

My concern is that in refusing to discuss the broader question of whether we, as individuals, have a right to make intimate decisions free from Government intrusion, I can not begin to understand how Judge Thomas would approach any number of cases in which the Court will determine the future relationship of individuals and Government in our society.   Considering his testimony on the issues of family and personal privacy as a whole, I am not comfortable that Judge Thomas would strike an appropriate balance between the right of individuals and the Government as we move into the next century.

C.   Judge Thomas Did Not Explain How He Would Use History
and Tradition to Determine Whether an Asserted Liberty
Interest Is Constitutionally Protected

Judge Thomas was similarly reluctant to expound the general methodology he would use to determine whether an asserted liberty interest is protected by the Constitution.   Judge Thomas told the committee that the meaning of the Constitution's broad phrases—like "liberty"—are not "self-defining" and must be interpreted based on the Framers' intent and our history and traditions.   (Transcript, Sept. 12, at 27.)   Again, this answer does not really say much about Judge Thomas' approach. All the Justices now on the Court look to history and tradition in evaluating asserted rights, but they do so in different ways, with radically different results.   The key question is whether the Court will protect only those interests supported by a specific and longstanding tradition, or whether a less constricted view of liberty will govern.

This debate was most clearly framed in the case of *Michael H. v. Gerald D.,* 491 U.S. 110 (1989), involving the asserted liberty interest of a biological father to see his child.   There, Justice Scalia, in a footnote joined only by Chief Justice Rehnquist, argued that the Constitution protects an interest only if it has been recognized at "the most specific level at which a relevant tradition can be identified." (Id. at 127 n. 6.) Thus, Justice Scalia looked at whether the asserted interest fit within a tradition of protecting what he called the "marital family"; he expressly rejected the idea that the interest be more broadly defined in terms of "parenthood" or "personal relationships." (Id.)

Justices O'Connor and Kennedy rejected this portion of Justice Scalia's opinion, expressly because they found this methodology overly constricting:

> [Justice Scalia] sketches a mode of historical analysis to be used when identifying liberty interests protected by the Due Process Clause of the Fourteenth Amendment that may be somewhat inconsistent with our past decisions in this area. [Citing *Griswold v. Connecticut* and *Eisenstadt v. Baird*]. On occasion the Court has characterized relevant traditions protecting asserted rights at levels of generality that might not be "the most specific level" available. *I would not foreclose the unanticipated by the prior imposition of a single mode of historical analysis.* (Id. at 132, O'Connor, J., concurring, (citations omitted) (emphasis added).)

Referencing this case, I asked Judge Thomas how he would define the interest at stake or use history and traditions to help give meaning to the broad phrases of the Constitution:

> The CHAIRMAN. * * * do you concur with the rationale offered by Justice Scalia [in *Michael H. v. Gerald D.*] as to how one is to determine whether or not an interest asserted by a person before the Court? * * *
>
> JUDGE THOMAS. Senator, again, that is a very recent case and I am in the position of not wanting to comment on that specifically, but I am very skeptical—

> * * *

> I am skeptical, when one looks at tradition and history, to narrow the focus to the most specific tradition. I think that the effort should be to determine the appropriate tradition or the tradition that is most relevant to our inquiry, and to not take a cramped approach or narrow approach that could actually limit fundamental rights.

> * * *

> The CHAIRMAN. * * * as I understand it, you are not taken with the Scalia approach.
>
> JUDGE THOMAS. Skeptical.

> * * *

Judge Thomas' failure to expressly reject Justice Scalia's methodology—stopping at expressing his "skepticism"—is unfortunate. I note that Justice Souter, when asked this same question last year, stated emphatically that he "would not accept" Justice Scalia's approach, and he explained how he would instead seek out the most "reliable evidence" including evidence of "great generality." His response on this point played an important role in my decision to support his nomination. (See S.Exec.Rep. 101–32, Additional Views of Chairman Biden at 18–19.)

PART THREE: JUDGE THOMAS' VIEWS ON THE CONSTITUTIONAL PROTECTION OF ECONOMIC AND PROPERTY RIGHTS

The Framers thought that the protection of private property was an essential ingredient in the maintenance of a free society. The Constitution protects private property in several places perhaps most significantly in the so-called takings clause of the 5th amendment of the Constitution, which states, "nor shall private property be taken for public use, without just compensation," and in the due process clauses of the 5th and 14th amendments, which stipulate that no government shall deprive any person of "life, liberty or property, without due process of law."

* * *

In the modern era, the Court has applied "rational basis" review to economic or property regulation challenged on due process grounds, meaning that it has broadly construed the legitimate objectives of government and has largely deferred to the legislature the question of whether the regulation serves one of those objectives. So long as a rational legislature might have concluded that the regulation advances a legitimate objective, under rational basis review the regulation will stand. This contrasts with "strict scrutiny" and "middle tier scrutiny," more stringent standards of review that are reserved for issues of race discrimination, gender discrimination, interference with fundamental interests such as free speech, the free exercise of religion, and privacy.

With respect to the takings clause, the prohibition against the taking of private property has never been understood to prohibit the legitimate regulation of private property in the public interest. To be sure, it is not possible to locate the exact dividing line between the realm of valid regulation from the realm in which the government may act, if it can at all, only upon the payment of just compensation. As the Supreme Court has said, "the question of what constitutes a 'taking' of property for purposes of the Fifth Amendment has proved to be a source of considerable difficulty. * * * [T]his court has, quite simply, been unable to develop any 'set formula' for determining when 'justice and fairness' require that economic injuries caused by public action be compensated by the government." *Penn Cen. Transp. Co. v. New York City*, 438 U.S. 104, 123 (1978).

This said, it is still possible to advance several generalizations about the current interpretation of this clause of the Constitution. First, the analysis of when property has been "taken," instead of legitimately regulated, focuses on the nature of the government's action and on the grievousness of the impact of that action on the complaining owner. See e.g., *Penn Central Transp. Co.*, 438 U.S. at 124. Second, as our Nation has become an increasingly industrialized, urbanized, and populated society, the Court has recognized that society's capacity, through its elected officials, to regulate corporate and commercial behavior in the interests of such concerns as worker health and safety, environmental protection, economic stability, minimum wages, consumer protection, Social Security, and public health has had to grow apace. Id. * * *

Until recently, this general outline was so widely accepted that an examination of a nominee's views on the constitutional treatment of economic and property rights played virtually no role in Supreme Court confirmations. However, if we go back in our country's history, we can find a different approach to the due process jurisprudence that some energetic scholars on the far right are attempting to reinvigorate. If they succeed, the Court will begin to strike down economic regulatory statutes under that clause of the Constitution. In the takings clause area, similar efforts are being made to persuade the Court that many more laws and regulations should be struck down. In both cases, the agenda of this group of scholars and others is to create an activist court in the areas of economic and property rights.

* * *

Charles Fried, the Solicitor General during the last years of the Reagan administration, [is a conservative observer of this phenomenon.] In his book, "Order and Law" (1991), he describes the agenda of a powerful minority within the Republican party. One aspect of that agenda relates to the takings clause. General Fried reports that the Attorney General and "his young advisers,"

> many drawn from the ranks of the then fledgling Federalist Societies and often devotees of the extreme libertarian views of Chicago law professor Richard Epstein—had a specific, aggressive, and, it seemed to me, quite radical project in mind: to use the takings clause of the Fifth Amendment as a severe brake upon federal and state regulation of business and property. The grand plan was to make government pay compensation as for a taking of private property every time its regulations impinged too severely on a property right—limiting the possible uses for a parcel of land or restricting or tying up a business in regulatory red tape. If the government labored under so severe an obligation, there would be, to say the least, much less regulation. ("Order and Law" (1991) at 183.)

This agenda will not be accomplished primarily by persuading existing judges to change their views. Instead, as with other aspects of the agenda, such as increasing the state's authority to regulate in areas currently protected by constitutional privacy doctrine, including matters of family values and norms, the most significant strategy is to appoint judges and Justices sympathetic to the agenda.

* * *

If the ultra-conservative agenda succeeds, the consequences would be enormous, as General Fried suggests. * * *

A. Judge Thomas' Speeches on Economic and Property Rights Suggested He Held Ultra–Conservative Views

Judge Thomas' speeches gave the committee several reasons to believe he was sympathetic to the views just described. To begin with, several of the prominent scholars promoting an activist Court in the area of economic and property rights employ natural law terminology, similar to that which Judge Thomas has embraced. * * *

Judge Thomas had expressly said he has admired these arguments. In a speech to the Pacific Research Institute, Judge Thomas had announced that:

> I find attractive the arguments of scholars such as Stephen Macedo who defend an activist Supreme Court, which would strike down laws restricting property rights. (Speech to the Pacific Research Institute, August 10, 1987, at 16.)

He immediately followed this endorsement with a qualifying statement: "But the libertarian argument [of Macedo and others] overlooks the place of the Supreme Court in a scheme of separation of powers. One does not strengthen self-government and the rule of law by having the non-democratic branch of the government make policy." (Id.) Before the hearings, however, it was difficult to know how significant a qualifying statement this was. After all, the "libertarian argument" for an activist Supreme Court is opposed to judges making "policy," too. That argument asserts that economic and property rights are protected as a matter of natural and constitutional law—it seeks to remove its conception of economic and property rights from the realm of governmental policy-making, and to put them beyond the reach of policy-makers.

The day after the Pacific Research Institute Speech, Judge Thomas gave another speech on this theme. In it, he criticized government's lack of respect for economic rights:

> My point is not to denigrate the Fourteenth Amendment. Rather, what we need to emphasize is that the entire Constitution is a bill of rights; and economic rights are protected as much as any other rights. (Speech to the ABA Business Law Section, August 11, 1987, at 9.)

This last statement is, of course, not the current law, as Judge Thomas quite explicitly acknowledged in an exchange during his testimony involving myself, Senator Brown and Judge Thomas. (Transcript, Sept. 13, 63–70, 120–27.) It is, however, quite consistent with the rhetoric of the ultra-conservative activists, who want to jettison the "double standard" and produce a jurisprudence in which the same heightened judicial scrutiny applicable to free speech and privacy claims is also applicable to takings or economic due process claims.

B. Judge Thomas Disavowed any Agenda in the Areas of Property and Economic Rights

In my view, Judge Thomas' testimony put to rest suspicions that he would begin his service on the Court with a conscious agenda to change the current law as it pertains to economic due process.

With respect to the due process jurisprudence and the *Lochner* era, questions on this subject represented one of the few times during the hearings when Judge Thomas declared his present view that a case or cases were "correctly decided," as opposed to more equivocal replies, such as that he had no reason to challenge them, or that he did not quarrel with them.

In an exchange with Senator Metzenbaum, Judge Thomas said:

No, Senator.   * * * [L]et me address the constitutional point first. I have indicated that I believe that the Court's post-*Lochner* decisions are the correct decisions; that those cases were appropriately decided; that the Court is not a super-legislature to second-guess the very complicated social and economic decisionmaking of the legislative and executive branches. (Transcript, Sept. 16, at 21.)

* * *

His testimony with respect to the takings clause is somewhat more ambiguous. In several exchanges, Judge Thomas acknowledged that here, unlike the due process area, there is an ultra-conservative movement underway in the judicial system, and not just in academic writings. What is more, in these exchanges, he reverted to more equivocal statements, such as "I have no quarrel with," perhaps suggesting more willingness to change the law in these areas than in the due process area.

In an exchange with Senator Brown, Judge Thomas discussed the current law respecting economic and property rights.

SENATOR BROWN. I guess I would like an indication from you as to whether or not you think property rights deserve a lesser protection in the Constitution, greater protection under the Constitution than other rights, or whether it is a balancing between rights when these questions arise. Would you share with us your view on that?

JUDGE THOMAS. Senator, my point has been that property rights, of course, deserve some protection, and I think they are, as are our other rights, important rights. The Court in looking at the economic regulations of our economy and our society has attempted to move away from certainly the *Lochner* era cases and not act as a super-legislature. And I indicated that that is appropriate, particularly in the area as I have noted—the health and welfare, wage and hour cases.

I think that some of those cases, the area, I think there is some developing in the taking area, and perhaps if I am fortunate enough to be confirmed to the Court, perhaps I would be called upon to rule on those issues. But I would be concerned about the diminishment or the diminishing, diminution of any rights in our society. But that is not to say in any way that I disagree with the standards that the Court applies to protecting those rights today (Transcript, Sept. 11, at 154–155.)

Senator Brown returned to this line of questioning later in the hearings.

SENATOR BROWN. Do you find laid out in our Constitution language that calls for a second-class level of protection for property rights?

JUDGE THOMAS. Senator, I think that we have certainly—as we have discussed in these hearings, I have said in my own writings that there should be a recognition of property rights—economic rights, and I was talking in that case more about my grandfather and his ability to, as you say, earn his living, not be denied that.

But I think what the courts have done in the regulation of the social and economic affairs of our country has been—and I think appropriately so. As I have noted, I have no quarrel with the equal protection analysis that the Court uses. The Court has tried to defer to the decision of the legislature. In other words, the balances should be struck by this body or by the political branches and not second-guessed by the courts. I have no reason to quarrel with that approach. It recognizes that the considerations are very complex and involve any number of factors that are best left to the legislative branch.

* * *

This exchange led me to return once more to the takings clause issue, because it was unclear whether Judge Thomas meant to say that he had no quarrel with the Court's current equal protection analysis, as it applies to economic regulation, or whether he meant to include the takings clause analysis, too.

THE CHAIRMAN.

* * * [Y]ou said you have no quarrel with what the Court does, how the Court deals now with regard to regulations of property.

* * *

Now, Judge, the Court's current approach is to give the legislature a broad latitude in both these areas—the area of determining whether or not the means is an appropriate means and whether or not the objective being served is an objective that falls within the police power. That is the state of the law now, and they essentially [use] a rational basis test [ ] or a much lower standard.

So my question is this: Do you agree with the state of the law as it is now with regard to property, as I understood you to say it? Or do you agree with Senator Brown who said it is wrong the way we are doing it now; property and the test applied to the taking of property should be elevated to the same level as other constitutional rights—i.e., the case he cited, the right to privacy in Moore?

What is your position?

Judge Thomas. Senator, I think that I indicated * * * that the current manner of equal protection analysis I have no quarrel with. * * * With respect to the area of the current law, in the area of taking, I have no basis to quarrel with that either. (Transcript, Sept. 13, at 120–125.)

On the basis of this testimony, it amounts to mere guesswork to try to determine whether Judge Thomas rejects the ultra-conservative approach to the takings clause being promoted by Professor Epstein and others, or whether he is being abundantly cautious because he is aware that takings clause cases come to the Court with some regularity—a caution I believe is unnecessary, but which would be consistent with his other testimony.

* * *

My conclusion is that here, as in other areas, Judge Thomas simply has not worked through his views in any systematic way. As a result, he was unable to engage the committee in an extended discussion of those views. So what are we to make of this state of affairs?

In his speeches and writings, Judge Thomas has expressed an attraction to some extreme views. * * *

Judge Thomas says he has no current agenda here, and that he is not a member of this school of thought, and I believe him. In this, as in other areas, Judge Thomas will have to develop a judicial philosophy. The question is: will he grow in the direction of the systematic agenda and program of the ultra-conservative right? While no one can know for sure, we can know that Judge Thomas's exposure to and his publicly stated affinity for these ideas have laid an intellectual foundation upon which he might well build. That foundation is already a part of his own process of maturation. Once he is on the Court, he will be free to call on that foundation in building a full blown judicial philosophy.

* * *

Were Judge Thomas's judicial philosophy more developed, I might have had less reason for concern in this area. As it is, the very lack of its firm development raises the prospect that turning this way is a possibility. It is a turn that would be extremely hazardous for the country.

Part Four: Judge Thomas' Views on the Separation of Powers and the Role of Congress

The doctrine of separation of powers refers to the concept that each branch of our tripartite government has its own role, and that no branch shall exercise the powers of the other two. The separation of powers, and the system of checks and balances of each branch over the others, is a central feature—and a critical safeguard—of our constitutional Government.

Coming into the hearings, I was profoundly troubled by Judge Thomas' apparent support of a radical view of separation of powers, accompanied by a strong hostility to Congress. Just as Judge Thomas had seemingly aligned himself with those who seek to use the takings clause of the fifth amendment to limit the power of society to regulate business, he appeared also to join those seeking to limit the power of society to regulate by revitalizing the doctrine of separation of powers.

This group believes that our current governmental structure permits agencies that are not under the President's control to exercise "Executive" power. Because these independent agencies may act·contrary to the President's desire, executive power is, in their view, "diluted." According to this school of thought it is imperative not only that executive power be kept from the other two branches of government, but that it be exercised only by the President or those directed by him.

Former Solicitor General Charles Fried has written about his years inside the Reagan Justice Department, and—to use his word—the "revolutionaries" who have a specific agenda with respect to separation of powers:

> To the revolutionaries in the Reagan administration, the independence of the independent regulatory commissions (for instance, the ICC, FTC, FCC, SEC, and, most imposingly, Federal Reserve Board) was an offense against the principles of the unitary executive and of the separation of powers. (Fried, C., Order & Law (1991) at 154.)

Judge Thomas appeared to share this view that independent agencies violated the doctrine of separation of powers. In a 1988 speech, he said:

> Unfortunately, conservative heroes such as the Chief Justice [Rehnquist] failed not only conservatives but all Americans in the most important court case since *Brown v. Board of Education.* I refer of course to the independent counsel case, *Morrison v. Olson.* As we have seen in recent months, we can no longer rely on conservative figures to advance our cause. Our hearts and minds must support conservative principles and ideas. * * * Justice Antonin Scalia's remarkable dissent in the Supreme Court case points the way toward those principles and ideas. He indicates how again we might relate natural rights to democratic self-government and thus protect a regime of individual rights. (Speech to the Pacific Research Institute, August 4, 1988, at 6–8.)

At the hearing, I asked Judge Thomas about his statement:

> "The CHAIRMAN. * * * do [you] consider *Morrison v. Olson* the most important case since *Brown v. Board of Education?*

> JUDGE THOMAS. I think it is one of the most important cases. * * * I say that because I think the cases that deal with the structure of our government are important cases.

* * *

The CHAIRMAN. * * * If Justice Scalia's opinion, the lone dissent that you found so remarkable—and that is your word, remarkable—in the *Morrison* case, had been the majority opinion, all of these agencies would be unconstitutional, * * * including the Federal Reserve Board, * * * because the rationale of Scalia's opinion does not stop at the independent counsel statute, it would outlaw all independent agencies.

Now, Judge, do you believe that the separation of powers requires the abolition of independent agencies in the Federal Government?

JUDGE THOMAS. Senator, I have not thought that. * * *

I was not involved in that debate and was not aware that there was a relationship or there was a second agenda to *Morrison v. Olson*. This is news to me, as you explain it today (Transcript, Sept. 16, at 153–58.)

Having offered the highest praise to Justice Scalia's argument on this most important of cases—important according to Judge Thomas for the very reason that it dealt with the structure of government—Judge Thomas did not appreciate the radical change this argument would have, if given effect, on our Government's current structure.

While I accept his statement that he was not aware of this aspect of the radical right's agenda, I remain troubled by the consequences should Judge Thomas apply these views as a member of the Court. In sum, Judge Thomas left me without any sense of how he would approach cases determining the future structure of our Government.

* * *

PART FIVE: JUDGE THOMAS' VIEWS ON CIVIL RIGHTS

A. Judge Thomas' Views on Gender Discrimination

1. Some of Judge Thomas' views, as expressed prior to the hearings, could appear hostile to issues of gender discrimination

In an article based on interviews with Thomas, published in 1987, Juan Williams wrote that Thomas said "blacks and women are generally unprepared to do certain kinds of work by their own choice. It could be that blacks choose not to study chemical engineering, and that women choose to have babies instead of going to medical school." ("A Question of Fairness," The Atlantic Monthly, February 1987 at 79.)

In a 1988 article in the Lincoln Review, Thomas implied that women should not be able to take advantage of anti-discrimination laws. In discussing a recent book by Thomas Sowell, who argues that the absence of women in certain jobs is due to their choice rather than to discrimination, then head of EEOC Thomas wrote:

> [Sowell's book] has a useful, concise discussion of discrimination faced by women. We will not here attempt to summarize it except to note that by analyzing all the statistics and examining the role of marriage on wage earning for both men and women, Sowell presents

a much-needed antidote to cliches about women's earnings and professional status. In any event, women cannot be understood as though they were a racial minority group, or any kind of minority at all. ("Thomas Sowell and the Heritage of Lincoln: Ethnicity and Individual Freedom," Lincoln Review (Winter 1988).)

* * *

2. *In his testimony, Judge Thomas expressed no hostility toward the middle-tier standard of review*

At the hearings, Judge Thomas was asked specifically about the statement just quoted:

> SENATOR DECONCINI. Sowell also explained pay inequities between the genders by claiming that "Women are typically not educated as often in such highly paid fields of mathematics, science, and engineering, nor attracted to physically taxing and well-paid fields such as construction work, lumber-jacking, coal mining and the like."

> What are your thoughts about that conclusion?

> JUDGE THOMAS. Well, I can't say whether or not women are attracted or not attracted to those areas. I think that is a normative comment there.

* * *

> Again, my point in saying that his argument could be an anecdote to the debate is because he attempts to disaggregate and to not simply say all of the reasons. It is not to say that I adopted * * * all of his conclusions and his assertions. I simply don't and did not at that time. (Transcript, Sept. 11, at 64–65.)

When asked specifically about the standard of review for claims of gender discrimination, Judge Thomas said "Senator, I have no reason and had no reason to question or to disagree with the three-tier approach." (Transcript, Sept. 11, at 59.)

These answers once again express Judge Thomas' recurring theme: He has no reason to question, or disagree with, or quarrel with current constitutional interpretation. Yet this is not particularly reassuring given his strongly expressed views before the hearings began. Unfortunately, here as elsewhere, we are left to speculate about the direction in which Judge Thomas will move once he begins to give life to his dispositions and inchoate judicial inclinations.

* * *

C. *Judge Thomas' Pronouncements Prior to the Hearings Suggested He Was Hostile to the Court's Traditional Jurisprudence in the Area of Race Discrimination*

As Chairman of the EEOC, Judge Thomas was a strong supporter of stiff penalties for individuals who had been found guilty of discrimination, as well as for remedies that would make whole individuals who could prove that they themselves had been victims of discrimination. However, some of his statements raised the concern that he would limit Congress' power to formulate permissible responses to societal discrimination. For example, in a 1988 book, Thomas characterized congressional attempts to remedy discrimination as ignoring constitutional mandates:

> Not that there is a great deal of principle in Congress itself. What can one expect of a Congress that would pass the ethnic set-aside law the Court upheld in *Fullilove v. Klutznick.* What the two branches were saying is this: the Court can reinterpret civil rights laws to create schemes of racial preference where none was ever contemplated. And Congress can devise laws justifying racial and ethnic set-asides on the basis of its powers to regulate interstate commerce. Any "equal protection component" of the Fifth Amendment due process clause is irrelevant. ("Civil Rights as a Principle Versus Civil Rights as an Interest," "Reassessing the Reagan Years" (1988) at 396.)

Judge Thomas also specifically criticized the Supreme Court's decisions acknowledging the constitutionality of appropriately drawn affirmative action programs.

* * *

D.   *Judge Thomas' Testimony Left Unanswered Questions as to His Judicial Approach to Race Discrimination Cases*

In part, Judge Thomas responded to questions about his prior views by emphasizing that they were policy positions, not the products of judicial reasoning. Even so, it was evident that in this one area of jurisprudence, he does have some considered views, and that they diverge from those of important Supreme Court decisions. For example:

> SENATOR BROWN. Judge, in the past you have expressed some concerns about racial quotas. If I understand your position as it has been articulated at this hearing, it has been an interest or an advocacy of affirmative action, but an opposition to racial quotas as a method of achieving those advances. I wonder if you could articulate the differences you see and the reasons for them.

> JUDGE THOMAS. As I indicated earlier, Senator, throughout my adult life, I have advocated the inclusion of those who have been excluded.

* * *

> The difficulty comes with how far do you go without being unfair to others who have not discriminated or unfair to the person who is excluded, and at that range I thought—and, again, this was the policy position that I advocated—that it was appropriate to draw the line at preferences and goals and timetables and quotas. (Transcript, Sept. 11, at 164–65.)

Asked further about the issue, Judge Thomas had the following exchange:

SENATOR SPECTER. * * * In a context where blacks have been egregiously discriminated against, it is clear that that is going to happen in the future under the same circumstances, and the way to prevent future victims is to set the goal, and my question to you is, isn't that a reasonable course which the Federal courts followed and the Supreme Court upheld, and, of course, which you disagreed with?

JUDGE THOMAS. It is certainly the course that the Supreme Court has upheld, and I disagree with that as certainly a policy-maker. (Transcript, Sept. 13, at 27.)

Then, the pertinent questions for a nominee become: Does he or she agree with the policies that have been enacted? Will he or she be faithful to and give effect to those policies? In the past, the Court has recognized that Congress's legitimate authority to enact remedial legislation under the commerce clause, as well as under section 5 of the 14th amendment, extends beyond both the power of a court of law and beyond whatever the Justices themselves might consider wise policy.

At the hearing, Judge Thomas was asked his opinion of the Court's interpretation of both the commerce clause and *Katzenbach v. Morgan,* in which the Court held Congress had broad powers under section 5 of the 14th amendment, extending even to a power to invalidate state laws that did not violate the equal protection clause as a matter of judicial enforcement. And with respect to both clauses, Judge Thomas said he had no "quarrel" or "objection" to the Court's current interpretation. (Transcript, Sept. 13, at 69, 148–49; and see part 4 above.)

This testimony amounts to a softening of Judge Thomas' earlier quoted views, which purported to criticize on constitutional grounds some of the Supreme Court decisions upholding affirmative action, such as *Bakke, Fullilove,* and *Weber.* It should, however, be read cautiously, for all Judge Thomas said in his testimony is that he has "no quarrel" with current interpretations of Congress' authority, interpretations which may well become crucial in the future, because it is pursuant to that authority that revisions to the civil rights statutes must be made.

In sum, the testimony provided by Judge Thomas continues to evidence some cause for concern as to how he as a justice would address issues of race discrimination.

* * *

CONCLUSION

A year ago, during the Senate's consideration of Justice Souter's nomination, I made it clear that, with respect to judicial philosophy, the "burden of proof" was on the nominee to demonstrate his or her suitability for the Court and clearly lay out for us his or her methodology for interpreting the Constitution.

Just as the nominee must persuade the President that he or she is the "right person for the job" before winning the nomination, the nominee must persuade the Senate that he or she is the right person for the Court before receiving our votes for confirmation.

In my view, Judge Thomas has not met this burden. It is not that I know for certain that he will take the Court in troubling new directions; rather, it is that I have too many doubts about his judicial philosophy to be confident that he will not. Given what is at stake, and where the Court currently stands, it is a risk we cannot afford to take, in my view.

How did we arrive at this particular juncture? There is no question that the aggressive agenda of ultra-conservatives in the Reagan and Bush administrations—an agenda of remaking the Court's protection for individual and property rights, and for fundamentally altering the balance of power between the branches of government—lies at the core of the dilemma. The result is that Judge Thomas is the seventh consecutive conservative Republican nominated to the Court over the past decade.

Most of our other Presidents have taken a far different approach to filling vacancies on the Court. While they have all tried to shift the Court by virtue of their power to nominate, they have also been guided by historical responsibilities to moderate their selections, and protect a diversity of views on the Court.

In this century, this tradition extends back as far as the Presidency of Herbert Hoover, a conservative Republican, who, after consulting with Senators of all views, nominated the liberal Benjamin Cardozo to the Court.

The tradition continued with Presidents Franklin Roosevelt and Harry Truman. As noted by Guido Calabresi, the Dean of the Yale Law School, who testified in favor of Judge Thomas' nomination:

> MR. CALABRESI. I just want to say that this is an extraordinary time in the history of the Court. * * * [It] is as long a time, perhaps as there has ever been in the history of this country, certainly since the Civil War, from 1860 to 1884 was a period of equivalent time.

> At other times when there has been such an extended period of time [when one party controlled the White House], the President has attempted to name people to the Court whose views are very different from his own. Presidents Roosevelt and Truman, for what seemed an eternity but was only 20 years, named all the Justices and made a point of naming some Justices who were very conservative and some from the other party. Justice Reed and Justice Byrne were Democrats and very conservative; Justice Burton was a Republican.

* * *

This pattern of moderation and balance continued into the Presidencies of Eisenhower, whose appointments included the moderate conservatives, John Harlan and Potter Stewart, as well as Democrat William Brennan and moderate Republican Earl Warren; Kennedy, whose appointments included the conservative Byron White, as well as the liberal Arthur Goldberg; Nixon, whose appointments included the moderate conservatives, Lewis Powell and Warren Burger, the more conservative William Rehnquist, and also the liberal Harry Blackmun; and Ford, whose sole appointment was the moderate John Paul Stevens.

The pattern stopped with the Reagan administration, and it has yet to be restored, as Dean Calabresi noted.

Dean Calabresi also noted that it is the right of a President to nominate whomever he chooses to the Court. It is not, however, an obligation of the Senate to confirm anyone whom he nominates. Under the "Advice and Consent" clause of the Constitution, the Senate is an equal partner in the job of filling Supreme Court vacancies.

When the President has selected nominees without regard to ideology, the Senate has generally deferred to the President's selections, so long as they met professional qualifications. On the basis of the evidence provided by those Justices who have been confirmed in the past decade, this and the previous administration have decided to repudiate this pattern.

Over the past decade, the Court overall has moved decidedly to a very conservative position, more conservative than the country as a whole. It is therefore the responsibility of nominees to make plain to the Senate how they will shape the current trend. This is why it is so important that nominees be prepared to discuss with the Judiciary Committee, candidly and forthrightly, what their fundamental judicial philosophy is.

In this regard, Judge Thomas' responses to the questions of the committee were inadequate. Many have expressed frustration at Judge Thomas' lack of responsiveness to the committee's questions. Others have said that vagueness and imprecision in responding is inevitable, because such an approach has become the most likely path for the nominee to win confirmation.

* * *

Throughout his testimony, Judge Thomas gave us many responses—but too few real answers.

* * *

I believe Judge Thomas when he says he has no checklist of cases to be overruled, and when he says that he never meant to advocate the full range of implications one could draw, and would have to draw, from his remarks.

The question about Judge Thomas—to use one of the favorite phrases of his supporters—is what views will he grow into at the Court?

I believe that Judge Thomas does not now have an agenda; but with these predispositions, I wonder what sort of an approach he will have as a Justice once he acquires a point of view. And this is a point that I found to be of constant concern during the hearings.

Would Judge Thomas take the views hinted at in his speeches and writings, and apply them to their full extent and conclusion as a Justice of the Supreme Court? * * * The major object of Judge Thomas' testimony was to reassure us that we need not worry; unfortunately, the major effect of his writings on these matters is to give great cause for concern.

Where such doubts exist, I cannot vote to confirm the nominee. * * *

I asked about the right to privacy at such length, not in a result-oriented effort to determine how Judge Thomas might rule on *Roe v. Wade,* nor because I think that there is any real chance that any state might ban the use of contraceptives in 1991. Rather, I made these inquiries because it is important that we place on the Court an individual who has an expansive view of personal freedom with respect to issues that will arise at the Court in the future, some we can not now even contemplate.

So it is not good enough that a nominee begrudgingly pledges not to reverse the battles already fought and won; rather, I am looking for a nominee's disposition with respect to questions of personal freedom not yet even framed.

* * *

I can best summarize my views on Judge Thomas' writings and speeches as follows: It seems to me that the major focus of these works was the construction of an intellectual framework for an approach to the question of civil rights and equality that would be a marked departure from the prevailing view—an approach that is one I generally do not accept, but does have a growing number of adherents.

In the process of developing this philosophy with respect to civil rights, Judge Thomas referenced theories being developed by other writers, for other purposes. These theories, as I have pointed out in detail above, would have devastating consequences if taken to the conclusion that their authors intend for them.

Perhaps Judge Thomas did not intend to embrace the conclusions of these theories, and instead, meant only to endorse them so far as they supported his views on civil rights. But the litany of speeches and writings Judge Thomas has made in the past, the consistency with which they have appeared to embrace ultraconservative views, the state of the current Supreme Court—and the danger to the fabric of our laws if these views were implemented—make this a risk that I cannot accept.

* * *

So we have come to this difficult juncture, and all of us have come to it—the Senate, the President's nominee, and the President. This confrontation was not inevitable; it could have been avoided. I say respectfully to the President of the United States that he must shoulder a major share of the responsibility for bringing us to this place, because he has created a real dilemma for the Senate, one in which we are forced to demand a very high degree of certainty about the President's nominee before we can give our consent.

The dilemma has been created by two facts: a fervent minority within the President's party is engaging in an open campaign to shift the Court dramatically to the right; and the President has not been willing to engage in the kind of consultation with the Senate that would give this body more assurance that his nominees are not participants in that campaign.

In the future, we need to pursue a course of moderation in judicial selections—not a course in which the Senate insists on someone of its own choosing, but a course of genuine moderation and genuine consultation and cooperation among the branches. Such a process could result in the selection and confirmation of the kind of Justices I spoke of earlier—justices who, regardless of their stand on the contemporary, politicized issues facing the Court, are the kind of individuals who share a sound vision of the Constitution.

I hope the President will join in breaking this cycle of political skepticism, because without him it will be impossible to make that break. * * *

ADDITIONAL VIEWS OF SENATOR METZENBAUM

* * *

A. RECORD AT THE EEOC

Clarence Thomas was chairman of the Equal Employment Opportunity Commission from 1982 to 1990. He was the chief law enforcement official responsible for protecting women, minorities, and the elderly from discrimination. But as Chairman of the EEOC, Judge Thomas pursued policies which undermined legal protections for minorities, women, and the elderly—the very people who are most in need of protection by the Supreme Court.

Judge Thomas' record with respect to age discrimination is particularly troubling. During his tenure as EEOC Chairman, thousands of older workers who believed that they were victims of age discrimination lost their right to bring age bias suits in Federal court because of the negligence of his agency.[1] Despite assurance from Clarence Thomas

---

1. The Age Discrimination in Employment Act (ADEA) requires older workers to file their age bias claims with the EEOC. The Commission is authorized to investigate the claim, and if it has merit, attempt to work out a settlement or file a lawsuit on behalf of the older worker. The ADEA has a 2–year statute of limitations, meaning that either the EEOC or the older worker who brings the age discrimination charge to the EEOC's attention, must file a lawsuit within 2 years of the alleged act of discrimi-

that he would correct the problem, Congress found it necessary on two separate occasions—in 1988 and again in 1990—to pass legislation to restore the rights of these older workers to file age discrimination suits in Federal court.

Judge Thomas' record with respect to sex discrimination in employment is also particularly troubling. During the past 15 years, a number of American companies adopted policies which barred women from certain jobs unless the women could prove they were not capable of bearing children. These so-called fetal protection policies left working women in the unconscionable position of having to undergo irreversible sterilization if they wanted to keep their jobs. Tragically, that's just what happened to a number of women, at companies such as American Cyanamid and Johnson Controls.

Six months ago, the Supreme Court completely banned these policies as illegal sex discrimination.

Judge Thomas, as head of the EEOC from 1982 to 1990, had the responsibility for protecting the millions of working women in this country against sex discrimination. Shortly before he became the Chairman, the EEOC decided not to resolve allegations of sex discrimination involving these fetal protection policies until it developed a formal position on the issue. * * *

Under Judge Thomas' command, the EEOC failed to address this intolerable situation for over 6 years. During this entire period, dozens of charges involving fetal protection policies sat at headquarters without resolution. * * *

Under increasing pressure from a House Education and Labor Committee investigation, the EEOC finally took a position in 1988, and began to resolve these charges in 1989. By that point, over 100 charges had piled up. The EEOC couldn't even find many of the women who had filed the charges, so their cases were thrown out. For these women, justice delayed was justice denied.

EEOC documents indicate that Judge Thomas was personally involved in the EEOC's default on this issue (Tr., September 16, 1991 at 40–41).

Judge Thomas' unrelenting hostility toward effective civil rights enforcement tools such as class action suits and affirmative action remedies hurt women and minorities. These proven enforcement mechanisms—which have been continually upheld by the Supreme Court—are capable and cost-effective means of obtaining and ensuring compliance with antidiscrimination laws. But largely for political reasons, reliance

nation. Otherwise, the older worker loses his or her right to seek redress under the law.

Unfortunately, during Judge Thomas' tenure as head of the EEOC, thousands of age bias claims sat languishing in the EEOC for over 2 years. As a result, thousands of older workers lost their right to bring lawsuits under the ADEA.

on these effective law enforcement tools dropped significantly during Judge Thomas' tenure at EEOC.

Judge Thomas' supporters suggest that his childhood experiences of surmounting poverty and segregation demonstrate that, if confirmed, he would show sensitivity and concern regarding civil rights cases that come before the Court. But Judge Thomas does not appear to have brought that experience to bear during his 8 years as the Nation's top civil rights law enforcement official. While Judge Thomas' background and life-story are both impressive and inspiring, his track record at the EEOC is the single best indicator of his approach to civil rights issues should he be confirmed for the Court.

* * *

B.   JUDGE THOMAS' LEGAL CREDENTIALS

Judge Clarence Thomas simply does not have the exceptional and distinguished legal credentials which one expects to find in a Supreme Court nominee. He practiced law for only 5 years, stopping at age 31. In his questionnaire, he did not identify a single case which he had argued in Federal court. By his own admission, he did not play a significant role in drafting any briefs filed by the EEOC during his tenure there. In addition, he does not have an extensive record of scholarship or expertise in an area of law, and he has served as a judge for a mere 17 months.

Julius Chambers, the director of the NAACP Legal Defense and Educational Fund, testified that Judge Thomas "does not meet the standards for elevation to the United States Supreme Court." The Legal Defense Fund reviewed the legal and related law and Government experience of Judge Thomas and compared his credentials with those of the other 48 Justices who were appointed to the Court in this century. The NAACP Legal Defense Fund found that virtually every Supreme Court Justice appointed in the 20th century possessed at least two of seven basic qualifications for the Court.[2] The Legal Defense Fund found that, at this stage of his career, Judge Thomas has not yet shown any of these fundamental qualifications. The review noted that all but 8 of the 48 Justices in this century had at least 10 years experience practicing law.[3] Of the 26 Justices appointed to the Supreme Court with prior

---

2. In prepared testimony submitted to the Judiciary Committee, the Legal Defense Fund identified the following seven basic qualifications: "(1) a substantial law practice either in the private or public sector, generally covering more than 10 years, (2) extensive legal scholarship or teaching, (3) significant experience as a judge, generally for five or more years, (4) the highest level of expertise in a particular area of the law, (5) superior intellect, (6) ability to persuade and lead, and (7) generally outstanding achievement over the course of their career." Prepared statement of Julius Chambers on behalf of the NAACP Legal Defense Fund, at 12.

3. The eight exceptions are: William Howard Taft, Felix Frankfurter, William O. Douglas, Francis William Murphy (who practiced law for 9 years, served as attorney general for 1 year, and a judge for 7 years), James Francis Byrnes (who served as a Congressman for 24 years and a Senator for 10 years), Wiley Blount Rutledge (law school professor for 13 years, 9 years judicial experience), Sandra Day O'Connor (practiced law for 8 years, State court judge for 7 years, State senator for 6 years), Anto-

judicial experience, only 5 had less than 4 years experience as a judge; but each of those 5 had spent at least 26 years practicing law.

Judge Thomas' supporters recognize that his legal and judicial record are not strong reasons to vote in his favor. Accordingly, they stress his capacity for growth. I do not believe that Justices who need to grow into the job should be put on the Supreme Court. If, as his supporters claim, Judge Thomas has the potential to be an outstanding judge, we should give him a few more years on the D.C. Circuit Court of Appeals to see if he lives up to that potential.

* * *

ADDITIONAL VIEWS OF SENATOR PATRICK J. LEAHY

* * *

THE SENATE SHOULD NOT CONSENT TO JUDGE THOMAS' NOMINATION

After considering Judge Thomas' record and his testimony before this committee, I cannot consent to his nomination to be an Associate Justice of the Supreme Court. * * * After reviewing his past record and listening to his testimony, I am left with too many doubts to vote in favor of Judge Thomas' confirmation. I have doubts about his legal ability, which, at this early stage in his career, is largely untested. I have doubts raised by his refusal to answer questions and his repeated disavowals of his earlier speeches and writings.

Furthermore, I have doubts about how Judge Thomas views the fundamental constitutional right to privacy, including a woman's right to choose. The most astonishing statement in these hearings was Judge Thomas' claim that he has never discussed the merits of *Roe v. Wade*, 410 U.S. 113 (1973), the most controversial Supreme Court case of the last quarter-century. Transcript of the Confirmation Hearings of Judge Clarence Thomas To Be an Associate Justice of the Supreme Court of the United States, hereinafter "Transcript," Sept. 11, 1991 at 102–05.

In the face of these doubts, the fact that Clarence Thomas is a fine person who has overcome what for many have been insurmountable obstacles is not a sufficient justification for a lifetime appointment to the Supreme Court.

* * *

PRIVACY

Most of the troubling issues about this nomination—ambiguous testimony, repudiations of prior statements and nonresponses to fair questions—coalesce in the area of privacy.

Judge Thomas' refusal to answer questions on privacy was especially difficult to understand because Judge Thomas opened the door to them. Unlike now-Justice Souter, Judge Thomas came before the Committee

---

nin Scalia (9 years of legal practice, 9 years as a law professor, 4 years judicial experience). *Id.* at 13.

having made statements that raised questions about his views on the right of privacy. He praised the Lehrman article [See Speech to the Heritage Foundation, June 18, 1987; Lehrman, "The Declaration of Independence and the Right to Life," The American Spectator, April 1987]; he participated in the White House Working Group on the Family which called for overturning *Roe* and other privacy cases [White House Working Group on the Family, "The Family: Preserving America's Future (1986)]; he favored a narrow reading of the ninth amendment and cited *Roe* in a footnote in an article on the privileges or immunities clause [Thomas, "The Higher Law Background of the Privileges or Immunities Clause of the Fourteenth Amendment," 12 Harv. J.L. & Pub. Pol. 63 (1989)]; and he specifically referred to abortion in a column in the Chicago Defender. Thomas, "How Republicans Can Win Blacks," Chicago Defender, Feb. 21, 1987. Given these statements, Judge Thomas did not enter the hearings with the appearance that he truly had no position on abortion and privacy rights.

As I said at the outset of this process, Judge Thomas' embrace of Lewis Lehrman's article—"The Declaration of Independence and the Right to Life"—was of particular concern to me. The consequence of Lehrman's thesis that a fetus has an inalienable right to life beginning at conception is that any termination of a pregnancy would constitute murder. That radical position goes far beyond the views of most conservatives that abortion is a political issue best left to the determination of legislative bodies.

Despite repeated questions from me and other members of the Committee, Judge Thomas did not categorically state that he disagreed with the Lehrman article. Instead, he explained that he invoked the article in his speech to a conservative audience to find "unifying principles in the area of civil rights" [Transcript, Sept. 11, 1991 at 96] and that he does "not endorse" Lehrman's conclusion. Transcript, September 13, 1991 at 21. These responses left me with more questions than answers.

The Lehrman article makes only one argument concisely and powerfully, and that argument is antithetical to a woman's fundamental right of choice. At the time Judge Thomas embraced the Lehrman article, did he understand its implications? Was he not sufficiently concerned about its conclusion to think twice about calling it a "splendid example" regardless of the audience he was trying to sway? If Judge Thomas did not agree with the radical position advocated in the Lehrman article, why could he not state his position unequivocally when asked about it repeatedly at the hearings?

Finally, nothing disturbed me more than Judge Thomas' statement that he has never discussed the merits of *Roe v. Wade* with anyone:

> SENATOR LEAHY. Judge, you were in law school at the time *Roe v. Wade* was decided. * * * You would accept, would you not, that in the last generation *Roe v. Wade* is certainly one of the more important cases to be decided by the U.S. Supreme Court.

JUDGE THOMAS. I would accept that it has certainly been one of the more important, as well as one that has been one of the more highly publicized and debated cases.

SENATOR LEAHY. So, * * * it would be safe to assume that when that came down, you were in law school [where] recent case law is oft[en] discussed, [and] that *Roe v. Wade* would have been discussed in the law school while you were there?

JUDGE THOMAS. The case that I remember being discussed most during my early part of law school was I believe * * * *Griswold* * * * and we may have touched on *Roe v. Wade* at some point and debated that, but let me add one point to that. Because I was a married student and I worked, I did not spend a lot of time around the law school doing what the other students enjoyed so much, and that is debating all the current cases and all of the slip opinions. My schedule was such that I went to classes and generally went to work and went home.

SENATOR LEAHY. Judge Thomas, I was a married law student who also worked, but I also found at least between classes that we did discuss some of the law, and I am sure you are not suggesting that there wasn't any discussion at any time of *Roe v. Wade?*

JUDGE THOMAS. Senator, I cannot remember personally engaging in those discussions.

SENATOR LEAHY. Have you ever had discussion of *Roe v. Wade*, other than in this room, in the 17 or 18 years it has been there?

JUDGE THOMAS. Only, I guess, Senator * * * in the most general sense that other individuals express concerns one way or the other, and you listen and you try to be thoughtful. If you are asking me whether or not I have ever debated the contents of it, [the] answer to that is no, Senator.

SENATOR LEAHY. Have you ever, [in] private gatherings or otherwise, stated whether you felt that it was properly decided or not?

JUDGE THOMAS. Senator, in trying to recall and reflect on that, I don't recollect commenting one way or the other. There were, again, debates about it in various places, but I generally did not participate. I don't remember or recall participating, Senator.

SENATOR LEAHY. So you don't ever recall stating whether you thought it was properly decided or not?

JUDGE THOMAS. I can't recall saying one way or the other, Senator.

Transcript, September 11, 1991 at 102–05.

I have given a lot of thought to this exchange. It is deeply troubling. It is hard to believe that there is a thoughtful lawyer in this country—much less a federal judge or a nominee to the Supreme Court—who has not discussed or expressed his view on *Roe v. Wade.*

Judge Thomas' assertion was even more baffling given his record of specific references to abortion and *Roe.*

CONCLUSION

As my views set forth above indicate, I am left with too many doubts to vote in favor of Judge Thomas' confirmation. I am concerned that he lacks the legal wisdom and judicial experience necessary to take the lead in grappling with the momentous constitutional issues he would face as a Supreme Court Justice. I am concerned that Judge Thomas has left us with no clear view of his constitutional philosophy. I am concerned about the differences between his hearing testimony and his prior speeches and writings. I am concerned by his refusal to answer significant and legitimate questions. Finally, based on the record as it was presented to the Committee, I am concerned that Judge Thomas will be a less than vigilant guardian of the fundamental right to privacy.

It may be that at some time in the future Judge Thomas will show himself prepared for a seat on the Supreme Court. But based on my review of Judge Thomas' record and his testimony before the Judiciary Committee during this hearing, I am not confident that he is ready now, and therefore, I cannot vote to confirm him.

ADDITIONAL VIEWS OF MESSRS. THURMOND, HATCH, SIMPSON, GRASSLEY AND BROWN

We strongly support Judge Clarence Thomas' nomination. * * *

JUDGE THOMAS' BACKGROUND AND QUALIFICATIONS

Judge Clarence Thomas was born June 23, 1948, in Pin Point, GA, a rural community near Savannah. His father left the family when Judge Thomas was still a small child. For the first years of his life Judge Thomas lived in a house with no indoor plumbing, moving at one point to a cramped tenement in Savannah. At the age of 7, he went to live with his maternal grandparents, Myers and Christine Anderson.

His grandfather, though barely literate, owned and managed an ice and fuel oil delivery business for which Judge Thomas worked after school. Mr. Anderson was also active in the local chapter of the NAACP. Judge Thomas learned many important lessons such as hard work and discipline from his grandparents and he has applied these lessons throughout his life.

The Andersons sent Judge Thomas to schools in Savannah, where he was taught by Franciscan nuns. The nuns underscored his grandparents' teaching about the importance of education.

In 1964, Judge Thomas transferred to St. John Vianney Minor Seminary near Savannah, where for most of the succeeding three years he was the only black student in his class. At this point in his life, Judge Thomas intended to become a priest. However, after spending several months at Immaculate Conception Seminary in Missouri, he changed his mind and transferred to Holy Cross College in Massachusetts. He supported his education through a combination of scholarships, loans, and jobs. He worked in the free breakfast program and tutored in the local community. He graduated with honors in 1971.

Judge Thomas then went to Yale Law School. While a law student, he worked summers for New Haven legal assistance and for a small civil rights law firm in Savannah. He graduated from law school in 1974.

Throughout his life, Judge Thomas has seized the opportunities that the American system offers to all. As Judge Thomas said on being nominated by President Bush, "only in America could this have been possible," for someone born in poverty and segregation to be nominated to the Supreme Court. In the President's words, Judge Thomas exemplifies "the endless possibilities of the American dream."

Judge Thomas' legal career is a long record of accomplishment. Most of his life he has been dedicated to public service. In 1974, John C. Danforth, then the attorney general of Missouri, hired him as an assistant attorney general. Judge Thomas practiced in both the trial and appellate courts, and argued several cases before the Missouri Supreme Court. In 1977, he joined the legal staff of the Monsanto Co. where he was involved in matters relating to contracts, antitrust law, environmental regulation and products liability. In 1979, he became a legislative assistant to Senator Danforth.

In 1981, Judge Thomas was appointed by President Reagan to be the Assistant Secretary for Civil Rights at the United States Department of Education. One year later, he was again nominated by President Reagan to be the Chairman of the Equal Employment Opportunity Commission; he was reappointed to that position in 1986. The EEOC, an agency that employs more than 3100 persons and has an annual budget of $180 million, enforces title VII of the Civil Rights Act of 1964, which prohibits discrimination based on race, color, religion, sex, or national origin. The EEOC also enforces laws against discrimination based on age or disability. During Judge Thomas' tenure at the EEOC, he performed a management miracle, transforming an inefficient and dispirited agency into an effective and dynamic enforcer of the civil rights laws. Judge Thomas emphasized the need to provide specific relief for individual victims of discrimination. Judge Thomas' tenure as Chairman was the longest in the history of the Commission. A strong indication of the success of his tenure and the respect that he engendered among his coworkers is that the employees of the EEOC have named the Commission's new headquarters building after him.

On March 12, 1990, Judge Thomas assumed his present position on the United States Court of Appeals for the District of Columbia Circuit, to which he was appointed by President Bush. During his time on the bench, he has written opinions in such areas as criminal law, antitrust law and trade regulation, constitutional law, and administrative law. He has participated in more than 140 decisions of the court. His opinions have been lucid and scholarly. None of his decisions has been reversed, either by the District of Columbia Circuit en banc or by the Supreme Court.

Throughout his confirmation hearing, we believe that Judge Thomas demonstrated the qualifications of character necessary for an Associate Justice of the Supreme Court of the United States. As well, he is highly qualified professionally. Simply said, he is intelligent, decent, honest, openminded, and fair. He brings to his judicial office a willingness to listen, to consider, and to analyze carefully.

In addition to Judge Thomas being highly qualified, we believe that he will bring a unique perspective of life that has required him, as he stated, to "touch on virtually every aspect, every level of our country, from people who couldn't read and write to people who were extremely literate, from people who had no money to people who were very wealthy." (Tr., 9/12/91, at 59.) Members of this committee, from both sides of the aisle, have called the story of Judge Thomas' life "impressive and truly inspiring" (Tr. 9/10/91, at 44, remarks of Sen. Simpson); "admirable" (id., at 18, remarks of Sen. Thurmond); and "an uplifting tale of a youth determined to surmount the barriers of poverty, segregation and discrimination" (id. at 53–54, remarks of Sen. Metzenbaum).

When Judge Thomas was before the Judiciary Committee regarding his nomination to be a judge of the U.S. Court of Appeals, he explained why he pursued the law as a profession:

> [T]he reason I became a lawyer was to make sure that minorities, individuals who did not have access to this society gained access. Now, I may differ with others as to how best to do that, but the objective has always been to include those who have been excluded.

* * *

No sitting Senator or other member of the Supreme Court has a background that is even remotely similar. Judge Thomas, as he has promised, would "bring to th[e] Court * * * an understanding and the ability to stand in the shoes of other people across a broad spectrum of this country." (Tr., 9/12/91, at 59–60.) The Court—and the country—will benefit from that understanding.

PRESUMPTION IN FAVOR OF THE NOMINEE

We believe that the President's nominee to the Supreme Court comes before the Judiciary Committee and the Senate with a presumption in his or her favor.

* * * Presidential primacy in making judicial appointments is reflected in the structure of the Constitution itself: the appointment power is assigned in Article II's enumeration of executive powers, not in the legislative powers of article I. The advice and consent function was never intended to permit substitution of the Senate's judgment for the President's in determining who should be selected from among the qualified and fit. Performance of the Senate's duty in accordance with the Constitution requires that the Senate as a whole respect the President's preeminent role in this process by according the President's nominee a presumption of qualification, and fitness.

Of course, this presumption of fitness may be overcome in individual cases if a nominee's character is found to be seriously flawed, that a nominee lacks integrity or judicial temperament, or that a nominee is deficient in professional qualifications. In historical context, the Senate's role is properly viewed as a vigorous check against any "spirit of favoritism" and the appointment of "unfit characters." "The Federalist" No. 76 (J. Cooke ed. 1961), at 513. Short of such potentially disabling infirmities, the burden rests on those who would challenge the President's nominee to expose disqualifications to that nominee's confirmation.

As well, a nominee should not be rejected for any alleged failure to assure this committee about his or her positions on specific, controversial issues. Those who would have Judge Thomas demonstrate his fitness by meeting certain specific, substantive litmus tests misunderstand the role of the Senate in the advise and consent process. The failure to meet substantive standards would disqualify countless otherwise intelligent, fair, and capable individuals from serving on the Supreme Court.

These "burdens of proof," whether general or specific, represent an "unwarranted, and in our view inappropriate, attempt to redefine the roles of the President and the Senate as they are now defined in the Constitution." S.Exec.Rep. No. 32 at 75. We believe the imposition of such burdens threatens the integrity of the confirmation process, denigrates the dignity of the Supreme Court as an institution, and impugns the integrity of nominees to that Court as individuals.

* * *

JUDGE THOMAS WAS APPROPRIATELY RESPONSIVE
TO THE COMMITTEE'S QUESTIONS

We believe that Judge Thomas responded openly, thoughtfully, and responsibly to the wide range of questions propounded to him during the hearings. Judge Thomas properly declined to express an opinion or position on particular issues that he could be required to resolve as a member of the Court or in his present role as a circuit judge. In this regard, he adhered to a long-standing tradition that is absolutely essential to the maintenance of an independent judiciary.

Judge Thomas was questioned extensively by some Committee members regarding his views on the various abortion-related issues raised by *Roe v. Wade* and its progeny. In all, Judge Thomas was asked more than ninety questions on the abortion issue. In response, Judge Thomas repeatedly explained the well-established principles that make such testimony improper. For example, in response to a question from Senator Leahy, Judge Thomas explained:

> [F]or me to respond to what my views are on those particular issues would really undermine my ability to be impartial in those cases. I have attempted to respond as candidly and openly as I

possibly can, without in any way undermining or compromising my ability to rule on these cases. (Tr., 9/11/91, at 99.)

If Supreme Court nominees could be forced to stake out their positions on the crucial legal issues of the day under the pressure of the confirmation process, the principle of judicial independence would be irreparably compromised. As former Chief Justice Burger explained the problem in a 1990 article:

> To expect a nominee to make commitments, or even to engage in substantive discussion of a case yet unseen, borders on the preposterous. * * * To call on a nominee for advance views as to questions that may come before the Court is really not unlike asking a potential juror how he or she will decide a particular case that the jury has not yet heard. A trial judge would reprimand a lawyer for such conduct. (Burger, "How Far Should the Questions Go?," Parade Magazine, Sept. 16, 1990, at 10, 14.)

Senator Hatch stressed Judge Thomas' current status as a sitting Federal judge when he raised his deep concerns on the subject of case-specific questioning:

> So, you are a sitting judge on one of the Nation's highest courts, and whatever the outcome of these hearings may be, you are still going to be a judge for the rest of your life, for the rest of your professional life, if you so choose to be.

> You simply do not have the freedom to answer every question as a sitting judge, every question that every Senator might have on this panel or might wish to be answered, and that goes for questions from both sides of the aisle, not just the other side of the aisle. (Tr. 9/12/91, at 87.)

These principles are fully consistent with the standard of responsiveness traditionally adopted by previous Supreme Court nominees. For example, Justice Thurgood Marshall was reticent in questioning during his confirmation hearing. Whereas today some believe the most controversial constitutional issues are the abortion issues raised by Roe v. Wade, at the time of Justice Marshall's confirmation hearings in 1967 the burning issue concerned the Supreme Court's decision in Miranda v. Arizona and related rulings expanding the rights of criminal suspects and defendants. Some Judiciary Committee members were just as anxious to extract Thurgood Marshall's views on Miranda in 1967 as some current committee Members are to learn Clarence Thomas' views on Roe today.

The exchanges on the Miranda decision between Thurgood Marshall and various Senators bear a remarkable resemblance to the questioning of Clarence Thomas with respect to Roe v. Wade and the abortion issue. In both instances, Senators pressed the nominee to disclose his views and opinions on a prominent holding that was certain to be revisited in future cases; in both instances the nominee steadfastly refused to compromise his capacity to participate impartially in such future cases by signalling his approach to such cases as a condition of confirmation; and in both cases the nominee was legally and ethically correct in resisting the pressure to telegraph his views.

Supreme Court nominees such as, Abe Fortas, Sandra Day O'Connor, Antonin Scalia, and David Souter consistently refused to answer questions on specific issues likely to come before the Court in future cases. In particular, nominees appearing before the Judiciary Committee in the "post-Roe" era have properly declined to respond to relentless efforts to elicit their views on the evolving and unsettled legal questions raised by the abortion controversy.

* * *

The Role of an Executive Branch Policymaker Is Fundamentally Different From That of a Judge

In the Department of Education and as Chairman of the Equal Employment Opportunity Commission [EEOC], Judge Thomas was a powerful advocate for policy positions advanced by the executive branch. Some members of the committee felt that certain positions Judge Thomas had proposed in his prior speeches were controversial. These included, for example, certain statements in speeches that were critical of affirmative action programs that involve preferences for one racial group over another. We believe the positions Judge Thomas advocated were always within the mainstream of public debate and were perfectly appropriate for an executive official holding an important and high-profile office. Furthermore, we believe that Judge Thomas' record on the District of Columbia Court of Appeals is an illustration that he has not advocated political policy as a member of the court. We have reviewed his record on the court and find no evidence that he injected any hint of political ideology into the judicial opinions he has authored or joined. In his testimony before the committee, Judge Thomas stated clearly that his views on policy are wholly distinct from his responsibilities and actions as a judge.

As his testimony makes abundantly clear, Judge Thomas is keenly aware that when he donned the robes of a Federal judge, he entered upon a new role, one that is and must remain independent from any policymaking agenda the judge may have advanced in an earlier career. In response to a question from Senator DeConcini, Judge Thomas testified:

> I think it is important for judges not to have agendas or to have strong ideology or ideological views. * * *

> I believe one of the Justices * * * spoke about having to strip down, like a runner, to eliminate agendas, to eliminate ideologies, and when one becomes a judge, it is an amazing process, because that is precisely what you start doing. You start putting the speeches away, you start putting the policy statements away. You begin to decline forming opinions in important areas that could

come before your court, because you want to be stripped down like a runner. So, I have no agenda, Senator. (Tr., 9/11/91, at 60–61)

* * *

If policy positions taken in speeches are to be overscrutinized and held against the nominee as evidence of prospective judicial opinions, many well-qualified candidates, who have served in the executive branch or in the Congress and have taken part in vital debate on the policy issues that face the country, will no longer be eligible for the Court.

* * *

As Senator Hatch cogently explained:

If there was a central theme to Judge Thomas' testimony, it was this: the roles of the judge and the policy maker are wholly and completely distinct. * * *

This distinction—between the judge as interpreter of the written law and the legislator as the author of the written law—appears to be wholly lost on some of Judge Thomas' critics. They are incredulous that Judge Thomas could, as a policymaker, have taken strong positions, and then, as a judge, forswear any policy agenda. For them, apparently, adjudication in the courts is nothing more than a continuation of politics by other means. Put more bluntly, some of the critics of Judge Thomas would collapse the distinctly different functions of adjudication and policymaking into an approach that simply reaches a preferred policy result, whatever the violence done to the written law. (Statement of Sen. Orrin Hatch, 9/27/91, at 2.)

* * *

JUDGE THOMAS POSSESSES APPROPRIATE JUDICIAL TEMPERAMENT

During Judge Thomas' appearance before the committee, he exhibited an exceptional temperament. Throughout his testimony, Judge Thomas consistently demonstrated the characteristics we consider crucial in any nominee: Openmindedness, impartiality, integrity, independence, and fairness.

Judge Thomas' willingness to listen to those who come before him shows us the most critical of qualities needed in a member of the Nation's highest court. It confirms that Judge Thomas will not pursue an agenda on the Court, but will simply go about the job of being a good and fair judge for the parties involved. In his opening statement, Judge Thomas explained:

I have learned to listen carefully, carefully to other points of view and to others, to think through problems recognizing that there are no easy answers to difficult problems, to think deeply about those who will be affected by decisions that I make and decisions made by others.

* * *

A judge must be fair and impartial. A judge must not bring to his job, to the court, the baggage of preconceived notions, of ideology, and certainly not an agenda, and the judge must get the decision right. Because when all is said and done, the little guy, the average person, the people of Pin Point, the real people of America will be affected not only by what we as judges do, but by the way we do our jobs. (Tr., 9/10/91, at 132–33.)

* * *

We are also impressed that Judge Thomas makes a conscious effort not to lose touch with the people who will be affected by his decisions. Judge Thomas told the committee:

[I]n my job, my current position on the Court of Appeals, one of the things that I always attempt to do is to make sure that in that isolation that I don't lose contact with the real world and the real people—the people who work in the building, the people who are around the building, the people who have to be involved with that building, the people who are the neighborhood, the real people outside. Because our world as an appellate judge is a cloistered world, and that has been an important part of my life, to not lose contact. (Tr., 9/13/91, at 84.)

* * *

JUDGE THOMAS FAITHFULLY ENFORCED THE LAW AS CHAIRMAN OF THE EQUAL EMPLOYMENT OPPORTUNITY COMMISSION

As Chairman of the EEOC, Judge Thomas faithfully enforced the employment discrimination laws. As Senator Hatch observed in his opening statement:

The Washington Post, no shill for the Reagan administration civil rights record, praised "the quiet but persistent leadership of Chairman Clarence Thomas" in an editorial on May 17, 1987, entitled "The EEOC is Thriving." The July 15, 1991, U.S. News and World Report wrote, "Overall, it seems clear that he left the [EEOC] in better condition than he found it." (Tr., 9/10/91, at 29.)

* * *

A. Judge Thomas' Record on Age Discrimination Reflects His Candor, Integrity, and Respect for the Law

Although the issue had been fully aired upon Judge Thomas' appointment to the court of appeals, allegations involving the lapse of age discrimination charges beyond the statute of limitations provided by the Age Discrimination in Employment Act [ADEA] were again raised in these hearings.

As he did in his court of appeals confirmation hearing, Judge Thomas accepted responsibility for the lapse, calling it "the low point of my tenure." (Tr., 9/12/91, at 120). Judge Thomas noted that, during his chairmanship of the EEOC, he promptly disclosed to Congress the existence of the lapse, and he took steps to prevent recurrence of the problem:

> [W]hat we attempted to do was, as soon as I found out [about the lapsed charges], * * * to not only inform Congress, but to make it public. I found out in December of 1987 and reported to Congress the day Congress returned for the next term in January. * * * If I could have investigated every one of those cases, I would have. There were approximately 2,000 * * * charges within EEOC which had missed the statute [of limitations] over a four-year period out of the approximately 50,000 or 60,000 that we receive a year. * * * But even one * * * is too many.

> We took steps to solve the problem. We * * * completed * * * the automation of the agency, so that the cases could be more accurately tracked, that is both at headquarters and in the field offices. We sent notices to the individuals, so that they would know when the statute was approaching. We held managers more accountable. We had done that before, but we redoubled our efforts. (Tr., 9/12/91, at 126–27.)

JUDGE THOMAS KNOWS THAT DISCRIMINATION EXISTS IN THE UNITED STATES AND HE IS COMMITTED TO ELIMINATING IT IN ALL OF ITS PERNICIOUS FORMS

Judge Thomas has been concerned throughout his career with improving the lives of those who have been disadvantaged, dispossessed, and victims of discrimination. Upon entering the executive branch of the Federal Government, Judge Thomas tried to identify and use "all avenues of inclusion." (Tr., 9/13/91, at 37.) At the EEOC, he stressed the importance of strong remedies for victims of discrimination, rather than reliance on quotas. But while recognizing the absolute necessity for government action to correct discrimination, he also advocated self-help and self-reliance. Judge Thomas' record illustrates that his aim was to end discrimination and to give all Americans an equal chance to succeed in the workplace.

Judge Thomas has supported constructive forms of affirmative action for the disadvantaged in our society. As he explained to Senator Brown, "throughout my adult life, I have advocated the inclusion of those who have been excluded." (Tr., 9/11/91, at 164.) And in response to a question from Chairman Biden, Judge Thomas stated clearly that "from a policy standpoint, I agree[ ] with affirmative action policies that focus[ ] on disadvantaged minorities and disadvantaged individuals in our society." (Tr., 9/13/91, at 44.) Judge Thomas' record and testimony reflect the efforts that he has made during his career to open the doors to advancement for those who have previously been left out.

* * *

In response to a question from Senator Simon on educational scholarships, Judge Thomas noted that:

When I had the opportunity to establish a program at EEOC that provided scholarships for minorities and women, I did. And it is a program that I think now has about $10 million in endowments. When I had an opportunity to establish a program or to participate in the establishment of a program here in Washington for minority interns, I did. I think that it is important for them to be here, to participate in this process, to learn from this process, to grow. I wish that when I was a kid I had had this opportunity also. (Tr., 9/11/91, at 173.)

As a policymaker, Judge Thomas did not endorse the use of quotas and preferences based on race or gender. As his testimony made clear, Judge Thomas developed his views only after careful consideration of the tension between the desire to remedy past discrimination against women and minorities and the desire to avoid unfair discrimination against innocent third parties:

I wrestled with that tension and I think others wrestled with that tension. The line that I drew was a line that said that we shouldn't have preferences or goals or timetables or quotas. I drew that line personally, as a policy matter, argued that, advocated that for reasons that I thought were important.

One, I thought it was true to the underlying value in [Title VII of the Civil Rights Act of 1964] that would be fair to everyone, and I also drew it because I felt and I have argued over the past 20 years and I felt it important that, whatever we do, we do not undermine the dignity, self-esteem and self-respect of anybody or any group that we are helping. That has been important to me and it has been central to me.

* * *

Judge Thomas' objections to race or group based preferences is well founded. As he stated to Senator Specter:

* * * I think we all know that all disadvantaged people aren't black and all black people aren't disadvantaged. The question is whether or not you are going to pinpoint your policy on people with disadvantages, or are you simply going to do it by race. (Tr. 9/13, a.m., p. 36.)

* * *

Some have intimated that Judge Thomas does not appreciate the reality of job discrimination against women. We believe any such suggestion is completely unfounded and contradicts Judge Thomas' clear record in this area.

In one colloquy, Senator Kennedy referred to a 1987 article in the Atlantic Monthly in which Judge Thomas is described as stating that some statistical hiring disparities could be due to cultural differences between men and women, including personal choices made by some women to take time away from their education to raise families. When asked if he believes these cultural differences fully explain the underrepresentation of women in the workplace, Judge Thomas stated:

> * * * I think it is important to state this unequivocally, and I have said this unequivocally in speech after speech. There is discrimination. There is sex discrimination in our society. My only point in discussing statistics is that I don't think any of us can say that we have all the answers as to why there are statistical disparities.

* * *

> I am not justifying discrimination, nor would I shy away from it. But when we use statistics I think that we need to be careful with those disparities. (Tr., 9/10/91, at 189–90.)

* * *

JUDGE THOMAS HAS ACKNOWLEDGED THE VALUABLE CONTRIBUTIONS OF THOSE IN THE CIVIL RIGHTS MOVEMENT

After outlining his childhood, education, and career in his opening statement, Judge Thomas reflected on how he made it from Pin Point, GA, to the U.S. Senate Caucus Room: "But for the efforts of so many others who have gone before me, I would not be here today. It would be unimaginable. Only by standing on their shoulders could I be here. At each turn in my life, each obstacle confronted, each fork in the road someone came along to help." (Tr., 9/10/91, at 130.) Judge Thomas expressly acknowledged the efforts of civil rights groups and their leaders:

> The civil rights movement, Reverend Martin Luther King and the SCLC [Southern Christian Leadership Conference], Roy Wilkins and the NAACP, Whitney Young and the [National] Urban League, Fannie Lou Haemer, Rosa Parks and Dorothy Hite, they changed society and made it reach out and affirmatively help. I have benefited greatly from their efforts. But for them there would have been no road to travel. (Tr., 9/10/91, at 131.)

* * *

Judge Thomas has consistently recognized his personal debt to the civil rights community. "I also experienced the progress brought about as a result of the civil rights movement," he said at the Wharton School of Business on January 18, 1983. "Without that movement and the laws it inspired, I am certain that I would not be here tonight." (Tr., 9/16/91, at 86.) On October 21, 1982, he described himself as "a beneficiary of the civil rights movement." (Id.) Similarly, Judge Thomas wrote in 1983: "Many of us have walked through doors opened by civil rights leaders, and now you must see that others do the same." (Id.) In these speeches, Judge Thomas praised the heroes and giants of the civil rights movement including Thurgood Marshall.

* * *

With respect to the contentious issue of affirmative action, Judge Thomas testified:

> I think that there is a need for debate. * * * [T]hese issues are so difficult, and the problems are so bad, that we need all of the talent, that we needed all of the ideas possible, not just one point of view.

> I did not feel that * * * I had the chance personally to engage in that debate, and I thought it was a lost opportunity, and I said [so] * * * to the civil rights community. * * * (Tr., 9/16/91, at 78–79.)

As Senator Grassley stated, "it may seem more newsworthy to report the Judge's remarks only when they have been critical of traditional civil rights leadership * * * but it is a false portrait of character being drawn." (Tr., 9/16/91, at 87–88.) That is because "some of [Judge Thomas'] critics who object to his expressed views against reverse discrimination and preference wish to make him look ungrateful." (Tr., 9/16/91, at 87–88.)

* * *

JUDGE THOMAS RECOGNIZES A CONSTITUTIONAL RIGHT OF PRIVACY

Certain members of the committee were keenly interested in Judge Thomas' views on unenumerated rights, most particularly privacy. Although we believe the committee's recommendation should not depend exclusively upon the nominee's opinions concerning any particular issue of substantive law, Judge Thomas' approach to this area clearly fell within the jurisprudential mainstream.

Judge Thomas testified that he believes "there is a right to privacy in the Fourteenth Amendment." (Tr., 9/10/91, at 149.) Following the position staked out by Justice Harlan, Judge Thomas would be inclined to locate the right of privacy specifically in the liberty component of the due process clause. He recognizes that "the marital right to privacy * * * is at the core" of the protections provided by the Due Process Clause and is "a fundamental right" (Tr., 9/11/91, at 178) upon which "the State cannot infringe * * * without a compelling interest" (Tr., 9/10/91, at 149.) More generally, he acknowledged that under the Supreme Court's privacy cases, "the notion of family is one of the most personal and most private relationships that we have in our country." (Id. at 156.)

On the issue of whether the Constitution provides a fundamental right of privacy for nonmarried individuals, Judge Thomas was equally forthcoming. He repeatedly stated that he agreed with the Supreme Court's leading precedent in this area, *Eisenstadt v. Baird,* which found such a right based on application of the equal protection clause in light of the privacy decision in *Griswold v. Connecticut.* The *Eisenstadt* decision also noted, that "[i]f the right to privacy means anything, it is the right of the *individual,* married or single, to be free from unwarranted governmental intrusion into matters so fundamentally affecting a person as the decision whether to bear or beget a child." (Emphasis in original.) * * *

Judge Thomas' endorsement of the privacy rationale of *Eisenstadt* was not a simple reliance on the value of precedent without any independent endorsement of the reasoning in the case or of other rationales for the result. Rather, it was an explicit endorsement of the "privacy rationale" for the result.

We note that Judge Thomas emphasized that in defining the contours of unenumerated rights, like privacy, the Court must proceed with deliberate caution and restraint. Referring to the liberty component of the due process clause, Judge Thomas firmly stated that when judges are "interpreting the more open-ended provision[s] of the Constitution," they "must restrain themselves from imposing their personal views"; rather, such interpretation should be rooted in the "history and tradition of this country." (Tr., 9/13/91, at 117–18.) He pointed out that the importance of looking to history and tradition "is not so much to restrain or constrain * * * the development of important rights and freedoms in our society, but rather to restrain judges so that they do not impose their own will or their own views or their own predispositions in the adjudication process." (Tr., 9/12/91, at 54.)

Some members of the committee pressed Judge Thomas to speculate on the furthest reaches of the right of privacy and to disclose his position on one of the most controversial issues likely to come before the Court— the issue raised in *Roe v. Wade.* Judge Thomas appropriately declined to answer these questions. He recognized, as do we, that any statement to the committee on this hotly contested issue could threaten his ability to remain impartial and could compromise the independence of the judiciary. * * * At the same time, Judge Thomas assured the committee more than once that he would bring an open mind to any privacy case involving abortion: "I have no reason or agenda to prejudge the issue or * * * to rule one way or the other on the issue of abortion." (Id. at 9.) * * *

JUDGE THOMAS SUPPORTS SEPARATION OF POWERS AS PROTECTIVE OF INDIVIDUAL LIBERTY

Judge Thomas was questioned closely by several Senators on the subject of separation of powers. His testimony shows that he attributes a significant value to the doctrine of separation of powers as a bulwark of individual liberty against governmental encroachment. Thus, in connection with the proper roles of the legislature and the judiciary within the scheme of separation of powers, Judge Thomas made clear that he would resist unconstitutional attempts to deprive the Federal courts of the power to review the constitutionality of such asserted encroachments. At the same time, he saw as dangerous the assertion by the judiciary of the power to tax, which traditionally belongs exclusively to the legislative branch.

In connection with questioning about a speech he had made that referred approvingly to the dissent in the independent counsel case, *Morrison v. Olson,* Judge Thomas made plain that he had been concerned to emphasize the importance to individual liberty of well-defined powers and clear lines of accountability for the political branches of the Government. The focus of separation of powers analysis, he explained, should be on the effect that governmental structures had upon individual rights:

> In speech after speech, I talked about the ideals and the first principles of this country, the notion that we have three branches, so that they can be in tension and not impede on the individual. That is what this case is about. At bottom, the case is about an individual who could be in some way, whose rights could be impeded by an individual who is not accountable to one of the political branches. That was the sole point. (Tr., 9/12/91, at 29).

* * *

JUDGE THOMAS UNDERSTANDS THE PROPER ROLE OF THE COURTS

* * *

Judge Thomas' view of the essentially interpretative, nonpolicy-making function of the courts was made clear throughout his testimony. For instance, in response to Senator Thurmond's questioning about the proper role of the judiciary in the scheme of separation of powers, Judge Thomas replied:

> I think, Senator, that the role of a judge is a limited one. It is to interpret the intent of Congress, the legislation of Congress, to apply that in specific cases, and to interpret the Constitution, where called upon, but at no point to impose his or her will or his or her opinion in that process, but, rather, to go to the traditional tools of constitutional interpretation or adjudication, as well as to statutory construction, but not, again, to impose his or her own point of view or his or her predilections or preconceptions. (Tr., 9/10/91, at 167–68.)

* * *

Chairman Biden expressed concerns that Judge Thomas may take an inappropriate, activist approach to economic regulation. We found that Judge Thomas has never indicated that he would be a judicial activist in striking down economic regulations. Such a course would be inconsistent with his approach to judging, discussed above; more specifically, in both his public speeches and his Senate testimony, Judge Thomas has made clear that he does not believe that the Supreme Court should take an activist course to invalidate economic regulations.

For example, in a 1987 speech before the Pacific Research Institute Judge Thomas criticized academics who have argued that the Supreme Court should be more activist in striking down laws that restrict property rights. In his testimony before this committee, Judge Thomas repeated that he did not agree with the activist approach. Responding to Senator Hatch's question as to whether he was going "to go on the bench to be a conservative judicial activist," Judge Thomas testified:

> I do not think the role of the Court is to have an agenda to say, for example, that you believe the Court should change the face of the earth. That is not the Court's role.

> There are some individuals who think, for example, as the Chairman mentioned earlier, that the whole landscape with respect to economic rights should be changed, and I criticize that. (Tr., 9/10/91, at 211.)

* * *

The following statements by Senators Byrd and DeConcini were made on the floor of the Senate after a special Judiciary Committee hearing held to explore Professor Anita Hill's allegations of sexual harassment.

STATEMENT OF SENATOR BYRD
Congressional Record S 14630–14634 October 15, 1991

* * *

MR. BYRD. Mr. President, I do not come to the floor today to debate the confirmation of the nomination of Judge Thomas. I come, rather, to state my viewpoint, believing that I have a responsibility to my constituents, a responsibility to Judge Thomas, a responsibility to my colleagues in the Senate, a responsibility to the people of the United States, and a responsibility to myself, to do so.

I have not previously spoken on this subject. I have indicated from the very beginning to the President and to one or two Senators—Senator Dole in particular—that it was my inclination to vote for the confirmation of Judge Thomas. And my inclination was based on my support of conservative nominees to the courts.

I believe that if there is to be a liberal body it should be the legislative body. I believe that the courts should be conservative. Several days ago, I was impressed to hear Judge Thomas say, as reported in the newspapers, that he believed his role as a judge to be that of interpreting the Constitution and the laws of the United States, not that of rewriting or remaking the laws. I did not like the Warren court, and have so stated many times on this floor, because, in my view, it sought to fulfill the functions of the legislature instead.

I prepared a statement in support of the confirmation of Judge Thomas. And when I left the Hill on last Thursday evening, after working in the Interior Appropriations conferences for 2 days, I left my speech in support of Judge Thomas on my desk, prepared to state today that I was going to vote for Judge Thomas to be an Associate Justice on the U.S. Supreme Court.

Mr. President, I watched the [Hill–Thomas] hearings at home on my television set. I know I have previously said that if we want to improve the education of our young people, we should throw out the television sets, or at least cut down the time that our youngsters view them. But in this instance my daughter asked me what I was going to do with my television set because I sat there glued to that television set all of Friday, into the wee hours of the night Saturday, into the wee hours of the morning. I watched every minute of the hearings with the exception of 15 minutes.

On Sunday Mr. Dole and Mr. Mitchell were on one of the programs, and they went over 15 minutes beyond 12 noon, and that was the reason I missed 15 minutes of what was happening in the large caucus room in the Russell Building.

I taped the testimony of Anita Hill, and I taped the testimony of Judge Thomas. I taped their appearances and I have replayed them.

This is a very extraordinary case. I know of no precedents of this kind; nothing similar, certainly on all fours, or even approaching that.

Millions of eyes all over this country have been watching the hearings. Millions of ears have been listening to the hearings. And, in listening to the call-in shows, C–SPAN, I have listened to what the people are saying. They are interested. They are watching. They are listening. And they have been quick to say that they have made up their minds, in most instances, one way or the other. I have read about the polls indicating what the people out beyond the Beltway are thinking.

Mr. President, I have concluded that I shall vote against the nomination of Judge Thomas.

Before going into the reasons, let me compliment Joe Biden— Senator Biden and Senator Thurmond on the fairness which they demonstrated throughout the televised hearings to the witnesses, to the nominee, and to their colleagues. It was a very difficult position that Senator Biden, as chairman of the committee in particular, had to maintain: Fairness, patience under great pressure, and in some cases under provocation. And so I do want to commend the chairman and ranking member.

I was formerly a member of the Judiciary Committee for several years. I am no longer a member. I am concerned about the atrocious, abominable leak that occurred.

It was a detestable thing. I do not know who is responsible, whether it is a Senator or a staff person. That is not my province, to make a judgment in that situation. But it reflected very adversely upon the committee, and I am sorry that it has reflected on the Senate as a whole. * * *

Now as to my reasons for the conclusion that I have reached to vote against Judge Thomas. I believe Anita Hill. I believe what she said. I watched her on that screen intensely and I replayed, as I have already said, her appearance and her statement. I did not see on that face the knotted brow of satanic revenge. I did not see a face that was contorted with hate. I did not hear a voice that was tremulous with passion. I saw the face of a woman, 1 of 13 in a family of southern blacks who grew up on a farm and who early in her life belonged to the church, who belongs to the church today, and who was evidently reared by religious parents. We all saw her family as they came into the hearing room—the aging father, the kind mother, hugging their daughter, giving her solace and comfort in her hour of trial.

I saw an individual who did not flinch, who showed no nervousness, who spoke calmly throughout, dispassionately and who answered difficult questions. Some thought there were inconsistencies, but a careful reading of the exact language of the questions that were put to her can, at least in one case, and perhaps in others, explain away the appearance of an inconsistency in what she was saying in response to that question—about which some loose talk was subsequently made about possible perjury.

I will not go into further details here, but it is very easy to charge inconsistencies in answering questions. But I thought that Anita Hill was thoughtful, reflective, and truthful. That was my impression. Granted, let us say, that there may have been a few seeming inconsistencies. * * * That does not mean that she was lying; that does not mean that her charges were not true. Perhaps longer hearings would have given her the opportunity and the committee the opportunity to clarify whatever seeming inconsistencies there may have been, to the satisfaction of those who held them.

She was a reluctant witness. There are those who ask why did she not come forward in the previous confirmation hearings? She simply was not contacted in the previous hearings. They ask, why did she wait 10 years? The fact that she waited 10 years does not negate the truth of her assertions. She explained the reasons why she waited. She explained that she was reluctant to come forward, she explained that she did not want to go forward. She explained that she did not even want to be there in that large chamber in the Russell Building that day and at that time. She explained that she had spoken to other individuals very early on—1981, 1982, 1983, 1987—and those same persons came forward later in the hearings and corroborated the fact that she had, indeed, talked about this several years ago.

Why did she not file a claim? She stated her reasons. She said that perhaps she used poor judgment. How many in this Chamber have not used poor judgment in the past?

* * *

There has been loose talk about fantasies. The former dean of Oral Roberts University explained that he had regretted the use of the word "fantasy." * * * It was just a word that he had used on the spur of the moment.

This woman was not fantasizing. As one who has lived a long life and who has had the opportunity to see many people in my life, in all walks of life, I think I have some ability to form an opinion of another person when I listen to that person, when I look into his eyes, to determine in my own view whether he may be fantasizing, whether he is out of his mind, whether he is some kind of nut, whether he is a psychopath. It comes through. None of that came through to me in Anita Hill's statements.

There have been theories about a conspiracy, special interest groups got to her, or she invented this, just something that she made up. A woman spurned, a woman scorned. I do not believe that any reasonable man could carefully look at that woman's face, listen to what she had to say, set in the whole context of the circumstances, and believe that she was inventing her story—suddenly, at the very last moment. She had no knowledge that anyone was going to contact her about this. This came out of the blue.

Truth is a powerful thing, and sometimes it is a strange thing. To those who wish to think of a confirmation hearing as a court case, as having the surroundings and carrying the environment of trial, one may see things perhaps differently. This is not a court case. This is a confirmation hearing. They say, well, there was nobody else who said this; there was no pattern. Would it not be reasonable to believe that there would be a pattern if this man were like this? Would he not be saying this thing to others?

Well, who knows? Perhaps he did. I am not going to say he did. I do not know. But since the flights of imagination seemed to be rampant around here, one might imagine there was somebody else. And even so, if there were no others, is it not possible that this could have happened in this case, that this could have happened just this once? Of course, it is possible.

One may say, well, it was not probable. One does not know about that.

Mr. President, what are my other reasons, aside from believing Anita Hill? I was offended by Judge Thomas' stonewalling the committee. He said he wanted to come back before the committee and clear his name. That is what I heard. He wanted to "clear his name." Well, he was given the opportunity to clear his name, but he did not even listen to the principal witness, the only witness against him. He said he did not listen to her. He was "tired of lies."

What kind of judicial temperament does that demonstrate? He did not even listen to her. What Senator can imagine that, if he were the object of scrutiny in such a situation, he would not have listened to the witness so that he would know how best to respond, how to defend himself, how to clear his name? But, instead, Judge Thomas came back and said he did not even listen. He set up a wall when he did that, because it made it extremely difficult for members of the committee to ask him what he thought about this or that which she said?

He wanted to clear his name, he said. I know that hindsight is great, and I would imagine that most of the Members of that committee now wished they had asked for a week's delay. That should have been done. That opportunity is gone. Perhaps much of this travail could have been avoided with a week's delay and by calling in the two persons—principal persons here—and talking with them in private.

But again, that is water over the dam. We now have only what happened, the circumstances, to deal with. Judge Thomas asked to come back to clear his name. I was extremely disappointed and astonished, as a matter of fact, when he came back to the committee and said he had not listened—had not listened—to Anita Hill.

By refusing to watch her testimony, he put up a wall between himself and the committee. How could the committee question him? How could the committee learn the truth if the accused refused even to listen to the charges? What does this say about the conduct of a judge? He is a judge now, a circuit court of appeals judge.

What does this say about him, the conduct of a judge, a man whose primary function in his professional life is to listen to the evidence, listen to both sides, whether plaintiff or defendant in a civil case, or a prosecutor and the accused in a criminal case?

I have substantial doubts after this episode about the judicial temperament of Judge Thomas, doubts that I did not have prior to last weekend's hearings. How can we have confidence if he is confirmed that he will be an objective judge, willing to decide cases based on the evidence presented if, in the one case that will matter most to him in his lifetime, he shut his eyes and closed his ears and closed his mind, and did not even bother to watch the sworn testimony of Anita Hill?

She was testifying under oath. He professed to want nothing more than to clear his name. Yet he could not be bothered to even listen to the allegations from the person making the allegations.

Another reason why I shall vote against Judge Thomas: He not only effectively stonewalled the committee; he just, in the main, made speeches before the committee; he managed his own defense by charging that the committee proceeded to "high-tech lynchings of uppity blacks."

Mr. President, in my judgment, that was an attempt to shift ground. That was an attempt to fire the prejudices of race hatred, and shift the debate to a matter involving race.

I frankly was offended by his injection of racism into the hearings. This was a diversionary tactic intended to divert both the committee's and the American public's attention away from the issue at hand, the issue being, which one is telling the truth? I was offended. I thought we were past that stage in this country.

So instead of focusing on the charges and attempting to be helpful to the committee in clearing his name, he invoked racism. Of course, he was embittered by the leak, and he was justified to so state. But, instead, he indicted the whole committee, he indicted the Senate, and he indicted the process. Not everybody in the Senate is guilty of leaking material. I did not leak it; I did not leak anything to the press. But he impugned me. And he impugned you, Senator Sasser; you are not on the committee; he impugned you, Senator Pryor, and you are not on the committee; and you Senator Bradley, and you are not on the committee. He did not make any distinctions. He did not discriminate among us. We were all guilty. He was bitter at the Senate, at the committee, at the process.

He should have been bitter at the person or persons who leaked whatever it was that was leaked, and he could have so stated in the strongest terms. But instead, he lectured the committee. He found fault with the "process." The process is a constitutional process that was determined by our forefathers in Philadelphia in 1787. That is the process.

And it is because of that process that Judge Thomas was given his day to clear his name. It is because of the process that he was able to overcome poverty. It was because of the process that he was able to stay out of prison in this country, that he was able to get that fine education. It was because of the process. It was because of the process that he was heard before the committee and given an opportunity to answer questions, given an opportunity to clear his name. That is the process.

If we are only talking about a leak, then that is something else. But one can condemn leaks without condemning the committee, without condemning the Senate, and without condemning the process.

He tried to shift ground. I think it was blatant intimidation, and, I am sorry to say, I think it worked. I sat there and I wondered: Who is going to ask him some tough questions? Are they afraid of him?

He said to Senator Metzenbaum, "God is my judge; you are not my judge, Senator." Well of course, God is also my judge. I am not God. But I do have a vote. And I have a responsibility to make a determination as to how I shall vote. That kind of talk, that kind of arrogance will never get my vote.

* * *

Leaks are deplorable. They are reprehensible, and I know we all are going to say, let us do something about it. But human nature has never changed. * * *

There will always be leaks.

We ought to do whatever we can to prevent them. And if we can find the Senator who, if, let us say, if it was a Senator, and that can be proved, I will be among the first to vote to expel him. If it was a staff member, I cannot vote to expel him. I simply think he ought to be fired.

But there will always be leaks—always. But the unfortunate way in which this information has come to light should not be enough to cause us to disregard the possible relevancy * * * and the possible accuracy of a charge which so pertains to the character and the temperament of an individual being considered for this august and powerful position.

Let me say, Mr. President, to my colleagues, this is a powerful position to which he is being appointed, if he is appointed, and I do not have any doubt that the Senate will confirm him. I said I did not come here to debate the matter. I do not think I am going to change anyone's minds. But I am going to make my statement. Judge Thomas made his statements in no uncertain terms. So I am going to make mine.

I want to compliment the chairman. I do not think the chairman was intimidated. I watched him carefully. If a person wants to clear his name, why should the committee members be intimidated by that person? If I had previously said that I would vote for him, I would have changed my position on that committee.

But so many of the Democrats had already said they were against him. They had already voted against him. So they could not help that. They did not realize at the time that this was coming. But to an extent, their previous vote had put them in a difficult position to question because everybody knew where they were coming from. * * *

I am very sorry that the matter of race was injected, not in an effort to clear one's name, but in an effort to shift the ground. So that, instead of making an effort to clear his name in the minds of the committee members and in the minds of Senators who were not on the committee, he shifted the blame to the process and to race prejudice.

I think it is preposterous. A black American woman was making the charge against a black American male. Where is the racism? Nonsense; nonsense!

* * *

Mr. President, this question of giving the benefit of the doubt, I have heard it said, well, if you have a doubt against this—and it is obvious nobody can really say with certitude as to which one is telling the truth, the whole truth, and nothing but the truth, so help him or her God—then you should give the benefit of the doubt to Judge Thomas. He is the nominee.

Mr. President, of all the excuses for voting for Judge Thomas, I think that is the weakest one that I have heard. When are Senators going to learn that this proceeding is not being made in a court of law? This is not a civil case; it is not a criminal case wherein there are various standards of doubt, beyond a reasonable doubt, so on and so on; if you have a doubt, it should be given to Thomas.

Why? This is a confirmation process, not a court case. We are talking about someone who was nominated for one of the most powerful positions in this country. Some say, he will only be one of nine men. But suppose it is a divided Court, four to four in a given case. That one man will make the difference. Suppose it is a divided Court and he does not show up for some reason, he does not vote on a matter. A tie is in essence a decision in some cases.

His decision will affect millions of Americans, black, white, minorities, the majority, women, men, children, in all aspects of living, Social Security, workmen's compensation, whatever it might be that might come to the Supreme Court of the United States. That one man in such an instance will have more power than 100 Senators, more power in that instance than the President of the United States. This is not a justice of the peace. This is a man who is being nominated to go on the highest court of the land. Give him the benefit of the doubt? He has no particular right to this seat. No individual has a particular right to a Supreme Court seat. Why give him the benefit of the doubt?

Such an honor of sitting on the Supreme Court of the United States should be reserved for only those who are most qualified and those whose temperament and character best reflect judicial and personal commitments to excellence.

A credible charge of the type that has been leveled at Judge Thomas is enough, in my view, to mandate that we ought to look for a more exemplary nominee. If we are going to give the benefit of the doubt, let us give it to the Court. Let us give it to the country. Judge Thomas professed, "You may kill me, look what you are doing to me," but "what you are doing to my country."

So, I will take that on. If Judge Thomas is rejected, he will not lose his life. He will not lose his property. He will not lose his liberty. He will go on being a judge of the appellate court, the youngest judge on the court, driving his car, mowing his grass, going to McDonalds, eating a Big Mac, and living his life, watching his son play football.

Now I do not say any of those things pejoratively, but those are his words. So why should we give the benefit of the doubt to him? He will not have to worry about a job. You cannot take his job away from him except through the impeachment process. He will be a judge for life. And his salary is inviolable. You cannot cut it.

But, he will be on that Court 30 years, if he lives out the psalmist's span of life. He will affect the lives of millions. He will make decisions which will impact on their ability to own a car or even to eat a Big Mac. Their liberty, their lives, their property, will be in his hands.

Now, if there is a cloud of doubt, this is the last chance. He is not running for the U.S. Senate, when there would be another chance in 6 years to pass judgment on him. He is not running for the House of Representatives, wherein there would be another chance in 2 years. He is not even running for office. He has been nominated to the Supreme

Court of the United States, and if he is not rejected—I believe he will not be rejected; I think too many have made up their mind, I think too many have been swayed with this argument about the benefit of the doubt—this is the last clear chance, to use a bit of legal terminology, this is it. The country will live with this decision for the next 30 years.

I realize it is possible that in the process a man could have been wronged. If it were a criminal trial, it would be different. That is what it is not.

Now then this final argument that I saw in the Washington Post editorial this morning to the effect that * * * in a case of treason, one witness is not enough. * * * You have to have two witnesses to a treasonous act. The editorial continues, we have a tradition "which holds that the unproven word of a single accuser is not enough to establish guilt." And the closing sentence, "But in these circumstances history gives us too many reasons not to act on the unproven word of a single accuser." Again, the editorial is confusing a confirmation process with a court setting.

I disagree with the statement, "History does not give us any reasons not to act on the unproven word of a single accuser in the confirmation of a nominee."

* * * Let us not get all confused about what we are doing. This is a confirmation process. And if there is a doubt, I say resolve it in the interest of our country and its future, and in the interest of the Court. Let us not have a cloud of doubt for someone who is going to go on that court and be there for many years.

* * *

Perhaps we need to clean up the process if we can. But the "process" is a constitutional process, and it has done us well for over two centuries. And as far as I am concerned the benefit of the doubt will go to the Court and to my children and to my grandchildren and to my country.

* * *

STATEMENT OF SENATOR DeCONCINI
Congressional Record S 14951–14953 October 22, 1991

* * *

THE NOMINATION OF JUDGE CLARENCE THOMAS

MR. DECONCINI. Mr. President, the following is a compilation of my statements regarding the nomination of Judge Clarence Thomas throughout the confirmation process.

As a result of the allegations of Professor Hill, the Senate, by unanimous consent, postponed the vote on the confirmation of Judge Thomas last week and directed the Senate Judiciary Committee to investigate and conduct hearings on the allegations.

The Judiciary Committee has been highly criticized for its action on these allegations before the Judiciary Committee vote on September 27. Let me just say that many have lost sight of the condition of confidentiality that Professor Hill demanded of Chairman Biden. Ultimately, the decision of her confidentiality was taken from Professor Hill when her confidential statement to the chairman was leaked to the press. Unfortunately, the process that ensued has, I fear, scarred Judge Thomas and Professor Hill for life—they have both been through a dreadful ordeal.

The allegations of Professor Hill are extremely serious: That Judge Thomas sexually harassed her—that he used vile, demeaning, and disgusting language with her in conjunction with his quest to date her while she was employed by him.

Unfortunately, despite the extensive investigation and exhaustive hearings—amounting to 32 hours and 23 witnesses, the results are inconclusive.

Claims of sexual harassment are difficult to prove because there are often no witnesses. However, by the same token, those accused of sexual harassment have virtually no defense because they cannot prove a negative. The claims of Professor Hill are egregious but so too is the injustice perpetrated when we attempt to adjudicate a 10–year–old claim through a political process that deprives an accused of the most basic safeguards of due process and fairness.

For this Senator, the burden of proof was on the accuser, Professor Hill. In this country, it is a basic right of our legal system that the benefit of the doubt rests with the accused. These are very serious allegations of personal conduct. This is not a question of ideology or judicial philosophy. It is for that reason that these charges must meet the burden of proof that we afford every defendant in our legal system.

Granted, this was not a court of law with the rules of evidence and the usual protection for a defendant. But that does not lessen the need to require these allegations to overcome the presumption that Judge Thomas is not guilty of these allegations. And those who suggest that the burden of proof is not on Professor Hill would have to deny that Judge Thomas was on trial this past week. Clearly Judge Thomas' integrity and reputation were on trial.

The evidence supporting the allegations of Professor Hill do not meet any reasonable burden of proof that they must overcome. The allegations cannot stand by themselves and what little supporting evidence that has been provided is inadequate.

The conclusion does not have to be made that one of the two is right and the other is wrong. The decision is whether the evidence that was presented over the last few days is conclusive. And here it is not.

I have not been convinced that Professor Hill's allegations occurred. And for that reason I cannot withdraw my support for the nomination of Judge Thomas to the U.S. Supreme Court. To do otherwise would open up the nominations process to all sorts of unsubstantiated allegations.

Professor Hill alleges that Clarence Thomas' sexual harassment commenced at the Office of Civil Rights for the Department of Education during the winter of 1981. In 1983, Clarence Thomas became the Chairman of the Equal Employment Opportunity Commission [EEOC]. Shortly thereafter, Anita Hill followed him to the EEOC. Professor Hill testified that after being subjected to his verbal assaults at the Office of Civil Rights she never sought alternative employment. Moreover, she asserted that when he left the Department of Education to become the Chairman of the EEOC that she would not have a job. Therefore, she had no recourse but to follow him to his new place of employment.

However, Ms. Berry, a personnel specialist at the Office of Civil Rights testified that as a "schedule A" employee Anita Hill had job security and was informed of her employment rights when she assumed the position. In addition, Mr. Singleton, Clarence Thomas' successor as the Assistant Secretary for the Office of Civil Rights, submitted an affidavit that stated that not only would Anita Hill continue to have a position she would have been able to maintain the same position that she occupied at the time of Clarence Thomas' departure. I wondered if perhaps she didn't realize that she had job security. However, Ms. Berry said that she was informed of her employment rights. Even if she didn't know wouldn't someone, who has been victimized by verbal assaults, ask?

* * *

One victim of sexual harassment testified that it is not unusual for a victim of sexual harassment to follow her harasser. However, another victim of sexual harassment, Ms. Brown, moved me very deeply when she testified most passionately:

> Let me assure you that the last thing I would ever have done is follow the man who did this to a new job, call him on the phone or voluntarily share the same air space ever again.

The claims of Professor Hill portrayed a very dark side of Clarence Thomas, a side that had not previously surfaced through five FBI background investigations and heated confirmation hearings for Government positions. If this dark side of Clarence Thomas existed, surely someone other than Anita Hill would have seen it. Surely someone, including Anita Hill who witnessed this dark side would have found him unsuitable to head the EEOC, the agency that is responsible for enforcing sexual harassment laws, or unsuitable for the Federal Court of Appeals of the D.C. Circuit that is responsible for adjudicating the rights of victims.

Due to Clarence Thomas' conservative ideology, his previous confirmations have been highly contested—this is not a man who has eluded scrutiny but rather has been in the public eye for quite some time. Why is Professor Hill the only one who witnessed his cruelty and abuse? Opponents of Clarence Thomas would say that Professor Hill is not alone; Angela Wright has also come forward, within the last week, and made allegations of sexual behavior in the office.

However, Angela Wright was fired by Clarence Thomas. By her own admission she was fired because she didn't accomplish the job that Clarence Thomas directed. Regarding her dismissal, Judge Thomas testified that he was dissatisfied with her job performance and he finally decided to fire her when she called someone a faggot, a slur that was unacceptable in the workplace. Moreover, after she came forward and requested to testify against Clarence Thomas she withdrew this request at the last minute. In my judgment, this places her credibility in serious doubt.

Many have attempted to reconcile these inconsistencies by second guessing Professor Hill's motivation to make a claim that is anything other than truthful. I leave such analysis to the experts. However, her behavior has placed, in this Senator, at least a shadow of a doubt regarding the weight of the evidence to substantiate her allegations.

I know that many women believe that we in the Senate, and men in general just don't get it—we don't understand. I for one agree that few men can truly understand the quiet desperation experienced by victims of sexual harassment. However, I believe that we do get it. My mother was a victim of sexual harassment and was fired for rejecting her boss' sexual overtures. Believe me, as a son knowing what happened to his mother, I get it. The use of power in the workplace over women in order to extract sexual gratification is despicable and must not be tolerated. The victimization of women at work, at home, and in the streets, is something that must be stopped.

* * *

I believe that Judge Thomas and Professor Hill have been pawns in a calculated game staged by interest groups that believe that the ends justify the means. If these groups are successful in their objective of defeating Judge Thomas, then these groups are the only winners—and the price for them was cheap because Professor Hill, Judge Thomas, and the American public are picking up the tab.

* * *

4. *The Nomination of Ruth Bader Ginsburg*

On March 19, 1993, Justice Byron White announced that he would be resigning at the end of the 1992 Term. By making his announcement several months before the end of the term, Justice White gave the newly-elected President the luxury of several months of deliberation. When resignations are announced at the end of the Term, Presidents frequently feel pressure to nominate someone quickly so that there is enough time to have the confirmation hearings and seat the new appointee before the start of the next term on the first Monday of October.[1]

1. Occasionally, Justices give the President advance, confidential notice several months before they publicly announce their retirement at the end of the term. Justice

President Clinton took advantage of the time allotted and on June 14, 1993 nominated Judge Ruth Bader Ginsburg, Circuit Judge on the U.S. Court of Appeals for the D.C. Circuit, the same court from which two of her to-be colleagues, Justices Scalia and Thomas, had come.

After a relatively short period, the Senate began its confirmation hearings on July 20, 1993. Judge Ginsburg, in her opening statement, gave her view of the proceedings.

SENATE HEARING, JULY 20, 1993
OPENING STATEMENT BY RUTH BADER GINSBURG

We—this Committee and I—are about to embark on many hours of conversation. You have arranged this hearing to aid you in the performance of a vital task—to prepare your Senate colleagues for consideration of my nomination.

The record of the Constitutional Convention shows that the delegates had initially entrusted the power to appoint federal judges, most prominently, Supreme Court Justices, not to the President, but to you and your colleagues—to the Senate, acting alone. Only in the waning days of the Convention did the framers settle on a nomination role for the President, and an advice and consent role for the Senate.

The text of the Constitution, as finally formulated, makes no distinction between the appointment process for Supreme Court Justices, and the process for other officers of the United States, for example, cabinet officers. But as history bears out, you and Senators past have sensibly considered appointments in relation to the appointee's task.

Federal judges may long outlast the President who appoints them. They may serve as long as they can do the job, as the Constitution says, they may remain in office "during good Behaviour." Supreme Court Justices, particularly, participate in shaping a lasting body of constitutional decisions; they continuously confront matters on which the framers left many things unsaid, unsettled, or uncertain. For that reason, when the Senate considers a Supreme Court nomination, the Senators are properly concerned about the nominee's capacity to serve the nation, not just for the here and now, but over the long term.

You have been supplied, in the five weeks since the President announced my nomination, with hundreds of pages about me, and thousands of pages I have penned—my writings as a law teacher, mainly about procedure; ten years of briefs filed when I was a courtroom advocate of the equal stature of men and women before the law; numerous speeches and articles on that same theme; thirteen years of opinions—well over 700 of them—decisions I made as a member of the U.S. Court of Appeals for the District of Columbia Circuit; several

Potter Stewart, for example, told President Reagan on April 21, 1981 that he intended to retire at the end of the term; the public was not informed until June 18 of that year. Ed Magnuson, "The Brethren's First Sister: A Supreme Court Nominee and A Triumph for Common Sense," Time Magazine, July 20, 1981, at 8.

comments on the roles of judges and lawyers in our legal system. That body of material, I know, has been examined by the Committee with care. It is the most tangible, reliable indicator of my attitude, outlook, approach, and style. I hope you will judge my qualifications principally on that written record spanning thirty-four years, and that you will find in it assurance that I am prepared to do the hard work, and to exercise the informed, independent judgment that Supreme Court decisionmaking entails.

I think of these proceedings much as I do of the division between the written record and briefs, on the one hand, and oral argument on the other hand, in appellate tribunals. The written record is by far the more important component in an appellate court's decisionmaking, but the oral argument often elicits helpful clarifications and concentrates the judges' minds on the character of the decision they are called upon to make.

There is, of course, this critical difference. You are well aware that I come to this proceeding to be judged as a judge, not as an advocate. Because I am and hope to continue to be a judge, it would be wrong for me to say or preview in this legislative chamber how I would cast my vote on questions the Supreme Court may be called upon to decide. Were I to rehearse here what I would say and how I would reason on such questions, I would act injudiciously.

Judges in our system are bound to decide concrete cases, not abstract issues; each case is based on particular facts and its decision should turn on those facts and the governing law, stated and explained in light of the particular arguments the parties or their representatives choose to present. A judge sworn to decide impartially can offer no forecasts, no hints, for that would show not only disregard for the specifics of the particular case, it would display disdain for the entire judicial process.

Similarly, because you are considering my capacity for independent judging, my personal views on how I would vote on a publicly debated issue were I in your shoes—were I a legislator—are not what you will be closely examining. As Justice Oliver Wendell Holmes counseled: "[O]ne of the most sacred duties of a judge is not to read [her] convictions into [the C]onstitution[ ]." I have tried, and I will continue to try, to follow the model Justice Holmes set in holding that duty sacred.

I see this hearing, as I know you do, as a grand opportunity once again to reaffirm that civility, courtesy, and mutual respect properly keynote our exchanges. Judges, I am mindful, owe the elected branches—the Congress and the President—respectful consideration of how court opinions affect their responsibilities. And I am heartened by legislative branch reciprocal sensitivity. As one of you said two months ago at a meeting of the Federal Judges Association: "We in Congress must be more thoughtful and deliberate in order to enable judges to do their job more effectively."

As for my own deportment or, in the Constitution's words, "good Behaviour," I prize advice received on this nomination from a dear friend, Frank Griffin, a recently retired Justice of the Supreme Court of Ireland. Justice Griffin wrote: "Courtesy to and consideration for one's colleagues, the legal profession, and the public are among the greatest attributes a judge can have."

It is fitting, as I conclude this opening statement, to express my deep respect for, and abiding appreciation to Justice Byron R. White for his thirty-one years and more of fine service on the Supreme Court. In acknowledging his colleagues' good wishes on the occasion of his retirement, Justice White wrote that he expects to sit on U.S. Courts of Appeals from time to time, and so to be a consumer of, instead of a participant in, Supreme Court opinions. He expressed a hope shared by all lower court judges; he hoped "the [Supreme] Court's mandates will be clear [and] crisp, * * * leav[ing] as little room as possible for disagreement about their meaning." If confirmed, I will take that counsel to heart and strive to write opinions that both "get it right" and "keep it tight."

———

After three days of hearing, appropriately described as a "love-fest," the Senate Judiciary Committee voted unanimously to recommend the confirmation of Judge Ginsburg. As one of the members of the Senate Judiciary Committee, Senator Howell Heflin, noted: "Back-slapping ha[d] replaced back-stabbing." [2] Even Senator Strom Thurmond, who had voted against Ruth Ginsburg's confirmation to the U.S. Court of Appeals thirteen years earlier, agreed to this nomination. One week after the committee's vote, Judge Ginsburg was confirmed by the whole Senate by a vote of 96–3, joining Sandra Day O'Connor to become the second woman to serve on the Supreme Court.

In reading the following excerpts from the Report of the Judiciary Committee, examine Judge Ginsburg's method of dealing with the difficult question of how someone with a substantial track record who has written numerous controversial academic articles, legal briefs, and judicial opinions can answer substantive questions without impairing her ability to make independent judgments once on the high court. In particular, compare her answers regarding the death penalty with those regarding abortion.

Also consider Senator Pressler's separate statement concerning his disappointment with Judge Ginsburg's lack of knowledge concerning "Indian Country issues." Is it reasonable to expect knowledge in all areas that come before the Court, before one votes to confirm a nominee? Is his threat concerning future nominees appropriate?

2. Joan Biskupic, "Ginsburg Stresses Value of Incremental Change; Nominee's First Day of Hearings Is Relaxed," Washington Post, July 21, 1993, at A6.

Also explore what Senator Cohen might have in mind when, in his separate statement, he suggests that the committee "work on a bipartisan basis to establish responsible guidelines for what will be expected of future nominees." What might such guidelines look like? Would they be useful? Constitutional?

Does Judge Ginsburg's successful confirmation process belie the predictions made after the hearings of Judge Bork and Judge Souter that henceforth only "stealth candidates" with little or no paper trails can be successfully confirmed? Or was this "lovefest" simply the result of a Democratic President facing a Democratic Senate? Are there lessons that future Presidents and Senators can and should draw from this experience?

NOMINATION OF RUTH BADER GINSBURG TO BE AN ASSOCIATE JUSTICE OF THE UNITED STATES SUPREME COURT

August 5, 1993 (legislative day, June 30), 1993.—Ordered to be printed
S.Exec.Rep. 103–6, 103d Cong., 1st Sess. (1993)

MR. BIDEN, from the Committee on the Judiciary,
submitted the following
REPORT
together with
ADDITIONAL VIEWS

The Committee on the Judiciary, to which was referred the nomination of Judge Ruth Bader Ginsburg to be an Associate Justice of the U.S. Supreme Court, having considered the same, reports favorably thereon, a quorum being present, by a vote of 18 yeas and 0 nays, with the recommendation that the nomination be approved.

CONTENTS

INTRODUCTION

The Senate Judiciary Committee unanimously recommends the confirmation of Judge Ruth Bader Ginsburg to be an Associate Justice of the U.S. Supreme Court. This unanimity results from two facts: First, Judge Ginsburg's qualifications and judicial temperament are indisputable. Second, and most important, Judge Ginsburg's extensive judicial record and style mark her as a true consensus candidate.

Judge Ginsburg is a nominee who holds a rich vision of what our Constitution's promises of liberty and equality mean, balanced by a measured approach to the job of judging. She accepts the Constitution as an evolving charter of government and liberty—as a limited grant of power *from* the people *to* the government—not a narrow list of enumerated rights. At the same time, she speaks and practices judicial restraint, understanding that a judge must work within our constitutional system—respecting history, precedent, and the respective roles of the other two branches.

The balance that Ruth Bader Ginsburg achieves—between her vision of what our society can and should become, and the limits on a judge's ability to hurry that evolution along—will serve her well on the Supreme Court.

II. THE NOMINEE

Judge Ginsburg was born on March 15, 1933, in Brooklyn, NY. She received her bachelor of arts degree from Cornell University in 1954. Judge Ginsburg pursued her legal education, first at Harvard Law School and then at Columbia Law School, receiving her juris doctor in 1959.

From 1959 to 1961, the nominee served as law clerk to Judge Edmund L. Palmieri, U.S. district court judge for the Southern District of New York.

From 1961 to 1962, the nominee was a research associate for the Project on International Procedure at Columbia Law School, and from 1962 to 1963, she served as the associate director of that program.

From 1963 to 1966, the nominee was an assistant professor at Rutgers, the State University School of Law. From 1966 to 1969 she was an associate professor and from 1969 to 1972, the nominee was a full professor at Rutgers.

From 1972 to 1980, the nominee was a professor at Columbia University School of Law.

From 1973 to 1974, she was a consultant to the U.S. Commission on Civil Rights.

From 1972 to 1973, Judge Ginsburg was the director of the Women's Rights Project at the American Civil Liberties Union; from 1973 to 1980, she served as a general counsel.

From 1977 to 1978, the nominee was a fellow at the Center for Advanced Study in Behavioral Sciences in Stanford, CA.

In 1980, President Carter nominated Judge Ginsburg to the U.S. Court of Appeals for the District of Columbia. She has served on that court from 1980 to the present. President Clinton nominated her to the Supreme Court on June 14, 1993.

III. THE AMERICAN BAR ASSOCIATION'S EVALUATION

A. *The Standing Committee unanimously gave Judge Ginsburg its highest rating of "Well Qualified"*

The American Bar Association's (ABA) Standing Committee on the Federal Judiciary, chaired by William E. Willis, Esq., unanimously found Judge Ginsburg to be "Well Qualified," its highest rating. (Letter from William E. Willis to Chairman Biden at 1 (July 15, 1993) (on file with the Senate Committee on the Judiciary).) * * *

PART 2: JUDGE GINSBURG'S JUDICIAL PHILOSOPHY AND CONSTITUTIONAL METHODOLOGY

I. JUDGE GINSBURG BELIEVES THE CONSTITUTION IS AN EVOLVING DOCUMENT

Judge Ginsburg's written record and testimony before the committee amply demonstrate that she believes the Constitution is a living document that adjusts to modern notions of ordered society to retain its vitality. She rejects any formulation of original intent that would freeze the Constitution in time, limiting its broad clauses to situations specifically contemplated by the framers. For example, in a speech given to the Eighth Circuit Judicial Conference, she said:

"[A] too strict 'jurisprudence of the framers' original intent' seems to me unworkable, and not what Madison or Hamilton would espouse were they with us today. It cannot be, for example, that although the founding fathers never dreamed of the likes of Dolly Madison or even the redoubtable Abigail Adams ever serving on a jury, we would today say it is therefore necessary or proper to keep women off juries.

"We still have, cherish, and live under our eighteenth century Constitution because, through a combination of three factors or forces— change in society's practices, constitutional amendment, and judicial intepretation—a broadened system of participatory democracy has evolved, one in which we take just pride. (Ruth Bader Ginsburg, Remarks on Women Becoming Part of the Constitution, Address Before the Eighth Circuit Judicial Conference (July 17, 1987), in 6 Law & Ineq.J. 17, 17 (1988) [hereinafter cited as 'Remarks'])."

Judge Ginsburg recognizes that our Constitution has grown from a document with a cramped view of "We, the People" to one increasingly inclusive of traditionally excluded social groups, including women and racial minorities. In her view, this evolution toward a more inclusive understanding of our Constitution's meaning is consistent with the broad intent of the framers. She believes that judges do their jobs properly when they act in accordance with the framers' "original understanding," but she does not find that "understanding" confining.

The nominee believes the framers understood that the Constitution would not remain static, constrained by the specific notions of the framers themselves. She believes they intended the Constitution to be subject to a careful process of extension—either through amendment, interpretation, or social practice. (Ginsburg, The James Madison Lecture on Constitutional Law, Speaking in a Judicial Voice, Address Before the New York University School of Law (March 9, 1993) in N.Y.U.L.Rev. (forthcoming 1993) (manuscript on file with the Senate Commission on the Judiciary) [hereinafter cited as "Madison Lecture"].) Supporting her view is her recitation of the history of our Nation. That history is one in which the framers contemplated continued slavery, refused women the franchise, and imposed property qualifications on men seeking to vote. Through the process of extension she describes, however, the Constitution grew—ultimately abolishing slavery and giving women the right to vote through amendment, recognizing women's equality through interpretation, and eliminating most voting qualifications other than age and citizenship through a combination of amendment, legislation, and social convention.

The nominee further articulated her view of the framers' original understanding in testimony before the committee. Judge Ginsburg testified in response to a question from the Chairman:

"[T]he immediate implementation in the days of the Founding Fathers in many respects was limited. 'We the People' was not then what it is today. The most eloquent speaker on that subject was Justice Thurgood Marshall when, during the series of Bicentennials when songs of praise of the Constitution were sung, he reminded us that the Constitution's immediate implementation, even its text, had certain limitations, blind spots, blots on our record. But he said that the beauty of this Constitution is that, through a combination of interpretation, constitutional amendment, laws passed by Congress, 'We the People' has grown ever larger. So now it includes people who were once held in bondage. It includes women who were left out of the political community at the start.

"So I hope that begins to answer your question. The view of the Framers, their large view, I think was expansive. Their immediate view was tied to the circumstances in which they lived. (Transcript, July 20, at 112.)"

When Senator Hatch asked the nominee whether she agreed with the statement, "the only legitimate way for a judge to go about defining the law is by attempting to discern what those who made the law intended," the nominee replied:

"I think all people could agree with that, but as I tried to say in response to the Chairman * * *, trying to divine what the Framers long ago intended, at least I have to look at that two ways. One is what they might have intended immediately for their day, and one is their larger expectation that the Constitution was meant to govern, not for the passing hour, but for the expanding future. And I know no better illustration of that than to take the great man who wrote the Declaration of Independence, who also said, for our state, a pure democracy, there would still be excluded from our deliberations women who, to prevent depravation of morals or ambiguity of issues, should not mix promiscuously in gatherings of men.

"Now I do believe that Thomas Jefferson, were he alive today, would say that women are equal citizens. * * * So I see an immediate intent about how an ideal is going to be recognized at a given time and place, but a larger aspiration as our society improves. I think the Framers were intending to create a more perfect union that would become ever more perfect over time. (Transcript, July 20, at 131–32)."

In short, Judge Ginsburg believes that the effort to divine the framers' specific original intent is an appropriate starting point in constitutional review, but she rejects the notion that the inquiry ends where it begins.

II. JUDGE GINSBURG ADVOCATES JUDICIAL RESTRAINT

One theme that emerged from the committee's extensive review of Judge Ginsburg's written record, as well as her testimony, is her belief in a judicial branch that moves incrementally. A careful adherent to a case-by-case method of gradual evolution in the law, Judge Ginsburg believes the Court should move in "measured motions." This view is exemplified by the following testimony from her opening statement:

"My approach [to judging], I believe, is neither liberal nor conservative. Rather, it is rooted in the place of the judiciary, of judges, in our democratic society. The Constitution's preamble speaks first of 'We, the People,' and then of their elected representatives. The judiciary is third in line and it is placed apart from the political fray so that its members can judge fairly, impartially, in accordance with the law, and without fear about the animosity of any pressure group.

"In Alexander Hamilton's words, the mission of judges is 'to secure a steady, upright, and impartial administration of the laws.' I would add that the judge should carry out that function without fanfare. She should decide the case before her without reaching out to cover cases not yet seen. She should be ever mindful, as Judge and then Justice

Benjamin Nathan Cardozo said, 'Justice is not to be taken by storm. She is to be wooed by slow advances.' (Transcript, July 20 at 91–92.)"

Judge Ginsburg has written extensively about how the judicial branch should take incremental steps, allowing legislatures and society to address and respond to court-ordered changes. In her Madison Lecture, she articulated a view about how judges should go about interpreting our evolving Constitution to accommodate modern circumstances. There is one overarching theme: the Court should generally lay markers along the road to doctrinal change, allowing public debate and legislative acceptance to occur, rather than making abrupt changes that lack secure foundations. She wrote, "[W]ithout taking giant strides and thereby risking a backlash too forceful to contain, the Court, through constitutional adjudication, can reinforce or signal a green light for a social change." (Madison Lecture at 36–37.)

As an example of this process at work, the nominee cited the gender equality cases of the 1970's, from *Reed v. Reed,* 404 U.S. 71 (1971), through *Craig v. Boren,* 429 U.S. 190 (1976). Prior to *Reed,* the Supreme Court had never found gender discrimination unconstitutional under the 14th amendment. In this line of cases, however, the Court developed a new theory of gender equality under the Constitution—ultimately concluding in *Craig* that gender classifications would be subjected to an intermediate standard of equal protection scrutiny. Each of these cases, beginning with *Reed* and culminating in *Craig,* was, in her view, a "pathmarker" toward the constitutional principle of gender equality. The nominee wrote of this development:

"For the most part, the Court was neither out in front of, nor did it hold back, social change. Instead, what occurred was what engineers might call a 'positive feedback' process, with the Court functioning as an amplifier—sensitively responding to, and perhaps moderately accelerating, the pace of change, change toward shared participation by members of both sexes in our nation's economic and social life. (Remarks at 24.)"
She stated further:

"The ball, one might say, was tossed by the Justices back into the legislators' court, where the political forces of the day could operate. The Supreme Court wrote modestly, it put forward no grand philosophy; but by requiring legislative reexamination of once customary sex-based classifications, the Court helped to ensure that laws and regulations would 'catch up with a changed world.' (Madison Lecture at 31–32 (footnotes omitted).)"

* * *

At least in part, Judge Ginsburg's prescription for cautious judicial advances reflects a recognition of the limitations under which the Court operates. The judiciary lacks a "sword" with which to enforce its pronouncements. She has written:

"With prestige to persuade, but not physical power to enforce, with a will for self-preservation and the knowledge that they are not 'a bevy of Platonic Guardians,' the Justices generally follow, they do not lead, changes taking place elsewhere in society. But without taking giant strides and thereby risking a backlash too forceful to contain, the Court, through constitutional adjudication, can reinforce or signal a green light for a social change. (Madison Lecture, at 36–37 (footnotes omitted).)"

III. Judge Ginsburg Acknowledges That Courts Must Act Boldly Where the Political Process Will Not Admit Constitutionally Necessary Change

In her Madison Lecture, Judge Ginsburg wrote:

"I do not suggest that the Court should never step ahead of the political branches in pursuit of a constitutional precept. *Brown v. Board of Education* [347 U.S. 483], the 1954 decision declaring racial segregation in public schools offensive to the equal protection principle, is the case that best fits the bill. Past the midpoint of the twentieth century, apartheid remained the law enforcement system in several states, shielded by a constitutional interpretation the Court itself advanced at the turn of the century—the 'separate but equal' doctrine. (Madison Lecture at 33–34 (footnotes omitted).)"

She wrote that "prospects in 1954 for dismantling racially segregated schools were bleak." (Madison Lecture at 34.) To paraphrase her argument: political actors were unlikely to be moved to desegregate the schools because a national consensus to support such bold legislative initiatives was lacking.

The nominee's generally cautious approach to judging stands in balance with her belief that our understanding of the Constitution's meaning evolves over time. Judge Ginsburg suggests that judges walk a fine line. In the context of discussing her litigation attacking laws that discriminated based on gender, she wrote, "Challenges to [gender-based] laws put the courts in the sticky marshland between constitutional *interpretation* in our system, a proper judicial task, and constitutional *amendment,* a job reserved to the people's elected representatives." (Ginsburg, The Meaning and Purpose of the Equal Rights Amendment, Address Before the Colloquim on Legislation for Women's Rights, Ocsterbeek, Netherlands 10 (September 27, 1979) [hereinafter, Meaning and Purpose].)

On the one hand, the nominee believes the Constitution to be an evolving document—a belief she ascribes to the framers as well. On the other hand, she believes judges can go too far, actually amending the Constitution when their job is to interpret only. She summarized this tension in her writings: "[T]he genius of our eighteenth century Constitution is its supple capacity to serve through changing times if supported by judicial interpretations that are neither 'mushy' nor too 'rigid.'" (Ginsburg, The Ben J. Altheimer Lecture, On Amending the Constitution: A Plea for Patience, Address Before the University of Arkansas at Little Rock School of Law (February 7, 1990) in 12 U.Ark. Little Rock L.J. 677, 693 (1989–90) (footnote omitted).)

In part because the nominee herself acknowledged a tension between the notion of an evolving Constitution and the principle of judicial restraint, several members of the committee sought to determine the nominee's view on the proper methodology for recognizing previously acknowledged rights.

During the hearing, the chairman asked the nominee to reconcile her position that courts must move incrementally with her support for a case like *Brown* where the Court took a bold step. In response, the nominee first reconciled her approval of *Brown* with her view of judicial restraint by pointing out that *Brown* "wasn't born in a day," even though it produced change "perhaps a generation before state legislators in our southern states would have budged on the issue." (Meaning and Purpose at 2.) Judge Ginsburg testified:

"Thurgood Marshall came to the Court showing it wasn't equal, in case after case, in four cases, at least, before he wanted to put that before the Court, *Sweatt v. Painter,* [339 U.S. 629 (1950)], *McLaurin* [*v. Oklahoma State Regents,* 339 U.S. 639 (1950)], *Gaines* [*v. Canada,* 305 U.S. 337 (1938)]. He set the building blocks, until it was obvious to everyone that separate couldn't be equal."

* * *

"But *Brown* itself * * * didn't say racial segregation * * *, is going to be ended [root and] branch by one decision. *Brown* was in 1954, and it wasn't until *Loving v. Virginia* [388 U.S. 1] in 1967 that the job was over, even at the Supreme Court level, even at the declaration level. (Transcript, July 20, at 123–124.).''

But Judge Ginsburg then did acknowledge that there are some cases in which the Court appropriately may lead society in bold new directions—even where there are no "pathmarkers" to show the way, and no "dialogue" with the political branches. She mentioned as examples *Worcester v. Georgia,* 31 U.S. 515 (1932), and *Dred Scott v. Sandford,* 60 U.S. 393 (1857).

Senator DeConcini pursued this issue in an effort to discern the methodology she would employ to recognize a case in which it is appropriate for the Court to lead society. The nominee stated, "[W]hen political avenues become dead-end streets judicial intervention in the politics of the people may be essential in order to have effective politics." (Transcript, July 21, at 13.) She gave as an example the legislative reapportionment case of *Baker v. Carr,* 369 U.S. 186 (1962), in which the Court established the principle of one person, one vote. In further response to this line of questioning by Senator DeConcini, the nominee indicated that courts should move with restraint, but that, where legislatures fail to resolve important questions, courts must step in to supply a remedy if a case demanding a remedy is before them. (*Transcript,* July 21, at 17–18.)

IV.   Judge Ginsburg's Theory of *Stare Decisis*

The committee is satisfied that Judge Ginsburg holds an appropriate respect for the principle of *stare decisis* and abiding understanding of the value of precedent. At the same time, she recognizes the importance of achieving the correct result in matters of constitutional interpretation, where the Court is the final arbiter. She distinguishes the somewhat diminished importance of *stare decisis* in the constitutional context from statutory interpretation, when stability becomes more important and errors by courts can be corrected by legislatures.   * * *

Judge Ginsburg rejects the view of some theorists that the doctrine of *stare decisis* is of less importance in areas such as criminal law. These theorists believe *stare decisis* applies with the most force with respect to contract or property rights, where, according to the theory, stability is more important because of the public's reliance on settled law.

* * *

Judge Ginsburg's testimony in other contexts exemplified her respect for precedent and inclination to adhere to the principle of *stare decisis*. She agreed with Senator Hatch's assertion that the abortion funding cases of *Maher v. Roe,* 432 U.S. 464 (1997), and *Harris v. McRae,* 448 U.S. 297 (1980), were the Supreme Court's precedent. She stated that she had no "agenda to displace them." (Transcript, July 22, at 28.) Likewise, in response to Senator Grassley, she expressed the view that the Supreme Court's decision in *Planned Parenthood v. Casey,* 112 S.Ct. 2791 (1992), reflected the importance of precedent.   * * *

PART 3: JUDGE GINSBURG'S VIEWS ON UNENUMERATED RIGHTS, PRIVACY, AND REPRODUCTIVE FREEDOM

Judge Ginsburg's testimony and writings on unenumerated rights, the right of privacy, and reproductive freedom set her apart from all other recent nominees to the Supreme Court. Judge Ginsburg enthusiastically embraced the concept of unenumerated rights and the right of privacy. She also forthrightly supported a woman's right to reproductive freedom, under either a privacy or an equal protection analysis.

I.   Judge Ginsburg Embraced the Concept of Unenumerated Rights, Including a Right of Privacy

A.   *Judge Ginsburg supports the concept of unenumerated rights*

In clear and unequivocal terms, Judge Ginsburg expressed support for and appreciation of the concept of unenumerated rights—the view that each American citizen has rights independent of and apart from those specifically listed in the Constitution. She stated, in response to the very first question of the hearings, by Chairman Biden:

"I think the Framers are shortchanged if we view them as having a limited view of rights, because they wrote, Thomas Jefferson wrote, 'We hold these truths to be self-evident, that all men are created equal, that they are endowed by their Creator with certain inalienable rights, that among these'—among these—'are life, liberty, and the pursuit of happiness,' and that Government is formed to protect and secure those rights.

"Now when the Constitution was written, as you know, there was much concern over a Bill of Rights. There were some who thought a Bill of Rights dangerous because one couldn't enumerate all the rights of the people; one couldn't compose a complete catalogue. * * *

"But there was a sufficient call for a Bill of Rights, and so the Framers put down what was in the front of their minds in the Bill of Rights.

"* * * And then * * * the Framers were fearful that this limited catalogue might be understood, even though it is written as a restriction on Government rather than a conferring of rights of people, that it might be understood as skimpy, as not stating everything that is. And so we do have the Ninth Amendment stating that the Constitution shall not be construed to deny or disparage other rights. So the Constitution * * * the whole thrust of it is people have rights, and Government must be kept from trampling on them. (Transcript, July 20, at 110–11.)"

Judge Ginsburg here compared the American Constitution to the French Declaration of the Rights of Man, which confers rights, rather than restricting government, and thus (unlike the Constitution) presupposes a world in which citizens have no rights other than those specifically given. (Transcript, July 20, at 111.)

Elaborating further on this view, Judge Ginsburg testified that "the Ninth Amendment is part of the ideal that people have rights, the Bill of Rights keeps the government from intruding on those rights. We don't necessarily have a complete enumeration here." (Transcript, July 21, at 112.)

B.   Judge Ginsburg subscribes to the views of Justice Harlan and Justice Powell with respect to when the Court should recognize an unenumerated right

Judge Ginsburg testified that in determining whether an asserted unenumerated right is protected by the Constitution—in particular, by the broadly worded Due Process Clause of the 14th Amendment—she would follow the approach articulated by Justice Harlan in *Poe v. Ullman,* 367 U.S. 497 (1961), and by Justice Powell in *Moore v. City of East Cleveland,* 431 U.S. 494 (1977).

Justice Harlan wrote in *Poe,* in arguing for a flexible conception of due process, not limited by the specific rights granted elsewhere in the Constitution:

"Due process has not been reduced to any formula; its content cannot be determined by reference to any code. The best that can be said is that through the course of this Court's decisions it has represented the balance which our Nation, built upon the postulates of respect for the liberty of the individual, has struck between that liberty and the demands of organized society. If the supplying of content to this Constitutional concept has of necessity been a rational process, it has certainly not been one where judges have felt free to roam where unguided speculation might take them. The balance of which I speak is the balance struck by this country, having regard to what history teaches are the traditions from which it developed as well as the traditions from which it broke. That tradition is a living thing. A decision of this Court which radically departs from it could not long survive, while a decision which builds on what has survived is likely to be sound. No formula could serve as a substitute, in this area, for judgment and restraint. (367 U.S. at 542 (Harlan, J., dissenting).)"

Judge Ginsburg testified that "I associate myself with *Poe v. Ullman* and the method that is revealed most completely by Justice Harlan in that opinion." (Transcript, July 22, at 62.)

Similarly, Judge Ginsburg read from Justice Powell's opinion in *Moore* in response to Senator Hatch's characterization of the dangers of substantive process. In *Moore,* Powell wrote:

"There *are* risks when the judicial branch gives enhanced protection to certain substantive liberties without the guidance of the more specific provisions of the Bill of Rights. As the history of the *Lochner* era demonstrates, there is reason for concern lest the only limits to such judicial intervention become the predilections of those who happen at the time to be Members of this Court. That history counsels caution and restraint. But it does not counsel abandonment.

* * *

"Appropriate limits on due process come not from drawing arbitrary lines but rather from careful 'respect for the teachings of history [and] solid recognition of the basic values that underlie our society.' (431 U.S. at 502–03.)"

Judge Ginsburg described this passage as the "most eloquent statement" of her own position after *Poe.* (Transcript, July 22, at 33.)

Significantly, Judge Ginsburg rejected the method adopted by Justice Scalia to identify interests protected by the Due Process Clause. In what Judge Ginsburg termed in her testimony "the famous Footnote Six" of *Michael H. v. Gerald D.,* 491 U.S. 110, 127, n. 6 (1989), Justice Scalia proposed limiting the scope of the due process clause to those interests which, most specifically defined, received the historic protection of the Government. Justices O'Connor and Kennedy, who joined most of Justice Scalia's opinion, declined to join this footnote, explaining that under the proposed method "many a decision would have reached a different result." Id. at 132. In response to a question from Chairman Biden, Judge Ginsburg associated herself with the views of Justices O'Connor and Kennedy on this subject, as opposed to those of Justice Scalia.

* * *

In adopting Justice Harlan's approach, and rejecting Justice Scalia's, Judge Ginsburg has selected a method for identifying unenumerated rights in keeping with the Constitution's majestic and capacious language. As Justices O'Connor and Kennedy recognized in *Michael H.*, "requiring specific approval from history before protecting anything in the name of liberty" effectively "squashes * * * freedom." 491 U.S. at 132. It is Justice Harlan's approach—an approach of measured change and rooted evolution—that comports with both the intent and the draftsmanship of the Constitution. Judge Ginsburg's embrace of this approach provides excellent reason to support her.

C. *Judge Ginsburg recognizes a right to privacy*

Judge Ginsburg's testimony left no doubt that she supports the Supreme Court's recognition of a general, unenumerated right to privacy. Her views were evident in an exchange with Senator Leahy:

"SENATOR LEAHY. Is there a constitutional right to privacy?

"JUDGE GINSBURG. There is a constitutional right to privacy which consists I think of at least two distinguishable parts. One is the privacy expressed most vividly in the Fourth Amendment, that is the government shall not break into my home or my office, without a warrant, based on probable cause; the government shall leave me alone.

"The other is the notion of personal autonomy; the government shall not make my decisions for me, I shall make, as an individual, uninhibited, uncontrolled by my government, the decisions that affect my life's course. Yes, I think that whether it has been lumped under the label, privacy is a constitutional right, and it has those two elements, the right to be let alone and the right to make basic decisions about one's life course. (Transcript, July 21, at 54–55.)"

* * *

Although Judge Ginsburg never explicitly referred to the right to privacy as a "fundamental right"—a term the Court commonly has used—she made clear that the Government must meet a very high burden before interfering with the right. In response to a question of the chairman, Judge Ginsburg stated:

"The line of cases that you just outlined, the right to marry, the right to procreate or not, the right to raise one's children, the degree of justification that the State has to have to interfere with that is very considerable. (Transcript, July 22, at 53.)"

Judge Ginsburg thus indicated that the right to privacy protected by the Constitution is a right of real meaning and consequence.

Judge Ginsburg's willing acknowledgment of the right to privacy, her characterization of the strength of that right, and most of all, her understanding of the values underlying that right—all of these set Judge Ginsburg apart from most recent nominees to the Supreme Court. Her testimony shows that she appreciates the importance of preventing government from controlling or burdening an individual's most central and personal decisions. Her testimony shows that she believes this restraint on government to be a central aspect of freedom.

II.   JUDGE GINSBURG SUPPORTS THE RIGHT OF
WOMEN TO REPRODUCTIVE FREEDOM

Prior to her nomination, Judge Ginsburg discussed her views on reproductive rights in two speeches, reprinted as articles; the most recent of these, presented in March 1993, is generally known as the Madison Lecture. (Madison Lecture; *see also* Ginsburg, William T. Joyner Lecture on Constitutional Law, Some Thoughts on Autonomy and Equality in Relation to *Roe v. Wade,* Address before the University of North Carolina School of Law (April 6, 1984) *in* 63 N.C.L.Rev. 375 (1985).) During her hearings, Judge Ginsburg clarified and expanded on her thoughts on this subject.

The premise of the Madison Lecture is that the Constitution protects in some measure the right of women to choose for themselves whether or not to terminate a pregnancy. Judge Ginsburg thus wrote that the Court should have struck down the extreme anti-abortion law under review in *Roe v. Wade*—a law she characterized as "intolerably shackl[ing] a woman's autonomy." (Madison Lecture at 23.)

Similarly, in her testimony, Judge Ginsburg left no doubt of her conviction that the Constitution protects the right to choose. In her most strikingly articulated of many statements on the issue, Judge Ginsburg told Senator Brown:

"This is something central to a woman's life, to her dignity. It is a decision that she must make for herself. And when government controls that decision for her, she is being treated as less than a fully adult human responsible for her own choices. (Transcript, July 21, at 106.)"

In response to another question of Senator Brown, exploring whether fathers may have rights relating to the decision to terminate a pregnancy, Judge Ginsburg added that "in the end it's [a woman's] body, her life. * * * [I]t is essential * * * that she be the decision maker, that her choice be controlling." (Transcript, July 21, at 108.)

In the Madison Lecture, Judge Ginsburg seemed to argue that the right to terminate a pregnancy arose from the equal protection guarantee, rather than from the right to privacy. There, Judge Ginsburg stated that the *Roe* Court should have "homed in more precisely on the women's equality dimension of the issue," arguing that "disadvantageous treatment of a woman because of her pregnancy and reproductive choice is a paradigm case of discrimination on the basis of sex." (Madison Lecture at 24, 28.)

In her testimony, Judge Ginsburg repeatedly stated that her emphasis on the equality aspect of reproductive freedoms was meant to supplement, rather than supplant, the traditional privacy rationale for the right to terminate a pregnancy. This point emerges clearly in the following exchange between Judge Ginsburg and Senator Feinstein:

"SENATOR FEINSTEIN. If I understand what you are saying you are saying that *Roe* could have been decided on equal protection grounds rather than the fundamental right to privacy. * * *

"JUDGE GINSBURG. Yes, Senator, except in one respect. I never made it either/or. * * * I have always said both, that the equal protection strand should join together with the autonomy of decision making strand; so that it wasn't a question of equal protection or personal autonomy, it was a question of both.

* * *

"So I would have added another underpinning, one that I thought was at least as strong, perhaps stronger. But it was never equal protection rather than personal autonomy. It was both. (Transcript, July 21, at 193–94.)"

* * *

Judge Ginsburg's effort to highlight the equality dimension of reproductive freedoms thus serves to enhance, rather than diminish, these important rights. Judge Ginsburg's analysis focuses on an aspect of reproductive rights the Court recently hinted at in *Casey v. Planned Parenthood,* 112 S.Ct. 2791 (1992)—the effect of these rights on the status of women in our society. In Judge Ginsburg's view, this analysis need not result in a weaker level of constitutional scrutiny than that demanded by the Court in *Roe.* It is true that gender discrimination currently receives only intermediate scrutiny, whereas the recognition of a fundamental right of privacy, as occurred in *Roe,* provokes strict scrutiny. But Judge Ginsburg made clear that equality is but one aspect of reproductive freedom; and she further noted on several occasions that the Court may yet hold sex distinctions to demand strict scrutiny.

In another aspect of her Madison Lecture, as well as in an earlier article, Judge Ginsburg suggested that the Court in *Roe* went too far too fast—that it should have struck down only the extreme anti-abortion law before it, leaving for another day the question of the constitutionality of other, more moderate abortion restrictions. Such an approach, Judge Ginsburg posited in the Madison Lecture, "might have served to reduce, rather than to fuel controversy." (Madison Lecture at 23.) According to Ginsburg, quoting *Roe* itself, "there was a marked trend in state legislatures 'toward liberalization of abortion statutes.' " (*Id.* at 32 (footnote omitted).) If *Roe* had limited its ruling—if it had, in Judge Ginsburg's words, "invited * * * dialogue with legislators"—that trend might well have continued. (Id.) By issuing its decision in *Roe,* Ginsburg argued, the Court halted this process, provoked popular backlash, and "prolonged divisiveness." (Id. at 37.)

Senator Metzenbaum and Judge Ginsburg engaged in an exchange on this subject:

"SENATOR METZENBAUM. Would you not have had some concern, or do you not have some concern, that had the gradualism been the reality, that many more women would have been denied an abortion or would have been forced into an illegal abortion and possibly an unsafe abortion?

"JUDGE GINSBURG. Senator, we can't see what the past might have been like. I wrote an article that was engaging in what if. I expressed the view that if the Court had simply done what courts usually do, stuck to the very case before it and gone no further, then there might have been a change, gradual changes.

* * *

"There was the one thing that one can say for sure: There was a massive attack on *Roe v. Wade*. It was a single target to hit at. I think two things happened. One is that a movement that had been very vigorous became relaxed * * *.

"So one side seemed to relax its energy, while the other side had a single target around which to rally, but that is my 'what if,' and I could be wrong about that. My view was that the people would have accepted, would have expressed themselves in an enduring way on this question. And as I said this is a matter of speculation, this is my view of what if. Other people can have a different view. (Transcript, July 20, at 183–84.)"

Judge Ginsburg's testimony on this matter—as well as the two articles it is based on—reflect her broad judicial philosophy: most notably, her commitment to gradual change and her respect for the political process. But Judge Ginsburg's testimony and articles do not call into question her fundamental commitment to reproductive rights. The committee understands her articles as presenting a view of how such rights can best be achieved and maintained—of how *any* rights can best be achieved and maintained—in a democratic society, rather than as expressing doubts about the rightful place of these rights in the constitutional order.

Questions remain open as to the approach Judge Ginsburg would follow, if confirmed, in cases soon to come before the Court involving abortion regulations. Judge Ginsburg, in responding to questions posed by Senator Metzenbaum, would not comment on whether the right to choose remains a fundamental right after *Casey;* neither would she comment on the level of scrutiny that should be applied to abortion regulations or on the permissibility of any particular regulations. (Transcript, July 20, at 184–85; July 21 at 196.) These questions are of obvious importance with respect to the future scope of reproductive freedoms.

But the committee knows far more about Judge Ginsburg's views on reproductive rights than it has known about any previous nominee's. Judge Ginsburg's record and testimony suggest both a broad commitment to reproductive freedoms and a deep appreciation of the equality and autonomy values underlying them.

PART 4: JUDGE GINSBURG'S VIEWS ON EQUAL
PROTECTION AND CIVIL RIGHTS

Judge Ginsburg came to the Committee with a long and impressive record in equal protection and civil rights law. As a lawyer, she led the effort to bring women within the coverage of the equal rights clause of the 14th amendment. Her continued work in the field, as a scholar and a judge, and her testimony before the committee evidences Judge Ginsburg's deep and principled commitment to the ideal of equal protection of the laws.

I.   JUDGE GINSBURG'S CAREER MARKS HER AS A LEADING SCHOLAR
AND ADVOCATE IN THE AREA OF EQUAL PROTECTION

A. Judge Ginsburg's record as an advocate

Before her appointment to the circuit court, Judge Ginsburg worked as an advocate to provide women with equal protection of the laws. Her work is justly renowned. As much as any other advocate, Judge Ginsburg is responsible for the celebrated Supreme Court decisions of the 1970's guaranteeing women's rights—decisions which still comprise the mass of governing constitutional law in this area. * * *

B. Sex discrimination

Judge Ginsburg has written dozens of law review articles on the topic of equal rights for women. She also wrote, with two co-authors, the leading law school casebook in this area: K. Davidson, R. Ginsburg, and H. Kay, Sex–Based Discrimination (1st ed. 1974). Just as Judge Ginsburg's advocacy and scholarship helped to create this new field, so too did her pedagogy help to transmit her learning to most of those who work in the field today.

In all of this material, Judge Ginsburg has made the case for treating women as full and equal citizens under the laws and Constitution. She describes the injury to both sexes from unequal treatment based on gender stereotypes. As an advocate, Judge Ginsburg often selected cases in which the gender differential most obviously penalized men, as a way of awakening an all-male bench to the reality of harm. Tradition portrayed these sex-based classifications as shelters for women, but Judge Ginsburg insisted that this portrayal was flawed. She explained how stereotypical thinking tends to become self-fulfilling, as when a law offers women fewer employment opportunities in the name of protection, but in reality serves to bar women from economic equality and independence.

In a closely related vein, some of Judge Ginsburg's writing set forth the case for an equal rights amendment to the Constitution. In her testimony, she explained that she continued to support an equal rights amendment:

"I remain an advocate of the Equal Rights Amendment, I will tell you, for this reason: because I have a daughter and a granddaughter, and I know what the history was, and I would like the legislature of this country and of all the States to stand up and say we know what that history was in the 19th century and we want to make a clarion call that women and men are equal before the law, just as every modern human rights document in the world does since 1970. (Transcript, July 21, at 65.)"

Judge Ginsburg's view is that passage of the ERA would have clarified the meaning of the 14th amendment without the need for what she has described as the Burger Court's "bold and dynamic" interpretation in the gender cases. Given that the ERA would have served in her view only to clarify the meaning of the 14th amendment, Judge Ginsburg stated she does not view defeat of the ERA as incompatible with the 14th amendment's extension of equal rights to women. (Transcript, July 21, at 65, 72–75, 75–76, and 143–44.)

A recent criticism of Judge Ginsburg's approach asserts that formal equality under the laws will not serve to achieve real equality for women. This criticism contends that Judge Ginsburg and others of her generation have not appreciated that sex-based laws can benefit women, whose different situation—both biological and social—demands not identical but different treatment.

Senator Specter spelled out this scholarly criticism and asked Judge Ginsburg for her reaction to it. Judge Ginsburg said that "[w]hat you discuss, Senator Specter, I think reflects largely a generation[al] difference." (Transcript, July 21, at 70.) She stated that she continues to bring "a certain skepticism" to supposed legislative protection of women. Judge Ginsburg observed, for example, that in the hearing room "most of the faces that I see are not women's faces." (Id.) Judge Ginsburg explained that she would moderate her skepticism about special legislative protection for women "if the legislature were just filled with women and maybe one or two men." * * * (Id. at 70–71.)

In her testimony, Judge Ginsburg repeatedly mentioned the possibility of applying a "strict scrutiny" standard of review to gender-based distinctions, rather than the current intermediate standard. Use of a strict scrutiny standard would represent a significant doctrinal shift, making almost all sex-based distinctions unlawful. * * * Judge Ginsburg did not specifically advocate this change. But her remarks suggest her openness to its consideration.

Judge Ginsburg told the committee that the Court had not settled the question of whether strict scrutiny should apply to gender-based distinctions:

"[H]eightened scrutiny, as I said before, for sex classifications is not necessarily the stopping point, as O'Connor made clear in the *Mississippi University For Women* case. [*Mississippi University For Women v. Hogan,* 458 U.S. 718 (1982).] Sex as a suspect classification remains open. It wasn't necessary for the Court to go that far in that case. * * * It is just that the Court has left that question open, and it may get there. (Transcript, July 21, at 195; see also Transcript, July 20, at 123; Transcript, July 22, at 185–91.)"

Here, Judge Ginsburg refers to a suggestive footnote in *Mississippi University For Women* (1982), in which the Court concluded: "We need not decide whether classifications based upon gender are inherently suspect." 458 U.S. at 724 n. 9.

Most observers have not taken this footnote as proof that the question of strict scrutiny remains an open one. Most have instead accepted the view that the Supreme Court in the 1976 case of *Craig v. Boren* decided that a middle-tier standard is appropriate for gender cases. *See* 429 U.S. at 190. This conclusion seems particularly valid in light of the Supreme Court's reiteration of the *Craig* standard in *Heckler v. Mathews,* 465 U.S. 728 (1984)—2 years *after* its 1982 footnote in *Mississippi University For Women.* 458 U.S. at 724 n. 9. The Supreme Court then described the middle tier standard as "firmly established." It entirely ignored the 1982 footnote to which Judge Ginsburg referred. 465 U.S. at 744.

Judge Ginsburg's testimony, highlighting the *Mississippi University for Women* footnote, thus seems to indicate her openness to continue doctrinal change—in particular, heightening the scrutiny for gender-based distinctions. This stance would comport with her historic support for the equal rights amendment—a link that she herself twice drew to Senator DeConcini. (Transcript, July 21, at 6–7.) Still, Judge Ginsburg declined to commit herself definitively when Senator DeConcini pressed her about whether "strict scrutiny should be the beginning point on any gender issue brought before the Court." (Id.).

C. Race discrimination and affirmative action

Judge Ginsburg's record and testimony demonstrate an awareness of the lingering effects of our national history of racism and racial discrimination. She also accepts the continued need to remedy the effects of racial discrimination in appropriate cases. She offered no hints of how she would rule in specific cases, but her testimony expressed support for continued efforts to root out discrimination. Her record as a judge suggests she will take a generous approach to possible remedies.

In the case of *O'Donnell v. District of Columbia,* 963 F.2d 420, 429 (D.C.Cir.1992), Judge Ginsburg concurred in a decision of the U.S. Court of Appeals for the District of Columbia Circuit striking down the District of Columbia minority set-aside program in construction. The court made clear in *O'Donnell* that this result was compelled by the Supreme Court's 1989 decision in *City of Richmond v. Croson,* 488 U.S. 469 (1989), in which the Court declared that even benign State and local racial classifications would be subjected to strict constitutional scrutiny under the Equal Protection Clause of the 14th amendment. Under this test, even a remedial affirmative action plan must be justified by a compelling governmental interest. One such interest is that of remedying past discrimination; a jurisdiction offering such a rationale is compelled to document with specificity its history of discrimination.

Concurring in the decision in *O'Donnell,* Judge Ginsburg expressed her view that a history of discrimination was not the only interest that a governmental entity might assert to justify the use of remedial affirmative action plans.   In her view, other interests, such as a desire to achieve diversity, might also suffice.

Under questioning by Senator Simon during the confirmation hearing, Judge Ginsburg explained her view in *O'Donnell.* She cited approvingly Justice Powell's opinion in the landmark case of *University of California Bd. of Regents v. Bakke,* 488 U.S. 265 (1978),[1] in which the Court affirmed the right of governmental entities to take race into account for certain purposes in a way consistent with the equal protection clause.   Citing Justice Powell, she stated that a governmental actor might well offer a sufficient rationale for an affirmative action program even if the rationale is not specifically tied to past discrimination.   Asked by Senator Simon whether she had any philosophical objection to the use of set-asides, the nominee stated:

"[I]n many of these cases, there really is underlying discrimination, but it's not easy to prove, and sometimes it would be better for society if we didn't push people to the wall and make them say, yes, I was a discriminator, that the kind of settlement that is encouraged in these plans is a better, healthier thing for society than to make everything fiercely adversarial, so that it becomes very costly and bitter.

"In many of these plans, there is a suspicion that there was underlying discrimination.   * * * But rather than make it a knock-down-drag-out fight, it would be better for there to be this voluntary action, always taking into account that there is an interest, as there was in the *O'Donnell* case, of the people who say but why me, why should I be the one made to pay, I didn't engage in past discrimination, and that's why these things must be approached with understanding and care. (Transcript, July 21, at 133–34.)"

Under questioning by Senator Feinstein, the nominee expressed a preference for goals and timetables, rather than rigid quotas. * * * Her record and testimony document Judge Ginsburg's recognition of the continued reality of race and sex discrimination, both overt and subtle. She has demonstrated an open-minded approach to finding solutions for this ongoing national problem.

D. *Discrimination based on sexual orientation*

The nominee did not indicate in any way how she might rule on the assertion that discrimination based on sexual orientation violates the Constitution.   She refused to comment on the issue in response to Senators Thurmond, Brown, and Cohen on the grounds that the question would undoubtedly come before the Court. (See Transcript, July 20, at 177; Transcript, July 22, at 191–92; Transcript, July 22, at 146.)

---

1. As an advocate, the nominee submitted a brief *amicus curiae* in *Bakke,* supporting the university's admissions program.

In her testimony, the nominee spoke broadly about our country's abhorrence of discrimination of any sort, including discrimination based on sexual orientation. In response to a question by Senator Kennedy, she said, "I think rank discrimination against anyone is against the tradition of the United States and is to be deplored. Rank discrimination is not part of our nation's culture. Tolerance is, and a generous respect for differences based on—this country is great because of its accommodation of diversity." (Transcript, July 22, at 10–11; see also id. at 146 (questioning by Senator Cohen).)

* * *

PART 5: JUDGE GINSBURG'S VIEWS ON RELIGIOUS FREEDOM

Few areas of constitutional law are in such ferment as that involving the first amendment's two guarantees of religious freedom—the free exercise clause and the establishment clause. In the free exercise area, the Court recently approved by a 5–4 vote a major doctrinal shift giving government greater leeway to apply laws interfering with religious practice. *Employment Division v. Smith,* 494 U.S. 872 (1990). Although the Court by now has lost two of the original dissenting Justices, its most recent free exercise decision suggests continued dissatisfaction and division over the new free exercise standard. *Church of the Lukumi Babalu Aye v. City of Hialeah,* 113 S.Ct. 2217 (1993). In addition, several Justices have expressed disagreement with the test traditionally used to review establishment clause claims; although a majority has not voted to depart from this approach, it sometimes appears to be hanging by a thread. See, e.g., *Lamb's Chapel v. Center Moriches Union Free School District,* 113 S.Ct. 2141 (1993).

Judge Ginsburg's vote in each of these areas might well prove crucial in marking the future direction of the Court. Although she has authored opinions only on the free exercise clause, and although her testimony with respect to each clause left important questions unanswered, her written record and congressional testimony in conjunction give reason to believe that Judge Ginsburg will respect both aspects of the first amendment's guarantee of religious freedom: tolerance of religious practice and separation of church and state.

* * *

PART 7: JUDGE GINSBURG'S VIEWS ON SEPARATION OF POWERS

Judge Ginsburg has a moderate and pragmatic view of the constitutional separation of powers. Recognizing that ours is "a system of separate branches of government," Judge Ginsburg also acknowledges the needed and complementary principle that "each branch is given by the Constitution a little space in the other's territory." (Transcript, July 20, at 166.) As Judge Ginsburg described the fundamental nature of our system of government, "the Constitution has divided government, but it also has checks and balances, and it makes each [branch] a little dependent on the other." (Transcript, July 20, at 166.) This under-standing of our constitutional order—as opposed to a rigid and formalistic notion of complete separation between branches—allows for some needed flexibility in our processes of government.

Judge Ginsburg's opinion in what is commonly known as the independent counsel case comports with the broad views she stated to the committee on separation of powers principles—and also illustrates the importance of those views. *In re Sealed Case,* 838 F.2d 476, 518 (D.C.Cir.1988) (Ginsburg, J., dissenting). The case involved a constitutional challenge to the Ethics in Government Act, which provided for the appointment of an independent counsel in cases of alleged misbehavior by members of the executive branch. Judge Ginsburg argued in dissent that the statute accorded with the Constitution even though it effectively transferred part of the prosecutorial function outside the executive branch. She reasoned that the statute combatted Watergate-style "abuses of executive power, abuses which themselves threatened the balance among the three branches of government." Id. at 527. Judge Ginsburg's position ultimately was adopted by the Supreme Court in *Morrison v. Olsen,* 487 U.S. 654 (1988), over a long dissent by Justice Scalia.

* * *

PART 10: JUDGE GINSBURG'S VIEWS ON CRIMINAL LAW AND PROCEDURE

Judge Ginsburg's record and testimony in the area of criminal law is reasonable and balanced, combining recognition of the need for effective law enforcement with concern for the constitutional rights of criminal defendants.

* * *

Judge Ginsburg has never ruled on death penalty questions and, like Justice Kennedy before her, declined to take a firm position on these questions during the hearing. (See Hearings on nomination of Anthony Kennedy, Tr. 12/15/87, at 208, where then Judge Kennedy refused to discuss the constitutionality of the death penalty on the ground that the issue involved a "constitutional debate of ongoing dimension.") Judge Ginsburg stated in response to questioning by Senator Hatch:

"At least since 1976, the Supreme Court, by large majorities, has rejected the position that the death penalty under any and all circumstances is unconstitutional. I recognize that there is no judge on the Court that takes the position that the death penalty is unconstitutional under any and all circumstances. * * *

"There are many questions left unresolved. They are coming constantly before that Court. * * *

"I can tell you that I do not have a closed mind on this subject. I don't want to commit—I don't think it would be consistent with the line I have tried to hold to tell you that I will definitely accept or definitely reject any position. I can tell you that I am well aware of the precedent, and I have already expressed my views on the value of precedent. (Transcript, July 22, at 16.)"

The Committee believes that Judge Ginsburg's approach to issues of criminal law and procedure is reasoned and balanced. Her opinions and her testimony reflect a respect both for the practical realities of law enforcement and the constitutional rights of the accused.

Conclusion

This report summarizes the extensive record before the Judiciary Committee and the Senate as it prepares to exercise its constitutional duty to consent to the President's choice of a Supreme Court nominee. The record amply demonstrates that Ruth Bader Ginsburg merits the support of the committee and the entire Senate.

Some members of the committee have expressed concern that Judge Ginsburg answered fewer questions during the hearings than they would have liked. But a careful comparison of Judge Ginsburg's answers with those of other recent nominees reveals that Judge Ginsburg supplies as much—or more—information about her views as anyone who has appeared before the committee in the last 5 years. During the course of her testimony, Judge Ginsburg in fact told the committee a great deal—most particularly about her approach to constitutional and statutory interpretation and her views on unenumerated rights, the right to privacy, and reproductive freedoms.

Judge Ginsburg's refusal to answer all the committee's questions also should be viewed in light of her substantial judicial record. In this respect, Judge Ginsburg's nomination might be contrasted to that of David Souter. Almost nothing was known about Justice Souter's constitutional philosophy or his approach to judging at the time of his nomination. By contrast, each member of the committee had ample means, prior to Judge Ginsburg's hearing, to discover much pertinent information—indeed, the most pertinent information—about Judge Ginsburg's judicial approach and method. In more than 300 signed appellate opinions, and more than three score articles, Judge Ginsburg told the Senate and the American people an enormous amount about herself even before the hearings opened.

None of this is to say that the committee is fully satisfied with the responsiveness of Judge Ginsburg's answers. But we have not been fully satisfied for many years, and perhaps will not be for as many longer. Given Judge Ginsburg's extensive written record and her willingness to answer questions at least as fully as other recent nominees, the committee sees no reason for this issue to bar her appointment.

Judge Ginsburg is open-minded, nondoctrinaire, fair, and independent. She respects and loves the law. She honors the concept of individual rights. She brings to constitutional interpretation an understanding that the Constitution is an evolving document, together with an appreciation that the most secure evolution is also the most rooted. She will be a fine Associate Justice of the United States Supreme Court.

* * *

ADDITIONAL VIEWS OF SENATOR PRESSLER

This was the first confirmation hearing of a Supreme Court nominee in which I participated. Because of this fact, I have considered carefully my vote on Judge Ginsburg's confirmation. Our vote today is a recommendation to the rest of our colleagues in the Senate whether or not they should confirm Judge Ginsburg. Prior to joining the committee, I always placed great weight on the committee's recommendations. I believe other Senators do also.

On one basic point, there is no argument: Judge Ginsburg is exceptionally well-qualified to be an Associate Justice of the U.S. Supreme Court. Her background is impressive. * * *

However, having said all this, I must express my disappointment with the nominee's responses to my questions during the hearings. Almost exclusively, I used my questioning periods to explore her understanding of Indian Country issues, which routinely come before the Court. My purpose in doing so was not to elicit a promise or commitment from her, or even an idea of how she would decide these issues so crucial to people in my part of the country. Rather, I had hoped to be satisfied that Judge Ginsburg had a good understanding and solid grasp of this complex and murky area of the law. Unfortunately, I was not satisfied.

While not as glamorous as other issues, Indian cases do frequently come before the Court. In the last decade, the Court has accepted approximately 40 cases dealing with the sovereignty, civil rights, law enforcement, or jurisdiction of American Indians and their tribes. I understand such cases never come before the D.C. Circuit Court of Appeals. Therefore, I did not expect Judge Ginsburg to be an expert on Indian law prior to her nomination. In an attempt to impress upon her the importance of these issues, I told Judge Ginsburg of my intent to inquire into her understanding of Indian Country law when she visited my office the day after her nomination. Additionally, I sent her references to several key Indian law cases a few weeks ago as well as a copy of the questions I intended to ask during the hearings.

Therefore, I was disappointed with Judge Ginsburg's answers to my questions. I felt they were largely nonresponsive and somewhat simplistic. She failed to demonstrate a basic or general philosophy toward, or even an interest in, Indian Country issues. To her credit, she did promise to approach these cases in the same thorough, meticulous way she prepares for all cases. I commend her for that. But I disagree with her if she believes a Supreme Court Justice really does not need to possess knowledge of Indian Country issues and the problems of the West prior to taking the bench. It is exactly that lack of an overall philosophy that has led to the patchwork of court decisions which characterizes Indian law today.

As I have stated before, Congress certainly shares equally in the blame for this situation. All too often, this body has failed to act in a responsible and sensible manner regarding the congressional action or clear intent; the Supreme Court must make the law that Congress is unwilling or unable to make. Through its decisions, the Supreme Court has the responsibility of providing guidance for lower courts on Indian Country matters. It is therefore easy to see the importance of selecting nominees who have a basic understanding of the complex history of the American Indians and their unique relationship with the U.S. Government.

Though I am not yet convinced that Judge Ginsburg has this understanding, I am voting for her confirmation. But I also want to put future Supreme Court nominees on notice that I will insist they have an interest and understanding of Indian Country law. After today, I will not vote for a nominee unless I am satisfied that they have demonstrated this concern.

But I am not here to make threats. I do wish Judge Ginsburg all the best. I hope she has a long and productive career on the highest Court in the land.

ADDITIONAL VIEWS OF SENATOR COHEN

Members of this committee have expressed the hope that soon-to-be Justice Ginsburg will exercise restraint on the Court. Other members pray that her past activism as an advocate will be revived on the Court. Both groups are likely to be disappointed. Nothing that has been said during the committee's deliberations and nothing that will be said on the Senate floor during the debate on the nomination will have a scintilla of influence upon her performance as a Justice on the Supreme Court. She is going to follow her own inner guides without regard to any of our importuning.

Judge Ginsburg indicated during the course of the hearings that she is a student and great admirer of Justice Holmes. He reminded us that the "history of the law is not logic but experience and that a page of experience is worth more than a volume of logic." Judge Ginsburg has demonstrated that she will bring not only a formidable intellect but also a great deal of experience to the Court, and this experience will serve the Court and the country well.

As the committee's unanimous vote on the nomination indicated, we all believe Judge Ginsburg meets the highest standards of professional competence and integrity, that she has a highly disciplined mind and a distinguished record as a jurist and an advocate, and should be confirmed overwhelmingly.

The hearings on the Ginsburg nomination, however, have highlighted concerns about the role of the Judiciary Committee in the "advice and consent" process and the expectations of the public about that role.

Editorial writers in major newspapers characterized the committee as a band of Lillputians who tried vainly to tie up a legal giant with trivial and petty pursuits. Others have suggested that Judge Ginsburg is "a methodical, passionless technician," and that what is really required on the Court is a "radical maverick" to cancel the radicalism of conservative justices.

Whatever one's characterization of Judge Ginsburg, only a single view of the committee emerged from the hearings and it was not a complimentary one. Members were accused of asking the wrong questions, failing to ask tough questions, or crossing the line between exploring judicial philosophy and that of social and legal policy.

Judge Ginsburg declared in her opening statement that she was setting the guidelines for the scope of her testimony. She indicated that any subject on which a nominee had written, lectured or taught was, in her view, open to inquiry but that other areas were not, particularly if they involved issues that might come before the Court at some future (however remote) time.

To allow a nominee to decide what he or she will testify to during the course of a hearing puts the members of the committee in the position of either having to accept the nominee's terms as dictated or vote against the nomination. I believe it is incumbent upon the committee to work on a bipartisan basis to establish responsible guidelines for what will be expected of future nominees. Nominees can, of course, decide whether they will abide by those rules and the committee members can then decide what action to take in response.

Finally, I want to commend the chairman for instituting reforms in committee procedures on Supreme Court nominations and, specifically, for his decision to hold a closed hearing on every nominee to review any allegations of a personal nature, even if no negative statements have been made. During my tenure in both the House and Senate, I have seen too many people have their lives destroyed by allegations, rumors, and outright lies before the appropriate congressional committee has had an opportunity to scrutinize such allegations for their veracity.

Part of the problem is the result of a great deal of misapprehension about what is commonly referred to as FBI reports. The FBI does not make reports. The FBI simply releases files which contain the questions that were put to certain witnesses and their responses. Those witnesses may remain anonymous. Their statements are not taken under oath. Their statements are not subject to scrutiny by the FBI. The statements are simply included in the file and those files are turned over to the committee.

When information is leaked from the FBI files, we have witnessed how easy it is to destroy a totally innocent individual. Such a situation casts great disrepute upon this committee or any other committee that allows character assassination to take place.

As a committee, we have a responsibility to a nominee to scrutinize any allegation of impropriety made against that individual and to test its validity. Such allegations should not be made public unless and until it is determined they have some foundation and, even then, only after we have confronted the nominee with them and given the individual a chance to either rebut them or to remove his or her name from consideration. It is important in my view, even though there were no allegations whatsoever against Judge Ginsburg, that we adopt the same process for all future nominees.

D. REFORMING THE PROCESS

In response to the emotionally charged, politically divisive confirmation battles over the Bork and Thomas nominations, commentators have offered a variety of reform proposals. The first three articles reprinted herein offer several suggestions for generally overhauling the nomination and confirmation process. In the second set of readings, the authors each propose a single relatively simple change that, in the author's view, will significantly improve the process.

In reading these articles, consider what the role of the Senate at the confirmation phase should be and whether the hearing process should be reformed in some way. Note that the custom of having the nominee testify before the Senate is relatively recent and that of televising the procedures even more recent. Should we reverse that trend and take the television out of the hearing room? Should there at least be a closed executive session for the initial examination of any allegations of intimate wrong-doings? Note Senator Biden's statement regarding the new procedures to be followed by the Senate Judiciary Committee for dealing with "investigative matters." Are these useful? Adequate?

Should more than a majority of Senators be required to confirm Supreme Court nominees? What would be the likely effect of amending the Constitution to require a ⅔ vote of the Senate for confirmation and is that effect desirable?

Consider whether all this concern with the confirmation process has been generated by problems with the nomination process. To the extent there has been a problem, has it been the kind or the quality of the nominee that has spawned doubts about the process? Should the President be required to consult with the Senate before making a judicial nomination? Does the Constitution contemplate such a role? Does it permit Congress to mandate such a role? If not, should the Constitution be amended to require consultation?[8]

Finally, consider whether we should change the nature of the position? Should the Constitution be amended to modify the life tenure given Supreme Court Justices, by, for example, giving them a term of years? How might that affect the appointment process? Would it

8. For readings related to this, see the articles in Section B, *supra,* especially the excerpts from Professors Strauss and Sunstein.

undermine the independence of the judiciary? Would it affect the attractiveness of the position?

STEPHANIE B. GOLDBERG, ED.,* WHAT'S THE ALTERNATIVE? A ROUNDTABLE ON THE CONFIRMATION PROCESS

ABA Journal, January 1992 (Stephanie B. Goldberg, ed.)

MODERATED BY MARTIN H. REDISH/EDITED BY STEPHANIE B. GOLDBERG

It was clear that something was terribly wrong with the process for confirming Supreme Court justices when, as Sen. John Danforth, R.–Mo., noted, many were clamoring for the nominee, Clarence Thomas, to take a lie detector test to resolve the doubts about his character.

Since then, almost every aspect of the process has been assailed, from the confidentiality of FBI reports to the scope of character inquiries to whether broadcasting the hearings has created a media circus.

Along with the criticisms has come an outpouring of suggestions: Get rid of the handlers, muzzle the special interest groups, beef up FBI investigations, and so on. None of this is likely to solve the fundamental problem, which is whether the Senate has the right to "play politics" and override candidates chosen by the executive branch to implement its own political agenda.

If so, then is a major overhaul necessary to resolve these bitter disputes, or is the existing machinery still serviceable?

In November, while the wounds from the Thomas confirmation were still healing, we asked a panel of scholars to share their impressions of the confirmation process and how it should be changed. Our moderator was Northwestern University Law Professor Martin H. Redish. He was joined by:

• R. Lea Brilmayer, who is Benjamin Butler Professor at New York University School of Law;

• Duke University Law Professor Walter Dellinger;

• Judge Alex Kozinski of the U.S. Court of Appeals for the Ninth Circuit; and

• University of Chicago Law Professor Michael W. McConnell.

* * *

Redish: Michael McConnell has suggested that the most important event in the Clarence Thomas confirmation process was not the second round of hearings, but the first, which focused on Thomas' background and philosophy.

He believes they have serious implications for judicial independence. Do others see that as the most important issue?

Brilmayer: I don't necessarily agree. The sexual harassment issue also is just as important—not to the confirmation process, but as a general issue in society.

Kozinski: The sexual harassment allegation raises the whole question of character and judicial temperament. Everyone agrees that there are certain things in a nominee's past that should raise doubts about his qualification to sit on the bench. That will and should always be with us. But it becomes troublesome when the character issue is used to disqualify someone for political or philosophical reasons.

Redish: Mike, was that your concern, too?

McConnell: I think there are two ways in which the independence of the judiciary is seriously compromised by the current confirmation process.

First, the adversarial nature of the hearings and their focus on specific legal issues throw the nominee into the arms of the Department of Justice for a two- or three-month indoctrination period.

He receives the department's views on every conceivable legal and constitutional issue and under circumstances when he is at his most receptive, because they are preparing him for a hostile assault.

It is outrageous that each new justice will have undergone that kind of "education."

The second problem is that nominees are inevitably going to be tempted to answer questions, not solely on the basis of their own good-faith evaluation of the legal issues, but according to how their answers will affect the Judiciary Committee and the public at large.

Redish: What's the alternative?

McConnell: We should return to a system in which the principal focus is on the nominee's past public record, including writings, opinions, acts and statements—preferably more formal statements, rather than informal after-dinner speeches.

I would like to see the senators engage, before they ever see the nominee, in a serious substantive discussion of the public record. First of all, they should insist that the nominee show some distinction. Then they should frame their arguments on the basis of what a nominee has done and said.

The appearance of the nominee before the committee, if he appears at all, ought to be a relatively minor footnote. Otherwise the principal attribute being judged is television style rather than a whole career.

Dellinger: I strongly agree. I believe that the hearing has come to play a far too prominent role in the process.

We went for 150 years without having nominees even appear before the Senate Judiciary Committee, and it did not become a settled practice until the nominations of Justices Stewart and Harlan in the late 1950s.

If I were to suggest a way to straighten out the process, I would have the Senate be more assertive about its policymaking judgments and, in a time of divided government, have it insist on consensus nominees.

I don't think the Senate should assess the worthiness of nominees by the kind of performance they put on for three days on television.

Redish: How would that have worked out in the case of Justice Souter?

Dellinger: Well, he would not have been confirmed unless there had been prior consultation and the Senate had been convinced of his accomplishments. The problem is this: If you compiled an honest list of the truly accomplished lawyers and judges, you'd find that most of them are not acceptable to this administration, although they are confirmable by the Senate.

There are a few exceptions, but generally the president essentially has allowed one part of his party to have a veto over Supreme Court nominations.

McConnell: Walter may overestimate the advantage of an aggressive Senate. We should recognize that distinction and confirmability are two different matters.

The problem is that we can't trust politicians in either branch to care much about distinction. Of course, they'll talk about it, but it's largely a smokescreen for other things.

Under those circumstances, I'm afraid that a more assertive role for the Senate merely creates the incentive for the president to find people who are non-controversial—hardly a good basis for distinction.

Brilmayer: I agree. It seems that a lot of questions the Senate asked didn't focus on distinction, but what positions the nominees were going to take on cases with political overtones.

Dellinger: Suppose the Senate or some other prominent group in the country suggested a list that included Dean Guido Calabresi, Professor Gerald Gunther, Chief Justice Ellen Peters, Judge Amalya Kearse, and William P. Coleman.

If the president ignored the list and came forward with somebody no one has ever heard of, at least it would put the nomination in perspective.

Redish: Can one argue that it is for the very reason that the judiciary is so independent after appointment that the confirmation process is necessary as the only political majoritarian check in the process?

Presumably, this is the stage where we don't want independence, where the political process is supposed to be performing its function.

And, given the nature of the communications media, isn't it perfectly appropriate to have the nominee appear on television, because the public's reaction is a perfectly sound influence at that time?

Dellinger: I agree that in a country that is otherwise committed to majoritarianism, judicial review is acceptable precisely because of the political nature of the confirmation process.

But I am still troubled by questions that seek to commit the nominee to a particular course of action.

Redish: Even if the commitment is unenforceable?

Kozinski: Even so, I would worry a lot if I were a lawyer appearing before a judge who had made that type of public statement.

Dellinger: Alex, why can't a nominee make any statement that a sitting justice can make? If Justice Stevens or Justice Scalia visits a law school, each is free to express his views on Roe v. Wade, although neither would be willing to comment on future cases.

Brilmayer: The real problem isn't whether people are going to be making statements that will cabin their judicial discretion, but whether political pressure will force people to make statements they don't actually believe.

Kozinski: When I speak publicly, I try to avoid questions on specific issues that may relate to pending cases in my circuit. I would suggest that Supreme Court justices have even less discretion to speak, because they get so many sensitive cases before them.

Redish: But no one has focused on the costs of not allowing the Senate to inquire in this manner. Walter, you described your ideal world, but what would be left for the Senate to do if it couldn't make those kinds of inquiries?

Dellinger: After the passage of the 17th Amendment providing for the election of senators, it is very difficult to argue that one of the Senate's most important functions should not be made on the basis of a very public record.

Partly, the process would be improved if we moved in the direction of a different nominee—a far more mature, distinguished person entering the final stage of a career.

I would suggest a lawyer who has had a full career, but not necessarily someone who has had occasion to think about burning social issues.

I believe, for example, that Lewis Powell's honest answer to most questions about privacy, abortion or unenumerated rights would have been: "Senator, I've never thought about that in my law practice." And that would be perfectly appropriate.

McConnell: I'd feel a little bit better about advice of that sort if some of Judge Bork's detractors were now saying that the failure to confirm him was a mistake.

To a large extent we are now reaping the unfortunate rewards of the Senate turning down someone of genuine distinction.

Dellinger: I think it's a false lesson to conclude that the Senate will not nominate someone with a major record of accomplishment.

I think the lesson was the Senate was not going to confirm someone who was so conservative that he essentially rejected all of the basic premises of the Warren Court.

It is quite clear that even after the Bork battle, someone like Gerald Gunther would be overwhelmingly confirmed.

McConnell: But it's also clear the Senate will confirm people like Anthony Kennedy, David Souter and Clarence Thomas, but not Robert Bork.

I don't think the difference between those individuals is that one is more conservative than the other three.

Dellinger: I agree.

Kozinski: Let me respond to the comment that we can't eliminate public hearings in a democracy. We don't live in a direct democracy, we live in a representative one. It is based, not only on the principle that we can't all get together in a big town hall and make decisions, but also that there are things in government that should not be decided by the rabble, because it does not always operate rationally.

What we saw with Bob Bork was an intrusion of direct democracy into a representative process. It was very troubling to those of us who suspect that, in addition to the full-fledged television campaign against him, Bork was defeated by the way he looks.

Getting back to Justice Thomas, it's equally distressing that the polls exerted as much influence as they did. It seemed to me that the tide turned on the less significant issue, as Michael identified it, but one that really could have defeated the nomination until the polls came out supporting Clarence Thomas over Professor Hill. I don't think that is a good way to conduct public business.

Redish: Why not, Alex? You're clearly correct to say we don't have a pure democracy, but I think Judge Bork would agree that popular sovereignty underlies the essence of our political system.

Why is it inappropriate for, say, Sen. Dixon from Illinois to vote the way his mail is going? Isn't that what the process is really all about?

Kozinski: The Constitution is an anti-democratic instrument. It is a check on absolute and direct democracy. We have built this structure in order to avoid the adverse effect of direct democracy.

Redish: But that's a red herring. This wasn't direct or absolute democracy. This was representative democracy acting in accordance with the structure of the Constitution.

Kozinski: I really don't know how the senators made their decisions, but whether Bob Bork looks cute should not have mattered.

Redish: I really don't think his looks were the major issue.

Kozinski: I heard a lot of comments like "I just don't trust him." I think it played a substantial role.

Brilmayer: Could I make a point on whether these things should be televised or not? At the end of the Anita Hill escapade, many people were very unhappy about the way things had worked out, the circus atmosphere and so forth.

But think back to the reaction the week before that when the allegation first surfaced. Imagine if those allegations hadn't come out, if they had been swept under the rug and then came out a year or two later. That would have created an enormous crisis in public confidence in the Court.

One reason it's good to have some publicity is that there were a lot of people in the country who felt they couldn't trust the Senate Judiciary Committee and the Senate to take their interests to heart.

Kozinski: If you don't trust your public officials, throw the rascals out.

Brilmayer: How can you do that if the information on their performance is withheld from you?

Kozinski: I don't see how you benefit from holding a televised hearing on Professor Hill's charges. I'm not saying they shouldn't have been looked into. But that's a different question altogether.

Brilmayer: But exactly the point I'm making is that they would not have been looked into, if there were no public outcry.

I also was extremely unhappy about this public spectacle. I don't like the way it turned out. But I'm not talking about whether the hearing should have been private. I'm talking about whether, if the whole proceedings had been private, there would have been any investigation of these charges.

McConnell: By that, you mean the charges would only have been investigated by the FBI.

Brilmayer: Yes.

McConnell: That would have happened even without the leak.

Brilmayer: I'm not standing up for the leak, but if the entire process was secret, people would have to worry about whether this sort of thing was being covered up.

McConnell: Let's not forget who was the victim of the public process after the leak. It was Anita Hill who was the principal victim, after she came to the committee on the understanding that her name would not be made public.

The committee staff egged her on to tell her story to them and the FBI on that basis. And then they turned around and leaked it in order to flush her out and put her in a situation where she could not maintain her privacy. I see no virtue in that at all.

Brilmayer: I don't disagree with most of what you said.

But can you imagine a confirmation process in which it would be possible for somebody to come forward with allegations without any public pressure to take the allegations seriously?

Rightly or wrongly, the reaction of most women was, "You guys don't take these things seriously because you're a bunch of men." I think that's a cost to be considered.

Dellinger: Do we all agree that a Senate Judiciary Committee is not a very effective forum for evaluating charges based on misconduct? That this should not be a model for the future?

Redish: As compared to what?

Dellinger: I'm inclined to think the only proper way to do it is to have an investigation, which is submitted for resolution to an appropriate body that has prescribed rules.

I understand the inevitability of the Anita Hill hearings. But surely it is not the appropriate forum for evaluating allegations of this kind.

McConnell: This goes way back in our history. As you know, Alexander Hamilton was one of the first to face it, and it's happened repeatedly since then to people from Alger Hiss and Jimmy Hoffa to John Tower and Ollie North.

Redish: But we're talking about a situation in which the alternative isn't a criminal forum, as it was in the Oliver North case.

To turn to another question, is it clear the senators properly perceived their roles? It's been suggested that the Republicans on the committee saw themselves as Clarence Thomas' defense counsel, while, as far as anyone could make out, the Democrats saw themselves as factfinders. Did they correctly understand their roles?

Kozinski: We're used to resolving things by the adversary process. So it was natural, I thought, that those on the committee who supported the nominee would take on the role of advocate, which creates some obvious tension because they're also judges.

Nevertheless, I think it worked fairly well.

Dellinger: I think the dual role of investigation and evaluation was a problem for the committee. It could have been avoided if the bulk of the questioning had been done by majority and minority counsel.

The questioning would have been considerably improved, and the senators could have played a more evaluative function.

Kozinski: What do you mean, "improved"? I thought the questioning was pretty good and I watch a lot of trials.

Dellinger: One problem was the Democrats did not attempt to oppose Judge Thomas as vigorously as the Republicans worked at discrediting Professor Hill.

McConnell: What's wrong with that?

Redish: Can you conceive of any testimony that would have gotten either Sen. Simpson or Sen. Hatch to say, "By God, it's true. He did do it"?

McConnell: I think they viewed their role as defending his innocence up until the point it became untenable.

It reminds me of the Watergate impeachment hearings, where a number of Republicans continued to defend President Nixon up until a certain point, when it became impossible for them.

I don't think that's a mixture of roles. I think that's rather natural. Furthermore, I'm surprised you think the Democrats on the committee did not go on the offensive.

Other than those who attempted to draw as little attention to themselves as possible, it seemed that's exactly what they were doing.

Dellinger: I think that staff counsel doesn't have to worry as much as senators about maintaining an appearance of impartiality or about asking questions that are potentially politically embarrassing. In that respect, I think the questioning could have been a little sharper.

McConnell: I agree the senators were more restrained in questioning Judge Thomas and Professor Hill, but I'm not convinced that is a bad thing.

Redish: Any final points?

McConnell: For the first time the public has been exposed to the kind of process we have, and there seems to be major dissatisfaction.

To some extent, it's misplaced, but I would still love to see the dissatisfaction channeled into genuine reform. The current process threatens judicial independence and undermines the quality of our Court to boot.

We now are in a period of divided government, which hasn't existed for most of our history. There are some things that have to be worked out afresh. This is one of them.

Dellinger: Some of the problems we see in the confirmation process actually originate in the nomination process, which is closed off from public view.

If the president would come forward with individuals whose nomination would be greeted with widespread acclaim, I think you would see a much prettier confirmation process.

Kozinski: Any attempt at sweeping reform is going to be hard to come by and is likely to backfire. I like the suggestion of de-emphasizing the hearings and re-emphasizing the public record.

That, of course, takes care of how you deal with nominees with no public record. Televising the hearings also leads to too much pain and too much unpredictability. I don't think it serves the American public well.

Brilmayer: We're not going to get anywhere with this problem, until we resolve whether we want the Senate to have the same sort of power in the confirmation proceedings as the president does in the nomination process.

Nomination is a quiet and essentially unreviewable process. You have no way of knowing who was passed over and for what reasons.

The Senate would like to have that kind of power also, but the way things are set up strategically, they simply can't do it. So the Senate is trying to reclaim some of the power it feels the president has.

I think I would disagree that it's really a problem of the president coming forward with consensus-oriented candidates. I'm not really convinced that's what the Senate votes for, and I'm also sort of puzzled about where the consensus should be determined.

A lot of the candidates on Walter's list would win a consensus from lawyers and academics, but is that really the group we want to look to?

The problem is I don't think we have a clear sense of what we want out of this process.

REPORT OF THE TWENTIETH CENTURY FUND TASK FORCE ON JUDICIAL SELECTION*
8–11 (1988)

A little over two years ago, the staff and Trustees of the Twentieth Century Fund decided that the way in which the federal judiciary was selected needed review. After some deliberation, it was decided that the issue was so timely and controversial that it warranted discussion and evaluation by a Task Force. A group of experts who could knowledgeably examine a system of judicial selection that seemed to be growing ever more political was thus brought together to explore the ways in which candidates for the federal bench—both the lower federal courts and the Supreme Court—are selected, nominated, and confirmed. [The Task Force made the following recommendations vis a vis the Supreme Court:] * * *

* From Judicial Roulette: *Report of the Twentieth Century Fund Task Force on Judicial Selection,* © 1988, The Twentieth Century Fund, New York. Reproduced with permission of the Twentieth Century Fund.

*The Task Force believes that the fundamental problem with the confirmation process for Supreme Court nominees is just the opposite of that for lower-court nominees: it is too visible and attracts too much publicity.** In some cases, such as the nominations of Louis Brandeis, John Parker, Felix Frankfurter, Justice Abe Fortas to be chief justice, and Robert Bork, the confirmation process has come dangerously close to looking like the electoral process. It has become very much a national referendum on the appointment, with media campaigns, polling techniques, and political rhetoric that distract attention from, and sometimes completely distort, the legal qualifications of the nominee.****

Since the appointment of Justice Sandra Day O'Connor in 1981, confirmation hearings on Supreme Court nominees have been televised. Media coverage may have a salutary effect in informing and educating the public about the nominee, the Court, and the Constitution. But it has also invited abuse of the confirmation process. The White House, the Department of Justice, senators, witnesses, and even nominees now seem tempted to use televised hearings as a forum for other purposes, ranging from self-promotion to mobilizing special interest groups in order to influence public opinion. Witnesses are called to testify not principally for their legal expertise, but as advocates for and against the nominees and as representatives of competing interests and constituencies. The confirmation process, in short, has become extremely politicized in a way that denigrates the Court and serves to undermine its prestige as well as public respect for the rule of law.

The Task Force recognizes that nominations to the Supreme Court have long had, and will continue to have, high visibility. The clock on

---

** Joseph A. Califano, Jr., dissents:* I disagree with the conclusions of the Task Force Report that the confirmation process for Supreme Court nominees is too visible and attracts too much publicity. I also disagree with the conclusion that Supreme Court nominees should no longer be expected to appear as witnesses during the Senate Judiciary Committee hearings on confirmation. Accordingly, I dissent from most of the discussion and other conclusions in the Task Force discussion of the confirmation process for Supreme Court nominees.

Much of the Supreme Court portion of the Task Force report is a thinly tailored argument to repeal the First Amendment to the Constitution as it might apply to hearings on Supreme Court nominees. The public scrutiny of Supreme Court nominees during their testimony before the Senate Judiciary Committee and such scrutiny of the testimony of other witnesses before the committee are essential in our society.

Each of the 9 members of the Supreme Court has far more power than any one of the 100 senators and certainly any one of the 435 representatives. Each Supreme Court nominee should be subjected to widespread public scrutiny before confirmation.

This is of the essence in a free society in which one of the branches exercises an enormous amount of power—indeed, final power in some matters—with respect to the other two branches and to the people of the country.

As Congress legislates in more detail, it puts more and more issues into our federal judiciary. As science raises to the level of constitutional dispute a host of issues that involve life and death—abortion is the most explosive one today, but surely euthanasia lurks in the wings—it puts more and more issues before our federal judiciary. As a citizen, I want to know as much as possible about each of the nine people who are going to decide such issues for me and my country.

Therefore, I believe that Senate confirmation hearings and the entire selection process for Supreme Court Justices should be as public and as publicized as modern communications can make them.

*** Philip B. Kurland strongly dissents* both from the conclusion of this paragraph and from the implication that these five hearings are analogous in any relevant way.

media coverage, especially television coverage, cannot and should not be turned back. But in light of that extensive media coverage, *the confirmation process needs to be depoliticized by minimizing the potential for participants to posture and distort the basic purpose of the proceedings.* *

Except in cases where a candidate's personal conduct—what the Constitution terms the "good behavior" requisite for all federal judges—is at issue, the Task Force recommends that Supreme Court nominees *should no longer be expected to appear as witnesses during the Senate Judiciary Committee's hearings on their confirmation.* ** (If they ask to do so, they should, of course, be permitted to appear.)

This recommendation calls for the Senate once again to adhere to the practice that it followed for most of its history. Throughout the past century, Supreme Court nominees did not appear as witnesses. It was not until 1925, when Harlan F. Stone made an appearance before the Judiciary Committee, that a Supreme Court nominee did so. In 1939, Felix Frankfurter was the second Supreme Court nominee to appear and to answer senators' questions, though he pointed out that it was "not only bad taste but inconsistent with the duties of the office for which I have been nominated for me to attempt to supplant my past record by personal declaration." A decade later, Sherman Minton repeatedly refused to appear before the committee, explaining that his "record speaks for itself."

The practice of Supreme Court nominees appearing and answering questions before the Senate Judiciary Committee is a relatively recent one. It is one that now ought to be abandoned. But *if nominees continue to appear before the committee, then the Task Force recommends that senators should not put questions to nominees that call for answers that would indicate how they would deal with specific issues if they were confirmed.* This was the practice until quite recently. During the confirmation hearings on Justice O'Connor and Judge Bork, the questions and answers sometimes crossed this line. Unfortunately, this change contributes further to the politicization of the process. In the Task Force's view, when nominees give answers indicating how they will vote once confirmed, they destroy the public's belief in the fairness of those on the bench, and thereby undermine confidence in the Court.

The Task Force further recommends that the Judiciary Committee and the Senate base confirmation decisions on a nominee's written record and the testimony of legal experts as to his competence.† The hearings, the witnesses called to testify, and the questions asked of them should be confined to the ability and capacity of the nominee to carry out the high tasks of serving on the Supreme Court.

* *Walter Berns comments:* I suggest further that television cameras be banned from the hearings. This would go some way toward getting the senators to attend to the business at hand instead of striking poses to please their favorite constituents.

** *Lloyd N. Cutler dissents.*

† *Lloyd N. Cutler dissents.*

The members of the Task Force are aware that these recommendations are controversial. The politics of judicial selection are such that any attempt to interfere with the procedures that have evolved also will interfere with the prerogatives of well-established political interests. Moreover, there was and continues to be considerable debate, and differences of opinion, among members of the Task Force on several important issues. But it is the view of the Task Force that the recommendations made in this report can contribute to restoring the basic purpose of confirmation hearings: to ensure that we select competent, impartial, and thoughtful judges. In addition, the Task Force believes that its recommendations, if adopted, could do much to rebuild public confidence in the appointment process, the Supreme Court, and the federal judiciary. We speak with one voice in acknowledging the importance of the issues raised in this examination of the politics of judicial selection and in affirming, with Hamilton, that "the complete independence of the courts of justice" is an indispensable prerequisite for the judiciary in a democratic polity.

ROBERT BORK,* THE SENATE'S POWER GRAB
N.Y. Times, June 23, 1993 at A23

[T]he Senate Judiciary Committee's [current practice of asking] detailed questions about [a nominee's] legal opinions on many divisive political issues * * * is a relatively new practice for the committee. For most of U.S. history, the nominee did not even appear before the committee: It was considered beneath the dignity of the office of a Justice. (As the Clarence Thomas hearings showed, that belief has some merit.) Even when the practice began in the 1930s, the questioning was usually perfunctory or nonexistent. In 1962, Byron R. White was asked only about a dozen questions. William O. Douglas waited outside the hearing room and was finally dismissed without being asked anything in 1939.

Two factors have changed all that. One is the presence of television in the hearing room. So long as the cameras are there, confirmations will be drawn-out photo opportunities.

The other is the politicization of the process. The Court is no longer primarily a legal institution but rather a political and cultural power—in one sense, the supreme political and cultural power, because its mandates are difficult to override and will not be ignored or disobeyed. Perhaps it was inevitable that an institution with such power would come to be viewed as a political prize and a political weapon.

What can stem this politicization? Practically speaking, only the citizens' and the Court's understanding of the difference between judges and legislators. But devotion to the morality of process turns out to be a paper obstacle to those who are very sure about the morality of results.

For example, if, as the National Abortion Rights Action League and the American Civil Liberties Union feel, morality demands the right to abortion, there is simply no point in demonstrating to them that, the Constitution being utterly silent on the question, abortion is a question for debate by the American people and elected officials, not by the Supreme Court.

The purpose of today's televised inquisitions concerning every thought a nominee ever had about the minutiae of constitutional law is the same no matter which side mounts the inquisition. Either nominees can be induced to give answers that will be used against them, or they can be forced into promises that they are likely to keep once on the Court lest they embarrass themselves.

There are two disastrous consequences of the judiciary's meticulous parsing of a nominee's views. First, the televised hearings have become a referendum on whether Americans approve of particular constitutional interpretations. The prohibitions of the Constitution were put in place precisely to prevent majority opinion from ruling certain areas of life. That purpose is defeated if majorities decide what they want the Constitution to mean.

An equally anticonstitutional consequence is the Senate's crossing of the line that separates its powers from those of the judiciary and the executive branches. For example, during the Clarence Thomas hearings, Democratic Senator Herb Kohl complained about the executive branch's assistance to Justice Thomas in preparing for the hearings. Of course, removing executive branch support for the nominee would be fatal to any confirmation: the amount of material that must be located, classified and analyzed in preparation for the hearings is staggering.

Senator Kohl said he was concerned about the constitutional principle of the separation of powers. He hinted that it was improper executive branch influence for the President's men and women to assist the nominee to prepare for the confirmation hearings. It is a wonder the Senator did not object to the President choosing the nominee in the first place.

Actually, some Senators did just that. Democrats Joseph Biden and Paul Simon said afterward that President Bush should have to clear future nominations with the committee—which effectively meant with the Democrats—before advancing a name. The Constitution states that the President shall nominate and, with the advice and consent of the Senate, appoint judges. These Senators suggested that they assume both functions. So much for the separation of powers.

That is not the design of our Government. Federal judges, alone among public officials, are given life tenure precisely so that they will not be accountable to the people. They must consider themselves bound by law that is independent of their own views of what is desirable. That is why an exploration of judicial philosophy, and not of political ends, is important in the confirmation process.

What kinds of questions might properly be put to a nominee to reveal their judicial philosophy? It is possible to explore a nominee's views without requiring a commitment from the nominee to vote a particular way in the future. * * *

[Instead of asking:] "Are you now or have you ever been, critical of the reasoning of Roe v. Wade?" [t]he question about Roe v. Wade could be put this way: "If a claim for a constitutional right to abortion came before the Court, how would you reason about it and what materials would you think relevant?" Or, for other subjects, "What bearing does the fact that the first Congress—which proposed the religion clauses of the First Amendment—provided paid chaplains for the House, the Senate and the military have on questions of the relation of religion to government?" Or, "Does the Ninth Amendment's statement that 'the enumeration in the Constitution, of certain rights, shall not be construed to deny or disparage others retained by the people' authorize judges to strike down legislation by finding and enforcing unmentioned rights?"

If questions like these are posed to * * * future nominees, the Senators and the public will learn how the nominees understand the role of a Justice, without requiring from them a commitment to vote any particular way on a specific issue.

* * *

[I]f Senators ask questions about judicial philosophy rather than seeking commitments to particular decisions, it would make a significant contribution to the American understanding of the Supreme Court's legitimate role in governing us.

LLOYD CUTLER,* WHY NOT EXECUTIVE SESSIONS?
Wash. Post, Oct. 17, 1991, at A23

Although millions of Americans were riveted to their TV sets over the past weekend, most of us agree that despite its entertainment value, such a public spectacle should never happen again. Is there a better way to deal with charges of personal misbehavior against nominees for high government office?

I think there is. The Constitution entrusts the Senate with the duty of advice and consent to treaties with foreign nations and to the president's appointment of "officers of the United States." The Framers selected the Senate, not the House, to approve treaties because they believed the smaller Senate could be entrusted to keep secrets and could hear the most delicate aspects of the reasons for and against a treaty without making them public.

In fact, the Senate has done well in keeping diplomatic and national security secrets. The Senate Intelligence and Armed Services committees conduct many secret hearings in executive session, and their record for being leakproof has been quite good, even when the subject is as politically controversial as support of the contras in Nicaragua. The entire Senate has also met in executive session—most recently in debating its consent to the Intermediate Nuclear Forces Treaty in 1988—and no damaging leaks have occurred. The Senate also goes into executive session when it acts as a jury in impeachment proceedings.

As Sen. Sam Nunn recommended yesterday, the same principle should be considered when the Senate's other "advise and consent" function, the confirmation of presidential appointments, involves issues of a confidential nature. Indeed, the Senate Armed Services Committee did just this in dealing with some of the personal-behavior accusations against John Tower.

When a charge of personal misconduct is made, especially sexual misconduct, and the responsible Senate committee decides that the charge is substantial enough to require an evidentiary hearing, the committee should invoke Senate Rule XXVI.5(b) and conduct the hearing in a secret executive session. Only a single copy of the transcript should be made, and, following the practice of the Senate Intelligence Committee, it should be kept under lock and key for senators only to examine in the committee's office.

After the hearing, the committee should file a report with the full Senate summarizing the gist of the testimony and any committee findings and conclusions on the issue. In the discretion of the committee, the report would be published and debate on the Senate floor would be in open session, or the report itself would be secret and would be presented to the full Senate in executive session.

True, there are so many Senate staffers and investigative reporters, and they exert such strong hydraulic pressure on one another, that what happens behind closed doors might leak out anyway, especially if the nomination is politically controversial and the charge is highly explosive. But even if a leak occurred, we would still be better off than now for several reasons:

The leak could only be of the committee report, or of second-hand accounts of who said what at the hearing or on the Senate floor. There would be no videotape to be televised in vivid sound and pictures.

The hearing itself would be much shorter and to the point. Deprived of their 12-camera TV studio and their national audience of millions, senators would waste much less time in irrelevant discourses on their own sensitivity and thoughtfulness and could concentrate on developing the facts.

The accuser and the accused would suffer less humiliation and invasion of their privacy than a televised public hearing entails.

The Senate would avoid confirming the prevalent low public opinion of those we have elected to high office.

The circus atmosphere of last weekend would not be repeated, and the standards of what can be said on daylight television to family audiences would not fall even lower than they are today. When a televised Senate Committee hearing contains explicit material that even Phil Donahue and Geraldo Rivera would think twice about using, the government itself is contributing to the cheapening and coarsening of public taste.

Let's give executive sessions a try. They may make things better and could hardly make them worse.

The writer, a Washington lawyer, was counsel to the president in the Carter administration.

UNITED STATES SENATE
COMMITTEE ON THE JUDICIARY
PREPARED REMARKS OF SENATOR JOSEPH R. BIDEN JR. ON THE CONFIRMATION PROCESS FOR JUDGE RUTH BADER GINSBURG
JULY 15, 1993

To improve public confidence in our investigations, we have changed certain policies concerning Supreme Court nominees. I laid out these investigatory reforms, which I now intend to follow, after the Thomas hearings last year.

First, as in the past, the committee will receive a full FBI report on the nominee. Staff with security clearance will review that file and other investigative material on a confidential and bipartisan basis.

An important change in procedure has been adopted to ensure that the Judiciary Committee will not again be placed in the difficult position, of possessing information about a Supreme Court nominee from a source unwilling to share that information with *all* other Senators.

Any source who comes to the committee with allegations against a Supreme Court nominee is now notified that all information will be placed in the nominee's confidential file, and shared on a confidential basis with *all* Senators, before the Senate votes on a Supreme Court nomination.

Second, because, ultimately, the question with respect to investigations of a Supreme Court nominee is the credibility and character of that nominee, the committee will conduct a closed session with Judge Ginsburg—and with all future nominees.

No issues of policy or jurisprudence will be discussed in this closed portion of the hearing.

The purpose of the session is to ask the nominee—face-to-face, on the record, under oath—about any investigative issues.

The hearing will be conducted in accordance with Senate Rule 25, which permits the committee to go into closed session to protect the privacy of the nominee in considering confidential information.

A closed hearing will be conducted for every Supreme Court nominee, so that the holding of such a session can not be taken to demonstrate that the committee has received adverse confidential information about the nominee.

The transcript of that session will be part of the confidential record of the nomination made available to all Senators.

Third, to insure that all Senators are aware of any charges in our possession, the committee will hold a closed, confidential briefing session for Senators only on all Supreme Court nominations.

At this briefing, all Senators will be invited, under rigorous restrictions to protect confidentiality, to inspect all documents and reports we compile.

The briefing will be offered following the completion of committee action and before the nomination goes to the floor.

I intend these three steps to help restore confidence in our investigative procedures, and to reassure the public about the seriousness with which we take such matters as part of the confirmation process.

I also hope that the whole of this nomination and confirmation process will contribute to enhancing the confidence of the American people in the *women and men* who will serve on the Supreme Court.

I intend in these next few weeks to do all that I can to further these goals.

I ask my colleagues in the Senate and on the Judiciary Committee to join me in considering the nomination of Ruth Bader Ginsburg fairly, efficiently, and with the public good foremost in our minds.

HENRY MONAGHAN,*
THE CONFIRMATION PROCESS: LAW OR POLITICS? **

101 Harv.L.Rev. 1202, 1203–1212 (1988)

In this commentary, I want to submit two claims—one normative, the other empirical—and to raise one question. The normative claim is that the Senate's role in the appointment of Supreme Court judges is properly viewed as largely "political" in the broadest sense of the term: no significant affirmative constitutional compulsion exists to confirm any presidential nominee. So viewed, the Senate can serve as an important political check on the President's power to appoint. Moreover, the political nature of the Senate's role, like that of the President, helps ameliorate the "countermajoritarian difficulty": by increasing the likelihood that Supreme Court judges will hold views not too different from those of the people's representatives, the Senate can reduce the tension between the institution of judicial review and democratic government.

* Harlan Fiske Stone Professor of Constitutional Law, Columbia University School of Law.

The empirical claim is that, at least for the foreseeable future, the overriding political power of the modern Presidency will continue to confine the Senate's actual role in the appointment process to its current dimensions. The Senate is incapable of systematically assuming any role greater than that of providing a check against the appointment of nominees perceived to be morally unworthy or too radical. In this respect, the unanimous confirmations of Judges Kennedy and Scalia reveal far more than does the rejection of Judge Bork.

Finally, the question I wish to raise is suggested by the nomination (not the withdrawal) of Judge Douglas Ginsburg. Should limits be imposed on the tenure of persons appointed judges of the Supreme Court?

* * *

II.

The Senate's actual role in the confirmation process depended upon the shifting balance of political power between Congress and the President. The Senate's significant nineteenth-century role reflected the general congressional dominance of that era. Scarcely one hundred years ago, Woodrow Wilson argued that national government was congressional government—more precisely, "government by the chairmen of the Standing Committees of Congress." Wilson put aside the President with the dismissive observation that his "business * * * occasionally great, is usually not much above routine." Although some such model of congressional government could be defended as late as the beginning of the New Deal, modern government is presidential government, at least in its most important aspects. Presidential ascendancy in the appointment process reflects this fact.

The modern Presidency, even a lame-duck Presidency facing a Senate controlled by the opposite party, has enormous resources for mobilizing support and for disciplining those senators who refuse to go along. Such resources—party discipline, ideology, and various carrots and sticks—can be concentrated on any issue of significant importance to the President. One could speculate extensively about why those resources failed in the case of Judge Bork. For us it suffices that the Bork proceedings themselves arose in a special context, one in which the administration's hard-line attitude on judicial nominations had left a bitter residue. Many parties were spoiling for a fight, and Judge Bork, who was perceived as far outside the mainstream of legal thinking, was the perfect catalyst to provoke one. Such a configuration is unlikely to be repeated frequently, suggesting Judge Bork's rejection portends no important institutional changes in the President's ability to win confirmation of nominees.

The institutionally important point is that it takes enormous energy for senators to unite in order to resist the President.[31] Once undertak-

---

31. It is no accident that in his book on the Supreme Court Chief Justice Rehnquist barely mentions the Senate's role in the chapter on the appointment process. *See*

en, such conduct cannot easily be sustained, as evidenced by the relief with which the Senate greeted Judge Kennedy's nomination. The senators made every effort to see him as different from Judge Bork, regardless of whether he actually was. Commenting on Judge Kennedy's "smooth sailing" on his initial Senate visit, Senator John McCain, a conservative Republican from Arizona, put the point well: the Senate was simply "weary" of fighting. "Nobody wants to go through that again. There's just too much blood on the floor." At most, Judge Bork's hearings may have established a tradition of more probing Senate interrogation of a nominee, but the political background in which the entire confirmation process functions remains one with a powerful Presidency. To be sure, the rejection reminds us that periodically the American people seem to need a battle over a Supreme Court appointment. But symbolism aside, the hard fact is that the President's vision of what is proper judicial philosophy ultimately will prevail, as Judge Kennedy's confirmation demonstrates.

Nonetheless, some believe that Judge Bork's rejection shows that the Senate's role is less marginal than I have argued. The Senate's failure to confirm Judge Bork is said to reflect popular rejection of original understanding theory and popular acceptance of a general constitutional right to privacy. Although these contentions initially appear plausible, when carefully analyzed their flaws become apparent. In fact, Judge Bork did not avow original understanding as the sole basis for legitimate judicial decisionmaking. Moreover, the abortion cases, the most frequently cited illustration of Judge Bork's rejection of a constitutional right to privacy, actually involve autonomy or freedom from regulation, not privacy. Furthermore, the claim that, at least in exceptional circumstances, the Senate acts as a court of popular opinion endorsing or rejecting certain constitutional views is unpersuasive.[35] Confirmation proceedings cannot be construed as referenda of any sort on judicial philosophies—except perhaps at the far margins—because the Senate is simply not equipped to proffer or register constitutional judgments of such magnitude. This is particularly true when, as in the case of Judge Bork, commentators seek to extract such judgments from a bitter, wide-ranging, and complex nomination proceeding that focused upon a multitude of issues involving the Reagan Presidency and a number of Supreme Court decisions.

W. REHNQUIST, *supra* note 6, at 235–51. On this issue, at least, *The Federalist* correctly predicted our present: the Senate's role is marginal, and "[i]t is not very probable that [the President's] nomination would often be overruled." The Federalist No. 76, at 512 (A. Hamilton) (J. Cooke ed. 1961).

35. Those who would argue otherwise must explain why Judge Bork's rejection implicitly endorses a liberal judicial philosophy, whereas the Senate's rejection of Jus-

tice Fortas as Chief Justice did not repudiate the same philosophy. Not surprisingly, claims of this nature tend to reflect the ideological commitments of their advocates. *Compare* Dworkin, *From Bork to Kennedy*, N.Y.Rev. of Books, Dec. 17, 1987, at 36, 38 *passim* (stating that liberals contend that Judge Bork's rejection was a declaration of popular will) *with* H. Abraham, *supra* note 3, at 43–45 (arguing that the rejection of Justice Fortas' nomination as Chief Justice reflected a referendum on the Warren Court).

III.

The events surrounding President Reagan's efforts to fill the vacancy left by Justice Powell's retirement raise an additional question. When nominated, Judge [Douglas] Ginsburg was 41 years old. His relative youth cannot by itself be treated as a disqualification. Benjamin Curtis was 41 when nominated, and Judge Story only 32. Because confirmation effectively carries life tenure, Judge Ginsburg might well have served for four decades. The nomination for such a potentially lengthy period of service provides a singular occasion for reexamining the advisability of life tenure for Supreme Court judges. For some, the same premises that justify the free play of politics in the confirmation process might also weigh against life tenure. Also some limits on judicial tenure would help reconcile judicial review with democratic government. My concerns lie elsewhere, however.

The most common defenses of life tenure, contained in Hamilton's writing in *The Federalist,* are not fully persuasive. In *Federalist* No. 78, Hamilton argued that life tenure is indispensable to insulate the judiciary from the other branches of government, and thus to ensure its independence. But even assuming that such complete judicial independence is desirable, eliminating life tenure need not materially undermine it. Presumably, what relieves judges of the incentive to please is not the prospect of indefinite service, but the awareness that their continuation in office does not depend on securing the continuing approval of the political branches. Independence, therefore, could be achieved by mandating fixed, nonrenewable terms of service. Hamilton's objection in *Federalist* No. 79 to a state constitutional provision imposing mandatory retirement on judges at sixty is similarly unpersuasive. He stated that such a provision was unsound in "a republic, where fortunes are not affluent, and pensions not expedient." Given the current prevalence of pensions, however, Hamilton's argument no longer carries weight.

I propose the consideration of two kinds of limitations on judicial tenure. The first is an age limit. I think it quite astounding that a majority of Supreme Court judges bordered on eighty years of age before Chief Justice Burger and Justice Powell retired. The Court's workload is very heavy, and it is doubtful that many octogenarians would be able to devote the energy necessary to the task. As Aristotle said, "that judges of important causes should hold office for life is a disputable thing, for the mind grows old as well as the body." The graying of the Court can only work to ensure even greater delegation of responsibility to law clerks.

My second suggestion is premised on a distrust of relatively unaccountable powerholders. The suggestion is that no one be permitted to serve for more than some fixed and unrenewable term, such as fifteen or twenty years. Governor Winthrop once described judges as "gods upon earth," and that surely is true of the Supreme Court judges. It seems dubious policy to leave such power in any person's hands for too long. In light of these concerns, and of the defects in the original justifications for life tenure, the burden should be on those who favor the continuation of the present arrangement to come forth with their argument. Or is the short response to both of my suggestions, "If it ain't broke, don't fix it"?

LEE EPSTEIN,* A BETTER WAY
TO APPOINT JUSTICES
The Christian Science Monitor,** Mar. 17, 1992 at 19

* * * As the confirmation proceedings for Clarence Thomas * * * indicated, something is seriously wrong with the way we appoint justices to the nation's highest court. We need to take a radical step to alter the entire nomination and confirmation process—and thus the political calculus of the president and the Senate: Let's amend the Constitution and require two-thirds of the Senate to confirm Supreme Court justices. This is a drastic proposal. No one likes to tinker with the Constitution. The framers erected an intricate system of government in which manipulation of one part inevitably affects the way another functions.

But the framers had little idea of the role the Supreme Court would come to play in United States politics. Nor did they envision the role politics would play in the court's decisions. Rather they imagined, as Alexander Hamilton wrote, a court full of principled justices who would "declare the sense of the law" through "inflexible and uniform adherence to the rights of the Constitution and of individuals."

That is why the framers developed the unique system of nomination, confirmation, and life tenure: to keep justices above partisan politics. Had they foreseen courts of recent eras, courts composed largely of legal activists eager to see their values etched into law, they would have devised a different scheme.

From the beginning, presidents have tried to pack the court with partisan or ideological soulmates. After his party lost the election of 1800, President John Adams and lame-duck Federalist senators hastily appointed a host of like-minded federal judges before the Jeffersonians came into power.

Although neither the confirmation process nor the court itself has ever measured up to the Constitution's lofty expectations, at no time in the past were they simultaneously so out of control. Requiring a two-thirds confirmation vote for justices would start to realize the framers' vision.

● A two-thirds vote would change, for the better, the political calculations of the president. Presidents—be they Democrats or Republicans—would have to rethink whom they nominated to the court. To gain approval of their nominees, they would need true bipartisan sup-

* Lee Epstein, associate professor of political science at Washington University in St. Louis, studies judicial politics.

** Excerpts from "*A Better Way to Appoint Justices*," by Lee Epstein, Professor of Political Science; Copyright © 1992 by Lee Epstein and the Christian Science Monitor. Reprinted by permission of the author and the Christian Science Monitor.

port, not just a few crossover votes. That would require them to place far more stock in candidates' legal credentials. It also would compel presidents to seek the advice of senators of both parties before making nominations.

• A two-thirds vote would also change, for the better, thinking in the Senate. If presidents gave senators a greater role at the "advice" stage, it would help to eliminate the sort of proceedings we have experienced in recent years—unacceptable candidates would never make it that far. Confirmation hearings would serve as forums to discern nominees' legal qualifications to sit on the Supreme Court, rather than as showcases for senators on the Judiciary Committee.

• A two-thirds vote is required for the approval of treaties (by the Senate) and the proposal of constitutional amendments (both Houses); who sits on the Supreme Court is today of similar importance. The framers required two-thirds votes for matters of great national importance. What has become more important—at least on domestic matters—than decisions of the US Supreme Court? Courts of the last three decades have enunciated public policy on reapportionment, affirmative action, and abortion.

• A two-thirds vote would not eliminate qualified candidates. Since the emergence of the modern Supreme Court (a date scholars fix at around 1937), only one successful nominee to be an associate justice might have failed to gain 67 Senate votes—Mr. Thomas. William Rehnquist might still have attained confirmation as an associate justice (he had 68 votes in 1971), but he might not have been able to ascend to the chief justiceship (he received only 65 votes in 1986).

I stress the word "might," because a change in the rules would significantly alter the calculus of both the president and the Senate. With a two-thirds requirement, Ronald Reagan might not have sought to elevate Mr. Rehnquist (or pursued the confirmation of Robert Bork), nor might President Bush have nominated Thomas. Alternatively, Rehnquist might have received more votes from the Senate if it was operating under the constraints of a two-thirds rule.

My point is not to second-guess past votes; it is to suggest that a two-thirds requirement would not restrict the pool of serious candidates. It may, though, reduce it just enough to eliminate those who have no business sitting on the most important judicial body in our nation.

Chapter Three

SETTING THE COURT'S AGENDA

The Supreme Court has virtually complete discretion to pick and choose, from the cases presented to it, which cases the Court will review and adjudicate on the merits. The Court, in effect, sets its own agenda as it decides which cases it will decide.

From an advocate's viewpoint, then, the first job is to convince the Court to hear the case, not necessarily to persuade the Court to a particular view of it. To the student of the Court, its discretion over its agenda means that the law the Court makes through its published opinions must be influenced, in some substantial manner, by the standards the Court employs at the screening stage—deciding which petitions for a writ of certiorari to grant. As it selects a comparative handful from the thousands of cases offered for review each year, the Court sends very strong signals about the kinds of cases, types of issues, and classes of litigants it favors.[1] For these reasons, a study of the Supreme Court's case selection process should be a central feature of an analysis of the institutional processes of constitutional lawmaking.

A central question, raised by all these materials, is the extent to which the Court's agenda-setting function is dictated by institutional concerns, on the one hand, or by the various justices' preferences for different constitutional law rules, on the other. Certainly, given the fact that the Court receives almost 6,000 petitions for review every year and typically grants fewer than 150, the principal function of the process is to weed out the vast majority of cases and deny them further review. Thus, most petitions must be denied without regard to the ideology or status of the petitioning party. In this sense, the certiorari process certainly is governed by institutional concerns.

With respect to those cases that are granted or are seriously considered as potentially "certworthy", however, the Court (or any particular justice who voted on the matter) may be predominantly motivated by either of two distinct goals. First, the decision whether or not to grant

---

1. These arguments have been forcefully voiced by Justice Brennan. See William J. Brennan, *The National Court of Appeals:* *Another Dissent,* 40 U.Chi.L.Rev. 473, 482–85 (1973) (excerpted in Section B. of this chapter, infra).

cert in close cases might be governed principally by a desire to further ideologically neutral institutional goals. Thus, for example, the Court or the justice might be searching for cases that reflect conflict among the lower courts that cannot be resolved except at the Supreme Court level. Alternatively, however, in such cases the Court or the justice might be seeking primarily to further the Court's (or that justice's) policy preferences. For example, the Court or the justice might be searching for cases that would be good vehicles for cutting back on the scope of the First Amendment's protection of freedom of religion. Just how large a role ideology, or value preferences, or judicial politics, plays in making up the Court's agenda remains a tricky question.[2]

The materials that follow are divided into four sections. Section A sets out the formal rules—the provisions of the U.S. Code governing Supreme Court jurisdiction and the central portions of the Supreme Court's own rules concerning the disposition of petitions for review. The central points are: Except for the very rare case that falls within the Supreme Court's original jurisdiction,[3] the Court hears only cases that it is requested to adjudicate by a party seeking review of an adverse decision by a lower state or federal court. Although, until recently, the jurisdictional statutes obliged the Court to consider a fair number of cases on the merits, this is no longer the case. Almost all cases now fall within a discretionary (or "certiorari"), rather than an obligatory (or "appeal"), category.[4] Supreme Court Rule 10 purports to describe the various factors that predominantly influence the Court's decision whether or not to grant a writ of certiorari, but this appears to be at best a checklist of certain relevant variables.

Section B describes the processes by which the Court receives, considers, and votes on petitions for writs of certiorari ("cert petitions") and oppositions to those petitions ("opp certs" or "cert opps"). Because the Court is asked to review about 6,000 cases each year and typically

---

2. We offer some further thoughts on this issue in a brief concluding note at the end of section C of this chapter, below.

3. Article III grants the Supreme Court original jurisdiction over a small class of cases. See U.S. Constitution art. III, § 2. Most cases that fall within the scope of this grant may also be (and usually are) filed originally in federal district courts. See 28 U.S.C. § 1251 (giving federal district courts concurrent jurisdiction over many cases falling within the Supreme Court's constitutionally conferred original jurisdiction). Of the original jurisdiction cases filed in the Supreme Court, most are rather boring (except to the litigants) boundary disputes between states. For an exception to the rule that original jurisdiction cases are boring, see Katzenbach v. Morgan, 384 U.S. 641, 86 S.Ct. 1717, 16 L.Ed.2d 828 (1966) (holding constitutional federal statute overriding certain English literacy voting qualifications in the States).

4. Appeals, rather than certiorari, to the Supreme Court still lie from decisions of three-judge federal district courts. Many cases involving the Voting Rights Act of 1965 still arise in three-judge district courts and Congress will occasionally direct that a new statute, whose constitutionality is obviously suspect, should be adjudicated in the first instance before a three-judge court. See, e.g., United States v. Eichman, 496 U.S. 310, 110 S.Ct. 2404, 110 L.Ed.2d 287 (1990) (direct appeal from district court as provided by Flag Protection Act of 1989); Thornburgh v. Gingles, 478 U.S. 30, 106 S.Ct. 2752, 92 L.Ed.2d 25 (1986) (direct appeal from district court as provided by Voting Rights Act of 1965). But, in general, such courts are now employed very rarely and, therefore, very few cases come to the Supreme Court as appeals.

agrees to give full, on the merits ("plenary") consideration to fewer than 150, these processes are designed to facilitate denials, not grants, of cert.

Section C of these materials reports the best empirical research on what actually goes on during the agenda setting process. We excerpt reports of two studies, analyzing different data, and describe the results of another study from yet a different data source.

Section D presents the very thoughtful conclusions of Professors Estreicher and Sexton for reforming the process. These conclusions are based on the authors' voluminous and painstaking analysis of every cert petition filed with the Court during the 1982 Term. (Chapter Six, Section A, below, considers more far-reaching proposals for redefining the Court's role in the national process of lawmaking. These materials also may be consulted at this point, because they concern some proposals for reducing the Court's responsibility for case screening and selection.)

All these materials, we believe, are worth reading and studying as they are presented below. Readers will learn even more, we have discovered, if they also engage themselves somewhat in the actual process. Those with access to the Supreme Court can study cert petitions pending before the Court and try to predict their outcome (or join with others to conduct a mock "cert conference"). Alternatively, one can read lower court opinions in cases for which cert petitions are pending, try to construct the arguments for and against granting cert, and then try to predict the outcome or conduct a mock conference.

A. GOVERNING STATUTES AND RULES

28 U.S.C. §§ 1251–1259 contain the federal statutes defining the Supreme Court's jurisdiction. They are set out below. [Sections 1252, 1255, and 1256 have been repealed in the past decade. One result of these changes is that the only instances in which the Court continues to have mandatory, not discretionary, jurisdiction over lower court decisions are those cases specified in § 1253.]

§ 1251. Original jurisdiction

(a) The Supreme Court shall have original and exclusive jurisdiction of all controversies between two or more States.

(b) The Supreme Court shall have original but not exclusive jurisdiction of:

(1) All actions or proceedings to which ambassadors, other public ministers, consuls, or vice consuls of foreign states are parties;

(2) All controversies between the United States and a State;

(3) All actions or proceedings by a State against the citizens of another State or against aliens.

* * *

§ 1253. Direct appeals from decisions of three-judge courts

Except as otherwise provided by law, any party may appeal to the Supreme Court from an order granting or denying, after notice and hearing, an interlocutory or permanent injunction in any civil action, suit or proceeding required by any Act of Congress to be heard and determined by a district court of three judges.

* * *

§ 1254. Courts of appeals; certiorari; certified questions

Cases in the courts of appeals may be reviewed by the Supreme Court by the following methods:

(1) By writ of certiorari granted upon the petition of any party to any civil or criminal case, before or after rendition of judgment or decree;

(2) By certification at any time by a court of appeals of any question of law in any civil or criminal case as to which instructions are desired, and upon such certification the Supreme Court may give binding instructions or require the entire record to be sent up for decision of the entire matter in controversy.

* * *

§ 1257. State courts; certiorari

(a) Final judgments or decrees rendered by the highest court of a State in which a decision could be had, may be reviewed by the Supreme Court by writ of certiorari where the validity of a treaty or statute of the United States is drawn in question on the ground of its being repugnant to the Constitution, treaties, or laws of the United States, or where any title, right, privilege, or immunity is specially set up or claimed under the Constitution or the treaties or statutes of, or any commission held or authority exercised under, the United States.

(b) For the purposes of this section, the term "highest court of a State" includes the District of Columbia Court of Appeals.

* * *

§ 1258. Supreme Court of Puerto Rico; certiorari

Final judgments or decrees rendered by the Supreme Court of the Commonwealth of Puerto Rico may be reviewed by the Supreme Court by writ of certiorari where the validity of a treaty or statute of the United States is drawn in question or where the validity of a statute of the Commonwealth of Puerto Rico is drawn in question on the ground of its being repugnant to the Constitution, treaties, or laws of the United States, or where any title, right, privilege, or immunity is specially set up or claimed under the Constitution or the treaties or statutes of, or any commission held or authority exercised under, the United States.

* * *

§ 1259. Court of Military Appeals; certiorari

Decisions of the United States Court of Military Appeals may be reviewed by the Supreme Court by writ of certiorari in the following cases:

(1) Cases reviewed by the Court of Military Appeals under section 867(a)(1) of title 10.

(2) Cases certified to the Court of Military Appeals by the Judge Advocate General under section 867(a)(2) of title 10.

(3) Cases in which the Court of Military Appeals granted a petition for review under section 867(a)(3) of title 10.

(4) Cases, other than those described in paragraphs (1), (2), and (3) of this subsection, in which the Court of Military Appeals granted relief.

———

Supreme Court Rules 10–16 govern the procedures for filing petitions for certiorari. They are presented, in somewhat edited form, below. Of particular interest is Rule 10, which contains the Court's statement of the criteria employed in ruling on cert petitions.

Rule 10. Considerations Governing Review on Writ of Certiorari

1. A review on writ of certiorari is not a matter of right, but of judicial discretion. A petition for a writ of certiorari will be granted only when there are special and important reasons therefor. The following, while neither controlling nor fully measuring the Court's discretion, indicate the character of reasons that will be considered:

(a) When a United States court of appeals has rendered a decision in conflict with the decision of another United States court of appeals on the same matter; or has decided a federal question in a way in conflict with a state court of last resort; or has so far departed from the accepted and usual course of judicial proceedings, or sanctioned such a departure by a lower court, as to call for an exercise of this Court's power of supervision.

(b) When a state court of last resort has decided a federal question in a way that conflicts with the decision of another state court of last resort or of a United States court of appeals.

(c) When a state court or a United States court of appeals has decided an important question of federal law which has not been, but should be, settled by this Court, or has decided a federal question in a way that conflicts with applicable decisions of this Court.

2. The same general considerations outlined above will control in respect to a petition for a writ of certiorari to review a judgment of the United States Court of Military Appeals.

Rule 11. Certiorari to a United States Court of Appeals Before Judgment

A petition for a writ of certiorari to review a case pending in a United States court of appeals, before judgment is given in that court, will be granted only upon a showing that the case is of such imperative public importance as to justify deviation from normal appellate practice and to require immediate settlement in this Court. 28 U.S.C. § 2101(e).

Rule 12. Review on Certiorari; How Sought; Parties

1. The petitioner's counsel, who must be a member of the Bar of this Court, shall file, with proof of service as provided by Rule 29, 40 copies of a printed petition for a writ of certiorari, which shall comply in all respects with Rule 14, and shall pay the docket fee prescribed by Rule 38. [For in forma pauperis filings, docket fees are waived and certain other technical rules are different.] The case then will be placed on the docket. It shall be the duty of counsel for the petitioner to notify all respondents, on a form supplied by the Clerk, of the date of filing and of the docket number of the case. * * *

2. Parties interested jointly, severally, or otherwise in a judgment may petition separately for a writ of certiorari; or any two or more may join in a petition. * * *

3. Not more than 30 days after receipt of the petition for a writ of certiorari, counsel for a respondent wishing to file a cross-petition that would otherwise be untimely shall file * * * 40 printed copies of a cross-petition for a writ of certiorari, which shall comply in all respects with Rule 14, except that materials printed in the appendix to the original petition need not be reprinted, and shall pay the docket fee pursuant to Rule 38. * * *

5. The clerk of the court having possession of the record shall retain custody thereof pending notification from the Clerk of this Court that the record is to be certified and transmitted to this Court. When requested by the Clerk of this Court to certify and transmit the record, or any part of it, the clerk of the court having possession of the record shall number the documents to be certified and shall transmit therewith a numbered list specifically identifying each document transmitted. * * *

Rule 13. Review on Certiorari; Time for Petitioning

1. A petition for a writ of certiorari to review a judgment in any case, civil or criminal, entered by a state court of last resort, a United States court of appeals, or the United States Court of Military Appeals shall be deemed in time when it is filed with the Clerk of this Court within 90 days after the entry of the judgment. A petition for a writ of certiorari seeking review of a judgment of a lower state court which is subject to discretionary review by the state court of last resort shall be deemed in time when it is filed with the Clerk within 90 days after the entry of the order denying discretionary review.

2. A Justice of this Court, for good cause shown, may extend the time to file a petition for a writ of certiorari for a period not exceeding 60 days.

3. The Clerk will refuse to receive any petition for a writ of certiorari which is jurisdictionally out of time.

4. The time for filing a petition for a writ of certiorari runs from the date the judgment or decree sought to be reviewed is rendered, and not from the date of the issuance of the mandate (or its equivalent under local practice). However, if a petition for rehearing is timely filed in the lower court by any party in the case, the time for filing the petition for a writ of certiorari for all parties (whether or not they requested rehearing or joined in the petition for rehearing) runs from the date of the denial of the petition for rehearing or the entry of a subsequent judgment. A suggestion made to a United States court of appeals for a rehearing in banc pursuant to Rule 35(b), Federal Rules of Appellate Procedure, is not a petition for rehearing within the meaning of this Rule.

5. A cross-petition for a writ of certiorari shall be deemed in time when it is filed with the Clerk as provided in paragraphs 1, 2, and 4 of this Rule, or in Rule 12.3. * * *

6. An application to extend the time to file a petition for a writ of certiorari must set out the grounds on which the jurisdiction of this Court is invoked, must identify the judgment sought to be reviewed and have appended thereto a copy of the opinion and any order respecting rehearing, and must set forth with specificity the reasons why the granting of an extension of time is thought justified. * * * An application to extend the time to file a petition for a writ of certiorari is not favored.

Rule 14. Content of the Petition for a Writ of Certiorari

1. The petition for a writ of certiorari shall contain, in the order here indicated:

(a) The questions presented for review, expressed in the terms and circumstances of the case, but without unnecessary detail. The questions should be short and concise and should not be argumentative or repetitious. They must be set forth on the first page following the cover with no other information appearing on that page. The statement of any question presented will be deemed to comprise every subsidiary question fairly included therein. Only the questions set forth in the petition, or fairly included therein, will be considered by the Court.

(b) A list of all parties to the proceeding in the court whose judgment is sought to be reviewed, unless the names of all parties appear in the caption of the case. * * *

(c) A table of contents and a table of authorities, if the petition exceeds five pages.

(d) A reference to the official and unofficial reports of opinions delivered in the case by other courts or administrative agencies.

(e) A concise statement of the grounds on which the jurisdiction of this Court is invoked showing:

(i) The date of the entry of the judgment or decree sought to be reviewed;

(ii) The date of any order respecting a rehearing, and the date and terms of any order granting an extension of time within which to file the petition for a writ of certiorari;

(iii) Express reliance upon Rule 12.3 when a cross-petition for a writ of certiorari is filed under that Rule and the date of receipt of the petition for a writ of certiorari in connection with which the cross-petition is filed; and

(iv) The statutory provision believed to confer on this Court jurisdiction to review the judgment or decree in question by writ of certiorari.

(f) The constitutional provisions, treaties, statutes, ordinances, and regulations involved in the case, setting them out verbatim, and giving the appropriate citation therefor. * * *

(g) A *concise* statement of the case containing the facts material to the consideration of the questions presented.

(h) If review of a judgment of a state court is sought, the statement of the case shall also specify the stage in the proceedings, both in the court of first instance and in the appellate courts, at which the federal questions sought to be reviewed were raised; the method or manner of raising them and the way in which they were passed upon by those courts; and such pertinent quotation of specific portions of the record or summary thereof, with specific reference to the places in the record where the matter appears (*e.g.,* ruling on exception, portion of court's charge and exception thereto, assignment of errors) as will show that the federal question was timely and properly raised so as to give this Court jurisdiction to review the judgment on a writ of certiorari. * * *

(i) If review of a judgment of a United States court of appeals is sought, the statement of the case shall also show the basis for federal jurisdiction in the court of first instance.

(j) A direct and concise argument amplifying the reasons relied on for the allowance of the writ. See Rule 10.

(k) An appendix containing, in the following order:

(i) The opinions, orders, findings of fact, and conclusions of law, whether written or orally given and transcribed, delivered upon the rendering of the judgment or decree by the court whose decision is sought to be reviewed.

(ii) Any other opinions, orders, findings of fact, and conclusions of law rendered in the case by courts or administrative agencies, and, if reference thereto is necessary to ascertain the grounds of the judgment or decree, of those in companion cases.
* * *

5.   The failure of a petitioner to present with accuracy, brevity, and clearness whatever is essential to a ready and adequate understanding of the points requiring consideration will be a sufficient reason for denying the petition.

Rule 15.   Brief in Opposition; Reply Brief; Supplemental Brief

1.   A brief in opposition to a petition for a writ of certiorari serves an important purpose in assisting the Court in the exercise of its discretionary jurisdiction.   In addition to other arguments for denying the petition, the brief in opposition should address any perceived misstatements of fact or law set forth in the petition which have a bearing on the question of what issues would properly be before the Court if certiorari were granted.   Unless this is done, the Court may grant the petition in the mistaken belief that the issues presented can be decided, only to learn upon full consideration of the briefs and record at the time of oral argument that such is not the case.   Counsel are admonished that they have an obligation to the Court to point out any perceived misstatements *in the brief in opposition,* and not later.   Any defect of this sort in the proceedings below that does not go to jurisdiction may be deemed waived if not called to the attention of the Court by the respondent in the brief in opposition.

2.   The respondent shall have 30 days (unless enlarged by the Court or a Justice thereof or by the Clerk pursuant to Rule 30.4) after receipt of a petition within which to file 40 printed copies of an opposing brief disclosing any matter or ground as to why the case should not be reviewed by this Court.   See Rule 10.   * * *

5.   Upon the filing of a brief in opposition, the expiration of the time allowed therefor, or an express waiver of the right to file, the petition and brief in opposition, if any, will be distributed by the Clerk of the Court for its consideration.   However, if a cross-petition for a writ of certiorari has been filed, distribution of both it and the petition for a writ of certiorari will be delayed until the filing of a brief in opposition by the cross-respondent, the expiration of the time allowed therefor, or an express waiver of the right to file.

6.   A reply brief addressed to arguments first raised in the brief in opposition may be filed by any petitioner, but distribution and consideration by the Court under paragraph 5 of this Rule will not be delayed pending its filing.   * * *

7.   Any party may file a supplemental brief at any time while a petition for a writ of certiorari is pending calling attention to new cases or legislation or other intervening matter not available at the time of the

party's last filing. A supplemental brief must be restricted to new matter. * * *

Rule 16. Disposition of a Petition for a Writ of Certiorari

1. After consideration of the papers distributed pursuant to Rule 15, the Court will enter an appropriate order. The order may be a summary disposition on the merits.

2. Whenever a petition for a writ of certiorari to review a decision of any court is granted, the Clerk shall enter an order to that effect and shall forthwith notify the court below and counsel of record. The case will then be scheduled for briefing and oral argument. If the record has not previously been filed, the Clerk of this Court shall request the clerk of the court having possession of the record to certify it and transmit it to this Court. A formal writ shall not issue unless specially directed.

3. Whenever a petition for a writ of certiorari to review a decision of any court is denied, the Clerk shall enter an order to that effect and shall forthwith notify the court below and counsel of record. * * *

B. MECHANICS OF THE CERTIORARI PROCESS

In its 1953 Term, the Supreme Court received 1,302 petitions and granted review in 115 cases.[1] In the 1963 Term, it received 2,294 and granted 142; for 1973, the figures were 3,943 and 169; and for 1983, 4,201 and 180. During the 1989 Term, the Court received 4,917 petitions and granted 122; for 1990, it received 5,865 petitions, granting 141; and in 1991, 5,865 petitions arrived while 120 were granted. In forty years, petitions have increased more than four-fold, while the number of cases adjudicated has remained rather constant.[2]

How does the Court decide which of almost 6,000 petitions should become one of the 125 or 150 cases set for plenary consideration? What steps are followed in judging which cases merit further review?

1. The data in this paragraph are taken from Arthur D. Hellman, *Case Selection in the Burger Court: A Preliminary Inquiry,* 60 Notre Dame L.Rev. 947, 951 (1985) (for 1953–83) and from a telephone conversation with the Clerk of the Court (for 1989–91). Prior to 1988, many of the filings invoked the Court's "appeal" rather than its "certiorari" jurisdiction. The data lump both kinds of cases together. Since 1988, virtually all of the cases that come to the Court come through its certiorari (discretionary) jurisdiction. The data in this paragraph reflect in forma pauperis filings as well as those for which the normal fee is paid.

2. It is too early to determine whether a new trend has begun, but, at this writing, the Court's docket of argued cases seems to be diminishing. Although the Court decided 127 cases in the 1991 Term, it decided only 116 in the 1992 Term. 61 Law Week 3124 (Aug. 17, 1993). (The number of cases decided in one Term does not necessarily match the number of cases granted in that Term because some cases are granted in one Term and adjudicated in the next.) Further, the Court's docket was so low at the outset of the 1993 Term that during the five days in October 1993 set aside for oral arguments, the Court scheduled oral arguments in only twelve cases. 62 U.S.Law Week 3149 (August 31, 1993). Because each argument day is long enough to accommodate the argument of four cases the Court might have heard twenty cases in the first month. Some observers wonder whether the Court is deliberately and systematically reducing the average number of cases per Term to which it gives plenary consideration.

Petitions for writs of certiorari ("cert petitions") and oppositions to the granting of such writs ("opp certs"), along with any amicus briefs in support of or in opposition to granting certiorari ("cert") are filed with the Clerk of the Supreme Court.[3] Once a week, the Clerk's Office distributes to each justice's chambers copies of those cert petitions [4] for which opp certs have been received or for which the time to file an opp cert has expired.[5]

Each justice then follows his or her own practice for determining how the justice will vote on the cert petition. The standard practice has varied over the years. Until about the 1920s, each justice studied by himself each petition for review (at that time, these were usually appeals). Congress converted most of the Court's jurisdiction to the discretionary certiorari with the "Judges' Bill" of 1925 and the justices soon developed a new practice in which each justice had his law clerks provide one or two page summaries of the cert petitions and opp certs, and made his judgment largely on the basis of these clerks' memos.

That practice persisted until the mid–1970s when, largely at the urging of Justice Powell, several justices formed a "cert pool." Initially, only a few justices—mostly those most recently arrived at the Court—

3. The Clerk of the Court is not to be confused with the justices' law clerks. The former is a senior professional full-time permanent employee, with a large staff, who manages all aspects of the Court's litigation docket.

4. Those reading literature about the Court's certiorari practice should be aware that this sentence reflects two relatively recent changes. First, until 1988, many cases came to the Court on appeal, rather than on certiorari. Although in fact the Court exercised great discretion in deciding which appeals it would set for oral argument and plenary consideration, when the Court declined to hear an appeal it technically had to rule on the merits of the case. An affirmance or reversal or a dismissal for want of a substantial federal question, albeit summary, had legal significance. Hicks v. Miranda, 422 U.S. 332, 95 S.Ct. 2281, 45 L.Ed.2d 223 (1975). A denial of certiorari carries no technical legal significance.

Second, a fee is charged for filing cert petitions with the Court and those who pay the fee must also supply enough copies of the petition to give one to each chambers. Those who cannot afford these costs, principally prisoners seeking direct or collateral review of their convictions, file "in forma pauperis" (IFP) and supply only one copy of their petition. [People sometimes take advantage of the "free ride" that IFP procedure allows. In In re McDonald, 489 U.S. 180, 109 S.Ct. 993, 103 L.Ed.2d 158 (1989)

the Court, over four dissents, refused to permit Jessie McDonald to file IFP and directed the Clerk not to receive any further IFP filings from him, finding that his 73 IFP filings from 1971 to 1989 constituted an abuse of the process. To the justices' law clerks, Mr. McDonald was known as the "frequent filer."] Before the introduction of the mass photocopying machine, these "IFPs" were sent only to the Chief Justice's chambers, where the Chief's law clerks prepared summaries and circulated them to the other chambers. Today, the Court provides each justice a photocopy of each IFP.

Additional copies of IFPs are not, however, made available to be supplied to the Court's depository libraries around the country. Consequently, virtually all retrospective academic research on the Court's cert practice has been limited to the study of paid petitions, which are permanently stored in public libraries.

5. Parties who prevailed below are not required to file opp certs, although most do. Occasionally, however, the prevailing party will acquiesce in the granting of certiorari (although the Court, of course, remains free to deny). Somewhat more frequently, the prevailing party will believe that the cert petition is so evidently frivolous that it needs no response. While the Court retains the power to grant or deny a petition without waiting for a response, it typically will call for a response ("CFR") if it is inclined to grant.

joined the pool. Others, like Justices Brennan, Douglas, Marshall, and Stewart, believed it was dangerous for all the chambers to be working from the same memo. Nevertheless, as these more senior justices retired, most of their successors joined the pool. Today, most of the justices belong to the pool.

Under the cert pool system, a week's petitions are divided evenly among all the law clerks whose justices belong to the pool. These clerks prepare memos on the cases assigned to them and all justices who participate in the pool receive these "pool memos." The justices then base their individual votes on the pool memo (with or without supplementation from their own clerks). As its name suggests, the point of the pool is to reduce the number of cert petitions that each pool clerk must review, thus freeing up law clerk time for other tasks. From discussions with former clerks, it is clear that, in most cases, the pool memo is the sole document on which those justices belonging to the pool base their judgment. Going behind the memo to examine the petitions themselves is rare. Justices who do not join the pool will usually have their own clerks prepare cert memos, either on every case or on selected cases.[6]

Petitions distributed during the summer are disposed of in a conference devoted solely to cert petitions that takes place at the end of September (just before the opening of the Court's Term on the first Monday in October). Such conferences may go on for several days and typically dispose of over one-quarter of all cases presented to the Court in a calendar year. During the Term, cases distributed to chambers during one week are put on a list to be disposed of at the next week's conference. Those conferences are likely to include discussion of and voting on argued cases as well.

Prior to 1930, it was customary for the justices to vote, in conference, on each petition. Chief Justice Hughes, however, initiated the "dead list," a list of cert petitions that he deemed not worthy of discussion, which he circulated to the entire Court before the conference. Such cases were to be denied without conference discussion absent objection from any other chamber. Today, the "dead list" has evolved into a "discuss list." The Chief Justice now circulates before the conference a list of those petitions that he believes merit discussion and voting. Each of the associate justices may then add any other case(s) to the discuss list. Once the discuss list is compiled in this fashion, all other petitions set for that week's conference will be automatically denied at the conclusion of the conference. Usually, fewer than 30 percent of the petitions scheduled for disposition at a conference appear on the discuss list.

Chapter Four, which reviews the Court's methods of adjudicating cases on the merits after cert has been granted, contains detailed

---

6. The excerpt from an article by Justice Brennan, which immediately follows this note, describes in greater detail the rather unique method of screening cert petitions that was followed in his chambers.

descriptions of the Court's conference procedures. We summarize here only those features relevant to the disposition of cert petitions.

The conference takes place in a room next to the Chief Justice's office. During these conferences, no one other than the justices is permitted to be present.[7]

The petitions on the discuss list are taken up one by one. The Chief Justice will state the case summarily and announce his vote. Discussion and voting then proceeds by seniority, from most senior to least senior. Seniority is calculated by number of years served on the Supreme Court except that the Chief Justice is always regarded, for purposes of ordering discussion and voting, as most senior. All sources agree that the workload, especially regarding cert, is so heavy that discussions at this stage are usually quite perfunctory; most justices, when their time comes, simply announce their vote.

The usual choice is between granting and denying cert. Many years ago, the Court adopted the so-called Rule of Four.[8] That is, if four justices vote to grant cert, cert is granted—even if five vote to deny. For those conscious of strategic options, the Rule of Four presents both opportunities and risks. A justice who wants to advance the law in a certain direction may be able to get an issue on the Court's agenda by persuading only three others of its importance. On the other hand, if four justices join to grant cert in order to seek a particular outcome in a particular case, they may wind up losing a five to four vote on the merits, thus enshrining in the U.S. Reports a precedent they do not favor and might have been able to avoid.

"Grant" and "deny" are not the only options available. Here are some other choices that occur at least once every Term:

(1) A justice may cast a "Join 3" vote. This means that the justice will provide a fourth vote if three others vote to grant, but is otherwise to be considered as voting to deny. Obviously, such a vote reveals that the justice casting it finds the question of whether to grant cert very difficult to resolve or believes the matter is sufficiently certworthy that three other justices who want to hear the case should not be deprived of

---

7. This is one reason why Justice Brandeis reportedly once said that the reason why the Court is so respected is that "We do our own work."

To get a message into the justices while the Court is in conference, one must knock on the door and wait for the most junior justice to answer. This led Justice Rehnquist, when he occupied that position, to describe himself as "the highest paid messenger in town."

8. This practice is usually traced to 1925, when Congress gave the Supreme Court largely discretionary (certiorari) in-

stead of mandatory (appeal) jurisdiction. The Court represented to Congress that it followed a Rule of Four and this is frequently said to be a reason why Congress agreed to give the Court more control over its own agenda. There is some evidence, however, that the Court during the 1930s followed a practice in which cert might be granted if only two or three justices strongly urged that course. See David M. O'Brien, *Storm Center: The Supreme Court in American Politics* 247 (3d ed. 1993). For at least the past 25 years, however, four has meant four.

that opportunity. Just as obviously, the system will not work if such a vote is cast frequently.[9]

(2) Justices typically vote to "Hold" a petition if it raises an issue that is likely to be resolved by, or substantially affected by, a case in which cert has already been granted. When the Court votes to hold a petition, no further action is taken at that time. Rather, the petition will be relisted for a conference decision after the case for which it was being held is decided.[10] Sophisticated litigants, such as the Solicitor General, who are aware of this option will often suggest it themselves in appropriate cases.

(3) The Court will occasionally decide to adjudicate a case summarily, on the merits, without further briefing or oral argument. It then grants cert and affirms (or reverses) simultaneously. This route is taken only when the petition concerns a case which a large majority of the Court quite confidently believes was rightly (or wrongly) decided below.

(4) The Court can ask for further assistance or input. Such input may come from any of several sources: (a) If some justices think the petition should be granted, but no opp cert has been filed, the Court is likely to vote first to request such a filing. (b) If the case involves a significant issue of federal law, but the federal government is not a party to the lawsuit and has not yet offered its view, the Court may ask the Solicitor General to file an amicus brief expressing the views of the United States. (c) If the Court believes that precedent relevant to the disposition of the case has intervened between the decision below and the consideration of the cert petition, it may grant cert, vacate the decision below, and remand to the lower court with instructions to reconsider its judgment in light of the intervening precedent.

The Supreme Court's decision whether or not to grant cert is almost totally unconstrained. For the Court to have authority to resolve a case, certain minimum conditions must be met. The case must be controlled by an issue of federal law; the Supreme Court is not authorized to review Judge Wopner's interpretation of local consumer protection statutes. The case must come from the highest ranking lower court from which review was available;[11] one cannot appeal a ruling from a state trial court directly to the U.S. Supreme Court if the state provides intermediate appellate review. The controversy must have been finally

---

9. Imagine the petition for which the votes are two to grant, four to deny and three to "Join 3."

10. Usually, the justice who wrote the majority opinion will be charged with making a recommendation to the conference as to how to dispose of the "held" petitions in light of the new precedent.

11. Strictly speaking, this requirement operates with the force of law only with respect to review of state court judgments. The Supreme Court is empowered to grant cert in federal cases before the relevant circuit court has ruled on the matter (i.e., issue "cert before judgment") and has done so in some cases of great public interest. These include Youngstown Sheet & Tube Co. v. Sawyer, 343 U.S. 579, 72 S.Ct. 863, 96 L.Ed. 1153 (1952) (The Steel Seizure Case) and United States v. Nixon, 418 U.S. 683, 94 S.Ct. 3090, 41 L.Ed.2d 1039 (1974) (Nixon Tapes Case). The norm, however, is to wait until the circuit court has ruled.

adjudicated in the courts below; one cannot halt a state trial in mid-course in order to ask the Supreme Court to review a ruling on the admissibility of evidence. And the cert petition must be filed within the established time limits and in proper form.

So long as these minimal requirements are met, the Court is free to grant or deny cert—or to choose another option, such as those outlined above—as it chooses, by whatever standards it prefers. Although its standards are self-generated, all observers agree that there is little overt politicking in the process. Communication among the justices, in advance of the conference, on whether or not to grant cert in particular cases is quite rare.[12] Discussion at the conference, because time is so limited, is very brief. Attempts at persuasion, apart from these conference discussions, usually take the form of opinions dissenting from the denial of cert. These are circulated among the justices before a final vote is announced and occasionally lead the justices to change their minds and agree to grant cert.

Notwithstanding the absence of definitive standards, all observers also agree that there are unarticulated standards, although they cannot be stated with precision and always admit of exceptions.[13] The overriding fact is that, absent major changes in the Court's schedule for disposing of adjudicated cases, the Court cannot conceivably adjudicate on the merits more than approximately three percent of the cases for which cert petitions are filed.[14] Consequently, every justice has to approach virtually every single cert petition with a strong presumption that it will be denied. One simply has to trust that state courts and lower federal courts are conscientiously examining the contentions advanced by litigants before them. One who looks at a cert petition and asks, initially, what was the proper resolution of this lawsuit almost certainly will not be able to keep up with the flow of cert petitions for a month.[15]

12. The justices' law clerks more frequently engage in discussion and debate, across chambers, as to which cases seem certworthy.

13. Section A., supra, of this chapter includes Supreme Court Rule 10 which lists some of the factors the Court takes into account. Section C., infra, of this chapter discloses the results of careful empirical research into the question of what factors appear highly correlated with a decision to grant or to deny.

14. As noted earlier, the Court now receives around 6,000 cert petitions each year. Were the justices to grant three percent, they would have to adjudicate fully 180 cases annually. The schedule, processes, and methods of adjudication employed by the Court have never proved capable of handling more than 180 fully adjudicated cases.

15. Considerations such as these explain why the justices are usually careful to assert that the denial of certiorari should not be taken as an indication of the Court's views on the merits of a case. Legally, denial of cert has no meaning or consequence. Yet, the fact that the Court for at least the past 30 years has rather consistently reversed the judgment below in over two-thirds of the cases it has heard on the merits, combined with the common sense observation that no one can be completely comfortable voting to deny cert in a case she or he thinks was wrongly decided, tells us that "cert denied" frequently does intimate something about the merits of the case. See Stephen L. Wasby, *The Supreme Court in the Federal Judicial System* 219 (4th ed. 1993). It remains, however, a very difficult task to figure out, from the outside, specifically which cert dispositions do and do not rest substantially on consideration of the merits of the judgment below.

Sometimes the Court becomes convinced, after reading the briefs and hearing the oral argument in a case, that it was a mistake to have granted cert and would be a further mistake to proceed to adjudicate the case. When this occurs, it is usually because the Court discovers on plenary review that the case lacks a particular fact or issue that was assumed to be present when cert was granted. The usual procedure in such cases is to DIG (Dismiss as Improvidently Granted) the writ of certiorari and thus be rid of the case. The Rule of Four limits this option. So long as four justices want to hear a case, it is supposed to be heard. Indeed, it can be argued that so long as any justice who voted to hear the case does not want it DIG'd the case should be heard.

Before turning to academic examinations of the results of the certiorari process, we present an excerpt from an article by Justice Brennan. With refreshing candor, he describes his views of the importance of the Court's screening or agenda-setting function and explains how he reviewed cert petitions.[16]

WILLIAM J. BRENNAN, JR.,* THE NATIONAL COURT OF APPEALS: ANOTHER DISSENT
40 U.Chi.L.Rev. 473, 477–483 (1973)

* * *

The method of screening the cases differs among the individual Justices, and thus I will confine myself to my own practice. That practice reflects my view that the screening function is second to none in importance—a point I shall touch upon more fully a little later. I try not to delegate any of the screening function to my law clerks and to do the complete task myself. I make exceptions during the summer recess when their initial screening of petitions is invaluable training for next Term's new law clerks. And I also must make some few exceptions during the Term on occasions when opinion work must take precedence. When law clerks do screening, they prepare a memorandum of not more than a page or two in each case, noting whether the case is properly before the Court, what federal issues are presented, how they were decided by the courts below, and summarizing the positions of the parties pro and con the grant of the case.

For my own part, I find that I don't need a great amount of time to perform the screening function—certainly not an amount of time that compromises my ability to attend to decisions of argued cases. In a substantial percentage of cases I find that I need read only the "Questions Presented" to decide how I will dispose of the case. This is certainly true in at least two types of cases—those presenting clearly frivolous questions and those that must be held for disposition of

---

16. The title of the article stems from its broader purpose: to discuss then-current proposals to create a new federal appellate court that would take over much of the Supreme Court's screening function.

Chapter Six, Section A., infra, examines this and related issues in detail.

* Reprinted by permission of the University of Chicago Law Review.

pending cases. Because of my familiarity with the issues of pending cases, the cases to be held are, for me, easily recognizable. For example, we heard argument early this Term in eight obscenity cases because we decided to undertake a general re-examination of that subject. Every agenda since then has included several cases of conviction or injunction under state obscenity laws and I simply mark those cases "hold." Similarly, with other cases I can conclude from a mere reading of the question presented that for me at least the question is clearly frivolous for review purposes. For example, during recent weeks, I thought wholly frivolous for review purposes questions such as: "Are Negroes in fact Indians and therefore entitled to Indians' exemptions from federal income taxes?" "Are the federal income tax laws unconstitutional insofar as they do not provide a deduction for depletion of the human body?" "Is the 16th Amendment unconstitutional as violative of the 14th Amendment?" and only last week, "Does a ban on drivers turning right on a red light constitute an unreasonable burden on interstate commerce?"

Nor is an unduly extended or time-consuming examination required of many of the cases that present clearly nonfrivolous questions. For very often even nonfrivolous questions are simply not of sufficient national importance to warrant Supreme Court review. And after a few years of experience, it is fair to say that a Justice develops a "feel" for such cases. For example, when the question is whether a court of appeals in a diversity case correctly applied governing state law, or correctly directed entry of a judgment notwithstanding the verdict, the question of error, if any, ordinarily does not fall within the area of questions warranting Supreme Court review. As to cases where my initial reading of the questions presented suggests to me that the case may merit Supreme Court review—the special "feel" one develops after a few years on the Court enables one to recognize the cases that are candidates for such review. I need not spend much time examining the papers in depth when the questions strike me as worthy of review, or at least as warranting conference discussion.

* * *

I should emphasize here that the longer one works at the screening function, the less onerous and time-consuming it becomes. I can state categorically that I spent no more time screening the 3,643 cases of the 1971 Term than I did screening half as many in my first Term in 1956. Unquestionably, the equalizer is experience, and for experience there can be no substitute—not even a second court. I subscribe completely to the observation of the late Mr. Justice Harlan that "Frequently the question whether a case is 'certworthy' is more a matter of 'feel' than of precisely ascertainable rules." A commentator expressed the same thought this way: "[The Court's] present monitoring of all cases on the docket gives the Court a feel for the subjects of its ultimate judicial administration powers and an intuitive knowledge of when and where it is necessary to execute those powers." * * *

[A]pproximately 30 percent of all cases docketed annually (that means in this Term, 1,100 cases) are placed on the "Discuss List" each Term. Under this system, a single Justice may set a case for discussion at conference and, in many instances, that Justice succeeds in persuading three or more of his colleagues that the case is worthy of plenary review. Thus, the existing system provides a forum in which the particular interests or sensitivities of individual Justices may be expressed, and therefore assures a flexibility that is essential to the effective functioning not only of the screening process but also of the decisional process of which it is an inseparable part.

* * *

[A]n artificial limitation of the Supreme Court's docket [also] would seriously undermine the important impact dissents from denial of review frequently have had upon the development of the law. Such dissents often herald the appearance on the horizon of a possible reexamination of what may seem * * * to be an established and unimpeachable principle. Indeed, a series of dissents from denials of review played a crucial role in the Court's reevaluation of the reapportionment question and the question of the application of the Fourth Amendment to electronic searches. Actually, every Justice has strong feelings about some constitutional view that may not yet command the support of a majority of the Court. For example, I thought that the Court was quite wrong in adopting "same evidence" rather than "same transaction" as the test of "same offense" for the purposes of double jeopardy. The question has recurred in case after case since the Court made that choice a few years ago. In each instance I and two of my colleagues have recorded our continued adherence to my minority view. Another example is the view shared by Mr. Justice Douglas with the late Mr. Justice Black in obscenity cases. They dissented in 1957 from the holding that obscenity does not enjoy First Amendment protection, and in every obscenity case since then Mr. Justice Douglas and, until his death, Mr. Justice Black, recorded their dissent from applications of the holding that obscenity is not protected speech. Only a brave man would say that their view could never prevail in the Court. The history of their dissents that have become law in cases involving reapportionment, the right to counsel, and the application of the Bill of Rights to the States are too fresh in mind to ignore. * * *

For the more statistically oriented, the subjective nature of the decision whether a particular case is of sufficient "importance" to merit plenary consideration is amply demonstrated by the voting pattern of the Justices in the screening process. Under our rules, a case may be granted review only if at least four of the nine Justices agree that such review is appropriate. It is noteworthy that, of the cases granted review this Term, approximately 60 percent received the votes of only four or five of the Justices. In only 9 percent of the granted cases were the Justices unanimous in the view that plenary consideration was warranted. Thus, insofar as the key determinant is the "substantiality" of the question presented, there can be no doubt that the appraisal is necessarily a subjective one. * * *

Finally, it should be noted that the * * * recommendation that the breadth of the Court's screening function be curtailed rests in part upon what I consider to be the mistaken assumption that the screening function plays only a minor and separable part in the exercise of the Court's fundamental responsibilities. In my view, the screening function is inextricably linked to the fulfillment of the Court's essential duties and is vital to the effective performance of the Court's unique mission "to define the rights guaranteed by the Constitution, to assure the uniformity of federal law, and to maintain the constitutional distribution of powers in our federal union."

The choice of issues for decision largely determines the image that the American people have of their Supreme Court. The Court's calendar mirrors the everchanging concerns of this society with ever more powerful and smothering government. The calendar is therefore the indispensable source for keeping the Court abreast of these concerns. Our Constitution is a living document and the Court often becomes aware of the necessity for reconsideration of its interpretation only because filed cases reveal the need for new and previously unanticipated applications of constitutional principles.

For example, the Due Process Clauses provide that no person shall "be deprived of life, liberty or property without due process of law." The interest of the defaulting conditional sales purchaser in the refrigerator or kitchen stove or bedroom furniture that he bought on time clearly does not constitute "property" in the traditional sense of the word. Similarly, welfare benefits, automobile driver's licenses, retail liquor licenses, and the like were traditionally viewed as "statutory entitlements," rather than as "property." Vast societal changes over the past few decades, however, have substantially altered the function and importance to the individual of these previously unprotected interests. A long series of seemingly unimportant cases filed in the Court over a period of years gradually generated an awareness of these societal changes and of the consequent need for constitutional reinterpretation. As a result, recent construction of the Due Process Clause requires government to afford notice and hearing before terminating "statutory entitlements" or repossessing goods. Another example may be seen in the area of criminal procedure. The Sixth Amendment's guarantee of the "Assistance of Counsel for his defense" is in terms applicable "in all criminal prosecutions." Are police interrogations or preliminary hearings part of the "criminal prosecution" for the purposes of this guarantee? The Court has held that they are in light of the serious abuses revealed in cases that reached our docket.

* * *

The point is that the evolution of constitutional doctrine is not merely a matter of hearing arguments and writing opinions in cases granted plenary review. The screening function is an inseparable part of the whole responsibility. * * *

C. WHAT'S REALLY HAPPENING?

We know that the Court gets a lot of cert petitions and grants very few of them. We know the methods and procedures the Court employs in determining which petitions to grant and which to deny. But we do not know what is really happening in this process. What standards are justices employing when they cast their votes? What factors are present in cases that get granted and missing in those that do not? When they vote in conference on petitions for writs of certiorari, are the justices pursuing institutional goals that are ideologically neutral (such as looking for conflicts among the circuits) or are they behaving strategically (i.e., trying to shape the substance of the law to their value preferences)?

Supreme Court Rule 10, reprinted in Section A above, purports to describe the factors that influence the decision whether or not to grant cert. The materials in this section reflect the best empirical research on what actually happens during the agenda setting process. Professor Hellman, looking at the cert petitions and the Court's decisions, describes with great care the particular factors that evidently have influenced the Court in deciding which petitions it will grant. Professor Provine seeks to answer the same question, but uses different data. She draws on extensive records kept by Justice Burton that reveal each justice's vote on every cert petition filed over a ten-year period. Together, these materials cast a good deal of light on what factors best explain the Court's decisions to grant or deny cert. Finally, in a concluding note, we summarize briefly the results of Professor Perry's research, based on interviews with law clerks and justices, and offer some observations of our own.

ARTHUR D. HELLMAN,* CASE SELECTION IN THE BURGER COURT: A PRELIMINARY INQUIRY**
60 Notre Dame L.Rev. 947, 947–1042 (1985)

In examining the record of the Burger Court, it is only natural to concentrate on the results of the Court's decisions (has the Court expanded or narrowed the rights of criminal defendants?) and on the doctrines invoked (does the Court still adhere to the three-part test for establishment clause challenges?). We tend to take as a given the presence of the cases in the Court and to assume, if we think about it at all, that the only tasks for the Justices are to decide the cases and to write opinions explaining the decisions and their relation to existing precedent. But this picture of the Court's work is quite incomplete. With a few exceptions, the cases that become "Supreme Court cases" do

---

* Professor of Law, University of Pittsburgh. B.A., Harvard, 1963; LL.B., Yale, 1966.

** Reprinted by permission of the author, Arthur D. Hellman. © Copyright 1985 Arthur D. Hellman.

so as the result of a selection process that is no less interesting and important than the decisional process that follows.

To appreciate the significance of the selection process, it is only necessary to juxtapose two sets of numbers. In each of the last few Terms, the Court has received about 4,200 applications for review. The number of cases receiving plenary consideration has been about 180 per Term. Plenary consideration means that the case will get full briefing, oral argument, and, almost invariably, an opinion on the merits. * * *

How does the Court select, from among the 4,200 cases filed, the 180 that it will hear and decide? * * * [M]uch can be learned by studying the Justices' opinions and orders against the background of the parties' submissions, the holdings of lower courts, and developments elsewhere in the legal system and society generally. * * *

I. INTRODUCTION
A. Cases Filed: What the Numbers Mean

* * *

The total [number of cases filed in the Supreme Court] for the 1983 Term was only sixteen percent higher than the figure for 1971—an increase, on the average, of little more than one percent a Term. During the same period, filings in the federal courts of appeals nearly doubled.

The extremely modest rate of growth over the last decade represents a major change from what the Court experienced in the 1960's. In 1972, when the Freund Study Group issued an alarmist report on the Court's ability to cope with its docket, it did so at the end of a decade that saw an increase in the total caseload from 2,185 to 3,643.* If filings had continued to grow at that rate in the decade that followed, the number of cases confronting the Court in the 1981 Term would have been 6,074. Instead it was only 4,422. And in the following Term the number dropped substantially, to 4,201. * * *

E. The Criteria for Plenary Review

At first blush it might seem quite anomalous, and even unjust, that more than ninety-five percent of the cases that come to the Court are disposed of without full briefing, without oral argument, and without an opinion. The anomaly disappears, however, or at least is substantially mitigated, if one accepts the orthodox view of the Supreme Court's role in the American judicial system. In that view, the function of the Supreme Court is not to correct errors in the lower courts, but to "secur[e] harmony of decision and the appropriate settlement of questions of *general importance.*"

Underlying this view is the recognition that virtually every case that comes to the Supreme Court has already received at least one level of appellate scrutiny. Admittedly, it is possible that another look by another court might lead to a more "correct" or a more "just" result.

---

* [Ed.] This report, and several others reviewing the Court's caseload, are summa- rized and analyzed in Chapter Six, Section A, *infra.*

But that possibility alone is not a sufficient reason for the Supreme Court to hear a case. * * * [I]n the familiar words of Justice Jackson: "[R]eversal by a higher court is not proof that justice is thereby better done. There is no doubt that if there were a super-Supreme Court, a substantial proportion of [the Supreme Court's] reversals of [lower] courts would also be reversed." [53] Thus it is sound to say, as Chief Justice Hughes did, that litigants who have argued unsuccessfully in the federal courts of appeals or state appellate courts "have had their day in court. If further review is to be had by the Supreme Court it must be because of the public interest in the questions involved." [54]

The criterion of "public interest" is epitomized in a term first given general currency in a speech by Justice Harlan: "certworthiness." [55] In the orthodox view, a case is certworthy if it will enable the Court to hand down a decision that will provide authoritative guidance, substantially augmenting what is furnished by existing precedents, for the resolution of a recurring issue of federal law. Typical indicia of certworthiness would be the presence of an intercircuit conflict or an appellate decision that calls into question the lawfulness of government policy of wide applicability.

Rigid adherence to the orthodox view would mean that immediately upon determining that a certiorari petition raised no issue of general importance, the Justices would reject the case without further consideration. However, as might be expected, the orthodox view does not accurately reflect what the Court does in fact. Few human beings, confronted with error or unfairness that is within their power to correct, would invariably stand by and do nothing simply because the case has no importance to anyone but the litigants, and the evidence shows that in this regard as in others, the Justices are quite human.

* * *

Yet even if the Court were to reject the strictures of the orthodox view altogether, it is not clear that the results of the selection process would be significantly different. * * * In appellate courts today, a large proportion of the cases involve nothing more than the application of well-established principles to particular facts. Many appeals challenge rulings that are subject to reversal only if clearly erroneous or an abuse of discretion. In short, the vast majority of appellate decisions are clearly correct, or at least within the range of acceptability under the governing law.

These considerations help to explain why seventy percent of the cases filed with the Court are so obviously unworthy of review that not

---

53. Brown v. Allen, 344 U.S. 443, 540 (1953) (concurring opinion). Justice Jackson was referring to Supreme Court review of state court decisions, but the point is applicable to federal courts as well.

54. Letter from Chief Justice Hughes to Senator Wheeler (March 21, 1937), *reprinted in* S.Rep. No. 711, 75th Cong., 1st Sess. 38, 39 (1937).

55. *See* Harlan, *Manning the Dikes,* 13 Rec.A.B.City N.Y. 541, 549 (1958).

even one Justice requests that they be discussed at the Court's conference. * * *

II. THE CASES THE COURT DOES NOT TAKE

Research has identified six categories of cases that very seldom receive plenary consideration, even though they constitute a significant portion of the Court's overall caseload. Four of the categories are defined by the status of the party seeking review: indigent litigants; defendants in federal criminal prosecutions; defendants in state criminal prosecutions; and civil litigants representing themselves. The other two groups of cases are characterized by the nature of the issues presented: state court cases involving spurious federal claims and cases raising issues similar to those that have already been granted review in other cases.

A. Cases Filed in Forma Pauperis ("FP")

* * *

FP cases account for 2,000 of the total filings each year, but only a tiny fraction are given plenary consideration. The total for the first four Terms of the 1980's was 44, an average of 11 per Term. In contrast, paid cases, which generated about 2,200 filings per Term, contributed an average of 160 cases to the plenary docket.

This record is not surprising, nor is it the product of discrimination against the poor. The vast majority of FP cases are filed by indigent criminal defendants who have nothing to lose by seeking Supreme Court review even if their arguments are clearly unworthy of the Court's attention. And this is so whether the applications are judged by certiorari standards or from the more tolerant standpoint of review for error. Even Justice Brennan, who might be expected to have as much sympathy for indigent petitioners as any member of the Court, has written that "in all but a handful of" these cases, "the merits involved are almost certainly insufficient to demand full review."

The FP cases that do reach the plenary docket fall into two well-defined groups, depending on the court of origin. When the Court accepts an indigent's petition from a federal court, the reason almost always is to resolve an intercircuit conflict. Of the 17 federal court cases that received plenary consideration in the first four Terms of the 1980's, 13 involved acknowledged conflicts; in 3 others, strong but arguable claims of conflict were made. And most of the cases raised issues of statutory construction rather than constitutional law.

The state court cases are a very different breed. Few of them involved conflicts; rather, the dominant theme is one of concern that the state court has improperly rejected a federal constitutional claim. In 17 out of 27 cases in the 1980–1983 period the judgment was actually reversed. In 3 other cases there were four votes for reversal, and in 2 additional cases the opinions of the Justices gave reason to believe that members of the Court who did not ultimately vote to reverse might well have been concerned, at the certiorari stage, that federal rights had been denied. It is also worth noting that 3 of the 27 cases were dismissed on jurisdictional grounds; if we look only at the cases decided on the merits, the focus on review for error becomes even more evident.

* * *

B. Paid Petitions Filed by Federal Criminal Defendants

Most of the federal criminal defendants who seek Supreme Court review do so as indigents, but in each of the last few Terms the Court has also received between 320 and 400 paid petitions challenging federal criminal convictions. Few of these petitions are granted. In the first four Terms of the 1980's, the Court granted plenary consideration to only 9 paid cases filed by federal criminal defendants, an average of little more than 2 per Term. * * *

When the Court does grant a federal criminal defendant's petition, it usually does so in order to resolve an intercircuit conflict. In the last five years, the Court has never granted a petition of this kind except where a conflict was present. And one must go back to 1977 to find a Term in which more than a single petition was granted in the absence of a conflict.

C. Paid Petitions Filed by State Criminal Defendants

Like their federal counterparts, state criminal defendants generally appear in the Supreme Court in forma pauperis, but a substantial number of paid petitions are also filed. In recent years the figures have ranged from 125 to 195. The proportion of cases that receive plenary consideration is higher than it is for the federal defendants, but still very low. In the four Terms of the 1980's the total number of plenary decisions of this kind was 8, and in the last three Terms of the 1970's it was 7.

When review is granted in a paid case filed by a state criminal defendant, the reason generally is not to resolve a conflict, but rather to permit the vindication of a federal right. Although the judgments were actually reversed in only 4 of the 8 cases in the 1980–1983 period, there were at least four votes for reversal in all but 2. The pattern is even more pronounced if we look at the Court's work over a somewhat longer span of time. In 6 of the 7 cases that received plenary consideration in the last three Terms of the 1970's the judgments were reversed (5 unanimously), and in the remaining cases there were four votes for reversal. Thus, of the 15 cases of this kind that reached the plenary docket in the seven Terms 1977 through 1983, 10 were reversed and 3 others had four votes for reversal.

* * *

D. Civil Cases Filed by Pro Se Litigants

In each of the first four Terms of the 1980's, the Court received, on the average, 135 paid petitions filed by litigants in civil cases who were representing themselves. These pro se petitions complained of a wide range of grievances, most frivolous by any standard, some fantastic. For example, one litigant twice sought to set aside the 1980 presidential election. Another claimed damages for emotional pain and suffering as a result of injuries to his dog. Another asserted that land had been taken illegally from his aunt in 1921.

In this light, it is hardly surprising that during the four Terms 1980–1983, only 2 pro se petitions were granted, and neither was a typical example of the genre. * * *

E. Spurious Federal Question Cases From State Courts

Pro se litigants may not know that in reviewing cases from state courts the Supreme Court can consider only the federal questions.[80] But lawyers generally are at least dimly aware of this fact. Thus, when a lawyer loses a state court case that has been litigated and decided entirely on the basis of state law issues, he will recognize that the state court's rulings on these matters do not, of themselves, provide grounds for Supreme Court review. And at that point most lawyers will accept the reality that in our federal system the case has reached the end of the road. But some attorneys are not content to stop there. They attempt to argue that the substance of the state court's judgment or the manner in which it was reached violated some right under the federal Constitution. The due process and equal protection clauses are most often invoked, but inventive counsel have also cited the contract clause, the commerce clause, and the seventh amendment.

These are the cases that I have labeled "spurious federal question cases." Their numbers range from 30 to 60 each Term. It is almost needless to say that none of these cases receives plenary review. And until very recently one could have added confidently that the cases took virtually none of the Justices' time. Today, however, this conclusion must be reassessed in light of the fact that the Justices have begun to consider the possibility of awarding damages against litigants who file frivolous petitions.

From the standpoint of workload, the soundness of this approach is very much open to question. While one can understand the Justices' frustration at having to consider cases that clearly do not belong on their docket, the actual imposition on their time is de minimis if review is simply denied. But that will no longer be true if the Court undertakes the task of distinguishing between cases that are merely unworthy of review and those that are frivolous. That determination does involve a question of judgment on which reasonable persons can differ, and it can be expected to consume substantially more time than the cases would otherwise require.[87] Nor can it reasonably be thought that the Court's

---

80. According to a recent national survey, 77 percent of the American public "incorrectly believes the Supreme Court can review and reverse every decision made by a state court." Krasno, *National Survey Examines Public Awareness of Judicial System,* 67 JUDICATURE 309 (1984).

87. As four members of the Court have stated, "Any evenhanded attempt to determine which of the unmeritorious applications should give rise to sanctions, and which should merely be denied summarily, would be a time-consuming and unrewarding task." Talamini v. Allstate Ins. Co.,

overall workload will be reduced because fewer cases will be filed. The Court is not likely to impose sanctions very often, and in any event it is difficult to believe that the lawyers who file these petitions undertake a careful cost-benefit analysis before proceeding.

* * *

F. Cases Held for Plenary Decisions

As previously noted, when a case is filed that raises an issue similar or identical to an issue presented by a case already chosen for plenary consideration, the Court's practice is to put the new case aside rather than to either grant or deny review. Later, when the plenary decision is announced, the Court takes another look at the held case. At that time the Court could, of course, decide that the case warrants review in its own right, but study of the Court's practices shows that the Court rarely takes that course.

G. Conclusion

In summary, the six classes of cases discussed in the preceding pages accounted for an average of 2,800 petitions a Term during the first four Terms of the 1980's—two-thirds of the Court's total caseload. But in all four Terms they contributed only 72 cases to the plenary docket—not even eleven percent.

* * *

III. THE FORCES THAT SHAPE THE PLENARY DOCKET

With only 180 places on the plenary docket and 4,200 cases to choose from (1,260 if we exclude the petitions that are denied unanimously and without discussion); with federal law governing almost every aspect of American life; and with a system under which minority coalitions can control the agenda, it would hardly be surprising if the composition of the plenary docket reflected a degree of randomness and unpredictability. But these centrifugal forces are balanced by others that bring identifiable patterns of change and continuity to the work of the Court. Study of those patterns sheds light not only on the process of case selection, but also on the Court's interaction with the other forces that influence the development of American law.

To understand these relationships, it is helpful to divide the Court's work into four broad areas: civil rights, federalism and separation of powers, general federal law, and the jurisdiction and procedure of federal courts. * * *

Until the mid–1960's, matters of general federal law constituted the largest segment of the plenary docket. However, toward the end of the Warren Court that distinction was usurped by civil rights, and throughout the fifteen years of the Burger Court, civil rights cases have occupied

105 S.Ct. 1824, 1827 (1985) (Stevens, J., joined by Brennan, Marshall, and Black-   mun, JJ., concurring).

the dominant position. During the first half of the 1970's, issues of civil rights law actually accounted for more than half of all cases given plenary consideration. For a few years thereafter, the proportion diminished somewhat, but in the 1983 Term it was as close to 50 percent as it could be: in 78 out of 157 plenary decisions, the principal issue decided, addressed, or presented was an issue of civil rights.

The predominance of civil rights cases will come as no surprise to anyone who follows the work of the Court even in a casual way. What is less well known is that matters of federalism and separation of powers (mostly the former) also occupy a much larger segment of the plenary docket than they did in earlier years. Nearly all of the major areas of federalism litigation have experienced growth. For example, challenges to state regulatory laws based on the negative implications of the commerce clause, which accounted for only 9 decisions in all sixteen Terms under Chief Justice Warren, gave rise to 7 decisions in the last three Terms of the 1970's. Another 5 opinions were issued in the four Terms that followed. Cases involving state taxation of interstate commerce dwindled to a handful in the late 1960's, but in the 1980–1983 period alone there were 7 such decisions. These were augmented by 5 cases in which state tax laws were challenged on the basis of federal statutes. Even the full faith and credit clause, which disappeared entirely from the plenary docket between 1966 and 1979, generated 3 decisions in the later Burger Court. The Court also granted review in 2 additional cases, but dismissed the petitions without reaching the merits of the constitutional claims.

* * * I turn to an examination of the institutions and activities that have influenced the selection of cases for plenary consideration. I begin by looking at the effect of forces originating within the Court; thereafter, I note some of the many external influences.

A. *Forces Originating Within the Court*

In October 1972, the Court heard oral argument in two cases that attracted wide public attention. *Roe v. Wade* [114] presented the question whether the federal Constitution limits state power to prohibit abortions. *San Antonio Independent School District v. Rodriguez* [115] was a challenge to a school financing system that resulted in higher educational spending in rich districts than in poor ones. Later in the Term, the Court upheld the claims of the abortion plaintiffs and rejected the attack on school financing. In the decade that followed, the Court issued 11 more opinions dealing with abortion, but there were only 2 plenary decisions that involved school financing.

These outcomes underscore the fact that one of the most powerful forces shaping the plenary docket is the course of adjudication within the Court itself. Several patterns can be identified. They are not mutually exclusive; a particular area of doctrinal development may illustrate more than one pattern at different times in its history.

---

114. 410 U.S. 113 (1973).   **115.** 411 U.S. 1 (1973).

First and most obvious, decisions recognizing new constitutional rights typically require further attention by the Court to clarify the nature and scope of the right. Few rights are self-defining; even fewer are absolute. And because every holding that recognizes a constitutional right limits, pro tanto, the autonomy of the executive and the legislature to act in accordance with the desires of the majority (or the bureaucracy), governmental litigants will seek to cabin the holding in the narrowest way possible. At the same time, potential beneficiaries will seek to expand its contours. Almost invariably, the tensions created by the competing forces will be brought to the plenary docket for resolution.

Abortion is one prominent example of this phenomenon. *Roe v. Wade* and *Doe v. Bolton* struck down abortion statutes that were typical of those adopted by almost all of the states, but they did not put abortion off limits to government regulation. Within a few years many states had adopted new abortion legislation, and four years after *Roe* the Supreme Court took the first in what was to become a long series of cases treating the constitutionality of particular regulations. Some of the cases involved statutes requiring the consent of the parents or husband of the pregnant woman; some dealt with laws limiting state funding for abortions; others considered the constitutionality of laws regulating the procedures for conducting abortions. Abortion laws were directly at issue in 11 of the 31 decisions on substantive due process that were handed down by the Burger Court in the twelve Terms beginning in 1972.

Another example of this pattern is commercial speech. Until about ten years ago, commercial speech—speech that does no more than propose a commercial transaction—was excluded altogether from the protections of the first amendment. The Court repudiated that position in the mid–1970's, but did not assimilate commercial speech with other forms of expression. Commercial speech was accorded a lesser degree of protection, and a distinct mode of analysis was developed for testing the constitutionality of particular regulations. Not surprisingly, over the last decade the Court has taken a fair number of cases to define when, and to what extent, commercial speech will be protected.

The pattern is also exemplified, although in a more complex way, by the Court's decisions on capital punishment. For more than a decade, Justices Brennan and Marshall have argued that "the death penalty is in all circumstances cruel and unusual punishment prohibited by the Eighth and Fourteenth Amendments." If the full Court had adopted that position, the decision would have required little if any clarification; death penalty cases would have disappeared from the Court's docket altogether. If, on the other hand, the Court had adhered to its 1971 view that the procedures for imposing the death penalty were to be left largely to the discretion of the states, the Justices would probably have taken an occasional case to address the constitutionality of particular procedures, but it is unlikely that capital punishment issues would have come to occupy a major segment of the plenary docket.

In fact, the Court took neither of these approaches. The Court held that the death penalty was not per se unconstitutional, but that the standards and procedures for imposing it would be subjected to strict scrutiny under federal law. The result has been a long series of decisions considering the constitutionality of particular laws and their application to particular situations. * * *

These examples alone might suggest that no matter what the nature of the Court's rulings, their effect will be to create a need for further plenary activity to clarify the meaning of what has gone before. Fortunately, the adjudicative process also works in the other direction. A series of decisions may clarify the law to the point where the Court need intervene only at rare intervals, at least until an entirely new facet of the problem emerges. For example, in Chief Justice Warren's last Term the Court held for the first time that the fourteenth amendment limits the authority of states to impose limitations on access to the ballot by minor parties and independent candidates. The effect of the decision was to cast doubt on the validity of ballot access restrictions in every state. Thus, unless the Court meant to say that states would have "to place on [their ballots] all persons who claim to be candidates," it was inevitable that the Court would have to spend some time delineating the scope of the new right. And so it did; ballot access cases appeared on the plenary docket in almost every Term of the early Burger Court, with a trilogy of important decisions in the 1973 Term. More recently, however, the Court has given little attention to the topic. The probable reason is that the decisions of the early and middle 1970's have clarified the law to the point that most disputes (to the extent they arise at all) can be settled without resort to the Supreme Court.

* * *

A more subtle kind of internal force than those previously discussed is the occasional emergence of a collective sense (shared by at least four Justices) that the time has come to clarify or reshape the law in a particular area. Thus, in the mid–1970's, the Court handed down a cluster of decisions that addressed several important issues under the federal securities laws. These issues had been percolating for years in the lower courts, but the Court had shown little interest in resolving them. The 1976 Term brought an outpouring of cases interpreting Title VII's prohibition on employment discrimination. One commentator, surveying the results, suggested that "the law under Title VII [had been] completely rewritten." In the late 1970's the Court turned its attention to the double jeopardy clause of the fifth amendment. Several precedents were overruled, including one that had been on the books for only three years.

B. Other Influences

* * *

1. Congressional Legislation

The most obvious of the external influences is the legislation enacted by Congress. Several major areas of statutory interpretation either did not exist or had barely emerged onto the legal scene prior to 1969. For example, environmental protection laws, which generated 23 decisions in the decade that began in 1974, were largely a product of the late 1960's and early 1970's. The Freedom of Information Act ("FOIA"), which gave rise to 16 decisions in the same period, dates from 1966 but did not become a major subject of litigation until the 1970's.

A striking illustration of this phenomenon is found in the realm of labor law. For the Warren Court, "labor law" meant, more than anything else, review of decisions by the National Labor Relations Board ("NLRB"). The Burger Court has continued to scrutinize NLRB rulings, albeit at a slightly slower pace, but in the last few years NLRB cases have been outnumbered by decisions interpreting the federal employment discrimination law, Title VII of the Civil Rights Act of 1964. As with FOIA, Title VII litigation took some time to work its way up to the Supreme Court, but when it did the effect was dramatic. While no subsequent Term has matched the outpouring of 9 decisions in the 1976 Term, the average of 4 decisions a Term makes employment discrimination one of the few statutory areas that consistently receive extensive plenary attention from the Burger Court.

2. Other External Forces

When we leave the realm of congressional legislation and attempt to identify the other external forces that have helped to shape the composition of the plenary docket, the task becomes much more difficult. Congressional legislation tends to be quite particularized in its effect on the Court's business; thus, the impact of labor laws will be felt primarily (though not exclusively) in the labor segment of the docket. In contrast, the influence of political, economic, and social forces will often be spread widely, but thinly, among several areas of the Court's work. The effects may be less visible; they may also be more difficult to isolate. Yet even when these caveats are taken into account, it is surprising how seldom we find a simple pattern of change or expansion in an area of primary activity that correlates neatly with an increase or decrease in the number of plenary decisions growing out of that activity. Important developments in American life—computerization is one example—may scarcely be reflected on the plenary docket at all. Others will generate decisions in one or two areas of the law, but beyond them have little impact on the Court's work. In this section I can do no more than sketch some of the patterns I have discovered.

a. Economic Developments

I begin with one of the most important developments in the nation's economy during the Burger Court years. The Arab oil embargo that brought an end to the era of cheap energy left its mark on almost every institution in American life, and the Supreme Court is no exception. To be sure, energy law, in one form or another, has been part of the Court's work at least since the early years of this century, but the volume of decisions in the last few Terms manifests a degree of involvement not previously seen. The impact has been felt primarily in the federalism segment of the docket. For example, cases in which an exercise of state power was challenged on the ground of preemption by federal energy regulation laws constituted such a minor element of the Court's work in the 1960's and 1970's that it probably would never have occurred to anyone to identify them as a discrete category. But in the first four Terms of the 1980's, issues of this kind generated 6 plenary decisions. Disputes between state and federal governments over rights in land and other property seldom appeared on the plenary docket until the 1970's, but in recent Terms they have become a regular part of the Court's work. Five of the 11 decisions in the later Burger Court involved oil-bearing lands. Disputes arising out of the production or distribution of energy resources resulted in opinions dealing with other federalism issues as well: the delineation of interstate boundaries, limits on state powers under federal regulatory programs and other federal legislation, the scope of national powers, and limitations on state taxation of interstate commerce.

I do not suggest that the issues in these cases necessarily grew out of the energy shocks of the 1970's. * * * Rather, the increased cost of fuel and the heightened interest in finding alternate energy sources raised the stakes in almost every activity that involved the production or distribution of energy. As a result, disputes that might not have arisen at all became the subject of litigation; lawsuits that might have come to an end in the lower courts were brought to the Supreme Court. And with so much more at stake, either in the particular case or in the application of the challenged rule of law to other disputes, the Justices had much more reason to grant plenary review.

It is all the more surprising, therefore, that issues of energy law outside the context of federal-state relations received very little attention from the Court in the years following the oil embargo. In the seven Terms 1977–1983 there were only 6 plenary decisions arising out of rulings by the Federal Energy Regulatory Commission ("FERC") and its predecessor the Federal Power Commission ("FPC"). During that same period the Court denied review in 5 cases in which the lower court had rejected the agency's view of the law. This record contrasts sharply with that of the preceding seven Terms, when the Court handed down 12 plenary decisions growing out of FPC proceedings and denied review in only 3 FPC cases brought to it by the federal government. And the Court has consistently refused to hear energy regulation cases from the Temporary Emergency Court of Appeals ("TECA").

These patterns suggest that the legal rules governing the allocation of costs and opportunities among producers and consumers of energy do not, of themselves, rank high among the Court's concerns; it is only when the rules implicate federal-state relations that the Justices are likely to intervene. One possible explanation for this dichotomy is that a high proportion of the federalism cases are brought to the Court by appeal or as original jurisdiction cases, whereas the pure federal law disputes can be taken up only by petition for certiorari. However, in view of the broader pattern of interest in federalism issues that cuts across so many substantive areas of the law, I am inclined to think that a concern for preserving the balance between federal and state power is, as much as anything else, the dominant force here.

Other important economic developments have made even less of a mark on the plenary docket. The tremendous expansion in the portion of the nation's economy devoted to health care has been reflected in a booming segment of the legal profession, but for the Supreme Court the effects have been quite modest.   * * *

Of course, not all segments of the economy have been expanding during the last fifteen years, and some of the downward trends have been reflected in the composition of the plenary docket. For example, three of the mainstays of the statutory work of the Warren Court were the Interstate Commerce Act, the Railway Labor Act, and the Federal Employers' Liability Act ("FELA"). In the seven Terms of the later Burger Court, all three statutes accounted for only 8 decisions. There can be little doubt that this change resulted in large part from the greatly diminished role of the railroads in the national transportation system. But other forces were at work also. The reduction in the number of decisions reviewing ICC orders coincided almost exactly with the repeal of the legislation that required three-judge district courts, with a direct appeal to the Supreme Court, for challenges to ICC rulings. And the profusion of FELA cases on the plenary docket in the 1950's was not simply a reflection of the significance of railroad accidents in the nation's economy; rather, it was a product of the belief shared by a majority of the Justices that the Court had a special responsibility "to exercise its power of review in *any* [FELA] case where it appears that the litigants have been improperly deprived of" their right to a jury determination. That belief no longer holds sway within the Court.   * * *

b. Changes in Social and Political Life

Of the social and political developments that have marked the decade and a half since Chief Justice Burger took office, none have had as great an impact on the nation as the rise of the women's movement. The Supreme Court has played a major role in that revolution, and the effects can be seen in the composition of the plenary docket. Issues of sex discrimination, which with one exception were entirely absent from the Court's work under Chief Justice Warren, have become a major component of the civil rights docket in the Burger Court. Starting with the pathbreaking opinion in *Reed v. Reed* in the 1971 Term, the Court has issued a total of 21 decisions addressing the constitutionality of governmental distinctions based on gender. In the realm of statutory law, claims of sex discrimination accounted for 14 of the 28 Title VII decisions in the seven Terms 1977 through 1983.

It is true that the proliferation of constitutional cases resulted in part from the Court's own decisions—decisions that signalled an end to the long-held view that nothing in the fourteenth amendment "preclude[s] the States from drawing a sharp line between the sexes." But the Court would hardly have received (or taken) so many opportunities to mark out the limits of the new approach if the egalitarian forces represented by the feminist movement had not seized upon those initial decisions to challenge laws in every realm of human endeavor from marriage to military service. * * *

All but 3 of the Court's sex discrimination cases, including the first 9, were brought as appeals. As a result, the only way the Court could avoid granting plenary review was to affirm summarily. But the Justices were not likely to find that an attractive option. If the lower court had accepted the constitutional claim, summary affirmance would disable all governments from enforcing similar laws; if the constitutional claim had been rejected, summary affirmance would fly in the face of the Zeitgeist. Thus it was to be expected that the Court would grant plenary consideration and confront the constitutional arguments on the merits.

The Court's willingness to address, and largely accept, the claims of the feminists contrasts sharply with its response to the homosexual rights movement. During the past decade, numerous cases have been brought to the Court raising issues of homosexual rights in a variety of contexts, including criminal law enforcement, education, and public employment. The claimants have invoked the due process clause, the equal protection clause, and the first amendment. There can be no doubt that the issues are recurring, and the results in the lower courts have not been uniform. But * * * the Court has consistently refused to grant plenary consideration to any of the cases. * * *

Inability to invoke the obligatory jurisdiction may be one reason why homosexuals have been unable to secure the place on the plenary docket that fell so easily to the women's movement, but it is not the only reason. The critical distinction, I believe, is that in the view of the Justices the nation is not yet ready for a definitive ruling on homosexual rights. * * * If the Justices were confident of the proper resolution of the constitutional issues, concern about public reaction probably would not stand in the way, but if they regard the questions as open and difficult, deferring a definitive resolution has two important advantages. It gives the Justices a chance to observe what happens in those states and circuits where homosexual rights have been recognized to one degree or another, and it leaves open the possibility that at some later time the legal issues will be clearer or the attitudes of the public more relaxed.

IV. REASONS FOR GRANTING REVIEW IN PARTICULAR CASES

In the preceding pages I have identified some of the forces that play a role in determining the kinds of issues that will occupy a prominent position on the plenary docket in any given period. Analyzing the reasons for the grant of review in particular cases is a far more difficult task, involving a much greater element of speculation and subjective evaluation. To be sure, some Court opinions do provide an explanation for the decision to grant plenary consideration. But those cases are a minority. And the brief statements can hardly reflect the different and overlapping reasons that may have prompted individual Justices to vote to hear a case. For example, Justice White may have been swayed by the presence of an intercourt conflict; Justice Stevens may have been unwilling to summarily affirm a case within the obligatory jurisdiction; and Justice Brennan may have been concerned primarily with correcting an erroneous denial of a federal right.

The analysis is made still more problematic by the fact that it is *post hoc*. Almost any Supreme Court decision will have some precedential value (and thus will be cited and relied upon) simply because it *is* a Supreme Court decision. Thus, from a retrospective standpoint, the criterion of "general importance" is easily satisfied. But that kind of justification can be misleading when the object is to determine how a case looked to the Justices at the time the application for review and responsive papers were filed.

With these limitations taken into account, it is possible to identify four broad categories of reasons for the grant of plenary review. Three of them are relatively well defined (which is not to say that the classification of particular cases is always easy): intercourt conflicts, compelling interests of the federal government, and doubtful recurring issues. The fourth category embraces all other reasons for review. By definition, it is an unruly category; cases are consigned to it only when it appears that none of the other three features was present at the time review was granted.

* * *

A. Intercircuit Conflicts

Among the orthodox justifications for Supreme Court review, the most firmly established is the intercircuit conflict. For present purposes, a conflict exists when two or more appellate courts have attached different legal consequences to transactions that are identical in all relevant respects. Failure to resolve a conflict can have three undesirable consequences. First, efficient planning and negotiation are frustrated when lawyers, in formulating advice to their clients, must take account of multiple rather than single contingencies at key points in their analysis. Second, the existence of a conflict encourages people to litigate rather than settle their disputes; when each side can point to a favorable precedent that is squarely on point (albeit from a different jurisdiction), both sides are likely to exaggerate the probability of ultimate vindication and thus to resist compromise. Finally, the simultaneous proclamation of inconsistent interpretations of federal law by appellate courts in different parts of the country tends to cast doubt on the rationality and evenhandedness of the legal system.

In this light, it is not surprising that the largest segment of the plenary docket is devoted to the resolution of intercourt conflicts. Specifically, conflicts were present in more than one-third of the 593 cases

that received plenary consideration in the first four Terms of the 1980's.
* * *

In several important areas of statutory law, the Court almost never grants review except to resolve a conflict. For example, the Court handed down 20 decisions on federal tax liability in the decade 1974–1983. All but one resolved intercircuit conflicts. During that same period the Court heard 28 cases involving the interpretation of substantive federal criminal statutes. All but 2 or 3 resolved intercircuit conflicts. The Court has given plenary consideration to only 10 bankruptcy cases in the last ten years. Intercircuit conflicts were present in all but one of those cases. Other areas dominated by conflict resolution include tax procedure, admiralty and maritime law, Federal Tort Claims Act litigation, and private civil rights litigation.

B. Compelling Interests of the Federal Government

In the second group of plenary decisions, about one-third the size of the first, the Court granted review in response to a compelling interest of the federal government. Most prominent are the cases in which the lower court had held a federal statute unconstitutional. In the four Terms of the 1980's there were 33 cases of this kind. All but 3 were brought to the Court by appeal, and in all but 3 the United States government was the party seeking review. Of equal importance, there were no cases during this period in which the Court refused to consider a properly presented government claim that a lower court had erred in striking down an act of Congress.

As this discussion suggests, lower court decisions holding federal statutes unconstitutional are usually easy to identify, and the grant of plenary review can be predicted with great confidence. When the subject of an invalidating decision is not an act of Congress but a policy or program of an executive department or administrative agency, and the basis for the ruling is not the Constitution but a statute, analyzing the operation of the certiorari practice becomes somewhat more difficult. The reason lies in the process that brings federal government cases to the Supreme Court. When a government agency loses a case in a court of appeals, it can seek review in the Supreme Court only if the Solicitor General agrees to file the petition. The Solicitor General carefully screens agency requests and files only those he thinks are truly worthy of the Court's attention.[395] Thus the narrow holding or the judgment resting on an unusual set of facts is not likely ever to reach the Court (except perhaps in the realm of criminal procedure), and the cases that do come before the Justices almost always involve issues that at least arguably implicate government policies of some general importance.

In this light, it would be quite defensible to simply assume that every government petition reflects a compelling governmental interest,

---

395. Rex Lee, who served as Solicitor General during the 1981 through 1984 Terms, stated that his office sought review in "about one of six cases" that government agencies asked him to take to the Supreme Court. Lauter, *Lee Reflects on His Tenure as Solicitor General,* Nat'l L.J., May 13, 1985, at 5.

and leave it at that. However, in classifying the cases in the study, I have taken a more skeptical approach, asking whether the lower court's ruling, if followed, would require the government to revise a policy of general applicability or modify the operation of a national program. In the four Terms of the 1980's, between 25 and 35 plenary decisions appeared to fit this description.

For the Justices themselves, the government's portrayal of the likely consequences of the decision below carries great weight—more so in some areas of federal regulation than in others. At one extreme is environmental law. In the seven Terms of the later Burger Court there were 14 plenary decisions interpreting modern environmental legislation. All but 2 of these were heard at the behest of the Solicitor General. During this same period the Court did not reject a single government petition in an environmental case. In other words, this segment of the docket was shaped almost entirely by the decisions of the Solicitor General.

No other area of the law quite matches this record, but a few come close. In the same seven Terms the Court handed down 9 decisions involving the rights of armed forces personnel and other issues relating to government employment. All but one had been brought to the Court by the government. And no government petitions were rejected.

* * * Five Social Security cases reached the plenary docket in the first four Terms of the 1980's. All were brought to the Court by the government, and all resulted in government victories. Four additional government cases were reversed or vacated summarily during this period; there were none in which review was denied.

Litigation arising out of proceedings in the Federal Energy Regulatory Commission ("FERC") and its predecessor the Federal Power Commission ("FPC") presents a somewhat more equivocal picture. In the seven Terms 1977–1983, all 6 of the Court's decisions reviewing FERC rulings came in cases brought to the Court by the government. And the government won at least a partial victory in 5 of the 6 cases— the exception being an affirmance by an equally divided Court. But the Court turned down 5 additional cases in which the lower court had overturned a FERC decision and the Solicitor General sought review. These data suggest that on the basis of the petition and response the Justices make a preliminary determination of the correctness of the judgment below, and that ordinarily review is granted only if five or more Justices believe that the lower court erred in rejecting the government's position.

Freedom of Information Act litigation presents an interesting variation on this pattern. From 1977 through 1983 the Court rejected only 2 government petitions involving FOIA issues. And the 5 FOIA cases that reached the plenary docket in the 1980's were all brought to the Court by the government. In the last three Terms of the 1970's only 2 out of 6 decisions were generated by government petitions, but in 3 of the 4 other cases the government supported the private party's application for review (and in the fourth case it supported the petitioner on the merits). In other words, there was only one case in all seven Terms in which certiorari was granted over the government's opposition. And in all but one of the plenary decisions the government won at least a partial victory. Thus, with FOIA as with FERC, the Court seldom grants review except when it is prepared to sustain the government's position.

* * *

These areas, of course, do not mark the full extent to which the composition of the plenary docket is shaped by the Solicitor General's perceptions of what issues require a decision at the national level. For example, in the preceding section of this article, I identified several segments of the Court's statutory work that are dominated by conflict resolution. The two largest of these are taxation and crimes. Only a minority of the cases in those areas were actually brought to the Court by the Solicitor General, but that fact does not tell the full story. In most of the other cases that reached the plenary docket, the government supported the petition for review filed by a private party. And only a handful of the petitions that the government did file failed to receive the requisite four votes.

Taken together, these data point to a recurring pattern that dominates the segments of the docket devoted to taxation and crimes; it can also be seen, less prominently, in other areas of statutory law. When the government's position on a recurring issue is rejected by a court of appeals, the government does not ordinarily ask the Supreme Court to grant review unless the decision creates an intercircuit conflict. Rather, the government adheres to its position until its view gains acceptance in another circuit. At that point a certiorari petition may well be filed by the party opposing the government. If that happens, the government will acquiesce in the grant of review. If it does not, the government will continue to litigate the issue, either in circuits where its position has already been rejected or in circuits that have not passed on the point. Sooner or later it will lose a case that can be taken to the Supreme Court so that the conflict will be resolved.

C. Doubtful Recurring Issues

In the third group of cases, constituting about one-sixth of the total, there was no acknowledged conflict, nor did the application for review invoke a compelling governmental interest. Rather, what could be found in each case was a discrete issue that was doubtful enough that there would be some efficiency in providing an authoritative resolution that would forestall further litigation or at least narrow the range of uncertainty.

Sometimes the issue had already given rise to two or more appellate decisions, though without a square conflict at the time review was granted. A good example is *Metropolitan Edison Co. v. NLRB,* a decision of the 1982 Term. The question was whether an employer commits an unfair labor practice by disciplining union officials more severely than other union employees for taking part in an unlawful work stoppage. The NLRB held that the employer had violated the Act, and the court of appeals enforced the Board's order. The employer filed a certiorari petition claiming an intercircuit conflict on the issue. The Solicitor General, in opposition, argued that the principle of the decision below had been accepted by all of the circuits that had considered the question.

Reasonable people can differ over whether there was a genuine conflict, or whether the various decisions could be reconciled on their particular facts. What could not be disputed was that the question was doubtful and recurring. Five years had passed since a seminal ruling by the NLRB, and in that time the issue had been the subject of several major appellate opinions and had generated substantial disagreement among the judges as to what considerations were relevant and how much weight they should be given. Thus, the case was certworthy irrespective of whether or not there was a true conflict.

In cases like *Metropolitan Edison,* review was justified because of disarray in the circuits that arguably stopped short of actual conflict. That kind of disharmony was not present in all of the multiple-appellate-decision cases, but sometimes the petitioner was able to point to other circumstances that pointed to the desirability of Supreme Court intervention. Consider, for example, *Morrison–Knudsen Construction Co. v. Director, OWCP,* another decision of the 1982 Term. In supporting the petition for certiorari, the Solicitor General (representing the nominal respondent) conceded that the decision below was the first to hold that fringe benefits are "wages" for the purpose of computing compensation benefits under the Longshoremen's and Harbor Workers' Compensation Act. But he urged the Court to hear the case anyway and to reverse the judgment. He noted that the court of appeals had "upset[ ] a long-established administrative construction of the LHWCA." This strongly suggested that the issue was at least doubtful. But the Benefits Review Board, acquiescing in the court of appeals decision, had announced its intention to apply the decision on a nationwide basis. The Solicitor General argued that this development "will require substantial efforts by insurers to readjust the workers' insurance program to account for the higher benefit payments that will result." Perhaps that prediction was overstated; even so, there could be no doubt that the question would recur, and in fact, while the petition was pending, another circuit endorsed the construction of the statute adopted by the lower court in *Morrison–Knudsen.*

D.   Other Reasons for Granting Plenary Review

Intercourt conflicts, compelling governmental interests, and doubtful recurring issues account for between two-thirds and three-quarters of the cases that receive plenary consideration. The remaining decisions are a heterogenous group, but several overlapping patterns can be identified.

* * *

[I]f there is a single theme that dominates the cases that do not readily appear to meet orthodox criteria for plenary review, it is that of resolving conflicts between state and national power. This theme finds its principal expression in two classes of decisions: those in which a state court rejected a federal claim, and those in which a federal court invalidated state official action.

* * *

Of the 199 general federal law cases in the first four Terms of the 1980's, 123 were filed by litigants other than the federal government. These petitions, in turn, were divided about equally between cases that presented intercircuit conflicts and cases that did not. The conflict cases ranged widely among the issues that occupy a substantial position on the plenary docket. But of the nonconflict cases, two-thirds involved issues of labor law or antitrust.

Two conclusions can be drawn from these data. First, in considering applications for review that raise questions of labor or anti-trust law, the Court employs a relatively flexible set of criteria. Cases will receive plenary consideration even though the need for an authoritative decision is, from the standpoint of the national law, less than overwhelming.

Second, in all other areas of federal regulation the Court will almost never grant a private petition in the absence of an intercircuit conflict. Moreover, of the 20 or so nonconflict petitions that did receive plenary consideration, about one-fourth had the support of the Solicitor General at the certiorari stage. The upshot is that in the absence of an intercircuit conflict or the backing of the Solicitor General, private litigants in all areas of statutory law other than labor and antitrust accounted for little more than a dozen plenary decisions in all four Terms.

D. MARIE PROVINE,* DECIDING WHAT TO DECIDE: HOW THE SUPREME COURT SETS ITS AGENDA**
64 Judicature 320, 320–333 (1981)

Since the passage of the 1925 Judiciary Act, the U.S. Supreme Court has enjoyed broad discretion to decide which cases it will resolve on their merits. As dockets have grown more crowded in recent decades, this discretion has become an increasingly significant feature of the Court's institutional power. * * *

Research on the Court, however, remains fixed almost exclusively upon the cases to which the justices have granted review. One explana-

* Excerpts from *Deciding What to Decide: How the Supreme Court Sets its Agenda,* by D. Marie Provine, copyright (c) 1981 by the American Judicature Society. Permission granted by Doris Marie Provine, Professor of Political Science, Syracuse University,

and "Judicature, the journal of the American Judicature Society."

** This article was adapted from the author's new book. *Case Selection in the United States Supreme Court* (Chicago: University of Chicago Press, 1980).

tion for the paucity of research on case selection is lack of data. The Court issues no opinions and releases no votes in denying or granting review. Traditionally, the only exceptions to complete secrecy in case selection have been occasional published dissents from denials of review, sporadic citations of reasons for granting review in opinions on the merits, general statements by justices and their law clerks on the case selection process, and the broadly-stated criteria of the Supreme Court Rules.

Scholars interested in analyzing case selection criteria with statistical tools had only the bare facts of grants and denials to work with until 1965, when the papers of Justice Harold H. Burton became available. Burton's papers, on file at the Library of Congress, include complete docket books recording the case selection votes of each justice for the 13 terms that Burton sat on the Court (1945–1957). These are the only complete records of case selection votes that are currently available for any period since the advent of discretionary review.

The Burton data make it possible to analyze case selection and its relationship to the more familiar work of the Supreme Court on the merits. Such an analysis suggests that the justices' conceptions of the proper role of the Court have a major impact on their votes to select cases for review. Consensus about the Court's role appears to have channeled and limited the expression of individual policy preferences and political attitudes in review decisions during the Burton period. Even when the justices disagreed in assessing review-worthiness, role perceptions seemed to be significant to their decisions. The only case selection records currently available thus suggest that, in agenda-setting, judicial sensitivity to the appropriate business of the Court is crucial.

I.   THEORIES OF CASE SELECTION

The case selection process, because of its secrecy, provides the justices with a special opportunity for favoring certain litigants or side-stepping volatile cases, possibilities that have been noted by scholars. Alexander Bickel, for example, suggested that Supreme Court justices should assess the political implications of the merits of cases and use case selection to limit "the occasions of the Court's interventions" in the political process.

* * *

Cue theory

Tanenhaus, Schick, Muraskin, and Rosen hypothesized that Supreme Court justices are concerned with reducing their workload, rather than with competing to get their policy preferences incorporated into decisions on the merits.[9] * * * The authors theorized that the justices cut down case-processing time by summarily eliminating much of the caseload from careful consideration. According to this hypothesis, they use a set of agreed-upon cues to differentiate cases that might be worthy of review from those they know they did not want to hear.

---

9. Tanenhaus, Schick, Muraskin, and Rosen, *The Supreme Court's Certiorari Jurisdiction: Cue Theory,* in Schubert (ed.), Judicial Decision-Making (New York: Free Press, 1963).

* * * Tanenhaus and his colleagues wrote before the release of the Burton papers, so they had only the pattern of grants and denials with which to work. * * *

The authors named three cues the Court used to select cases for careful scrutiny, and to eliminate summarily the remaining (cueless) 40 to 60 per cent of the caseload:

- the presence of the United States as petitioner;
- the existence of a civil liberties issue;
- disagreement among the lower courts.

Testing cue theory

The accuracy of cue theory can be assessed by examining the fate of cue-containing cases during the Burton period, which matches almost exactly the 1947–1958 period Tanenhaus examined. Burton's papers permit a test of cue theory because his records reveal that a significant proportion of cases were eliminated with only cursory analysis, while the remainder were given more careful attention. The separation was accomplished by special listing, an administrative convenience devised by Chief Justice Hughes before Burton joined the Court.

The practice while Burton sat on the Court was for the chief justice and his staff to prepare a special list, or dead list, of cases deemed unworthy of conference time. The list circulated among the justices each week, and unless one of them put a special-listed case up for conference consideration, it was denied review automatically. Burton filed each week's special lists, and he kept a record of any changes justices requested. These records show that such alterations were rare.

* * * [Burton's records show that cases with Tanenhaus cues] were significantly more likely to get case selection votes than others on the Appellate Docket. Clearly the cues, especially the U.S. as petitioner, are related to the concerns the justices have in selecting cases for review on the merits. This is not surprising, since Tanenhaus settled upon the cues by examining the statements of Supreme Court justices and others about the types of cases of particular interest to the Court.

Were the authors simply suggesting that some types of cases have a better chance of getting votes for review than others, the Burton data would tend to substantiate the hypothesis. Cue theory, however, purports to explain how the justices reduce the mass of petitions they receive to a more manageable number without actually considering the argument each petitioner makes for review on the merits. * * *

If the cues actually served this short-circuiting purpose, cases containing cues should not appear on the special lists. Yet * * * in all three categories, some cue-containing cases are special listed.

Not a mechanical process

This pattern of voting suggests that the case characteristics that Tanenhaus deemed cues may be significant to the justices in case selection decisions, but that the decisionmaking process is not as mechanical as the authors suggest. Of course, something differentiates special-listed cases from those discussed in conference. The memos Burton's clerks wrote for him on each case and the case selection voting patterns suggest that cases with jurisdictional defects, inadequate records, and no clearly presented issues were the most likely to be special listed.[12]

No easily identifiable case characteristics are invariably associated with special listing, however. This suggests that neither the justices nor the clerks rely on a fixed set of cues to separate cases into those worthy of scrutiny and those to be discarded summarily. With the assistance law clerks provide in digesting cases and writing memos, there is little reason to expect Supreme Court justices need such an abbreviated preliminary screening procedure.

It is more likely that the justices reduce the time they spend in evaluating petitions by relying on the clerks' memos. The justices may then reach a decision by engaging in a weighing process in which a few characteristics of cases—including probably the Tanenhaus cues—encourage at least some of the justices to vote for review, while many other characteristics act like demerits, preventing review in the absence of strong reasons in favor. The special-listed cases are those which contain one or more demerits and no countervailing considerations in favor of review.

The pattern of voting in U.S.-brought cases supports this interpretation. Because of the Solicitor General's careful screening, these cases seldom contain characteristics strongly discouraging review, so the Court seldom puts them on the special lists. In fact, * * * U.S. cases are sufficiently impressive that in the Burton period they usually received at least one justice's vote for review. The evidence does not suggest, however, that the justices initially separate U.S. cases from the rest in an attempt to save reading time.

The attitudinal hypothesis

Another approach for understanding how the Court selects cases for plenary review emphasizes judicial predispositions towards litigants and policies. Sidney Ulmer has actively promoted this perspective, using the Burton papers to test his attitudinal conception of the case selection process.

One of Ulmer's principal findings has been that a justice's votes to review and his later votes on the merits are strongly related to each other.[15] Ulmer was able to show, for example, that for eight of the 11 justices whose votes he examined, a justice's vote to review helped to

12. These were some of the considerations Tanenhaus hypothesized to control the review decision *after* the initial search for cues had occurred. *Id.,* at 118.

15. Ulmer, *The Decision to Grant Certiorari as an Indicator to Decision "On the*

Merits," 4 Polity 429 (1972); and Ulmer, *Supreme Court Justices as Strict and Not–So–Strict Constructionists: Some Implications,* 8 Law & Soc'y Rev. 13 (1973).

predict his vote on the merits. Votes to review were associated with votes to reverse on the merits.

* * *

Recently Ulmer has gone further, arguing that the justices sometimes try to disguise the extent to which they are influenced by their attitudes towards litigants in case selection. According to this hypothesis, when a justice suspects he cannot win review on the merits, he suppresses his ever present desire to vote for the underdog or the upperdog. * * *

Ulmer's finding that votes to review and votes to reverse were correlated suggests that the justices *do* let their assessment of the merits of cases influence their review decisions. * * *

II. An Overview of Voting Patterns

If case selection is functionally equivalent to decisionmaking on the merits, most case selection decisions should be non-unanimous, as most decisions on the merits are. Also, individual decisions to grant review should correlate highly with votes to reverse the lower court on the merits, and votes to reverse should be rare when a justice did not vote for review. Finally, the frequency with which a justice votes for review should be directly related to the level of his overall dissatisfaction with lower court results.

If attitudes towards litigants explain why individual case selection votes correspond with votes in fully considered cases, then the justices generally presumed to be the most politically liberal and the most conservative should seldom vote to review the same case. On the Court as a whole, disagreement among the justices should be parallel at both stages of decision, and this pattern should be consistent with the liberal-conservative spectrum we see in on-the-merits voting.

With the Burton records, we can determine whether or not these patterns existed during a significant portion of the modern Court's history. Analysis of case selection votes can thus contribute to our understanding of the relative significance of role constraints and attitude in judicial decisionmaking.

Unanimity in case selection

Contrary to what one would expect if judicial views of the merits alone determined review decisions, the prevailing pattern in case selection is unanimity. During the Burton period, 82 per cent of case selection decisions were unanimous: 79 per cent were unanimous denials of review, and three per cent were unanimous grants. Available evidence indicates that the level of unanimity in case selection has remained high since the Burton era. This numerical evidence alone suggests that case selection decisions are not functionally equivalent to decisions on the merits, and that some norm or norms guide the justices in deciding whether to vote for review.

Analysis of the types of cases decided unanimously during the Burton period suggests that the justices shared a conception of the work appropriate to the Court that overshadowed policy preferences and sympathies for certain litigants. Evidence of this is that the types of cases usually presumed to tap judicial attitudes most directly were the very types most often denied review unanimously: the petitions of prisoners and suits by business interests seeking relief from government regulation.

This pattern of unanimity in presumably ideologically-charged cases cannot be attributed to an unusual period of ideological uniformity on the Supreme Court. The Court's membership in this period included civil libertarians like Black and Douglas as well as non-libertarians like Reed and Vinson. Yet all of them were in agreement that most of these cases should not be reviewed. In other words, all of the justices seem to have been convinced that certain types of cases were not important enough to review, even if they touched the private sympathies of individual justices.

A review of memos written by Justice Burton's law clerks suggests that this consensus has both procedural and subject matter aspects. As noted earlier, cases with defective records from below or other weaknesses unrelated to the substance of their claims tended to be denied review unanimously, usually by special listing. Likewise, certain subject matters almost never got votes for review. Contract disputes, common law issues, and real property litigation were prime candidates for unanimous exclusion. Sixty per cent of these cases were special listed.

Unanimity in favor of review

The types of cases in which the justices were most often unanimous in favor of review also suggests the importance of shared views about the proper business of the Court. During the Burton period, * * * the justices tended to be unanimous in four types of cases which are related to basic areas of responsibility for the court of last resort in a federal system.

• U.S. petitions and labor claims which are similar in frequently raising issues concerning the proper scope of federal law-making authority.

• Civil rights and liberties petitions which usually claimed federal constitutional rights against asserted state and local authority.

• Federalism cases, which require the Court to adjust competing jurisdictional claims among governmental and quasi-governmental authorities and which are clearly a central function for the court of last resort in a federal system.

* * *

Frequency of votes for review

The significance of role perceptions in case selection decisions is also evident when the Burton period justices are compared according to the frequency with which they voted for review. * * *

Certain justices during the Burton period consistently voted more often for review than their colleagues. The justices often divided into two groups on this issue, with 20 percentage points or more separating them. * * * Black and Douglas were the long-standing members of the review-prone group, while Frankfurter and Burton were mainstays of the review-conservative group.

* * *

Changes in the membership of the Court did not disrupt voting propensities, even when they affected how a majority of the Court could be expected to vote on the merits. This suggests that those who voted often for review did so with little regard for probable outcome on the merits, and even without regard to marshalling enough votes to gain review. The review-prone justices, in other words, appear to have been unconcerned with the impact of their case selection votes in specific cases.

Propensity to vote for review

It seems likely that differences in the frequency with which individual justices voted for review are related to differences in the disposition of the justices to exercise Supreme Court power. Clearly the structure of case selection requires the justices to consider the proper scope of Supreme Court activity in voting for or against review. The identity of the most review-prone and the most review-conservative justices during the Burton period also suggests the relevance of such a concern.

Pritchett's discussion of differences among the justices in plenary decisionmaking is particularly useful in showing this connection. * * *

Those men whom Pritchett labelled "libertarian activists" in *Civil Liberties and the Vinson Court* were the most review-prone justices who sat during the entire Burton period.[26] Pritchett's "less libertarians" are among the least review-prone justices. Frankfurter, Pritchett's lone example of libertarian restraint, is somewhere near the middle in case selection, as he is in Pritchett's typology.

Pritchett described the libertarian activist as the judge whose sympathies are aroused by the underdogs in our society and for whom "the result is the test of a decision." A believer in libertarian restraint, on the other hand, emphasizes the process of judicial decisionmaking and the non-democratic basis of judicial power. For Pritchett, a justice's activism or restraint is a function of the interaction of two variables: his sympathies towards underdogs and "the conception which the justice holds of his judicial role and the obligations imposed on him by his judicial function."

Information about the frequency with which the justices vote for review is consistent with this two-dimensional interpretation of judicial

---

26. Pritchett, Civil Liberties and the Vinson Court (Chicago: University of Chi- cago Press, 1954).

motivation. Sympathy for underdogs and an expansive interpretation of the availability of Court-fashioned relief seemed to play a part in explaining voting frequency.

The Court's proper workload

Differing convictions among the justices about the workload appropriate to the Court, a question central to the role it should perform, also appear to have been crucial. This is particularly evident when differences in voting frequencies are examined in detail. [The study examines the four justices who sat throughout this period: Black, Burton, Douglas and Frankfurter.] * * *

Had two other justices consistently voted with them, Black and Douglas would have engaged the Court in several times as many cases as either Frankfurter or Burton. The willingness of Black and Douglas to involve the Court in this number of plenary decisions suggests that they placed little value on time-consuming methods of decisionmaking. These men exhibited in their case selection behavior a willingness to reach decisions quickly and to justify them without ado, characteristics that are also evident in their behavior on the merits.

* * * Black and Douglas participated in many more four-, five-, and six-vote grants than either Burton or Frankfurter. Only when seven or eight votes were cast were Burton and Frankfurter slightly more likely to have voted for review than Black or Douglas. This pattern indicates that Black and Douglas must have voted for review in many cases without paying much attention to the ideological similarities and differences with their colleagues that were usually in evidence in published decisions. Black and Douglas thus appear to differ from Burton and Frankfurter less in the types of cases they voted to hear than in the numbers they felt competent to decide on the merits.

In the weekly case selection conferences, the contrast between the two approaches must have been continually apparent and frequently irritating. To review-conservative justices like Frankfurter, the more review-prone justices must have seemed insensitive about the work-load they were willing to impose on the Court. To the review-prone justices, those who seldom voted for review must sometimes have seemed callous about the plights of petitioners and the development of legal rights.

Conclusion

This analysis suggests that Supreme Court justices during the Burton period shared a powerful conception of the role of their institution, which appears to have sharply limited the level of disagreement that could otherwise have been anticipated in case selection voting. Consensus on the norms of judicial behavior also appears to have discouraged these justices either from combining forces to achieve the results they preferred on the merits or from voting individually in a way that would indicate routine calculation of probable outcomes in the case selection process.

The voting patterns examined here thus suggest that role conceptions serve both a limiting and a liberating function. Judicial conceptions of appropriate behavior help to limit the expression of judicial predispositions towards litigants in voting. Yet role conceptions also operate to free the justices from ideological isolation, permitting them to vote routinely with ideologically dissimilar justices.

The evidence here also suggests that role conceptions can also be a source of disagreement in case selection. The considerable differences among the Burton period justices in their willingness to vote for review appear to be at least partly attributable to variation in conceptions of the Court's role.

* * *

For students of judicial decisionmaking, the significance of role conceptions in case selection has additional implications. The explanatory power of the concept in this context suggests that role perceptions deserve more attention in analyses of Supreme Court decisionmaking on the merits. Differences in role conceptions have, of course, been the focus of some research, but the phenomenon of consensus among justices has received too little attention.

Preoccupation with voting differences among the justices gives a misleading impression of judicial motivation. Differences in judicial attitudes and role conceptions tend to receive lopsided attention, while the influence of shared norms derived from legal and professional socialization tends to be ignored. This makes it difficult to determine the extent to which judicial decisionmaking parallels political decisionmaking in other contexts. A more accurate picture will emerge only when political scientists acknowledge that the work of Supreme Court justices includes more than nonunanimous decisions on the merits.

Further Reflections on Criteria for Cert Petitions

As noted at the outset of this chapter, a central question about the Court's agenda setting process is: What are the justices trying to accomplish? Is this a "legalistic" process in which each justice applies some objective, ideologically neutral standard—such as, is there a conflict among the circuits—in deciding how to vote on each cert petition? Or is this a "political" process, in which each justice is quite aware that setting the agenda greatly influences the outcome and so, when voting on cert petitions, is seeking to promote that justice's values and preferences for various rules of law?

The previous articles, by Hellman and Provine, use different methods to try to answer this question. Hellman looks at cert petitions and the subsequent disposition of them. Provine looks at cert petitions and the voting patterns of individual justices reflected in their docket books.

A provocative book by Professor H.W. Perry [1] reflects yet a third method of inquiry and arrives at results very similar to those Provine emphasizes.

Perry conducted detailed interviews about the Court's cert processes with, *inter alia,* five Supreme Court justices and sixty-four former Supreme Court clerks. After sifting through these interviews, Perry reached the conclusion that each justice employs two different approaches to voting on cert petitions.

In Perry's judgment, the threshold question for each justice is whether that justice cares strongly about the outcome of the case on the merits.[2] If the justice does not care strongly, then he or she will focus on such "jurisprudential" or "legalistic" issues as whether the decision below reflects a split among the circuits, whether it involves an important issue, and whether this is an appropriate time to resolve the issue.

Where the outcome of the case does matter to the justice, however, Perry concludes that he or she will shift to an "outcome" mode and exhibit "more strategic" behavior. In such cases, the justice will want to vote to grant cert if the justice anticipates winning on the merits and concludes that this case is a good vehicle for espousing her or his position. Conversely, in such cases, if the justice anticipates losing on the merits, the justice will vote to deny cert unless convinced, by very strong evidence, that it would be institutionally irresponsible to refuse to take the case. Based on his research, Perry concludes that "the strategic behavior in case selection [as opposed to the jurisprudential behavior] is the exception, even among the justices we would consider the most 'political'." [3]

It would appear, then, that the literature on the Court's agenda setting process is reaching a consensus that the process is both legalistic and political. Further, because different justices will care differently about the outcome of different cases, it will always be difficult to disentangle the factors that underlie decisions to grant or deny cert. Advocates will continue to be well advised to argue the merits of their cases in cert petitions and scholars will continue to find Supreme Court Rule 10 a most inadequate statement of the considerations that truly govern the disposition of cert petitions.

D. PROPOSALS FOR REFORM

This section consists of a single reading, which reports the conclusions Professors Estreicher and Sexton reached after a year-long study of every cert petition filed with the Court. They lay out several proposals for alterations in the Court's procedures that they expect would make

---

1. H.W. Perry, *Deciding to Decide: Agenda Setting in the United States Supreme Court* (1991). The book deserves careful study by those interested in these questions. Regrettably, its publisher, the Harvard University Press, refused to allow any portion of it to be reprinted in this volume.

2. *Id.* at 277–282.

3. *Id.* at 275 n. 5.

the process run more smoothly and produce more defensible results. Each of their proposals is worth careful review.

As further review of all the materials in Chapter Three, consider these additional questions. Has the Court's jurisdiction been made too discretionary; should the categories of cases coming to the Court on appeal (or "as of right") be expanded? Where the Court believes the decision below to be correct, under what circumstances (if any) should it nevertheless grant certiorari? Where it tentatively concludes the decision below was wrong, under what circumstances (if any) should the Court deny cert? What strategies are available to a justice who wishes to see certiorari granted or denied in a particular case?

SAMUEL ESTREICHER AND JOHN SEXTON,* IMPROVING THE PROCESS: CASE SELECTION BY THE SUPREME COURT
70 Judicature 41 (1986)

We have produced elsewhere our empirical assessment of the case for a new national court of appeals or intercircuit tribunal, concluding on the basis of a study of all the cases granted and denied review by the Supreme Court during the 1982 Term that the data do not support creation of a new tier of appellate review interposed between the present courts of appeals and the Supreme Court.[1] We do not propose to retrace that ground here. We do believe, however, that whether or not new courts are ultimately established, there are several reforms that should be put in place to enable the justices to manage better their scarce decisional resources. Most of the reforms we propose here could be effected by the justices themselves; one or two would require congressional action. Each would enable the Court better to perform its managerial functions and to fulfill its role as articulator of authoritative and uniform federal law.

ABOLISH MANDATORY JURISDICTION

All the justices and virtually all commentators endorse the proposal to abolish mandatory jurisdiction. The Court's mandatory appellate docket accounts for somewhere between 25 and 35 per cent of the Court's caseload (21 per cent in the 1982 Term).[2]

DEVELOP SPECIFIC CRITERIA

We urge the Court to develop more specific criteria for selecting cases for review. Supreme Court Rule 17,[3] we submit, offers no guid-

* Professors of Law, New York University. Reprinted by permission of the authors, Samuel Estreicher and John Sexton.

1. *See* Estreicher and Sexton, *A Managerial Theory of the Supreme Court's Responsibilities: An Empirical Study,* 50 N.Y.U.L.Rev. 681 (1984); *see generally, The New York University Supreme Court Project,* 59 N.Y.U.L.Rev., Nos. 4–6 (1984).

2. [Ed.] Since publication of this article, Congress has abolished most of the Court's mandatory jurisdiction.

3. [Ed.] Since publication of this article, the Rule has been renumbered as Rule 10 and slight stylistic changes made in it. The present Rule 10 is reprinted in section A of this chapter.

ance to the bar and unnecessarily exacerbates the Court's difficulties in managing its docket. Rule 17 reflects the tension between the promise that the Court may hear all important federal questions and the reality that it cannot do so:

> A review on writ of *certiorari* is not a matter of right, but of judicial discretion, and will be granted only when there are special and important reasons therefor. The following, while neither controlling nor fully measuring the Court's discretion, indicate the character of reasons that will be considered.
>
> (a) When a federal court of appeals has rendered a decision in conflict with the decision of another federal court of appeals on the same matter; or has decided a federal question in a way in conflict with a state court of last resort; or has so far departed from the accepted and usual course of judicial proceedings, or so far sanctioned such a departure by a lower court, as to call for an exercise of this Court's power of supervision.
>
> (b) When a state court of last resort has decided a federal question in a way in conflict with the decision of another state court of last resort or of a federal court of appeals.
>
> (c) When a state court or a federal court of appeals has decided an important question of federal law which has not been, but should be, settled by this Court, or has decided a federal question in a way in conflict with applicable decisions of this Court.

Presumably, conflicts—whether among the federal courts of appeals or the state courts of last resort, or between federal courts of appeals and state courts of last resort—present a strong claim for review. But in our study period, "conflict" appeared as a justification for a grant of *certiorari* in only about 35 per cent of the cases.

Rule 17 is indeterminate with respect to the other potential grounds for review. Conflict with Supreme Court precedent, if viewed in the narrow sense of head-on clash with prior rulings, would clearly warrant a grant of *certiorari*, but such cases are few and far between: we identified only five such cases out of the 164 on the docket during the 1982 Term. We are told that review is also appropriate in cases calling for "an extraordinary exercise" of the Court's power of supervision, but the very language used suggests that this is a narrow category of cases. Thus, Rule 17 accounts for most of the non-conflict cases heard by the Court under the open-ended residual category of "important question[s] of federal law which [have] not been, but should be, settled by this Court."

It is, of course, vaguely comforting that the Court is free to grant *certiorari* whenever a particular petition strikes it as meritorious, thus making the Court potentially available for all significant questions of federal law. But for the Court to assume, and for students of the Court to insist upon, an unrealistic set of responsibilities is to ensure dissatisfaction and, more importantly, to forestall careful thinking about what the Court should be doing with its limited decisional capacity.

A principled set of case selection criteria would send clearer signals to the bar. Definite criteria for "certworthiness" would enable practitioners to self-censor many petitions filed in full compliance with Supreme Court Rule 17 as presently written, but that clearly do not merit review. Moreover, the tendency to construe a denial of review as a judgment on the merits would be significantly diminished.

LINK PETITIONS TO THE CRITERIA

The rules governing petitions for *certiorari* should require petitioners to file a short supplemental statement—possibly on a checklist form developed by the Court—setting forth procedural information to facilitate the Court's evaluation of the certworthiness of each petition. This statement should indicate whether the petition is from a final judgment of the court below and should explicitly link the petitioner's request for review to the Court's articulated criteria.

When the basis of the request for review is an alleged conflict among the circuits, the statement should provide three additional pieces of information. First, the petitioner should identify the precise issue on which a conflict is alleged. Second, the petitioner should cite, say, at least three, but no more than six, cases presenting the conflict. Third, the petitioner should aver that the alleged conflict was brought to the attention of the court below.

ALERT LOWER COURT TO CONFLICTS

In order to promote intercircuit reconciliation, we recommend that a petitioner who alleges a conflict among the circuits be required to demonstrate that the conflict was considered by the lower court. The petitioner should be required to bring the conflict to the attention of the court of appeals. If the appeals panel does not acknowledge the existence of the alleged conflict in its opinion, the petitioner must again raise the issue in the petition for rehearing or suggestion for rehearing *en banc*. In the rare case in which a conflict arises after the petition for rehearing is filed, but before the last date for filing with the Supreme Court, the petitioner should be permitted—indeed, encouraged—to return to the court of appeals for reconsideration based on the allegedly conflicting decision.

PENALIZE FRIVOLOUS PETITIONS

We urge that the Supreme Court, on the model of Rule 11 of the Federal Rules of Civil Procedure, require certification that the petition for review is not frivolous under the Court's criteria. Costs or other sanctions should be imposed on attorneys who violate this procedure. An attorney would certify that he has examined the case selection criteria articulated by the Court and that he has in good faith a reasonable basis for urging Supreme Court review in a particular case. The Court could then impose sanctions (costs and attorney's fees involved in opposing the petition) if, under the Court's criteria, the attorney filed a frivolous petition.

A Second Look

Under the present procedures, once four justices vote to hear a case (the Rule of Four), review is granted. Usually the announcement is made by the Court on the Monday following the conference. The case is not studied again until the Court considers it on the merits.

Occasionally the justices dismiss a writ of *certiorari* as having been improvidently granted. [T]his practice wastes the Court's time and damages its credibility. Moreover, we suspect that the incidence of overt dismissals understates the justices' own tally of improvident grants, because the Court tends to decide a case once *certiorari* has been granted.

Relatively modest procedural changes could reduce the number of improvident grants. The justices at the initial conference should vote on each petition to grant or deny review, as they do now. However, the results of that vote should not be announced. Instead, petitions that receive at least four votes should be submitted to an independent staff of the caliber of the justices' clerks, headed by a leading member of the Supreme Court bar. The staff would evaluate each proposed grant under the Court's criteria to determine whether the case merited review. They would also inquire whether there were any procedural obstacles to consideration of the merits, such as the absence of a final judgment, and evaluate the state of the record to determine whether the case provided a suitable vehicle for review. Then the petitions, accompanied by the staff reports, would be returned to the justices for reconsideration and a final vote at a second conference. If the case still received at least four votes, review would be granted and the result announced.

We recognize that some critics will view this suggestion as a further step toward "bureaucratic justice," whereby the justices do not make the decisions themselves but merely manage a bureaucratic machine. Our proposal, in fact, involves no delegation of decisionmaking or loss of accountability, because the function of our proposed staff is purely advisory; its members would simply highlight difficulties with the tentatively granted petition, in light of the Court's case selection criteria, the state of the record, and the suitability of the case as a proposed vehicle. The justices would receive and act on the staff's recommendations, but they would not be bound by them in any way.

We urge that the screening process include another preliminary step when a petition is to be granted as a possible vehicle for announcing a major doctrinal shift or innovation. There is no point in a vehicle grant that will yield only a plurality opinion and a splintered Court. As former Secretary of Transportation William T. Coleman recently suggested, fragmented opinions encourage later litigants to seek review on the chance that a plurality or concurring opinion might presage a shift in the Court's position. Therefore, to better identify appropriate vehicles, the justices should take a straw vote or in some other way determine whether they will be able to unite on an opinion that authoritatively sets forth clear and easily applied rules and legal principles. Naturally, this straw vote would not (and should not) preclude a change of mind after briefs and argument. But if the justices' straw vote determines that there is no consensus on the structure or substance of an eventual Court opinion, then the justices will have had an advance notice that the case may prove to be an unsuitable vehicle.

LESS FREQUENT CONFERENCES

The justices presently vote on requests for review as part of their weekly conference. Consequently, most of the cases the Court selects come from relatively small and unrepresentative samples of the annual pool of filed cases. During these weekly conferences, case selection is conducted without any real sense of how the docket is evolving. By contrast, the justices' major conference each September, at which they have before them approximately one-fifth of the cases filed in a year, provides a striking lesson in how case selection might differ if the weekly conferences were dropped in favor of less frequent deliberations. Presumably, the cases at the September conference are representative of those filed throughout the year. Yet, over the last four terms, the ratio of cases granted *certiorari* to petitions considered at the September conference has been significantly lower than that for the rest of the year.[4]

If, by contrast, the justices were to review petitions on a monthly or semimonthly rather than weekly basis, they could gain a more accurate overview of the developing docket and the work of the lower courts. By locating each decision to grant or deny review in the context of a larger sample of the docket, monthly or semi-monthly review would reduce the incidence of improvident grants.

We also urge consideration of the suggestion that petitions be screened by panels of three justices, with only one vote necessary to bring a petition before all nine justices for review. This proposal would reduce substantially the screening burden; each justice would consider only the one-third of all petitions handled by his or her panel and those cases referred to the full Court by the other two panels.

FACILITATE FURTHER RESEARCH

The Court should facilitate empirical research by publishing the justices' votes on decisions to grant or deny review. Publication need not be simultaneous with the actual vote; records on votes to grant or deny review could be made available several years after the actual vote. Such information would be extraordinarily useful in discussing proposals

---

4. During the 1979 Term, for example, the ratio of granted cases to cases considered at the September conference was only 1 in 20 (22 of 391), whereas for the rest of the year it was 1 in 12 (110 of 1385). During the 1980 Term, the ratio was 1 in 23 at the September conference (21 of 458), 1 in 11 for the rest of the year (146 of 1541). During the 1981 Term, the ratio was 1 in 14 at the September conference (26 of 373), 1 in 10 for the rest of the year (177 of 1727). During the 1982 Term, the ratio was 1 in 24 at the September conference (16 of 412), and 1 in 10 for the rest of the year (153 of 1480). (Figures compiled from data in U.S.L.W. vols. 47–50.)

for reform. For example, it would provide a data base for assessing the operation of the Rule of Four, and for evaluating proposals for a Rule of Five. Similarly, publication of these votes would permit students of the Court to evaluate the contribution, if any, of the *cert* pool practice to the overgranting phenomenon.

MODIFY TRANSFER AND VENUE RULES

In our view, the mere fact that two circuits are in conflict presents no pressing reason for Supreme Court intervention, unless a party can take advantage of the conflict by forum shopping or unless the conflict stymies the planning of multi-circuit actors. Much can be done, however, to minimize these undesirable features of conflicts while preserving the benefits of intercircuit percolation and reducing significantly the number of conflict cases requiring the Court's attention.

The most promising approach, in our view, would be for Congress generally to restrict federal venue to the district or circuit where the claim or cause of action arose. Under a restrictive venue regime, parties would know with certainty the law that would govern their affairs. Moreover, they would be unable to bring themselves under a different set of legal rules by forum choice. We recognize that this approach raises difficult questions, such as the assignment of a *situs* to multi-district or multi-circuit transactions. Special rules might also be needed for cases involving challenges to government regulations or other decisions of national applicability; for example, venue could be restricted to the District of Columbia Circuit or to the principal place of business or the residence of the challenger. For actions originating at the district court level, provision for transfer of venue for reasons of litigation convenience would be necessary, but, by analogy to the rules governing transfer in federal diversity cases, the law of the transferor circuit would apply.

OTHER PROPOSALS

In our view, the proposals that follow should be adopted only as a last resort before the creation of a new intermediate appellate court. These cures pose difficulties or undermine important values and practices, yet are distinctly preferable to creation of a new national court of appeals or intercircuit tribunal.

Modification of the Rule of Four. Several commentators and at least one justice have suggested that the Rule of Four be replaced by a Rule of Five. This proposal's drawback is that it would enable an entrenched majority to foreclose even threshold consideration of issues of concern to a significant minority of justices. Moreover, although a Rule of Five might increase the reversal rate for cases on the *certiorari* docket, or reduce the aggregate number of grants per term, adoption of the proposal would provide no additional assurance of appropriate case selection.

Giving nationally binding effect to certain en banc *circuit court decisions.* Justice White and several commentators have proposed a novel way of addressing intercircuit conflicts. If, after a panel of one circuit decides a legal issue, a panel of a second circuit decides the same issue differently, the second circuit court must convene *en banc* to reconsider the issue. The resulting *en banc* decision would become a nationally binding rule that could be overturned only by the Supreme Court.[5]

Although this proposal appears at first glance to be an attractive way to dispose of intercircuit conflicts, we do not support it for several reasons. First, and foremost, it does not give sufficient weight to the value of percolation. For example, legal issues are susceptible of more than two polar resolutions; the Court should have the benefit of intermediate approaches. Second, this proposal would permit a circuit with little experience and knowledge in an area of law to overrule a circuit with widely acknowledged expertise (for example, the Second Circuit on securities regulation law or the District of Columbia on administrative law). Third, this proposal shares some of the difficulties that would beset an intercircuit tribunal. Because the *en banc* decision would purport to bind the nation yet be authoritative only if not overturned by the Supreme Court, litigants still would press further their claims, and the Court would be under considerable pressure to review the *en banc* ruling.

[O]ur study raises doubt about the alleged pressing need to free up additional docket capacity. According to our criteria, the cases requiring the Court's attention during the 1982 Term (what we call the "priority docket") accounted for only 48 per cent of the overall grants, and nearly one in four decisions to grant review was improvident.

Specialized appellate courts. Some commentators have suggested the creation of specialized appellate courts, on the model of the Court of Appeals for the Federal Circuit. These courts would eliminate intercircuit conflicts in areas over which they had exclusive jurisdiction. A specialized court for tax appeals is the most frequently suggested new tribunal. Critics of this proposal argue that a judge familiar with the full range of legal questions potentially implicated in a federal case will decide cases more soundly and creatively than a specialist judge, and that a court that deals exclusively with a governmental agency might become too deferential to the views of either the agency or a specialized segment of the bar. We doubt that specialized appellate courts can effectively reduce the Court's caseload. Such courts would sacrifice the benefits of percolation, are vulnerable to capture by special interest, and, if given responsibility over controversial subjects, would require greater Supreme Court supervision.

Courts of exclusive jurisdiction, if established, should be confined to areas that are not likely to generate wide controversy, to areas in which certainty and predictability in the law are paramount. Patent litigation

---

5. *See* White, *Challenges for the U.S. Supreme Court and the Bar: Contemporary* *Reflections,* 51 Antitrust L.J. 275 (1982).

is one such area, and thus assignment of patent cases to the Court of Appeals for the Federal Circuit was appropriate. We do not expect litigants in patent cases to seek Supreme Court review regularly. Similarly, we do not expect the justices to feel any strong temptation to intervene. Tax litigation might be another such area. To avoid the "captive court" problem, tax cases should also be assigned to the Court of Appeals for the Federal Circuit. This practice would expand the subject-matter responsibilities of that court, and, correspondingly, the breadth of perspective of its judges.

We do not at present urge the creation of additional specialized tribunals. Even in the tax area, the case has yet to be made with convincing clarity that such a change is needed.

Chapter Four

COLLEGIAL DECISION MAKING

Once a cert petition is granted and the case fully briefed, the Court is ready to consider the case on the merits. The materials in this chapter describe how the Court works its way from deciding that a case should be heard to publishing an opinion disposing of the matter.

In the first reading, Chief Justice Rehnquist describes how the Court functions, first in hearing oral argument, then in deliberating on these argued cases, and finally in assigning, drafting, circulating and responding to opinions resolving them. Next, a New York Times article recounts Justice Scalia's frustration with the brevity of the Court's conferences. The excerpt from Professor O'Brien gives specific illustrations, drawn from the justices' own papers, of the opinion writing process. He provides many concrete examples of the types of give and take that occur in the course of fashioning opinions.

Following these overviews are some more particular observations on the value of dissents by Supreme Court justices. Justice Brennan provides a classic definition and defense of the function of dissenting opinions in the process of constitutional adjudication. Justice Ginsburg (Judge Ginsburg, when she wrote this piece) tempers the Brennan article with some observations on the appropriate limits of style in concurring and dissenting opinions.

Finally, two readings describe, in detail, the internal deliberations of the Court in two landmark cases, *Roe v. Wade,* 410 U.S. 113, 93 S.Ct. 705, 35 L.Ed.2d 147 (1973) and *United States v. Nixon,* 418 U.S. 683, 94 S.Ct. 3090, 41 L.Ed.2d 1039 (1974). Together, these readings illustrate the very wide range of methods available to the justices to try to shape opinions of the Court. By explaining how the Court proceeded from argument to opinion in these dramatic and seminal cases, these readings vividly reveal the significance of factors the public usually cannot witness in the development of constitutional law.

A central conclusion of these materials is that, at least for the average case, the justices spend very little time deliberating on its outcome in each other's presence. Oral argument sometimes serves as a forum for exchanging views among the justices, but that does not appear

381

to be its principal purpose or focus. At the end of each week of oral argument, the Court holds a conference that is specifically designed for sharing views, but often entails little more than announcing votes and tallying who won and who lost.

Justice Scalia laments that the justices do not engage in more substantive exchanges in conference. What might account for the fact that conference discussions are so abbreviated? Suppose the justices' conference discussions on argued cases were longer and more intensive. Would that change results? Or opinions? Would it alter the actual or perceived influence of law clerks? Would the justices have to agree to hear fewer cases?

Short conferences put pressure on the opinion writing process. The materials as a whole explain the variety of options, or strategies, available to justices in the opinion writing process. The key point seems to be that it is in this period that true interaction and deliberation take place as opinions are drafted, circulated, studied and revised, adopted or rejected. Deliberation and negotiation do take place, then, but largely through written, arms' length exchange rather than through face-to-face oral communications.[1]

Why does this form of interaction dominate the Court's process of collegial decision making? By sweeping all previous negotiations and exchanges behind one set of formal published opinions, does the process unduly obscure the factors that guide the outcomes of cases? During these exchanges of drafts, is too little emphasis placed on shaping an opinion that many justices are likely to join (and too much on writing concurrences and dissents)? In those cases where, at the end of the process, a solid majority is massed behind a single opinion, what is the point of publishing a dissent or concurrence?

It is instructive to ponder these questions while reading the materials. Better yet, select a case pending before the Court. With a group, conduct a mock conference on the case and then assign, write and circulate opinions. Such a "mock" experience, which we have observed many times, will be remarkably similar to that described in these readings.

---

1. When we were law clerks, we observed the peculiar phenomenon that a justice, who wished to join an opinion authored by another justice, would write a note to the author saying, "Please join me." Grammatically, that seemed backward, but the style was employed universally. Recently, Justice Stevens observed that this habit of expression, which he recalled from his days as a law clerk to Justice Rutledge in 1947, traced back to the time when a single copy of a proposed opinion was circulated. When a justice received such a proposed opinion, and agreed with it, he would write "Please join me" on the back of the opinion and send it back to the author for circulation to the next chamber. Current practice is to send proposed opinions to all chambers simultaneously. Justice Stevens reported that, although he and justices senior to him observe this custom of expression even under the changed circumstances, more recently arrived justices—beginning with Justice O'Connor—now employ more precise instructions, such as "I am pleased to join your opinion." As Justice Stevens commented, on this matter of style "the textualists have taken over from the traditionalists." See Tony Mauro, *Please Join Me,* Legal Times, June 7, 1993, at 10.

WILLIAM H. REHNQUIST,* THE SUPREME COURT: HOW IT WAS, HOW IT IS
287–303 (1987)

How the Court Does its Work: Deciding the Cases

Potter Stewart, with whom it was my privilege to sit as a member of the Court for nearly ten years, passed on to me more than one bit of sound advice in the years when I was the junior member of the Court. I remember his saying that he thought he would never know more about a case than when he left the bench after hearing it orally argued, and I have found that his statement also holds true for me. When one thinks of the important ramifications that some of the constitutional decisions of the Supreme Court have, it seems that one could never know as much as he ought to know about how to cast his vote in a case. But true as this is, each member of the Court must cast votes in about one hundred and fifty cases decided on the merits each year, and there must come a time when pondering one's own views must cease, and deliberation with one's colleagues and voting must begin.

That time is each Wednesday afternoon after we get off the bench for those cases argued on Monday, and Friday for those cases argued on Tuesday and Wednesday. * * * A buzzer sounds—or, to put it more accurately, is supposed to sound—in each of the nine chambers five minutes before the time for conference, and the nine members of the Court then congregate in the Court's conference room next to the chambers of the Chief Justice. We all shake hands with one another when we come in, and our vote sheets and whatever other material we wish to have are at our places at the conference table. Seating at this long, rectangular table is strictly by seniority: the Chief Justice sits at one end of the table, and Justice Brennan, the senior associate justice, sits at the other end of the table. Unlike those ranged along the sides of the table, we have unrestricted elbow room. But even along the sides of the table, the seating remains by seniority: the three associate justices next in seniority sit along one side, and the four associates having the least seniority sit along the opposite side. * * *

To one and all familiar with the decision-making process in other governmental institutions, the most striking thing about our Court's conference is that only the nine justices are present. There are no law clerks, no secretaries, no staff assistants, no outside personnel of any kind. If one of the messengers from the Marshal's Office who guard the door of the conference knocks on the door to indicate that there is a message for one of the justices, the junior justice opens the door and delivers the message. The junior justice is also responsible for dictating to the staff of the clerk's office at the close of the conference the text of the orders that will appear on the Court's order list issued on the Monday following the conference.

I think that the tradition of having only the justices themselves present at the Court's conference is a salutary one for more than one reason. Its principal effect is to implement the observation of Justice Brandeis * * * that the Supreme Court is respected because "we do our own work." If a justice is to participate meaningfully in the conference, the justice must himself know the issues to be discussed and the arguments he wishes to make. Some cases may be sufficiently complicated as to require written notes to remind one of various points, but any extended reading of one's position to a group of only eight colleagues is bound to lessen the effect of what one says. * * *

In discussing cases that have been argued, the Chief Justice begins by reviewing the facts and the decision of the lower court, outlining his understanding of the applicable case law, and indicating either that he votes to affirm the decision of the lower court or to reverse it. The discussion then proceeds to Justice Brennan and in turn down the line to Justice Scalia. For many years there has circulated a tale that although the discussion in conference proceeds in order from the Chief Justice to the junior justice, the voting actually begins with the junior justice and proceeds back to the Chief Justice in order of seniority. I can testify that, at least during my fifteen years on the Court, this tale is very much of a myth; I don't believe I have ever seen it happen at any of the conferences that I have attended.

The time taken in discussion of a particular case by each justice will naturally vary with the complexity of the case and the nature of the discussion which has preceded his. The Chief Justice, going first as he does, takes more time than any one associate in a typical case, because he feels called upon to go into greater detail as to the facts and the lower-court holding than do those who come after him. Justice Brennan, who frequently disagrees with me (and also disagreed with Chief Justice Burger) in important constitutional cases, and is therefore the first to state the view of the law with which he agrees, also frequently takes more time than the other associates. The truth is that there simply are not nine different points of view in even the most complex and difficult case, and all of us feel impelled to a greater or lesser degree to try to reach some consensus that can be embodied in a written opinion that will command the support of at least a majority of the members of the Court. The lack of anything that is both previously unsaid, relevant, and sensible is apt to be frustrating to those far down the line of discussion, but this is one of the prices exacted by the seniority system. With occasional exceptions, each justice begins and ends his part of the discussion without interruption from his colleagues, and in the great majority of cases by the time Justice Scalia is finished with his discussion, it will be evident that a majority of the Court has agreed upon a basis for either affirming or reversing the decision of the lower court in the case under discussion.

When I first went on the Court, I was both surprised and disappointed at how little interplay there was between the various justices during the process of conferring on a case. Each would state his views, and a junior justice could express agreement or disagreement with views expressed by a justice senior to him earlier in the discussion, but the converse did not apply; a junior justice's views were seldom commented upon, because votes had been already cast up the line. Like most junior justices before me must have felt, I thought I had some very significant contributions to make, and was disappointed that they hardly ever seemed to influence anyone because people did not change their votes in response to my contrary views. I thought it would be desirable to have more of a round-table discussion of the matter after each of us had expressed our views. Having now sat in conferences for fifteen years, and risen from ninth to seventh to first in seniority, I now realize—with newfound clarity—that while my idea is fine in the abstract it probably would not contribute much in practice, and at any rate is doomed by the seniority system to which the senior justices naturally adhere.

Each member of the Court has done such work as he deems necessary to arrive at his own views before coming into conference; it is not a bull session in which off-the-cuff reactions are traded, but instead a discussion in which very considered views are stated. * * *

Until the past term, I had sat in conference only under Chief Justice Burger; three of the associate justices sitting at present—Justices Brennan, White, and Marshall—also sat in conference under Chief Justice Warren. Chief Justice Burger presided for seventeen years, and so all of us became used to a particular form and style of conference. But there is good reason to think that the conferences of past Courts may have been quite different from that of the Burger Court.

I have heard both Justice Felix Frankfurter and Justice William O. Douglas describe the conferences presided over by Chief Justice Charles Evans Hughes in which they sat, and I have heard Justice Douglas describe the conferences presided over by Chief Justice Harlan F. Stone. These two styles of conference were apparently much different. Chief Justice Hughes has rightly been described as Jovian in appearance, and, according to Frankfurter, he "radiated authority." He was totally prepared in each case, lucidly expressed his views, and said no more than was necessary. In the words of Justice Frankfurter, you did not speak up in that conference unless you were very certain that you knew what you were talking about. Discipline and restraint were the order of the day.

Understandably, some of the justices appointed by President Franklin Roosevelt in the last part of Hughes's tenure resented the tight rein imposed by the latter—imposed albeit only by example. Hughes was succeeded as Chief Justice by Harlan F. Stone in 1941. Stone was one of those who had disliked the taut atmosphere of the Hughes conference, and he opened up the floor to more discussion. But, according to Justice Douglas, Stone was unable to shake his role as a law-school professor, and as a result he led off the discussion with a full statement of his own views, then turned over the floor to the senior associate justice; but at the conclusion of the latter's presentation Stone took the floor once more himself to critique the analysis of the senior associate. The conference totally lost the tautness it had under Hughes, and on some occasions went on interminably.

The conferences under Chief Justice Burger were somewhere in between those presided over by Hughes and those presided over by Stone. Since I have become Chief Justice, I have tried to make my opening presentation of a case somewhat shorter than Chief Justice Burger made his. I do not think that conference discussion changes many votes, and I do not think that the impact of the Chief Justice's presentation is necessarily proportional to its length. I do not mean to give the impression that the discussion in every case is stated in terms of nine inflexible positions; on occasion one or more of those who have stated their views toward the beginning of the discussion, upon seeing that those views as stated are not in agreement with those of the majority, may indicate a willingness to alter those views along the lines of the thinking of the majority. But there is virtually no institutional pressure to do this; dissent from the views of the majority is in no way discouraged, and one only need read the opinions of the Court to see that it is practiced by all of us.

I feel quite strongly a preference for the Hughes style over the Stone style insofar as interruptions of conference discussion are concerned. I think it is very desirable that all members of the Court have an opportunity to state their views before there is any cross-questioning or interruption, and I try to convey this sentiment to my colleagues. But the Chief Justice is not like the speaker of the House of Representatives; it would be unheard of to declare anyone out of order, and the Chief Justice is pretty much limited to leading by example. On rare occasions questioning of a justice who is speaking by one who has already spoken may throw added light on a particular issue, but this practice carries with it the potential for disrupting the orderly participation of each member of the Court in the discussion. At the end of the discussion, I announce how I am recording the vote in the case, so that others may have the opportunity to disagree with my count if they believe I am mistaken.

The upshot of the conference discussion of a case will, of course, vary in its precision and detail. If a case is a relatively simple one, with only one real legal issue in it, it will generally be very clear where each member of the Court stands on that issue. But many of the cases that we decide are complex ones, with several interrelated issues, and it is simply not possible in the format of the conference to have nine people answering either yes or no to a series of difficult questions about constitutional law. One justice may quite logically believe that a negative answer to the very first of several questions makes it unnecessary to decide the subsequent ones, and having answered the first one in the negative will say no more. But if a majority answers the first question in the affirmative, then the Court's opinion will have to go on and discuss the other questions. Whether or not the first justice agrees with the majority on these other issues may not be clear from the conference discussion. The comment is frequently heard during the course of a discussion that "some things will have to be worked out in the writing" and this is very true in a number of cases. Oral discussion of a complex case will usually give the broad outlines of each justice's position, but it is simply not adequate to fine-tune the various positions in the way that the written opinion for the majority of the Court, and the dissenting opinions, eventually will. The broad outlines emerge from the conference discussion, but often not the refinements.

So long as we rely entirely on oral discussion for the exposition of views at conference, I do not see how the conference could do more than it now does in refining the various views on a particular issue in a case. I understand that judges of other courts rely on written presentations circulated by each judge to his colleagues before the conference discussion; this practice may well flush out more views on the details of a case, but the need to reconcile the differences in the views expressed still remains. There is also a very human tendency, I believe, to become more firmly committed to a view that is put in writing than one that is simply expressed orally, and therefore the possibility of adjustment and adaptation might be lessened by this approach. At any rate, we do not use it, and I know of no one currently on our Court who believes we should try it.

Our conference is a relatively fragile instrument, I believe, which works well for the purpose to which we put it, but which also has very significant limitations. Probably every new justice, and very likely some justices who have been there for a while, wish that on occasion the floor could be opened up to a free-swinging exchange of views with much give-and-take rather than a structured statement of nine positions. I don't doubt that courts traditionally consisting of three judges, such as the federal courts of appeals, can be much more relaxed and informal in their discussion of a case they have heard argued. But the very fact that we are nine, and not three, or five, or seven, sets limits on our procedure. We meet with one another week after week, year after year, to discuss and deliberate over some of the most important legal questions in the United States. Each of us soon comes to know the general outlook of his eight colleagues, and on occasion I am sure that each of us feels, listening to the eight others, that he has "heard it all before." If there were a real prospect that extended discussion would bring about crucial changes in position on the part of one or more members of the Court, there would be a strong argument for having that sort of discussion even with its attendant consumption of time. But my sixteen years on the Court have convinced me that the true purpose of the conference discussion of argued cases is not to persuade one's colleagues through impassioned advocacy to alter their views, but instead by hearing each justice express his own views to determine therefrom the view of the majority of the Court. This is not to say that minds are never changed in conference; they certainly are. But it is very much the exception, and not the rule, and if one gives some thought to the matter this should come as no surprise.

The justices sitting in conference are not, after all, like a group of decision-makers who are hearing arguments pro and con about the matter for the first time. They have presumably read the briefs, they have heard the oral arguments of the lawyers who generally know far more about the particular case than the justices do, and they have had an opportunity to discuss the case with one or more of their law clerks. * * * All in all, I think our conference does about all that it can be expected to do in moving the Court to a final decision of a case by means of a written opinion.

During a given two-week session of oral argument, we will have heard twenty-four cases. By the Friday of the second week we will have conferred about all of them. Now the time comes for assignment to the various members of the Court of the task of preparing written opinions to support the result reached by the majority.

In every case in which the Chief Justice votes with the majority, he assigns the case; where the Chief Justice has been in the minority at conference, the senior associate justice in the majority assigns the case. Although one would not know it from reading the press coverage of the Court's work, the Court is unanimous in a good number of its opinions, and these of course are assigned by the Chief Justice. Since the odds of his being in a minority of one or two are mathematically small, he assigns the great majority of cases in which there is disagreement within the Court but which are not decided by a close vote. When the conference vote produces three or even four dissents from the majority view, the odds of course increase that the Chief Justice will be one of the dissenters; I have during my tenure received assignments not only from the Chief Justice, but from Justice Douglas, Justice Brennan, Justice White, and Justice Marshall. Sometimes the assignments come around during the weekend after the second week of oral argument, but sometimes they are delayed until early the following week. Since there are nine candidates to write twenty-four opinions, the law of averages again suggests that each chambers will ordinarily receive three assignments.

I know from the time during which I was an associate justice how important the assignment of the cases is to each member of the Court. The signed opinions produced by each justice are to a very large extent the only visible record of his work on the Court, and the office offers no greater reward than the opportunity to author an opinion on an important point of constitutional law. When I was an associate justice I eagerly awaited the assignments, and I think that my law clerks awaited them more eagerly than I did. Law clerks serve for only one year, and if I was assigned seventeen or eighteen opinions during the course of the year, each of the law clerks would have an opportunity to work on five or six opinions. My law clerks were always in high hopes that one of the cases on which they had worked or in which they were really interested and regarded as very important would be assigned to me. Unfortunately, they were frequently disappointed in this respect, because not every one of the twenty-four cases argued during a two-week term is both interesting and important.

Now that I am Chief Justice, of course, I have the responsibility for assigning the writing of opinions for the Court in cases where I have voted with the majority. This is an important responsibility, and it is desirable that it be discharged carefully and fairly. The Chief Justice is expected to retain for himself some opinions that he regards as of great significance, but he is also expected to pass around to his colleagues some of this kind of opinion. I think it also pleases the other members of the Court if the Chief Justice occasionally takes for himself a rather routine and uninteresting case, just as they are expected to do as a result of the assignment process. At the start of the October 1986 term I tried to be as evenhanded as possible as far as numbers of cases assigned to each justice, but as the term goes on I take into consideration the extent to which the various justices are current in writing and circulating opinions that have previously been assigned.

* * *

When a case is assigned to me I sit down with the law clerk who is * * * responsible for the case, and go over my conference notes with him. * * * [T]he notes and my recollection of what was said at conference generally prove an adequate basis for discussion between me and the law clerk of the views expressed by the majority at conference, and of the way in which an opinion supporting the result reached by the majority can be drafted. After this discussion, I ask the law clerk to prepare a first draft of a Court opinion, and to have it for me in ten days or two weeks.

I know that this sort of deadline seems onerous to the new crop of law clerks when, after the October oral argument session, they undertake the first drafting of an opinion for me. I am sure that every law clerk coming to work for a justice of the Supreme Court fancies that the opinion he is about to draft will make an important contribution to the jurisprudence of the Supreme Court, and in the rare case he may be right. But with this goal in mind the law clerk is all too apt to first ponder endlessly, and then write and rewrite, and then polish to a fare-thee-well. This might be entirely appropriate if his draft were a paper to be presented in an academic seminar, or an entry in a poetry contest. But it is neither of these things; it is a rough draft of an opinion embodying the views of a majority of the Court expressed at conference, a rough draft that I may very well substantially rewrite. It is far more useful to me to get something in fairly rough form in two weeks than to receive after four or five weeks a highly polished draft that I feel obligated nonetheless to substantially revise. It is easy in October, when the work of the Court is really just starting up for the term, to imagine that there is an infinite amount of time in which to explore every nuance of a question and to perfect the style of every paragraph of the opinion.

But, as I learned long ago, and as the law clerks soon find out, there is not an infinite amount of time. By the last week in October, we are already busy preparing for the November oral-argument session, at the end of which we will be assigned two or three more cases in which to prepare opinions for the Court. I feel very strongly that I want to keep as current as I possibly can with my work on the Court, in order not to build up that sort of backlog of unfinished work that hangs over one as an incubus throughout the remainder of the term.

When I receive a rough draft of a Court opinion from a law clerk, I read it over, and to the extent necessary go back and again read the opinion of the lower court and selected parts of the parties' briefs. The drafts I get during the first part of the term from the law clerks require more revision and editing than the ones later in the term, after the law clerks are more used to my views and my approach to writing. I go through the draft with a view to shortening it, simplifying it, and clarifying it. A good law clerk will include in the draft things that he might feel could be left out, simply to give me the option of making that decision. Law clerks also have been exposed to so much "legal writing" on law reviews and elsewhere that their prose tends to stress accuracy at the expense of brevity and clarity. Frank Wozencraft, who was my predecessor as assistant attorney general for the Office of Legal Counsel in the Justice Department, imparted to me a rule of thumb that he used in drafting opinions, which I have used since: If a sentence takes up more than six lines of type on an ordinary page, it is probably too long. This rule is truly stark in its simplicity, but every draft I review is subjected to it. Occasionally, but not often, a draft submitted by a law clerk will seem to me to have simply missed a major point I think necessary to support the conclusion reached by the majority at conference; I will of course rewrite the draft to include that point.

* * *

I hope it is clear from my explanation of the way that opinions are drafted in my chambers that the law clerk is not simply turned loose on an important legal question to draft an opinion embodying the reasoning and the result favored by the law clerk. Quite the contrary is the case. The law clerk is given, as best I can, a summary of the conference discussion, a description of the result reached by the majority in that discussion, and my views as to how a written opinion can best be prepared embodying that reasoning. The law clerk is not off on a frolic of his own, but is instead engaged in a highly structured task which has been largely mapped out for him by the conference discussion and my suggestions to him.

This is not to say that the clerk who prepares a first draft does not have a very considerable responsibility in the matter. The discussion in conference has been entirely oral, and as I have previously indicated, nine oral statements of position suffice to convey the broad outlines of the views of the justices but do not invariably settle exactly how the opinion will be reasoned through. Something that sounded very sensible to a majority of the Court at conference may, when an effort is made to justify it in writing, not seem so sensible, and it is the law clerk who undertakes the draft of the opinion who will first discover this difficulty. The clerk confronting such a situation generally comes back to me and explains the problem, and we discuss possible ways of solving it. It may turn out that I do not share the clerk's dissatisfaction with the reasoning of the conference, in which event I simply tell him to go ahead. If the objection or difficulty he sees is also seen as such by me, we then undertake an exploration for alternative means of writing the same passage in the draft. Similarly, the conference discussion may have passed over a subsidiary point without even treating it; it is not until the attempt is made to draft a written opinion that the necessity of deciding the subsidiary question becomes apparent. Here again, we do the best we can, recognizing that the proof of the pudding will be the reaction of those who voted with the majority at conference when they see the draft Court opinion.

When I have finished my revisions of the draft opinion, I return it to the law clerk, and the law clerk then refines and on occasion may suggest additional revisions. We then send the finished product to the printer, and in short order get back printed copies with the correct formal heading for the opinion.

When the Supreme Court first began to hand down written opinions in the last decade of the eighteenth century, the author of the opinion was designated, for example, "Cushing, Justice." This style was followed until the February 1820 term of the Court when it was replaced by the form, for example, "Mr. Justice Johnson" as the author of the opinion. This style endured for more than one hundred and fifty years, indeed until a year or two before Justice O'Connor was appointed to the Court in 1981. In 1980 Justice White with great prescience suggested to the conference that since in the very near future a woman justice was bound to be appointed, we ought to avoid the embarrassment of having to change the style of designating the author of the opinion at that time by doing it before the event. The conference was in entire agreement, and very shortly thereafter, without any explanation, the manner of designating the author of the opinion became simply, for example, "Justice Brennan." Our desire to avoid later embarrassment was only partially successful, however; the very first day on which opinions in the new style were handed down, *The New York Times* carried a story devoted to the change of style under the by-line of its astute Supreme Court correspondent, Linda Greenhouse.

I have always felt that opinions coming back in printed form are vastly improved over the draft sent to the printer even though the latter has not changed a word in the draft. There is something about seeing a legal opinion in print that makes it far more convincing than it was in typescript. I have the feeling that if we circulated our drafts to the other justices in typescript, we might get many more criticisms than we do with the printed product.

At any rate, circulate them to the other chambers we do, and we wait anxiously to see what the reaction of the other justices will be, especially those justices who voted with the majority at conference. If a justice agrees with the draft and has no criticisms or suggestions, he will simply send a letter saying something such as "Please join me in your opinion in this case." If a justice agrees with the general import of the draft, but wishes changes to be made in it before joining, a letter to that effect will be sent, and the writer of the opinion will, if possible, accommodate the suggestions. The willingness to accommodate on the part of the author of the opinion is often directly proportional to the number of votes supporting the majority result at conference; if there were only five justices at conference voting to affirm the decision of the lower court, and one of those five wishes significant changes to be made in the draft, the opinion writer is under considerable pressure to work out something that will satisfy the critic, in order to obtain five votes for the opinion. Chief Justice Hughes once said that he tried to write his opinions clearly and logically, but if he needed the fifth vote of a colleague who insisted on putting in a paragraph that did not "belong," in it went, and let the law reviews figure out what it meant.

But if the result at conference was reached by a unanimous or a lopsided vote, a critic who wishes substantial changes in the opinion has less leverage. I willingly accept relatively minor suggestions for change in emphasis or deletion of language that I do not regard as critical, but resist where possible substantial changes with which I do not agree. Often much effort is expended in negotiating these changes, and it is usually effort well spent in a desire to agree upon a single opinion that will command the assent of a majority of the justices.

The senior justice among those who disagreed with the result reached by the majority at conference usually undertakes to assign the preparation of the dissenting opinion in the case if there is to be one. In the past it was a common practice for justices who disagreed with the opinion of the Court simply to note their dissent from the opinion without more ado, but this practice is very rare today. The justice who will write the dissent notifies the author of the opinion and the other justices of his intention to prepare a dissent, and will circulate that opinion in due course. Perhaps it would be a more rational system if, in a case where a dissent is being prepared, all of those, except the opinion writer, who voted with the majority at conference, as well as those who dissented, would await the circulation of the dissent, but in most cases this practice is not followed. One reason for the current practice is probably that for one reason or another dissents are usually circulated weeks, and often months, after the majority opinion is circulated. A justice who was doubtful as to his vote at conference, or who has reservations about the draft of the Court opinion, may tell the author that he intends to await the dissent before deciding which opinion to join. But this is the exception, not the rule; ordinarily those justices who voted with the majority at conference, if they are satisfied with the proposed Court opinion, will join it without waiting for the circulation of the dissent.

At our Friday conferences the first order of business is the decision as to what opinions are ready to be handed down. The Chief Justice goes in order, beginning with Justice Scalia, and will ask him if any of his opinions are ready to be handed down. If all of the votes are in in a case where he has authored the draft of the Court's opinion, he will so advise the conference, and unless there is some objection, his opinion for the Court will be handed down at one of the sittings of the Court the following week. On that day, the Clerk's Office will have available at 10:00 A.M. for anyone who wishes it copies of Justice Scalia's opinion in that particular case. Meanwhile, the first order of business after the Court goes on the bench will be the announcement by Justice Scalia of his opinion from the bench. He will describe the case, summarize the reasoning of the Court, announce the result, and announce whatever separate or dissenting opinions have been filed. The decision-making process has now run full circle: A case in which certiorari was granted somewhere from six months to a year ago has been briefed, orally argued, and now finally decided by the Supreme Court of the United States.

STUART TAYLOR, JR.,* RUING FIXED OPINIONS
N.Y. Times, February 22, 1988 at A16

Justice Antonin Scalia says one thing has disappointed him since he joined the Supreme Court in 1986: the absence of give and take among the Court's members when they meet in conference to discuss and vote in cases they have heard.

These conferences are the only occasions when the Justices all meet together without clerks or aides, and the confidentiality of what is said is closely guarded.

"Not very much conferencing goes on" at the conferences, Justice Scalia said at a question-and-answer session after delivering a speech at George Washington University's National Law Center on Tuesday. By "conferencing," he explained, he meant efforts to persuade others to change their views by debating points of disagreement.

"In fact," he said, "to call our discussion of a case a conference is really something of a misnomer. It's much more a statement of the views of each of the nine Justices, after which the totals are added and the case is assigned.

"I don't like that. Maybe it's just because I'm new. Maybe it's because I'm an ex-academic. Maybe it's because I'm right." In response to another question, Justice Scalia said the Court might improve the quality of its deliberations if it reduced the number of cases it hears to allow more time for each case.

* * *

DAVID M. O'BRIEN,* STORM CENTER: THE SUPREME COURT IN AMERICAN POLITICS

304–306, 314–327 (1993)

* * *

OPINION-WRITING PROCESS

Opinions justify or explain votes at conference. The opinion for the Court is the most important and most difficult to write because it represents a collective judgment. Writing the Court's opinion, as Holmes put it, requires that a "judge can dance the sword dance; that is he can justify an obvious result without stepping on either blade of opposing fallacies." Holmes in his good-natured way often complained about the compromises he had to make when writing an opinion for the Court. "I am sorry that my moderation," he wrote Chief Justice Edward White, "did not soften your inexorable heart—But I stand like St. Sebastian ready for your arrows."

* * *

WRITING AND CIRCULATING OPINIONS

* * *

The practice of circulating draft opinions began around the turn of the century and soon became pivotal in the Court's decision-making process. The circulation of opinions provides more opportunities for the shifting of votes and further coalition building or fragmentation within the Court. Chief Justice Marshall, with his insistence on unanimity and nightly conferences after dinner, achieved unsurpassed unanimity. Unanimity, however, was based on the reading of opinions at conferences. No drafts circulated for other justices' scrutiny. Throughout much of the nineteenth century, when the Court's sessions were shorter and the justices had no law clerks, opinions were drafted in about two weeks and then read at conference. If at least a majority agreed with the main points, the opinion was approved.

In this century, the practice became that of circulating draft opinions, initially carbon copies and now two photocopies, for each justice's examination and comments. Because they gave more attention to each opinion, the justices found more to debate. The importance of circulating drafts and negotiating language in an opinion was underscored when Jackson announced from the bench, "I myself have changed my opinion after reading the opinions of the members of the Court. And I am as stubborn as most. But I sometimes wind up not voting the way I voted in conference because the reasons of the majority didn't satisfy me." Similarly, Brennan noted, "I converted more than one proposed majority into a dissent before the final decision was announced. I have also, however, had the more satisfying experience of rewriting a dissent as a majority opinion for the Court." In one case, Brennan added, he "circulated 10 printed drafts before one was approved as the Court's opinion."

* * *

How long does opinion writing take? In the average case, Tom Clark observed, about three weeks' work by a justice and his clerks is required before an opinion circulates. "Then the fur begins to fly." The time spent preparing an opinion depends on how fast a justice works, what his style is, how much use of law clerks he makes, and how controversial the assigned case is. Holmes and Benjamin Cardozo wrote opinions within days after being assigned, with little assistance from law clerks. Even into his eighties, Holmes "thirsted" for opinions. Chief Justice Hughes held back assignments from Cardozo because the justice's law clerk, Melvin Segal, complained that Cardozo would spend his weekends writing his opinions and thus he had little to do during the week. Cardozo later gave his clerk responsibility for checking citations and proofreading drafts. But Cardozo still overworked himself, and Hughes continued to hold back assignments for fear that the bachelor's health would fail. By comparison, Frankfurter relied a great deal on his clerks and was still notoriously slow. As he once said, in apologizing to his brethren for the delay in circulating a proposed opinion, "The elephant's period of gestation is, I believe, eighteen months, but a poor little hot dog has no such excuse."

A comparison of the Warren and Burger Courts during the 1964 and 1973 terms provides one indication of the amount of time involved in writing and circulating opinions. In the tradition of Holmes and Cardozo, Black and Douglas expeditiously completed their opinions in about twenty-two days, whereas others took an average of thirty-nine days. Unlike some who acquired more law clerks, Douglas used about the same amount of time to complete his opinions. During the Warren Court, it took an average of thirty-five days for justices to complete their opinions, but it took Douglas only twenty-seven. The Burger Court averaged fifty-two days, but Douglas averaged twenty-five. Both Warren and Burger took longer than other justices when completing their opinions, doubtless because of their additional responsibilities as chief justice. Warren took fifty-two days, whereas Burger took about eighty-two to complete his opinions.

A number of factors affect how long it takes a justice to complete opinion assignments for the Court. Some justices work quickly, as already noted, while others are notoriously slow. In a study of the Vinson Court (1946–1952), Jan Palmer and Saul Brenner found further confirmation for Black's and Douglas's reputation as expeditious opinion writers, and that Frankfurter consistently took more time than his colleagues to complete his opinions. They also found that over the years Chief Justice Vinson, while striving to equalize his opinion assignments, tended to favor "speedy" writers like Black and Douglas, despite his ideological disagreements with them. Among other factors associated with prolonging the time taken to produce an opinion for the Court are (1) the importance and divisiveness of a case, (2) the size of the voting majority at conference, (3) whether the initial vote was to affirm rather than reverse a lower court, (4) whether one or more of the justices later switched their votes, and (5) whether a case had to be reassigned or carried over for another term.

The interplay of professional and psychological pressures on a justice writing the Court's opinion is a complex but crucial part of the Court's decision making. When the practice, in the 1920s and 1930s, was to return comments within twenty-four hours after receipt of a draft, the pressures were especially great. There are no time limits now, but the pressures persist, especially during the last two months of a term, when the justices concentrate on opinion writing. Burger recalled how late one term Black insisted on changes in one of Brennan's opinions and the latter became very curt on the telephone with his esteemed friend, whereupon Black came into Brennan's chamber and told him, "this place can be a pressure cooker and it can beat the strongest of men. You should get out of here and forget it for a few days." Brennan did.

Whether drafting or commenting on a proposed opinion, justices differ when trying to influence each other. They look for emotional appeals, sometimes personal threats. Justice Clark thought that Warren was the greatest chief justice in the history of the Court and sought his approval of a revised opinion. But he received this disturbing response: "Tom: Nuts. E.W." Shortly after coming to the Court, Brennan wrote Black, "I welcome, as always, every and any comment you will be good enough to make on anything I ever write—whether we vote together at the time or not." On the back of Stone's draft opinion in *United States v. Darby* (1941), Douglas wrote, "I heartily agree. This has the master's touch." "This is grand plum pudding," Frankfurter added. "There are so many luscious plums in it that it's invidious to select."

Douglas could be a real charmer—if he wanted to be—when appealing for modifications in proposed opinions. "I would stand on my head to join with you in your opinion," he told James Byrnes, though continuing, "I finally concluded, however, that I cannot." * * *

By contrast, the style of McReynolds was abrupt—sometimes rude— and usually left little room for negotiation. "This statement makes me sick," he once observed. Frankfurter's approach also could be irritating. He was not above making personal attacks. To threaten his ideological foe Hugo Black, Frankfurter circulated but did not publish the following concurring opinion:

> I greatly sympathize with the essential purpose of my brother (former Senator) Black's dissent. His roundabout and turgid legal phraseology is a *cris de coeur*. "Would I were back in the Senate," he seems to say, "so that I could put on the statute books what

really ought to be there. But here I am, cast by Fate into a den of judges devoid of the habits of legislators, simple fellows who have a crippling feeling that they must enforce the laws as Congress wrote them and not as they ought to have been written * * *."

Frankfurter nonetheless usually tempered his criticisms by making fun of his own academic proclivities: "What does trouble me is that you do not disclose what you are really doing." He wrote Douglas, "As you know, I am no poker player and naturally, therefore, I do not believe in poker playing in the disposition of cases. Or has professing for twenty-five years disabled me from understanding the need for these involutions?"

More typically when commenting on circulated drafts, justices appeal to professionalism and jurisprudential concerns. Even McReynolds, perhaps at the prompting of Taft, once appealed to Stone's basic conservatism: "All of us get into a fog now and then, as I know so well from my own experience. Won't you 'Stop, Look, and Listen'?" Such appeals may carry subtly or explicitly the threat of a concurring or dissenting opinion. Stone, in one instance, candidly told Frankfurter, "If you wish to write [the opinion] placing the case on the ground which I think tenable and desirable, I shall cheerfully join you. If not, I will add a few observations for myself."

Justices may suggest minor editorial or major substantive changes. Before joining one of Arthur Goldberg's opinions, Harlan requested that the word "desegregation" be substituted for "integration" throughout the opinion. As he explained, " 'Integration' brings blood to Southerners' eyes for they think that 'desegregation' means just that—'integration.' I do not think that we ought to use the word in our opinions." Likewise, Stewart strongly objected to some of the language in Abe Fortas's proposed opinion in *Tinker v. Des Moines School District* (1969), which upheld the right of students to wear black armbands in protest of the government's involvement in Vietnam. "At the risk of appearing eccentric," Stewart wrote, "I shall not join any opinion that speaks of what is going on in Vietnam as a 'war' [since Congress never formally declared a war in Vietnam]." * * *

Editorial suggestions may also be directed at a justice's use of precedents and basic conceptualization. Douglas, for instance, sent Brennan a letter outlining fourteen changes he thought necessary in the proposed opinion for the watershed reapportionment decision in *Baker v. Carr* (1962). Likewise, Brennan sent a twenty-one-page list of revisions on Earl Warren's initial draft of *Miranda v. Arizona* (1966), which upheld the right of criminal suspects to remain silent at the time of police questioning. At the outset, Brennan expressed his feeling of guilt "about the extent of the suggestions." But he emphasized the importance of careful drafting. Brennan explained, "[T]his will be one of the most important opinions of our time and I know that you will want the fullest expression of my views."

Occasionally, proposed changes lead to a recasting of the entire opinion. Douglas was assigned the Court's opinion in *Griswold v. Connecticut* (1965), in which he announced the creation of a constitutional right of privacy based on the "penumbras" of various guarantees of the Bill of Rights. His initial draft, however, did not develop this theory. Rather, Douglas sought to justify the decision on the basis of earlier cases recognizing a First Amendment right of associational privacy. The analogy and precedents, he admitted, "do not decide this case." "Marriage does not fit precisely any of the categories of First Amendment rights. But it is a form of association as vital in the life of a man or a woman as any other, and perhaps more so." Both Black and Brennan strongly objected to Douglas's extravagant reliance on First Amendment precedents. In a three-page letter, Brennan detailed an alternative approach, as the following excerpt indicates:

> I have read your draft opinion in *Griswold v. Connecticut,* and, while I agree with a great deal of it, I should like to suggest a substantial change in emphasis for your consideration. It goes without saying, of course, that your rejection of any approach based on *Lochner v. New York* is absolutely right. [In *Lochner* (1905), a majority read into the Fourteenth Amendment a "liberty of contract" in order to strike down economic legislation. Although the Court later abandoned the doctrine of a "liberty of contract," *Lochner* continues to symbolize the original sin of constitutional interpretation—that is, the Court's creation and enforcement of unenumerated rights.] And I agree that the association of husband and wife is not mentioned in the Bill of Rights, and that that is the obstacle we must hurdle to effect a reversal in this case.

> But I hesitate to bring the husband-wife relationship within the right to association we have constructed in the First Amendment context. * * * In the First Amendment context, in situations like *NAACP v. Alabama* [1964], privacy is necessary to protect the capacity of an association for fruitful advocacy. In the present context, it seems to me that we are really interested in the privacy of married couples quite apart from any interest in advocacy * * *. Instead of expanding the First Amendment right of association to include marriage, why not say that what has been done for the First Amendment can also be done for some of the other fundamental guarantees of the Bill of Rights? In other words, where fundamentals are concerned, the Bill of Rights guarantees are but expressions or examples of those rights, and do not preclude applications or extensions of those rights to situations unanticipated by the Framers.

The restriction on the dissemination and use of contraceptives, Brennan explained,

> would, on this reasoning, run afoul of a right to privacy created out of the Fourth Amendment and the self-incrimination clause of the Fifth, together with the Third, in much the same way as the right of

association has been created out of the First. Taken together, those amendments indicate a fundamental concern with the sanctity of the home and the right of the individual to be alone.

"With this change of emphasis," Brennan concluded, the opinion "would be most attractive to me because it would require less departure from the specific guarantees and because I think there is a better chance it will command a Court." Douglas subsequently revised his opinion and based the right of privacy on the penumbras of the First, Third, Fourth, Fifth, and Ninth Amendments.

In order to accommodate the views of others, the author of an opinion for the Court must negotiate language and bargain over substance. "The ground you recommend was not the one on which I voted 'no'—But I think that, as a matter of policy, you are clearly right; and I am engaged in redrafting the opinion on that line," Brandeis wrote to the respected craftsman Van Devanter, adding, "May I trouble you to formulate the rule of law, which you think should be established?"

At times, justices may not feel that a case is worth fighting over. "Probably bad—but only a small baby. Let it go," Sutherland noted on the back of one of Stone's drafts. * * * Similarly, Pierce Butler agreed to go along with one of Stone's opinions, though noting, "I voted to reverse. While this sustains your conclusion to affirm, I still think reversal would be better. But I shall in silence acquiesce. Dissents seldom aid in the right development or statement of the law. They often do harm. For myself I say: 'Lead us not into temptation.'"

* * *

In major cases, compromise becomes more difficult. In 1967, for instance, the Court agreed to decide two important cases, *Marchetti v. United States* and *Grosso v. United States*. Both raised the issue of whether requiring gamblers to register with the Internal Revenue Service and pay an occupational tax on their gambling earnings violates the Fifth Amendment privilege against self-incrimination. By registering with the IRS, a gambler becomes open to state and federal prosecution for engaging in organized gambling and thus incriminates himself.

Harlan's first draft on *Marchetti* met with opposition from Brennan and Douglas. Initially, Brennan sought accommodation:

I think your conclusion is fully supported without that part of your Part III. * * * I expect, however, that you'd rather not omit that portion. Could you stop at Part III at page 10, and make a new section IV beginning with the [next] full paragraph. * * * If so, I could file a concurrence stating that I join the judgment of reversal for the reasons expressed in Parts I, II, IV and V of your opinion.

Douglas, however, immediately circulated a concurrence for *Marchetti* and a dissenting opinion for *Grosso*. Although Brennan preferred these drafts, he thought it wiser to try to mediate the growing dispute within the majority. "Is there anything about Parts I, II, IV and V which you can't join?" Brennan gently pushed Douglas, emphasizing that "it might be helpful on this prickly problem if we could join as much as possible of what John has written." Black, the senior associate who assigned the opinion, agreed. But he told Harlan; "With my constitutional beliefs I could not possibly agree with any part of subdivision III of your opinion except the next to the last sentence in the last paragraph."

After thinking it over for two days, Harlan offered a compromise:

Because of the fact that you, Bill Douglas and Bill Brennan feel so strongly that Part III of my opinion in this case contains implications that were never intended on my part—namely that the taxing power may in some circumstances override the protections afforded by the Fifth Amendment privilege—I have decided to delete that section of my opinion, and am recirculating accordingly.

With his revised draft of *Marchetti*, Harlan was able to hang on to a bare majority, but found himself completely alone on his *Grosso* draft.

Discouraged by the growing dissension, Harlan wrote Black:

I am faced with the unusual experience of having to withdraw from the opinion which I prepared for the Court in this case under your assignment. I intend to propose at next Thursday's Conference that this case, and also No. 181, *Grosso v. United States*, be set for reargument next Term, as suggested by Brother White in his separate opinion, dissenting in *Marchetti*, and concurring in the Judgment in *Grosso*.

The proposal was accepted, and both cases were reargued the next term. Tempers cooled, and Harlan further modified his approach; this eventually enabled him to command a majority on both cases. In the end, only Chief Justice Warren dissented from the ruling striking down the statute as a violation of the Fifth Amendment.

* * *

WILLIAM J. BRENNAN, JR.,* IN DEFENSE OF DISSENTS**
37 Hastings L.J. 427, 427–438 (1986)

* * *

Why do judges dissent? Not many years ago, the writer Joan Didion * * * wrote an elegant essay for the New York Times. The question she addressed, and the title of her essay, was "Why I Write." She said:

Of course I stole the title * * * from George Orwell. One reason I stole it was that I like the sound of the words: *Why I Write*. There you have three short unambiguous words that share a sound, and the sound they share is this:

* Associate Justice, Supreme Court of the United States.

** © 1986 by University of California, Hastings College of Law. Reprinted from Hastings Law Journal, Vol. 37, No. 3, pp. 427–438, by permission.

I

I

I

In many ways writing is the act of saying I, of imposing oneself upon other people, of saying *listen to me, see it my way, change your mind.*[6]

No doubt, there are those who believe that judges—and particularly dissenting judges—write to hear themselves say, as it were, I I I. And no doubt, there are also those who believe that judges are, like Joan Didion, primarily engaged in the writing of fiction. I cannot agree with either of those propositions.

Of course, we know why judges write *opinions*. It is through the written word that decisions are communicated, that mandates issue. But why *dissent*? * * * After all, the law is the law, and in our system, whether in the legislature or the judiciary, it is made by those who command the majority. As the distinguished legal philosopher H.L.A. Hart declared, "A supreme tribunal has the last word in saying what the law is and, when it has said it, the statement that the court was 'wrong' has no consequences within the system: no one's rights or duties are thereby altered." In view of this reality, some contend that the dissent is an exercise in futility, or, worse still, a "cloud" on the majority decision that detracts from the legitimacy that the law requires and from the prestige of the institution that issues the law. Learned Hand complained that a dissenting opinion "cancels the impact of monolithic solidarity on which the authority of a bench of judges so largely depends." Even Justice Holmes, the Great Dissenter himself, remarked in his first dissent on the Court that dissents are generally "useless" and "undesirable." And more recently, Justice Potter Stewart has labeled dissents "subversive literature." Why, then, does a judge hold out?

Very real tensions sometimes emerge when one confronts a colleague with a dissent. After all, collegiality *is* important; unanimity *does* have value; feelings *must* be respected. * * *

It seems that to explain why a dissenter holds out, we should examine some of the many different functions of dissents. Not only are all dissents not created equal, but they are not intended to be so. In other words, to answer "why write," one must first define precisely what it is that is being written. I do not have an exhaustive list, but let me at least suggest some diverse roles that may be served by a dissent. * * *

In its most straightforward incarnation, the dissent demonstrates flaws the author perceives in the majority's legal analysis. It is offered as a corrective—in the hope that the Court will mend the error of its ways in a later case. Oliver Cromwell captured the thrust of that type of dissent when he pleaded to the General Assembly of the Church of Scotland in 1650, "Brethren, by the bowels of Christ I beseech you,

6. N.Y. Times, Dec. 5, 1976, § 7 (Book   Review), at 2 (emphasis in original).

bethink you that you may be mistaken." But the dissent is often more than just a plea; it safeguards the integrity of the judicial decision-making process by keeping the majority accountable for the rationale and consequences of its decision. Karl Llewellyn, who was critical of the frequency with which Supreme Court Justices, of all courts, dissented, grudgingly acknowledged the importance of that role, characterizing it as "rid[ing] herd on the majority." At the heart of that function is the critical recognition that vigorous debate improves the final product by forcing the prevailing side to deal with the hardest questions urged by the losing side. In this sense, this function reflects the conviction that the best way to find the truth is to go looking for it in the marketplace of ideas. It is as if the opinions of the Court—both for majority and dissent—were the product of a judicial town meeting.

The dissent is also commonly used to emphasize the limits of a majority decision that sweeps, so far as the dissenters are concerned, unnecessarily broadly—a sort of "damage control" mechanism. Along the same lines, a dissent sometimes is designed to furnish litigants and lower courts with practical guidance—such as ways of distinguishing subsequent cases. It may also hint that the litigant might more fruitfully seek relief in a different forum—such as the state courts. I have done that on occasion. Moreover, in this present era of expanding state court protection of individual liberties, in my view, probably the most important development in constitutional jurisprudence today, dissents from federal courts may increasingly offer state courts legal theories that may be relevant to the interpretation of their own state constitutions.

The most enduring dissents, however, are the ones in which the authors speak, as the writer Alan Barth expressed it, as "Prophets with Honor." These are the dissents that often reveal the perceived congruence between the Constitution and the "evolving standards of decency that mark the progress of a maturing society," and that seek to sow seeds for future harvest. These are the dissents that soar with passion and ring with rhetoric. These are the dissents that, at their best, straddle the worlds of literature and law.

While it is relatively easy to describe the principal functions of dissents, it is often difficult to classify individual dissents, particularly the great ones, as belonging to one category or another; rather, they operate on several levels simultaneously. For example, the first Justice Harlan's remarkable dissent in *Plessy v. Ferguson* [15] is at once prophetic and expressive of the Justice's constitutional vision, and, at the same time, a careful and methodical refutation on the majority's legal analysis in that case.

In this masterful dissent, the Justice said that "in view of the Constitution, in the eye of the law, there is in this country no superior, dominant, ruling class of citizens. There is no caste here. Our Constitution is color-blind * * *." Justice Harlan also foretold, with unfortu-

15. 163 U.S. 537, 552 (1896) (Harlan, J., dissenting).

nate accuracy, the consequences of the majority's position. Said he, the *Plessy* decision would:

> not only stimulate aggressions, more or less brutal and irritating, upon the admitted rights of colored citizens, but will encourage the belief that it is possible, by means of state enactments, to defeat the beneficent purposes which the people of the United States had in view when they adopted the recent amendments of the Constitution * * *.

He addressed, and dismissed as erroneous, the majority's reliance on precedents. "Those decisions," he declared:

> cannot be guides in the era introduced by the recent amendments of the supreme law, which established universal civil freedom, gave citizenship to all born or naturalized in the United States and residing here, obliterated the race line from our systems of governments * * * and placed our free institutions upon the broad and sure foundation of the equality of all men before the law.

Justice Harlan, in that dissent, is the quintessential voice crying in the wilderness. In rejecting the Court's view that so-called separate but equal facilities did not violate the Constitution, Justice Harlan stood alone; not a single other justice joined him. In his appeal to the future, Justice Harlan transcended, without slighting, mechanical legal analysis; he sought to announce fundamental constitutional truths as well. He spoke not only to his peers, but to his society, and, more important, across time to later generations. He was, in this sense, a secular prophet, and we continue, long after *Plessy* and long even after *Brown v. Board of Education*,[19] to benefit from his wisdom and courage.

From what source did Justice Harlan derive the right to stand against the collective judgment of his brethren in *Plessy*? We may ask the same question of Justice Holmes in *Abrams;*[20] of Justice Brandeis in *Olmstead;*[21] of Justice Stone in *Gobitis;*[22] of Justice Jackson in *Korematsu;*[23] of Justice Black in *Adamson;*[24] or of the second Justice Harlan in *Poe v. Ullman;*[25] to name but a few of the most famous and powerful dissents of this century. And surely, you may ask the same question of me. How do I justify adhering to my essentially immutable positions on obscenity, the death penalty, the proper test for double jeopardy, and on the eleventh amendment? For me, the answer resides in the nature of the Supreme Court's role.

The Court is something of a paradox—it is at once the whole and its constituent parts. The very words "the Court" mean simultaneously

19. 347 U.S. 483 (1954).

20. Abrams v. United States, 250 U.S. 616, 624 (1919) (Holmes, J., dissenting).

21. Olmstead v. United States, 277 U.S. 438, 471 (1928) (Brandeis, J., dissenting).

22. Minersville School Dist. v. Gobitis, 310 U.S. 586, 601 (1940) (Stone, J., dissenting).

23. Korematsu v. United States, 323 U.S. 214, 242 (1944) (Jackson, J., dissenting).

24. Adamson v. California, 332 U.S. 46, 68 (1947) (Black, J., dissenting).

25. 367 U.S. 497, 522 (1961) (Harlan, J., dissenting).

the entity and its members. Generally, critics of dissent advocate the primacy of the unit over its members and argue that the Court is most "legitimate," most true to its intended role, when it speaks with a single voice. Individual justices are urged to yield their views to the paramount need for unity. It is true that unanimity underscores the gravity of a constitutional imperative—witness *Brown v. Board of Education* [26] and *Cooper v. Aaron.* [27] But, unanimity is not in itself a judicial virtue.

Indeed, history shows that nearly absolute unanimity enjoyed only a brief period of preeminence in the Supreme Court. Until John Marshall became Chief Justice, the Court followed the custom of the King's Bench and announced its decisions through the seriatim opinions of its members. Chief Justice Marshall broke with the English tradition and adopted the practice of announcing judgments of the Court in a single opinion. At first, these opinions were always delivered by Chief Justice Marshall himself, and were virtually always unanimous. Unanimity was consciously pursued and disagreements were deliberately kept private. Indeed, Marshall delivered a number of opinions which, not only did he not write, but which were contrary to his own judgment and vote at conference.

This new practice, however, was of great symbolic and practical significance at the time. Remember the context of the times when the practice was introduced. As one commentator has observed, when Marshall delivered the opinion of the Court, "[h]e did not propose to announce only the views of John Marshall, Federalist of Virginia." Rather, "he intended that the words he wrote should bear the imprimatur of the Supreme Court of the United States. For the first time, the Court as a judicial unit had been committed to an opinion—a ratio decidendi—in support of its judgments." This change in custom at the time consolidated the authority of the Court and aided in the general recognition of the Third Branch as co-equal partner with the other branches. Not surprisingly, not everyone was pleased with the new practice. Thomas Jefferson, who also was a lawyer, was, of course, conversant with the English custom, and was angrily trenchant in his criticism. He wrote that "[a]n opinion is huddled up in conclave, perhaps by a majority of one, delivered as if unanimous, and with the silent acquiescence of lazy or timid associates, by a crafty chief judge, who sophisticates the law to his own mind, by the turn of his own reasoning." In other words, Marshall had shut down the marketplace of ideas.

Of course, Jefferson was overstating matters a bit. In fact, unanimity remained the rule only for the first four years of Marshall's Chief Justiceship, and during that period only one, one-sentence concurrence was delivered, and that by Justice Chase. But, in 1804 Justice William Johnson arrived on the Court from the state appellate court of South Carolina. He tried to perpetuate the seriatim practice of his state court

26. 347 U.S. 483 (1954).   **27.** 358 U.S. 1 (1958).

and issued a substantial concurrence in one of the first cases in which he participated. And his colleagues were stunned. Johnson later described their reaction in a letter to Jefferson. "Some Case soon occurred," he wrote:

> in which I differed from my Brethren, and I felt it a thing of Course to deliver my Opinion. But, during the rest of the Session I heard nothing but lectures on the Indecency of Judges cutting at each other, and the Loss of Reputation which the Virginia appellate Court had sustained by pursuing such a Course.

Nonetheless, the short-lived tradition of unanimity had been broken, and, in 1806, Justice Paterson delivered the first true dissent from a judgment and opinion of the Court in *Simms v. Slacum.* As one historian has observed, considerably understating the case, since that time "dissents were never again a rarity." Even Chief Justice Marshall filed nine dissents from the opinions of the Court during his closing years on the Bench.

What, then, should we make of modern critics of dissents? Charles Evans Hughes answered that question sixty years ago and I think what he said then is as true today. He said:

> When unanimity can be obtained without sacrifice of conviction, it strongly commends the decision to public confidence. But unanimity which is merely formal, which is recorded at the expense of strong, conflicting views, is not desirable in a court of last resort, whatever may be the effect upon public opinion at the time [the case is announced]. This is so because what must ultimately sustain the court in public confidence is the character and independence of the judges. They are not there simply to decide cases, but to decide them as they think they should be decided, and while it may be regrettable that they cannot always agree, it is better that their independence should be maintained and recognized than that unanimity should be secured through its sacrifice.

In Chief Justice Hughes' view, and in my own, justices do have an obligation to bring their individual intellects to bear on the issues that come before the Court. This does not mean that a justice has an absolute duty to publish trivial disagreements with the majority. Dissent for its own sake has no value, and can threaten the collegiality of the bench. However, where significant and deeply held disagreement exists, members of the Court have a responsibility to articulate it. This is why, when I dissent, I always say why I am doing so. Simply to say, "I dissent," I will not do.

I elevate this responsibility to an obligation because in our legal system judges have no power to *declare* law. That is to say, a court may not simply announce, without more, that it has adopted a rule to which all must adhere. That, of course, is the province of the legislature. Courts *derive* legal principles, and have a duty to explain *why* and *how* a given rule has come to be. This requirement serves a function within the judicial process similar to that served by the electoral process with regard to the political branches of government. It restrains judges and keeps them accountable to the law and to the principles that are the source of judicial authority. The integrity of the process through which a rule is forged and fashioned is as important as the result itself; if it were not, the legitimacy of the rule would be doubtful. Dissents contribute to the integrity of the process, not only by directing attention to perceived difficulties with the majority's opinion, but, to turn one more time to metaphor, also by contributing to the marketplace of competing ideas.

* * * A dissent challenges the reasoning of the majority, tests its authority and establishes a benchmark against which the majority's reasoning can continue to be evaluated, and perhaps, in time, superseded. This supersession may take only three years, as it did when the Court overruled *Gobitis* [42] in *Barnette;* [43] it may take twenty years, as it did when the Court overruled *Hammer v. Dagenhart* [44] in *Darby;* [45] it may take sixty years as it did when we overruled *Plessy* in *Brown.* The time periods in which dissents ripen into majority opinions depend on societal developments and the foresight of individual justices, and thus vary. Most dissents never "ripen" and do not deserve to. But it is not the hope of eventual adoption by a majority that alone justifies dissent. For simply by infusing different ideas and methods of analysis into judicial decision-making, dissents prevent that process from becoming rigid or stale. And, each time the Court revisits an issue, the justices are forced by a dissent to reconsider the fundamental questions and to rethink the result.

I must add a word about a special kind of dissent: the repeated dissent in which a justice refuses to yield to the views of the majority although persistently rebuffed by them. For example, Justice Holmes adhered through the years to his views about the evils of substantive due process, as did Justices Black and Douglas to their views regarding the absolute command of the first amendment. * * * I adhere to positions on the issues of capital punishment, the eleventh amendment, and obscenity, which I developed over many years and after much troubling thought. On the death penalty, for example, as I interpret the eighth amendment, its prohibition against cruel and unusual punishments embodies to a unique degree moral principles that substantively restrain the punishments governments of our civilized society may impose on those convicted of capital offenses. * * * For me * * * the fatal constitutional infirmity of capital punishment is that it treats members of the human race as nonhumans, as objects to be toyed with and discarded. * * *

42. Minersville School Dist. v. Gobitis, 310 U.S. 586 (1940), *overruled,* West Virginia State Bd. of Educ. v. Barnette, 319 U.S. 624 (1943).

43. West Virginia State Bd. of Educ. v. Barnette, 319 U.S. 624 (1943).

44. 247 U.S. 251 (1918), *overruled,* United States v. Darby, 312 U.S. 100 (1941).

45. United States v. Darby, 312 U.S. 100 (1941).

This is an interpretation to which a majority of my fellow justices—not to mention, it would seem, a majority of my fellow countrymen—do not subscribe. Perhaps you find my adherence to it, and my recurrent publication of it, simply contrary, tiresome, or quixotic. Or perhaps you see in it a refusal to abide by the judicial principle of stare decisis, obedience to precedent. * * * Yet, in my judgment, when a justice perceives an interpretation of the text to have departed so far from its essential meaning, that justice is bound, by a larger constitutional duty to the community, to expose the departure and point toward a different path.

This kind of dissent, in which a judge persists in articulating a minority view of the law in case after case presenting the same issue, seeks to do more than simply offer an alternative analysis—that could be done in a single dissent and does not require repetition. Rather, this type of dissent constitutes a statement by the judge as an individual: "Here I draw the line." Of course, as a member of a court, one's general duty is to acquiesce in the rulings of that court and to take up the battle behind the court's new barricades. But it would be a great mistake to confuse this unquestioned duty to obey and respect the law with an imagined obligation to subsume entirely one's own views of constitutional imperatives to the views of the majority. None of us, lawyer or layman, teacher or student in our society must ever feel that to express a conviction, honestly and sincerely maintained, is to violate some unwritten law of manners or decorum. We are a free and vital people because we not only allow, we encourage debate, and because we do not shut down communication as soon as a decision is reached. As law-abiders, we accept the conclusions of our decision-making bodies as binding, but we also know that our right to continue to challenge the wisdom of that result must be accepted by those who disagree with us. So we debate and discuss and contend and always we argue. If we are right, we generally prevail. The process enriches all of us, and it is available to, and employed by, individuals and groups representing all viewpoints and perspectives.

I hope that what I have said does not sound like too individualistic a justification of the dissent. No one has any duty simply to make noise. Rather, the obligation that all of us, as American citizens have, and that judges, as adjudicators, particularly feel, is to speak up when we are convinced that the fundamental law of our Constitution requires a given result. I cannot believe that this is a controversial statement. The right to dissent is one of the great and cherished freedoms that we enjoy by reason of the excellent accident of our American births.

Through dynamic interaction among members of the present Court and through dialogue across time with the future Court, we ensure the continuing contemporary relevance and hence vitality of the principles of our fundamental charter. Each justice must be an active participant, and, when necessary, must write separately to record his or her thinking. Writing, then, is not an egoistic act—it is duty. Saying, "listen to me, see it my way, change your mind," is not self-indulgence—it is very hard work that we cannot shirk.

RUTH BADER GINSBURG,* SPEAKING IN A JUDICIAL VOICE

1–19 (Madison Lecture, New York University School of Law,
March, 1993) (on file with the NYU Law Review)

INTRODUCTION

James Madison's forecast still brightens the spirit of federal judges. In his June 1789 speech introducing to Congress the amendments that led to the Bill of Rights, Madison urged:

> [If a Bill of Rights is] incorporated into the [C]onstitution, independent tribunals of justice will consider themselves in a peculiar manner the guardians of those rights; they will be an impenetrable bulwark * * * naturally led to resist every encroachment upon rights * * * stipulated for in the [C]onstitution by the declaration of rights.

Today's independent tribunals of justice are faithful to that "original understanding" when they adhere to traditional ways courts realize the expectation Madison expressed.

In Federalist No. 78, Alexander Hamilton said that federal judges, in order to preserve the people's rights and privileges, must have authority to check legislation and acts of the executive for constitutionality. But he qualified his recognition of that awesome authority. The judiciary, Hamilton wrote, from the very nature of its functions, will always be "the least dangerous" branch of government, for judges hold neither the sword nor the purse of the community; ultimately, they must depend upon the political branches to effectuate their judgments. Mindful of that reality, the effective judge, I believe and will explain why in this lecture, will strive to persuade, and not to pontificate. She will speak in "a moderate and restrained" voice, engaging in a dialogue with, not a diatribe against, co-equal departments of government, state authorities, and even her own colleagues.

* * *

Collegiality in Appellate Decisionmaking

I turn now to the first of the two topics this lecture addresses—the style of judging appropriate for appellate judges whose mission it is, in Hamilton's words, "to secure a steady, upright, and impartial administration of the laws." Integrity, knowledge and, most essentially, judgment are the qualities Hamilton ascribed to the judiciary. How is that essential quality, judgment, conveyed in the opinions appellate judges write? What role should moderation, restraint, and collegiality play in the formulation of judicial decisions? As background, I will describe

---

* Reprinted by permission of Ruth Bader Ginsburg.

three distinct patterns of appellate opinion-casting: individual, institutional, and in between.

The individual judging pattern has been characteristic of the Law Lords, who serve as Great Britain's Supreme Court. The Lords sit in panels of five and, traditionally, have delivered opinions seriatim, each panel member, in turn, announcing his individual judgment and the reasons for it.

In contrast to the British tradition of opinions separately rendered by each judge as an individual, the continental or civil law traditions typified and spread abroad by France and Germany call for collective, corporate judgments. In dispositions of that genre, disagreement is not disclosed. Neither dissent nor separate concurrence is published. Cases are decided with a single, per curiam opinion generally following a uniform, anonymous style.

Our Supreme Court, when John Marshall became Chief Justice, made a start in the institutional opinion direction. Marshall is credited with establishing the practice of announcing judgments in a single opinion for the Court. The Marshall Court, and certainly its leader, had a strong sense of institutional mission, a mission well served by unanimity. Marshall was criticized, in those early days, for suppressing dissent. Thomas Jefferson complained:

> An opinion is huddled up in conclave, * * * delivered as if unanimous, and with the silent acquiescence of lazy or timid associates, by a crafty chief judge, [a majority of one,] who sophisticates the law to his own mind, by the turn of his own reasoning.

But even Marshall, during his long tenure as Chief Justice, ultimately dissented on several occasions and once concurred with a separate opinion. We continue in that middle way today. Our appellate courts generally produce a judgment or opinion for the court. In that respect, we bear some resemblance to the highly institution-minded civil law judges, although our judges individually claim authorship of most of the opinions they publish. In tune with the British or common law tradition, however, we place no formal limit on the prerogative of each judge to speak out separately.

To point up the difference between individual and institutional modes of judging, I have drawn upon a 1989 letter from a civilian jurist. The letter came from a member of the Conseil d'Etat, the illustrious body created by Napoleon that still serves, among other functions, as Supreme Administrative Court for France. The conseiller who wrote to me had observed, together with several of his colleagues, an argument in the D.C. Circuit. The appeal was from a criminal conviction; the prime issue concerned the Fifth Amendment's double jeopardy ban. When the case was decided, I sent our French visitors copies of the slip sheet. It contained the panel's judgment, and three opinions, one per judge. I paraphrase the conseiller's reaction:

The way the decision is given is surprising for us according to our standards. The discussion of theory and of the meaning of precedents is remarkable. But the divided opinions seem to me very far from the way a judgment should issue, particularly in a criminal case. The judgment of a court should be precise and concise, not a discourse among professors, but the order of people charged to speak in the name of the law, and therefore written with simplicity and clarity, presenting short explanations. A judgment that is too long indicates uncertainty.

At the same time, it is very impressive for me to see members of a court give to the litigants and to the readers the content of their hesitations and doubts, without diminishing the credibility of justice, in which the American is so confident.

The conseiller seems at first distressed, even appalled, at our readiness to admit that legal judgments (including constitutional rulings) are not always clear and certain. In his second thought, however, the conseiller appears impressed, touched with envy or admiration, that our system of justice is so secure, we can tolerate open displays of disagreement among judges about what the law is.

But overindulgence in separate opinion writing may undermine both the reputation of the judiciary for judgment and the respect accorded court dispositions. Rule of law virtues of consistency, predictability, clarity, and stability may be slighted when a court routinely fails to act as a collegial body. Dangers to the system are posed by two tendencies: too frequent resort to separate opinions and the immoderate tone of statements diverging from the position of the court's majority.

Regarding the first danger, recall that "the Great Dissenter," Justice Holmes, in fact dissented less often than most of his colleagues. Chief Justice Stone once wrote to Karl Llewellyn (both gentlemen were public defenders of the right to dissent): "You know, if I should write in every case where I do not agree with some of the views expressed in the opinions, you and all my other friends would stop reading [my separate opinions]." In matters of statutory interpretation, Justice Brandeis repeatedly cautioned: "[I]t is more important that the applicable rule of law be settled than that it be settled right." "This is commonly true," Brandeis continued, "even where the error is a matter of serious concern, provided correction can be had by legislation." Revered constitutional scholar Paul A. Freund, who clerked for Justice Brandeis, recalled Justice Cardozo's readiness to suppress his dissent in common law cases (the Supreme Court had more of those in pre-*Erie v. Tompkins* days), so that an opinion would come down unanimous.

Separate concurrences and dissents characterize Supreme Court decisions to a much greater extent than they do court of appeals three-judge panel decisions. In the D.C. Circuit, for example, for the statistical year ending June 1992, the court rendered 405 judgments in cases not disposed of summarily; over 86% of those decisions were unanimous. During that same period, the Supreme Court decided 114 cases with full opinions; only 21.9% of the decisions were unanimous. A reality not highlighted by a press fond of separating Carter from Reagan/Bush appointees accounts in considerable measure for this difference: the character of cases heard by courts of appeals combines with our modus operandi to tug us strongly toward the middle, toward moderation and away from notably creative or excessively rigid positions. * * *

Concerning the character of federal cases, unlike the Supreme Court, courts of appeals deal far less frequently with grand constitutional questions than with less cosmic questions of statutory interpretation or the rationality of agency or district court decisions. In most matters of that variety, as Justice Brandeis indicated, it is best that the matter be definitively settled, preferably with one opinion. Furthermore, lower court judges are bound by Supreme Court precedent more tightly than is the High Court itself.

Turning to the way we operate, I note first that no three-judge panel in a circuit is at liberty to depart from the published decision of a prior panel; law of the circuit may be altered only by the court en banc. To assure that each panel knows what the others are doing, the D.C. Circuit, and several other federal circuit courts of appeals, circulate opinions to the full court, once approved by a panel, at least a week in advance of release.

Second, in contrast to district judges, who are the real power holders in the federal court system—lords of their individual fiefdoms from case filing to first instance final judgment—no single court of appeals judge can carry the day in any case. To attract a second vote and establish durable law for the circuit, a judge may find it necessary to moderate her own position, sometimes to be less bold, other times to be less clear. We can listen to and persuade each other in groups of three more effectively than can a larger panel.

On the few occasions each year when we sit en banc—in the D.C. Circuit, all twelve of us when we are full strength—I can appreciate why unanimity is so much harder to achieve in Supreme Court judgments. Not only do the Justices deal much more often with constitutional questions, where only overruling or constitutional amendment can correct a mistake. In addition, one becomes weary after going round the table on a first ballot. It is ever so much easier to have a conversation—and an exchange of views on opinion drafts—among three than among nine or twelve.

In writing for the court, one must be sensitive to the sensibilities and mindsets of one's colleagues, which may mean avoiding certain arguments and authorities, even certain words. Should institutional concerns affect the tone of separate opinions, when a judge finds it necessary to write one?

I emphasize first that dissents and separate concurrences are not consummations devoutly to be avoided. As Justice Brennan said in thoughtful defense of dissents: "None of us, lawyer or layman, teacher or student in our society must ever feel that to express a conviction, honestly and sincerely maintained, is to violate some unwritten law of manners or decorum." I question, however, resort to expressions in separate opinions that generate more heat than light. Consider this sample from an April 1991 D.C. Circuit decision. The dissenter led off:

> Running headlong from the questions briefed and argued before us, my colleagues seek refuge in a theory as novel as it is questionable. Unsupported by precedent, undeveloped by the court, and unresponsive to the facts of this case, the * * * theory announced today has an inauspicious birth.

That spicy statement, by the way, opposed an en banc opinion in which all of the judges concurred, except the lone dissenter.

It is "not good for public respect for courts and law and the administration of justice," Roscoe Pound decades ago observed, for an appellate judge to burden an opinion with "intemperate denunciation of [the writer's] colleagues, violent invective, attributi[on]s of bad motives to the majority of the court, and insinuations of incompetence, negligence, prejudice, or obtuseness of [other judges]." Yet one has only to thumb through the pages of current volumes of U.S. Reports and Federal Reporter Second to come upon condemnations by the score of a court or colleague's opinion or assertion as, for example, "folly," "ludicrous," "outrageous," one that "cannot be taken seriously," "inexplicable," "the quintessence of inequity," a "blow against the People," "naked analytical bootstrapping," "reminiscent * * * of Sherman's march through Georgia," "Orwellian."

* * *

The most effective dissent, I am convinced, "stand[s] on its own legal footing"; it spells out differences without jeopardizing collegiality or public respect for and confidence in the judiciary. I try to write my few separate opinions each year as I once did briefs for appellees—as affirmative statements of my reasons, drafted before receiving the court's opinion, and later adjusted, as needed, to meet the majority's presentation. Among pathmarking models, one can look to Justice Curtis' classic dissent in the *Dred Scott* case, and, closer to our time, separate opinions by the second Justice John Marshall Harlan.

* * *

BERNARD SCHWARTZ,* THE ASCENT OF PRAGMATISM: THE BURGER COURT IN ACTION
297–307 (1990)

ROE v. WADE: CONFERENCE AND ASSIGNMENT

* * *

Roe v. Wade came before the Court with a companion case, *Doe v. Bolton*. In both cases, pregnant women sought relief against state abortion laws, contending that they were unconstitutional. At issue in *Roe* was a Texas statute that prohibited abortions except to save the mother's life. The statute in *Doe* was a Georgia law that proscribed an abortion except as performed by a physician who felt, in "his best clinical judgment," that continued pregnancy would endanger a woman's life or injure her health; the fetus would likely be born with a serious defect; or the pregnancy resulted from rape. In addition, the Georgia statutory scheme posed three procedural conditions: (1) that the abortion be performed in an accredited hospital; (2) that the procedure be approved by the hospital staff abortion committee; and (3) that the performing physician's judgment be confirmed by independent examinations by two other physicians.

* * *

Roe v. Wade and *Doe v. Bolton* were both discussed at the same postargument conference in December 1971. [At this time, the Court was composed of only seven Justices. Harlan and Black had died recently and neither Powell nor Rehnquist had yet been confirmed.] The Chief Justice devoted much of his *Roe v. Wade* discussion to the question of standing. On the merits, Burger said, "The balance here is between the state's interest in protecting fetal life and the woman's interest in not having children." In weighing these interests, the Chief Justice concluded, "I can't find the Texas statute unconstitutional, although it's certainly archaic and obsolete."

Douglas, who spoke next, declared categorically, "The abortion statute is unconstitutional. This is basically a medical and psychiatric problem"—and not only to be dealt with by prohibitory legislation. Douglas also criticized the statute's failure to give "a licensed physician an immunity for good faith abortions." Brennan, who followed, stressed even more strongly the right to an abortion, which should be given a constitutional basis by the Court's decision.

Stewart, next in order of seniority, stated, "I agree with Bill Douglas." He did, however, indicate that there might be some state power. "The state can legislate, to the extent of requiring a doctor and that, after a certain period of pregnancy, [she] can't have an abortion."

White said, "On the merits I am on the other side. They want us to say that women have a choice under the Ninth Amendment." White said that he refused to accept this "privacy argument." Marshall, on the other hand, declared, "I go with Bill Douglas, but the time problem concerns me." He thought that the state could not prevent abortions "in the early stage [of pregnancy]. But why can't the state prohibit after a certain stage?" In addition, Marshall said that he would use "liberty" under the Fourteenth Amendment as the constitutional base.

Blackmun, then the junior Justice, spoke last. Blackmun displayed an ambivalence that was to be reflected in his draft *Roe v. Wade* opinion. "Can a state properly outlaw all abortions? If we accept fetal life, there's a strong argument that it can. But there are opposing interests: the right of the mother to life and mental and physical health, the right of parents in case of rape, the right of the state in case of incest. I don't think there's an absolute right to do what you will with [your] body." Blackmun did, however, say flatly, "This statute is a poor statute that * * * impinges too far on her."

The conference outcome was not entirely clear; the tally sheets of different Justices do not coincide. What was clear, however, was that a majority were in favor of invalidating the laws: in *Roe v. Wade,* it was five (Douglas, Brennan, Stewart, Marshall, and Blackmun) to two (the Chief Justice and Justice White) according to one tally sheet, and four to three (with Blackmun added to the dissenters) according to a December 18, 1971, Douglas letter to the Chief Justice. Despite the fact that he was not part of the majority, Chief Justice Burger assigned the opinions to Blackmun.

Though the majority may have disapproved of the Burger assignment, only Douglas (whose tally sheet showed four votes for invalidating the laws, with himself as senior Justice in the majority) protested, in his December 18 "Dear Chief" letter: "As respects your assignment in this case, my notes show there were four votes to hold parts of the * * * Act unconstitutional * * *. There were three to sustain the law as written. I would think, therefore, that to save future time and trouble, one of the four, rather than one of the three, should write the opinion."

The Chief Justice replied with a December 20 "Dear Bill" letter. "At the close of the discussion of this case I remarked to the Conference that there were, literally, not enough columns to mark up an accurate reflection of the voting in either the Georgia or the Texas cases. I therefore marked down no votes and said this was a case that would have to stand or fall on the writing, when it was done. That is still my view of how to handle these two * * * sensitive cases, which, I might add, are quite probably candidates for reargument."

* * * Douglas and Brennan, who had led the proabortion bloc at the conference, decided to wait to see the Blackmun drafts before doing anything further. Though Douglas had tallied Blackmun with the minority, others had noted his vote with the majority. This might well mean Blackmun opinions agreeable to Douglas and Brennan, and make either a confrontation with the Chief Justice or a separate majority draft unnecessary.

Roe v. Wade: Blackmun Draft

Justice Blackmun has termed *Roe v. Wade* "a landmark in the progress of the emancipation of women." That could hardly have been said had his original draft become the final opinion of the Court. The draft did strike down the abortion statute, but it did so on the ground of vagueness—not because it restricted a woman's right to have an abortion. The draft expressly avoided the issue of the state's substantive right to prohibit abortions or "imply that a State has no legitimate interest in the subject of abortions or that abortion procedures may not be subject to control by the State."

The abortion opinion had been assigned in December 1971. Blackmun was the slowest worker on the Court, and the abortion cases were his first major assignment. He worked at them mostly alone.

Finally, on May 18, 1972, Blackmun sent around his draft *Roe v. Wade* opinion. "Herewith," began the covering memo, "is a first and tentative draft for this case * * *. [I]t may be somewhat difficult to obtain a consensus on all aspects. My notes indicate, however, that we were generally in agreement to affirm on the merits. That is where I come out on the theory that the Texas statute, despite its narrowness, is unconstitutionally vague.

"I think that this would be all that is necessary for disposition of the case, and that we need not get into the more complex Ninth Amendment issue. This may or may not appeal to you * * *. I am still flexible as to results, and I shall do my best to arrive at something which would command a court."

In *United States v. Vuitch,* decided the year before, the Court had upheld a similar District of Columbia abortion law against a vagueness attack. The Blackmun draft distinguished *Vuitch* on the ground that the statute there prohibited abortion unless "necessary for the preservation of the mother's life or health," while the Texas statute only permitted abortions "for the purpose of saving the life of the mother." Thus *Vuitch* "provides no answer to the constitutional challenge to the Texas statute."

In the Texas statute, "Saving the mother's life is the sole standard." This standard is too vague to guide physicians' conduct in abortion cases. "Does it mean that he may procure an abortion only when, without it, the patient will surely die? Or only when the odds are greater than even that she will die? Or when there is a mere possibility that she will not survive?"

"We conclude that Art. 1196, with its sole criterion for exemption as 'saving the life of the mother,' is insufficiently informative to the physician to whom it purports to afford a measure of professional protection but who must measure its indefinite meaning at the risk of his liberty, and that the statute cannot withstand constitutional challenge on vagueness grounds."

Blackmun's vagueness analysis was extremely weak. If anything, the "life saving" standard in the *Roe v. Wade* statute was more definite than the "health" standard upheld in *Vuitch.* But the draft's disposition of the case on vagueness enabled it to avoid the basic constitutional question. As the Blackmun draft stated, "There is no need in Roe's case to pass upon her contention that under the Ninth Amendment a pregnant woman has an absolute right to an abortion, or even to consider the opposing rights of the embryo or fetus during the respective prenatal trimesters.''

Indeed, so far as the draft contained intimations on the matter, they tended to support state substantive power over abortions. "Our holding today does not imply that a State has no legitimate interest in the subject of abortions or that abortion procedures may not be subjected to control by the State * * *. We do not accept the argument of the appellants and of some of the amici that a pregnant woman has an unlimited right to do with her body as she pleases. The long acceptance of statutes regulating the possession of certain drugs and other harmful substances, and making criminal indecent exposure in public, or an attempt at suicide, clearly indicate the contrary." This was, of course, completely different from the approach ultimately followed in the *Roe v. Wade* opinion of the Court.

The *Roe v. Wade* draft did not deal at all with the right of privacy. It was, however, discussed in Blackmun's *Doe v. Bolton* draft, which he circulated on May 25, 1972. As summarized in the covering memo, his draft "would accomplish * * * the striking of the Georgia statutory requirements as to (1) residence, (2) confirmation by two physicians, (3) advance approval by the hospital abortion committee, and (4) performance of the procedure only in [an] accredited hospital."

Blackmun's *Doe* draft dealt specifically with the claim that the law was an "invalid restriction of an absolute fundamental right to personal and marital privacy * * *. The Court, in varying contexts, has recognized a right of personal privacy and has rooted it in the Fourteenth Amendment, or in the Bill of Rights, or in the latter's penumbras." The draft flatly rejected the assertion "that the scope of this right of personal privacy includes, for a woman, the right to decide unilaterally to terminate an existing but *unwanted* pregnancy without any state interference or control whatsoever." As the draft put it, "Appellants' contention, however, that the woman's right to make the decision is absolute—that Georgia has either no valid interest in regulating it, or no interest strong enough to support any limitation upon the woman's sole determination—is unpersuasive."

The draft rejected as "unfair and illogical" the argument that "the State's present professed interest in the protection of embryonic and fetal 'life' is somehow to be downgraded. That argument condemns the State for past 'wrongs' and also denies it the right to readjust its views and emphases in the light of the more advanced knowledge and techniques of today."

The *Doe* draft, utterly unlike the final Blackmun opinions, stressed the countervailing interest in fetal life. "The heart of the matter is that somewhere, either forthwith at conception, or at 'quickening,' or at birth, or at some other point in between, another being becomes involved and the privacy the woman possessed has become dual rather than sole. The woman's right of privacy must be measured accordingly." That being the case, "The woman's personal right * * *, is not unlimited. It must be balanced against the State's interest." Hence, "we cannot automatically strike down the remaining features of the Georgia statute simply because they restrict any right on the part of the woman to have an abortion at will."

The implication here was that substantial state power over abortion existed. Under the *Doe* draft, as the Blackmun covering memo pointed out, the state may provide "that an abortion may be performed only if the attending physician deems it necessary 'based upon his best clinical judgment,' if his judgment is reduced to writing, and if the abortion is performed in a hospital licensed by the State through its Board of Health." This was, of course, wholly inconsistent with the Court's final decision in *Roe v. Wade*.

ROE V. WADE: REARGUMENT AND SECOND CONFERENCE

It soon became apparent that the Blackmun drafts were not going to receive the five-Justice imprimatur needed to transform them into Court opinions. On May 18 and 19, 1972, Brennan and Douglas sent "Dear Harry" letters urging, in Brennan's words, "a disposition of the core constitutional question. Your circulation, however, invalidates the Texas statute only on the vagueness ground * * *. I think we should dispose of both cases on the ground supported by the majority." Douglas agreed. "That was the clear view of a majority of the seven who heard the argument * * *. So I think we should meet what Bill Brennan calls the 'core issue.' " Douglas also referred to the fact that, at the conference, "the Chief had the opposed view, which made it puzzling as to why he made the assignment at all."

The conference minority now sought to delay—and perhaps reverse—the abortion decisions. *Roe* and *Doe* had come before a seven-Justice Court. The two vacancies were not filled until Powell and Rehnquist took their seats in January, 1972. After the Blackmun drafts were circulated in May, the Chief Justice directed his efforts to securing a reargument in the cases, arguing that the decisions in such important cases should be made by a full Court.

At this point White sent around a brief draft dissent. Circulated May 29, it effectively demonstrated the weakness of the Blackmun vagueness approach in striking down the Texas law. Referring to the *Vuitch* decision that a statute that permitted abortion on "health" grounds was not unconstitutionally vague, the White draft declared, "If a standard which refers to the 'health' of the mother, a referent which necessarily entails the resolution of perplexing questions about the interrelationship of physical, emotional, and mental well-being, is not impermissibly vague, a statutory standard which focuses only on 'saving the life' of the mother would appear to be a fortiori acceptable * * *. [T]he relevant factors in the latter situation are less numerous and are primarily physiological."

On May 31, Chief Justice Burger circulated a Memorandum to the Conference favoring reargument—"[T]hese cases * * * are not as simple for me as they appear to be for others. The states have, I should think, as much concern in this area as in any within their province; federal power has only that which can be traced to a specific provision of the Constitution * * *. I want to hear more and think more when I am not trying to sort out several dozen other difficult cases * * *. I vote to reargue early in the next Term."

The Burger move to secure reargument was opposed by the Justices who favored striking down the abortion laws. They feared that the two new Justices would vote for the laws. In addition, the White draft dissent might lead another Justice to withdraw his support from the Blackmun *Roe* draft—maybe even Blackmun himself whose position had been none too firm. Indeed, he had become convinced that the cases should be reargued and circulated a May 31 Memorandum to the Conference to that effect. "Although it would prove costly to me personally, in the light of energy and hours expended, I have now concluded, somewhat reluctantly, that reargument in *both* cases at an early date in the next term, would perhaps be advisable * * *. I believe, on an issue so sensitive and so emotional as this one, the country deserves the conclusion of a nine-man, not a seven-man court, whatever the ultimate decision may be."

Douglas replied to Justice Blackmun the same day, "I feel quite strongly that they should not be reargued." The next day, June 1, an angry Douglas wrote to the Chief Justice, "If the vote of the Conference is to reargue, then I will file a statement telling what is happening to us and the tragedy it entails."

The Douglas statement was never issued even though the Justices did vote to set the abortion cases for reargument. Only Douglas was listed as dissenting.

* * *

The abortion cases were reargued on October 11, 1972. At the conference, the Justices who had participated in the earlier conference took the same positions as before. The two new Justices took opposing positions. Powell said that he was "basically in accord with Harry's position," while Justice Rehnquist stated, "I agree with Byron" White— who had declared, "I'm not going to second guess state legislatures in striking the balance in favor of abortion laws."

Several Justices agreed with Justice Stewart when he stated, "I can't join in holding that the Texas statute is vague." Stewart was for striking that law, but urged a different approach. He said that he would "follow John Harlan's reasoning in the Connecticut case and can't rest there on the Ninth Amendment. It's a Fourteenth Amendment right, as John Harlan said in *Griswold*."

ROE V. WADE: SECOND DRAFT AND FINAL OPINION

The most important part of Blackmun's postreargument conference presentation was his announcement, "I am where I was last Spring." However, he made a much firmer statement this time in favor of invalidating the abortion laws. He also said, "I'd make Georgia the lead case." But he was opposed on this by several others, particularly Powell, who felt that "Texas should be the lead case."

Most important of all, during the summer, Blackmun had completely rewritten the abortion opinions. On November 21, he circulated the revised draft of his *Roe v. Wade* opinion. "Herewith," began the covering memo, "is a memorandum (1972 fall edition) on the Texas abortion cases."

He expressly abandoned the vagueness holding. The holding on the constitutional merits "makes it unnecessary for us to consider the attack made on the Texas statute on grounds of vagueness."

The new Blackmun draft contained the essentials of the final *Roe v. Wade* opinion, including its lengthy historical analysis. In particular, Blackmun now grounded his decision upon *Griswold v. Connecticut.* According to Blackmun, "the right of privacy, however based, is broad enough to cover the abortion decision." In addition since the right at issue was a "fundamental" one, the law at issue was subject to strict-scrutiny review: the state regulation of the fundamental right of privacy "may be justified only by a 'compelling state interest.'"

The Blackmun privacy-strict scrutiny approach was substantially influenced by a Douglas draft opinion in *Doe v. Bolton,* which had been prepared in January, 1972. The Douglas draft had expressly invalidated the abortion law as violative of the right of privacy and adopted the strict-scrutiny review standard. There is a note in Douglas's hand, dated March 6, 1972, indicating that a copy of his draft had been "sent * * * to HB several weeks ago."

At the postargument conference, the Chief Justice had asked, "Is there a fetal life that's entitled to protection?" Justice Stewart said that the Court should deal specifically with this issue, saying, "it seems essential that we deal with the claim that the fetus is not a person under the Fourteenth Amendment." The *Roe v. Wade* opinion met this Stewart demand with a statement that the word "person" in the Fourteenth Amendment does not include a fetus—a point that is said to have been added at Justice Stewart's insistence.

The second draft also adopted the time approach followed in the final opinion. However, it used the first trimester of pregnancy alone as the line between invalid and valid state power. "You will observe," Justice Blackmun explained in his covering memo, "that I have concluded that the end of the first trimester is critical. This is arbitrary, but perhaps any other selected point, such as quickening or viability, is equally arbitrary."

The draft stated that, before the end of the first trimester, the state "must do no more than to leave the abortion decision to the best medical judgment of the pregnant woman's attending physician." However, "For the stage subsequent to the first trimester, the State may, if it chooses, determine a point beyond which it restricts legal abortions to stated reasonable therapeutic categories."

Later drafts refined this two-pronged time test to the tri-partite approach followed in the final *Roe* opinion. In large part, this was in response to the suggestion in a December 12 letter from Justice Marshall: "I am inclined to agree that drawing the line at viability accommodates the interests at stake better than drawing it at the end of the first trimester. Given the difficulties which many women may have in believing that they are pregnant and in deciding to seek an abortion, I fear that the earlier date may not in practice serve the interests of those women, which your opinion does seek to serve."

The Marshall letter stated that his concern would be met "If the opinion stated explicitly that, between the end of the first trimester and viability, state regulations directed at health and safety alone were permissible."

Marshall recognized "that at some point the State's interest in preserving the potential life of the unborn child overrides any individual interests of the women." However, he concluded, "I would be disturbed if that point were set before viability, and I am afraid that the opinion's present focus on the end of the first trimester would lead states to prohibit abortions completely at any later date."

Blackmun adopted the Marshall suggestion, even though Douglas and Brennan wrote expressing their doubts about the "viability" approach.

In a December 14, 1972, letter, Stewart delivered a more fundamental criticism of the Blackmun approach: "One of my concerns with your opinion as presently written is the specificity of its dictum—particularly in its fixing of the end of the first trimester as the critical point for valid state action. I appreciate the inevitability and indeed wisdom of dicta in the Court's opinion, but I wonder about the desirability of the dicta being quite so inflexibly 'legislative.'" This is, of course, the common criticism that has since been directed at *Roe v. Wade*. The high bench was acting like a legislature; its drawing of lines at trimesters and viability was, in the Stewart letter's phrase "to make policy judgments" that were more "legislative" than "judicial." Stewart worked on a lengthy opinion giving voice to this criticism, but in a December 27 letter he informed Blackmun that he had decided to discard it and "to file instead a brief monograph on substantive due process, joining your opinions."

* * *

BOB WOODWARD & SCOTT ARMSTRONG,*
THE BRETHREN

308–347 (1979)

* * *

The [day following oral argument in *United States v. Nixon*, 418 U.S. 683 (1974),] the eight Justices met in conference to vote on the case. [Justice Rehnquist recused himself.] Everyone was well prepared. The memos [dealing with many of the legal questions and circulated before oral argument] from the chambers of Douglas, Powell, Brennan and Stewart had defined the scope of the case. Dealing first with the technical questions, they all agreed that the ruling [by federal district court Judge Sirica] on the subpoena was of sufficient constitutional significance to be appealed to the Supreme Court. It was properly before them.

The first disagreement arose when Powell held firm to the position he had expressed in his memo on Rule 17(c), [which sets the standards for issuing subpoenas in federal cases,] that there was a need for a higher standard of evidence for presidents than for other people.

White disagreed completely. The Court should ensure that the President was treated like any citizen, no more, no less. * * * Thus, White said, he would be forced to dissent on that point if the others supported Powell's position.

The discussion was sharp and heated. The question of the standard was only one possible sticking point. The difficult questions revolving around the grand jury's naming of the President as an unindicted coconspirator should be sidestepped, they all agreed.

On the central question of executive privilege, the Justices agreed that the judiciary's specific need for sixty-four particular tapes for a criminal trial outweighed the President's generalized claim of confidentiality. At the same time, they all acknowledged that some form of executive privilege existed, at least implicitly.

Brennan saw the consensus immediately. The President did not have a single vote. Even more encouraging, there was reason to believe that the gaps among the Justices could be bridged. A single opinion seemed within reach. That would be the greatest deterrent to a defiant President. * * *

Marshall was afraid a single opinion would never attract all eight votes. The Justices were agreed on the result, but not on the reasoning. The discussion in conference had been odd. Conversation at conference normally focused on a case in light of the Constitution. This discussion had centered more on the Court's role and power than on the case.

The Chief [, who announced he would assign the opinion to himself,] got right to work with two of his clerks. This would be his most historic opinion, perhaps the Court's most momentous opinion. This was an opinion that would establish the Chief's independence from Richard Nixon. And, like Earl Warren before him, he would pull together and hold a unanimous Court on an extraordinarily divisive issue.

* * *

This would be the opinion that would give the Chief a chance to draw on his legal knowledge about the separation of powers, an expertise he had refined in the Adam Clayton Powell case, when he was on the Court of Appeals, and which had been reversed by the Warren Court.

* * *

Seated at the ceremonial desk in the conference room, the Chief told his clerks to pull up the two black leather chairs. They would work right there. He jotted down an outline in large block letters. Each of them would take one section and begin drafting. Then they would reconvene, read through the work line by line, and correct as they went. It was a tedious approach, but it was the Chief's style. He worked best talking out the question, with someone to keep him company. * * * The three men worked late into the night.

* * *

The Chief felt pressured. He had spent hours at his desk with his two clerks. The work was going smoothly. * * * [H]e decided that the first two sections of the draft were ready to circulate. One dealt with the facts, the other with the technical, though uncontroversial, question of appealability. Just over a week had passed since conference. Perhaps now he would convince the skeptics of his ability to turn out an opinion in timely fashion. Burger read the material over and decided to add a brief cover memo.

MEMORANDUM TO THE CONFERENCE

The enclosed material is not intended to be final, and I will welcome—indeed I invite—your suggestions. Regards, WEB.

Though the job had eluded him, or he it, Potter Stewart knew what it meant to be a Chief Justice. A Chief must be a statesman, a master of the Court's internal protocols, able to inspire, cajole and compromise, a man of integrity, who commanded the respect of his colleagues. But, most of all, a Chief Justice had to be a student of the nation's capital, able to see the politically inevitable, willing to weigh the Court's destiny against other Washington institutions. A Chief Justice, Stewart believed, should be a man not unlike himself.

Warren Burger was none of these things. He was a product of Richard Nixon's tasteless White House, distinguished in appearance and bearing, but without substance or integrity. Burger was abrasive to his colleagues, persistent in ignorance, and, worst of all, intellectually dishonest. "On ocean liners," Stewart told his clerks, "they used to have two captains. One for show, to take the women to dinner. The other to pilot the ship safely. The Chief is the show captain. All we need now is a real captain." Stewart was convinced that the Chief could never lead them to a safe, dignified opinion befitting one of the most important cases in the Court's history.

When the Chief's first two sections came in, Stewart read them carefully. The facts section was poorly written, dashed off with little care. There was not enough attention to the sequence of events or to the key issues.

The section on appealability was not much better. It offered no cogent response to St. Clair's argument that Sirica should first have held Nixon in contempt before the case could be brought to the Court. This should not have become a complicated section to draft. Douglas's draft had already included two simple reasons why the Court could and had to intervene: the risk of a constitutional confrontation between the two branches of government; and the protracted litigation that might result if normal contempt procedures were followed.

The next afternoon, July 11, Stewart and Powell talked about what should be done with the Chief's sections. The two men agreed that they were awful. If they were not vastly improved, the sections would be an embarrassment to the Court. Even worse, if they foreshadowed the quality of what was to come, the opinion not only would hurt the Court's reputation, but could damage its future relations with the other branches of the government. This opinion would be analyzed and dissected for years to come.

All of the eight Justices seemed to be in general agreement on the basic outline. It would be a shame not to produce the best possible piece of legal work, which the Chief could not conceivably do alone. Despite what he said about welcoming comments from the rest, they knew Burger rarely incorporated individual suggestions unless he saw a risk of losing his majority.

Stewart and Powell talked strategy. Brennan's suggestion of a joint opinion could be implemented, but they would have to work behind the Chief's back. Each of the other Justices would systematically propose alternative drafts to various of the Chief's sections. They all could then express their preference for the substitute sections. Seeing that he was outnumbered, the Chief would be forced to capitulate. They would have to gauge White's thinking and see if he could be brought along. Blackmun would have to be won over at once. Although he had broken with Burger in the past and was disgusted by Watergate, Blackmun might support Burger here. They would have to enlist him quickly, tactfully, somewhat indirectly. They knew that Blackmun enjoyed preparing the detailed facts sections in cases. If he could be persuaded to redo the facts section, the others could praise it, suggest it be incorporated, in reality substituted. That would cement an alliance with Blackmun. In turn, he would support the alternative drafts on the other sections. Once committed, Blackmun could oppose the Chief as forcefully as any of them. Stewart left the discussion convinced that the center could once again control the outcome, though it would not be easy.

* * *

Later that afternoon, Powell and Stewart approached Blackmun. The Chief's facts were inadequate. Only Blackmun could repair the damage, they said. Blackmun readily agreed. He would do his best with the facts. He certainly could do better than the Chief had done. He gathered all the relevant material and headed for the Justices' library.

When Brennan heard of the Stewart–Powell plan, he thought it was magnificent. He was also delighted to learn that Blackmun had so enthusiastically expressed his independence. Brennan agreed that Blackmun should handle the facts. He thought the rest of the lineup equally obvious. Douglas should take on appealability; he himself standing; White the 17(c) rule on admissibility and relevance; and Powell and Stewart, together, the extremely sensitive executive privilege section. Marshall, the Court's least productive worker, could be mollified without giving him a section.

Stewart took the first step. "Dear Chief," he wrote, "Responding to your circulation of yesterday, I think, with all due respect, that Bill Douglas's draft on appealability is entirely adequate. * * * "

Brennan quickly followed with a similar memo to the Chief praising Douglas's section.

Powell dictated a single cautious sentence: "Dear Chief: Potter's suggestion as to Bill Douglas's draft on appealability is entirely acceptable to me. Sincerely, Lewis."

Douglas sent his own "Dear Chief" memo saying Brennan had shown him a proposal on the standing section: " * * * It seems to me to be adequate and might put us quickly another rung up the ladder if the other Brethren agree."

When a copy of Douglas's memo arrived in his chambers, Brennan was afraid that it might appear that he was circulating sections privately. He immediately sent his standing section, previously given only to the Chief and Douglas, to all the others.

The four memos from Stewart, Powell, Brennan and Douglas were greeted by the Chief with some consternation. He had hardly begun and four of his colleagues were already criticizing his work. Everyone seemed to be in such a hurry. Deciding to meet what he thought they saw as the major problem—a possible delay of the opinion—Burger gathered together his drafts of the standing and 17(c) sections for circulation. In a cover memo, he said: "I believe we have encountered no insoluble problems to this point."

The Chief then decided to confront the others' concern about delay in a second memo:

MEMORANDUM TO THE CONFERENCE

I have received various memos in response to preliminary and partial sections circulated.

With the sad intervention of Chief Justice Warren's death [shortly after oral argument in the case], the schedules of all of us have been altered. I intend to work without interruption (except for some sleep) until I have the "privilege" section complete and the final honing complete on all parts.

I think it is unrealistic to consider a Monday, July 15, announcement. This case is too important to "rush" unduly although it is in fact receiving priority treatment.

I would hope we could meet an end-of-the-week announcement, i.e., July 19 or thereabouts.

Brennan was extremely frustrated by the Chief's memo. Certainly there was agreement that July 15 was not a realistic announcement date, but not for the reasons Burger gave. The Chief simply did not perceive the problem: all of his sections needed major rewriting.

The next morning, Friday, July 12, Douglas was appalled at the Chief's standing section which dealt with the question of whether [Special Prosecutor Leon] Jaworski could sue the President. It borrowed from the Brennan draft, but contained neither a satisfactory explanation of the regulations governing the prosecutor's office nor the fact that those regulations had the force of law. In Douglas's view, the Chief had failed to fully and conclusively establish that the courts often resolved disputes within other branches of government. Obviously the Chief didn't really believe the courts should get involved in such disputes. Burger still believed he was right and Warren wrong in the Adam Clayton Powell case.

The day before, Douglas had told the Chief that Brennan's standing section was "adequate." Now Douglas decided to be more explicit. Putting his felt-tip pen to paper again, he wrote to Burger that he had just reread Brennan's suggestions and "would, with all respect, prefer it over the version which you circulated this morning."

* * *

For three days, White had said little, lying in wait. He saw the Rule 17(c) section as the key. That was what the case was about. Would the existing rules and law be applied to the President in the same manner as they would be to any other citizen? The Chief's answer was ambiguous. He had tilted toward raising the standard. So White rewrote the section to enhance the importance of Rule 17(c) as a simple application of *existing law*.

* * *

White had his suggestions retyped and took them to Stewart, who liked the approach. It answered questions that the White House could raise in order to keep the tapes from being used at trial.

With that, White decided to circulate his proposal. "Dear Chief," he wrote, "The attached is the bare bones of an alternative treatment which I am now embellishing to some extent. Sincerely, Byron."

Douglas got his copy and pounced at once. He agreed with White's proposed 17(c) section, he declared in a memo to the Chief. Brennan was also pleased with White's proposal. It seemed wholly in line with his own suggestions on Rule 17(c) that had circulated the day of orals. In order to preserve his position with Powell, he decided not to endorse White's memo formally.

Powell was distressed at White's memo; the President was getting nothing, no extra consideration. Even Brennan had said the courts should be "particularly meticulous" to insure that Rule 17(c) had been correctly applied. Desiring to reach a middle ground, Powell circulated his own revised memo. He dropped his "necessity" standard and substituted a requirement that a "special showing" be made to establish that the material was essential. At the bottom of Brennan's copy, Powell wrote in his own hand, "I have tried to move fairly close to your original memo on this point, as I understand it, and what you said at conference. Lewis."

Brennan was confused by the personal note. In his own memo, Brennan had purposely steered clear of endorsing a higher standard, particularly a "special showing"—whatever that might be.

The Chief, who had at first been mildly bewildered by the sudden activity, was now angry. Brennan, Douglas, Powell, Stewart and now White—of all people—were sabotaging his work. Marshall had been silent, but he would certainly follow Brennan. Burger had an insurrection on his hands. He decided to waste no time in getting to Blackmun, his one remaining ally.

Blackmun had just finished his crash project of revising the statement of facts in the case when the Chief appeared at the door to his chambers. It was an awkward moment. Burger had no idea what Blackmun was preparing.

The Chief entered Blackmun's office and began complaining bitterly about the criticism he was getting on nearly all fronts. Ten critical memos had flown back and forth in the past two days. He could barely get a rough draft out of his typewriter before someone was circulating a counterdraft, suggestions or alternatives. It was amazing, he said. He could not get the counterdraft read before a barrage of memos arrived approving everyone's work but his own.

Blackmun listened.

Didn't the other Justices realize that he had been busy with the Warren funeral, the Chief said? He had his always-growing administrative duties, managing the building, the 600 federal judges. "It's my opinion," he finally asserted, "they are trying to take it away from me."

Blackmun hated scenes, and he disliked crossing the Chief. But it was time to tell the Chief where he stood.

"Before you go on, I think you should see this," Blackmun said, handing the Chief his revision of the facts section.

"What's this, Harry, a few suggested changes you'd like?"

"No," Blackmun said. "It's an entirely new section which I think you should substitute for your initial draft."

"Well," said the Chief, flustered, "it's too late now for such major revisions."

"Would you at least please read the new draft?" Blackmun asked.

Burger's eyes flashed. He turned and stormed out the door without a word.

Blackmun wanted to calm the Chief. He picked up one of the perfectly sharpened pencils on his desk and wrote a cover memo for his facts section.

"Dear Chief, With your letter of July 10 you recommended and invited suggestions. Accordingly, I take the liberty of suggesting herewith a revised statement of facts and submit it for your consideration."

He continued in a more personal vein. "Please believe me when I say that I do this in a spirit of cooperation and not of criticism. I am fully aware of the pressures that presently beset all of us." The draft was circulated. The tone of the cover memo signaled several of the Justices that something had happened. Blackmun told them about his encounter with the Chief. The incident became known as the "Et Tu Harry" story.

When the clerk network passed word that Blackmun had agreed to draft a counterstatement of the facts, several clerks joked that Blackmun would write it like his *Flood v. Kuhn* baseball antitrust opinion. He would begin the facts, "There have been many great Presidents," and then list thirty-six Presidents, leaving out the thirty-seventh, Richard Nixon.

Brennan was elated both by the revised Facts section and by word that Blackmun had stood up to the Chief. He wrote a memo that rubbed salt in the wound. "Dear Chief: I think that Harry's suggested revision of the Statement of Facts is excellent and I hope you could incorporate it in the opinion."

Stewart, too, was quite happy to see the Blackmun section. To one degree or another, all seven Justices were now confronting the Chief. But Burger's position could harden in the face of such pressure. Stewart had three minor points he wanted to add to Blackmun's section, to show that he was not just criticizing the Chief's work. He wrote Burger: "I think Harry Blackmun's revision of the statement of facts is a fine job, and I would join it as part of the Court opinion, with a couple of minor additions."

* * *

Stewart saw that White had dug in on 17(c). White could be as inflexible as the Chief. In addition to his original reservations about the other Justices developing substitute opinions and trying to force them on the Chief, White now had second thoughts about substituting sections one at a time. * * * The Chief would see Brennan's hand in this if he hadn't seen it already. White was loath to have it appear that he had drifted under Brennan's influence. He had to prove his independence both to the Chief and to Brennan.

White swiveled to the right for his typewriter.

Dear Chief: Your statement of the facts and your drafts on appealability and (standing) are satisfactory to me, although I could subscribe to most of what is said in other versions that have been submitted to you.

My views on the Rule 17(c) issue you already have.

With respect to the existence and extent of executive privilege * * * I cannot fathom why the President should be permitted to withhold the out-of-court statements of a defendant in a criminal case * * *. For me, the interest in sustaining confidentiality disappears when it is shown that the President is in possession of out-of-court declarations of those, such as [Charles W.] Colson and Dean, who have been sufficiently shown to be co-conspirators * * *. Shielding such a conspiracy in the making or in the process of execution carries the privilege too far.

White had the memo retyped and sent simultaneously to the Chief and to all the other Justices. * * *

Brennan had to get White back in the fold. He jotted out a memo: "Dear Byron: I fully agree with your expanded Sec. 17(c) treatment, recirculated July 13, 1974, and hope it can serve to cover that issue in the Court's opinion." He specified that copies be sent to all the others, including the Chief. Maybe that would appease White.

Stewart followed with a similar memo to the Chief.

"I agree with Byron's revision of the discussion of the Rule 17(c) issues," Stewart said.

* * *

Brennan * * * undertook in some detail to bring Marshall up to date. His support was crucial, particularly given the widening difficulties with White and Powell. Douglas had deserted to Goose Prairie. And you could never tell when Blackmun would bolt to the Chief. Perhaps White had already done so.

Marshall said that he would go along. His clerks drafted a short memo for him to sign. It was the coldest prose they could fashion.

Dear Chief:

1. I agree with Byron's recirculation * * * of the section on 17(c).

2. I agree with Harry's Statement of Facts.

3. I agree with Bill Brennan's treatment of the section on [Standing].

4. I agree with Potter's memorandum on the question of appealability.

Sincerely,
T.M.

Brennan was relieved. The memo was more direct than he expected. TM was back on the team.

Marshall's memo went off like a grenade in the Chief's chambers. Of all the memos this was the most combative. It obviously reflected the sentiments of Marshall's clerks, and the fact that Marshall was giving them free rein. It would be hard to budge that chambers.

It wasn't only Marshall's chambers. The Chief's clerks could see the hands of their fellow clerks in other chambers in all the various alternative drafts and supporting memos. They realized that because the seven other Justices had no other cases to work on, their clerks had little to do. So the Justices and the clerks spent their time cutting the Chief's rough, preliminary drafts to ribbons.

* * *

But the Chief decided to fight back with a memo to the conference on the nature of his prerogatives as the designated author.

My effort to accommodate everyone by sending out "first drafts" is not working out.

I do not contemplate sending out any more material until it is *ready*. This will take longer than I had anticipated and you should each make plans on an assumption that no more material will be circulated for at least one week.

* * *

At [a luncheon with Brennan and White,] Stewart had offered to redraft Powell's section on executive privilege, and now he got down to work. Altering Powell's deferential language, Stewart wrote that confidentiality in government was important, but he stated firmly that in every case, the Courts, never the executive, would make a final determination. Stewart chose a simpler argument than Powell. He adapted and enlarged upon the argument already made by Douglas, that due process would be denied everyone—prosecutors, defendants, witnesses, the public at large—if all the evidence was not turned over.

More importantly, on the sticky issue of the Rule 17(c) standard, Stewart lowered Powell's standard from "compelling justification" to a milder "sufficient justification." That might safely allow him to walk the line between Powell and White.

On Tuesday, July 16, Stewart privately sent his redraft to Powell, and Powell said it was acceptable. Stewart concluded that Powell had given up on the higher standard. Buttressed by Powell's support, Stewart sent copies to White, Brennan and Marshall. Those three then met to review Stewart's section and passed word to Stewart that it was acceptable. White and Powell had finally found a point of agreement, Stewart hoped.

As best he could tell, Stewart now had five votes for the section. Rather than further aggravate the Chief, Stewart decided not to send his own substitute draft to the Chief but to wait for the Chief's circulation on the privilege section.

Of all the Justices, Stewart was at once the most desirous of confrontation and the most committed to compromise. The tension between the two impulses at times seemed to exhilarate him.

The Chief spent the day grinding out his privilege section. The work went faster than he had expected. He tried to borrow generously from some of the ideas provided by Powell, Douglas, and even Brennan, and the pieces fell together nicely.

* * *

By early evening, the Chief had what he felt was a satisfactory draft. He resolved to make an appeal to perhaps the most obviously conspiratorial of the Justices. He reached Brennan by phone at home.

Burger told Brennan he had finished a draft of the privilege section and would like him to have a copy before Brennan left for Nantucket for the weekend.

Brennan said he would be delighted to see it.

Telling him that things were moving faster than he had indicated the day before, the Chief hinted that the opinion could come down shortly after the weekend—perhaps on Monday, July 22.

That indeed would be good, Brennan said. The Chief was obviously in an excellent mood. They fell into an animated discussion of non-Watergate matters.

Early the next morning, Wednesday, July 17, Brennan received his copy of the executive-privilege section. On initial reading, Brennan thought it was in better shape than the Chief's other sections. There were, however, some problems. First, the Chief was not emphatic in meeting the White House challenge by restating the ultimate responsibility of the courts to decide all such constitutional disputes. Second, the Chief talked of the "competing demands" of the executive and judicial branches, which had to be weighed in order to determine which would prevail. That determination turned on the extent to which each branch's "core functions" were involved. Such functions for the executive included war powers, the conduct of foreign relations, and the veto power. On the other hand, one of the "core functions" of the judiciary was ensuring that all evidence was available for a criminal trial.

The Chief then reasoned that in the tapes case a "core function" of the judiciary was clearly involved, whereas none was for the President. Under that reasoning the President lost. The Chief had also sidestepped Powell's demand for a higher standard by simply saying that the special prosecutor had shown "a sufficiently compelling need" for the material to be inspected by Judge Sirica.

Brennan assumed that the core functions formulation—a potentially vague and expandable creation—could probably be rendered harmless by limiting its meaning to foreign affairs, military or state secrets. It was doubtful, he felt, that the Chief would balk at that.

Though it was rough, Brennan felt that the draft was adequate and immediately told the Chief so. He recommended that Burger circulate it.

Encouraged by this response, Burger sent the section around. A full opinion draft, he told the others, would be ready by the end of the week.

The other Justices were not happy with the Chief's privilege section. Stewart didn't trust it. He particularly did not like the core functions analysis. Even if more narrowly defined than in the Chief's draft, the term implied that a President had an absolute constitutional prerogative over his core functions. These "core" functions were very loosely outlined as the Chief named them—war, foreign relations, the veto power or, as the Chief had written, whatever was implied when the President was "performing duties at the very core of his constitutional role."

* * *

Powell agreed with Stewart. When they met with Brennan and Marshall, Stewart made his case, and Powell supported him. Marshall agreed.

Brennan, however, disagreed. The term could be rendered harmless by narrowing the definition. It was more important to keep the Chief on track.

No, Stewart argued. The Chief had moved into dangerous territory.

Brennan saw the others were flatly opposed and was embarrassed by his initial enthusiasm. They might well be right about core functions. Brennan, holding out for a compromise, said he was sure the Chief was not wedded to the term or the analysis.

The four decided to nibble at the Chief's privilege section a subsection at a time. Stewart should circulate only the portions of his substitute section that might be added to the Chief's, particularly the *Marbury v. Madison* restatement—the portion that forthrightly and definitively ruled that the courts had absolute authority to resolve the dispute. They would wait until the Chief circulated his full opinion, all sections from facts to privilege, to attack the concept of *core functions*.

Before leaving for Nantucket on Thursday, July 18, Brennan dictated a memo to Burger.

Dear Chief,

This will formally confirm that your "working draft" circulated July 17, of "The Claim of Executive Privilege" reflects for me a generally satisfactory approach. * * * I do however agree with Potter, that St. Clair's argument, that the President alone has the power to decide the question of privilege, must be dealt with. Potter's suggested way is satisfactory to me.

Brennan closed by saying that he expected to have some more suggestions and would pass them on.

Marshall's memo to the Chief was even fainter in its praise of Burger's draft. "I agree with its basic structure, and believe that it provides a good starting point with which we can work." But, he added, he agreed with Stewart that the White House position that the President should ultimately decide what is privileged should be "firmly and unequivocally" rejected.

* * *

White did not like what he had seen. The Chief was creating too much law to dispose of the case. He sat down at his typewriter and composed another message.

Dear Chief:

I am in the process of considering your draft on executive privilege.

I am reluctant to complicate a difficult task or to increase your labors, of which I am highly appreciative, but I submit the following comments for your consideration.

First, he said, "I do not object to Potter's suggestion. * * *" Then came the real message. There was too much discussion of executive privilege and a construction of newly defined power for the courts to decide these issues. Too little was being made of Rule 17(c). All citizens, Presidents among them, were obligated equally to cooperate in criminal trials. That was the heart of the case. In this case,

The courts are playing their neutral role of enforcing the law already provided them, either by rule, statute, or Constitution. * * * I doubt, therefore, that we need discover or fashion any inherent powers in the judiciary to overcome an executive privilege which is not expressly provided for but which we also fashion today.

* * *

As the latest wave of memos arrived at his desk, Burger saw that large accommodations would be necessary. He decided first to add four long paragraphs at the front end of the privilege section, incorporating Stewart's suggestion. *Marbury v. Madison* * * * was cited at the beginning and the end—"It is emphatically the province and duty of the judicial department to say what the law is." It was rather obvious, but if Stewart, Brennan and Marshall thought it was important, so be it.

Now for White. White's multiple memos on one subject were clear. Rule 17(c) was what concerned him. The Chief took his own 17(c) section, cast it aside, rearranged some of the paragraphs in White's 17(c) proposal, and incorporated it almost verbatim. Keeping only three of his own sentences on the admissibility of recorded conversations and one of his own footnotes, the Chief dropped only one of White's sentences, one that he deemed redundant, given what would follow in the executive privilege section. Several of White's footnotes were dropped as unnecessary. The Chief was now certain that each of White's major points was included in some form. White would have to join. And with White neutralized, and the others accommodated on the *Marbury v. Madison* issue, the Chief decided to phone Nantucket and talk to Brennan.

Brennan was surprised to get the call.

Burger said the entire opinion would be circulated in draft form by the weekend; sufficient revisions had been made to meet White's objections. He was hopeful that the opinion might come down by the next Wednesday. It would be helpful if Brennan could return to Washington by Monday to help finish work.

Brennan agreed and hung up. He was both pleased and disappointed. At last there would be a complete draft from which to work. But Brennan did not see how White could have been so easily accommodated. He also thought the Chief did not yet understand how profound were the disagreements. White's draft represented a full-fledged renewal of his debate with Powell over the standards applicable to a presidential subpoena. Skeptical, Brennan made arrangements to return to Washington.

* * *

The Chief spent the next day, Friday, July 19, in his chambers, working with his clerks to pull the opinion together for the first time. Though he tried to incorporate any reasonable suggestion from the memos of the other Justices, the Chief still had to modify the language in several of the memos. Powell's proposal that the courts show "solicitous concern" was changed to "great deference."

Brennan's repeated invitation to the White House to withhold national security material as privileged was also altered.

In the last ten days the Chief had tried to accommodate nearly all the others. He used some of Powell's language on the importance of confidentiality, and the need for deference and restraint by the courts. He simply incorporated Stewart's *Marbury v. Madison* section. He inserted almost verbatim White's section on Rule 17(c). He picked up some ideas from Douglas, particularly his appealability section. He used some of Brennan's standing section. And he tried to accommodate Marshall's objection to two footnotes: one was deleted completely, the other was modified.

That left Blackmun. The Chief used large parts of his statement of the facts. What difference did it make anyway? * * *

The Chief was in his chambers early Saturday. He was in an excellent mood. He read over the draft one last time and was proud of the work. Though the others had tried to pick the opinion to death, it was solid, complete, straightforward and well reasoned. The rest of them had gone over every word he had written, demanding changes. But they had essentially acceded to what he felt sure would be the most important part of the case—the part with the most far-reaching implications. The key sentence was still there. "The protection of the confidentiality of presidential communications has * * * constitutional underpinnings." Nixon was going to lose the case, but the larger principle he claimed to be fighting to protect would be upheld.

The Chief finally sent the draft down to the printer. With nothing more to do, he proposed that his clerks join him for lunch. * * *

Stewart had arrived at the Court that Saturday morning thinking that the first official full draft would come around. When it was brought to him, he read the twenty-nine pages slowly. As he had expected, the core functions analysis was there, the central part of the section on executive privilege that the Chief had labeled Part C. Stewart was uneasy. As inelegant as the writing was, something else worried him. The tone was odd, the references somehow stilted, the citations of cases slightly off the mark. Could there be some subtle meaning beneath the words that he was missing? Could the Chief be slipping something in to sabotage the opinion? Could he be omitting something to create a loophole?

Nixon was desperate. Surely he would look for any ambiguity or favorable point on which to base a last-ditch defense. He might accept the Court's judgment on the law but reinterpret some obscure reference in the opinion. Could there be a bubble of imprecision that would give the President the "air" he needed?

Stewart realized he might be getting too suspicious or paranoid, but the simple fact was that he just didn't trust the Chief, particularly on this case. * * * Stewart's instinct was to drop as much as possible from the Chief's draft and substitute his own analysis and language. If Stewart could not locate the loopholes, at least he might remove some of them, if only accidentally, by putting the argument in his own words. The best way to get the Chief to adopt changes was to go slowly, item by item. Once the Chief accepted a change, he generally forgot where it had come from and became certain it had been his idea.

But now there was not much time. The Chief was talking about an announcement in four days, and Stewart had not even told Burger his major complaint about the core function analysis. An early announcement looked impossible. However awkward, there was no choice but to move a step at a time even if the deadline had to be pushed back. Stewart could at least count on support from the others who had approved his version; at a minimum that included Powell, Brennan, and Marshall.

Then there was the matter of control. Since Burger had come to the Court, the major opinions had been the achievement of the center coalition. There was no reason that this opinion should be any different. To a great degree it was rightfully theirs. The Chief had to be reminded of this fact of life. It was not the Chief's Court, or a Nixon Court.

* * * After the Chief's draft had circulated, [White and Marshall] stopped by Stewart's chambers. Stewart was sitting at his desk in a polo shirt. White was still pleased that the Chief had adopted his 17(c) section. He and Marshall sat at the left end of the desk, and a small group of clerks hovered at the front and right side.

They went through the draft line by line. Stewart made his case against the core functions analysis, restating every argument. White and Marshall agreed that it would be better to substitute Stewart's simpler alternative. Powell and Brennan also agreed, Stewart reminded them, so they had five votes. There were other minor problems. *President* should be capitalized. Then they decided to list their nonnegotiable demands.

The door to Stewart's inner office was open, and they heard someone come into the outer office. There was a second of silence, and Marshall turned toward the door. "Hi, Chief," he boomed.

Burger hesitated in the doorway. He just wanted to make sure that everyone had received a copy of the full draft, he said. The printers, he said apologetically, had forgotten to heat the lead to set type that morning so the draft had been delayed until midday.

It was obvious what Stewart, White and Marshall were doing.

It looks good, Stewart said. His hands working furiously, he picked up a rubber band, put it in his mouth and began to chew it—an old nervous habit.

White was more direct. He said there were still some problems and they were trying to isolate the main ones.

Yeah, the Chief responded. He appeared tense, but he was gracious. Well, he said, he was still shooting for a Wednesday announcement. He said goodbye and left.

The group waited in silence as Burger closed the outer door behind him.

"Jesus," Marshall said, "it's like getting caught with the goods by the cops."

Stewart was visibly distressed. This could make the Chief more intractable.

In any event, they told each other, the Chief's little visit had changed things. Their small intrigue, or what remained of it, was no more. Before the Chief put a more sinister interpretation on the meeting than was warranted, they had to do something, and at once. They had to lay out their demands clearly.

Stewart said maybe they could turn the incident to their advantage. The Chief's discovery had given their convocation legitimacy. Burger would be expecting them to come to him with suggestions. It was important to find a way to present their demands with the force but not the appearance of an ultimatum.

With Stewart orchestrating, they singled out the necessary modifications. It boiled down to some changes in wording and the core functions problem.

"Well, Potter," White remarked, "I'm going home. You go tell him." Everyone laughed.

"I'm not going by myself," Stewart said to more laughter.

"Oh yes," White replied. Stewart was definitely the man for the job. Given his close relationship with the Chief, he would be most effective.

After some more moments of teasing, White agreed to go with Stewart and Marshall. They walked down the hall to Burger's office.

The Chief greeted them. They outlined their suggestions.

It all sounds fine with me, the Chief responded, except the elimination of the core functions analysis.

But that was the biggest problem they had, Stewart said.

Well, the Chief replied, he preferred his core functions section, and he was going to keep it. In fact, this was the part of the opinion that offered the most explicit reason for why the President had to lose—an essential core function of the judiciary was pitted against a general need for confidentiality.

Stewart could see that the Chief was growing increasingly adamant. Instead of debating it right now, Stewart suggested that perhaps he should go back to his office and draft an alternative subsection C along the lines that he and the others had been talking about. He would have it ready for the Chief's consideration by Monday.

The Chief had little choice but to agree. He would look over Stewart's proposal.

After the three Justices left, the Chief vowed to his clerks that he would hold his ground. He could see that Stewart was the leader. His suggestions were the most sweeping and unacceptable; Stewart was not going to carry it off. No way, the Chief said.

Back in his chambers, Stewart got out his uncirculated version of the privilege section. Brennan, Marshall and Powell had already approved it.

The fault in the Chief's reasoning lay in his effort to balance the President's interests against those of the courts. On one side, the Chief put the Article II powers of the President, which he said contained executive privilege. On the other side of the scale, the Chief put the Article III power of the courts. Since there was a specific demonstrated need for evidence in a criminal trial, the weight was on the Judiciary's side of the scale. Burger's conclusion in this case was that there was an imbalance. Little or nothing of weight on Nixon's side, and great weight on the Court's.

Stewart was opposed to creating new constitutional concepts such as core functions, but he had other important problems with this section as well. The definition of executive core functions was too broad and too vague. The term was an open door for a defiant reinterpretation by the President. And the definition of judicial core functions was apologetic. The judicial interest seemed manufactured. The Chief's opinion smacked of judicial legislation, as if the Court were conjuring new constitutional grounds for compelling the production of evidence as a special indulgence for fellow judges. Burger had dismissed Stewart's constitutional due process basis for the need for evidence in a footnote rather than in the text.

Also, Burger's effort to balance the needs of one branch of the federal government against the interests of another, raised the separation-of-powers question. Since such questions were generally left to the head of the affected branch rather than the courts, the Chief was simply asking for trouble.

Perhaps there was an easy way of handling this, Stewart thought. The Chief had balanced the needs of the President against those of the Court. Why not balance them against the Constitution? The Fifth and Sixth Amendments guaranteed due process and a fair trial with all the evidence. Taking some language from the memos of Douglas and White to develop a constitutional foundation for a subpoena, Stewart wrote that "the needs of due process of law in the fair administration of criminal justice" required the evidence. This line of argument would force Nixon to pit his claims against the Bill of Rights, the commitment to the rule of law, and the concept of due process.

* * *

Now that he had his foundation, Stewart began tinkering with both drafts, trying to develop an alternative that would change the thrust of the opinion but least challenge the Chief. He kept the Chief's first two paragraphs, and the next long paragraph except for the last sentence, which said the courts must have standards and procedures to ensure that the "legitimate confidentiality" of the executive is preserved. That sentence had originally come from Powell's pre-argument memo. Stewart then substituted a new line of reasoning for the Chief's core functions analysis. He wrote seven paragraphs in place of the Chief's final four, keeping only Burger's last sentence, which summarized the decision. Stewart had his clerks come in on Sunday, July 21, to type the new version, twelve pages, triple-spaced.

Early Monday morning, July 22, Stewart went over the draft. He was satisfied that it gave the tapes subpoena a firm constitutional basis while giving executive privilege a very limited constitutional status. He then went to White and Marshall and went over it with them in detail. They agreed that they would join the Chief only if he accepted Stewart's substitute. Afterward, Stewart sent a copy to the Chief. That still left four Justices out of the picture—Douglas, Brennan, Blackmun and Powell.

Stewart decided to make sure that everyone understood they were on a one-way street; there was no turning around. He wrote:

Re: Nixon cases
Memorandum to: Mr. Justice Douglas
                        Mr. Justice Brennan
                        Mr. Justice Blackmun
                        Mr. Justice Powell

Byron, Thurgood, and I were here in the building on Saturday afternoon when the printed draft of the tentative proposed opinion was circulated. After individually going over the circulation, we collected our joint and several specific suggestions and met with the Chief Justice in order to convey these suggestions to him.

[O]ur joint suggestions were too extensive to be drafted on Saturday afternoon, and I was accordingly delegated to try my hand at a draft over the weekend. The enclosed draft embodies the views of Byron, Thurgood, and me, and we have submitted it to the Chief Justice this morning.

As of now, Byron, Thurgood, and I are prepared to join the proposed opinion, if the recasting of [the section] is acceptable to the Chief Justice.

At this late stage it seems essential to me that there be full intramural communication in the interest of a cooperative effort, and it is for this reason that I send you this memorandum bringing you up to date so far as I am concerned.

P.S.

Copies to: The Chief Justice
                Mr. Justice White
                Mr. Justice Marshall

P.S. As you will observe, the enclosed draft borrows generously from the draft of the Chief Justice as well as Lewis Powell's earlier memorandum.

Blackmun was pleased to see someone stand up to the Chief. Stewart's proposal was far superior, if for no other reason than the weight and authority of the language. Blackmun made it known that he was now prepared to join if the substitution were made.

Powell also found Stewart's version preferable and gave his tentative approval. But he was not deluded. Very little had been taken from his early memo.

Brennan flew in from Nantucket later that afternoon and read the proposal. Though he thought it overly generous in its use of the Chief's language, there were no apparent major changes from the first version he had approved. He quickly called Stewart to say that he agreed strongly that the substitution was essential.

Douglas was scheduled to return from Goose Prairie that afternoon. The Chief sent a messenger to the airport to give Douglas a copy of the full draft he had circulated two days earlier. If Douglas ratified his version, it could puncture the counterdraft movement. Brennan, however, made sure that a copy of Stewart's proposal was also at the airport. He also took the precaution of sounding out Douglas before the Chief could get to him. Douglas agreed that the substitution should be made. That was seven votes, according to Brennan's count. The Chief was the only holdout to his own opinion.

Burger was exhausted. In addition to closing a Court term and attending his official functions, he had worked for more than two straight weeks without a day off. Burger felt the others had been merciless. And Stewart's memo calling for future "full intramural communication" was a joke, after the way he had operated behind his back for weeks. This was all particularly ironic given the Saturday meeting. The Chief didn't think the little gathering in Stewart's chambers he had wandered into on Saturday was in the spirit of "full intramural communication." Each of them had taken a section of his draft and chewed it to bits. If he had written only an eighth of the opinion, he too could have fussed over every word and each comma.

But what would the others do? The Chief had talked to some of them. All, to one degree or another, seemed sympathetic to Stewart's proposal. Burger felt he had been sandbagged; he needed time to consider his options. He dashed off a quick "Personal" memo to the conference.

> Potter's memo of July 22, 1974, enclosing a revision of Part "C" prompts me to assure you that I will work on it promptly with the hope to accommodate those who wish to get away this week.
>
> The two versions can be accommodated and harmonized and, indeed, I do not assume it was intended that I cast aside several weeks work and take this circulation as a total substitute.
>
> I will have a new draft of Part "C" along as soon as possible. I take it for granted voting will be deferred until the revised opinion is recirculated.

Once again, Brennan saw, Burger had not even understood the vast difference between the two approaches. The two simply could not be "accommodated and harmonized" as the Chief had proposed. Any attempt by the Chief to accomplish that would inevitably result in another half-baked, paste-up job.

At least the Chief finally perceived that he was up against the wall. For Burger to plead that any vote be deferred meant that they were gaining some ground.

Burger knew that he faced a tough choice. There was no "give" in Stewart's posture, and Stewart seemed to have lined up all the others. Burger read through the alternative drafts. They were really two different ways of saying the same thing; the approaches were different but the bottom line was the same. The President would have to turn over his tapes. Whichever version they used would not make any difference to history or constitutional law. Burger was sure his version was better, but the others thought differently. What was the big deal? It came down to three pages out of a thirty-page opinion. All of them, living day and night with the case for weeks, had become wrapped up in each word and phrase. Did the difference have any substance? Burger could find none. It would all seem silly in a few weeks. But the Chief knew that making concessions was part of holding the Court together. The main thing was to get the opinion delivered. He wanted it unanimous. They were on the final leg. The only thing holding them up seemed to be this section. Stewart had left the first two paragraphs the same. That was settled. The Chief then took Stewart's next two paragraphs about the rule of law and compressed them, shifting some of the sentences around, dropping others.

* * *

He then switched around and condensed some of the next four Stewart paragraphs—the central basis of Stewart's argument that due process and the fair administration of justice required the President's relevant evidence.

Burger did not find it particularly painful to make the alterations. Stewart's draft didn't really say anything he would not have written himself. The core functions approach was just one of several possible lines of reasoning. Also, he had improved on Stewart's prose.

Late in the day, Burger had a rough draft of this amalgamation typed, and took it to Douglas, who now seemed the most reasonable of his colleagues. Douglas was happy with the new section and told the Chief it would win quick approval from the others.

Meanwhile Brennan had gone to dinner and returned to the Court. Having initially expressed fairly strong support for the Chief's privilege section, including the analysis of core functions, he felt guilty now. Perhaps the Chief didn't understand that Stewart's version was a necessary improvement. With his clerk, Brennan had begun writing a detailed letter to the Chief spelling out why Stewart's constitutionally based approach was better.

Fortified by Douglas's support, the Chief walked over to Brennan's chambers about 9 P.M. Burger was in an effusive mood. The last problem surely was solved. He told Brennan he had revised the "C" section and had just shown it to Douglas, who liked it.

Brennan was alarmed. The first vote for a draft was often the most important psychologically. Douglas's vote could make the other six appear to be the holdouts.

The effort of harmonizing the two versions, the Chief said, had been very difficult. Stewart's draft proposal could not be accepted as a substitute because it was so poorly written.

This remark struck Brennan as almost comic, but he decided that the time was ripe to step forward. He preferred Stewart's version, he said, and had just drafted a note explaining why. The core functions argument would not do.

Burger was surprised. *That* has been dropped in the new harmonized version, he said.

What was *that?* Brennan asked incredulously.

Core functions was dumped, Burger replied.

But of course, Brennan said, *that* was the dispute.

That, Burger said, was nothing more than "the little word discrepancies" between the two versions.

Brennan was skeptical. He asked to see the latest revision.

Sure, Burger said. They returned to Burger's chambers to get a copy.

Brennan read it quickly. Though still in rough form, the new version made no mention whatsoever of core functions. The whole notion had been jettisoned. Even more intriguing, Brennan thought he recognized whole sections, apparently verbatim, from Stewart's draft.

Though Burger's new version was not perfect, Brennan thought it was acceptable.

Brennan told the Chief he was delighted. If *this* is it, he would go along.

That is my compromise, the Chief said.

Brennan bid him a very pleasant goodnight and walked out. He reread the draft to make sure there were no hidden meanings, and he compared it carefully with Stewart's. He did not want to rush to accept something the others would oppose; it had been, after all, his initial encouragement of the Chief on the core functions argument that had slowed down the efforts to win concessions from Burger.

Brennan went to see Douglas. Was he right? It seemed like a capitulation by the Chief.

Douglas agreed.

Brennan was amazed. There were nine paragraphs in the section, some of them long. Only two, the introductory and least important paragraphs, were from the original. The other seven were from Stewart's draft. More than three quarters of the language was Stewart's. Most importantly, the basis was due process and not core functions. And all four footnotes in the section were Stewart's.

Brennan and Douglas decided that Brennan should phone the others that night. Brennan called Stewart first to tell him of the victory.

Stewart was dubious.

Brennan read every word of that section of the modified draft to Stewart.

If *that* was it, Stewart agreed, the Chief had caved in. Of course, he would join.

Unable to contain his enthusiasm, Brennan phoned White, then Marshall and finally Blackmun. It was a victory both in principle and for their strategy. They all three agreed that they could join if it turned out to be final.

Brennan could not reach Powell by telephone, but he conveyed the outcome of the calls to Douglas, who phoned the Chief to suggest a conference the next day in order to ensure that they were all on track.

The Chief agreed. His coalition was building.

By 10 A.M. the next morning, Tuesday, July 23, the Chief had formally circulated his revised section C as seven double-spaced pages.

Brennan read over Burger's cover memo. "As I view this revised Section 'C,' it does not differ in substance from the original circulation." Incredible, Brennan thought. Was it a face-saving rationalization, or did the Chief not comprehend what had been forced on him?

* * *

The Chief followed with a memo saying there would be a conference at 1:30. At 1:25, the conference bell rang. The tension was more pronounced than ever. Various pieces of the opinion draft had been okayed, but this was really their first look at the whole. It was now virtually impossible to trace the turns and twists the opinion had taken: ideas articulated by Douglas and Powell, modified by Brennan, quickly sketched by the Chief; a section substituted by White; a footnote dropped for Marshall; Blackmun's facts embroidered over the Chief's; Stewart's constant tinkering and his ultimatum. Still hanging over them all was the possibility that the President of the United States might ignore them.

Since the printed draft was not yet ready, they sat down and made sure that each had a complete typed draft. They discussed a few minor changes. All seemed to agree that they could join the Chief's opinion.

The eight Justices were exhausted. Summer was slipping away. As they proceeded, the tensions were replaced by a slightly self-conscious notetaking, as if they were preparing for some further drafts.

Douglas, just back from Goose Prairie, suddenly spoke up from his end of the table. There were too many changes that he had not seen or approved. The opinion had drifted in too many directions. Many elements were not derived from their original conference discussion, or from the Chief's initial work. If all these changes were left in, Douglas said, he would file a separate opinion, a concurrence.

Brennan felt helpless. It had been settled, but now, as in hundreds of cases over the years, Douglas was going to do his own thing. Before Brennan could say anything, Powell said that he too was considering a separate opinion. Through many small subtle changes, the Chief's opinion had shifted from the middle course he thought they had agreed upon. The notion of deference to presidential confidentiality, and the need for a higher standard to be applied for subpoenas to an incumbent President, had not been given real consideration in the opinion. They were ruling that any grand jury could subpoena material from the President in a criminal investigation. That was too sweeping. They could, and they should, rule more narrowly, fitting the circumstances to this unique case. Their job was, in part, to ensure that the presidency and the chief executive's decision making were protected from unwarranted intrusions. This opinion failed to do so.

The room erupted. The tentative unanimity that had prevailed only a few minutes before had evaporated.

White was sitting quietly for the moment, but Brennan thought he would probably be next. A separate opinion by Powell would likely touch him off and compel him to respond.

Brennan made an impassioned plea for unanimity. Everyone had problems with the opinion, he said. He too had problems. But it was a compromise document and it was essential both to the Court and to the nation. They might not be able to imagine what was at stake in this case, nor could they predict the consequences of their action. The Court must speak with one voice. He turned to Powell and Douglas. The opinion is fine, he pleaded. Please let it go, he beseeched them.

* * *

As Powell listened to Brennan's appeal, he could see that, like the others, Brennan was overwrought and frantic. Brennan spoke with a tremor in his voice. He was not expressing an ordinary argument, but a conviction. Powell had a nearly inflexible rule: If at all possible, never let a separate opinion or concurrence jeopardize personal relations. Brennan might be right. The need for one voice possibly outweighed the need to precisely state and limit the opinion. Certainly it was not an outrageous opinion. The corporate product was bland enough; and it would not be an embarrassment. Powell might have fought Brennan alone, but Brennan had support. Most significantly he had the Chief's.

Okay, Powell said, he would go along. He withdrew his threat graciously. He would accede to the majority.

Douglas also backed off, and the room itself seemed to cool.

* * *

The next morning, July 24, the Court convened at 11 A.M. Rehnquist was not present. Once on the bench, the Chief took a few moments to pay tribute to Earl Warren, since there had been no meeting of the Court since his death two weeks before. Then Burger announced the case and began reading a summary of its major points in his best, most forceful voice. A silent, unanimous Court sat on either side of him.

* * *

In San Clemente, California, President Nixon picked up his bedside phone. His Chief of Staff, Alexander M. Haig, told him that the Supreme Court decision had just come down. Nixon had seriously contemplated not complying if he lost, or merely turning over excerpts of the tapes or edited transcripts. He had counted on there being some exception for national-security matters, and at least one dissent. He had hoped there would be some "air" in the opinion.

"Unanimous?" Nixon guessed.

"Unanimous," Haig said. "There is no air in it at all."

"None at all?" Nixon asked.

"It's tight as a drum." *

After a few hours spent complaining to his aides about the Court and the Justices, Nixon decided that he had no choice but to comply.

Seventeen days later, he resigned.

* See *RN: The Memoirs of Richard Nix-on, pp. 1051–52.*

Chapter Five

THE ROLES OF THE PARTICIPANTS

The Supreme Court is more than a collection of nine justices. It is an institution, a bureaucracy. The Court has an extensive support staff, its own cafeteria and police force, a printing shop, and a basketball court (which is located directly above the courtroom where the justices hear oral arguments and, hence, is the highest court in the land).

In this chapter we consider the roles of certain people or offices that are closely connected to the Court's substantive decisional processes. Section A reviews the office of the Chief Justice, focusing principally on what sets the Chief Justice apart from the others, formally termed the "Associate Justices." Section B presents materials on the justices' law clerks, explaining who they are and what they do. Section C describes the advocates before the Court. We break these readings into three topics: (1) the general quality of advocacy before the Court; (2) the special roles played by the Solicitor General, the federal government's advocate before the Court; and (3) the use of the amicus curiae (literally translated as "friend of the court") brief by partisans seeking to influence the Court's rulings in particular areas.

A. THE CHIEF JUSTICE

Historians have adopted the convention of designating periods of the Supreme Court's history by the name of the person who served as Chief Justice at the time. Thus, we have witnessed the "Taft Court," the "Warren Era," and the "Burger Court." Is this manner of reference simply convenient, or does it reflect an important insight? What, except the title, is special about being Chief Justice?

The initial articles in this section do two things simultaneously. First, they acquaint us with the character and methods of our more recent Chief Justices, from Hughes through Rehnquist. The reader will gain a fairly rich historical overview of the Court and its Chief Justices during the past sixty years through these materials.

Additionally, the readings review and explain what we know about the two unique features of the Chief Justice's office that clearly affect the decisional process. These are the Chief Justice's responsibilities to preside at conferences and to determine who will write the Court's opinion in cases in which the Chief Justice is in the majority.

The opinion assignment role, in particular, may be quite powerful. Can the Chief Justice influence colleagues' votes by rewarding them with plum assignments? What assignments might constitute such plums? What factors have Chief Justices usually employed in assigning opinions? How might research to date on these questions be improved?

The final article in this section examines the recent tendency of Congress to place more and more administrative responsibilities on the Chief Justice.[1] Consider whether this is a wise trend and, if not, what might be done about it. Does the federal judiciary need a figurehead, a "legal chancellor," to take on some of the administrative and ceremonial tasks that now burden the Court (and especially its Chief Justice)?

Putting all these materials together, one should consider such over-arching questions as precisely what makes the position of Chief Justice distinctive? Should a President, in nominating someone to serve as Chief Justice, use criteria different from those employed in selecting an Associate Justice? Such large questions might lead to somewhat more refined issues, such as why does the President designate who shall serve as Chief Justice? Could the justices take on this task themselves? Why does the position not go by seniority or rotate among the entire Court for specified terms? Could Congress limit the number of years any justice may serve as Chief Justice? Should it?

ALPHEUS T. MASON,* THE CHIEF JUSTICE OF THE UNITED STATES: PRIMUS INTER PARES**
17 J.Pub.L. 20 (1968)

President Washington offered John Jay whatever place in the new government he might prefer. Jay's choice of the Chief Justiceship apparently confirmed the President's belief that the judiciary would be "the keystone of our political fabric." In the long view, Washington's expectations have not been disappointed.

Popular interest in the Supreme Court centers around its titular head, the Chief Justice of the United States. The Court is often referred to by the name of the man who occupies the center chair, implying that he puts his peculiar stamp on the Court's work. The custom continues,

1. This is, in fact, part of a wider trend in which Congress has been giving more administrative, non-judicial tasks to the federal judiciary. See, e.g., Morrison v. Olson, 487 U.S. 654, 108 S.Ct. 2597, 101 L.Ed.2d 569 (1988) (judicial appointment of certain federal prosecutors); Mistretta v. United States, 488 U.S. 361, 109 S.Ct. 647, 102 L.Ed.2d 714 (1989) (U.S. Sentencing Commission located in judicial branch, al-though composed of both judges and non-judicial personnel).

* McCormick Professor of Jurisprudence, Princeton University.

** Excerpts from *The Chief Justice of the United States: Primus Inter Pares,* by Alpheus T. Mason, pp. 20–60. Copyright 1968 by Emory Law Journal, Atlanta, Georgia, reprinted by permission of the publisher.

although Chief Justice Marshall's regime is the only one that clearly sustains it. Chief Justices Waite, Fuller, White and Vinson were overshadowed by one or more eminent colleagues.

Reference is sometimes made to the "Stone" and "Vinson" Courts, but the identification suggests weakness, rather than persuasive command. Though a gifted administrator, Fred Vinson left no distinctive mark on American jurisprudence, while Harlan Fiske Stone suffered from administrative ineptitude. Certain Courts have been called by the name of a President. Chief Justice Chase's tenure was designated "Lincoln's Court"; the court during the years 1941–1946, covering Stone's Chief Justiceship, has been labeled the "Roosevelt Court." But, the label was affixed only to indicate that the President had appointed a majority of the Court's Members. All such labels are of limited usefulness and are often misleading. The times in our history when the Chief Justice epitomized the entire Court, especially at the high level of constitutional doctrine, are the exception rather than the rule.

"[T]here have been great leaders on the bench," Charles Evans Hughes wrote in 1928, "who were not Chief Justices." The center position has been occupied occasionally by jurists of high distinction, but "they gained nothing by virtue of their headship of the Court." Justice Holmes, who served under four Chief Justices, declared that "the position of Chief Justice differs from that of the other Judges only on the administrative side." "[B]eing Chief Justice of the Supreme Court," Chief Justice Stone remarked, "is a good deal like being Dean of the law school—he has to do the things that the janitor will not do." The Supreme Court, Justice Frankfurter has written, is "an institution in which every man is his own sovereign." During most of our history, the Chief Justice has been *primus inter pares,* the first among equals.

Though James Wilson and John Rutledge unblushingly appealed to President Washington for appointment to the position, the Chief Justiceship had relatively little prestige before John Marshall. Such distinction as it first enjoyed was diluted by the attitude of early incumbents toward it. John Jay resigned the Chief Justiceship for the governorship of New York; Associate Justice William Cushing, suffering from "impaired mental faculties," refused President Washington's offer of promotion to it. Jay was adamant in 1800 when President Adams begged him to return to his old station and thus save the country from President-elect Jefferson's "visionary schemes and fluctuating theories." "I left the Bench," Jay wrote Adams, "perfectly convinced that under a system so defective it would not obtain the energy, weight, and dignity which was essential to its affording due support to the national government; nor acquire the public confidence and respect which, as the last resort of the justice of the nation, it should possess."

Even after Marshall and Taney had raised the office to the most distinguished judicial position in the world, Chief Justice Chase declared:

> The extent of the power of the Chief Justice is vastly misconceived. In the Supreme Court he is but one of eight judges, each of whom

has the same powers as himself. His judgment has no more weight, and his vote no more importance, than those of any of his brethren. He presides, and a good deal of extra labor is thrown upon him. That's all.

* * *

By the end of the [nineteenth] century, despite the blemish Chief Justice Taney's Dred Scott ruling inflicted, the office still enjoyed prestige considered worth preserving. Chief Justice Fuller declined to accept President Cleveland's offer of Secretary of State. The Chief Justice told the President, that "surrender of the highest judicial office in the world for a political position, even though so eminent, would tend to detract from the dignity and weight of the tribunal. We cannot afford this." Like his father Alphonso Taft, William Howard Taft prized the office even beyond that of President. "To be Chief Justice," Alphonso Taft wrote in 1864, "is more than to be President." On two occasions prior to his election to the Presidency in 1908, William Howard Taft refused to accept offers of a place on the Court as Associate Justice. After four years in the White House he still wanted to be Chief Justice of the United States. When, in 1921, his life-long ambition was finally realized, he considered it a step up, not only because the Court is "the most powerful instrumentality in carrying into execution the written will of the sovereign people," but also because he had been "less than four per cent of the Presidents" and "more than eleven per cent of the Chief Justices."

* * *

Taft made clear to President-elect Harding "that now under the circumstances of having been President and having appointed three of the present bench and three others and having protested against Brandeis, I could not accept any place but the Chief Justiceship."

Charles Evans Hughes, at 68, accepted President Hoover's offer of the Chief Justiceship, though this meant ending the career of his son as Solicitor General.

Ambitious for the Chief Justiceship, Robert H. Jackson was twice almost in possession of it. When one or more of his colleagues intervened to prevent it, Associate Justice Jackson, then Chief Prosecutor at the Nuremberg Trials, precipitated one of the ugliest feuds in judicial history. "It is," Jackson commented, "the most sought after, the longest living office." "[S]ince Marshall's time," Justice Frankfurter observed, "only a madman, a certified madman, would resign the Chief Justiceship to become governor [as John Jay did] * * *."

The Chief Justice has only one power comparable in explicitness to certain of those of the President. Article I, section 3, declares that "[w]hen the President of the United States is impeached the Chief Justice shall preside." Exercised only once in nearly two centuries, this special function has proved to be of relatively small importance. In playing roles, large and small, not formally designated by the Constitution, the Chief Justice exerts influence unmatched by that of any of his colleagues. * * * Certain of the functions he discharges as head of his Court and of the federal judicial system belong to him alone. He is the Court's chief administrative officer; he presides over the secret conferences of the Justices and in open Court. He is Chairman of the Judicial Conference of the United States. He administers the oath of office to the President and speaks in the Court's behalf to other organs of government. He announces its orders. * * * As sole spokesman for the federal judiciary, his opportunities for influencing Congress, the President, and the public are incalculable, limited only by his desire and capacity to avail himself of them.

The opinion assigning function offers almost boundless possibilities for the Chief Justice to exert his influence. He can use it to advance his own prestige, taking the plums for himself, leaving the dry, inconsequential cases to his colleagues. The Chief Justice may exercise it so as to exploit the special talents of his Associate Justices, or use it in such a way as to develop specialties they do not already possess. He can use the opinion assigning function to give added weight to a particular decision, or to enhance his own public image. In a controversial case, he can use the assignment power to promote harmony by selecting a writer other than the obvious spokesman of the Court's divergent wings, or add to judicial asperities by singling out the previously vehement dissenter to voice the view now held by a majority. He may pick the man "who will write in the narrowest possible way * * * [or] * * * take the chance of putting a few seeds in the earth for future flowering." Responsibility for these choices rests solely with the Chief Justice. The use he makes of them will not only affect the dispatch of judicial business but may vitally influence the course of law and history.

Without thought of possible consequences, Chief Justice Stone selected Justice Frankfurter as the Court's spokesman in *Smith v. Allwright,* the decision which outlawed the white primary in the face of a comparatively recent precedent. Certain Justices had misgivings, and Justice Jackson spelled these out to the Chief Justice in persuasive detail.

> I hope you will forgive me for intruding into the matter of assignments, the difficulties of which I feel you generally resolve with wisdom and always with fairness, but I wonder if you have not overlooked some of the ugly factors in our national life which go to the wisdom of having Mr. Justice Frankfurter act as the voice of this Court in the matter of *Smith v. Allwright.* It is a delicate matter. We must reverse a recent, well-considered, and unanimous decision. We deny the entire South the right to a white primary, which is one of its most cherished rights. It seems to me very important that the strength which an all but unanimous decision would have may be greatly weakened if the voice that utters it is one that may grate on Southern sensibilities. Mr. Justice Frankfurter unites in a rare degree factors which unhappily excite prejudice. In the first place, he is a Jew. In the second place, he is from New England, the seat

of the abolition movement. In the third place, he has not been thought of as a person particularly sympathetic with the Democratic party in the past. I know that every one of these things is a consideration that to you is distasteful and they are things which I mention only with the greatest reluctance and frank fear of being misunderstood. I have told Mr. Justice Frankfurter that in my opinion it is best for this Court and for him that he should not be its spokesman in this matter and that I intend to bring my view of it to your attention. With all humility I suggest that the Court's decision, bound to arouse bitter resentment, will be much less apt to stir ugly reactions if the news that the white primary is dead, is broken to it, if possible, by a Southerner who has been a Democrat and is not a member of one of the minorities which stir prejudices kindred to those against the Negro.

I have talked with some of them [the other Justices] who are still in the building, and they feel as I do.

I rely on the good understanding which I have always felt existed between us and upon our mutual anxiety for the welfare and prestige of the Court to excuse my intrusion in a matter which, having spoken my piece, is solely for your judgment.

Stone retreated at once, withdrawing the case from Frankfurter and reassigning it to Reed.

Even before the assignment stage of a case is reached, the Chief Justice has opportunities to make his influence felt. He presents the case in conference and selects the lines along which it may be argued. "You can see," Frankfurter writes,

the important function that rests with the Chief Justice in determining who should be spokesman of the Court in expressing the decision reached, because the manner in which a case is stated, the grounds on which a decision is rested—one ground rather than another, or on one ground rather than two grounds—how much is said and how it is said, what kind of phrasing will give least trouble in the future in a system of law in which as far as possible you are to decide the concrete issue and not embarrass the future too much—all these things matter a great deal. The deployment of his judicial force by the Chief Justice is his single most influential function.

The way in which the Court does its work, the customary reliance on precedent, the large part that may be played by discussion, debate and compromise at every stage of the judicial process, impose on the Chief Justice responsibilities and opportunities not shared by his colleagues. Of the Chief Justice's strategic position, Justice Frankfurter has written:

An important thing in the work of a Chief Justice which distinguishes his from other members of the Court, is that he is the presiding officer, and has guidance of the business of the Court in his hands. It isn't what he says in his opinions that is more important than what his brethren say, but what he advises on the mechanics of doing the job—should we give a lawyer extra time, should we hear this case now or later, should we grant a rehearing if the Court is divided; things that pertain to the way that the business should be done, things that cannot properly be managed without knowledge of the nature of the business, or, since you deal with eight other human beings, without knowledge of the ways of the other eight Justices.   * * *

Essential to the Chief Justice's leadership, along with command of administrative detail, is familiarity with technical matters of procedure and jurisdiction.   On this score, Hughes stands pre-eminent.   Taft, on the other hand, confessed his inadequacy, and relied on Justice Van Devanter's knowledge of the authorities, procedure and practice, all necessary for keeping the Court consistent with itself.

A task no Chief Justice can delegate is the role of moderator, the job of guiding and directing.   By smoothing troubled waters, the Chief Justice may prevent the Conference from degenerating into a row. Fuller did this with marked success.   So did Taft.   So does the present Chief Justice.   "His friendliness, obvious decency, and personality," a former Warren law clerk writes, "brought a coherence heretofore lacking in the Court."   Stone, on the other hand, suffered not only from an inability to master the routine details of life and work, but also as a moderator.   Outspoken himself, he would "descend to theatre, fight with the gladiators, needle one phalanx or the other * * *."

Justice Frankfurter vividly described Hughes at Conference, surrounded by a mound of thick volumes, all flagged at points likely to arouse controversy.   When a colleague raised a question, the Chief Justice's confident reach for the volume containing the answer was calculated to discourage interruption.   By employing the methods of a military commander, Hughes made the Chief Justiceship a symbol of efficiency—"the very model of the master of his craft and office."   In Conference, as in open Court, discussion was rationed, "lasting six hours," Justice Brandeis recalled, "and the Chief Justice did all the speaking."   John W. Davis reports that "[A]t the close of the hour allotted for oral argument he would cut off counsel in the middle of the word 'if' * * *."

Hughes succeeded in getting the jump on the brethren by his quickness in selecting the issue.   Rarely did anyone speak out of turn. For him, Frankfurter recalled, "the Conference was not a debating society but a place where nine men do solos."   If difference of opinion disclosed itself between two liberal members of the Court, the Chief Justice would put "his big toe in and widen the cleavage."   When differences threatened to produce dissents or concurrences, the Chief Justice would blow his whiskers straight out and say, "Brethren, the only way to settle this is to vote."

Once, at a Saturday Conference, Stone asked permission to read an opinion he had not had time to print and circulate, expecting full discussion, followed by the Chief Justice's recommendation that the case go over a week. Not so; when Stone finished reading, Hughes commented: "Very powerful memorandum. Case goes down on Monday."

Stone's Chief Justiceship furnishes sharp contrasts to that of Hughes. After the first Conference, Justice Frankfurter mixed feelings of relief with words of caution: "I should like to say to you how much I enjoyed the relaxed atmosphere and your evident desire to have our Conference an exchange of responsible views of nine men, led by a considerate moderator, and so I am full of happy days ahead." "Of course I understand," Frankfurter went on, "that you did not want to pull at the reins with our brethren their first day in harness. But the deviations from the tradition of speaking out of turn only prove to me overwhelmingly how important that tradition is for the wise and effective conduct of the Court's business."

Believing profoundly in freedom of expression for others no less than for himself, Stone would not budge. The Saturday Conferences usually dragged on into the middle of the following week. Efficiency, in the narrow sense, suffered. But there were compensations. "Long before I came down here," Frankfurter observed, "I thought that Chief Justice Hughes was unduly emphasizing keeping the dockets clear as against the quality of the clearing." "Any Justice who kicks about the amount of time given to conference," Justice Jackson commented, "ought to resign." "Whatever the ultimate verdict," Justice Douglas wrote, "those who stand at close range know that the Court as an institution grew in stature under the influence of Harlan Fiske Stone."

After exploring the differing methods of Hughes and Stone, Professor Walter Gellhorn is not convinced of the superiority sometimes accorded the former.

> * * * I am shocked by the decisional process in the Supreme Court of the United States as it proceeded under Hughes. The judges heard arguments throughout the week on cases that had been for the most part carefully selected as the sort of cases that required the judgment of our highest Court. Few of the judges made any extensive notes about the cases they had heard; few of them made any careful study of the records or briefs of the cited authorities before they went to conference. Then in the space of four hours the Court decided not only the cases that it had heard, but also voted on the pending petitions for certiorari, jurisdictional statements, and other materials on the docket. This meant that the discussion in conference was perforce a statement of conclusions more than an exchange of mutually stimulating ideas. Some of the apparent unanimity in the Hughes Court derived, in my estimation, from the superficiality of the discussion which glossed over rather than illuminated difficulties in the path. If judging is as important a governmental task as we lawyers assert it to be, I am not at all inclined to say that extended conferences about the matters being judged should be viewed as a deficiency in a Court * * *. Hughes

used to believe in the appearance of unanimity regardless of the reality. As a consequence of his policy, opinions were often published without the actual but with the apparent concurrence of the brethren. Hughes himself often switched his own vote in order to give a larger measure of apparent support to an opinion with which he did not in fact agree. I am dubious that this sort of intellectual flexibility is a sign of better judging than would be a more candid reflection of division when division exists.

The use a Chief Justice makes of his office depends in part on his concept of it, and on his determination to use it to accomplish results he considers desirable. William Howard Taft entertained a truly magisterial conception of the Chief Justiceship. Under him the Chief Justice was more than *primus inter pares.* * * * Enamored of "the executive principle" and the need for "teamwork," and frowning on dissent unless "absolutely necessary," he set out to maximize the limited powers of the Chief Justice in a way that contrasts sharply with his failure to exercise the actual powers of the Presidency. * * *

Taft brought to the Court a clear image of the Chief Justiceship— the office and its powers. Motivating his tenure was a passion for "teamwork"; it alone would give "weight and solidarity" to judicial decisions. "Massing the Court" was a consuming ambition. To this end, he persuaded by example, discouraged dissents, exploited personal courtesy and charm, maximized the assignment and reassignment powers and relied on the expertise of his Associate Justices.

Under Chief Justice Taft's leadership, a firmly united judicial majority envisioned itself in the van of national progress. The laissez-faire dogma, glorified in the writings of Herbert Spencer and William Graham Sumner, was the principal avenue to wealth and social happiness. Taft believed that courts were society's assurance that the sober second thought of the community would prevail. Viewing the Supreme Court as the last bastion against "Bolsheviks," "Socialists" and "progressives," he was determined to head it. Thanks to the judiciary, "[t]he leviathan, the people," he declared, "cannot * * * be given a momentum that will carry them in their earnestness and just indignation beyond the median and wise line." "The Constitution was intended, [and] its very purpose was to prevent experimentation with the fundamental rights of the individual."

Soon after his appointment, the Chief Justice announced at Conference that he had "been appointed to reverse a few decisions," and with his famous chuckle, "I looked right at old man Holmes when I said it." To this end, Taft exerted influence on the White House to win appointment of those he favored, and to discourage selection of any "off-horse" whose mind might not go along with his own.

During the early years of his regime, Taft's success was remarkable. Wielding power far beyond that represented by his vote, Taft appears to have taken even Brandeis into his camp. Disappointing former President Wilson's hopes that Justices Clark and Brandeis would "restrain the Court in some measure from the extreme reactionary course," Clark resigned, explaining that "Justice Brandeis and I were agreeing less and less frequently in the decision of cases involving what we call * * * liberal principles."

As a judicial architect, Taft is without a peer. * * * On his own initiative, the tenth Chief Justice pressed for revisions in the judicial organization and administration. To his credit is the Act of September 14, 1922, establishing the judicial conference, the Judges Bill of 1925, giving the Justices considerable control over their docket, and the palatial Supreme Court Building. It may be that only one man, Senator Thomas J. Walsh, aided by sympathetic colleagues, kept Taft from winning the revised federal rules of procedure.

Taft's successor, former Associate Justice Charles Evans Hughes, singled out and deplored trends Chief Justice Taft had long combatted. * * * Hughes furnishes us this clue in his book on the Supreme Court, published two years before his appointment to the Chief Justiceship:

> The existence of the function of the Supreme Court is a constant monition to Congress. A judicial, as distinguished from a mere political, solution of the questions arising from time to time has its advantages in a more philosophical and uniform exposition of constitutional principles than would otherwise be probable. Moreover, the expansion of the country has vastly increased the volume of legislative measures and there is severe pressure toward an undue centralization. In Congress, theories of State autonomy, strongly held so far as profession goes, may easily yield to the demands of interests seeking Federal support. Many of our citizens in their zeal for particular measures have little regard for any of the limitations of Federal authority. We have entered upon an era of regulation with a great variety of legislative proposals, constantly multiplying governmental contacts with the activities of industry and trade. These proposals raise more frequently than in the past questions of National, as opposed to State, power. If our dual system with its recognition of local authority in local concerns is worth maintaining, judicial review is likely to be of increasing value.

Anticipated was the impasse between Court and Congress in the crucial term, 1935–1936, when the New Deal floundered on the shoals of constitutionality.

* * *

Some of the fiercest battles in American constitutional history feature the President and the Chief Justice as antagonists—Jefferson and Marshall, Lincoln and Taney, Roosevelt and Hughes. But none is so dramatic or revealing as the drawn-out contest between the New Deal President and Charles Evans Hughes. * * *

The major antagonists during the first quarter of the nineteenth century, as in the nineteen thirties, were the Chief Justice and the President. The burden of Jefferson's complaint was national supremacy; of Roosevelt's judicial supremacy. Marshall used the judicial forum to enlarge national power. Hughes joined in judicial decisions that defeated the power to govern. * * *

Both Marshall and Hughes proved more than a match for their politically resourceful antagonists. The contemporary significance of *Marbury v. Madison,* declaring for the first time an Act of Congress unconstitutional, is the stern lecture Chief Justice Marshall gave President Jefferson and Secretary of State Madison concerning the proper discharge of official duties. Similarly, in the Gold Clause cases, Chief Justice Hughes lectured President Roosevelt, expressing shock at the Government's repudiation of its promise to liquidate Liberty Bonds in gold. Though knowing, as did Marshall in *Marbury,* that the moral imperatives he espoused were unenforceable, Hughes solemnly declared that "The United States are as much bound by their contracts as are individuals." In the eyes of their critics, both Marshall and Hughes were addicted to the habit, as Jefferson said, "of going out of the question before them, to throw an anchor ahead and grapple further hold for future advances of power." * * *

As judicial strategists, Marshall and Hughes were astute. Just as Federalist Chief Justice Marshall scored in his encounters with Democratic–Republican President Jefferson, so Republican Chief Justice Hughes was more than a match for Democratic President Roosevelt, the most astute politician of modern times. Certain observers thought the outcome in the Court-packing struggle was due, not to the merits of the issue, but to Chief Justice Hughes' superior skill as a political strategist. "Chief Justice Hughes," Harold Ickes recorded, "played a bad hand perfectly while we [the President and his advisers] have played a good hand badly." To defeat the President's plan, the Justices retreated. Roosevelt never doubted that his own "clear-cut victory on the bench" did more than anything else to bring about defeat of the plan in the halls of Congress.

Hughes' political victory in 1937 is comparable to that Marshall scored over Jefferson in 1803. Marshall's triumph was recognized by his contemporaries and credited in the perspective of history. No such accolade has yet been accorded Hughes. It seems odd that Hughes' admirers and apologists should be at great pains to note other similarities between the two Chief Justices, yet reluctant to portray their hero in the role that most closely resembles Marshall—that of political strategist. After the dust of battle had settled, Professor Frankfurter made this appraisal: "I learnt from Holmes that White C.J., had his ear to the ground, and Marshall was not without guile, nor was Taney naive—but no doubt the present Chief will be accorded the highest rank for cunning."

* * *

The qualities that make for greatness in a judge are no sure index of success as Chief Justice. Only two Associate Justices in our history, Edward Douglass White and Harlan Fiske Stone, have been promoted.

In neither case did elevation add cubits to their respective statures as jurists. Stone appears to have lost, rather than gained. President Lincoln, believing that appointment of the Chief Justice from within the Court would stir political rivalries, had refused to follow this course. President Grant accepted Lincoln's reasoning. In 1910, President Taft, breaching a century-old tradition, elevated Associate Justice White, a Democrat. President Roosevelt promoted Justice Stone, a Republican. In 1949 retired Justice Roberts, with fresh examples in mind of bitter rivalry among the Justices for promotion to the center chair, said, "as a matter of personal belief, I do not think an associate justice ought to be eligible to be Chief Justice * * *."

* * * A Chief Justice with little or no claim to distinction as a jurist, who brings to his task no judicial experience, may make his mark. * * * Morrison R. Waite came to the Chief Justiceship a relatively obscure lawyer, without judicial or other public experience, except a short stint as presiding officer in the Ohio State Constitutional Convention. Wanting to be helpful, Justice Clifford suggested that he preside until the new Chief Justice caught on to the ropes. Profoundly aware of his own shortcomings, Waite though troubled, was not offended. "Those fellows up there," he told Benjamin Rush Cowen, "want to treat me as an interloper." Waite solicited Cowen's advice. "I would go up there tomorrow," Cowen declared firmly, "get on the box, gather up the reins and drive; and give them to understand that I was Chief Justice." Waite listened without comment. The next day he returned to Cowen's office in very good humor. The advice had been carried out; it worked "splendidly, splendidly! * * * [I] am going to drive and those gentlemen know it."

Chief Justice Fuller, a man of diminutive stature, faced a Court made of intellectual and physical giants, two of them—Harlan and Matthews—were over six feet tall; two others—Gray and Bradley—were intellectuals; all were confident, self-assured personalities. Fuller, who came to the Court without public experience of any sort, was so short, five and one-half feet, that while sitting on the bench he had to use a hassock to keep his feet from dangling. At first his towering colleagues regarded him with doubt and suspicion. However, self-effacing courtesy, unimpeachable integrity, a strong sense of fairness and disarming humor made Melville W. Fuller one of the most successful presiding officers in the Court's history. Justice Holmes accorded him high praise. Fuller "had the business of the Court at his finger ends"; he was perfectly courageous, prompt, decided and able to turn off "matters that daily called for action easily, swiftly, with the least possible friction, with inestimable good humor and with a humor that relieved tension."

In the end, a Chief Justice's "actual influence will depend upon the strength of his character and the demonstration of his ability in the intimate relations of Judges." It will also depend on his conception of the office, and on the role he thinks the Court should occupy in the American structure of government. John Marshall, a robust nationalist, pursued a systematic course, using every opportunity to anchor national power in authoritative judicial decisions. * * *

Roger Brooke Taney had at least one thing in common with his distinguished predecessor. Like Marshall, he moved against the dominant political trend. Confronted with the abolitionist movement and national action designed to destroy slavery, Taney interposed constitutional roadblocks and finally brought down on his head a storm of protest. The Court became the focus of fierce controversy, the Chief Justice being featured as the villain in the plot.

* * *

Marshall and Taney demonstrated that, in the hands of one having the will and the capacity to exercise it, the office of Chief Justice affords opportunity to determine the course of history unequaled by that of any other, save the Presidency. John Quincy Adams credited John Marshall with giving "a permanent and systematic character to decisions of the Court," cementing "the Union which the crafty and quixotic democracy of Jefferson had a perpetual tendency to dissolve." The office of Chief Justice, Adams explained, is more important than that of the President

> because the power of constructing the law is almost equivalent to the power of enacting it. The office of Chief Justice of the Supreme Court is held for life, that of the President of the United States only for four, or at most for eight, years. The office of Chief Justice requires a mind of energy sufficient to influence generally the minds of a majority of his associates; to accommodate his judgment to theirs, or theirs to his own; a judgment also capable of abiding the test of time and of giving satisfaction to the public.

* * * Of all major governmental officials, none can compare in length of service with our Chief Justices. "Presidents come and go," Taft remarked in 1916, "but the Court goes on forever." It may be significant that two of our greatest judicial heads served a total of sixty-three years, Marshall from 1801 to 1834, Taney, from 1835 to 1864. * * * The Chief Justice's tenure being for life, it is not surprising that none of our Presidents, not even Franklin D. Roosevelt, matched the service records of Marshall, Taney, Waite and Fuller. Four Chief Justices—Chase, White, Taft and Hughes—exceeded or equaled the usual Presidential term of eight years. * * *

We have had fourteen Chief Justices and thirty-six Presidents. Aside from President Washington, who appointed three (Jay, Rutledge and Ellsworth), no President has named more than one Chief Justice. John Adams appointed John Marshall to combat Democratic–Republicanism. Andrew Jackson selected his former Attorney General and close adviser, Roger Brooke Taney. With full knowledge of Salmon P. Chase's deep conviction that "rebellion could not be crushed with one hand while slavery was protected with the other," Lincoln appointed his political opponent Chief Justice. Grant, after two attempts to fill the office, turned to obscure Morrison R. Waite. Those close to the administration accepted him "with a sense of relief but no enthusiasm." Cleveland surprised the legal profession and the country by choosing his unknown and untried friend, Melville W. Fuller. Taft, looking ahead, perhaps, to possible fulfillment of his own ambition, passed over Charles Evans Hughes, age 48, and, for the first time in history, promoted an Associate Justice, sixty-five-year-old Edward Douglass White. President Hoover, conscious of the Republican party's debt to Charles Evans Hughes, and apparently wary of Justice Stone's "liberal tendencies," called the former Associate Justice from a lucrative Wall Street law practice to head the Court. Franklin D. Roosevelt, convinced that his action would contribute to national unity in the trying war years ahead, promoted Associate Justice Harlan Fiske Stone, a Republican. Truman, desirous of quelling unseemly bickerings within the Court, called on easy-going Fred Vinson to serve as peacemaker. President Truman tells an incredible story concerning the considerations that moved him to appoint Fred Vinson Chief Justice of the United States. The President did it on the advice of former Chief Justice Hughes and Justice Roberts. Both told him: "You don't need to look any further. The Chief Justice is administrator. He's administrator of the courts; he's got to be a man who can make the Court get along together, and everybody likes. You've got the man in your cabinet"—Fred Vinson. Eisenhower, breaking what became his unbroken policy of appointing to the Supreme bench only those having previous judicial experience, honored Thomas E. Dewey's 1948 running mate, Earl Warren.

* * *

No one function, nor all combined suffice to explain the office and power of the Chief Justice. Besides the functions themselves, the incumbent's influence depends on the use he makes of them and the manner in which they are discharged. Beyond all this is the human factor, the intangibles, the personality—the moral energy the man at the center releases. One may say of the office of Chief Justice of the United States what Woodrow Wilson said of the Presidency: his office "is anything he has the sagacity and force to make it." The Chief Justice, like the President, "is entitled to be as big a man as he can."

DAVID O'BRIEN, STORM CENTER: THE SUPREME COURT IN AMERICAN POLITICS *
(3rd Ed.) 306–314 (1993)

OPINION ASSIGNMENT

The power of opinion assignment is perhaps a chief justice's "single most influential function" and, as Tom Clark has emphasized, an exercise in "judicial-political discretion." By tradition, when the chief justice is in the majority, he assigns the Court's opinion. If the chief justice

* Reprinted from STORM CENTER, The Supreme Court in American Politics, Third Edition, by David M. O'Brien, by permission of the author and W. W. Norton & Company, Inc. Copyright © 1993, 1990, 1986 by David M. O'Brien.

did not vote with the majority, then the senior associate justice who was in the majority either writes the opinion or assigns it to another.

* * * In unanimous decisions and landmark cases, the chief justice often self-assigns the Court's opinion. "The great cases are written," Justice John Clarke observed, "as they should be, by the Chief Justice." But chief justices differ. Fuller, even against the advice of other justices, frequently "gave away" important cases; Taft, by contrast, retained 34 percent, Hughes 28 percent, and Stone 11 percent of "the important cases." Various considerations may lie behind a chief justice's self-assignment, such as how much time he has already invested in a case and how he finally decides to vote. Warren explained his self-assignments in two cases as follows:

> Because I prepared a memorandum in No. 15—*Yellin v. United States*—before our Conference discussion, I thought it would be advisable for me to assign the case to myself.

> You will recall that when we discussed No. 24—*Halliburton Oil Well Cementing Co. v. Reily*—I did not vote because I was uncertain as to what my decision would be, and Justice Black assigned the case further, I have decided to vote to reverse. I am, therefore, reassigning the case to myself.

Chief justices approach opinion assignment differently. Hughes tended to write most of the Court's opinions and was "notoriously inclined to keep the 'plums' for himself." Between 1930 and 1938, Hughes wrote an average of twenty-one opinions for the Court, while other justices averaged only sixteen each term. * * * Like Hughes, Stone tended to take more of the opinions for himself. He averaged about nineteen, whereas other justices each wrote only about fifteen opinions for the Court every term.

The inequities in opinion assignments by Hughes and Stone angered some justices. When Vinson became chief justice, he strove to distribute opinions more equitably. * * * On a large chart, he kept track of the opinions assigned, when they were completed, and which remained outstanding. Vinson was remarkably successful in achieving parity in opinion assignments. All justices on the Vinson Court averaged about ten opinions for the Court every term. Warren followed that practice and achieved the same result. Warren "was the Super Chief," in Brennan's view, and "bent over backwards in assigning opinions to assure that each Justice, including himself, wrote approximately the same number of Court opinions and received a fair share of the more desirable opinions. Burger likewise paid attention to equity in opinion writing, but tended to write slightly more opinions for the Court each term than the other justices. During his years as chief justice (1969–1986), Burger averaged 15.3 opinions for the Court each term, whereas the other justices averaged 13.9 opinions. By comparison, in his first three years as chief justice, Rehnquist appeared to strive for an even more equal distribution of the workload: he averaged 15.6 opinions for the Court, while other members averaged 15.3 opinions per term.

Parity in opinion assignment now generally prevails. But the practice of immediately assigning opinions after conference, as Hughes did, or within a day or two, as Stone did, was gradually abandoned by the end of Vinson's tenure as chief justice. Following Warren and Burger, Rehnquist assigns opinions after each two-week session of oral arguments and conferences. With more assignments to make at any given time, they thus acquired greater flexibility in distributing the workload. Chief justices also enhanced their own opportunities for influencing the final outcome of cases through their assignment of opinions.

Assignment of opinions is complicated in controversial cases. Occasionally, a justice assigned to write an opinion discovers that it "just won't write," and it must then be reassigned. Reassignment of opinions occurs infrequently. In the 1964 and 1973 terms, from 1 to 3 percent of the cases were reassigned. This was due to sharp divisions among the justices. When the Court first tackled the controversy over televising criminal trials, in *Estes v. Texas* (1965), for example, the justices were deeply split. Stewart's initial draft failed to command a majority. He was relegated to writing a dissenting opinion, joined by three others. Clark wrote the Court's final opinion, holding that the cameras in the courtroom were too disruptive and denied the defendant's right to a fair trial. Later, when the Burger Court reexamined the constitutionality of the death penalty in *Gregg v. Georgia* (1976), White found that "his approach to the capital cases may no longer command a majority." He accordingly gave *Gregg* and its companion cases back for reassignment. After holding a conference in early May to "clear the air," Burger reassigned the opinions to Stewart, who wrote the Court's opinion upholding capital punishment.

Sometimes justices switch votes after an opinion has been assigned, and thus necessitate reassignment. The "cases of the Murdering Wives," as Frankfurter referred to them, illustrate the consequences of switching votes and the effect of changes in the Court's composition. Both cases, *Reid v. Covert* (1956) and *Kinsella v. Krueger* (1956), involved women who had allegedly killed their husbands stationed abroad in the military. They raised the issue of the constitutionality of subjecting civilians living abroad with military personnel to courts-martial under the Uniform Code of Military Justice, which does not extend the same guarantees as those in the Bill of Rights for criminal trials. Warren initially assigned the opinions, but Stanley Reed changed his vote. The decision went the other way, and the opinion was reassigned to Clark. He held that the women could be tried under military law. In the next year, though, Sherman Minton retired and William Brennan took his place on the bench. The Court reconsidered the issue in *Reid v. Covert* (1957) and reversed its earlier decision. This time the Court enforced the protections of the Bill of Rights.

The justice assigned to write an opinion for the Court occasionally decides that the case should go the other way. Taft once assigned himself an opinion, but wrote it reversing the vote taken at conference. He explained to his brethren, "I think we made a mistake in this case and have written the opinion the other way. Hope you will agree."

Rather dramatically in the course of writing an opinion for a bare majority in *Garcia v. San Antonio Metropolitan Transit Authority* (1985), Justice Blackmun changed his mind and wrote the opinion so as to reach the opposite result. Instead of extending an earlier controversial five-to-four ruling handed down by Rehnquist in *National League of Cities v. Usery* (1976), Blackmun wrote his *Garcia* opinion the other way and expressly overturned *Usery*. Rehnquist's opinion in *Usery* was divisive because the Court had not limited Congress's power under the commerce clause since striking down much of the early New Deal legislation, which precipitated the "constitutional crisis" of 1937. Yet Rehnquist had managed to persuade Blackmun, along with three others, to strike down Congress's setting of minimum wage and maximum hour standards for all state, county, and municipal employees under the Fair Labor Standards Act. He did so on a novel reading of the Tenth Amendment guarantee that powers not delegated to the federal government "are reserved to the States" and by claiming that the Court should defend states' sovereignty against federal intrusions on their "traditional" and "integral" state activities. The justices remained sharply divided on Rehnquist's position in *Usery*. Finally, when assigned *Garcia*, Blackmun was to write an opinion striking down the extension of federal wage and overtime standards to municipal transit workers. But he changed his mind about the wisdom of Rehnquist's earlier opinion and attempt to draw a line between "traditional" and "nontraditional" state activities in limiting congressional power. So he wrote his *Garcia* opinion in line with the views of the four dissenters in *Usery,* upholding Congress's power and overturning Rehnquist's earlier ruling.*

Dramatic instances of vote switching and opinion reassignment, however, are rare. Changes in voting alignments usually only increase the size of the majority. * * *

* Notably, seven years later, after four appointees of Reagan and Bush joined the Court and only three justices who made up the majority in *Garcia* remained on the bench, the Court again reconsidered *Usery* and *Garcia*. At issue in *New York v. United States* (1992) was the constitutionality of Congress's imposing in 1985 a deadline for each state to provide disposal sites for all low-level radioactive waste generated within its borders by 1996. New York authorities contended that Congress had infringed on states' rights under the Tenth Amendment, but an appellate court rejected that argument on the basis of the ruling in *Garcia*. On appeal, moreover, the Rehn-quist Court declined to reconsider and overrule *Garcia*. While strongly defending federalism in her opinion for the Court, Justice O'Connor tried to set that controversy aside. In a narrowly drawn opinion, O'Connor upheld all of the requirements imposed on the states by Congress except for a provision requiring states that failed to provide for radioactive waste disposal sites by 1996 to take title of and assume all liability for wastes generated and not disposed within their jurisdictions. That requirement intruded on states' sovereignty, O'Connor claimed, though dissenting Justices Blackmun, Stevens, and White sharply disagreed.

Since justices may switch their votes and since opinions for the Court require compromise, chief justices may assign opinions on the basis of a "voting paradox" or, as David Danelski has explained, "assign the case to the justice whose views are closest to the dissenters on the ground that his opinion would take a middle approach upon which both majority and minority could agree."

Some chief justices employ the strategy of assigning opinions to pivotal justices more than others do. Hughes, Vinson, and Warren tended to favor justices likely to hold on to a majority, and perhaps even win over some of the dissenters. Taft and Stone were not so inclined. Assigning opinions to pivotal justices presents a chief justice with additional opportunities for influencing the Court's final ruling. Because votes are always tentative, a chief justice may vote with a majority and assign the case to a marginal justice, but later switch his vote or even write a dissenting opinion.

Chief justices may take other factors into account in assigning opinions. What kind of reaction a case is likely to engender may be important. Hughes apparently took this into account when giving Frankfurter the first flag-salute case, *Minersville School District v. Gobitis* (1940) because he was a Jewish immigrant. There the Court, with only Stone dissenting, denied the Jehovah's Witnesses' claim that requiring schoolchildren to salute the American flag at the start of classes violates the First Amendment. But three years later, in a second case, the Court reversed itself. In *West Virginia Board of Education v. Barnette* (1943), the Court held that the First Amendment guarantee of freedom of religion prohibits states from compelling schoolchildren to recite the pledge of allegiance to the flag.

Hughes was also inclined to give "liberal" opinions to "conservative" justices in order to defuse opposition to rulings striking down early New Deal legislation. Later, when the Court decided the Texas *White Primary* case, *Smith v. Allwright* (1944), ruling that blacks may not be excluded from voting in state primary elections, Stone assigned the Court's opinion to Frankfurter. But Jackson immediately expressed his concerns about the assignment. Frankfurter was a Vienna-born Jew, raised in New England, and a former professor at the elite Harvard Law School. Stone and Frankfurter were persuaded of the wisdom of reassigning the opinion to Reed, a native-born Protestant from Kentucky, long associated with the Democratic party. The justices thought that they might thereby diminish some of the opposition in the South to the ruling.

A number of other cases illustrate that public relations may enter into a chief justice's calculations. The leading civil libertarian on the Court, Hugo Black, wrote the opinion in *Korematsu v. United States* (1944), upholding the constitutionality of the relocation of Japanese–Americans during World War II. A former attorney general experienced in law enforcement, Tom Clark, wrote the opinion in the landmark exclusionary rule case, *Mapp v. Ohio* (1961), holding that evidence obtained in violation of the Fourth Amendment's requirements for a reasonable search and seizure may not be used against criminal suspects at trial. And a former counsel for the Mayo Clinic, experienced in the law of medicine, Harry Blackmun, was assigned the abortion case *Roe v. Wade* (1973).

These examples also suggest that chief justices may look for expertise in particular areas of law. Taney gave Peter Daniel a large number of land, title, and equity cases, but few involving constitutional matters. Taft was especially apt to assign opinions on the basis of expertise: John Clarke and Joseph McKenna wrote patent cases; Louis Brandeis, tax and rate opinions; and James McReynolds was "the boss on Admiralty," while Willis Van Devanter and George Sutherland, both from "out West," were given land and Indian disputes. Burger tended to give First Amendment cases to Byron White and Potter Stewart and those involving federalism to Lewis Powell or William Rehnquist, depending on the size of the conference vote. By contrast, Warren expressly disapproved of specialization. He thought that it both discouraged collective decision making and might make a "specialist" defensive when challenged. Yet Brennan wrote the watershed opinions on the First Amendment and became a kind of custodian of obscenity cases during the Warren Court.

The power of opinion assignment invites resentment and lobbying by the other members of the Court. Justice Frank Murphy, for instance, was known within the Court to delegate his opinion writing largely to his clerks. Neither Stone nor Vinson had much confidence in his work. Accordingly, he received few opinions in important cases from either chief justice. Murphy once complained to Vinson, when tendering back his "sole assignment to date": "I have done my best to write an opinion acceptable to the majority who voted as I did at the conference. I have failed in this task and a majority has now voted the other way." Only when Murphy's ideological ally, Hugo Black, as the senior associate, assigned opinions did he receive major cases.

"During all the years," Warren claimed, "I never had any of the Justices urge me to give them opinions to write, nor did I have anyone object to any opinion that I assigned to him or anyone else." Warren's experience was exceptional, but he also often conferred with other justices before making his assignments. Black and Douglas, for instance, urged Warren to assign Brennan the landmark case on reapportionment, *Baker v. Carr* (1962). They did so because Brennan's views were closest to those of Stewart, the crucial fifth vote, and his draft would be most likely to command a majority. Most chief justices find themselves lobbied, to a greater or lesser degree, when they assign opinions.

* * *

G. EDWARD WHITE, EARL WARREN: A PUBLIC LIFE *
159–171, 188–190 (1982)

The Crucible of Brown v. Board of Education

Of all the journeys made by Earl Warren during his public career, that from the governorship of California to the Supreme Court of the United States was the most wrenching. There was, first of all, Warren's realization that he was about to occupy a position that must have seemed, for most of his working life, unfathomably remote and munificent. A Bakersfield iceman's delivery boy, Ezra Decoto's assistant, Culbert Olson's frustrated attorney general, and Thomas Dewey's spear carrier was becoming Chief Justice of the United States.

There was, in addition, the stark contrast between the office Warren was relinquishing and the office he was about to occupy. The Supreme Court sat in Washington, a city with which he was not familiar; its members engaged in tasks that he had apparently not performed before; the Court personified a professional world in which he had not immersed himself for ten years and with whose uppermost echelons he was barely familiar. On becoming attorney general and governor he had brought along his own staff to smooth the transition: In October, 1953 he was alone, not even, after his induction, accompanied by Nina, who returned to California to supervise the move east.

* * *

The characteristic caution with which Warren approached new experiences surfaced as he assumed the office of Chief Justice. He asked Hugo Black, the senior associate justice, to "manage a few of the conferences until I could familiarize myself with proceedings." He observed as the rest of the Court disposed of certiorari petitions that had been filed over the summer, taking no part in the deliberations. He assigned himself a case "of no notoriety" for his first opinion, interpreting the Federal Longshoremen's and Harbor Workers' Compensation Act for the benefit of workers whose job-incurred injuries had not been adequately reported. * * *

Within a few months, however, Warren's presence as Chief Justice emerged rapidly and decisively. This development was striking, because Warren was not able, as Chief Justice, to make the typical changes in an office he had made as a California public official. While he retained a keen interest in such administrative matters as the Court's docket, the schedule of arguments and conferences, and the internal workings of the Court's permanent staff, he could not replace older, incompatible justices with new ones more aware of his executive style, as he had done with personnel in California. He could not cultivate the press; judges did not hold press conferences. He had no powers of the purse, being beholden

---

to Congress for appropriations, no ability to expand his personal staff, few perquisites of office.

Warren's position as Chief Justice gave him no formal powers that his associates lacked, only informal opportunities to exercise leadership. He had no experience in being a judge; he had given little attention to the principal work of the Court, deciding complicated issues of constitutional law. He had no reputation as a legal scholar; he was expected to be a conciliatory, "middle-of-the-road" chief, overshadowed by such influential associates as Hugo Black, William O. Douglas, Felix Frankfurter, and Robert Jackson.

Despite these obstacles, and the relatively low expectations of performance that accompanied Warren's appointment, he soon became a formidable presence on the Court. The most important feature of Earl Warren's chief justiceship, in fact, was his presence. By the time of his retirement Warren was ranked with John Marshall, Roger Taney, and Charles Evans Hughes as the most influential Chief Justices in the history of the Supreme Court. This ranking was all the more surprising because, unlike those other occupants of the chief justiceship, Warren was not regarded as a judge possessing considerable intellectual talents or conspicuous analytical abilities. He was regarded as one of the great Chief Justices in American history because of the intangible but undeniable impact of his presence on the Court.

The episode that enabled Warren to establish his presence on the Supreme Court was the decision in the five segregation cases, which were handed down under the name of the Kansas case, *Brown v. Board of Education,* on May 17, 1954. The segregation cases, which had been set down for reargument in June, 1953, were reargued in December of that year, after Warren had become Chief Justice, and voted upon in March, 1954. Warren's opinion for the Court was approved by all the justices on May 15. The story of Warren's role in the *Brown* case is now a familiar one; my interest here is in examining *Brown* as a means by which Warren established his personal imprint on his new office and as a formative experience in his career as a judge.

Warren had been neither an outspoken supporter nor a vocal opponent of segregation during his California career. * * * At the time he came to consider the *Brown* decision in 1953, Warren's views on race relations seem to have been relatively undeveloped, as were his views on many other issues he would be facing as a judge.

 The Court, meanwhile, was deeply split on the *Brown* case, as revealed by its inner history in the 1952 term. Four justices—Black, Harold Burton, Douglas, and Sherman Minton—had in that term declared themselves personally opposed to racial segregation and in favor of overruling *Plessy v. Ferguson,* the Court's 1896 precedent maintaining that "separate but equal" racially segregated public facilities did not violate the Fourteenth Amendment's Equal Protection Clause. Three justices—Tom Clark, Stanley Reed, and Chief Justice Fred Vinson— favored retaining *Plessy,* with varying degrees of enthusiasm, and two justices—Frankfurter and Jackson—were hard-pressed to find an adequate rationale for overruling *Plessy,* although personally unsympathetic to enforced racial segregation.

In response to repeated prodding by Frankfurter, the Court finally resolved to put the *Brown* case over for rehearing in the 1953 term. * * * The major purpose of the reargument was to give the justices more time to congeal their positions on the segregation cases. Frankfurter and Jackson, especially, were fearful that an opinion that invalidated segregation but did so in a strident or unreasoned fashion would do greater harm than the continuance of the practice.

Those supporting reargument had not anticipated, of course, that Chief Justice Vinson would die of a heart attack in September, and that the man who replaced him would take a different position toward the segregation cases. From the beginning Warren saw *Brown* as a comparatively simple case. He felt that Stone and Vinson Court precedents had crippled the separate but equal doctrine. He believed that "separate but equal" systems rarely resulted in comparable educational facilities for whites and blacks and thought that such a showing would be comparatively easy to make. He also believed, despite his ambivalent experience with racism in California, that the injustice of an enforced separation of human beings based on their color was apparent. Unlike Vinson, who worried about Congress's reluctance to change segregated practices, the entrenched practices of segregation in the South, and the longstanding existence of the *Plessy* principle, Warren was mainly concerned with the problem of how a decision to eradicate segregation in the public schools could be effectively implemented.

Warren's forging of a unanimous majority for the *Brown* decision established his presence on the Court. The task was one especially suited to his skills: It involved convincing others of the necessity for an arm of government to act decisively and affirmatively where a moral issue was at stake. The eradication of segregation, in his mind, was comparable to the establishment of compulsory health insurance. Both were responses to an injustice; both sought to prevent humans from being disadvantaged through no fault of their own. A difference between the two responses was that Warren the judge did not need to rely upon another branch of government to make the response for him, as Warren the governor had had to rely upon the California legislature. But Warren the judge faced two problems of comparable difficulty. He needed to convince persons affected by the Court's response that they should accept it, and he needed to enlist support for his position on the segregation cases within the Court itself.

In the *Brown* case the fortuity of Warren's being appointed to the chief justiceship rather than to an associate justiceship first assumed significance. The protocol of the Court is based on seniority: The Court's most junior member states his views last in conference debate and has no power to assign opinions for authorship. But the Chief Justice is treated differently: He is ranked first in protocol and in formal privileges notwithstanding his seniority. Thus, new associate justices tend to receive insignificant opinions their first term, but not necessarily new Chief Justices, since the Chief Justice assigns opinions when he is in the majority. It would have been inconceivable for Warren to have written the opinion in *Brown v. Board of Education* if he had been an associate justice. Moreover, associate justices have no control over the internal management of cases: when they are argued, discussed in conference, and so on. That administrative task is reserved for the chief. Warren could not have carried out his strategy for bringing about a unanimous decision on the *Brown* case had he been an associate justice.

In addition, despite the convention that the Chief Justice has only one vote among nine justices and thus has no more power than any other justice, a Chief Justice has opportunities to exercise leadership not possessed by associate justices. * * * A person, such as Warren, who was accustomed to chairing meetings, managing agendas, and assigning office tasks, might find that the chief justiceship gave him ample opportunities to exercise power and to make his presence felt. If some of the tasks of a Chief Justice can be likened to those of a chairman of a small group called on regularly to make decisions, those were tasks that Warren had performed for much of his public life.

During the oral reargument of *Brown,* which took place in October, 1953, Warren remained largely silent, in keeping with the low profile of his first months as chief. He then delayed putting *Brown* on the conference agenda for two months, and by December 12, 1953, when the first Court conference on *Brown* was held, he was ready to declare his views. He began by stating that in his judgment one could not sustain *Plessy* unless one granted the premise that blacks were inferior to whites. He did not grant that premise, and consequently he was prepared to invalidate segregation and to insure equal treatment of all children in the public schools. But while he had no doubts about the principle of *Brown,* he had not resolved how it was to be implemented, and he suggested that the Court take some time and care in the framing of a decree, being sensitive, especially, to conditions in the Deep South. He suggested that no vote on the segregation cases be taken that day, but that the case be "talk[ed] over, from week to week * * * in groups, over lunches, in conferences."

With this statement Warren communicated three messages to his colleagues. The first was that if there had been any doubt as to whether the Court would invalidate *Plessy,* that doubt was foreclosed. At least five justices would so vote, Warren being the fifth. The second was that Warren viewed the segregation cases as separable into two components: the framing of an opinion overruling or emasculating *Plessy* and the framing of a decree implementing the Court's decision. Warren's preliminary strategy on the segregation cases was, according to Justice Burton, to "direct discussion towards the decree—as probably the best chance of unanimity." In this strategy he had the enthusiastic support of Felix Frankfurter, who had resolved to work behind the scenes for a decision invalidating segregation and may have suggested the strategy to Warren.

Warren's remarks communicated one other message. The message was that those on the Court who remained prepared to defend the "separate but equal" doctrine would have to confront Warren's assertion that segregation and the idea that blacks were inferior to whites were intimately linked. Without labeling defenders of the *Plessy* decision white supremacists, he conveyed that association. This was a familiar Warren technique, the argument to induce shame. Opponents of Warren in California had repeatedly had their positions labeled immoral, unethical, or unjust by Warren, and found that they were forced to defend themselves against such alleged polarizations of their views. Warren continued this practice in his oral questioning of counsel in arguments before the Supreme Court. In cases, for example, where the police from a given state had allegedly intimidated a person suspected of committing a crime, Warren would occasionally ask the lawyer arguing the case for the state why he "had treated [the suspect] this way." The lawyer, of course, had not participated in the alleged intimidation and perhaps had not even met the state law enforcement officers whose conduct was being scrutinized. Warren, however, identified him with the practices and asked him to justify them.

Within a short time after Warren's remarks in conference, two additional justices on the Court revealed themselves as now prepared to support a majority opinion invalidating segregation. Clark, whom others in the 1952 term had thought to oppose a reversal of *Plessy*, identified himself in the December conference as prepared to declare segregation unconstitutional, although he remained concerned about the mechanics of implementation. Frankfurter, who a year earlier had suggested that nothing in the Fourteenth Amendment prevented racial segregation in the states, now made an ambiguous statement in conference that stopped short of committing himself to any majority opinion but indicated that he favored overruling *Plessy*, and followed his remarks with a memorandum to the justices supporting Warren's position.

* * *

Warren next let the segregation cases simmer among his colleagues. On January 15, 1954, the day that Frankfurter circulated his memorandum on the cases, Warren scheduled a luncheon at which the cases were discussed. Throughout January and February the justices continued to discuss the case informally, all save Frankfurter and Jackson meeting regularly for lunch. In late February or March a formal vote was taken. Eight justices voted to invalidate segregation; Reed voted to uphold it. Of the eight, Jackson had indicated that he would probably write a concurrence and had, as early as February 15, drafted a memorandum that was to be its basis. Warren assigned the majority opinion to himself and began to work on it in early April.

The Court had by now agreed on the strategy of separating its response to the cases into an opinion, which would invalidate segregation on principle, and a decree, which would implement the decision. The justices had also agreed to delay formulation of the decree another year, so that affected states could be invited to participate in its framing the following term. The hand of Frankfurter was visible here: His January memorandum had contained the phrase "all deliberate speed," which was later to be pivotal in the decree, and the Court had endorsed his and Warren's belief that implementation should be gradual and mindful of local conditions. Warren had only two hurdles left—the achievement of unanimity, including the suppression of concurrences, and the production of an opinion that was, as he put it, "non-rhetorical, unemotional, and, above all, non-accusatory."

In securing the first of these goals Warren was aided, it appears, by Jackson's heart attack on March 30, which left Jackson hospitalized and was to lead to his death. Warren produced an opinion on May 7, which shortly secured the consent of all the justices except Jackson and Reed. On May 10 Warren visited Jackson in the hospital and delivered his draft opinion. Jackson, whose condition had prevented him from working on any cases and who was therefore disinclined to develop his February memorandum into a concurrence, resolved to join the majority, making only minor suggestions. While Warren's opinion satisfied Jackson in its moderate tone and its absence of pretense, Jackson might well have written separately had he been in full health.

Meanwhile, Warren had a conversation with Reed between the seventh and the twelfth of May. One of Reed's law clerks, who was present at the conversation, reported that Warren said, "Stan, you're all by yourself in this now. You've got to decide whether it's really the best thing for the country." The issues for Reed, Warren suggested, were issues of conscience and of the effect of a southern justice's dissent on a matter so pivotal to the South. Reed eventually capitulated. Formal unanimity was secured on May 15, with Warren making another visit to Jackson on that day. The decision in the segregation cases was announced on May 17, with Jackson leaving the hospital to appear in the courtroom with the rest of the justices.

* * *

The plan of separating the opinion from the decree may have been Frankfurter's; the decision to reargue the case and avoid the deadlock forming on the Vinson Court was prompted by Frankfurter.

But the step-by-step process of converting recalcitrant justices to the majority position was formulated and carried out by Warren. Warren made the decision not to take a formal vote but to meet in informal lunches and conversations; Warren produced a draft opinion that won the consent of his colleagues without major alterations; Warren convinced Jackson and Reed of the importance of a unanimous opinion; Warren took special pains to conceal the decision from all but the participating justices until the moment it was announced. No justice on the Warren Court that had witnessed the new Chief Justice's handling of the segregation cases could fail to sense his presence. James Reston, in a March, 1954 column, reported that other justices had found in the new chief "a sensible, friendly manner," a "self-command and natural dignity," a "capacity to do his homework," and "an ability to concentrate on the concrete."

The *Brown* case, however, was more than an episode that conveyed to other justices the fact that Earl Warren was a person to be reckoned with. It was also a catalyst in helping Warren crystallize his thinking about the new office he held. There were two dimensions to *Brown,* and the case was susceptible to two different jurisprudential interpretations. One dimension of *Brown* was its short-range politics. Viewed from this perspective, it was a moderate, compromising decision, delaying action on its implementation, confining its impact to the public schools, avoiding emotional language or the stigmatization of segregationists, inviting representatives of the states to participate in the formulation of a forthcoming decree. * * *

Another dimension of *Brown,* however, was its meaning as a philosophical statement. This dimension became apparent in the Court's treatment of racial segregation cases after *Brown,* in which segregation in other public facilities was summarily declared unconstitutional by unanimous per curiam opinions that cited *Brown.* As a philosophical statement—that racial segregation in public facilities was inherently unfair and unjust, whatever the context—*Brown* became an example of the use of the Constitution by the Supreme Court to compel action by other branches of government. The states and Congress (which had permitted segregation in the District of Columbia) were told by the Warren Court in *Brown* and its progeny that many of their existing practices were illegal, that they had to change those practices, and that if they did not, the Court would support those persons—whom everyone understood to be hitherto disadvantaged blacks—who pressed for change. Seen from this perspective, *Brown* ushered in a new role for the Supreme Court in the twentieth century, that of an active enforcer of fairness and justice as embodied in the Constitution.

The feature of *Brown* that most clearly identified the emergence of the Court in this new role was the absence of conventional constitutional analysis in the *Brown* opinion. Warren's opinion for the Court invalidated segregation as a violation of the Equal Protection Clause not through any analysis of the historical meaning of that clause (the history was dismissed as inconclusive) or through a close analysis of precedents in the race relations area (they were treated summarily). Warren's opinion invalidated segregation on the basis of two findings. First, he found that "today" education was "perhaps the most important function of state and local governments," and that the Equal Protection Clause consequently required that "the opportunity of an education * * * be made available to all on equal terms."

Second, he found that "[racially] separate educational facilities [were] inherently unequal," because "segregation of white and colored children in public schools has a detrimental effect on the colored children," being "interpreted as denoting the inferiority of the negro group." The basis for Warren's first finding was his own conviction of the importance of education; the basis for his second finding was social science literature of the 1940s and fifties on racial prejudice and its effects. The opinion in *Brown,* in short, declared racial segregation unconstitutional through appeal to contemporary social perceptions rather than to constitutional doctrine.

The ideal behind *Brown*—the intuitive justice of equality of opportunity—was an ideal not explicitly codified in the Constitution. The force of the case was in the decisive, almost summary fashion with which Warren's opinion announced the Court's dedication to that ideal in the race relations area. When coupled with the per curiams after *Brown,* the decision conveyed a jurisprudential message: The Warren Court, at least in race relations cases, was going to fuse constitutional interpretation with a search for justice, reading constitutional language in a way that could make the Constitution harmonize with current perceptions of what justice required. And if the Court's readings compelled a change in the practices of other branches of government, the Court was not going to avoid insisting on that change merely because those branches were purportedly more democratic in composition than it.

In *Brown,* then, can be seen the seeds of an activist support for "liberal" policies, such as equality of opportunity, that was to constitute an important theme of the Warren Court. The *Brown* decision was a classic manifestation of mid-twentieth-century liberal theory in its effort, through the affirmation of principles such as equality of opportunity, to fuse the idea of affirmative, paternalistic governmental action with the idea of protection for civil rights and civil liberties. * * *

The two dimensions of *Brown* had suggested two possible roles for Warren the Chief Justice. One was as temporizer and compromiser, avoiding open confrontations on politically sensitive issues, burying internal differences beneath a hard-won statement of unanimity. Another was as activist promoter of the cause of justice, particularly justice for those who had been denied equal opportunities in American life. Both roles were consistent with Warren's California experience. He had been measured in his rhetoric and careful in the timing of his actions as a California public official; he had chosen, for the most part, not to polarize issues and to justify his decisions on the basis of propositions that had widespread public support. On the other hand he had been continually interested in having his offices take decisive action on issues, and he had not been deterred by the reluctance of other governmental institutions to be comparably activist. Warren had functioned, in California, as both the artfully "moderate" politician and the determinedly activist officeholder.

As Chief Justice of the United States, Warren was eventually to discard the role of temporizing politician for the role of activist judge. The subsequent course of his tenure revealed *Brown* to have been the seedbed of his activism. The momentum of the Court's mission in *Brown*, which came to be seen by Warren as a mission to vindicate ethical principles that were embodied in the Constitution, even if this meant dramatically expanding the Court's jurisdictional reach and power, eventually grew to the point where *Brown* now appears as the case where the Warren Court's ultimate character was first revealed.

* * *

As Warren began to move away from the cautious posture of his first years on the Court he became inclined to trust his instincts, to emphasize the significance of getting "good" results as a judge. He came to see Frankfurter's purported subordination of personal preferences to a theory of judicial restraint as regularly resulting in decisions that were obfuscated by a flood of academic language, or unnecessarily self-conscious, or sometimes simply misguided. * * *

Underneath Warren's hearty, pleasant persona, then, his peers on the Court confronted a Chief Justice who had confidence in his intuitive reactions, who had formed his own judgments about his peers, separating those he saw as potential supporters from those who appeared to be antagonists, who was used to getting his own way, and who was not afraid to speak his mind. They also confronted a Chief Justice willing to compromise on matters he regarded as relatively insignificant—technical language in a given opinion—to prevail on matters he thought important, such as decent and just results. This was the same Earl Warren contemporaries had confronted as governor, attorney general, and district attorney. If there was a continual discrepancy between Warren's persona and his composite personality, the discrepancy remained constant over time.

* * *

This posture—impatience with obstructionist doctrine when justice called out to be done—was to become identified with Earl Warren's chief justiceship; it was to serve as a powerful alternative jurisprudence to that of Frankfurter. Most of Warren's energy on the Court was directed toward achieving the "right" results. He did not often agonize, as did Frankfurter, over an outcome in a case, nor did he despair of finding an adequate constitutional basis for justifying his intuitions, nor did he worry about being overly activist. He spent his time on discerning results that seemed just and on marshaling support for those results by attempting to convince others of their inherent justice. * * *

BERNARD SCHWARTZ, THE ASCENT OF PRAGMATISM: THE BURGER COURT IN ACTION *

1–15 (1990)

Chief Justice Burger and His Court

"Don't let them push you around." Chief Justice Burger once told me this was the principal advice given him by his predecessor, Earl Warren. But the leadership role of a Chief Justice depends more on his abilities than his position, and in the Supreme Court it is difficult for a Chief Justice to assert a *formal* leadership role. Aside from his designation as Chief of the Court and his slightly higher salary, the Chief Justice is not superior to his colleagues—and certainly is not legally superior.

The Justices themselves have always been sensitive to claims of Chief Justice superiority. As Justice Tom C. Clark said, "The Chief Justice has no more authority than other members of the court." And Justice Felix Frankfurter wrote "that any encouragement in a Chief Justice that he is the boss * * * must be rigorously resisted * * *. I, for my part, will discharge what I regard as a post of trusteeship, not least in keeping the Chief Justice in his place * * *."

The Chief Justiceship should not, however, be approached only in a formalistic sense. The greatest Chief Justices have known how to make the most of the extralegal potential inherent in their position. The Chief Justice may be only *primus inter pares;* but he is *primus.* Somebody has to preside, both in open court and in the even more important work of deciding cases in the conference chamber. The Chief Justice controls the discussion in conference; his is the prerogative to call and discuss cases before the other Justices speak. A great Chief Justice leads the Court with all the authority, all the *bravura,* of a great maestro.

Yet even a strong Chief Justice is limited. The Supreme Court is a collegiate institution, which is underscored by the custom of the Justices calling each other "Brethren." The Justices can only be guided, not directed. As Frankfurter stated, "Good feeling in the Court, as in a family, is produced by accommodation, not by authority—whether the authority of a parent or a vote."

* * *

In many ways, the individual Justices operate like "nine separate law firms." Justice Stewart told me that even Chief Justice Warren "came to realize very early * * * that this group of nine rather prima donnaish people could not be led, could not be told, in the way the Governor of California can tell a subordinate, do this or do that."

* * *

* Excerpts from *The Ascent of Pragmatism,* © 1990 by Bernard Schwartz. Reprinted with permission of Addison–Wesley Publishing Company.

BURGER ON OLYMPUS

Earl Warren brought more authority to the position of Chief Justice than had been the case for years, and the Warren Court bore his image as unmistakably as the earlier Courts of John Marshall and Roger B. Taney. The high bench was emphatically the *Warren* Court, and he and the country knew it.

This was plainly not as true under Warren E. Burger. The Burger tenure was not marked by strong leadership in molding Supreme Court jurisprudence.

Burger himself was cast from a different mold than Warren. Although, as a reporter pointed out, his "white maned, broad-shouldered presence on the bench is very reminiscent of his predecessor's," the men beneath the dignified exteriors were completely dissimilar. Burger's background was mostly in a law firm in St. Paul. He had nothing like the spectacular career and broad experience in politics of Warren, although he had been active in the Republican party. He worked in Harold E. Stassen's successful campaign for governor, and in 1952 he was Stassen's floor manager at the Republican convention when Minnesota's switch supplied the necessary votes for Eisenhower's nomination.

After the election, Burger was appointed assistant attorney general in charge of the Claims Division of the Department of Justice. * * *

In 1956, Burger was named to the U.S. Court of Appeals in Washington, D.C., where he developed a reputation as a conservative, particularly in criminal cases. He was sworn in as Chief Justice in June 1969 and headed the Court until 1986.

Burger's critics contend that he stood too much on the dignity of his office and was aloof and unfeeling. Intimates stress his courtesy and kindness and assert that the office, not the man, may have made for a different impression. "The Chief," says Justice Blackmun, who grew up with him, "has a great heart in him, and he's a very fine human being when you get to know him, when the tensions are off. One has to remember, too, that he's under strain almost constantly."

Burger, not a person to develop intimate relations with colleagues, was as close to his law clerks as to anyone. And law clerks, in particular, speak of him with affection. One of them worked all day doing research for a conference that evening. She brought her work to the Chief Justice's home after 6:00 P.M. He asked her if she had eaten. "That's not important," she replied. "The main thing is to finish before the conference." At this Burger said, "You can't work if you don't eat." He brought in tomatoes from his garden and made her a sandwich. Later, just before the conference, Burger said, "You see, we finished on time."

Every Saturday at noon, Burger made soup in his tiny office kitchen for his clerks. Then Burger would sit and talk with them informally for hours, usually with colorful reminiscences about his career. The one rule was that no one could talk about the cases currently before the Court.

Another clerk recalls how one day Burger decided to eat in the Court cafeteria and after a few moments found himself posing for pictures with tourists and their children. "He seemed entirely comfortable, just like a politician, even though he never got his lunch."

Others picture the Chief Justice as a petty pedant, not up to the demands of his position and most concerned with minor details and the formal dignity of his office. Burger himself undertook the redecoration of the Supreme Court cafeteria and personally helped choose the glassware and china. He also redesigned the Court bench, changing it from a traditional straight bench to a "winged," or half-hexagon shape.

Burger was dismayed to find that his Supreme Court office was smaller than the one he had had at the court of appeals. Next door was the elegant conference room, which could serve admirably as a ceremonial office for the Court head. Burger did not go so far as to take over the conference room; instead, he placed an old desk in the room and moved the conference table to one side. Thus the conference room also became the Chief Justice's reception room.

Burger's use of the conference room irritated the others. Justice Hugo L. Black's wife noted in her diary that she was told "that C.J. Burger had decided to take the *Conference* Room for *his office!* Funny thing. Isn't that a kick! Hugo says he will not quarrel with him about such an insignificant matter but John Harlan called from Connecticut and was red-hot about it."

Burger was also criticized for his treatment of those who disagreed with him. Lewis Powell at one time cast a critical fifth vote in an emotional criminal case. Burger tried hard to get Powell to change his vote, and, after resisting weeks of pressure, Powell told another Justice: "I'm resigned to writing nothing but Indian affairs cases for the rest of my life." Or as Justice Blackmun said, "If one's in the doghouse with the Chief, he gets the crud."

Yet Burger himself could wryly refer to his reputation in this respect. During one term, the Chief Justice had had a number of disagreements with John Paul Stevens. One of the Court secretaries was taking a course in cake decorating, and each week she brought in the fancy cake she had baked. At the end of the course, she made a cake in the shape of a bench, with realistic figures of the Justices. There was a chocolate Thurgood Marshall and a Stevens with bow tie and glasses. It was decided that the cake should be sent up to the Justices, but the clerks had eaten the Stevens figure. When the cake was brought in, the Chief Justice turned to Stevens and declared with mock solemnity, "You see what happens when you disagree with me!"

* * *

Burger was always sensitive to what he perceived to be slights to his office and to himself; throughout his tenure he had an almost adversarial relationship with the press. According to one reporter, "He fostered an atmosphere of secrecy around the court that left some employees terrified of being caught chatting with us." When a network asked permission to carry live radio coverage of the arguments in what promised to be a landmark case, the Chief Justice replied with a one-sentence letter: "It is not possible to arrange for any broadcast of any Supreme Court proceeding." Handwritten at the bottom was a post-script: "When you get the Cabinet meetings on the air, call me!"

Burger was particularly concerned about leaks to the press. He once circulated a memorandum to the conference headed "*CONFIDEN-TIAL* " because a reporter had attempted to interview law clerks. "I have categorically directed," Burger declared, "that none of my staff have any conversation on any subject with any reporter. This directive was really not necessary since this is a condition of employment. I know of no one who is skilled enough to expose himself to any conversation with a reporter without getting into 'forbidden territory.' The reporter will inevitably extract information on the internal mechanisms of the Court, one way or another, to our embarrassment."

The Chief Justice was deeply hurt by derogatory accounts about his performance, particularly in the best seller *The Brethren,* and was gleeful when he told me that copies of the book were remaindered at ninety-eight cents in a Washington bookstore. * * *

Burger's critics often singled out his concern with food and attire. Author Lincoln Caplan quotes Burger as saying "that he himself should be in a wig and gown, and had been cheated out of it by Thomas Jefferson." Early Supreme Court Justices did wear wigs and gowns, but the practice was soon abandoned, in part at least because of Jefferson's opposition. Caplan does state that he "wasn't sure whether [Burger] was being humorous or not."

It cannot be denied that, from his "Middle Temple" cheddar, made according to his own recipe, to the finest clarets, Burger is somewhat of an epicure. One of the social high points of a 1969 British–American conference at Ditchley, Oxfordshire, was the learned discussion about vintage Bordeaux between Burger and Sir George Coldstream, head of the Lord Chancellor's office and overseer of the wine cellar at his Inn of Court. The Chief Justice was particularly proud of his coup in snaring some cases of a rare Lafite in an obscure Washington wine shop.

The effectiveness of a Chief Justice is, of course, not shown by his epicurean tastes. Indeed, the one Justice who was willing to talk to me frankly about Burger's professional performance was most uncompli-mentary.

Burger, according to this Justice, "will assign to someone without letting the rest know, and he has five [votes] before the rest of us see it." The Justice also complained about the Burger conduct of conferences in criminal law cases. "If it's a case in which a warden is the petitioner, the Chief Justice goes on and on until the rest are driven to distraction."

The Chief Justice's votes were based upon his own scale of values, which were different from those that had motivated members of the Warren Court. When he considered a fundamental value to be at stake, Burger could be as stubborn as his predecessor. "Someone," he insisted to a law clerk, "must draw the line in favor of basic values and, even if the vote is eight-to-one, I will do it." * * *

Among the things the Chief Justice felt strongly about was the dignity of the legal profession. * * * In one case, he wrote to the others, "The petitioner's counsel was somewhat above mediocre but the State's case was *miserably* presented." Because of this, the Court should "at least appoint amicus curiae for California and begin our drive to force the States to abandon their on-the-job training of their lawyers in this Court." In a case involving a doctor, he urged that the opinion should contain "a few well chosen (?) comments about the gross fraud perpetrated by this 'quack.' "

* * *

Burger was greatly offended when the Court reversed the conviction of a young man for wearing a jacket emblazoned with the words "Fuck the Draft" in a courthouse. The Chief Justice was particularly upset by the opinion's quoting the offensive four-letter word. He prepared a two-paragraph dissent, ultimately withdrawn, which, according to the covering memo, "is the most restrained utterance I can manage." In the draft dissent, Burger wrote, "I, too, join a word of protest that this Court's limited resources of time should be devoted to such a case as this. It is a measure of a lack of a sense of priorities and with all deference I submit that Mr. Justice Harlan's 'first blush' was the correct reaction. It is nothing short of absurd nonsense that juvenile delinquents and their emotionally unstable outbursts should command the attention of this Court."

Even though the Chief Justice may have felt strongly about them, these were relatively minor matters. On more important concerns Burger came to the Court with an agenda that included a massive dismantling of the jurisprudential edifice erected by the Warren Court, particularly in the field of criminal justice. In large part, Burger owed his elevation to the highest judicial office to his reputation as a tough "law and order" judge. He had commented disparagingly on the Warren Court decisions on the rights of criminal defendants. As Chief Justice, he believed that he now had the opportunity to transform his more restrictive views into positive public law.

Burger expressed opposition during most of his tenure to *Mapp* and *Miranda* —the two landmark criminal procedure decisions of the Warren Court—but he was never able to persuade a majority to cast those cases into constitutional limbo. The same was true of other aspects of Burger's anti-Warren agenda. No important Warren Court decision was overturned by the Burger Court. If Burger hoped that he would be able to undo much of the Warren "constitutional revolution," he was clearly to be disappointed.

Burger was more effective as a court administrator and as a representative of the federal courts before Congress than as a leader and molder of Supreme Court jurisprudence. Looking back at the Warren years, Byron White told me that, as far as relations with Congress were concerned, "Things have changed * * * for the better as far as I can see * * *. Chief Justice Warren did have such a problem with the civil rights thing, and with prayers and reapportionment. Congress was in such a terrible stew that his name was mud [there], which rubbed off on all of us." Under Burger the situation was different. Few Chief Justices have had better relations with Capitol Hill.

As for court administration, Burger played a more active role than any Court head since Chief Justice Taft. His administrative efforts ranged from efforts at fundamental changes, such as his active support of the creation of a new court of appeals to screen cases that the Supreme Court would consider, to attention to such petty details as the shape of the bench.

One must conclude that Burger was miscast in the role of leader of the Court—a harsh but fair description of a man who devoted so much of his life to the bench and worked as hard as he could to improve the judicial system and one who also could be warm and charming in his personal relationships. Yet his personality was, in many ways, contradictory—"at once gracious and petty, unselfish and self-serving, arrogant and insecure, politically shrewd yet stupid and heavy-handed at dealing with people."

Of course it was more than these personality contradictions that damaged Burger's effectiveness as a leader of the Court. A major part of his failure may be attributed to the manner in which he presided at conferences and assigned opinions. But an important factor was his inadequacy as a judge. One who examines the decision process in important cases must reluctantly conclude that Burger was out of his depth. Although the picture in some accounts of his intellectual inadequacy is certainly overdrawn, most of his colleagues could run intellectual rings around the Chief Justice.

Burger's ineffectiveness as a judge was particularly striking in the *Nixon* case. The Chief Justice's draft opinion was so inept that it had to be completely rewritten by the other Justices. The final opinion was described by a Justice as an "opinion by committee," instead of one written by its nominal author.

There was a comparable situation in the last important case decided by the Burger Court—*Bowsher v. Synar*. The Burger draft opinion contained a far more expansive view of presidential power than the other Justices were willing to accept. It was only after the Chief Justice revised his draft in accordance with the Justices' suggestions that the draft could come down as the *Bowsher* opinion.

Similarly, in the *Swann* school-busing case, the Chief Justice's opinion had to be substantially revised before it could come down as the opinion of the Court. His draft was not supported by the law or the rationale behind the decision itself. * * *

CONFERENCES AND ASSIGNING OPINIONS

Traditionally the most important work of the Supreme Court has been done in private, particularly in the conference sessions that take place after cases have been argued. It is in the conference that the Court decides, and the primary role at the conference is exercised by the Chief Justice, who leads the discussion. He starts the conference by discussing the facts and issues involved. He then tells how he would vote. Only after his presentation do the other Justices state their views, in order of descending seniority.

The manner in which he leads the conference is the key to much of a Chief Justice's effectiveness. His presentation fixes the theme for the discussion that follows and, if skillfully done, is a major force in leading to the decision he favors.

The two strongest leaders of the conference during this century were Charles Evans Hughes and Earl Warren. Most students of the Court rank Hughes as the most efficient conference manager in the Court's history. He imposed a tight schedule on case discussions. * * *

If Hughes was the most efficient, Warren may have been the most effective in presiding over the sessions—the "ideal" conference head, Justice Stewart said to me. His forte was his ability to present cases in a manner that set the right tone for discussion. He would state the issues in a deceptively simple way, one stripped of legal technicalities, and, where possible, relate the issues to the ultimate values that concerned him. Opposition based upon traditional legal-type arguments seemed inappropriate, almost pettifoggery. As Justice Fortas once told me, "Opposition based on the hemstitching and embroidery of the law appeared petty in terms of Warren's basic-value approach."

Conference notes show that when Warren sought to lead the Court in a particular direction, he was usually able to do so. Conference notes taken during the Burger tenure do not give the same impression. Burger did not have anything like the Warren ability to state cases succinctly, to lead the discussion along desired lines. Burger was too often turgid and unfocused, with emphasis upon irrelevancies rather than central points. It was said that Burger's discussion of cases at conference left the Justices with the feeling that he was "the least prepared member of the Court." In a comment on Chief Justice William H. Rehnquist, Thurgood Marshall said, "He has no problems, wishy-washy, back and forth. He knows exactly what he wants to do, and that's very important as a chief justice." There is little doubt that Marshall was contrasting the Rehnquist conference approach with Burger's.

More important was Burger's lack of leadership. The conference notes in hundreds of cases reveal how frequently the lead was taken by the Associate Justices—particularly so in the major cases. It was not the Chief Justice who usually played the crucial role in the decision process.

One must also fault him for his use of the power to assign the writing of opinions—aside from managing the conference, the most important function of the Chief Justice. In discharging it, a Chief Justice determines what use will be made of the Court's personnel; the particular decisions he assigns to each Justice in distributing the work load will influence both the growth of the law and his own relations with his colleagues.

The power of the Chief Justice to assign the opinions probably goes back to John Marshall's day. During Marshall's early years, it is probable that he delivered the opinion of the Court even in cases where he dissented. Apparently the practice then was to reserve delivery of the opinion of the Court to the Chief Justice or the senior Associate Justice present on the bench and participating in the decision. But as time went on, other Justices also began to deliver opinions. By Chief Justice Taney's day, the Chief Justice assigned each opinion.

In the early years of opinion assignment by the Chief Justice, he may well have assigned all opinions. It was not very long, however, before the Chief Justice's assigning power was limited to cases where he had voted with the majority.   * * *

Chief Justice Burger did not always follow the established practice. According to an English comment, "Chief Justice Burger would sometimes vote against his instincts in order to preserve his prerogative of assigning the majority opinion." In other words, Burger would vote with the majority in order to control the assignment of opinions.

The one Justice who was willing to talk to me frankly about Burger's assignment practice spoke of it in a most denigratory fashion. "The great thing about Earl Warren was that he was so considerate of all his colleagues. He was so meticulous on assignments." Now, the Justice went on, "all too damned often the Chief Justice will vote with the majority so as to assign the opinion, and then he ends up in dissent."

* * *

Of course, Chief Justice Burger also made use of more traditional assignment techniques. He took many of the most important cases, such as the *Nixon* case, since the Court in such cases should speak through its head; he assigned the more significant cases to his allies, such as Blackmun in his earlier years and Rehnquist more recently; and left lesser cases to his opponents on the Court, notably Brennan.

The Chief Justice also employed the technique of assigning a case to the most lukewarm member of the majority. An illustration can be found in a November 14, 1978, Burger letter to Justice Brennan: "Apropos your opinion (I believe at lunch Monday) whether Bill Rehnquist was an appropriate assignee of the above case, I had discussed this with Bill. He prefers his first choice disposition, i.e., no judicial review, but he was willing to write the holding to reflect the majority view otherwise. There were 8 to affirm and he fits the old English rule-of-thumb as the 'least persuaded,' hence likely to write narrowly."

SUE DAVIS,* POWER ON THE COURT:
CHIEF JUSTICE REHNQUIST'S
OPINION ASSIGNMENTS**

74 Judicature 66 (1990)

By the spring of 1989 it was clear that the Supreme Court had shifted to the right.[1] As observers proclaimed the arrival of a genuine Rehnquist Court, they seemed to take as a matter of faith that the leadership of the Chief Justice was instrumental in cementing the conservative majority. Although his clearly established record for fourteen-and-a-half years as the Burger Court's most conservative member made William H. Rehnquist seem to be the ideal choice to carry out the legacy of Ronald Reagan's presidency, a Chief Justice's ability to shape the Court's decisions is always constrained by the other members of the Court. By 1988, the replacement of Lewis Powell by Anthony Kennedy and the presence of two other justices appointed by Ronald Reagan, combined with Justice White, made the emergence of a cohesive conservative majority quite likely. Indeed, the dynamic of the eight associate justices could have been as crucial to building a conservative majority to fulfill the goals of the Reagan Administration as the chief justiceship of William Rehnquist.

This article examines the role that Rehnquist, in his capacity as Chief Justice, has played in the Supreme Court's turn to the right. Although he has one vote as do each of the eight associate justices, the Chief Justice who wishes to maximize his position as a policy leader has a number of devices. He has the opportunity to influence the outcome of cases in the leadership roles and strategies he adopts in conference, the strategy he uses in opinion assignments, in circulating the "discuss list" for petitions for certiorari, in the crafting of his own opinions, in

* Sue Davis is an associate professor of political science at the University of Delaware.

** Excerpts from *Power on the Court: Chief Justice Rehnquist's Opinion Assignments,* pp. 66–72. Copyright © 1990 by Judicature, Chicago, Illinois, reprinted with permission of the author.

1. *See for example,* Patterson v. McLean, 109 S.Ct. 2363 (1989) (narrowing the application of civil rights laws that prohibit discrimination in employment); Wards Cove Packing Co. v. Atonio, 109 S.Ct. 2115 (1989); Richmond v. Croson, 109 S.Ct. 706 (1989); Martin v. Wilks, 109 S.Ct. 2180 (1989) (curtailing affirmative action); National Treasury Employees Union v. Von Raab, 109 S.Ct. 1384 (1989); Skinner v. Railway Labor Executives' Association, 109 S.Ct. 1402 (1989) (upholding drug testing for federal employees); Duckworth v. Eagan, 109 S.Ct. 2875 (1989); Arizona v. Youngblood, 109 S.Ct. 333 (1988); U.S. v. Sokolow, 109 S.Ct. 1581 (1989); Florida v. Riley, 109 S.Ct. 693 (1989) (making further exceptions to the rules established by the Warren Court that protect the rights of the accused); Penry v. Lynaugh, 109 S.Ct. 2934 (1989); Stanford v. Kentucky, 109 S.Ct. 2969 (1989) (upholding the death penalty for convicted murderers who committed the crime at the age of sixteen and convicted murderers who are mentally retarded); Webster v. Reproductive Health Services, 109 S.Ct. 3040 (1989) (approving state restrictions on abortion).

the image he presents to the public, and in his personal interaction among the other justices.

In this article I examine one instrument of the Chief Justice's power—the assignment of majority opinions—in order to begin to assess the extent to which Rehnquist is acting as a policy leader. In cases in which the Chief Justice votes with the majority, the rules of the Court provide that he assign the writing of the opinion either to himself or to one of the other justices who voted with him. David J. Danelski explained that the selection of the author of the majority opinion is important because the opinion determines not only the value of a decision as a precedent, but also how acceptable it will be to the public.[2] The author of the opinion, moreover, may be responsible for holding the majority together in a close case, and may persuade would-be dissenters to join the majority.

David W. Rohde underlined the importance of the assignment of majority opinions by identifying two sets of concerns: intra-Court and extra-Court factors.[3] The first set of concerns includes holding together a tenuous majority, increasing the size of a solid majority, and promoting harmony among the justices. Walter F. Murphy pointed to an intra-Court factor when he reflected that a Chief Justice might reward his coalition within the Court by assigning the interesting and important cases to those "who tend to vote with him, leaving the dregs for those who vote against him on issues he thinks important."

Extra–Court factors include those that involve the relationship between the Court and the rest of the political system. The Chief should be sensitive to "public relations" in assigning opinions, particularly those that will be unpopular to a large segment of the public. Further, as Elliot Slotnick noted, the Chief Justice may be the most appropriate member of the Court to author the majority opinion in critical cases because of his symbolic status.[4] Rohde also pointed to a third factor that "has to do with the personal policy preference of the assigner." The Chief Justice can make assignments strategically to members of the Court whose views are most similar to his own in order to maximize the likelihood that the majority opinion will further his objectives.

ASSIGNMENT STRATEGIES

Seeking to further an understanding of the Supreme Court as a collegial decisionmaking body, scholars have formulated and tested a number of hypotheses concerned with the strategies used by the assigners of majority opinions. Danelski formulated two assignment rules

2. Danelski, *The Influence of the Chief Justice in the Decisional Process of the Supreme Court,* in Goldman and Sarat, American Court Systems: Reading in Judicial Process And Behavior (San Francisco: W.H. Freeman and Company 1978).

3. Rohde, *Policy Goals, Strategic Choice and Majority Opinion Assignments in the*

U.S. Supreme Court, 16 Midwest J. of Pol. Sci. 652–682, 679 (1972).

4. Slotnick, *Who Speaks for the Court? Majority Opinion Assignment from Taft to Burger,* 23 Am.J. of Pol.Sci. 60–77, at 75 (1979).

that a Chief Justice might use to influence others to join the majority. First, he might assign the opinion to the justice whose views are the closest to the dissenters in the belief that the justice would take an approach upon which both majority and minority could agree. Second, where there are blocs on the Court and a bloc splits, the Chief Justice might assign the case to a majority member of the dissenters' bloc. Danelski found that of the three Chief Justices he studied only Hughes appeared to follow such rules.

A number of scholars, attempting to determine whether assigners followed Danelski's first rule, have found a pattern of overassignment to the justice closest to the dissenters in cases in which a change in one vote would have altered the outcome.[5] Saul Brenner and Harold J. Spaeth found that assigning the majority opinion to the marginal justice * * * did not actually help to maintain an original minimum winning coalition.[6] Thus, it is not clear what an assigner accomplishes by favoring the justice closest to the dissenters over the other members of the majority.

Rohde hypothesized that the justice who assigns the majority opinion will either write the opinion himself or assign it to the justice whose position is closest to his own on the issue in question. Analyzing civil liberties cases decided during the Warren era, he found that the pattern of opinion assignments supported his hypothesis. Moreover, the assigner's tendency to give opinions to the justice closest to him increased in important cases, and as the size of the majority increased.

When Gregory Rathjen replicated Rohde's study using economics rather than civil liberties cases he found that the pattern of assigning opinions to the closest justice disappeared.[7] While Rathjen endorsed the theory that justices assign opinions on the basis of policy preferences, he suggested that Rohde's hypothesis was most viable in cases that involved issues of primary concern to the Chief. He surmised that the issues presented in economics cases were less salient to Warren than those of individual rights, so that the Chief Justice may have placed policy concerns aside in those cases in order to assign in a manner that would help to equalize the workload.

Slotnick explored an alternative to ideological concerns in assigning opinions: equality of workload. Examining two models of opinion assignment—the opinion assignment ratio (OAR), which is conditioned on the frequency with which each justice is a member of the majority, and the model of absolute equality of caseloads, whereby all justices would have substantially the same number of majority opinions regardless of how often they agreed with the majority—he found that the six chief justices from Taft through Burger followed a norm of absolute

5. Ulmer, *The Use of Power in the Supreme Court,* 30 J.Pub.L. 49–67 (1970).

6. Brenner and Spaeth, *Majority Opinion Assignments and the Maintenance of the Original Coalition on the Warren Court,* 32 Am.J. of Pol.Sci. 72–81, 77–78 (1988).

7. *Policy Goals, Strategic Choices, and Majority Opinion Assignments in the U.S. Supreme Court: A Replication,* 18 Am. J.Pol.Sci. 713–724 (1974).

equality rather than the OAR model. Moreover, it was Chief Justice Burger's behavior that most closely approximated the model of absolute equality. Likewise, Spaeth found that Burger practiced equal distribution to an extent that was unmatched by any of his five predecessors.[8]

Slotnick discovered that chief justices departed from the norm of equality in important cases, assigning opinions to themselves at a substantially higher rate than they did for the universe of cases. That pattern of self-assignment in important cases was most pronounced in highly cohesive cases—in cases where the Court was divided the Chief tended to avoid writing the opinion. Slotnick found those who most often voted with the Chief Justice were favored in the assignment of opinions in important cases. Spaeth's analysis of Burger's assignments revealed the same pattern.

HYPOTHESIS

The theory and methods developed in previous judicial research provided the basis for the four hypotheses tested here. The hypotheses reflect the two expectations that Rehnquist has assigned opinions with a goal of equal distribution of workload and that he has also attempted to assign opinions so as to further his policy preferences.

Rehnquist can be expected to continue the tradition of distributing opinions on the basis of absolute equality that Slotnick found to be the norm for Chief Justices from Taft through Burger. By the Chief Justice's own account:

> [Assigning opinions] is an important responsibility, and it is desirable that it be discharged carefully and fairly. At the start of the October 1986 term I tried to be as evenhanded as possible as far as numbers of cases assigned to each justice, but as the term goes on I take into consideration the extent to which the various justices are current in writing and circulating opinions that have previously been assigned.

The Chief Justice's comments suggest that "evenhandedness" rather than ideology would be the dominant factor in his assignments. Accordingly, Hypothesis 1 states that the opinions have been evenly distributed among the nine justices.

Studies of opinion assignment decisionmaking by previous Chief Justices have revealed a departure from the norm of equality in important cases. Thus, Hypothesis 2 posits that in important cases the Chief Justice has overassigned opinions to himself but that evenhandedness has prevailed to the extent that he has not kept the important cases for himself at a significantly higher rate than his predecessors.

Rohde's theory, based on the assumption that "justices are rational and that their primary motivation in making decisions is their own personal preferences about what is good public policy," is considered in

---

8. Spaeth, *Distributive justice: majority*   67 Judicature 299–304 (1984).
opinion assignments in the Burger Court,

Hypothesis 3. If the Chief's goal is to keep the majority and to have the opinion written in a way that is compatible with his preferences, he should assign opinions to the justice whose views most resemble his own. Thus, according to Hypothesis 3, Rehnquist has overassigned opinions to himself or to the justice whose position is closest to his on the issue in question.

Finally, I address the question of whether the Chief Justice uses his authority to assign opinions to hold a minimum winning coalition together by assigning the majority opinion to the justice closest to the dissenters. Specifically, Hypothesis 4 states that in cases decided by a minimum majority coalition Rehnquist has overassigned to the justice closest to the dissenters.

ANALYSIS AND RESULTS

The data used here are comprised of all cases decided with full opinion during the term 1986 through 1988—a total of 445 cases.[9] To test Hypothesis 1, the total number of opinions assigned to each justice were determined and OAR's for each justice for each of the three terms were calculated.[10] The results suggest that Rehnquist has taken the assignments made by others into account in order to achieve an equal distribution of opinions. Rehnquist has continued the tradition of absolute equality in opinion assignments. When the three years are considered together each justice wrote an average of 15.35 opinions per term with a standard deviation of only 1.57.

Rehnquist appears to be adhering to the norm of equality of workload in assigning opinions. The tests of the remaining three hypotheses should shed light on the extent to which he also uses policy considerations as a basis for allocating opinion assignments.

"IMPORTANT CASES"

Hypothesis 2 requires a definition of "important cases." Several methods of identifying such cases have been utilized in judicial research. For example, important cases may be identified as those that were cited most often by the Court in subsequent decisions, or those included in the leading constitutional law texts. All the methods share an element of arbitrariness and none of them take into account the importance of the cases to the Chief Justice at the time they were decided. I have chosen to utilize the method devised by Spaeth whereby the cases headlined in the *Lawyer's Edition* of the *United States Reports* are classified as "important cases." Spaeth's method has the advantage that it eliminates bias in favor of constitutional cases and makes it possible to

9. I used Harold Spaeth's United States Supreme Court Judicial Data Base, Phase I.

10. A justice's OAR is calculated by dividing the number of majority opinions by the number of his or her votes with the majority and multiplying the result by 100 to obtain a percentage. Slotnick, who devised the OAR, pointed out that it is a measure that is sensitive to a justice's availability for assignment of majority opinions. A justice who was in the majority infrequently would not be likely to write as many majority opinions as a justice who voted with the Chief a great deal of the time.

classify cases that have been decided so recently that they have not been included in any of the casebooks.

The *Lawyer's Edition* identified 48 [important] cases for the terms 1986 through 1988. Rehnquist assigned opinions in 36 of those cases, nine of which he assigned to himself (25 per cent). Both Spaeth and Slotnick found that Chief Justice Burger assigned about 25 per cent of the important cases to himself. Slotnick found the average self-assignment ratio for Chief Justices from Taft through the first five years of the Burger Court to be 24.8. The data support Hypothesis 2 insofar as Rehnquist clearly overassigned opinions to himself.

The most interesting finding with regard to important cases was that Rehnquist assigned more opinions to Justice White than he did to himself. The Chief Justice's apparent preference for White may be a result of the latter's increasing alignment with Rehnquist. During the last five terms of the Burger Court White and Rehnquist voted together in 65.6 percent of the cases in which they both participated. During the first three years of the Rehnquist Court, however, their percentage of interagreement rose to 74.6 per cent. It is possible, therefore, that Rehnquist assigned opinions to White with the goal of maximizing the prospects of cementing the alliance between them and, thus, of drawing White close to the conservatives.

Agreement

Tests of Hypotheses 3 and 4 mandate a technique to measure agreement between the Chief Justice and the other members of the majority. Following the example of previous studies, I used cumulative scaling to identify the "closest" justice to the opinion assigner. I constructed separate scales for the three issues of criminal procedure, civil rights, and the First Amendment and used the scale scores of the justices to determine their "closeness" to the Chief Justice. That is, in a given case the justice in the majority with the scale score nearest to Rehnquist's was considered to be the justice in the position closest to that of the Chief Justice. [Editors: Thus, on any given issue, Rehnquist occupied position one on the scale, the justice who most often voted with Rehnquist on that issue occupied position two, and the justice who voted least frequently with Rehnquist on that issue was in position nine.]

For Hypothesis 3 to be supported, Rehnquist's assignment of opinions should reveal a pattern of overassignment to himself (position 1) and to the justice in the majority with the scale score closest to his own (position 2). The distribution of opinions for the 1986 term, as well as previous research, suggests the existence of a "freshman effect" in opinion assignments. Accordingly, I excluded justices serving a first term on the Court from the analysis.

In order to measure "overassignment" I began with the assumption that in any case each justice in the majority has an equal probability of being assigned the opinion. That made it possible to compare the actual proportion of majority opinions Rehnquist assigned to a position to the proportion that could be expected if he were assigning randomly. Thus, for the hypothesis to be supported, the comparisons would have to reveal a substantially greater proportion of opinions Rehnquist assigned to Positions 1 and 2.

The [results show that the] difference between the actual and expected proportion of opinions assigned is in the predicted direction but the difference is not great enough to be statistically significant. Thus, the hypothesis that Rehnquist has assigned opinions to the justices whose views are most compatible with his own failed to be supported.

The Chief Justice's goal of maintaining an equal workload may have acted as a constraint on his ability to assign opinions ideologically. Additionally, as Rathjen suggested, an opinion assigner may utilize his discretion to assign opinions to the justices most likely to further his policy goals in areas that are most salient to him and in the other areas concentrate on equality of workload, thereby conserving his resources. If one of the three issues is more important to the Chief Justice than the others, he might assign opinions accordingly. But the pattern of Rehnquist's assignments in each of the three areas does not suggest that to be the case.

Rathjen's assertion concerning the importance of the issue to the assigner, Rehnquist's own statements regarding the importance of federalism, along with the lack of support for Hypothesis 3 lend credibility to the possibility that neither criminal procedure, civil rights, nor the First Amendment are particularly salient to Rehnquist. If federalism and/or economic issues are more important to Rehnquist than any sub-category of civil liberties, analysis may reveal a pattern of overassignment to the justice in the position closest to his in those areas. Unfortunately, attempts to scale both economics and federalism cases proved unsuccessful, rendering any identification of the closest justice to Rehnquist unreliable.

Hypothesis 4 predicts that in cases decided by a margin of one vote Rehnquist will assign the opinion to the justice in the majority whose scale score places him/her closest to the dissenters (the marginal position) in order to maintain the majority coalition. Thus, the data will support Hypothesis 4 if the results show that Position 5 received the assignment in a substantially greater proportion of cases than would have been expected by chance. It should be emphasized that the justice who occupies Position 5 varies according to the composition of the majority coalition—that is, Position 5 is not an individual justice. [The data show that] Position 5 received a greater proportion of assignments than the other positions and at a greater rate than was expected. Still, the difference between the actual and expected proportion was not statistically significant. Thus, Hypothesis 4 failed to be supported.

The lack of support for Hypotheses 3 and 4 indicates that Rehnquist did not favor the justice whom he believed would write an opinion that would further the Chief Justice's own policy goals, nor did he show a preference for the marginal justice in close cases. The failure of the analysis to reveal either that Rehnquist overassigned majority opinions to the justice closest to him or to the justice closest to the dissenters in close cases suggests that the Chief Justice has not used his discretion to assign opinions in order to advance his policy goals.

CONCLUSION

The results of the analysis of opinion assignments during the first three terms of the Rehnquist Court show that if the Chief Justice's goal has been to distribute the workload evenly he has been successful except with respect to the important cases. His assignments in important cases suggest that he combined a goal of equal workload with one of advancing his policy preferences by keeping opinions for himself and by assigning to White, thereby courting an increasingly close ally. But the assertion that he assigned opinions with an eye to advancing his policy preferences is not otherwise supported by the data. In short, the results suggest that Rehnquist has not fully utilized his opinion assigning prerogative as an instrument to shape the decisions of the Court.

This article, because it examines only one aspect of the Chief Justice's leadership, reveals nothing about Rehnquist's use of other resources that a Chief Justice may use to maximize his power. Moreover, it is important for the reader to be aware that the analysis, by necessity, is based only on the final vote of the Court, as conference votes are not available. Thus, it is impossible to take into account that in any given case Rehnquist may have voted with the minority in conference and then switched or that the members of a winning coalition in the final vote may not be the same as the original majority.

Still, the results are consistent with the assertion that Rehnquist's leadership has not been crucial to the emergence of a solid conservative majority. It is possible that the Chief Justice has not exercised the prerogatives of his office to their full extent simply because he has not needed to do so. The membership of the Court is such that opinion assignments may rarely make any difference to the outcome of the cases. If so, the Chief Justice has no need to act as a strong leader. The dynamic of a Court whose members consist of four conservatives in addition to the Chief Justice may have rendered it unnecessary for Rehnquist to draw on all the resources of his power.

ALAN B. MORRISON AND D. SCOTT STENHOUSE,* THE CHIEF JUSTICE OF THE UNITED STATES: MORE THAN JUST THE HIGHEST RANKING JUDGE **

1 Constitutional Commentary 57 (1984)

The Chief Justice has always been more than first among equals. His position as chair of the Supreme Court's weekly conferences, at

* Mr. Morrison, a Washington attorney, directs the Public Citizen Litigation Group, which he founded with Ralph Nader in 1972. The basic research for this article was done by Mr. Stenhouse, who now practices law in Atlanta, while he was a student and Mr. Morrison was a Visiting Professor at Harvard Law School.

** Excerpts from *The Chief Justice of the United States: More than Just the Highest Ranking Judge,* by Alan B. Morrison and D.

which tentative votes are taken on cases that have been argued, and decisions made on which cases will have full briefing and argument, is more than titular. His power to choose who will write the majority opinion, if he is on that side, can influence the course of the law, which depends at least as much on the rationale as on the result. And his symbolic function as the leader of our entire judicial system has always been important.

Such differences between his role and that of the other Justices are traditional and probably necessary. This article is about a more recent and more disturbing phenomenon: the plethora of nonjudicial responsibilities that modern Chief Justices have assumed or, more often, been assigned by Congress. Every Justice, and indeed every federal judge, has some administrative duties. But the Chief Justice has more of them, and on the whole his are more significant. Cumulatively, his responsibilities raise several serious questions.

The first is time. With increasing outside duties and an increasing caseload, is it possible for one person to continue to handle all of these tasks effectively? Or will nonjudicial activities detract from the Court's primary function?

As a result of these activities, there has also been a significant increase in the power of the Chief Justice. Some of his prerogatives are merely managerial. But many, such as the power to appoint important committees and to act as spokesman for the federal judiciary, entail significant policy-making functions. Should we be concerned about such concentrations of power in one individual? No Chief Justice has been accused of any scandalous improprieties. But scandal is not the only danger inherent in extra-judicial endeavors. The administrative work of every Chief Justice inevitably brings him or her into situations that could tarnish the image of the Court, to the point where it is seen as simply another participant in political disputes. If that were to occur, it might do serious damage to the confidence most Americans have in the fundamental fairness of our court of last resort.

A final reason for studying the Chief Justice's duties is to broaden our conception of the qualities that should be sought in those who are considered for the office. What does the job involve?

I. Time Commitments

"If the burdens of the office continue to increase as they have in the past years, it may be impossible for the occupant to perform all of the duties well and survive very long." Those words were spoken by Chief Justice Burger in December, 1978. Nearly ten years earlier, however, he endorsed the idea of judges serving on the boards of nonprofit groups "so long as the demands on their time and energy do not violate the absolute priority of their court duties."

Scott Stenhouse, pp. 57–76. Copyright 1984 by University of Minnesota Law School and Constitutional Commentary, Minneapolis, Minnesota, reprinted by permission of the publisher and the authors.

Are those statements consistent, and if so, where is the problem? To begin, most of the Chief Justice's nonjudicial duties have been imposed by Congress. Has this occurred too often? One standard by which to answer that question was supplied by Senator Ervin, who declared that a judge's first responsibility is to "be a full-time judge in his own court." The most time-consuming obligation of the Chief Justice, apart from judging, is his role as head of the Judicial Conference of the United States, which is, in essence, the policy-making body of the federal judiciary. It is comprised of the chief judges of all federal courts of appeals and a district judge from each of the circuits (other than the new Federal Circuit). The Conference is charged with supervision of the federal court system—trying to assure that cases are promptly decided, recommending rules changes, initiating or responding to legislation relating to virtually every aspect of what transpires in the federal courts, and the like. When it was created by Congress in 1922, the Conference met for one day each year. Now it has two two-day meetings, and according to the Chief Justice each of these requires an additional two or three days for preparation.

Besides serving as presiding officer, the Chief Justice appoints the chairmen of over twenty committees, dealing with subjects like court administration, the jury system, probation, and federal magistrates. Among the most important are those which consider possible changes in procedural rules. The Conference's committees on judicial conduct advise judges about the propriety of various activities, review their reports of extra-judicial income, and assist them with their financial disclosure forms required by the Ethics in Government Act. The Chief Justice also appoints the principal staff on several of these committees. Because of the key role played by the committees, he keeps in close touch with their chairs. In 1972, Congress authorized the appointment of an Administrative Assistant to the Chief Justice, in part to relieve him of some of the liaison functions with groups such as the Judicial Conference. But as Chief Justice Burger himself recognized, "there is a limit to the delegation of functions and a limit in delegating decisionmaking."

A second major responsibility is his position as chair of the Board of the Federal Judicial Center. Congress has directed that he, the six sitting federal judges, and the Director of the Administrative Office of the United States Courts, who comprise the Center's Board, meet quarterly to oversee its work. The Center, whose primary function is to engage in research, training, and education for the judicial branch, has a budget which has increased from $500,000 at its inception in 1967 to almost $8,600,000 today. It engages in a wide range of research projects, offers training sessions for judges and nonjudicial personnel in the system, and has committees on such topics as prisoners' civil rights suits, revising jury instructions, and conducting conferences for appellate judges. Like the committees of the Judicial Conference, those working under the Federal Judicial Center also require the time and attention of the Chief Justice.

A third duty concerns the Administrative Office of the United States Courts. This Office works closely with the Federal Judicial Center and the Judicial Conference in the broad area of judicial administration. It is almost impossible to assign many of the Chief Justice's duties to any one of the three because there is so much overlap. His specific responsibilities for the Administrative Office arise because its director and deputy are appointed by the Supreme Court and their work is under the direction of the Judicial Conference. Since courts or conferences cannot, as a practical matter, supervise individuals, much of the responsibility falls on the Chief Justice.

A great deal of what the Administrative Office does, such as handling pay and purchasing books and other supplies, is generally no burden to the Chief Justice. But the Office is also the major source of data for the Judicial Conference and the Congress about the use of the federal courts. These, in turn, are vital to the Chief because of his concerns about the increasing case load, the adequacy of judicial salaries, and the number of judges. For these reasons he has become involved, although probably to a lesser degree than in other areas of court administration, in the work of the Administrative Office.

Another major responsibility is what he has referred to somewhat facetiously as his "role of building manager of the Supreme Court building." Of course, the day to day operations are handled by the marshall, clerk, librarian, reporter of decisions, and the Chief's administrative assistant. They in turn are subject to the supervision of the whole Court. In some cases this is done by Court committees; in others the job has fallen to individual Justices, particularly the Chief Justice.

Chief Justice Burger has taken his duties in managing the Supreme Court building very seriously. He himself has mentioned the time that he spends in making decisions relating to the modernization of the Court's equipment. Other observers have mentioned his involvement in such details as ordering paint, planting flowers, having the reflecting pools painted blue, and installing exhibits for tourists. He has also changed the lighting of the courtroom, altered the shape of the Justices' bench, moved the journalists' location, and improved the cafeteria. Indeed, he is so well versed in the Court's budget that he was able to recite down to the last dollar the overtime charges that were being run up in the print shop in trying to have all the opinions ready for Monday morning before the practice was changed in the mid–1960s.

Congress has also required the Chief Justice to make various kinds of appointments. Many involve temporary or special purpose courts such as the Temporary Emergency Court of Appeals, which in recent years has concentrated on energy price litigation, and the Judicial Panel on Multi-district Litigation, which coordinates complex cases arising in various locations around the country. He is also empowered to assign judges within the federal system to fill temporary needs—with their consent and that of their chief judge—including trips to such places as the Northern Mariana Islands, Guam, and the Virgin Islands. These assignments do not comprise a significant portion of his work load, but they are one more straw on the camel's back. Equally important, they may permit the Chief to exercise extraordinary influence in certain areas of the law.

Congress has assigned to the Chief Justice many activities which are remote from judicial administration. In 1846 it made him a Regent of the Smithsonian and more recently a trustee of the National Gallery of Art and the Joseph M. Hirshhorn Museum and Sculpture Garden. Other outside positions, not congressionally imposed, include: Honorary Chairman of the Board of Trustees of the Supreme Court Historical Society (a group formed at his urging); Honorary Trustee of the National Geographic Society; and Honorary Chairman of the Institute on Judicial Administration and the National Judicial College. Some of these are pleasant diversions, yet they can become demanding. It is worth recalling that Chief Justice William Howard Taft resigned from the Board of Yale University because he felt the ten meetings a year did not permit him to maintain his work load on the Court.

There is a great deal that the Chief Justice has to do simply because he is the Chief Justice—the inevitable swearings-in, receptions, and attendance at joint sessions of Congress addressed by the president. While every other Justice is assigned to one federal judicial circuit for administrative and other duties, the Chief and two other Justices are assigned an additional circuit. Each year the circuit holds a conference which its Justice usually attends and often addresses. The Chief Justice also makes an annual address on the state of the judiciary to the American Bar Association, and frequently speaks before the American Law Institute, law schools, and other gatherings.

How much time does all this take? By one report, the Chief Justice has timed his own work week at seventy-seven hours, with about one-third devoted to non-case activities. He has also stated that no member of the Court works less than sixty hours a week. Surely, by any measure, his work load is considerable, and the burdens from his non-case activities are significant.

Some perspective can be gained by considering his extra-judicial duties in light of the Court's case load. For example, during the 1953 Term (Earl Warren's first) the Court issued sixty-five signed opinions; in the 1981–82 Term that figure was 141, or more than double the number thirty years before; in the same period, the number of cases on the Court's docket went from 1463 to 5311.

Have outside activities prevented the Chief Justice from writing a reasonable share of the Court's opinions? During the five terms ending in June, 1982, he averaged the same number of majority opinions as his colleagues. Yet he wrote far fewer concurrences and dissents than any other Justice, perhaps partly because he cast relatively few dissenting votes. This may reflect a conviction that, as Chief Justice, he should try to harmonize the Court's work and that therefore concurrences and dissents should be used sparingly. But there is at least some evidence that in a few cases each year there is not enough time for the Chief to add his concurring or dissenting views, and so he joins others rather than separately stating his own position.

Can a Chief Justice, despite considerable nonjudicial work, devote adequate thought to judging? Charles Evans Hughes and Joseph R. Lamar, who served on presidential commissions while they were Associate Justices, were reportedly unable to maintain their full judicial work loads. Indeed, Hughes acknowledged that he was so worn out by the added burdens that his work was impaired for several months even after the commission was concluded. This was during an era when the Court's case load was relatively light. Chief Justice Burger says that the Court should give full treatment to no more than 100 cases each year if it is to maintain adequate quality. The current level, including full per curiam opinions, is more than fifty percent beyond this figure.

Some of a Chief's activities will inevitably reflect personal interests. The incumbent, for instance, cares intensely about judicial administration. But most of his duties are mandatory and, since his successor will probably have some favorite causes, the work load of non-case activities is not likely to decrease substantially. As Chief Justice Burger put it, just "because the Chief Justices, up to now, have somehow managed to cope, we should not assume that these glacial pressures can always be kept under control."

II. POLITICAL POWER

It would be hard to find an educated American who does not realize that in making constitutional law the Supreme Court wields a significant kind of political power. The nonjudicial political powers of the Chief Justice are less well appreciated. Congress has assigned him a major role in three significant policymaking fields: creating rules for the federal courts, participating in the legislative process, and appointing judges to certain special courts.

The role of judges—and particular Supreme Court Justices—in fashioning or approving procedures derives from the common-sense notion that they are uniquely qualified for this task. In 1934 Congress gave the Court the job of writing federal rules of civil procedure, subject only to the right of Congress to override them by statute. Since then Congress has also given the Court responsibility for the criminal, appellate, and bankruptcy rules, and—subject to a veto by either house of Congress—the rules of evidence (except those relating to the law of privilege).[40]

As every attorney knows, procedural rules sometimes determine cases. Indeed, when the Court sent over its Rules of Evidence in 1972,

---

40. 18 U.S.C. § 3771 (1976) (criminal); 28 U.S.C. § 2072 (1976) (appellate); 28 U.S.C. § 2075 (1976) (bankruptcy); and 28 U.S.C. § 2076 (1976) (evidence). It is now clear that the veto over rules of evidence is void, Immigration & Naturalization Serv. v. Chada, 103 S.Ct. 2764 (1983), but perhaps this veto will be deemed severable from the grant of rulemaking authority.

they created such a controversy that Congress substantially rewrote them.

* * *

In theory, the power of the Chief Justice, as one of nine Justices who vote on all rule changes, is no greater than that of his colleagues. In fact, that is not the way the system works. Of necessity, the Justices give proposed rules only a cursory glance. This reality elevates the importance of the drafters. Rules proposals come from the Judicial Conference, headed by the Chief Justice, after passing through the Standing Committee on Rules of Practice and Procedure and the appropriate advisory committee, whose members are his appointees. In addition, the staff person who does the basic research for the advisory committee (known as the reporter) is selected by the Chief Justice. Since most potential reporters are academics, their views are often readily ascertainable, making it possible to ensure that appointees concentrate on areas of importance to the Chief and rarely suggest rule changes that are inconsistent with his philosophy. While the committee system is not simply an extension of the Chief Justice's personal staff, there is a close connection between them not readily apparent from the formal structure established by Congress. At the very least it provides a substantial protection against unfriendly rule changes reaching the Supreme Court where they would have to be formally voted down to be defeated.

One recent addition to the Chief Justice's powers in the rule-making process deserves special mention. In the Classified Information Procedures Act of 1980 Congress sought a solution to the problem of what to do with classified materials that become part of court proceedings, as well as the problem of "graymail"—the threat by a defendant in a criminal case to use classified information to defend himself. The job of writing the security procedures was given jointly to the Chief Justice, the Attorney General, the Director of the CIA, and the Secretary of Defense. Aside from any problems that may arise if the Supreme Court ever has to decide the validity of those rules, the notion that the Chief Justice and members of the Executive Branch should jointly issue regulations of this kind contradicts the basic tenets of separation of powers. Not only is the Chief Justice's role undesirable, it is also plainly unnecessary.

Another major source of the Chief's political power is his ability to influence legislation. The formal power to propose or evaluate bills resides in the Judicial Conference, not the Court or the Chief Justice. The Federal Judicial Center and the Administrative Office of the United States Courts also play a role through their research and the statistics they provide, which are often used by the Chief Justice in his speeches to support or oppose a given recommendation. Their evidence is especially influential in congressional decisions about the number of federal judges and support personnel and, less directly, on whether new kinds of cases should be allowed in the federal courts in light of the current case load. In addition, the Judicial Center's research "often involves matters that are subjects of legislative consideration—for example, criminal code revision, the Speedy Trial Act, or proposals to restructure judges' sentencing discretion * * *."

The influence of the Chief Justice himself on legislation may in some senses be more powerful than in rule making, even though the Conference can only make recommendations. Unlike rule making, in which every Justice has a vote, none of the remaining eight has a legislative role since the views are expressed by the Judicial Conference, not the Court. Some of the Conference's legislative recommendations come from standing committees over which the Chief Justice has the considerable powers described above; in other cases special committees are formed, where the Chief's decision to create a new group may be the single most important aspect of the process.

It is impossible to assess fully the Chief Justice's impact on legislation because his influence is often subtle. Perhaps more important, his role is unclear because the meetings of the committees, as well as of the Judicial Conference itself, are conducted behind closed doors—a prerogative the Conference fought hard to maintain in 1980 when Senator Dennis DeConcini proposed to open virtually all of them to the public.

Appointments are the third major source of the Chief Justice's political power. In addition to appointing committees and top staff for the Judicial Conference and the Judicial Center, he is authorized to select, from the federal judiciary, the chief judge and the members of several special courts. One of these courts—the Temporary Emergency Court of Appeals—is now responsible for appeals in all oil and gas pricing and allocation cases. Obviously, his choice of these judges can have a major impact on the development of the law. While no one has suggested that the Chief Justice has unfairly balanced TECA, the possibility nonetheless exists and warrants serious thought.

Another extremely important power that Congress has given the Chief Justice is the right to name the members of the trial and appellate benches of the Foreign Intelligence Surveillance Court, created by Congress to oversee the use of wiretaps by the executive branch in the foreign intelligence area. Most of the original appointees were judges with reputations for upholding the government's position in criminal cases; in 1981 they lived up to their reputations by approving all 431 Justice Department requests to start or continue electronic surveillance. Unlike the President's judicial appointments, these designations by the Chief Justice are not subject to Senate confirmation. While no one expected the present Chief Justice to fill the positions only with civil libertarians, it surely would be more consistent with stated congressional intentions to ensure better balance, perhaps by requiring that the assignments be approved by the Supreme Court as a whole.

In suggesting that the Chief Justice has political power, it is important not to overstate the case. He obviously does not possess nonjudicial power comparable to that of, say, a leader of Congress. But he has enough influence to justify a reevaluation of this aspect of the office.

III. Maintaining the Appearance of Impartiality

The Supreme Court has been called the "least dangerous branch" because it lacks the two great powers of the sword and the purse. Its power ultimately rests on public support. That in turn requires a popular belief that it is an impartial tribunal.

At least some of the Chief Justice's activities are potentially damaging to this aura of impartiality. One of the themes echoed by almost every witness at the 1969 Senate hearings on non-judicial activities of federal judges was that judges ought to stay out of controversial matters. As Senator Ervin said, "There seems to be widespread agreement with Chief Justices Hughes' statement that the business of judges is 'to hear appeals and not to make them.'"

The witnesses were aware of the contrary history, beginning with John Jay, who served as secretary of state, ambassador to Great Britain, and candidate for governor of New York, all while he was sitting as our first Chief Justice. A number of other Justices also served on non-judicial bodies, such as the postal investigation commission (Chief Justice Hughes) and the group, headed by Justice Lamar, that attempted to mediate the boundary dispute between Venezuela and British Guiana. In the period around World War II Justice Reed became chairman of the Committee to Improve the Civil Service, Justice Roberts investigated Pearl Harbor, and Justice Jackson took a year's leave to serve as the American prosecutor at Nuremburg. The most famous recent example of extra-judicial service was when Chief Justice Warren chaired the committee investigating the assassination of President Kennedy.

* * *

Whatever short-term benefit may have accrued as a result of Chief Justice Warren's service in the investigation of the Kennedy assassination seems to be outweighed by the doubts that have arisen about that investigation. In his memoirs Warren recalled his initial reservations about serving: it would be inconsistent with the principle of separation of powers; it would take time away from his work on the Court; it might cause him to disqualify himself from litigation arising out of the investigation. Yet he took the job, and his memoirs reflect no sense that this was an unwise decision. Justice Roberts, in contrast, confessed that he had made a mistake in accepting outside appointments while on the Court. In retrospect it seems that none of these assignments of sitting Justices to presidential commissions turned out well, either for the work of their commissions or for the Court.

Today no active Justice sits on an investigative commission. However, the Chief Justice has become involved in several other endeavors that raise similar questions. For example, in Congress, the Judicial Conference and hence the Chief Justice speak for the federal judiciary. There are three dangers whenever a judge takes a legislative position on a controversial question: it may detract from his or her real or apparent impartiality in a subsequent case; the judge may be unable to limit himself to technical advice and thus become a special interest pleader like every other lobbyist; and, finally, it is hard to say what kinds of legislation are proper subjects of comment by the Justices.

* * *

Chief Justice Burger has twice been the center of the kind of controversy that is likely to recur when judges engage in lobbying. In one incident, he was reported to have sent Roland Kirks, then director of the Administrative Office, in the company of an influential Washington lawyer-lobbyist, to visit House Speaker Albert to campaign against some aspects of pending consumer legislation. Kirks subsequently denied that the Chief Justice even knew about the lobbying trip until after it occurred, yet the Chief felt constrained to issue his own statement, which did not actually deny that he had sent Kirks, although he subsequently took that position. It matters little who actually authorized whom to do what. What is significant is that the Chief Justice was so personally involved in the lobbying process that he had to defend his actions in the public press.

He also became very much involved with the Bankruptcy Reform Act of 1978, making extensive eleventh hour efforts to delay the bill, including telephone calls to its sponsors and to highly placed persons on the Senate Judiciary Committee. One of the bill's Senate supporters received a call from the Chief Justice in which Burger reportedly "not only lobbied, but pressured and attempted to be intimidating," calling the Senator "irresponsible" for approving the bill and threatening to get the President to veto it. Appeals Court Judge Ruggero Aldisert, Chairman of the Bankruptcy Committee of the Judicial Conference, defended the Chief Justice, arguing that he was merely fulfilling his statutory duty to report the adverse recommendations of the Judicial Conference. Even assuming that the Chief Justice was carrying out the will of the Judicial Conference, its position could readily have been communicated with far less direct personal involvement of the Chief Justice and consequent loss of prestige to the Court.

Such activities have led a popular network television news program to air a report about the Chief Justice, investigating his off-the-bench activities. In October 1980 *Congressional Quarterly* ran an article debating the wisdom of lobbying by federal judges and especially Chief Justice Burger. And the New York Times admonished that the duties of Chief Justice and lobbyist "sit uneasily in the same chair * * *; the need for prudence should be evident." Thus, it appears that it is news when a Supreme Court Justice engages in lobbying, and resultant media coverage is potentially damaging to the perceived neutrality of the Court.

Which legislative topics are out of bounds for judges? Chief Justice Burger has stated that he would not comment on any subject other than those relating to his "responsibilities for the administration of justice." Professor Bickel said that he would like the Court to comment only on jurisdictional statutes, because they are "highly technical" and, without judicial advice about them, legislatures would operate nearly blindly.

Limiting comments to legislation affecting the administration of justice has a neutral and self-defining ring, but its parameters are quite amorphous. The Chief Justice has regularly expressed his dislike of proposals which would have created additional work for the federal courts. Yet in a recent interview, when asked about a bill to prevent federal courts from proceeding in controversial areas such as busing and school prayer, he declined to offer an opinion, replying "[t]hat is a subject I will have to leave to others." The point is not that the Chief Justice was wrong to refuse to express his views in that instance, or that he should not have commented on other bills dealing with access to the federal courts. Rather, the two examples demonstrate that in some sense all these bills relate to "the administration of justice." Because the term is so potentially broad, it is an uncertain standard by which to decide which legislation is appropriate for judicial comment. Some topics are obviously too political, but the difficult question is, where should the line be drawn and who should draw it? One answer, of course, is to stay out of the legislative arena entirely. At most, the judiciary should answer legislative requests for its views, keeping replies as technical and objective as possible.

Whenever the Chief Justice ventures beyond his judicial role, the possibility of creating an appearance of impropriety exists. One such opportunity is provided in the numerous appointments that he makes to committees of the Judicial Conference. Students of the Conference have recognized that these committee assignments, though often arduous and always unremunerated, are coveted by judges because they are one of the few means of status differentiation within the judiciary. The assignment power enables a Chief Justice to reward friends and allies. Consider this letter from Chief Justice Taft to a retired district judge, discussing legislation that would give the Chief more power regarding the assignment of judges to other locations: "[I]t may be that you and I can agree occasionally on your hearing cases in one of the Southern Districts in the winter time when the beauties of living in Maine are a matter of retrospect or prospect." Such a tiny reward is unlikely to destroy the judiciary's moral fiber, but one wonders whether the Chief Justice should be a part of this sort of petty patronage system.

Consider also the role of Chief Justice Burger in the formation of the Supreme Court Historical Society, whose purpose is to promote the presentation of the history of the Court. Unlike the National Geographic Society, on whose board he also serves, the Chief Justice has not had to disqualify himself from any cases involving the Historical Society. Still, his participation has raised questions about his role in the Society's fund raising, which involves soliciting money from lawyers who appear before the Court and from litigants whose cases may be there. Some observers believe that he unnecessarily damages the prestige of the Court by serving on the Society's board with, for example, Robert Stevens, the retired head of a textile firm that is frequently involved in extremely bitter litigation, some of which reaches the Court. The situation is further clouded by Stevens's additional gift of $8,500, beyond his $5,000 lifetime membership in the Society, which was used to commission a portrait of the Chief Justice for the National Portrait Gallery. Although these kinds of activities may produce only a faint whiff of impropriety, even that minimal damage is an excessive price to pay for the Chief's participation.

Even the Chief Justice's role as chancellor of the Smithsonian Institution causes problems that may reflect on the Court and may cause him to have to recuse himself in a tax case involving the valuation of gems given to that Institution. A recent newspaper story reported that the Internal Revenue Service has cracked down on what the Service alleges are "sham" valuations of gifts to the Smithsonian for which the donors deducted five times the amount they paid for them. The Chief Justice is involved because he and the Smithsonian's Secretary hosted a black tie dinner honoring two of the four donors, a fact that appeared in the third paragraph of the article. Although there is not even a hint of wrongdoing on the part of Chief Justice Burger, the incident cannot have helped his image or the Court's and, if the tax case goes to the Supreme Court, it will at least cause some concern over whether the Chief Justice can hear it.

Even as seemingly innocuous a task as "building manager," has produced unwanted litigation and publicity. Two individuals carrying signs (one of which merely recited the first amendment) on a sidewalk outside the Court were threatened with arrest because a federal statute made such conduct on the Court's grounds illegal. They brought suit under the first amendment against the Supreme Court marshal, who is responsible for supervising the building under the direction of the entire Court, and Chief Justice Burger, who has the statutory duty of approving regulations governing the security and decorum of the Court's property. Eventually, the case went to the Court, but despite his status as a named defendant the Chief Justice did not recuse himself. The fact that eventually the Court unanimously upheld the challenge did not prevent a columnist from highlighting the arguable conflict of interest in banner headlines in Sunday papers around the country: "Suing Burger in the Burger Court." While some might lift an eyebrow whenever the Justices are called upon to decide a case involving protests on the Court's grounds, the problem would surely have been diminished if Congress had not made the Chief Justice responsible for the regulations, but instead had assigned the job to the General Services Administration, which manages most federal property, so that it rather than he had been named as a defendant.

A recent series of events offers further evidence that the problems created by the multiple roles of the Chief Justice are not merely theoretical. On June 28, 1982, the Supreme Court declared that the provisions of the bankruptcy law which allowed bankruptcy judges, who were not appointed for life, to decide certain kinds of cases, were unconstitutional. The Chief Justice cast one of three dissenting votes. Recognizing that the entire bankruptcy system could be seriously disrupted, the Justices agreed to suspend the effect of their ruling until October 4, 1982, to enable Congress to remedy the matter.

At that point, exit the Chief Justice as adjudicator, and enter the Chief Justice as lobbyist and administrator. One solution to this problem would be to make all bankruptcy judges lifetime federal judges. The Judicial Conference apparently saw the addition of 227 bankruptcy judges as a diminution of the prestige of the current district judges and spoke out against it. At one point the Chief Justice even considered appearing on television to express his opposition to the proposal.

Meanwhile, as the October 4 deadline approached, it became apparent that Congress was unlikely to act. In early September the Conference, charged by Congress with overall responsibility for the smooth operation of the federal courts, decided to do something if Congress did not act. With no opportunity for public comment, it issued rules, which it recommended to all federal courts, on how to handle the problem if Congress continued to procrastinate.

Whether because of doubts about the rules' legality or for some other reason, the Justice Department asked the Court to give Congress more time—until December 24, 1982, when the lame-duck session was expected to be over. The Court agreed, and the problem was avoided for another two and a half months. But once again Congress could not agree on a solution, once again the Conference's interim solution was sent out, and once again the Department of Justice asked for more time. This time the Court, with the concurrence of the Chief Justice, said no. That left the federal courts with only the interim rules suggested by the Conference, with the Chief Justice's blessing.

It is unclear whether the interim rules are valid. Even if Congress eventually acts, the saga is not likely to end since some of those who lost cases under the interim rules will seek reversals on the ground that the Conference had no authority to issue them.

If such a case goes to the Court, the Chief Justice will be hard put to maintain a semblance of judicial detachment. Indeed, he is not likely to be the only one with a predilection on the issue. He may well have talked to his colleagues when the second request for more time was denied in December and told them that doom would not truly result from the denial of the stay because the Judicial Conference rules would prevent chaos. Hence anyone challenging the rules could hardly be accused of being cynical if he felt that the judicial deck was stacked against him.

The point is not that anyone did anything wrong or assumed roles not specifically authorized by Congress in trying to cope with this genuine problem. The difficulty arose because Congress had assigned nonjudicial functions to the Chief Justice which are plainly inconsistent with his judicial role.

IV. WHAT CAN BE DONE?

No single additional duty of the Chief Justice takes enough time away from deciding cases so that it can be described as interfering with his judicial responsibilities. Nor will any single foray into the rule-making or legislative arena destroy the impartial image of the Court. But cumulatively the accretion of duties in the office of the Chief Justice is an alarming phenomenon.

The first remedy should be a moratorium on new duties for the Court or the Chief Justice. A recent proposal illustrates just how urgently we need this moratorium. However painful it may be for members of Congress to set their own salaries and decide how much of their expenses of living in Washington should be deductible on their federal tax returns, it surely turns the notion of separation of powers upside down to propose, as did the Senate majority and assistant majority leaders, that the job be turned over to the Supreme Court. Unless Congress stops looking to the Court to solve every difficult problem, the rest of the effort to reduce the power of the Chief Justice will almost certainly fail.

We also should recognize that all of the Chief Justice's added duties do not cause equally severe problems of time commitment, political influence, and apparent prejudice. Unfortunately, the easier solutions don't often match the more serious problems. For instance, a retired Justice could replace the Chief on the boards of various institutes and societies, but this would have scarcely any effect on the Chief's work week or on his influence over important policy matters. The Chief Justice also could abandon his role as ultimate supervisor of the Court's print shop, physical plant and support staff, with no great loss to the Court, but also no great gain.

Finding a replacement for the Chief Justice as the head of the federal judiciary is much harder, partly because the position has so many components. One idea, proceeding from the opposite direction, is to reduce the Court's work load, perhaps by establishing a new court to handle some of the cases that now go to the Supreme Court. Even if there were sufficient support for such a change, it would address only one aspect of the problem of nonjudicial activities.

Developing an earlier suggestion of Chief Justice Burger, Professor Daniel Meador urged that the administrative functions of overseeing the work of the committees of the Judicial Conference, supervising the Administrative Office, and heading the Federal Judicial Center be assigned to a newly created post called "Chancellor of the United States Courts." Creating that job, which might well be filled by a sitting federal judge who would assume the duties on a full-time, but temporary basis, would relieve the Chief Justice of most of his administrative duties pertaining to the federal judicial system. As Meador recognizes, the basic idea has several possible variants, each with its own advantages and disadvantages, but with none likely to replace all of the Chief Justice's obligations. Yet the concept deserves further study.

If one of our concerns is the amount of power possessed by Chief Justices, then one way to attack the problem would be to limit the time that any person may serve as Chief Justice. The Constitution gives all federal judges life tenure; it does not require that the Justice who is also designated as Chief must remain in that position as long as he or she remains on the Court. Since 1958, the chief judges of the district and circuit courts have been required to step down at the age of seventy, although they may remain active judges. In 1982 Congress further reduced the period that any person may serve as chief judge to seven years or the age of seventy, whichever comes first. The same approach makes even more sense for the Chief Justice of the United States. Not only does he have more nonjudicial duties than do most lower court judges, but his influence is far greater than the leader of any circuit or district court. A fixed term, whether determined by age or years of service in the job, would militate against the possibility that any Chief Justice would wield too much power or become out of touch with the political mood of the country. And to the extent that nonjudicial obligations drain the Chief's energy, relieving him of his special duties as Chief will help in the later years when even the most vigorous tend to slow down.

In the meantime, we need to acknowledge that the job of being Chief Justice is not simply that of the highest judge in the land. It seems unlikely that any Chief Justice could greatly reduce his nonjudicial activities merely by eliminating the relatively few tasks that Congress has not imposed. It should be apparent that the position calls not only for a superior lawyer, but also an able administrator, an extraordinarily energetic individual with a broad view of our system of justice and a commitment to exercise the powers of the office in an even-handed manner.

The full scope of the Chief Justice's duties is of more than academic concern, since Chief Justice Burger has recently celebrated his seventy-fifth birthday. When the search for his successor is undertaken, it should be done with a greater appreciation than in the past of the power and scope of the Chief Justice's duties. For if the search is not premised on an accurate assessment of the position, we will never find a person who can perform its functions adequately. If our Chief Justices are going to do much more than decide cases, we need to be sure that they are qualified for their whole job.

B. THE LAW CLERKS

Our experience has been that law clerks, in describing themselves, often inflate their importance and power. But there can be no doubt that these young lawyers do have some influence. Typically, law clerks are the only people trained in law (other than the justices) to whom a justice can talk candidly and conveniently about pending cases.

The readings that follow describe the origins and evolution of the role of the law clerk. Do the clerks have too much power? How could we tell? What seems to explain why the justices typically choose as clerks people who are only a year or two out of law school and hire them for only one or two years? Is experience a disqualification for the job? If you were a Supreme Court justice, what tasks do you think you would assign to your clerks?

DAVID M. O'BRIEN,* STORM CENTER: THE SUPREME COURT IN AMERICAN POLITICS
164–177 (3rd ed. 1993)

JUSTICE AND COMPANY—NINE LITTLE LAW FIRMS

When Potter Stewart joined the Court in 1958, he expected to find "one law firm with nine partners, if you will, the law clerks being the associates." But Justice Harlan told him, "No, you will find here it is like nine firms, sometimes practicing law against one another." Each justice and his staff work in rather secluded chambers with virtually none of the direct daily interaction that occurs in lower federal appellate courts. No one today follows Frankfurter's practice of sending clerks—"Felix's happy hotdogs"—scurrying around the building. "As much as 90 percent of our total time," Powell underscored, "we function as nine small, independent law firms."

> I emphasize the words *small* and *independent*. There is the equivalent of one partner in each chamber, three or four law clerks [eight of the justices each use four clerks, while Justice John Paul Stevens relies on three], two secretaries, and a messenger. The informal interchange between chambers is minimal, with most exchanges of views being by correspondence or memoranda. Indeed, a justice may go through an entire term without being once in the chambers of all of the other eight members of the Court.

A number of factors isolate the justices. The Court's members decide together, but each justice deliberates alone. Their interaction and decision making depend on how each and all of the nine justices view their roles and common institutional goals. According to John Harlan, "decisions of the Court are not the product of an institutional approach, as with a professional decision of a law firm or policy determination of a business enterprise. They are the result merely of a tally of individual votes cast after the illuminating influences of collective debate." By contrast, Burger emphasized, "In this Court we only act together, even when we do not agree. To do our task, we must consult on each step and stage, and almost daily, as the decisions evolve." Intellectual and personal compatibility and leadership may determine whether justices embrace an institutional, consensual approach to their work or stress their own policy objectives. More recently Rehnquist has said, "When one puts on the robe, one enters a world * * * which sets great store by individual performance, and much less store upon the virtue of being a 'team player.' " At worst, as Harry Blackmun observed, the justices are "all prima donnas."

Today, justices "stay at arm's length," in Byron White's view, and rely on formal printed communications partly because the workload discourages justices "from going from chamber to chamber to work things out." Powell also remarked that "collegiality diminishes as the caseload increases." This is particularly troubling for new members of the Court.

The growing caseload has affected the contemporary Court in several ways. By Chief Justice Stone's time, it was well established for each justice to have one law clerk and for the chief justice to have one additional clerk. During Fred Vinson's chief justiceship, the number increased to two and more or less remained the same through the years of the Warren Court. Beginning in 1970, the number gradually grew to three and to four, with Burger having a fifth senior clerk. But see pg. 503. The number of secretaries likewise increased, at first in place of additional clerks and later to help the growing number of clerks. The Legal Office was created in 1975 to assist the justices; subsequently, the staff of research librarians was increased and the secretarial pool was enlarged.

Computer technology also affects the operation of the chambers. In the late 1970s, each chamber acquired a photocopying machine and five or more terminals for word processing and computerized legal research in the library. * * *

The justices' chambers tend to resemble, in Chief Justice Rehnquist's words, "opinion writing bureaus." * * *

Law Clerks in the Chambers

Law clerks have been in the Court just over a century. As the Court's caseload increased, the justices acquired more clerks and delegated more of their work. But in addition to relieving some of the justices' workload pressures, clerks bring fresh perspectives to the Court. For young lawyers one or two years out of law school, the opportunity of clerking is invaluable for their later careers. After their year at the Court, clerks have gone on to teach at leading law schools or to work for prestigious law firms.

On his appointment in 1882, Horace Gray initiated (at first at his own expense) the practice of hiring each year a graduate of Harvard Law School as "secretary" or law clerk. When Oliver Wendell Holmes succeeded Gray, he continued the practice, and other justices gradually followed him. Most justices have had clerks serve for only one year. There are some notable exceptions: one clerk for Pierce Butler served sixteen years; McKenna's first clerk worked for twelve; Frank Murphy kept Eugene Gressman for six; and Owen Roberts had a husband-and-wife team as his permanent clerk and secretary. * * * Burger had his special legal assistant sign on for three to four years.

The selection of clerks is entirely a personal matter and may be one of the most important decisions that a justice makes in any given year. The selection process varies with each justice. But four considerations appear to enter into everyone's selection process: the justice's preference for (1) certain law schools, (2) special geographic regions, (3) prior clerking experience on certain courts or with particular judges, and (4) personal compatibility.

Following Gray and Holmes, Brandeis, Frankfurter, and William Brennan, in their early years on the bench, chose graduates of Harvard Law School. Taft and Vinson tended to select graduates from their alma maters, Yale and Northwestern, respectively. Other justices likewise have tended to draw on their alma maters. Though graduates from Ivy League schools still continue to be selected in disproportionately large numbers, there is now a greater diversity.

Several justices have favored particular geographic regions when selecting clerks. Douglas and Warren tended to select individuals from the West, Charles Whittaker those from the Midwest, and Black those from the South and, in particular, from Alabama. As one former clerk remarked, "The perfect clerk for Justice Black was an Alabama boy who went to Alabama Law School. If that wasn't possible, then someone from the South who went to a leading law school."

As the Court's caseload and involvement with constitutional and statutory interpretation grew, the justices started drawing clerks from lower federal or state courts. Consequently, clerking for a respected judge or on a leading court in the country may now be as important as attending a top law school. Most justices choose clerks for their legal training and experience and not because of ideological affinity with particular federal judges. However, Scalia tends to favor those who in law school belonged to the Federalist Society, a national conservative legal fraternity that he helped found in 1979 while teaching at the University of Chicago Law School.

The position and duties of clerks naturally vary with the justice. Oliver Wendell Holmes initially had little casual contact with his clerks, but when his eyesight began to fade in his later years, they served as companions and often read aloud to him. According to Walter Gellhorn, Stone "made one feel a co-worker—a very junior and subordinate co-worker, to be sure, but nevertheless one whose opinions counted and whose assistance was valued." Likewise, Harold Burton told his law clerks that he wanted each "to feel a keen personal interest in our joint product," and he encouraged "the most complete possible exchange of views and the utmost freedom of expression of opinion on all matters to the end that the best possible product may result." Earl Warren's law clerks communicated with him almost always by memorandum. Some justices prefer to work more or less alone, and some like Douglas and Burger simply did not establish relationships easily. By contrast, Brennan, Blackmun, Powell, Rehnquist, Scalia, and John Paul Stevens set up rather warm working relationships with their clerks. The level of work and responsibility depends on the capabilities and the number of the clerks and varies from justice to justice and over the course of the clerkship year.

At one extreme, perhaps, is Dean Acheson, who said of his working with Brandeis, "He wrote the opinion; I wrote the footnotes." At the other are clerks like Butler's, Byrnes's, and Murphy's who drafted almost all of a justice's written work. Indeed, within the Court, Murphy's law clerks were snidely referred to as "Mr. Justice Huddleson" and "Mr. Justice Gressman." In one instance, Wiley Rutledge wrote to the chief justice, "After discussion with Justices Black and Douglas and Justice Murphy's clerk, Mr. Gressman, it has been agreed that I should inform you that the four of us" agree that the petition should be granted review and that "the case should be set for argument forthwith." On another occasion, Gressman wrote Rutledge, "I have tried in vain to reach Justice Murphy. But I know that he would want to join Black's statement if he files it. It certainly expresses his sentiments. I feel it perfectly O.K. to put his name on it—he would want it that way, especially since you are putting your name on it."

Most clerks' roles fall somewhere between these two extremes. Stone let his clerks craft footnotes that often announced novel principles of law. * * * Frankfurter had his clerks prepare lengthy memoranda, such as the ninety-one-page examination of segregation prepared by Alexander Bickel in 1954, as well as some of his better-known opinions, such as his dissent in the landmark reapportionment case, *Baker v. Carr* (1962).

From the perspective of other justices, Frankfurter "used his law clerks as flying squadrons against the law clerks of other Justices and even against the Justices themselves. Frankfurter, a proselytizer, never missed a chance to line up a vote." * * *

Most justices now delegate the preliminary writing of opinions to their clerks. Earl Warren's practice, for instance, was to have one of his clerks do a first draft of an opinion. Warren would meet with the clerk and sketch an outline of the main points to be included in the opinion. Later he would give the clerk's draft a "word for word edit" in order to get his own style down. * * *

Even though they delegate the preliminary opinion writing, justices differ in their approach when revising first drafts. If a clerk's draft is "in the ball park," they often edit rather than rewrite. But some, like Burton, virtually rewrite their clerks' drafts, while others, like Reed, tend to insert paragraphs in the draft opinions prepared by their clerks. As one former clerk recalled, Reed simply "didn't like to start from the beginning and go to the ending." Consequently, his opinions tend to read like a dialogue with "a change of voice from paragraph to paragraph." * * *

Though there are differences in the duties and manner in which clerks function, certain responsibilities are now commonly assigned in all chambers. Clerks play an indispensable role in the justices' deciding what to decide. As the number of filings each year rose, justices delegated the responsibility of initially reading all filings: appeals, which required mandatory review, and petitions for *certiorari*—"pets for *cert.,*" as Justice Holmes referred to them—which seek review but may be denied or granted at the Court's own discretion. Clerks then write a one- to two-page summary of the facts, the questions presented, and the recommended course of action—that is, whether the case should be denied, dismissed, or granted full briefing and plenary consideration.

This practice originated with the handling of indigents' petitions—*in forma pauperis* petitions, or "Ifp's"—by Chief Justice Hughes and his clerks. Unlike paid petitions and appeals, which are filed in multiple copies, petitions of indigents are typically filed without the assistance of an attorney in a single, handwritten copy. From the time of Hughes through that of Warren, these petitions were solely the responsibility of the chief justice and his law clerks (and this also explains why the chief justice had one more law clerk than the other justices). Except when an Ifp raised important legal issues or involved a capital case, Chief Justice Hughes as a matter of course neither circulated the petition to the other justices nor placed it on the conference list for discussion. Stone, Vinson, and Warren had their law clerks' *certiorari* memos routinely circulated to the other chambers. Chief justices, of course, differ in how carefully they study Ifp's. Hughes and Warren were especially conscientious and scrupulous about Ifp's; the latter told his clerks, "[I]t is necessary for you to be their counsel, in a sense." As the number of Ifp's and other filings grew, they became too much for the chief's chambers to handle alone. They were thus distributed along with other paid petitions and jurisdictional statements to all chambers for each justice's consideration. Accordingly, almost all filings, with the exception of those handled by the Legal Office, are now circulated to the chambers, where clerks draft short memos on most.

With the mounting workload in the 1970s, the role of law clerks in the screening process changed again. In 1972, at the suggestion of Lewis Powell, a majority of the Court's members began to pool their clerks, dividing up all filings and having a single clerk's *certiorari* memo then circulate to all those participating in the "*cert.* pool." Eight justices—Rehnquist, White, Blackmun, O'Connor, Scalia, Kennedy, Souter, and Thomas—now share the memos prepared by their pool of clerks. * * *

Those justices who objected to the establishment of the *cert.* pool and who refuse to join nevertheless find it necessary to have their clerks prepare memos on the most important of those one hundred or more filings that come in each week. * * *

* * *

Stevens's three clerks write memos on only those petitions they deem important. He reviews those and reads the lower-court opinions on all cases to be discussed at conference. For Stevens, the preliminary screening of cases consumes about a day and a half per week.

After the justices vote in conference to hear a case, each usually assigns that case to a clerk. The clerk then researches the background and prepares a "bench memo." Bench memos outline pertinent facts and issues, propose possible questions to be put to participating attorneys during oral arguments, and address the merits of the cases. The clerk stays with the case as long as the justice does, helping with research and draft opinions. The nature of the work at this stage varies with the justice and the case, but it includes research, a hand in drafting the opinion and in commenting on other justices' responses to it, and the subsequent checking of citations and proofreading of the final version. Justices may also tell their clerks to draft concurring or dissenting opinions, while they themselves concentrate on the opinions they are assigned to write for the Court. As each term draws to a close and the justices feel the pressure of completing their opinions by the end of June or the first week of July, clerks perhaps inevitably assume an even greater role in the opinion-writing process.

Has too much responsibility been delegated to law clerks? Do they substantively influence the justices' voting and the final disposition of cases? After thirty-six years on the bench, Douglas claimed that circumstances were such that "many law clerks did much of the work of the justices." Rehnquist has provided one perspective on the function of law clerks: "I don't think people are shocked any longer to learn that an appellate judge receives a draft of a proposed opinion from a law clerk." He added, however:

> I think they would be shocked, and properly shocked, to learn that an appellate judge simply "signed off" on such a draft without fully understanding its import and in all probability making some changes in it. The line between having law clerks help one with one's work, and supervising subordinates in the performance of *their* work, may be a hazy one, but it is at the heart * * * [of] the fundamental concept of "judging."

Some thirty-five years ago, Rehnquist, who clerked for one-and-a-half years with Robert Jackson, had charged that law clerks—who he also claimed tended to be more "liberal" than the justices for whom they worked—had a substantive influence on the justices when preparing both *certiorari* memos and first drafts of opinions. The degree to which law clerks substantively influence justices' voting and opinion writing is difficult to gauge, and it certainly varies from justice to justice. With the increasing caseload, justices have perhaps inevitably come to rely more heavily on their law clerks' recommendations when voting in conference. Yet even when Rehnquist served as a clerk and the caseload was less than a third of its present size, justices no doubt voted overwhelmingly along the lines recommended by their law clerks. Vinson, for one, tallied the number of times he differed with his clerks. There were differences in less than 5 percent of the cases.

Clerks would look very powerful indeed if they were not transients in the Court. Clerks, as Alexander Bickel once noted, "are in no respect any kind of a powerful kitchen cabinet. * * *"

As part of the institutionalization of the Court, law clerks have assumed a greater role in conducting the business of the Court. Their role in the justices' screening process is now considerably greater than it was in the past. At the stage of opinion writing, the substantive influence of law clerks varies from justice to justice, and from time to time in each chamber, as well as from case to case. No less important, the greater numbers of law clerks and of delegated responsibilities contribute to the steady increase in the volume of concurring and dissenting opinions written each year and to the justices' production of longer and more heavily footnoted opinions.

BERNARD SCHWARTZ,* THE ASCENT OF PRAGMATISM: THE BURGER COURT IN ACTION
35–39 (1990)

JUNIOR SUPREME COURT

In a congratulatory letter to Justice Rehnquist, Justice Douglas wrote, "I realize that you were here before as a member of the so-called Junior Supreme Court." Douglas was referring to service as a law clerk to Justice Jackson. Once upon a time, the Douglas characterization of the clerk corps might have been taken as one made wholly in jest, but that was no longer the case.

Over half a century ago, Justice Louis D. Brandeis stated, "The reason the public thinks so much of the Justices of the Supreme Court is that they are almost the only people in Washington who do their own work." The legend that this remains true is still prevalent, and in his book on the Court, even Chief Justice Rehnquist tells us that "the individual justices still continue to do a great deal more of their 'own work' than do their counterparts in the other branches of the federal government."

The Rehnquist-type account has been accepted both by the press and the public. "Alone among Government agencies," Anthony Lewis wrote in the *New York Times,* "the court seems to have escaped Parkinson's Law. The work is still done by nine men, assisted by eighteen young law clerks. Nothing is delegated to committees or ghostwriters or task forces." In an earlier day, the law clerk would perform only the functions of an associate in a law firm, i.e., research for senior members and assistance generally in the firm's work. It may be doubted that Justices such as Holmes or Brandeis used their clerks as more than research assistants. More recently, however, the Justices have given their clerks an ever-larger share of responsibility, including even the writing of opinions.

Complaints against the clerks' role have been common, including a noted 1957 article in *U.S. News & World Report* by William H. Rehn-

* *The Ascent of Pragmatism,* © 1990 by Bernard Schwartz. Reprinted with permis-   sion of Addison–Wesley Publishing Company.

quist himself. Rehnquist stated that the Justices were delegating substantial responsibility to their clerks, who "unconsciously" slanted materials to accord with their own views. The result was that the liberal point of view of the vast majority of the clerks had become the philosophy espoused by the Warren Court.

A reply to Rehnquist was made, largely under Justice Frankfurter's instigation, by Alexander M. Bickel, a former Frankfurter clerk and a leading constitutional scholar. In a 1958 article in the *New York Times,* Bickel asserted that "the law clerks are in no respect any kind of a kitchen cabinet." Their job is only to "generally assist their respective Justices in researching the law books and other sources for materials relevant to the decision of cases before the Court." They also "go over drafts of opinions and may suggest changes."

In the Burger Court, the truth was closer to the Rehnquist than the Bickel picture. "In the United States," notes a recent *London Times* article, "judges have 'clerks', i.e., assistants who prepare and frequently write judgments which their masters often merely adopt and which a qualified observer can easily recognize as the work of a beginner."

An even harsher view of the clerk system was expressed the year after Chief Justice Burger retired by Professor Philip B. Kurland, a leading constitutional scholar. As he notes, the law clerks now exercise a major role in the two most important functions of the Justices: (1) the screening of cases to determine which the Court will hear and decide; and (2) the drafting of opinions. "I think Brandeis would be aghast."

A few years ago, Justice Stevens publicly conceded that he did not read 80 percent of the certiorari petitions presented to the Court. Instead his clerks prepare memoranda summarizing those cases and issues and recommending whether or not certiorari should be granted. The Justice reads only those where the granting of certiorari is recommended. The only member of the Burger Court who personally went over petitions for review was Brennan, who customarily shared the work with his law clerks. * * *

While the Justices make the final decision on what certiorari petitions to grant, *the* work on the petitions is done by the law clerks. In the vast majority of cases, the Justices' knowledge of the petitions and the issues they present is based on the clerks' cert memos, and they normally follow the recommendations in the memos. Sheer volume, if nothing else, has made this the prevailing practice.

The Justices themselves have expressed qualms about this delegation of the screening task. In declining to join the cert pool, Douglas wrote to the Chief Justice: "The law clerks are fine. Most of them are sharp and able. But after all, they have never been confirmed by the Senate." Some years earlier, Justice Frankfurter wrote to Justice Stewart, "The appraisal and appreciation of a record as a basis for exercising our discretionary jurisdiction is, I do not have to tell you, so dependent on a seasoned and disciplined professional judgment that I do not believe that lads—most of them fresh out of law school and with their present tendentiousness—should have any routine share in the process of disemboweling a record, however acute and stimulating their power of reasoning may be and however tentative and advisory their memos on what is reported in the record and what is relevant to our taking a case may be." * * *

An even more important delegation to the clerks involves the opinion-writing process itself. "As the years passed," says Douglas in his *Autobiography,* "it became more and more evident that the law clerks were drafting opinions." Even the better Justices have made more extensive use of their clerks in the drafting process than outside observers have realized. In the Burger Court, indeed, the routine procedure was for the clerks to draft virtually all opinions.

As one federal judge put it, "What are these able, intelligent, mostly young people doing? Surely not merely running citations in *Shepard's* and shelving the judge's law books. They are, in many situations, 'para-judges.' In some instances, it is to be feared, they are indeed invisible judges, for there are appellate judges whose literary style appears to change annually."

* * *

It is, of course, true that the decisions are made by the Justices— though, even with regard to them, the weaker Justices have abdicated much of their authority to their clerks. In most chambers, the clerks are, to use a favorite expression of Chief Justice Warren, not "unguided missiles." The Justices normally outline the way they want opinions drafted. But the drafting clerk is left with a great deal of discretion. The Justices may "convey the broad outlines," but they "do not invari-ably settle exactly how the opinion will be reasoned through." The details of the opinion are left to the clerk, in particular the specific reasoning and research supporting the decision. The technical minutiae and footnotes, which are so dear to the law professor, are left almost completely to the clerks. Thus, footnote 11 of the *Brown* school segrega-tion opinion—perhaps the most famous footnote in Supreme Court history—was entirely the product of a Warren law clerk.

To be sure, the Justices themselves go over the drafts, and, said Justice Rehnquist, "I may revise it in toto." But, he also admits, "I may leave it relatively unchanged." Too many of the Justices circulate drafts that are almost wholly the work of their clerks.

The growing number of law clerks has naturally led to an increase in the length, though plainly not the quality, of opinions. What Douglas once wrote about Court opinions has become increasingly true: "We have tended more and more to write a law-review-type of opinion. They plague the Bar and the Bench. They are so long they are meaningless. They are filled with trivia and nonessentials."

The product of the Douglas animadversion has been one result of the burgeoning bureaucratization of the Court. Law clerks have a similar academic background and little other experience. For three years they have had drummed into them that the acme of literary style is the law review article. It is scarcely surprising that the standard opinion style has become that of the student-run reviews: colorless, prolix, platitudinous, always erring on the side of inclusion, full of lengthy citations and footnotes—and above all dull.

The individual flair that makes the opinions of a Holmes or a Cardozo literary as well as legal gems has become a thing of the past. There is all the difference in the world between writing one's own opinions and reviewing opinions written by someone else. It is hard to see how an editor can be a great judge. Can we really visualize a Holmes coordinating a team of law clerks and editing their drafts?

* * * In the Supreme Court, as in most institutions, the balance of power has shifted increasingly to the bureaucrats and away from the nominal heads. Law clerks now have tremendous influence. All too often the clerk corps sets the tone in the Marble Palace. Asked about the shrillness that some observers perceived in Burger Court opinions, Rehnquist said, "It may reflect conflict among law clerks rather than acerbity or lack of civility among the judges."

C. THE ADVOCATES

1. *The General Quality of Supreme Court Advocacy*

In the beginning, advocates could argue for as long as they wanted. The argument in *Gibbons v. Ogden,* for example, went on for five days; [1] the advocates in *Trustees of Dartmouth College v. Woodward* argued for three days.[2] But, as the Court's calendar became more crowded and concern for efficiency increased, the Court began to consider limiting the time allotted for oral argument. In 1849, the Court imposed time-limits, allocating two hours to each side.[3] The limits were subsequently reduced so that by 1970, the norm had become one-half hour per side.[4]

Today the limit remains at thirty minutes per side, with exceptions made for extraordinary cases. Although the lawyer for each side usually uses his or her full thirty minutes, occasionally the Solicitor General or other amicus curiae is given a slice, usually ten or fifteen minutes, of the allotted thirty minutes. *See e.g., Barefoot v. Estelle,* 460 U.S. 1067, 103 S.Ct. 1519, 75 L.Ed.2d 944 (1983) in which the NAACP was given a portion of the petitioner's time. In special cases, the Court may give both sides additional time. In the *United States v. Nixon,* 417 U.S. 927, 94 S.Ct. 2637, 41 L.Ed.2d 231 (1974), for example, each side was

1. George Dangerfield, "The Steamboat Case," in *Quarrels That Have Shaped the Constitution,* (John Garraty, ed.) (1987), p. 67. The opinion in Gibbons v. Ogden may be found at 22 U.S. (9 Wheat.) 1, 6 L.Ed. 23 (1824).

2. Maurice G. Baxter, *Daniel Webster and the Supreme Court,* (1966), pp. 80–88. The opinion in The Trustees of Dartmouth College v. Woodward may be found at 17 U.S. (4 Wheat.) 518, 4 L.Ed. 629 (1819).

3. 7 How. v (1849).

4. Boskey and Gressman, *Changes in Supreme Court Rules,* 49 F.R.D. 679, 689 (1970). In the 1950s, the Court had two different dockets: the "regular" and the "summary" docket. The more difficult cases were assigned to the regular docket and were given one hour per side; the cases thought to be more simple were allotted only one-half hour per side. W. Rehnquist, *The Supreme Court,* p. 274.

allocated one and one-half hours for its argument. Similarly, in *Bowsher v. Synar,* 475 U.S. 1009, 106 S.Ct. 1181, 89 L.Ed.2d 298 (1986), each side was permitted one hour for oral argument. Occasionally, one or both sides allocate some of the additional time to an amicus. In *Wheeler v. Barrera,* 414 U.S. 1140, 94 S.Ct. 891, 39 L.Ed.2d 97 (1974), for example, each side was given an extra fifteen minutes and the petitioner gave the United States its extra fifteen minutes.

In the reading that follows, Chief Justice Rehnquist describes a variety of types of oral advocates, including the "lector," the "debating champion," the "Casey Jones," the "spellbinder," and finally the "all American oral advocate." While he notes that almost all oral arguments are useful, he urges lawyers to emulate the "all American oral advocate."

Consider, as you read this, whether the United States would be well-advised to establish a more specialized "Supreme Court bar." At present, the only requirement for becoming a member of the "Supreme Court bar" is to be a member in good standing of, and to have been admitted to practice in, an organized bar for three years.[5] Should the qualifications for admission to the Supreme Court bar be tightened? Would the quality of oral advocacy be enhanced if the standards were stricter?

WILLIAM H. REHNQUIST,* THE SUPREME COURT: HOW IT WAS, HOW IT IS
271–283 (1987)

HOW THE COURT DOES ITS WORK: ORAL ARGUMENT

The time that elapses between the grant of certiorari in a case and its oral argument depends upon the time of year at which certiorari is granted and the state of the Court's calendar. Usually a case granted review in September will be argued in January or February, but a case granted review in June will not be argued until December. Several weeks before the oral argument is scheduled, the briefs filed by the parties are available to the justices to read. * * *

Each justice prepares for oral argument and conference in his own way. Several of my colleagues get what are called bench memos from their law clerks on the cases—bench memos being digests of the arguments contained in the briefs and the law clerk's analysis of the various arguments pro and con. I do not do this, simply because it does not suit my own style of working. When I start to prepare for a case that will be orally argued, I begin by reading the opinion of the lower court which is to be reviewed. * * * I then read the petitioner's brief, and then the respondent's brief. Meanwhile, I have asked one of my law clerks to do the same thing, with a view to our discussing the case.

---

5. Supreme Court Rule 5.
* Text: Copyright © 1987 by William H.

Rehnquist. By permission of William Morrow & Company, Inc.

I let my law clerks divide up the cases among themselves according to their own formula. Since there are usually twenty-four cases for each two-week session of oral argument, this means that each law clerk will end up with eight cases for which that clerk is responsible. I think that most years my clerks have divided up the cases with a system something like the National Football League draft, in which those morsels viewed as more choice are taken first in rotation, with the cases viewed as the dregs left until the end.

When the law clerk and I are both ready to talk about the case, we do just that. * * * I tell the law clerk some of my reactions to the arguments of the parties, and am interested in getting the clerk's reactions to these same arguments. If there is some point of law involved in the case that doesn't appear to be adequately covered by the briefs, I may ask the law clerk to write me a memorandum on that particular point. Either before or after I talk about the case with the law clerk, I also go back and read several of our previous opinions that are relied upon by one side or the other. If it is a recent opinion, it is quite easy to imagine that you remember what was said without having to look at it again, but this often turns out to be exactly that: imagination, rather than reality.

I have used this process pretty much since the time I first came to the Court, but when the process I have just described came to an end, I used to wonder what I should do next. If it was an important constitutional question, it obviously deserved extended and deliberate consideration, and I felt there was obviously more that I should do. I would then begin reading decisions from other courts, and cases from our Court that were only tangentially related to the one to be argued; I even set aside a particular time at which I would simply sit down and "think" about the case. None of these backup procedures seemed to advance me much toward my goal; it is much easier to read what someone else has said about a particular legal problem than to try to figure out what *you* think about it. Then I began to realize that some of my best insights came not during my enforced thinking periods in my chambers, but while I was shaving in the morning, driving to work, or just walking from one place to another. This phenomenon led me to revise my approach to preparation for argued cases by sharply cutting down on collateral reading in most of them, and simply allowing some time for the case to "percolate" in my mind.

After I finished reading the lower-court opinion and briefs, reading the controlling precedents, and talking to the law clerks, I would simply go on to the next item of business. I did that not because I had finally reached a conclusion about the case, but with the idea that I now knew enough that thoughts about it would probably occur between then and the time for conference discussion and voting. They might come in a chance bit of conversation with a colleague; they might come some night while I was lying awake in bed; they might come during oral argument. But once I had made myself sufficiently familiar with the case, come they inevitably did. Probably the most important catalyst for generating further thought was the oral argument of that *case*.

The only publicly visible part of the Supreme Court's decision process is the oral argument. It is the time allotted to lawyers for both sides to argue their positions to the judges who will decide their *case*. In our Court, it takes place in the courtroom of the Supreme Court building fourteen weeks out of each year; two weeks each in the months of October through April. During weeks of oral argument, the Court sits on the bench from ten o'clock in the morning until noon, and from one o'clock until three, on Monday, Tuesday, and Wednesday. On each of these days it hears four cases, allotting one half hour to the lawyers for each side in the four cases that it will hear that day. Oral arguments are open to the public, and one can generally find in the newspaper what cases are going to be argued on a particular day.

In the fifteen years that I have been on the Court, the presentation of each side of a case has been limited to one half hour except in cases of extraordinary public importance and difficulty. * * * My experience * * * as a justice convinces me that by and large our present rules for oral argument are about right. There may be an extremely rare case which because of both its importance and its complexity requires more than an hour for oral argument, but in such cases the Court is generally willing to grant additional time. The Supreme Court of the United States does not generally review evidentiary matters, and so the only questions before us in a given case are pure questions of law. Even these are sometimes limited to one or two in number by the order granting certiorari. A good lawyer should be able to make his necessary points in such a case in one half hour.

* * *

Lawyers often ask me whether oral argument "really makes a difference." Often the question is asked with an undertone of skepticism, if not cynicism, intimating that the judges have really made up their minds before they ever come on the bench and oral argument is pretty much of a formality. My answer is that, speaking for myself, it does make a difference: I think that in a significant minority of the cases in which I have heard oral argument, I have left the bench feeling different about the case than I did when I came on the bench. The change is seldom a full one-hundred-and-eighty-degree swing, and I find that it is most likely to occur in cases involving areas of law with which I am least familiar.

There is more to oral argument than meets the eye—or the ear. Nominally, it is the hour allotted to opposing counsel to argue their respective positions to the judges who are to decide the case. Even if it were in fact largely a formality, I think it would still have the value that many public ceremonies have: It forces the judges who are going to decide the case and the lawyers who represent the clients whose fates will be affected by the outcome of the decision to look at one another for an hour, and talk back and forth about how the case should be decided.

But if an oral advocate is effective, how he presents his position during oral argument *will* have something to do with how the case comes out. Most judges have tentative views of the case when they come on the bench, and it would be strange if they did not. * * *

But a second important function of oral argument can be gleaned from the fact that it is the only time before conference discussion of the case later in the week when all of the judges are expected to sit on the bench and concentrate on one particular case. The judges' questions, although nominally directed to the attorney arguing the case, may in fact be for the benefit of their colleagues. A good oral advocate will recognize this fact, and make use of it during his presentation. Questions may reveal that a particular judge has a misunderstanding as to an important fact in the case, or perhaps reads a given precedent differently from the way in which the attorney thinks it should be read. If the judge simply sat silent during the oral argument, there would be no opportunity for the lawyer to correct the factual misimpression or to state his reasons for interpreting the particular case the way he does. Each attorney arguing a case ought to be much, much more familiar with the facts and the law governing it than the judges who are to decide it. Each of the nine members of our Court must prepare for argument in four cases a day, on three successive days of each week. One can do his level best to digest from the briefs and other reading what he believes necessary to decide the case, and still find himself falling short in one aspect or another of either the law or the facts. Oral argument can cure these shortcomings.

On occasion of course we get lawyers who do not come up to even the minimum level of competence in representing their client before our Court, either from lack of training and ability or, even worse, lack of preparation. But the great majority of advocates who appear before us exceed the minimum level of competence one might expect, and most of them are far above average in the profession. In my day as a law clerk, it seemed to me that criminal defendants were not as capably represented as they might have been, because at that time the so-called "criminal lawyer" was often possessed of a second-rate education and second-rate abilities. But that is no longer true today with the proliferation of public defender and similar offices which attract bright and able younger lawyers. The truly outstanding advocate before our Court is still a great rarity: * * * the lawyer who knows the law, knows the facts, can speak articulately, but who knows that at bottom first-rate oral advocacy is something more than stringing together as many well-constructed relevant sentences as is possible in one half hour.

We who sit on the bench day after day to hear lawyers practice this art are bound to become, whether we like it or not, connoisseurs of its practitioners. Rather than try to draw up a long list of do's and don'ts for the oral advocate, I have tried in the following paragraphs to catalog some of the species of practitioners who have argued before the Court in my time.

The first is the lector, and he does just what his name implies: He reads his argument. The worst case of the lector is the lawyer who actually reads the brief itself; this behavior is so egregious that it is rarely seen. But milder cases read paraphrases of the brief, although they train themselves to look up from their script occasionally to meet the judges' eyes. Questions from the judges, instead of being used as an opportunity to advance one's own arguments by response, are looked upon as an interruption in the advocate's delivery of his "speech," and the lawyer after answering the question returns to the printed page at exactly where he left off; returns, one often feels, with the phrase "as I was saying" implied if not expressed. One feels on occasion that at the conclusion of his argument the lector will say, "Thus endeth the lesson for today."

The lector is very seldom a good oral advocate. It would be foolish for a lawyer to stand before an appellate court with *nothing* written out to guide his presentation, but the use of notes for reference conveys a far different effect from the reading of a series of typed pages. The ultimate purpose of oral argument, from the point of view of the advocate, is to work his way into the judge's consciousness and make the judge think about the things that the advocate wishes him to think about. One of the best ways to begin this process is to establish eye contact with as many of the judges as possible, and this simply can't be done while you are reading your presentation.

An oral advocate should welcome questions from the bench, because a question shows that at least one judge is inviting him to say what he thinks about a particular aspect of the case. A question also has the valuable psychological effect of bringing a second voice into the performance, so that the minds of judges, which may have momentarily strayed from the lawyer's presentation, are brought back simply by this different sound. But the lector is apt to receive fewer questions than a better advocate just because he seems less willing than other lawyers to take the trouble to carefully answer the questions. When he has finished reading a presentation to the Court, all he has done is to state a logical and reasoned basis for the position he has taken on behalf of his client before the Court; but this much should have been accomplished in his briefs. If oral argument provides nothing more than a summary of the brief in monologue, it is of very little value to the Court.

The second species of oral advocate who comes to my mind is what I shall call the debating champion. He has an excellent grasp of his theory of the case and the arguments supporting it, and with the aid of a few notes and memorization can depart from the printed page at will. But he is so full of his subject, and so desirous of demonstrating this to others, that he doesn't listen carefully to questions. He is the authority, and every question from the bench is presumed to call for one of several stock answers, none of which may be particularly helpful to the inquiring judge. He pulls out all the stops, welcomes questions, and exudes confidence; when he has finished and sat down, one judge may turn to another and say, "Boy, he certainly knows his subject." But simply showing how well you know your subject is not the same as convincing doubters by first carefully listening to their questions and then carefully answering them.

The third species of oral advocate I shall simply call "Casey Jones." This lawyer has a complete grasp of his subject matter, *does* listen to questions, tries to answer them carefully, and does not read from any prepared text. He is a good oral advocate, but falls short of being a top-notch oral advocate because he forgets about the limitations of those he is trying to convince. The reason I call him Casey Jones is because he is like an engineer on a nonstop train—he will not stop to pick up passengers along the way.

He knows the complexities of his subject, and knows that if he were permitted to do so he could easily spend an hour and a half arguing this particular case without ever repeating himself. He is probably right. For this reason, in order to get as much as possible of his argument into half an hour, he speaks very rapidly, without realizing that when he is arguing before a bench of nine people, each of them will require a little time to assimilate what he is saying. If the lawyer goes nonstop throughout the thirty minutes without even a pause, except for questions, even able and well-prepared judges are going to be left behind. To become a truly first-rate oral advocate, this lawyer must simply learn to leave the secondary points to the brief, to slow down his pace of speaking, and to remember that the lawyer who makes six points, of which three are remembered by the judges, is a better lawyer than a lawyer who makes twelve points, of which only one is remembered by the judges.

Next we come to the spellbinder, who is fortunately today much more of a rara avis than even in the days when I was a law clerk. The spellbinder has a good voice, and a good deal of that undefinable something called "presence" which enables him to talk *with* the Court rather than talk *to* the Court. This species of oral advocate has much going for him, but he tends to let his natural assets be a substitute for any careful analysis of the legal issues in the case. He is the other side of the coin from Casey Jones, who won't let up on legal analysis long enough to give the judges even a mental breathing spell. The spellbinder's magniloquent presentation of the big picture could be copied in part with profit by Casey Jones, but the thorough attention to the subject of the latter could be copied by the spellbinder. The spellbinder's ultimate weapon is his peroration, or at least so he thinks. A florid peroration, exhorting the Court either to save the Bill of Rights from the government or to save the government from the Bill of Rights, simply does not work very well in our Court.

These are but a few of the varied species of oral advocates that have come before our Court in my time. If we were to combine the best in all of them, we would of course have the All American oral advocate. If the essential element of the case turns on how the statute is worded, she will pause and slowly read the crucial sentence or paragraph. She will realize that there is an element of drama in an oral argument, a drama in which for half an hour she is the protagonist. But she also realizes that her spoken lines must have substantive legal meaning, and does not waste her relatively short time with observations that do not advance the interest of her client. She has a theme and a plan for her argument, but is quite willing to pause and listen carefully to questions. The questions may reveal that the judge is ignorant, stupid, or both, but even such questions should have the best possible answer. She avoids table pounding and other hortatory mannerisms, but she realizes equally well that an oral argument on behalf of one's client requires controlled enthusiasm and not an impression of *fin de siècle* ennui.

One of the common misapprehensions about practice before the Supreme Court, which I heard often during my days in private practice in Phoenix and still hear since I have been on the Court, is that if one has business before the Supreme Court of the United States it is best to retain a "Washington lawyer" or a "Supreme Court specialist." The first of these statements is simply not true, and the second is true only in a very limited sense.

During particular times in the history of the Supreme Court, there has been a very definite "Supreme Court bar," consisting of lawyers who follow the work of the Court closely, and appear before the Court regularly year in and year out. Daniel Webster and his colleagues at the bar did this in the days of John Marshall and Roger Taney; Reverdy Johnson, William Evarts, and Matthew Carpenter did it in the days of Salmon P. Chase and Morrison Waite; and Charles Evans Hughes and John W. Davis did it in the days of William Howard Taft. Whether any of these lawyers had any special influence upon the Court I do not know, but apparently a number of clients thought so or they would not have been retained in so many cases.

Based on personal observation during my sixteen years of service on the Court, I am quite firmly of the belief that there is no such Supreme Court bar at the present time. With the exception of the attorneys in the office of the solicitor general of the United States, who of course are not available to represent private clients, it is quite remarkable if a single lawyer argues more than one or two cases a year before us. * * *

I do *not* mean to say that it makes no difference whom a client retains to represent him before our Court. It makes a great deal of difference, but that difference lies not in the geographic location of the lawyer, or his reputation, but in the kind of performance he puts on in any particular client's behalf. A lawyer in Prescott, Arizona, who knows very little about Supreme Court cases and makes equally little effort to find out about them in the process of preparing a brief in the Supreme Court will be of little use to the client. But a Washington lawyer of similar ignorance and laziness will be of equally little use to the client. Every lawyer who stands up and begins to argue orally before our Court is presumed by us to be capable of doing full justice to the client's cause. That presumption may be rebutted, but if so it will be only as a result of the lawyer's performance, and not because of any lack of reputation or experience as a Supreme Court advocate.

* * *

2. *The Solicitor General*

In 1870, Congress decided that the Attorney General needed more permanent assistance and therefore created both the Office of Solicitor General and the Department of Justice.[1] The responsibility of the Solicitor General, or "SG" as the position has come to be called, is "to assist the Attorney General in the performance of his duties."[2] As the readings indicate, those responsibilities are extensive.

The first two readings by Lincoln Caplan and Rebecca Salokar describe the various functions of the SG. Primarily, the Solicitor General is responsible for all government litigation before the Supreme Court. Because the United States is the most frequent litigant to appear before the Court, this responsibility is considerable. The SG decides whether a case in which the United States has lost should be appealed to the Supreme Court. Occasionally, the SG will even "confess error," when he or she believes a government victory in the lower court was erroneous.

In this capacity as the United States' "gatekeeper" to the Court, the SG is often called upon to resolve conflicts among various governmental agencies. The excerpt by Professor Salokar explores the SG's gatekeeper function well. If and when the Supreme Court grants review in a case in which the government is a party, it is the SG's responsibility to decide what position the United States will take, to write the brief, and ultimately to argue the case.

The SG also frequently participates as amicus curiae ("friend of the court"), at both the certiorari stage and the merits phase. Often that participation comes at the invitation of the Court. The Court may invite the SG to give its opinion on the "certworthiness" of a petition being considered by the Court or to file an amicus brief in a case in which cert has already been granted, invitations the SG finds difficult to refuse. As the excerpt from Professor Salokar indicates, a petitioner's chances of persuading the Court to grant cert rise substantially when the SG files in support of a petition, whether the SG's opinion comes by invitation or on its own initiative. To what extent is the SG's success rate at the certiorari stage due to the fact that the SG is a "repeat player" who knows what factors the Court considers important and may be acting essentially as a super law clerk in advising the Court? To what extent is the SG's success rate due to the fact that the Court is likely to ask the SG for its opinion only in cases that have a good chance of being heard?

---

1. Act of June 22, 1870, ch. 150, 16 Stat. 162 (1870). The statute is presently codified at 28 U.S.C. §§ 501, 505.

2. *Id.* Prior to this legislation, the Attorney General operated without any official department and often relied on ad hoc appointments to argue cases on behalf of the United States. See Bloch, *The Early Role of the Attorney General in Our Constitutional Scheme: In the Beginning There Was Pragmatism,* 1989 Duke L.J. 561.

Whatever the reasons for the SG's rate of success, advocates believe they are well-advised to try to get the Solicitor General on their side.

The articles by Richard Wilkins and Michael McConnell, and the formal opinion issued by the Office of Legal Counsel under Attorney General Griffin Bell, explore the controversial question of the degree to which the Solicitor General is and/or should be directed by the political preferences of the Attorney General and President. The SG is a political appointee who serves at the pleasure of the President. At the same time, he or she has a special relationship to the Court. The Office of Solicitor General is the only litigant with a permanent office in the Supreme Court building and one of the few lawyers allowed to file a brief as a friend of the Court without the permission of the parties to the suit.[3] In addition, unlike other litigants who must color-code their briefs according to the document's role in the case—e.g., petitions for cert must be white, responses light orange, appellants' briefs on the merits light blue—the SG alone is permitted to file all its briefs in one color of its choosing, thus making the SG's briefs readily identifiable.[4] Moreover, as noted, the Court frequently asks the SG for its opinion on selected cases.

In reading these articles, consider to what extent this special relationship with the Court may present conflicts with the SG's relationship with the President. Should the Solicitor General be more independent of the President? Should Congress revise the position so as to make it more independent of the President, by, for example, giving the position a fixed term of years? Can Congress do so consistently with the Constitution? What should the SG do when a statute, disliked by the President, is challenged as unconstitutional? Must the SG defend it? If the alleged unconstitutionality is that the statute infringes on the executive branch? Only if the alleged unconstitutionality is something other than an intrusion on the executive branch? Would Congress be well-advised to establish its own counsel to defend its legislation before the Court? Note that the Senate in 1978 created the Office of Senate Legal Counsel for exactly this purpose.[5] The Senate had preferred to establish a joint Office of Congressional Legal Counsel, but the House of Representatives disagreed. Rather than setting up a joint office or a special office for itself, the House chose to have the Clerk of the House handle litigation that involves its members, officers, and staff.[6] Should Congress revisit this issue?

We believe the best way to get an understanding of the role of the Solicitor General is to examine current cases in which the United States

---

3. Sup.Ct.Rule 36.4.

4. The SG briefs today are gray. Caplan, at 21.

5. Title VII of the Ethics in Government Act of 1978, Pub.L. No. 95–521, § 701, 92 Stat. 1824 (codified at 2 U.S.C. § 288–288n).

6. H.R.Conf.Rep. No. 1756, 95th Cong., 2d Sess. 14, reprinted in 1978 U.S.Code Cong. and Admin.News 4381, 4396. For discussion of the House's decision not to agree to establish an Office of Congressional Legal Counsel to represent both houses, see Bloch, *The Early Role of the Attorney General in Our Constitutional Scheme: In the Beginning There Was Pragmatism*, 1989 Duke L.J. 561, n. 200.

is a party as well as cases in which it is amicus curiae. We therefore urge the reader to find such cases, study the SG's briefs, and assess their influence.

LINCOLN CAPLAN,* THE TENTH JUSTICE
3–13 (1987)

THE TENTH JUSTICE

The United States takes pride in its commitment to the rule of law, and during this century the individual who has best represented this dedication may be a little-known figure called the Solicitor General. The nation's constitutional government is distinguished by its need for the consent of the governed, and the law is the compact between the people and their representatives. Of all the nation's public officials, including the Attorney General and the Justices of the Supreme Court, the Solicitor General is the only one required by statute to be "learned in the law." Although he serves in the Department of Justice, and his title, like the Attorney General's, is displayed in large bronze letters on the facade of the Department's building, he also has permanent chambers in the Supreme Court. The fact that he keeps offices at these two distinct institutions underscores his special role. The Solicitor General's principal task is to represent the Executive Branch of the government in the Supreme Court, and when he takes the lectern before the Justices, his status is clear. With his assistants and other lawyers for the government, the Solicitor General is among the last attorneys to carry on the custom of arguing at the Court in formal garb of striped pants, dark vest, and tails. The Justices expect the substance of his remarks to be distinguished as well. They count on him to look beyond the government's narrow interests. They rely on him to help guide them to the right result in the case at hand, and to pay close attention to the case's impact on the law.

Because of what Justice Lewis Powell has described as the Solicitor's "dual responsibility" to both the Judicial and the Executive Branch, he is sometimes called the Tenth Justice. Although he operates in a sphere of government that is invisible to almost all citizens, his influence is undeniable. Some parts of it are not hard to measure. During the 1983 Term of the Supreme Court, of the 3,878 petitions for writs of certiorari (the form in which most parties ask the Court to review a case) submitted by lawyers across the country, the Justices granted only 3 percent. Of petitions from the Solicitor General, they approved 79 percent, or almost four out of five. Whenever the government supported a petition as amicus curiae, or friend of the Court, in a case where it was not directly involved, the chances that the Court would approve the petition rose from 2 percent to 78 percent—up thirty-nine times. The Solicitor General, unlike the ordinary legal counsel, appeared to have almost a standing invitation to come to the Court, and was able to bring along most advocates he sponsored. Once he arrived before the Court, he was even more effective. Of the 262 cases the Justices considered that Term, the government took part in 150. The Solicitor General (or SG, as he is called) won 83 percent of his cases outright and partial victories in another 2 percent, for an exceptional overall success rate of 85 percent.

While the SG's performance has only rarely reached this level, it has been remarkably better than the record of nongovernmental attorneys in almost every year since the SG became the government's chief lawyer and began to do what most people assume falls naturally to the Attorney General. Until 1853, the Attorney General's was a part-time job. He had a smaller salary than the other members of the President's Cabinet, and was expected to supplement his income through the cases that he attracted in private practice because of his office. The government's modest amount of legal business was then managed by lawyers who did not work for the Attorney General, and its court appearances in civil suits were dealt with by a Solicitor in the Department of the Treasury.

In the mid-nineteenth century, as the country grew, the volume of official legal work expanded and became more than the government could handle. Private attorneys then took on the public's cases. But their judgments about the law were sometimes at odds with the government's, and their fees were high. As dissatisfaction with this arrangement spread, a congressional panel known as the Joint Committee on Retrenchment recommended that a Ministry of Justice be established to save money and consolidate the government's legal work under one master. The legislators also realized that the Attorney General was increasingly preoccupied with management and politics, and had little time for the intricacies of courtroom law.

In 1870, when Congress created the Justice Department, it drew on the model of Treasury's Solicitor and directed that "there shall be * * * an officer learned in the law, to assist the Attorney–General in the performance of his duties, to be called the solicitor-general * * *." Congressman Thomas Jenckes, a Republican from Rhode Island who sponsored the bill establishing the office, explained: "We propose to have a man of sufficient learning, ability, and experience that he can be sent to New Orleans or to New York, or into any court wherever the government has any interest in litigation, and there present the case of the United States as it should be presented." Though early SGs tried occasional cases before juries (the first Solicitor was Benjamin Bristow, who had made his reputation prosecuting the Ku Klux Klan), the people in the office have for many years concentrated on the government's appeals, especially to the Supreme Court.

In 1986, the Justice Department had 5,107 attorneys. The SG's office had only twenty-three, the size of a small law firm. The Solicitor's team has always been relatively tiny, but within the Executive Branch the SG has played a powerful and almost judicial role consistent with his standing as the Tenth Justice. For every petition the SG sends to the

Supreme Court, he rejects five from federal agencies with grievances they want the Justices to settle. Often he spurns an agency's request because he thinks it is wrong about the law. (A Solicitor General once wrote, "Government lawyers, like those in general practice, may experience that marvelous adjustment of perspective which often comes to the most ardent advocate when he loses—that is, the realization that he really should have lost.") Even if he thinks the agency is right, the SG is not easily persuaded to allow an appeal. As the then Associate Justice William Rehnquist noted with approval in a 1984 opinion, "The Solicitor General considers a variety of factors, such as the limited resources of the government and the crowded dockets of the courts, before authorizing an appeal." If the facts of a case that the government has lost are so unusual as to give it little weight as a precedent, or if there is general agreement among the dozen regional U.S. Courts of Appeals about the law under scrutiny, the SG will usually accept the defeat.

Lawyers on the Solicitor's team prefer to talk about the cases they present to the Supreme Court, but they spend half their time sifting through proposed appeals from trial-court rulings against the government. In a speech at the University of Oklahoma, one Solicitor General bragged, "If the district court in Oklahoma City makes a decision which the United States Attorney doesn't like, he may well tell the press, 'I am going to appeal.' When I see those statements in the press, I say to myself, 'Yes, he is going to appeal if I say he can.' But sometimes I don't." The SG and his staff have a reputation for stinginess, and the trait matters because they are in effect a court of last resort. By screening cases that they believe are not ready for hearing by the Courts of Appeals or the Supreme Court, the Solicitor General and his aides help assure that judges rule on those the SG does consider ripe for appeal.

* * *

The influence of the Solicitor at the Court goes beyond helping the Justices set their docket. The Justices also turn to the SG for help on legal problems that appear especially vexing, and two or three dozen times a year they invite him and his office to submit briefs in cases where the government is not a party. In these cases especially, the Justices regard him as a counselor to the Court. But in every case in which he participates, the Justices expect him to take a long view. The Solicitor General advises the Court about the meaning of federal statutes as well as about the Constitution, so his judgments regularly affect the work of the Legislature as much as the Executive and the Judiciary. Lawyers who have worked in the SG's office like to say that the Solicitor General avoids a conflict between his duty to the Executive Branch, on the one hand, and his respect for the Congress or his deference to the Judiciary, on the other, through a higher loyalty to the law.

LORE

In a corridor on the fifth floor of the Justice Department, where the lawyers in the SG's office work, photographs of thirty-six of the thirty-eight men who have served as Solicitor General hang in a kind of gallery. Aside from one in color and a sepia-toned print whose border seems tinged with gold, the photos are black-and-white. Like the reputation of the archetypical SG, the subjects of the pictures appear direct, upright, and somehow eccentric. Almost half wear mustaches. None is a woman, and two—Supreme Court Justice Thurgood Marshall and former appeals court judge Wade McCree—are black. Their average tenure has been three years.

Except for a few articles in law reviews, occasional mentions in books about other legal topics, and speeches by Solicitors reprinted in bar journals, little has been written about the SG. The history of the Solicitor General is passed on among the small circle of lawyers who know about it—usually by moving down the line of men pictured in the gallery and telling stories of what they and their teams contributed to the office. The stories are then retold to a new SG or lawyer in the office so he will know the tradition he's expected to uphold.

By most accounts, John W. Davis, who was SG from 1913 through 1918, was one of the truly distinguished Solicitors. He was then appointed Ambassador to Great Britain (in 1918), and ran for President (in 1924), but while he was SG he made the job more prestigious than the Attorney General's. As soon as Davis began his first argument before the Supreme Court as Solicitor General, Chief Justice Edward White sighed in relief: the government's brief was in good hands. As SG, Davis often took long walks with the Chief Justice, who used the chance to remind Davis about the Court's reliance on him. White generally did not say much about himself, but one day he stopped, planted his feet, and said, "You know, Mr. Davis, I'm not an educated man. Everything I get I've got to get through my ears. If you say that something happened in 1898, and the next time you say it happened in 1888, why Sir, it's just as if you'd stuck a knife in me!"

Thomas Thacher, SG from 1930 through 1933, perfected a technique that became an insider's signal of the Solicitor's views. Thacher had given up one judgeship to take the job, and subsequently filled another judgeship, and, perhaps because of his judicial temperament, he was reluctant to sign briefs whose legal validity he doubted; but he was also unwilling, on the other hand, to withhold from the Supreme Court arguments he could not fully discredit. In close cases, he decided, he would sign the government's brief, but tag on a disclaimer that became known among the SG's lawyers as "tying a tin can." "The foregoing is presented as the position of the Internal Revenue Service," the brief would clatter, letting the Justices know it was not the Solicitor General's view. Since the Court rarely subscribes to the arguments of a brief from any part of the government without the SG's sponsorship, the judgment that Thacher (and, later, others) expressed by tying a tin can was usually decisive.

One of the SG's more distinctive practices is known as "confessing error." If a private attorney wins a case he thinks he should have lost in a lower federal court, he is likely to accept his victory in diplomatic silence. But when the government wins on grounds that strike the Solicitor General as unjust, he may "confess error" and recommend that the Supreme Court overturn the flawed decision. Most confessions of error involve criminal convictions, and happen for a range of reasons: a jury was selected unfairly; a judge gave faulty instructions to the jury before asking its members to reach a verdict; there was scant evidence supporting the verdict.

Confessions of error please almost no one but the SG and the defendant, who goes free. The government lawyers who have tried the case feel betrayed. The judge whose decision the SG wants overturned thinks the rug has been pulled out from under him by a double-dealing government. Judge Learned Hand sometimes complained, "It's bad enough to have the Supreme Court reverse you, but I will be damned if I will be reversed by some Solicitor General." Some current members of the Supreme Court—Chief Justice Rehnquist and Justice Byron White, in particular—clearly dislike the practice, and browbeat the SG when he steps up to confess. Rehnquist has urged his colleagues that they should not "respond in Pavlovian fashion" when the SG confesses error, but should instead make their own ruling on the case.

But Archibald Cox, who was SG from 1961 to 1965 and who ranks with Davis and former Supreme Court Justice Robert Jackson as one of the three most respected Solicitors, has expressed a stalwart's faith in the practice of confessing error. "It tests the strength of our belief that the office has a peculiar responsibility to the Court," he told the Chicago Bar Association in 1962, during his tenure as Solicitor. "It affects the way all our other cases are presented. If we are willing to take a somewhat disinterested and wholly candid position even when it means surrendering a victory, then all our other cases will be presented with a greater degree of restraint, with a greater degree of candor, and with a longer view, perhaps, than otherwise." The view expressed by Cox was originally endorsed in 1942 by the Supreme Court, in an opinion that declared, "The public trust reposed in the law enforcement officers of the Government requires that they be quick to confess error when, in their opinion, a miscarriage of justice may result from their remaining silent."

The best-known instance of a Solicitor General acting with candor and disinterest, to use Cox's terms, occurred in 1955, when Senator Joseph McCarthy was just past his heyday and the influence of McCarthyism was still heavy. Someone accused John Peters, a physician, of disloyalty to the United States and membership in the Communist Party. Peters was a senior professor of medicine at Yale University, and had advised the Surgeon General for years as a consultant. The government found Peters innocent of the charges in eight separate hearings held over four years, but he was eventually judged unfit for government service by an agency known as the Loyalty Review Board. The board relied on confidential informers and would not let Peters know the identities of, or cross-examine, these witnesses. He claimed he had a constitutional right to confront them and to rebut the charges they made against him. At every stage of the board's hearings against him, the only evidence publicly introduced was favorable testimony from an ex-president of Yale, a distinguished federal judge, and others in the doctor's corner. The case against him was based on secret testimony—as the chairman of the review board put it, on "evidence given by confidential informants not disclosed" to Peters.

The Solicitor General was Simon Sobeloff, who held the post from 1954 to 1956. When Peters appealed, Sobeloff concluded that it would do no one any good for the Justice Department to oppose him in the Supreme Court. With the encouragement of Attorney General Herbert Brownell, Jr., the SG set out narrow grounds for siding with the doctor. As Sobeloff indicated, the case had "far-reaching importance." It was bad for Peters to be kept in the dark about his accusers, but it was worse that the members of the Loyalty Review Board, acting as judges, were also ignorant about the identities and, therefore, the reliability of some of the informants. The SG called this "well-nigh indefensible," and concluded. "The President recently said in his State of the Union Message: 'We shall continue to ferret out and to destroy communist subversion. We shall, in the process, carefully preserve our traditions and the basic rights of every American citizen.' Now is the time, and this case the appropriate occasion, I believe, for showing the country that the Administration is as firmly pledged to the second sentence as the first."

Brownell asked other senior officials at the Justice Department to consider Sobeloff's argument. FBI Director J. Edgar Hoover strongly disapproved, and Brownell rejected the Solicitor General's proposal. Sobeloff decided his only option was to withhold the SG's backing from the government's case. He refused to sign the government's brief or to argue its merits before the Supreme Court, and another Justice Department official took over the case. The Court ruled against the government and for Peters, though the Justices did not address the major constitutional question.

Outside the Court's rarefied circle, the idea of refusing to represent the government may sound like the gesture of a prima donna. If you do not like what the government stands for, why not quit? The answer lies in the SG's responsibility to the Court as well as the Executive, and, because of that, Sobeloff's decision set a standard of integrity for SGs to come. It also cost him considerably. Prior to Sobeloff's taking his stand, he had been promised a seat on the Court of Appeals for the District of Columbia, perhaps as a step to the Supreme Court. ("Every time Sobeloff comes to see me," said Justice Felix Frankfurter, "I feel as if he's taking my temperature.") Not long afterward, a seat on the appeals court came open, but Sobeloff was passed over in favor of the man who had taken on the Peters case for the government—Warren Burger. Burger made his name as a conservative foil to the liberal majority of the D.C. Circuit, and later was appointed Chief Justice of the

United States. Sobeloff eventually filled a seat on the federal Court of Appeals in Maryland.

Had Sobeloff gone on to the Supreme Court, he would have been one of a handful of SGs who have subsequently won such appointment. They include William Howard Taft, Stanley Reed, Robert Jackson, and Thurgood Marshall. Lloyd Wheaton Bowers would have been in this group, but he died before President Taft was able to appoint him. * * * With such other distinguished figures as Archibald Cox, the first Watergate Special Prosecutor, the SGs-turned-Justices lead a pantheon of highly respected lawyers who have served in the SG's office and gone on to positions of wide esteem in the law. Many of the more prominent former SGs may have become judges in part because the SG's office itself has a judicial cast. A young law professor who hopes to work there said, "It's the only spot, besides a judgeship, where your job is to figure out what you think is the right answer for the law and then to present your argument to the highest court in the land."

The post itself gets a lot of deference from members of the bar, whatever their station. In 1940, Frank Murphy, an experienced and vain politician then freshly appointed to the Supreme Court, asked a clerk if any member of that bench had ever held as many important public offices as Murphy himself. "Well, there was Taft," the clerk answered. "He was Solicitor General, he was a Circuit Court judge, he was president of the Philippines Commission, he was Secretary of War, he was President of the United States, and, of course, he was Chief Justice." Crestfallen, the new Justice asked, "He was Solicitor General, too?"

REBECCA SALOKAR,* THE SOLICITOR GENERAL: THE POLITICS OF LAW
12–14, 22–31, 130–150 (1992)

CHAPTER 1: OFFICE OF THE SOLICITOR GENERAL
RESPONSIBILITIES

The solicitor general of the United States wears many hats in the Department of Justice. In addition to being a part of the organizational chain of command for the department, the officeholder is tasked with a broad range of responsibilities that include work before the Supreme Court as well as any other court in the nation. The solicitor general must authorize the United States attorneys to proceed with an appeal in every case that the government loses in a lower court. Although this basic appellate work requires a significant amount of manpower within the office, most members of the solicitor general's staff see their work before the Supreme Court as the most important.

There are a variety of tasks managed by the solicitor general's office with respect to Supreme Court litigation. These responsibilities include the following:

* Excerpts from Rebecca Salokar, *The Solicitor General: The Politics of Law* © 1992 by Temple University. Reprinted by permission of Temple University Press.

— Deciding which cases warrant a petition for certiorari to the Supreme Court.

— Writing and revising briefs in support of or opposition to certiorari.

— Writing and revising briefs for cases selected by the Supreme Court for a decision on the merits in which the government is a participant.

— Presenting oral arguments in the Supreme Court, or authorizing another party to present arguments.

— Submitting amicus curiae briefs to the Supreme Court when the United States is an interested party.

— Authorizing others to intervene as amicus curiae in cases where the United States is a party.

— Deciding on intervention where the United States has a technical right to intervene.

— Mediating interdepartmental disputes that arise over matters of legal policy.

In short, the solicitor general is responsible for any and all actions on behalf of the United States government before the Supreme Court. Although some rare exceptions have been made to allow certain agencies of the government to argue cases without the solicitor general's assistance, the agencies will have had at least the solicitor general's approval to present their cases.

These mandated responsibilities are accomplished not only by drawing on the expertise of the staff within the solicitor general's office but through close cooperation with the various staff attorneys assigned to the other divisions of the Department of Justice (for instance, Civil, Civil Rights or Antitrust Divisions), the senior counsels of governmental departments (Labor, Transportation, et cetera) and with the lawyers for independent agencies (such as the National Labor Relations Board, Interstate Commerce Commission, or Federal Trade Commission). Because these other agencies have been working on the cases since the trial stage, they often provide the solicitor general with a thorough history of the cases, as well as insight on the contested legal issues. As Solicitor General Charles Fried noted in an oversight hearing before the House of Representatives, "We do not sit on the fifth floor of the Department of Justice, scan the legal universe, and then decide what will happen. Rather, they, divisions and departments of Government with programmatic responsibilities come to us with recommendations, which we approve, and then proceed, in the Supreme Court, to brief and argue for them." In essence, the Office of the Solicitor General is not insulated from other areas of government in accomplishing its work. Rather, it is subject to a range of influences from the executive branch, Congress, and even the Supreme Court, itself.

In 1987, Solicitor General Fried represented the government before the Supreme Court and performed the other appellate tasks required of his office with a budget of only $3,861,000. This included his own salary and the salaries of twenty-two staff attorneys, as well as technical and clerical support (personnel and equipment). When compared to some of the private law firms of this nation, the office is a relatively inexpensive operation. Yet it is one of the "finest law firms" in the nation, according to former Solicitor General Fried.

A closer examination of the total workload of the solicitor general sheds light on both the frequency with which the government appears before the Supreme Court and its overwhelming success in this arena. By focusing on the 1959 to 1989 Supreme Court terms, it is evident that the government is a decisive presence before the Court. More important, however, is the substantial success that this small "law firm" enjoys before the highest court in the nation.

THE SUCCESSFUL LITIGANT

The Supreme Court's jurisdiction, its power to hear cases, and decide controversies, is rooted in constitutional, legislative, and self-imposed rules and practices. This quagmire of standards permits the Court a wide range of discretion in deciding which cases it will hear each term. It is within this rather tentative and unpredictable scheme that the solicitor general of the United States must select the cases the government will pursue. Additionally, the government's attorney must also respond to suits in which a private litigant attempts to take the government to the Supreme Court. Just how successful is the government in getting on the Court's agenda when acting as a petitioner, getting off the Court's agenda when named as a respondent, and, most important, how often does the government prevail when the case is decided on the merits? The answers to these questions confirm that the Office of the Solicitor General is an exceptionally successful litigant before the Supreme Court.

Agenda Success

Most of the Supreme Court's workload involves cases appealing a lower-court decision, and the key means of gaining the Court's review is through the petition for a writ of certiorari.

* * *

The most frequent form of government participation in certiorari cases was as respondent, responding to a suit brought by an aggrieved private litigant or state against the United States. The solicitor general responded to 38,412 certiorari cases during the 1959 to 1989 terms.
* * *

The government was quite successful in having these cases dismissed early in the certiorari process. Over 96 percent of the cases naming the United States as respondent were eliminated at the first stage with the decision by the Court to deny certiorari or review. This is not surprising considering that the Court routinely dismisses 91 percent of all certiorari requests with or without government involvement. The government, although successful as a respondent at this first stage of litigation, does not seem to enjoy any special advantages over the private respondent.

As petitioner, however, the solicitor general has a significant advantage over private litigants. As the attorney for the United States, the solicitor general has available a large pool of possible certiorari requests and selects only a small number of cases that will most likely meet the standards of the Court in granting review and, subsequently, result in a decision favoring the government. And even if the government is denied review, it is likely that cases raising similar issues will flow into the office at a later time providing other opportunities for Supreme Court review. Private litigants, on the other hand, are usually involved in only one case and do not enjoy the same selection of opportunities. A denial of certiorari by the Court generally means the end of the litigation for the private petitioner.

The advantage that the solicitor general enjoys in his capacity as a petitioner is clear. The solicitor general sought certiorari in 1,294 cases between 1959 and 1989, and was successful in obtaining the Court's review 69.78 percent of the time. Certiorari requests were granted in only 4.9 percent of the private litigation. Given such poor odds, it is no wonder that private litigants seek the government's support through an amicus brief.

The amicus curiae or "friend of the court" brief permits the government (and other litigants) to participate in a case in which the United States is not formally named as a party. Amicus briefs may be filed either at the petition stage, when the Court is deciding whether or not to review a case, or at the stage when the justices are considering the merits or issues of a case. By filing an amicus brief, the solicitor general has the opportunity to present the government's views on a range of issues. The government may wish to express its support for, or opposition to, a petition for a writ of certiorari. Additionally, the solicitor general is likely to address the potential impact a decision will have on federal law and federal agency operations and programs or simply provide additional information and legal considerations not contained in the litigants' documentation. Finally, the amicus brief has served as a vehicle to express the administration's policy positions and goals on issues that have historically been considered outside the scope of federal law.

* * *

It is clear that the solicitor general's amicus support of petitioners significantly benefits the private litigant. When the government filed an amicus brief on behalf of the appellant or petitioner, the Court granted review in 87.6 percent of the cases. Surprisingly, this success is even greater than when the government sought the Court's review of its own cases.

More curious, however, is the government's apparent influence as an amicus on behalf of respondents. Of the 484 cases in which the United States sided with the respondent or appellee, the private litigant had only a 60 percent chance of getting the most favorable outcome, a denial of review. When we consider that nearly 95 percent of all certiorari cases and over 79 percent of appellate cases without government involvement are routinely denied review, the amicus support of the solicitor general appears to be detrimental to the private litigant trying to stay out of court.

* * *

These findings support the argument that the government's participation serves as a cue or signal to the Court in its search for cases that merit review. Unfortunately for private respondents, the cue is also used for their cases. The court may view the government's intervention as a red flag indicating executive interest or that the case is controversial and involves legal issues important enough to merit the solicitor general's attention and that, therefore, perhaps the Court should also give the case serious consideration.

An alternative explanation for the government's support of respondents and the apparently negative impact on those litigants may hinge on the Court's amicus invitation to the government, an invitation that is seen as an order. The *Annual Reports of the Attorney General of the United States* do not indicate which cases involved an invitation to the solicitor general. However, Puro found that nearly half of the solicitor general's amicus cases were the result of a Court request.*

Success in Merit Decisions

* * * [T]he grant of a writ of certiorari by the Supreme Court to the request of the United States, is only a partial victory. The agreement by the Court to review a lower-court decision against the government is not a guarantee that the final outcome of the case will reverse the lower-court's decision. * * *

During the 1959 to 1989 terms, the Court decided 8,926 cases on the merits. The government participated either as a party to the suit or as an amicus in 4,329 (47.5 percent) of these cases. * * *

The success that the solicitor general enjoys at the early stages of the Court's decision making continues in decisions on the merits. The government's position prevailed in 2,961 (67.6 percent) of the cases in which it participated. There were 1,159 decisions (26.8 percent) between 1959 and 1989, that were clearly against the government's position and 209 decisions (4.8 percent) that were unclassifiable. The decisions on the merits in favor of the government were the result of the solicitor general actually "going to the mat" with an opposing litigant and being declared the victor by the Supreme Court.

* Steven Puro, "The Role of the Amicus Curiae in the United States Supreme Court: 1920–1966" (Ph.D. Dissertation, State University of New York at Buffalo, 1971).

Two studies of interest group litigants provide the means to compare the success of the government in decisions on the merits. In an analysis of the Legal Services Program, Susan Lawrence found that this organization won 62 percent of its cases before the Supreme Court. According to Karen O'Connor and Lee Epstein, the Women's Rights Project of the American Civil Liberties Union was even more successful in its litigation before the Court, winning 66 percent of its cases. The success of these two interest groups clearly rivals that of the government, but the comparison is limited to this single category of cases and does not tell the whole story.

More revealing is to consider all of the "first-round knockouts" that the government enjoys, the early dismissals rendered by the Court through denials of certiorari and refusals to grant jurisdiction. The success rate of the government increases substantially when these early victories and losses are tabulated in conjunction with the decisions on the merits * * *.

When all of the "quick" victories and losses are considered, the government is successful in nearly 96 percent of the cases in which it participates. The core of this success rests on the more than 36,000 cases brought by private litigants against the government that were subsequently denied certiorari by the Supreme Court. * * *

In this respect, the United States enjoys unrivaled success. On the average, only one of every twenty-five private claims docketed before the Supreme Court against the United States is accepted for the Court's review. And even when these private cases are decided by the justices on the merits, only one of every four are held in favor of the private litigant. In essence, private litigants win a mere 1 percent of their cases against the United States before the Supreme Court.

THE DEFINITIVE "REPEAT PLAYER"

In a study of why certain litigants prevail in the courtroom over others, Marc Galanter recognized a distinction between "Repeat Players" and "One–Shotters." The Repeat Player enjoys a substantial measure of success over the less frequent litigant. He defines a Repeat Player as "a unit which has had and anticipates repeated litigation, which has low stakes in the outcome of any one case, and which has the resources to pursue its long-run interests."

Solicitors general are the definitive Repeat Players. They enjoy the numerous advantages of the Repeat Player including advance intelligence, access to specialists, a wide range of resources, expertise, opportunities to build informal relations with the Supreme Court, and a high degree of credibility before the Court. In addition, the government is more interested in the long-term development of the law and rules than in the immediate success of a particular case.

Institutional overload also favors the Repeat Player. According to Galanter, "Typically there are far more claims than there are institutional resources for full dress adjudication of each." The sheer number of cases on the Court's docket favors the solicitor general over the One–Shotter, the infrequent litigant who attempts to take her case before the Supreme Court. Lastly, Galanter has pointed out that the rules, "a body of authoritative normative learning," also favor Repeat Players since these litigants have "successfully articulated their operations to pre-existing rules."

The complicated nature of the rules further requires the resources of legal experts that One–Shotters do not traditionally have at their disposal. The solicitor general has access not only to a staff of professional lawyers who are skilled in the intricacies of Supreme Court adjudication, but to issue experts scattered throughout the Department of Justice and the executive branch. The solicitor general, Repeat Player par excellence, is highly successful before the Supreme Court.

* * *

Chapter 3: Untangling The Bramblebush
The Clients: Divisions, Departments, and Agencies

A significant portion of the solicitor general's work involves managing Supreme Court litigation on behalf of the various divisions within the Department of Justice, other executive departments, and the independent agencies. With few exceptions, all government entities must "hire" the government's lawyer in order to pursue their case before the Supreme Court. A lawyer's job is to advise his client of the best avenues of legal recourse, but the solicitor general does more than offer advice. He makes the decisions on behalf of the client. In this capacity, the solicitor general acts as a gatekeeper for the Court, selecting only the best government cases for the Court's review. The solicitor general is also a mediator, judge, broker, or "head basher" when conflicts arise between agencies, departments, or divisions. * * *

Much of the work of the solicitor general involves the various divisions within the Department of Justice. Since the department is charged with enforcement of the nation's laws, it only makes sense that many of the government's cases will emanate from these divisions. If the executive departments (such as the Departments of Transportation, Veterans' Affairs, and the Treasury) must be consulted on the policy (as opposed to the legal) aspects of a pending case, the solicitor general will usually work through the divisions of the Department of Justice to obtain the necessary information.

Recommendations on a range of legal activities flow into the solicitor general's office from the agencies. Using their own counsel, the agencies track cases in their areas of interest as litigation moves through the lower courts. Agency counsel must also be aware of the Supreme Court's docket, looking for cases in which the government might need to file an amicus brief in order to protect its interests. * * *

The agencies notify the solicitor general of their interest in a case through a memorandum that is screened by the assistants in the office. Some divisions and agencies even go so far as to send a prepared draft of the brief. When the Court invites the government to submit its views through an amicus brief, the divisions and agencies are asked for input.

The assistants in the solicitor general's office will work with the counsel of the various divisions in preparing the case once approval has been given by the solicitor general to go forward. Since most of the requests sent by the agencies will be rejected, conferences may be held between the general counsel of the agency or division and the solicitor general or one of his deputies.

* * *

[T]he solicitor general faces [considerable difficulty] when deciding which of the agencies' cases will reach the Court. The agencies' perspective is that they are responsible for developing the policies of the government and, as such, are in the best position to determine which issues are most important for judicial resolution. The solicitor general, on the other hand, is charged with ensuring that the cases taken to the Court can be won, are important enough for the Court's attention, and will result in "good law." * * *

Conflicts between the desires of an agency or division and the decisions of the solicitor general to block an agency's access to the Supreme Court can be resolved in a number of ways. On some occasions, the solicitor general will simply tell the agency, "No," and the issue is dead. A division or agency may attempt to go above the solicitor general to the attorney general or even the White House. * * * [Occasionally] the solicitor general has stepped aside and permitted an assistant attorney general to handle the case without his support or approval. In still other cases, the solicitor general may accept the agency's argument and prepare the brief including a footnote that states that the solicitor general does not subscribe to the argument presented. *Bob Jones University v. United States* * * * is one example.

The situation can be even more difficult for the government's lawyer when two agencies or divisions disagree in the same case. Due to these "accidents of litigation," cases come before the solicitor general in which agencies want to take opposing positions. The role that the solicitor general plays in resolving these conflicts depends upon who holds the office. In my interviews, the terms "broker," "mediator," and "judge" were used by former solicitors general to describe their approach to dispute resolution.

Rex Lee felt that he was more than a mediator; he felt he was acting as a judge in determining which position would be presented to the Court.

> When there was a conflict within government, as not infrequently happened, I would hold a hearing and hear the opposing points of view. And when I made the decision, that was the position that was taken by the federal government. And it usually meant that the opposite point of view simply would not be represented. It always sobered me because I realized that the decision I was making, unlike

the circumstance in private practice, precluded one of my clients from presenting that client's point of view to the Supreme Court. It not only meant that I would not present it, it meant that no one would.

Lee hesitated to resolve these conflicts by allowing both points of view to be presented to the Court, a practice that has occurred in the past. But he did recognize that occasionally he would act as a mediator, attempting to resolve the issue so that all sides were content. One such case involved the three bank regulatory agencies and the Securities and Exchange Commission (SEC). The compromise position presented by the government was ultimately accepted by the Court. Lee's successor, Charles Fried, also viewed his role in this light, serving as a broker between the agencies and divisions to negotiate a resolution to the impasse.

Cox was more adamant about his part in dispute resolution. "My view was that I would try to knock heads together and impose a unified position. I think there was only one instance in which I simply couldn't do it." That case was *St. Regis Paper Co. v. United States*. The issue involved a conflict over an attempt by the Federal Trade Commission (FTC) to force a manufacturer to submit file copies of census reports as part of an antitrust investigation, reports that the government had promised would be kept confidential. With the Census Bureau, the Department of Commerce, and the Bureau of the Budget on one side of the case and the FTC and Antitrust Division on the opposite side, Cox prepared a brief that addressed both positions. In an effort to dissuade the Court from reaching a decision on the merits, Cox also argued that the matter was rendered moot by the submission of the requested reports in conjunction with the judicial investigation. He wanted, if possible, to avoid a decision against either side. At oral argument, he presented the standing issue and argued both sides. The Court was not convinced by Cox's effort to avoid the merits and acknowledged the dispute within the executive branch in its decision for the FTC and Antitrust Division.

The question of whether the government can oppose itself before the Supreme Court came up years earlier in a case involving the Interstate Commerce Commission (ICC). The rules of the Court state that only cases of an adversarial nature will be accepted for review. In *United States v. Interstate Commerce Commission,* the government took both sides of the case; it would both win and lose. The issue came about as a result of the government's activities in the shipping industry, which made it subject to the rate-setting jurisdiction of the ICC. In an initial hearing before the ICC, the United States lost its case and subsequently sued the ICC in a special three-judge district court. Because of a statutory requirement that all suits against the ICC "shall be brought * * * against the United States," the United States named itself as both the plaintiff and the defendant in the lower court. The district court dismissed the suit since it lacked adversity: the government could not sue itself.

On direct appeal, the Supreme Court recognized that the issue was justiciable, that a real controversy existed. "Thus a suit filed by John Smith against John Smith might present no case or controversy which courts could determine. But one person named John Smith might have a justiciable controversy with another John Smith. This illustrates that courts must look behind names that symbolize the parties to determine whether a justiciable case or controversy is presented." The Court also dealt with the conundrum that each party was being represented by the same attorney, the attorney general of the United States. "Although the formal appearance of the Attorney General for the Government as statutory defendant does create a surface anomaly, his representation of the Government as a shipper does not in any way prevent a full defense of the Commission's order." This 1949 decision set the precedent for Cox's unique method of dispute resolution in the *St. Regis* case: let the courts decide.

Griswold's perspective on resolving agency conflicts suggests that he would attempt to get a consensus, but that, in the end, he would make his own decision. In one particular case that involved the rebroadcasting of television programs to remote locations, the Copyright Office of the Library of Congress, the Federal Communications Commission and the Antitrust Division of the Department of Justice each had their own position. "I found the problem far from easy to solve. I had a meeting with all of them together. Couldn't get any kind of agreement or hearing from any of them and finally decided to make my own decision. And my staff and I prepared a brief * * *. I've forgotten just how they [the Court] did decide it. But the Congress came along about four years later and passed a statute exactly that way."

In another instance, this one involving the patents office, Griswold was confronted by a former student who was representing the commissioner of patents. Griswold planned to argue against a rule that a licensee cannot dispute the validity of a patent. "And finally, Jim said to me, pounding the table, 'Well, I want to know who makes that policy in this government.' And I said, 'Well, Jim, when the case is in the Supreme Court, we do.'" Griswold's position was upheld by the Court and, years later, his former student conceded that the case did resolve some problems with the law.

The work with other areas of the executive branch becomes even more complicated when an independent regulatory agency seeks access to the Supreme Court. In the legislation establishing several of the regulatory agencies (particularly, the National Labor Relations Board [NLRB], the Securities and Exchange Commission [SEC], the Federal Trade Commission [FTC], Tennessee Valley Authority [TVA], and others), Congress specifically granted them the authority to litigate their own cases. Although the degree of this authority varies by agency and by the level of adjudication, Olson found that thirty-five agencies had been given this power by 1982. The question that has come up several times, but has generally been avoided, is whether or not the independent regulatory agencies have the right to take their own cases to the Supreme Court without the approval of the solicitor general.

Rather than address this potential conflict, the solicitor general traditionally has authorized the counsel of an independent agency to proceed with its own arguments. But this approval is only given when the agency counsel threatens to broach the controversy. "There was an occasion when a question came up with the SEC and where the SEC had been refused a number of times for filing petitions and decided at one point that they would then represent themselves and ask for authority from the solicitor general to do so. I don't know whether they needed it or not. In any event, they went ahead and they lost, huge losses, 9–0, 9–0, and I think that at some point along the line, they decided they better come back into the fold."

One former staff attorney suggested that the Court would probably refuse to hear a case that the solicitor general had not authorized. "At a minimum, if the petition were filed on behalf of a government agency without the solicitor general's name on it or authorization, it would immediately draw the conclusion that the solicitor general doesn't think much of this case."

* * *

In working with the agencies, the solicitor general also ensures that the legal positions the government takes are consistent over time. This is particularly difficult when there have been changes in administrations and in policies. Lee was confronted with such a case in 1982, *Utah Power and Light Company v. Federal Energy Regulatory Commission.* In the Federal Power Act of 1918, the Federal Energy Regulatory Commission (FERC) was permitted to favor publicly owned utilities over investor-owned companies when granting ownership licenses for hydro-electric dams. This policy had been followed through the Carter administration. With license renewals pending, private companies filed suit to block this preferential treatment. While the case was being litigated, however, the Reagan administration came into office. With new appointees to the FERC, the agency shifted its position on municipal preference and asked Lee to urge the Supreme Court to vacate the lower-court's decision. This lack of consistency was exactly what the solicitor general tried to avoid. Rather than filing a motion to vacate, Lee recommended that the Supreme Court remand the case to the court of appeals for further consideration. The Court denied certiorari, however, leaving the lower-court's decision intact.

In a second example of the solicitor general's efforts to maintain the consistency of the government's positions, the Court had invited the solicitor general to submit an amicus curiae brief. Solicitor General Bork and his staff took the issue to the State Department for their views: "When it [the State Department] finally did submit its views, they were contrary to statements that we had made on behalf of the State Department eight years earlier or some similar period of time. And we concluded, having advised the State Department eight years ago that the law should be 'x,' we couldn't turn around now just because there was a different legal advisor at the State Department who said that the law really should be 'y.' But that meant we had a tremendous conflict with the State Department which the solicitor general had to resolve and he resolved it in favor of what had been before." The case was *Alfred Dunhill of London, Inc. v. Republic of Cuba.* The position taken by the government as amicus urged reversal and was argued by Antonin Scalia. The Court ruled in favor of the petitioner and the United States.

The relationship of the agencies, divisions, and departments with the Office of the Solicitor General is an important one. The examples provided give credence to the argument that the solicitor general is a critical actor in the policy decisions of the executive branch. He determines exactly which policies will be taken to the Court and what the position of the government will be on that particular issue. Although the question of independent litigation authority has never been formally resolved, the agencies have tacitly acknowledged the right of the solicitor general to deny them access to the Supreme Court. Only in rare instances do they challenge the solicitor general's expertise and judgment as the government's lawyer.

* * *

CHAPTER 4: VESTED INTERESTS

TRANSITION CASES: A PROBLEM OF UNFINISHED BUSINESS?

* * *

[A]dministrations differ on policy issues, priorities, and their ideological beliefs about the role of government; cases [pending before the Court when a new Administration takes office] can pose a dilemma for the newly elected president and appointed solicitor general.

* * *

One of my early considerations in studying the Office of the Solicitor General was that transitional cases would pose great difficulty for the incoming appointee. In my interviews and research, I came across only one instance in which an administration was so disgruntled by a position taken before the Court by the previous administration that it tried to force the solicitor general to reverse the government's position. Transitional cases are simply not a problem.

The pressures to resist changing the position of the United States and to argue the case as it was filed are directly tied to the belief that the solicitor general must maintain his reputation before the Court. A blatant reversal of position "would not but undermine the respect traditionally accorded the Department of Justice and the Office of the Solicitor General by the justices on the Court." As a former staff member explained,

It is very, very difficult once a case has been filed in the Supreme Court involving the government, for the government to shift position because it kind of destroys its credibility with the Court. In other words, the factors that led the government to ask the Supreme Court to hear a case have not changed. If it turns out that there is a change in the administration and suddenly the new administration says, "Well, we don't think you should hear this case," you begin to wonder how correct the first one was. And then two years later when the new solicitor general says something, how accurate is that?

In short, any evidence of being a "wishy-washy" litigant can damage the reputation of the solicitor general and irritate the Court.

There are other reasons the government does not change its position when a new administration takes office. One has to do with timing. Because cases in which the government has filed a petition have usually been docketed, a new solicitor general would have to ask the Court to delay the oral arguments or even defer their decision and set the case for reargument in order to permit the new administration to file its views. "Such a move, however, would require lightning-fast coordination by the new and yet-to-be-coordinated team."

A second reason that transitional cases are not treated any differently than other cases is that, "Cases have a life of their own. There are too many people interested in succeeding." Deputy Solicitor General Lawrence Wallace explained that the solicitor general's office works closely with the career staff in the various divisions of the Department of Justice and the independent regulatory agencies. By the time the case gets to the solicitor general, the attorneys in these divisions and agencies as well as their "publics" have become careful watchdogs of the proceedings.

In my analysis of the Supreme Court decisions of cases in which the government was a participant, I isolated those cases that would have been filed by one administration and argued by another. I detected no differences in the success rates of the government in these transitional cases. In testing the hypothesis that an incoming administration might subtly try to "throw" the cases as a result of a disagreement with the former administration's positions, I found absolutely no evidence of such behavior. The cases that are inherited by an incoming administration are argued and briefed as diligently as the cases that are filed by the new administration.

There have been occasions in the past in which the government did switch sides during the judicial proceedings. However, this usually occurs during the trial stage or between the trial stage and the first appeal.

* * *

CHAPTER 5:

FRIEND OF THE COURT: THE GOVERNMENT AS AMICUS

Amicus participation is another facet of the solicitor general's work before the Supreme Court. As a "friend of the court," the government's lawyer can enter any case on the docket and submit the views of the executive branch for the justices' consideration. In this capacity, solicitors general are sometimes even more successful than when they argue on behalf of their own client. It has been suggested that solicitors general enjoy a greater degree of freedom in their amicus activity than when the government is a party to the case. This discretion extends not only to selecting the cases in which they will participate, but also to formulating the arguments that the government will present to the Court. The Court's practice of inviting the government to express its views is of particular interest since the "invitation" limits the discretionary nature of the solicitor general's decisions.

The amicus brief provides the government with an extra tool to gain access to the Court's docket. Unlike cases in which the government is a party, the outcome of an amicus case is less likely to have a direct impact on the executive branch. In some respects, amicus participation is a low-risk venture for the government. But more important, it allows the executive branch to further its political agenda before the Court.

WITH FRIENDS LIKE THIS, YOU CAN'T LOSE

The amicus curiae brief has historically been used to provide the Court with information that may not have been available or well developed in the briefs of the litigants. By allowing a third party to submit its views, the justices enjoy a diversity of perspectives, additional technical information, and even an insight into public opinion. * * *

The filing of an amicus brief is governed by Supreme Court rule 36. Private parties or interest groups who wish to present their views to the Court must first obtain the permission of both litigants in the case. The United States, by way of the Office of the Solicitor General, is specifically exempted from the consent requirement. In short, the solicitor general may submit the views of the government in any case on the docket. Amicus briefs can be submitted at the jurisdictional or petition stage, or when the case is set for plenary action.

The solicitor general can also request argument time from the Court in order to present the government's views. In practice, the solicitor general makes this request only when his arguments are substantially different from those of the litigants or when his participation is specifically requested by a litigant who is willing to forego a portion of its assigned time. In the mid–1980s, the solicitor general was denied permission by the Court to argue in several cases. Rumors around the Court were that the denials were the justices' way of telling the solicitor general that he had become "too political." "There was a time when there were rumors from the Court, from the clerks, that the Court had much less confidence in whatever the solicitor general might have to say about the agenda cases than everybody had thought was the case in prior years." There is no way to substantiate the story. However, it had an impact on the staff of the Solicitor General's Office. The message that was received was, "You can file a brief because the rules say that you don't need anybody's permission, so we've got your brief, but we really don't need to hear from you."

During the 1984 term, the solicitor general submitted six amicus briefs supporting petitions of certiorari and six in support of jurisdictional statements. Of these twelve cases, the Court agreed to set ten for plenary review. The solicitor general may also file an amicus brief to dissuade the Court from reviewing a case on behalf of a respondent. During that same year, the government urged the Court to deny review of eighteen lower-court decisions. The justices obliged in sixteen instances. Of cases granted oral argument time, the solicitor general had filed amicus briefs in forty-three cases (38 percent of all such cases).

Solicitors general view their role as amici in terms of the benefits the Court accrues from the government's submissions and participation. Former [Reagan Administration] Solicitor General Rex E. Lee was quite confident in stating, "In every single case the court would be better off if it had the benefit of my views." During the 1987 oversight hearings, Representative William Hughes of New Jersey offered Solicitor General Charles Fried a description that is particularly appropriate for amicus participation. "You more or less view your office as sort of a constitutional ombudsman, to make sure that all areas of public interest, particularly with regard to constitutional issues, are explored, debated and discussed, as issues are decided." In some respects, the amicus brief allows the solicitor general to be a dabbler, participating in cases over a range of issue areas and topics. The United States has used the amicus curiae brief as a ticket into some of the most important cases decided in contemporary history. *Brown v. Board of Education of Topeka, Baker v. Carr* and *Regents of the University of California v. Bakke* are but a few of the examples.

Since the outcomes of cases in which the government files an amicus brief may have little effect on the overall operation of government, the solicitor general feels more comfortable in advancing positions that are not likely to prevail on the merits. In *Hobbie v. Unemployment Appeals Commission of Florida,* then-Solicitor General Fried explained that he knew it was unlikely that the government's position would be accepted. "But it was a position which deserved to be put in front of the Court, deserved to be attended to and responded to, and there it was. Sometimes, even though you didn't think you were going to win, nevertheless, you did want to have a particular position put before the Court." In the oversight hearings, Fried further explained that even though the government loses some of these cases, the arguments of the solicitor general can still be useful to the Court.

Within the past two decades, there have been numerous studies on the amicus participation of the solicitor general. Steven Puro's extensive work on the use of the amicus brief seems to have sparked additional studies that focus exclusively on the solicitor general's use of the amicus brief. One of the assumptions, however, that is raised in nearly every study is that the solicitor general enjoys an extraordinary degree of independence in deciding to "be a friend." Given the complex environment in which solicitors general find themselves, the decision to submit an amicus brief must be understood in terms of demands and expectations.

THE DECISION TO BEFRIEND

Amicus cases provide an opportunity to study solicitors general in cases where their decisions to participate are, perhaps, the least constrained. This is not to suggest, however, that they are free of the external demands of their environment. Rather, the nature of amicus participation is such that the United States has not lost a suit in a lower court that it is seeking to remedy, nor is the government drawn into the case by an aggrieved litigant. The amicus brief simply allows solicitors general to present their views in someone else's case.

In Puro's research, which was based on interviews conducted during the summer of 1968, he identified three considerations used by the solicitor general when deciding to file an amicus brief.

(1) Is there a significant issue in the case concerning the federal government or the public interest?

(2) Is this a good case to present the issues raised?

(3) Would the participation of the Solicitor General be helpful to the Court or make any contribution to the case?

Although these criteria are still used, they have been expanded to encompass the more "politicized" use of the amicus brief. As Philip Kurland noted * * * the intervention by a third party is no longer for the purposes of enlightening the Court on issues of the law, but to show support in a very public way for a specific litigant. This change is not limited to the government's use of the tactic but can be seen in virtually all amicus submissions.

The presence of a federal issue is fairly easy to detect in cases pending before the Court. One of the divisions or agencies that watch the Court's docket will notify the solicitor general of their interest in a particular case. For example, litigation in the area of antitrust enforcement is predominately a matter between private parties. * * * But the Antitrust Division of the Department of Justice would be very interested in filing an amicus brief in an antitrust case that comes before the Supreme Court simply to ensure that the government's views are heard and its interests are protected. This may also apply to agencies who are tasked with administering a particular rule that comes under attack in private litigation.

Suits that involve matters of criminal procedure and imprisonment in which a state is a party are also important to the federal government. A ruling in these areas can have a direct or indirect effect on the federal criminal code and the operation of its prisons. As Lee noted, these cases might even have "a larger impact on the interests of the United States than it would on the immediate parties." He also mentioned Title VII cases, securities cases and voting cases as other areas that would fall into the federal sphere of interest.

Solicitors general consider the fact situation of a case when deciding whether or not to submit an amicus brief. During Fried's tenure, a minority set-aside suit from Dade County, Florida reached the Supreme Court, and the justices asked for the solicitor general's input on the case. In his brief, Fried pointed out that a better case, *City of Richmond v. J.A. Croson Co.*, was on its way to the Court. The *Croson* suit dealt with less complicated issues and would provide the justices with a more direct fact situation than the case from Dade County.

The final criterion that Puro identified was whether or not the government would make any contribution to the case by filing an amicus brief. In my discussions with former staff members, they recalled instances in which the decision not to file was based on the fact that there were a large number of amicus briefs submitted from other organizations and interest groups. Furthermore, the solicitor general just did not have anything to add to the discussion. The issue terrain had been covered by the litigants and other amicus briefs.

In discussing amicus participation, Lee suggests that there are two categories of cases eligible for briefs. The first category includes the cases that involve the federal interest. The second category are those cases, "which fall right at the core of the current administration's broader agenda. For me [Lee] these included cases involving obscenity, the religion clauses, and abortion." These latter cases have been dubbed the "agenda" cases and are evidence for those who point to the "politicization" of the office.

Lee pulled no punches in explaining his amicus participation in these types of cases. "One of the purposes of the solicitor general is to represent his client, the president of the United States. One of the ways to implement the president's policies is through positions taken in court. When I have that opportunity, I'm going to take it." Lee's desire to carry out the president's agenda was tempered, however, by his belief that "it is a mistake to file in too many * * *. This is one instance where precedent actually works in reverse. The fact that I had already filed several amicus briefs in the 'category two' cases during a particular term was a strong argument against doing it again. The reason is that while I think it is proper to use the office for the purpose of making my contribution to the President's broader agenda, a wholesale departure from the role whose performance has led to the special status that the solicitor general enjoys would unduly impair that status itself. In the process, the ability of the solicitor general to serve any of the President's objectives would suffer."

Former assistant Kathryn Oberly also noted the problem of agenda cases. "The question is whether you lose some of that credibility by filing briefs in cases where it is clear to everybody, including the Court, that the only interest is political, political in the sense that this is this administration's philosophy." As with cases in which the government is a party, a sensitivity to the reputation of the Office of the Solicitor General tempers the decisions of the officeholder and his staff.

The term, "agenda" case, was coined during the Reagan administration to refer to the cases in which Lee and Fried filed amicus briefs for the purpose of advancing the president's policies through the Court. Prior to the Reagan administration, the government had remained out of abortion cases and many of the establishment clause controversies that involved state governments. But abortion was a key issue for the administration and both Lee and Fried argued to weaken and, ultimately, to reverse the standards established in *Roe v. Wade.*

The Reagan administration's involvement in affirmative action cases has also been mentioned as an example of agenda pursuit. But it is just this example that gives Fried the opportunity to respond to his critics.

> Affirmative action cases are absolutely standard amicus cases and every administration would have gotten into them because there are at least three agencies which are in that business. There is equal opportunity because of the Equal Employment Opportunity Commission, the Civil Rights Division and the Civil Division, and they are all in those businesses. Anything the Supreme Court decides in that area is going to impact on their activities, so they are always going to want to get into those cases because they don't want to have decisions affecting their activities without them having had a voice. That's quite normal and you'll see that forever in discrimination cases. Administrations, all administrations, have participated in those cases.

In this observation, Fried is quite correct. Administrations have weighed in with amicus briefs in discrimination suits going back as far as the *Brown* decisions.

[President Kennedy's Solicitor General Archibald] Cox's recollection of his amicus filings follows more closely Puro's criteria for case selection. "The only amicus cases we went into that I can think of were where the construction of a federal statute was involved and the questions of preemption or civil rights. I extended it to reapportionment." But the amicus brief was not seen as the tool for advocacy that it is today as evidenced by its relatively infrequent use during the early part of my study. For Cox, agenda cases involved civil rights and reapportionment. He did not attract as much attention as Reagan's solicitors general since Cox's positions were a logical progression of the Warren Court's development of the law. Lee and Fried, however, brought a new agenda to the Court that urged wholesale reversal in established areas of the law, a request that was granted with increased frequency as Reagan exercised his opportunities to change the Court's membership. Not so long ago, two other solicitors general, Stanley Reed (1935–1938) and Robert H. Jackson (1938–1940), found themselves trying to "unsettle" the law in their pursuit of the New Deal agenda before the Supreme Court. In sum, agenda cases have always been a part of the solicitor general's work since he is responsible for defending the client's legal interests before the Court.

The decision to file a brief is tempered by the frequency with which the government has appeared as an amicus in the recent past. Lee's concern as solicitor general was that he not become involved in so many cases that the Court should begin to expect the government's views and, as a result, give them less weight. "It is almost as though I had a certain number of chips that I could play. Where was the best place to play them?" Lee also believed that the Court's tolerance of these agenda cases may be limited. "There's an inverse relationship between the effectiveness of that kind of advocacy and the frequency with which you use it." The decision to file an amicus brief in an agenda case was carefully considered in light of the credibility of the office and the potential gains that may result from the case.

Evidence that others believe in this reputation and the successes that the solicitor general enjoys before the Court is seen in the requests the office receives for amicus support. The private litigant who can persuade the solicitor general to weigh in on her side of the argument will have gained a tremendous advantage. Edward Leahy's "Ten Commandments of Certiorari," encourages the private litigant to find an ally in the government: "Your strongest potential ally is the solicitor general, who carries tremendous credibility with the court. If you think the solicitor general will support your position, you can make the approach either through the specific governmental agency or department that would have an interest in your case or directly to the Solicitor General's Office. The solicitor general, however, is unlikely to appear voluntarily in support of your petition unless a truly important issue is presented. If that is so, he undoubtedly will be aware of your case." * * * [C]ase studies on women's organizations' litigation strategies, the African–American civil rights movement, and others have shown that these groups sought out the solicitor general's support for their issues. [Erwin] Griswold [Solicitor General for Presidents' Johnson and Nixon] recalled that the National Association for the Advancement of Colored People (NAACP) was involved in several cases during his stint as solicitor general. "They [the NAACP] would be referred to the Civil Rights Division which at that time was taking fairly strong positions in support of civil rights."

The decision to befriend can take place either at the jurisdictional stage or once the Court has granted plenary review. In either event, the solicitor general does enjoy some freedom in determining what the position of the United States will be once he decides to file. [According to Griswold,] "In the end, it's necessary to make a choice and to choose, no doubt about that," and this responsibility falls to the solicitor general. Choosing sides, however, may be considerably more difficult when the government is invited by the Court to participate as an amicus.

THE ORDER TO BEFRIEND

The discretion that the solicitor general enjoys in selecting the cases for amicus participation is greatly reduced when the Supreme Court invites the government to present its views in a case that the solicitor general had no intention of entering. This invitation, as it is called, is viewed by the office as an order, and it is an order that all solicitors general have tacitly acknowledged. As Kurland noted, "Surely there is a difference between a volunteer amicus and one who is drafted."

* * *

In my discussions with former staff members and solicitors general, I sensed that there were mixed feelings about the amicus invitations. On the one hand, the staff view the Court's request as an acknowledgment of their expertise. However, others suggested that the Court would often turn to the government "to act as extra law clerks for the Court, because we couldn't figure out what they thought our interest, meaning the federal interest, was [in the case]. * * * There were some where I'd say we were just writing what we thought was the right thing, and I don't mean from an agenda or policy analysis * * * sort of a legal analysis, about whether the issues were important. Those were the cases where I thought we were serving as the Court's extra law clerks."

In many of the invitations, however, the federal interest was clear in that an agency of the government may have had a stake in the outcome. This type of case was referred to the appropriate division or agency for their input.

Fried acknowledged that the amicus invitations can make for a very awkward situation: "They are often cases in which you would really rather not say what you think. The best example of all is the *Beck* case, *Communication Workers of America v. Beck.* That was a Court request where the position we had to take, which supported the union, was a position that the administration was very uncomfortable with as a matter of policy. I didn't like it and I didn't feel very enthusiastic about helping it out. Had it not been for a Court request, we would have stayed out of it."

The fact situations of cases are a reason to avoid filing an amicus brief voluntarily. When the Court invites the government, the solicitor general must play the cards he has been dealt. The United States was invited in *Johnson Transportation Agency v. Santa Clara County, California,* a gender-based affirmative action case, where "the facts were terrible. We would have waited for a better case." Most of the amicus cases, however, were routine in that there was a clear federal interest, according to Fried.

Lee also expressed some discomfort with the amicus invitations, but they came as no surprise. If the Court was asking for the government's input, it usually meant that the justices were having trouble deciding whether or not to take the case. Additionally, Lee believes that the Court may simply have wanted to know what impact the case would have on government, "and we're the ones, of course, that can best give an answer to that. There are also other instances which are just so hard, I suspect, that the Court would like another dispassionate view by one who litigates in the federal courts frequently." Lee also revealed, however, that the invitations "raised the greatest tensions within the government itself."

Once the invitation has been issued, the solicitor general is responsible for fashioning the government's response. As noted above, cases that are clearly within the federal domain are referred to the appropriate agencies or divisions for comment. The government may be asked to file an amicus brief early in the life of a case prior to the certiorari determination. If this is requested and the Court accepts the case for plenary review, the government will usually maintain its amicus status during the consideration on the merits. The Court can also ask the solicitor general to file an amicus brief following the grant of certiorari.

In my study of the 1959 to 1986 Court terms, the government was invited to participate as an amicus in 440 cases. The trend toward increased use of the amicus brief is reflected in the number of invitations issued to the solicitor general. Over the first five years of my study, a total of thirty invitations were issued. Between 1981 and the conclusion of the 1985 term, 127 invitations had reached the solicitor general's office. In short, the Court has quadrupled its reliance on the solicitor general's expertise.

Fifty-six cases with invitations were decided on the merits and the government's position prevailed in 59 percent of the cases decided by plenary review. In perusing the cases that were decided on the merits, one has to wonder why the solicitor general did not voluntarily enter as an amicus. Nine of these cases involved matters concerning Native Americans. Rules of the Securities and Exchange Commission, National Labor Relations Board, and antitrust enforcement were issues in fifteen cases, and many of the others involved state and federal relations with respect to taxation and entitlement programs. It may well be, as Fried suggested, that the facts of these cases were not the best for Supreme Court decision.

Puro, in a study of cases involving economic issues, closely examined ten cases in which the government had been invited to participate as an amicus on the merits. He found that the position that the government offered was sustained by the Court in six of the ten cases. My research, which incorporates all amicus activity on the merits, confirms that the government does win nearly 60 percent of the time when it has been invited.

The Supreme Court's regular invitations to the solicitor general to join as an amicus is a unique practice. With the exception of the government's lawyer, it is rare that the Court will reach out and tap an attorney from whom it wants to hear. Despite the unusual nature of these invitations, these cases are treated by the Office of the Solicitor General the same way as any other case is treated. Finally, we have seen that there is no significant reduction in the office's success when it has been ordered to befriend the Court.

SUCCESS AS AMICUS

There is a growing body of literature on the role of the United States as amicus as befits the importance of the activity to the solicitor general's office. The United States was involved in 518 amicus cases decided by a full Supreme Court opinion between 1959 and 1986. More than half of these cases (305) were on behalf of the petitioner. The party that the government supported with an amicus brief won 71.9 percent of the time. This comports with the success rate of 75 percent determined by Puro in his study of the 1920–1966 terms and the 70.4 percent success rate reported by S. Sidney Ulmer and David Willison in their analysis of the 1969–1983 terms. In addition to the studies by Puro and Ulmer, research by Karen O'Connor and Jeffrey Segal has broadened our understanding of the Office of the Solicitor General.

What is interesting about the progression of studies on the government's lawyer is the various approaches the scholars have taken in examining the solicitor general's success. O'Connor focused on three solicitors general, Griswold, Bork, and McCree and their decisions in case selection by subject and argument position in three issue areas. Her findings point up the differences between officeholders on both measures. Ulmer and Willison found that success did not vary significantly between solicitors general or by whether the government had been invited to participate or had entered the case willingly. * * *

My examination of the success of the solicitor general as amicus between 1959 and 1986 confirms the findings of these scholars and expands the research base. We have seen that success in decisions on the merits depended on the side that the government took in the case. This holds true for amicus cases as well. * * * When the United States entered a case on behalf of the petitioner, the private litigant enjoyed a 78.36 percent chance of prevailing on the merits. This is almost as high as the government's own success on the merits when it is named as the petitioner (80.2 percent). More interesting is that the government's success as amicus supporting a respondent is slightly higher than in the government's own cases.

The results are not surprising when we once again consider that the Court does not grant review in order to affirm the decisions of the lower courts. However, what we can derive from this analysis is that the solicitor general's support as amicus benefits not only petitioners but also respondents who are the more disadvantaged litigants once the case has been set for consideration on the merits.

The party in the White House is the clearest political distinction between solicitors general and between administrations. In analyzing the success of the government as amicus, I separated cases by the party identification of the White House and found that the party of the administration was not significantly related to the side that the government assumed as amicus. Furthermore, Democrats and Republicans did not differ in their success as amici. Each supported the winning litigant in approximately 72 percent of the cases.

As I suggested in my earlier discussion, the nature of the beast has changed over time. The use of the amicus curiae as a tool for organized interest groups has also become a tool for the executive branch and even for the Court by its invitations. * * * [From 1959 through 1986,] the United States participated as amicus in an average of seventeen briefs per year. The early solicitors general did not submit amicus briefs nearly as often as recent officeholders have. In fact, Rankin filed in only seven cases during his final year as solicitor general (1959–1960) whereas Lee averaged just over seventeen cases per year during his four-year tour of duty as Reagan's solicitor general.

* * *

There are no significant differences in the outcome of cases with amicus participation during the various presidential administrations. * * * It is interesting to note that in spite of the charges of politicizing the Office of the Solicitor General, the Reagan administration was typical of all administrations in its successes as amicus. The government, regardless of who is at the helm, is truly a good friend to the private litigant.

Summary

The amicus brief provides the solicitor general and the president with yet another avenue to approach the Court. But the government's appearance can be coerced by the justices through their invitation to participate, making for some difficult situations within the executive branch. During the 1959–1986 terms, the use of the amicus brief by the government increased significantly. But the Court also took advantage of the amicus brief's popularity by asking for the solicitor general's expertise and participation with increasing frequency.

In many respects, amici are managed in the Office of the Solicitor General like the government's own cases. Agencies are contacted for information as the solicitor general is beset with requests for support from within government as well as from outside interest groups. The decision to befriend may rest with the solicitor general, but, like his decisions in government cases, external factors and the political environment play significant roles in decision making.

As an amicus, the government is helpful to the private litigant, especially petitioners, but also to respondents. Evidence uncovered by earlier research suggests that solicitors general differ in the way they employ the amicus brief, both in their case selection and in the nature of their arguments. However, those distinctions are not evident at this aggregate level of analysis. Additionally, differences in the success rates of administrations were not detected in my research.

* * *

MEMORANDUM OPINION FOR THE ATTORNEY GENERAL,* ROLE OF THE SOLICITOR GENERAL

21 Loy.L.A.L.Rev. 1089 (1988)
Reprinted from 1 Op. Off. Legal Counsel 228 (1977)

The purpose of this memorandum opinion is to discuss (1) the institutional relationship between the Attorney General and the Solicitor General, and (2) the role that each should play in formulating and presenting the Government's position in litigation before the Supreme Court.

I

The Judiciary Act of 1789 created the Office of the Attorney General and provided that the Attorney General would prosecute and conduct all suits in the Supreme Court in which the United States was "concerned." Act of September 24, 1789, ch. XX, § 35, 1 Stat. 73. The Office of the Solicitor General was created in 1870. Act of June 22, 1870, ch. CL, § 2, 16 Stat. 162. The statute provided that there should be in the Department of Justice "an officer learned in the law, to assist the Attorney General in the performance of his duties, to be called the Solicitor General * * * "; and it provided further that the Attorney General could direct the Solicitor General to argue any case in which the Government had an interest. *See* Fahy, "The Office of the Solicitor General," 28 A.B.A.J. 20 (1942).

The statute was enacted at the behest of Attorney General Henry Stanbery. Mr. Stanbery had argued that his work load was great and that he needed assistance in preparing opinions and arguing cases before the Supreme Court. He suggested that a new office be created for the purpose of discharging these functions. Congress, perceiving that the measure would make it possible to discontinue the expensive practice of retaining special counsel to represent the Government in cases argued before the Supreme Court, acceded to his request. *Id.*

In 1878 the language of the statute was partially revised. The language of the revision has survived to the present day. The modern statute, codified at 28 U.S.C. § 518, provides in pertinent part:

(a) Except when the Attorney General in a particular case directs otherwise, the Attorney General and the Solicitor General shall conduct and argue suits and appeals in the Supreme Court and suits in the Court of Claims in which the United States is interested.

(b) When the Attorney General considers it in the interests of the United States, he may personally conduct and argue any case in a court of the United States in which the United States is interested, or he may direct the Solicitor General or any officer of the Department of Justice to do so.

The Department's own regulations provide that the Solicitor General performs his duties "subject to the general supervision and direction" of the Attorney General. 28 CFR § 0.20. The same language is used to describe the relationship between the Attorney General and the offices that report directly to him, such as the Office of Legal Counsel. The Assistant Attorneys General in charge of the various divisions perform their duties subject to the Attorney General's supervision, but under the direction of the Associate or Deputy Attorney General. From a legal standpoint, the relationship between the Attorney General and the Solicitor General would thus appear to be substantially the same as that existing between the Attorney General and the Assistant Attorneys General.

II

We think it plain from the language and history of the relevant statutes that the Office of the Solicitor General was not created for the purpose of relieving the Attorney General of the responsibility for formulating or presenting the Government's case in litigation before the Supreme Court. Congress simply intended to provide the Attorney General with a learned helper who would perform these functions at the Attorney General's direction. We note in passing that at least one Solicitor General has adopted this view publicly. *See, Fahy, supra,* at 21. We know of no public utterance by a Solicitor General to the contrary. *See, generally,* Cox, "The Government in the Supreme Court," 44 Chi.B.Record 221 (1963); Sobeloff, "The Law Business of the United States," 34 Ore.L.Rev. 145 (1955); Stern, "Inconsistency in Government Litigation," 64 Harv.L.Rev. 759 (1951). The short of the matter is that under law the Attorney General has the power and the right to "conduct and argue" the Government's case in any court of the United States. 28 U.S.C. § 518(b).

III

Traditionally, however, the Attorney General has given the Solicitor General the primary responsibility for presenting the Government's views to the Supreme Court, and in the discharge of that function the Solicitor General has enjoyed a marked degree of independence. Indeed, his independence has been so great that one Solicitor General, Francis Biddle, was led to remark:

> He [the Solicitor General] determines what cases to appeal, and the client has no say in the matter, he does what his lawyer tells him, the lawyer stands in his client's shoes, for the client is but an abstraction. He is responsible neither to the man who appointed him nor to this immediate superior in the hierarchy of administration. The total responsibility is his, and his guide is only the ethic of his law profession framed in the ambience of his experience and judgment. (F. Biddle, In Brief Authority 97 (1962).)

Because the question of the "independence" of the Solicitor General has a direct and important bearing upon the general question to which this memorandum is addressed, we shall consider it in some detail.

Mr. Biddle's statement suggests that the Solicitor General has enjoyed two kinds of independence. First, he has enjoyed independence within the Department of Justice. It is he, of all the officers in the Department, who has been given the task of deciding what the Government's position should be in cases presented to the Supreme Court. The views of subordinate officers within the divisions of the Department are not binding upon him, and the Attorney General has made it a practice not to interfere. With respect to his relation to the Attorney General, we feel constrained to add, however, at the risk of repetition, that the Solicitor General's independent role has resulted from a convenient and necessary division of labor, not from a separation of powers required by law. Moreover, Francis Biddle may have overstated the case to some degree. Under the relevant statutes, as noted, the Attorney General retains the right to assume the Solicitor General's function himself, if he conceives it to be in the public interest to do so.

Secondly, the Solicitor General has enjoyed independence within the executive branch as a whole. He is not bound by the views of his "clients." He may confess error when he believes they are in error. He may rewrite their briefs. He may refuse to approve their requests to petition the Court for writs of *certiorari*. He may oppose (in whole or in part) the arguments that they may present to the Court in those instances where they have independent litigating authority.

The reasons for this independence are, for the most part, familiar:

First, it has been thought to be desirable, generally, for the Government to adopt a single, coherent position with respect to legal questions that are presented to the Supreme Court. Because it is not uncommon for there to be conflicting views among the various offices and agencies within the executive branch, the Solicitor General, having the responsibility for presenting the views of the Government to the Court, must have power to reconcile differences among his clients, to accept the views of some and to reject others, and, in proper cases, to formulate views of his own.

Second, as an officer of the Court and as an officer of Government, the Solicitor General has a special duty to protect the Court in the discharge of its constitutional function. He protects the Court's docket by screening the Government's cases and relieving the Court of the burden of reviewing unmeritorious claims. He prepares accurate and balanced summaries of the records in the cases that are presented for review; and within the limits of proper advocacy, he provides the Court with an accurate and expert statement of the legal principles that bear upon the questions to be decided.

Third, as an officer who plays an important role in the development of the law, he has a duty to protect the law from disorderly growth. He is called upon to decide questions of "ripeness" in the most general sense: on a case-by-case basis he must determine whether *this* is the appropriate time for presenting *this* issue to the Supreme Court on *this* record. *See* Cox, *supra,* at 226. In order to discharge that function, he must have, among other things, the power to refuse requests for petitions for *certiorari* and the power to decline to present the Government's views, as *amicus,* in cases in which the Government might otherwise have an interest.

Finally, and most importantly, the Solicitor General has assumed an independent status because of the prevalent belief that such independence is necessary to prevent narrow or improper considerations (political or otherwise) from intruding upon the presentation of the Government's case in the Nation's highest Court. It was a Solicitor General, Frederick W. Lehmann, who wrote that "the United States wins its point whenever justice is done its citizens in the courts"; and the burden of history is that justice is done most often when the law is administered with an independent and impartial hand. The Nation values the Solicitor General's independence for the same reason that it values an independent judiciary. The Solicitor General has been permitted his independence largely because of the belief, as Mr. Biddle put it, that "the ethic of his law profession framed in the ambience of his judgment and experience" should be his only guide.

IV

In what circumstances should the Attorney General exercise his right to "conduct" litigation before the Supreme Court? To the extent that the Solicitor General's traditional role reflects a simple division of labor within the Department, it is plain that the Attorney General may exercise his prerogative whenever it is administratively convenient for him to do so. The real question is to what extent he can intervene, in individual cases, without doing violence to the important principles or functions that have justified the Solicitor General's independence within the Government at large.

We have identified four such principles or functions: the Solicitor General must coordinate conflicting views within the executive branch; he must protect the Court by presenting meritorious claims in a straightforward and professional manner and by screening out unmeritorious ones; he must assist in the orderly development of decisional law; and he must "do justice"—that is, he must discharge his office in accordance with law and ensure that improper concerns do not influence the presentation of the Government's case in the Supreme Court.

In our opinion, there is no institutional reason why the Attorney General could not, in individual cases, discharge all four of these functions as well as the Solicitor General. However, in practice the Attorney General could never be sure that he was exercising the independent judgment essential to the proper performance of those functions if he acted alone without the advice of an independent legal adviser, *i.e.,* the Solicitor General.

The Attorney General is responsible for the objective and evenhanded administration of justice independent of political considerations or pressures. However, he is also a member of the President's Cabinet and responsible for advising the President on many of the most important policy decisions that are made in the executive branch. He is necessarily exposed repeatedly to nonlegal arguments and opinions from other Cabinet members. His is the difficult task of separating the different factors that might properly be considered in his role as a policy adviser from those relevant to his duties as the chief legal officer of the Government.

The Constitution requires the President, and thus the Attorney General, to execute the laws faithfully. It requires them to follow the law, even if that course conflicts with policy. For this reason alone, in our view, the tradition of the "independent" Solicitor General is a wise tradition. It has arisen because it serves a useful constitutional purpose. Very simply, an independent Solicitor General assists the President and the Attorney General in the discharge of their constitutional duty: concerned as they are with matters of policy, they are well served by a subordinate officer who is permitted to exercise independent and expert legal judgment essentially free from extensive involvement in policy matters that might, on occasion, cloud a clear vision of what the law requires. While it is doubtful whether either the President or the Attorney General could "delegate" to the Solicitor General the ultimate responsibility for determining the Government's position on questions of law presented to the Supreme Court, as a matter of practice, in the discharge of their offices, they can allow themselves the benefit of his independent judgment, and they can permit his judgment to be dispositive in the normal course.

The dual nature of the Attorney General's role as a policy and legal adviser to the President strengthens, in our view, the necessity for an independent Solicitor General. To the extent the Solicitor General can be shielded from political and policy pressures—without being unaware of their existence—his ability to serve the Attorney General, and the President, as "an officer learned in the law" is accordingly enhanced. For this reason we believe the Solicitor General should not be subjected to undue influence from executive branch officials outside the Department of Justice. The Solicitor General should not be viewed as having final, essentially unreviewable authority in controversial cases, because such a role would inevitably subject him to those policy pressures that can obscure legal insights. The Attorney General, we believe, reinforces the independence of the Solicitor General by allowing himself to act as the final legal authority in those small number of cases with highly controversial policy ramifications. As such, the Attorney General and not the Solicitor General will be the focus of policy pressures from both within and outside the executive branch.

We do not believe that the Attorney General's power to direct the prosecution of cases in the Supreme Court should never be exercised, but we do believe that the tradition of the independent Solicitor General is one that should be preserved. We think that the Attorney General can participate in the formulation of the Government's position before the Court in certain circumstances without doing violence to that tradition; but, because of the value of the Solicitor General's independence, there are procedural and substantive considerations that should guide and temper the exercise of that power.

V

Procedural Considerations. Undoubtedly, the working relationship between the Attorney General and the Solicitor General is one that will vary from Administration to Administration in accordance with the personalities of the individuals who hold these offices; but as we have said, the traditional pattern is one of noninterference. From this tradition we derive a rule of procedure: in our opinion, with respect to any pending case, the Solicitor General should be given the opportunity to consider the questions involved and to formulate his own initial views with respect to them without interference from the Attorney General or any other officer in the Administration.

There are at least two reasons for following a procedure of this kind. First, the procedure ensures that the Attorney General (and the President) will enjoy the benefit of the Solicitor General's independent judgment in every case. That independence would be compromised if the Solicitor General were subjected to frequent advice or suggestions from the President or the Attorney General before he is allowed to formulate his own position. Second, this procedure helps to ensure that the Attorney General will not exercise his supervisory powers gratuitously. No one can say what the Solicitor General's position will be before he has taken it.

This brings us to a related point. The Solicitor General should be allowed to formulate a position with respect to pending cases, and he should be allowed to act independently in the discharge of that function, but he should not be required to make his decision in an informational vacuum. He is not omniscient, and he should be free to consult the various offices and agencies in the executive branch that may have views on the questions presented by the case at hand. In fact, this is the traditional practice. The Solicitor General does consult and is consulted by other officers of Government. Far from detracting from his independent function, this practice enhances its value. It ensures that the Solicitor General's judgment will be informed judgment.

Substantive Considerations. Once the Solicitor General has taken a position with respect to a pending case, that position will, in most cases, become the Government's position as a matter of course. However, in some cases the Attorney General may need to determine whether or not the Government should adopt that position. Plainly, the Attorney General, as well as the President, have the power to decline to adopt it, but to exercise that power is to reject the Solicitor General's independent and expert legal counsel in favor of other legal advice or policy considerations.

We should make one observation at this point. We have said that an independent Solicitor General assists the Attorney General and the President in the discharge of their constitutional duty to put law before policy. It is our opinion that if the Solicitor General is to be of real value in that regard, his judgment must be permitted to be dispositive in the ordinary course. The Government's position should be changed by the Attorney General only in rare instances.

How does one identify the "rare instances" in which intervention by the Attorney General may be justifiable? We can offer no litmus test, but we wish to make several observations that bear upon the question.

First, in our opinion, the mere fact that the Attorney General may disagree with the Solicitor General over a question of law is not ordinarily a sufficient reason for intervention in a given case. If the Solicitor General has fallen into error, the Supreme Court will have an opportunity to correct the error, and the Government's ultimate interest in a just result will be vindicated. If the Court upholds his position, then all the better, for his legal judgment and not that of his superiors, was correct. In either case, for all of the reasons given above, the potential benefit of intervention is usually outweighed, in our view, by the mischief inherent in it.

There may be a case in which the Attorney General is convinced that the Solicitor General has erred so far in the legal analysis that intervention is required. We believe such cases will be quite rare, but when they arise the Attorney General must follow the rule of law himself and be guided by his own experience and judgment.

There is another category of questions that may be involved in cases presented to the Supreme Court with respect to which the Attorney General's or the President's judgment may be essential. Our analysis turns upon the uncertain but traditional distinction between questions of law and questions of policy.

All of the cases that are decided by the appellate courts can be said to involve "questions of law" in a technical sense. The outcome in each case must be justified by reference to rules or principles that are prescribed in the Constitution, statutes, regulations, ordinances, or in the previous decisions of the courts. In some cases, however, questions of "policy" are integrally intertwined with questions of law. In other cases the major decision may be a discretionary one such as filing of an *amicus* brief when there has been no request from the Court for the views of the Government.

The Solicitor General can and should enjoy independence in matters of legal judgment. He should be free to decide what the law is and what it requires. But if "law" does not provide a clear answer to the question presented by the case before him, we think there is no reason to suppose that he, of all the officers in the executive branch, should have the final responsibility for deciding what, as a matter of policy, the interests of the Government, the parties, or the Nation may require. To our knowledge, no Solicitor General has adopted a contrary view.

The short of the matter is that cases may arise in which questions of policy are so important to the correct resolution of the case that the principles that normally justify the Solicitor General's independent and dispositive function may give way to the greater need for the Solicitor General to seek guidance on the policy question. Questions of policy are questions that can be effectively addressed by the Attorney General, a Cabinet officer who participates directly in policy formation and who can go to the President for policy guidance when the case demands.

But the Attorney General and the President should trust the judgment of the Solicitor General not only in determining questions of law but also in distinguishing between questions of law and questions of policy. If the independent legal advice of the Solicitor General is to be preserved, it should normally be the Solicitor General who decides when to seek the advice of the Attorney General or the President in a given case.

JOHN M. HARMON
Assistant Attorney General
Office of Legal Counsel

RICHARD G. WILKINS,* AN OFFICER AND AN ADVOCATE: THE ROLE OF THE SOLICITOR GENERAL **

21 Loy.L.A.L.Rev. 1167, 1167–1177 (1988)

The Solicitor General and his staff of twenty-three attorneys occupy offices located on the fifth floor of the Department of Justice Building in Washington, D.C. The post of the Solicitor General, created in 1870 when Congress established the Department of Justice, has evolved from that of "a courtroom lawyer and the Attorney General's assistant" to that of the chief appellate litigation officer "responsible for conducting and supervising all aspects of government litigation in the Supreme Court of the United States." For the most part, the Solicitor General and his staff have performed their duties in distinguished obscurity, receiving generally high praise for professional comportment and rarely prompting public comment or attention. All that has changed. In 1982, the editorial staff of the *New York Times* blasted Solicitor General Rex E. Lee for presenting the Supreme Court with "political tract[s]" rather than "principled counsel." [7] More recently, Lincoln Caplan, author of *The Tenth Justice*, has charged that "the Reagan Administration has stripped the office of its traditional autonomy, debased its credibility and turned it into an ideological mouthpiece."

* * *

* Associate Professor of Law, Brigham Young University, B.A., 1976. Brigham Young University, J.D., 1979. The author served as an Assistant to Solicitor General Rex E. Lee from July 1981 to May 1984.

** Reprinted with the permission of the Loyola of Los Angeles Law Review and the author, Richard G. Wilkins.

7. N.Y. Times, Aug. 4, 1982, at A22, col. 1.

Although Caplan's critique of the Solicitor General's Office "is largely a polemic against the Reagan Administration," it raises serious questions. Has the Office of the Solicitor General been subjected to unusual political pressure? A review of the available literature, including articles by past Solicitors General and a comparative statistical study, suggests that the office has always responded to the political inclinations of then-current administrations. Thus, the assertion that the Solicitor General has lost his "independence" is something of an overstatement; he has never been completely autonomous. Nevertheless, the recently perceived political sensitivity of the Solicitor General prompts a more difficult inquiry: How should the Solicitor General respond to ideological demands? Here, no ready solution exists. Those who see the Solicitor General primarily as an advocate of the administration that appointed him will give one answer. Those—like Caplan—who see the Solicitor General primarily as an officer of the Court and an independent moderating force within the administration will give another.

I believe that the Solicitor General's proper role lies between that of unquestioning advocate and independent officer of the Court. While the Solicitor General appropriately serves as an advocate, his advocacy must be tempered by the realization that he occupies a unique position of influence with the Supreme Court of the United States. Thus, Mr. Caplan notwithstanding, the Solicitor General should support the administration's views on sensitive legal issues. However, in the course of that advocacy, the Solicitor General must never sacrifice his credibility and reliability as a trusted officer of the Court. Maintaining a balance between the sometimes conflicting duties of advocate and officer of the Court is a difficult and often thankless task. The recent experience of Rex E. Lee suggests that a person who accomplishes the feat may have few friends in any quarter—the administration may find the Solicitor General's reasoned advocacy too tame, while political opponents may find any such advocacy outrageous. Achieving and maintaining that balance, however, is the fundamental mission of the Solicitor General.

I. Pressure and Politics: The Independence of the Solicitor General

* * * The most visible responsibility of the [Solicitor General's Office] is the actual conduct of the government's appellate practice before the Supreme Court. That responsibility embraces several discrete steps, beginning with the decision "whether the government should petition the Supreme Court for certiorari, or acquiesce in or oppose the petitions filed by others," and concluding with the actual preparation and presentation of the government's cases before the Court. The confluence of these duties imposes a ponderous decision-making burden upon the Solicitor General.

In performing these day-to-day tasks, the Solicitor General and his staff have achieved "an exceptional degree of autonomy." Much of this autonomy derives from the simple fact that the bulk of the Solicitor General's staff consists of civil service employees who are not subject to removal for political or ideological reasons. Moreover, the workload within the office is assigned without regard to the ideological leaning of particular attorneys. Additionally, in the vast majority of cases, questions regarding "politics" never arise—the majority of the litigation passing through the office involves matters that simply do not attract political attention. Indeed, freedom from constant political scrutiny is essential to both the efficient functioning of the office and the broader litigation strategy of the government as a whole. The government loses "literally thousands" of cases in the lower courts each year, and the attorneys and officials involved often have strong opinions regarding the future course of those cases. Without a significant degree of independence from disappointed government officials, the Solicitor General would quickly lose the important ability to say "No."

* * *

The general independence so critical to the ongoing successful management of the government's Supreme Court litigation has always had limits, however. * * * Any assertion that the Solicitor General should be free of political suasion ignores the reality that he is an official within the executive branch who serves at the pleasure of the President who appointed him. An exhaustive student note, appearing eleven years ago in the Michigan Law Review, examined the statutory and constitutional foundations of the Solicitor General's power,[39] considered whether the Solicitor General could lay claim to any common law authority, and balanced the respective values of autonomy and political accountability as applied to his office. None of these bases was found to provide solid support for a totally independent Solicitor General. While applicable law may confer an important policy-making role upon the Solicitor General, he is not an elected official and "does not have the political legitimacy to advocate on behalf of 'the United States' independent of Congress and the President." The Solicitor General similarly cannot claim "common-law stature as advocate for the public interest" because he has no independent electoral mandate: he "serves as proponent of public interests only where authorized by Congress and as directed by the President." Finally, "[d]espite the apparent desirability of allowing the Solicitor General a great degree of autonomy," he "has no institutional warrant to oppose the President" and it is accordingly "difficult to support a claimed prerogative to defy the President." Thus, the note concluded, absent legislation designed to make the Solicitor "either truly autonomous or * * * accountable solely to Congress," the "Solicitor General operates in an executive capacity" and is "ultimately responsible to the President and must comply with his bidding." As Justice Sutherland once noted, "[i]t is quite evident that one who holds his office only during the pleasure of another, cannot be depended upon to maintain an attitude of independence against the latter's will."

Of course, the foregoing is only a partial answer to recent claims that the Reagan Administration has "turned the post of Solicitor Gener-

---

39. Note, 76 Mich.L.Rev. 324 (1977).

al from a position of independence into the job of a good-natured mouthpiece." It establishes that the Solicitor General cannot legitimately claim true independence from the President, but it does not refute the submission that the Reagan Administration has been unusually heavy handed in its dealings with its Solicitor Generals. The available evidence, however, suggests that recent events at the Office of the Solicitor General do not represent a radical departure from past practice. On the contrary, past Solicitor Generals have consistently reflected the position of the presiding administration in their presentations to the Court.

Erwin Griswold, who served as Solicitor General under Presidents Lyndon Johnson and Richard Nixon, and who is generally highly regarded even by recent critics, "tried to keep the Republicans as happy with his advocacy as he had the Democrats." Indeed, one scholar has noted that Griswold took explicit cues from the Nixon Administration regarding what the Solicitor's position should be in politically sensitive cases. Even Caplan, who tries mightily to downplay any political influence upon Griswold's decisions while Solicitor General, reports that Griswold filed a brief in the Pentagon Papers case [51] that was contrary to his own "judgments behind closed doors." Despite Griswold's own conclusion that "the government should stop objecting to publication of the history, because the only harm that would come of it was political embarrassment," he nevertheless filed a brief asserting that publication of the Pentagon Papers could cause "immediate and irreparable harm to the security of the United States." Moreover, while Griswold had consistently taken a strong pro-civil rights stand under President Johnson, he modified his views regarding appropriate civil rights remedies after President Nixon "publicly announced that his administration would no longer support forced busing to achieve integration."

Robert Bork, who was appointed by Nixon to succeed Griswold, and who served under Nixon and Gerald Ford, was likewise willing to tune his advocacy to reflect administration views. * * * Caplan summarized Bork's service as Solicitor as follows:

> Bork regularly found means to carry the Administration's message to the Court. He was a more enthusiastic advocate of Nixon's legal notions than Griswold had been (and, in the process, drove away one assistant who believed that the former Yale professor had compromised the integrity of the Solicitor General's judgment about the law), and he was equally forthright about making arguments favored by Ford.

Any given Solicitor General's enthusiastic sponsorship of administration goals, of course, may stem more from personal commitment to those goals than explicit pressure from the Oval Office. The President's careful selection of a person committed to the administration's agenda is, nevertheless, a plain example of political influence on the Office of the Solicitor General.

51. New York Times v. United States, 403 U.S. 713 (1971).

Jimmy Carter appointed Wade McCree as Solicitor General. McCree, like his predecessors, gave distinguished service during his four years in office. He also glanced toward Pennsylvania Avenue when preparing briefs in politically sensitive matters. When a draft of the government's brief in *Regents of the University of California v. Bakke*,[58] which supported Bakke and argued against affirmative action, was leaked to the press, substantial pressure to reverse that position—from the White House on down—was brought to bear upon the Department of Justice and McCree in particular. The brief ultimately filed with the Supreme Court did not support Bakke, but instead urged the Court to remand the matter to the California Supreme Court for further proceedings. Caplan asserts that the change in position did not result from political pressure, but rather occurred because "the Solicitor General knew about and shared the President's belief in affirmative action." The fact that McCree "shared" the President's beliefs, however, cannot avoid the pragmatic reality that he "knew about" them, too.

In any event, the *Bakke* matter is not the only known instance during the Carter Presidency when administration policy exerted substantial influence over the Solicitor's affairs. After heated public opposition greeted the government's presentation in *Personnel Administrator of Massachusetts v. Feeney*,[63] Attorney General Griffin Bell "institute[d] a policy requiring the solicitor to give notice to Bell of all cases involving policy issues. This policy permitted Bell to examine the matter, and if necessary, consult with the President *before* the solicitor's brief was written."

In addition to the preceding anecdotal evidence, a statistical study of the amicus curiae presentations of Solicitors Griswold, Bork and McCree confirms that they were sensitive to the ideological viewpoints of their respective administrations.[65] The study examined each case in which one of the three Solicitor Generals had participated as amicus curiae during the 1967 to 1979 Terms of the Court. The briefs were classified as "pro" or "anti" in each of three areas: personal liberties, civil equality and criminal rights. The study found that Griswold, under President Johnson, and McCree, under President Carter, "took decidedly more pronounced 'pro-rights' positions than did Bork" under Presidents Nixon and Ford. Moreover, during their tenure under President Nixon, both Griswold and Bork "adopted 'anti-rights' positions more frequently than McCree." McCree "advanced a pro-civil equalities claim in a slightly higher percentage of his amicus briefs than either solicitors Griswold or Bork." These results were explained, at least in part, by reference to the political agendas of the Johnson, Nixon, Ford and Carter presidencies. McCree's record on civil liberties, for example, "meshes

---

58. 438 U.S. 265 (1978).

63. 442 U.S. 256 (1979). The case involved a challenge to a statutory veteran's preference scheme. The government's stance angered many women's rights groups.

65. O'Connor, The Amicus Curiae Role of the U.S. Solicitor General in Supreme Court Litigation, 66 Judicature 256 (1983).

with his philosophy as a jurist, as well as those of the Carter administration generally." The study also concluded that "Griswold and Bork's 'anti-rights' position was probably rooted in the Nixon administration's strong law and order stance."

The records of Griswold, Bork and McCree are hardly ones of staid independence from presidential politics. And, while nothing in the foregoing details detracts from the professional integrity of any former Solicitor General, their records demonstrate that they consistently advocated views in sensitive cases that were consistent with those of their particular administrations. Thus, nothing terribly surprising—or new—arises from the fact that the Solicitors General in the current administration have similarly advocated President Reagan's views. The charge that President Reagan has "turned [the Solicitor] into an ideological mouthpiece" is decidedly overblown; the Solicitor General has always been a mouthpiece. The real question raised by the recent criticisms of the Office of the Solicitor General is not whether the Solicitor General should listen to the President or not. The evidence shows that he always has. The current debate, therefore, boils down to basic disagreement with the positions the Solicitor is advocating. Critics, such as Caplan, may couch their arguments in terms of "misuse" or "abuse" of the Solicitor General's office, but they are essentially champing at the fact that the Court is being presented with substantive legal arguments they strongly dislike.

MICHAEL W. McCONNELL,* THE RULE OF LAW AND THE ROLE OF THE SOLICITOR GENERAL **
21 Loy.L.A.L.Rev. 1105, 1105–1112 (1988)

I. THREE APPROACHES TO THE SOLICITOR GENERAL'S FUNCTION

Let us grant the attractive premise that the Solicitor General, more than the ordinary advocate, must comply with and promote the rule of law in his representation of the United States in the Supreme Court. The President is charged to "take Care that the Laws be faithfully executed";[1] the Solicitor General, as the executive officer entrusted with Supreme Court litigating authority, exercises the "take Care" responsibility in that sphere. But what does the rule of law mean in this context?

There are three prominent approaches to the Solicitor General's responsibility: (1) he must make only those arguments to the Court that he believes to be substantively valid, even if the interests of his client would be better served by other plausible legal arguments; (2) he must make only those arguments to the Court that are consistent with the Court's interpretation of legal requirements; and (3) he must make the

* Assistant Professor of Law, University of Chicago Law School. Formerly Assistant to the Solicitor General (1983–85). B.A. 1976, Michigan State University; J.D. 1979, University of Chicago Law School.

** Reprinted with the permission of the Loyola of Los Angeles Law Review and the author, Michael W. McConnell.

1. U.S. Const. art. II, § 3.

arguments with the best prospect of serving his clients' interests, that is, upholding government action.

Generally, the first approach—the "independence" approach—is invoked to criticize the Solicitor General when he allows the interests of the client agencies, the views of the President, or the opinions of other lawyers in and out of the Department of Justice to influence what arguments he will make to the Court. Generally, the second approach— the "precedent" approach—is invoked to criticize the Solicitor General for asking the Court to modify its precedents or for making an argument that the present nine Justices are unlikely to adopt. Generally, the third approach—the "government interests" approach—is invoked to criticize the Solicitor General for failing to defend federal statutes or government action, or for filing briefs not directly related to that end.

The "independence" and "precedent" approaches emphasize the distinction between the role of the Solicitor General and that of other advocates. They seem, at first blush, to have more to do with the rule of law than the "government interests" approach. The Solicitor General, it is said, has responsibilities to the rule of law that so far exceed the ordinary advocate that he can almost be called a "Tenth Justice." This title captures the view that the Solicitor General properly exercises a judicial-type function, accepting and rejecting legal arguments on the basis of his best understanding of what the Constitution and laws require rather than the interests of the client agencies. As expressed in an official memorandum on the role of the Solicitor General issued under Attorney General Griffin Bell, "the Solicitor General * * * must protect the Court by presenting meritorious claims in a straightforward and professional manner and by screening out unmeritorious ones[.]" [3] The same memorandum states that "[t]he Nation values the Solicitor General's independence for the same reason that it values an independent judiciary," and endorses former Solicitor General Francis Biddle's formulation that the Solicitor General's "only guide" should be " 'the ethic of his law profession framed in the ambience of his judgment and experience.' "

Alternatively, the Solicitor General is said to be like a "Tenth Justice" because his arguments are designed principally to be of service to the Court rather than to advance the interests of the executive or legislative branches. His name appears below those of the Justices in the front of each issue of U.S. Reports. He is not an outsider or a critic of the Court, but their partner in a common effort to uphold the Constitution and laws. To be useful, his arguments ought to proceed from the Court's recent precedents and help the Court to fit the current case into a settled framework of existing decisions. Just as continuity and stability are desirable features of the law, they are desirable features of the Solicitor General's argumentation.

3. Memorandum Opinion for the Attorney General: The Role of the Solicitor General, 1 Op.Off. Legal Counsel 228, 231–32 (1977) [hereinafter 1977 Memorandum].

The "government interests" approach to the Solicitor General's role is more modest. It treats the Solicitor General less like a "Tenth Justice" and more like an ordinary lawyer—more skilled, more distinguished, more responsible, perhaps, but still a lawyer for a client. Under this approach, it is the function of the adversary process, and ultimately of the Court, to uphold the rule of law. The Solicitor General best serves by making the best arguments he can for upholding government action, rather than by exercising independent opinions or by trying to "protect" the Court from arguments. Indeed, by failing to make the best possible case for the government's position—assuming the position is at least tenable—the Solicitor General makes the Court's job harder and vindication of the rule of law that much more difficult.

The "government interests" approach, like the others, recognizes the Solicitor General's responsibility to present the facts and legal background of a case with scrupulous accuracy and fairness. No responsible theory of the Solicitor General's function would tolerate shading or hiding the truth. Indeed, as the most common repeat player in the Supreme Court, the Solicitor General should feel these constraints more keenly than other lawyers, since his credibility in other cases will suffer if a brief is less than fully accurate. But this responsibility of full and fair appellate advocacy is shared, even if to a lesser degree, by all Supreme Court advocates.

The three approaches to the Solicitor General's function each contain a valuable insight. Unfortunately, they are in obvious conflict with one another. The first approach establishes the independent professional judgment of the Solicitor General as the criterion for fealty to the rule of law; the second establishes either judicial precedent or predictions about how the current nine Justices will decide a case as the criterion; the third leaves the rule of law to be achieved through the adversary process. Except in the happy event that the Solicitor General's own professional judgment on legal issues coincides perfectly with both the interests of the government and with precedent—or with his predictions about how the current Court would decide the question—he will be faced with a choice. Should he present the view he believes to be correct? Should he present the view that best accords with the Court's interpretations? Or should he present the view that most advances government authority?

Perhaps the three approaches should be viewed as tactical or strategic considerations—as part of a lawyerly prudence directed to winning cases. A Solicitor General is unlikely to win by tilting at precedents that command the support of a majority of the Justices. To put his argument in terms consistent with the Court's other recent decisions, rather than openly confronting the Court's recent errors, is plain good sense and good strategy. Similarly, for the Solicitor General to establish a reputation for presenting only "meritorious" arguments will increase his rhetorical effectiveness. If he can establish that he is more than a "hired gun," his arguments will carry greater weight and conviction. And finally, when the Solicitor General confines his arguments to the specific practical needs of the client agencies, rather than wasting precious time and resources on mere matters of constitutional principle, he will be less likely to ruffle feathers and more likely to win cases of immediate interest to his "clients."

Perhaps the entire professional tradition of the Solicitor General's office can be explained in terms of these prudential considerations, without reference to controversial propositions like the "rule of law." One could predict that the Solicitor General, as the only lawyer who frequently appears before the Court, would develop a strong tradition of following precedent, would exercise strong independent judgment, and would emphasize the interests of the government agencies. Seen as prudential considerations, there is little or no contradiction between the three approaches. Each is subsumed in the lawyer's creed: win as many cases as you can.

And yet, the dictates of prudence do not seem to exhaust the responsibilities of the Solicitor General. Prudence is an instrumental virtue, just as winning cases is instrumental. Great Solicitors General have not hesitated, in appropriate cases, to criticize precedent—even recent precedent; to offer arguments that are likely to be rejected; to spurn arguments that would foster greater governmental power and discretion; even to take positions that they would not agree with in their individual capacities. Following the dictates of prudence will help the Solicitor General and his Office to accumulate reputational capital with the Court; but cases will arise when the Solicitor General will, and should, choose to spend that capital.

The three commonly offered approaches to the Solicitor General's role thus do not offer a clear-cut basis for evaluating a particular decision, or even a particular Solicitor General. A Solicitor General's performance cannot be judged according to tidy criteria, for the available criteria are conflicting and require a different balance in different cases. One must understand the Solicitor General's function in light of his own assessment of what the times require. Substantive disagreement over the desirable direction of constitutional law should not be confused with transgression of the rule of law.

II. Illustrations of the Conflict

Any lawyer who has served in the Office of the Solicitor General could offer illustrations of cases in which these approaches conflict. I will describe three such cases during my tenure as Assistant to the Solicitor General, each of which presented a different combination of factors and in each of which the conflict was resolved in a different way.

In the October 1984 Term, the Supreme Court granted certiorari in *Tony and Susan Alamo Foundation v. Donovan.*[5] The case concerned application of federal minimum wage laws to a religious community in which all the members worked for the community and in return received housing, food, clothing, medical care, and other necessities of life. The

---

5. 471 U.S. 290 (1985).

members believed they were working for God and that acceptance of a wage would be an affront to God. They therefore sought an exemption under the free exercise clause. The Department of Labor defended the constitutionality of applying the minimum wage laws to the Alamo Foundation, and prevailed in the district court and the court of appeals.

My own assessment of the case was that the Alamo believers were right: they had an unquestionably strong and sincere belief that was frustrated by the government action, and the government's interest in forcing them to accept a wage was, in my judgment, far from compelling. Under the "independence" approach—assuming that the Solicitor General agreed with my assessment—the government should confess error. On the other hand, the Supreme Court had rejected every free exercise challenge to a neutral government action in the preceding fifteen years, except in the narrow context of unemployment compensation. If the question were how the Supreme Court would decide the case—the "precedent" approach—I thought that it was likely that the Court would uphold the government's action. Finally, the "government interest" was clear: Congress had passed the statute with no exceptions for religious accommodation, and the agency had enforced it.

After some agonizing, we filed a brief in defense of the Labor Department. So far as I can evaluate my own work, the brief was accurate and fair, and there was ample precedent for our position. I also continue to believe the brief was wrong on the merits. The Supreme Court decided the case unanimously in favor of the government, in an opinion that was singularly insensitive to the sincere religious interests of the petitioners. I took no pleasure in the victory; rather the opposite. The notion, fostered by the 1977 Memorandum to Griffin Bell, that when the Supreme Court accepts the Solicitor General's argument it proves "his legal judgment * * * was correct," obviously confuses winning with being right. The development of constitutional law would have been better served if the Alamo Foundation's legal position had been more forcefully presented. Yet it did not seem then, nor does it seem now, that that was *our* responsibility.

Estate of Thornton v. Caldor, Inc.[7] presented a different twist. In *Thornton,* a state supreme court had struck down under the establishment clause a state statute allowing workers who observe a sabbath day to designate that day as their day off. In *Thornton,* unlike *Alamo Foundation,* the real question was whether to file a brief, rather than what position the brief should take, since the United States was not a party. In my independent judgment, the state law fully comported with the first amendment. The federal government interest was that the reasoning of the lower court decision, if not reversed, could call into doubt the religious accommodation requirements of Title VII of the Civil Rights Act of 1964. Perhaps more important in our thinking, however, was that the case presented an attractive context for the "accommoda-

7. 472 U.S. 703 (1985).

tion" theory the Department of Justice was urging in a variety of establishment clause cases.

The problem was that the lower court opinion was a straightforward application of the Supreme Court's usual test for establishment clause violations. If one had to predict on the basis of precedent, it was likely that the Supreme Court would agree with the lower court. Should that factor be viewed, as it usually would, as a strong argument against participating in the case? Or should this be viewed as an opportunity to demonstrate to the Court, in an attractive context, why it should modify its approach to establishment clause cases?

Solicitor General Lee decided to file amicus curiae briefs urging the Court to grant certiorari in the case and reverse the lower court. We concluded that the important legal principle presented in *Thornton*, coupled with the substantial—even if not compelling—client interest, justified this course of action even though federal government programs were not directly involved. The brief on the merits devoted most of its attention to showing why a rigid application of the usual establishment clause test would be inconsistent with the overall purposes of the religion clauses. While it was respectful in tone, the brief forthrightly urged a significant reformulation of constitutional doctrine.

In *Thornton* and several other decisions handed down at about the same time, the Court reaffirmed its establishment clause precedents and affirmed the lower court. Rather than advancing the "accommodation" theory, it was a setback. With the benefit of hindsight, does this mean that our brief was irresponsible or that it violated the rule of law? I think not. I continue to believe that the government was right in the case, and the Court wrong. The only way for the Court to profit by attorneys' arguments is for attorneys to offer theories that may depart from current precedent. If every brief urges the Court to do what it is likely to do anyway, then briefs will not be a source of growth for the Court. A harder question is whether the *Thornton* brief, and others filed on related issues at about the same time, were strategic errors. In the fall of 1984, when these briefs were written, the time had seemed ripe for reconsideration of first amendment doctrine. By late spring, 1985, the Court's temper had shifted. Some have suggested that our briefs "scared" moderates on the Court, notably Justice Powell, and thus were counterproductive. My guess is that the real stimulus for the Court's shift was the divisive religious squabbling in the 1984 Presidential election; the Court may have judged it an unpropitious time to reconsider its separationist approach to church-state relations. Since that time, the Court's decisions have moved somewhat closer to the position we urged in *Thornton*.[10] Without access to the Court's inner councils we will never know.

---

10. *See* Witters v. Washington Dep't of Servs. for the Blind, 474 U.S. 481 (1986) (establishment clause does not preclude state from paying tuition for ministry train-ing under vocational education program for the blind); Corporation of Presiding Bishop of Church of Jesus Christ of Latter Day Saints v. Amos, 107 S.Ct. 2862 (1987) (es-

A final case from my years at the Solicitor General's Office, one in which I did not participate directly, rounds out the discussion. In *Garcia v. San Antonio Metropolitan Transit Authority*,[11] the question was whether application of federal wage and hour laws to a municipal transit authority was an unconstitutional infringement on state sovereignty under the doctrine of *National League of Cities v. Usery*.[12] Here the government interest was clear: to defend the statute. But the independent constitutional judgment of the Solicitor General was more sympathetic to state sovereignty. One of the central elements of the constitutional philosophy of the President and his chief lawyers was a return to more generous notions of federalism. Moreover, the precedents were equivocal: *Usery* stood for the principle of state sovereignty but subsequent decisions had eroded *Usery* in various contexts. The Court ordered reargument in the case on whether *Usery* should be overruled, which removed much of the usual prudential constraint against attacking precedents. Not surprisingly, the case generated strenuous debate and disagreement among lawyers in and out of the department.

The Solicitor General decided to file a brief defending the federal statute, but to do so on the basis of a strict reading of *Usery*. Other parties to the case urged that *Usery* be overruled—a position at once more radical and more consonant with the government's client interests. The brief made a persuasive case both that *Usery* was good law and that the San Antonio transit system could be subjected to federal regulation. The Court, however, overruled *Usery* in a sweeping five-four decision, with no Justice adopting the Solicitor General's approach to the case. Should this be seen as a rebuff? It seems to me the brief made a significant contribution: it provided the vehicle, had the Court wished it, to uphold the government's interests in the case without shutting off further doctrinal development of the *Usery* principle. It presented a plausible intermediate position. That the Justices did not adopt it does not mean that it was not the right position for the government to take.

The foregoing illustrations cast doubt on the notion that any single criterion can be substituted for the Solicitor General's admittedly subjective judgment of the needs and potentialities of a case. In *Alamo Foundation* the Solicitor General took the "government interest" approach where it conflicted with "independent" constitutional judgment; in *Thornton* he took the "independence" approach where it conflicted with precedent; and in *Garcia* he took the "precedent" approach where the other approaches tugged in opposite directions. In each of these cases the Solicitor General might be criticized, and probably has been. I suspect, however, that few fair observers—whatever their ideological persuasion—would consistently espouse any one of the three approaches

tablishment clause does not preclude Congress from carving out exception from religious antidiscrimination laws for protection of religious organizations).

11. 469 U.S. 528 (1985).

12. 426 U.S. 833 (1976).

across the full range of cases. Does this mean that the rule of law is an empty concept as applied to the role of the Solicitor General?

3. Amicus Curiae

Rule 37 of the Supreme Court's rules governs the filing of amicus curiae briefs.[1] Translated literally, "amicus curiae" means "friend of the court."[2] When not formally a party to a case, but concerned with its outcome or the kind of doctrine the opinion may embrace, a special interest group or a government official can use the vehicle of an amicus brief to inform the Court of its concerns.[3] The amicus is, in essence, a lobbyist before the Court.

Amicus briefs vary widely in their content, principally because the motives for filing them vary widely. At one extreme is the brief, filed solely to let the Court know that an organized group hopes for a particular outcome,[4] that contains no legal analysis and a scanty, one-sided policy argument. At the other extreme is the brief, filed by an expert, that is far superior to anything filed by either of the parties. Today, highly visible Supreme Court cases very often attract two or more amicus briefs of each type.

Unfortunately, the definitive work on amicus briefs has yet to be written. But the materials that follow describe in more detail how these amici lobby the Court. As a group, these materials suggest just how large a role amicus briefs now play in the strategy of an advocate presenting a major case to the Court.

The materials consist of four readings. The Ennis article sets the stage by describing the vast and varied volume of amicus activity in the Supreme Court today. He also summarizes three principal strategic purposes amicus briefs can serve.

Following Ennis, Professor Morris describes increasing amicus activity by states and steps taken to increase coordination among states in filing amicus briefs. He details the factors that go into a state attorney general's decision whether or not to file (or join in another state's brief) in particular cases and suggests that increased coordination among states has raised their success rates. The reader should also recall that

---

1. Supreme Court Rule 37 provides that amicus briefs may be filed supporting or opposing a petition for a writ of certiorari or in cases in which cert has already been granted. To file an amicus brief, one must seek consent from the parties to the case. If all parties consent, the brief may be filed, but if any party objects, the amicus may move the Court for permission to file. An important exception to these requirements is that consent is not required for an amicus brief submitted on behalf of the United States, an agency of the United States, a state or a subdivision of a state. In practice, in the large majority of cases, all parties routinely consent to requests to permit amicus briefs to be filed.

2. The plural is "amici curiae" or "friends of the court."

3. Occasionally, amici are permitted to join in oral argument as well. This happens very infrequently, however, and in the few cases in which it occurs, it is usually the U.S. Solicitor General who is allowed to participate.

4. To be completely candid about it, such briefs are often motivated principally by the desire to strengthen support for the organization among its members or to increase its membership.

the national government, through the Office of the Solicitor General in the Department of Justice, frequently files amicus briefs with the Court. These activities are treated in the previous readings in this chapter.[5]

Finally, we excerpt two studies of interest group amicus participation in highly visible law reform efforts. Professor Schubert, drawing heavily on the work of Professor Vose, details the NAACP's coordination of amicus briefs in *Shelley v. Kraemer,* 334 U.S. 1, 68 S.Ct. 836, 92 L.Ed. 1161 (1948). *Shelley* held unconstitutional the use of judicial enforcement of racially restrictive covenants to invalidate real property transfers. The NAACP's extensive effort to sponsor and control amicus activity in *Shelley* is commonly regarded as the starting point of the modern trend toward massive amicus participation in highly visible and controversial cases. Professor Behuniak–Long shows how this form of advocacy has evolved as she reviews the 78 amicus briefs filed in *Webster v. Reproductive Health Services,* 492 U.S. 490, 109 S.Ct. 3040, 106 L.Ed.2d 410 (1989), one of the recent controversial abortion cases. In *Webster,* the Court upheld several restrictions imposed by Missouri on the availability of abortions.[6]

The careful reader will note that the materials as a whole reveal that a particular amicus brief may be filed for any of several reasons. Further, although it is extremely difficult to gauge the impact amicus briefs have on the Court's decisions, it is nevertheless clear that many people think they can make a difference. Surely, the central fact that emerges from all these readings is that coordination of amicus activity is now a part of the established and accepted role of counsel for the parties in most major cases before the Court. Accordingly, in our experience, a good way to review these materials is to read and analyze several amicus briefs filed in a pending Supreme Court case.

BRUCE J. ENNIS,* EFFECTIVE AMICUS BRIEFS**
33 Cath.U.L.Rev. 603, 603–608 (1984)

I. THREE MISCONCEPTIONS ABOUT AMICUS BRIEFS

Let's begin by dispelling three common misconceptions about amicus briefs. The first is that amicus briefs are not very important; that they are at best only icing on the cake. In reality, they are often the cake itself. Amicus briefs have shaped judicial decisions in many more cases than is commonly realized. Occasionally, a case will be decided on

---

5. See Chapter 5, Section C. 2., supra.

6. Do not overlook a contrast between the two case studies. Schubert seems to regard the amicus brief as exceptional and questionable. For Behuniak–Long, it is an established practice. Undoubtedly, this reflects a shift in prevailing attitude between the times the two pieces were written.

* Mr. Ennis is a partner of Ennis, Friedman, Bersoff & Ewing. A.B. 1962, Dartmouth College, J.D., 1965, University of Chicago.

a ground suggested only by an amicus, not by the parties. Frequently, judicial rulings, and thus their precedential value, will be narrower or broader than the parties had urged, because of a persuasive amicus brief. Courts often rely on factual information, cases or analytical approaches provided only by an amicus. A good idea is a good idea, whether it is contained in an amicus brief or in the brief of a party.

The second misconception is that amicus briefs are not filed very often, and then only in great constitutional cases. That was not true twenty years ago, and is even less true today. Amicus briefs offer such enormous utility, flexibility and cost-effectiveness that their use is steadily and dramatically increasing. In the Supreme Court's 1965 Term, for example, of the 128 cases decided by opinion, 46 involved amicus briefs. Thus, even eighteen years ago, about a third of all opinion cases involved amicus participation. By the Court's 1980 Term, however, of the 137 cases decided by opinion, 97, or 71% of the total, involved amicus briefs.

Actually, the increasing and now quite common use of amicus briefs is even more dramatic than these figures suggest. In the earlier years, a case with amicus participation would usually involve only one amicus. In recent years, however, it has become common for several amicus organizations, sometimes dozens, to file briefs in a given case. Since amicus briefs are now filed in over two-thirds of all the Supreme Court cases decided by opinion, and since it is common for more than one amicus to participate in a given case, it is quite possible that the Supreme Court now reviews more briefs from amici than from parties.

These statistics indicate that if you have a case in the Supreme Court there is a good chance your opponent will be supported by an amicus brief. So it is no longer enough for you to write a first rate brief. In today's world, effective representation of your client requires that you at least seriously explore the possibility of enlisting persuasive amicus support on your client's behalf.

The third misconception is that amicus briefs are filed primarily by politically "liberal" public interest groups. That was largely true twenty years ago, but is not true today. There are now almost as many "conservative" public interest groups as liberal ones. Groups such as the Mountain States Legal Foundation, the Capital Legal Foundation, the Pacific Legal Foundation, and the New England Legal Foundation appear alongside the ACLU, the NAACP Legal Defense Fund, and the Natural Resources Defense Council in the lists of amici.

In addition, the United States frequently files amicus briefs. In fact, the Supreme Court *requests* the United States to participate as amicus "a couple of dozen" times each term.

Moreover, the amicus brief is not limited to public interest groups or the United States. Professional associations such as the American Bar Association and the American Psychological Association, other governmental entities, corporations, unions, and banks now appear regularly as amici.[3]

II. EFFECTIVE COOPERATION BETWEEN PARTY AND AMICUS

Of course, there does not have to be any cooperation. Amici frequently file briefs supporting neither side, but advancing their own positions and interests. The Court will occasionally request the participation of an amicus when it suspects collusion between the parties, or when the parties do not have an adversary posture with respect to certain issues in the case.[4] Let's assume, however, as is more common (and as the Supreme Court's rules contemplate) that the amicus will support one of the parties. In that case, there is a great deal of support that can be provided in addition to filing an amicus brief. The amicus and its counsel can help the party plan the *party's* strategy, and can provide research, drafting, and editorial assistance to the party. The amicus can organize one or more moot courts, etc. This assistance is a much neglected resource that can be extremely useful.

In the amicus brief itself, support for a party will usually take one of three forms:

A. *Helping the Party Flesh Out Arguments the Party is Forced to Make in Summary Form*

Because of page limits, or considerations of tone and emphasis, parties are frequently forced to make some of the points they wish to make in rather abbreviated form. A supportive amicus can flesh out those points with additional discussion and citation of authority. Or the amicus can support points the party is making by providing a detailed legislative or constitutional history, a scholarly exposition of the common law, or a nationwide analysis of relevant state laws.

---

3. Governmental entities, particularly states, frequently file amicus briefs. A small sample of other organizations filing Supreme Court amicus briefs during the 1980 Term includes:

American Bankers' Association; Securities Industry Association; U.A.W. Legal Services Plan; National Railway Labor Conference; AFL–CIO; Allegheny–Ludlum; Cummins Engine Co.; CBS, Inc.; TWA; National Steel Co.; Centex Corp.; National Semiconductor Corp.; Merck & Co.; Cessna Air; Georgia–Pacific; Mead Corp.; Chamber of Commerce of the United States; Boise–Cascade; Owens–Illinois; Safeway Stores; Weyerhaeuser Co.; American Insurance Association; Atlantic Richfield; American Bell International, Inc.; Sperry Corp.; Sylvania Technical Systems, Inc.; American Iron & Steel Institute; American Medical Association; American Association of University Professors; and Morgan Guaranty Trust Company of New York.

4. Perhaps the first amicus to appear in the United States Supreme Court was Henry Clay, who was allowed to appear as amicus because the Court suspected collusion between the parties. *See* Green v. Biddle, 21 U.S. (8 Wheat.) 1 (1823), mentioned in O'Connor & Epstein, *Court Rules and Workload: A Case Study of Rules Governing Amicus Curiae Participation*, 8 Justice J. 35, 36 (1983). Another example is Bob Jones Univ. v. United States, 103 S.Ct. 2017 (1983), in which both the United States and Bob Jones University, the nominal parties, took the position that the Internal Revenue Service lacked authority to issue a regulation which effectively denied tax exemptions for religious private schools which discriminated on the basis of race. *Id.* at 2025 n. 9. The Supreme Court appointed a distinguished private attorney, William T. Coleman, Jr., who successfully urged the position, as amicus, that the IRS had the authority to deny tax exemptions for private, racially discriminatory religious schools.

For example, in the recent case of *Toll v. Moreno,*[6] the World Bank submitted an amicus brief urging the Supreme Court to rule, on Supremacy Clause grounds, that certain state statutes which disadvantaged alien college students were unconstitutional. The alien students touched briefly on the Supremacy Clause, but the thrust and greater portion of their brief was necessarily concerned with their equal protection and due process arguments. The Court ruled for the students, but it chose to decide the case on the basis of the Supremacy Clause theory that had been advocated primarily by the amicus.

Similarly, in the Supreme Court's latest round of abortion decisions, the plaintiffs devoted only one paragraph in their brief to the argument that nonphysicians should be allowed to engage in abortion counseling because they thought they would probably lose that issue. Instead, the plaintiffs chose to stress other important issues they thought they had a better chance to win. But the American Psychological Association, as amicus, marshaled empirical studies to show why counseling by nonphysicians would help to promote truly informed consent, and the Court agreed.[7]

B.   Making Arguments the Party Wants to Make But Cannot Make Itself

It frequently happens that a party wants a particular argument to be made but is not in a position to make that argument itself. The party may simply lack credibility on that issue, or it may be unable to make the argument for political or tactical reasons. For example, governmental entities often feel compelled, for political reasons, to argue for very broad rulings: eliminate the exclusionary rule entirely, absolute immunity for all governmental employees, etc. But courts, including the Supreme Court, are institutionally conservative and usually prefer to decide cases on narrower grounds if possible. An amicus can suggest those narrower grounds: qualify the exclusionary rule rather than eliminate it, distinguish a prior case rather than overrule it, or dismiss certiorari as improvidently granted, among others.

A good example of this type of cooperation is *Metromedia, Inc. v. San Diego,*[8] in which San Diego sought to exclude most billboards from designated sections of the city, on grounds of traffic safety and aesthetics. The billboards carried primarily commercial messages, but they occasionally carried political messages as well. The billboard owners

---

6. 458 U.S. 1 (1982).

7. City of Akron v. Akron Center for Reproductive Health, 103 S.Ct. 2481 (1983). In addition, amicus groups can often supply relevant but specialized information not readily available to a party. For example, the majority opinion in Roe v. Wade, 410 U.S. 113 (1973), establishing a woman's constitutional right to effectuate her decision to have an abortion, expressly referred to positions urged by amicus groups, and relied heavily on historical, social and cru-

cial medical data presented to the Court by amicus groups. *Id.* at 148–52. In the companion case of Doe v. Bolton, 410 U.S. 179 (1973), the majority noted that "various amici have presented us with a mass of data" showing that "some facilities other than hospitals are entirely adequate to perform abortions" and expressly relied on that data to reject the state's contrary claim. *Id.* at 195.

8. 453 U.S. 490 (1981).

were represented by an experienced and extremely sophisticated Supreme Court advocate. He knew the Court would be closely divided, and would be more troubled by the regulation's prohibition of political speech than by its prohibition of commercial speech. The billboard owners, however, were not in a position to argue credibly on behalf of political speech because they did not themselves engage in political speech; they simply leased billboard space, primarily to commercial speakers. Their lawyer decided it would be important to demonstrate to the Court that organizations traditionally concerned with the protection of political speech were opposed to the San Diego ordinance, so he asked the ACLU if it would file an amicus brief emphasizing the political speech aspects of the case, and the ACLU agreed.

The Court, as expected, was closely divided. Although a majority of the Court agreed to a judgment striking down the San Diego ordinance, only three other Justices joined in Justice White's plurality opinion. Those four thought the ordinance was constitutional insofar as it regulated only commercial speech, but they struck down the entire ordinance because it unconstitutionally regulated political speech, and the commercial and political regulations were not severable. Given the closeness of this decision, it seems clear that the billboard owners advanced their interests by enlisting amicus support.

C. Informing the Court of the Broader Public Interests Involved, or of the Broader Implications of a Ruling

One of the most common forms of amicus support is to inform the court of interests other than those represented by the parties, and to focus the court's attention on the broader implications of various possible rulings. Governmental entities are uniquely situated to define and assert the "public interest," and their views as amicus will, therefore, carry substantial weight. If a governmental entity is already a party, amicus support from other governmental entities will enhance the credibility of the party's arguments.

* * *

THOMAS R. MORRIS,* STATES BEFORE THE U.S. SUPREME COURT: STATE ATTORNEYS GENERAL AS AMICUS CURIAE**
70 Judicature 298 (1987)

* * * [A]ny evaluation of governmental representation before the U.S. Supreme Court is incomplete without consideration of the litigation

* Thomas R. Morris is an associate professor of political science at the University of Richmond.

** Excerpts from *States before the U.S. Supreme Court: State Attorneys General as Amicus Curiae,* by Thomas R. Morris. Copyright © 1987 by Thomas R. Morris and the American Judicature Society. Permission granted by "Judicature, the journal of the American Judicature Society" and Thomas R. Morris, President and Professor of Political Science, Emory & Henry College, Emory, Virginia.

activities of state attorneys general and their staff attorneys. As a group, their rate of participation both as direct parties and *amici curiae* in Supreme Court cases is second only to the Solicitor General's Office. The reappearance of federalism as a dominant constitutional value makes the period of the Burger Court an appropriate one for examining representation of state interests.

* * *

The Solicitor General's Office submitted *amicus* briefs in 20 per cent of the cases argued before the Supreme Court during the 1974 through 1983 terms of the Court; state attorneys general, by comparison, participated as *amici curiae* in 13 per cent of the cases during that time period.
* * *

This article examines the *amicus* participation of the states before the nation's highest court for a ten-year period of the Burger Court era.
* * *

THE ROLE OF STATE ATTORNEYS GENERAL

The position of state attorneys general is unique in American government. It operates in the interstices of law and politics, on the front line of federal-state relations, and at the conjunction of the executive, legislative, and judicial processes. Prior to the 1970s, state attorneys general tended to look upon their role as being merely ministerial functionaries of the state administration; they were in office to do the bidding of other political executives and defend the state establishment from legal attacks. The size and responsibilities of state attorneys general's offices expanded in the 1970s to include public advocacy roles in such areas as consumer protection, antitrust enforcement, utility rate intervention, and environmental protection. Largely passive attorneys general's offices were transformed into activist ones. A new breed of state attorneys general, younger and better educated than their predecessors, increasingly exploited the political advantages of their offices. Popularly elected in 43 states, state attorneys general supplemented the traditional legal defense roles of the office with public advocacy activities that contributed to the growing perception of the office as a political stepping stone to higher elective office.

Initially appointed to the Minnesota attorney generalship in 1961 at the age of 32, Walter Mondale was one of the earliest of the new breed of state attorneys general. Declaring himself an "activist," Mondale sought "ways of using the office not in the old traditional passive way, but in an affirmative public protection role." Confronted with complaints of a furnace-repair hoax and initially stymied by the absence of a consumer fraud statute, Mondale's consumer protection unit took action against the company based on a public nuisance law originally written to protect citizens from barking dogs.

Mondale's service as attorney general is also remembered for his involvement in the landmark decision of the U.S. Supreme Court in *Gideon v. Wainwright* (1963). In the early summer of 1962, Florida

Attorney General Richard W. Ervin mailed a letter to his counterparts in the other states inviting them to submit *amicus* briefs supporting the 1942 precedent of *Betts v. Brady* on which Florida's restrictive right-to-counsel policy for indigents was based. His letter carried the familiar appeal to states as states by invoking "the right of states to determine their own rules of criminal procedure." [6]

Mondale's surprising response detailed his support of the policy followed by Minnesota and 34 other states to provide for the appointment of counsel for indigents in all felony cases. He sent a copy of his letter to Massachusetts Attorney General Edward J. McCormick, Jr., whose office took on the responsibility of drafting an *amicus* brief arguing for a change of the *Betts* precedent. Mondale and McCormick enlisted 21 other attorneys general, including three from states which had no such requirement for counsel, to join them in filing a brief with the Court opposing the existing policy in Florida. Only two states—North Carolina and Alabama—supported Florida's position. In his opinion for the Court, Justice Black took notice of the unexpected position of the states: "Twenty-two states as friends of the Court argue that *Betts* was an anachronism when handed down and that it should be overruled. We agree."

* * *

Unanimity of state legal positions, of course, does not assure supportive decisions by the Supreme Court. When the Court was faced with the extension of *Gideon* in *Argersinger v. Hamlin* (1972) nine years later, for example, all state participation supported the position taken by Florida, but the outcome was the same as before—the court ruled against Florida's policy. The attorneys general of ten states joined the respondent state of Florida and separate *amicus* briefs were filed by three states supporting Florida's practice of restricting right to counsel to offenses punishable by more than six months imprisonment.

COMPARISONS WITH SOLICITOR GENERAL

* * *

For complex political reasons, state attorneys general have not generally enjoyed the same degree of independence as the Solicitor General in deciding which cases to take to the Supreme Court. They interact with a wide array of officials at both the state and local levels of government, and most of them participate in campaigns for re-election or election to other offices in which litigation records (especially the failure to appeal cases) can become an issue. In 1984, for example, Dennis Roberts, Attorney General of Rhode Island, was locked in a close re-election contest with Arlene Violet, who had challenged him two years earlier. His decision to petition the U.S. Supreme Court for review of his state supreme court's decision to grant Claus von Bulow a new trial was dismissed by the accused's attorney as "political" and by Justice

6. Lewis, Gideon's Trumpet 142 (New York: Vintage Books. 1964).

Stevens as "frivolous." Roberts ultimately lost both the appeal and the election. A 1985 *National Law Journal* article also reported a sudden upsurge in petitions to the Supreme Court from Missouri during the period when the state's attorney general, John Ashcroft, was running for governor.

In the 1970s, the states were generally criticized by scholars and justices alike as poor litigators in the Supreme Court. In a 1975 address to the Fifth Circuit Judicial Conference, Justice Powell noted that "some of the weakest briefs and arguments came from * * * " assistant state attorneys general, especially when compared with the lawyers representing the advocacy groups most likely to oppose state governments.[12] The National Association of Attorneys General (NAAG) responded to the criticisms of state performance in the nation's highest court by designating a lawyer to work full-time as the Supreme Court counsel to the attorneys general. Prior to the fall of 1982, states participating as direct parties or considering an *amicus* brief would write other state offices they thought might be interested or occasionally put a notice in the NAAG's monthly newsletter. The counsel now arranges moot courts several days prior to scheduled arguments for attorneys general and their staff attorneys before the Court. The counsel also orchestrates a communications network among the state offices that informs them about pending litigation and *amicus* activity in other states. The network has been credited with more "effective coordination" of *amicus curiae* briefs filed by the states in some 100 cases.

The effort to provide more centralized coordination of state litigation since 1982 is an important development, but it cannot expect to match the tight control of the Solicitor General's Office. * * * Despite the modern trend encouraged by NAAG toward consolidation of all state legal authority in a centralized attorney general's office, some states permit local government attorneys and state agencies to initiate and appeal cases impacting on statewide interests without the approval, or even over the objection, of the state's chief legal officer.

In Texas, the attorney general decided it was in the best interests of the state not to appeal a federal trial court's decision invalidating a state sodomy statute. After unsuccessfully trying to have the state supreme court order the attorney general to pursue an appeal, a local prosecutor succeeded in his effort to have the U.S. Court of Appeals for the Fifth Circuit permit him to intervene and appeal the case over the objections of the attorney general. Texas' petition for *certiorari* to the Supreme Court was supported by the Attorney General of Oregon, who filed an *amicus* brief joined by 25 other states requesting reversal of the Fifth Circuit's inappropriate and potentially disastrous signal to lower echelon and nonlegal state policymakers: If you disagree with the Attorney

---

12. Quoted in Baker and Asperger. *Foreword: Toward A Center for State and*   *Local Advocacy,* 31 Cath.U.L.Rev. 368 (1982).

General's legal advice and litigation strategy, you may be treated as a spokesperson for the state in the federal courts.[14]

The high court denied *certiorari* on July 2, 1986, but an earlier case provided some support for the position of the *amici* states. When a New York district attorney appealed a decision by the state high court invalidating a state statute regulating deviant sexual behavior, the Supreme Court indicated that the determination of what state officials should represent the state is "wholly a matter of state concern." The New York Attorney General submitted an *amicus* brief in the case arguing that the statute as applied in the case violated free speech and privacy rights, but that it should not have been struck down on its face. The conflict in the positions taken by the attorney general and the district attorney was cited as one reason for dismissing the writ of *certiorari* as improvidently granted. In the process of explaining its decision, however, the Court did concede that "in addressing the constitutionality of a statute with statewide application we consider highly relevant the views of the State's chief law enforcement official." [15]

* * *

THE STATUS OF *AMICUS* BRIEFS

Rule 36.4 of the Supreme Court facilitates the filing of "friend of the court" briefs. States represented by their attorneys general, as well as any other public agency at any level of government represented by its appropriate legal representative, are exempt from the requirement imposed on private groups to secure the consent of other parties to the litigation or the approval of the Court before filing *amicus* briefs. In most instances, state officials merely file briefs with the Court, although on rare occasions they argue as *amici curiae*. For the ten terms of the Court examined in this study, state attorneys general or their staff attorneys argued as *amicus curiae* in only 14 cases, and five of those were the death penalty cases heard on March 30 and 31, 1976.

* * * The availability of attorneys otherwise committed to representing traditional clients in state legal offices becomes an important factor in *amicus* activity. Attorney General Dave Frohnmayer of Oregon estimated that five hours per case are necessary for the approximately eight requests each month for his office to write or join in an *amicus curiae* brief. Even though the briefs usually address the most important issues of the day, he notes that there is no way to charge the cost of the screening time to any particular client-agency. Finally, assuming the office files two major *amicus* briefs in the U.S. Supreme Court at 150

---

14. Brief Amici Curiae for the States, Texas v. Hill (No. 85–1251), Oct. Term. 1985, p. 2. On the issue of whether state attorneys general may appeal cases against the wishes of their state clients, state court precedents are divided. See Feeney v. Commonwealth, 373 Mass. 359, 366 N.E.2d 1262 (1977) for an example permitting such appeals and Santa Rita Mining Co. v. Department of Property Valuation, 111 Ariz. 368, 530 P.2d 360 (1975) denying that discretion.

15. New York v. Uplinger, 467 U.S. 246, 247, n. 1 (1984).

hours per case, 780 attorney hours would be necessary each year for *amicus* activity.

While it is difficult to determine how much effect *amicus* briefs have on Supreme Court decisions, the large number of *amicus* briefs submitted to the Court by government officials and private groups provides some indication of the importance attributed to them. Developments during the oral arguments in the short-lived precedent of *National League of Cities v. Usery* (1976) are instructive in this regard. Four states—Alabama, Colorado, Michigan and Minnesota—filed *amicus* briefs in opposition to the state position taken by California and 19 other states. The position of the four states was cited by the Solicitor General during oral argument as an indication that state sovereignty was not threatened, as the majority maintained, by the extension of the Fair Labor Standards Act to all state and local employees. The attorney for the majority state position replied that he had a letter from the Governor of Colorado instructing the attorney general of his state to withdraw his name from the brief referred to by the Solicitor General. Upon hearing about the Solicitor General's comment, Governor George Wallace of Alabama responded by immediately sending a telegram to the Supreme Court indicating his state supported the position taken by the majority of states participating in the case.

Opposing positions by the states before the Court was a rarity during the period of this study. Not counting original jurisdiction cases, where conflict among the states is much more likely, splits took place in only about two per cent of the cases. * * *

Commerce clause cases were most frequently the source of divisions among the states. In *Commonwealth Edison Co. v. Montana* (1981), Montana's 30 per cent severance tax on coal precipitated seven *amicus* briefs addressing the question of whether the tax constituted an unconstitutional burden on interstate commerce. Support for the tax came from states rich in energy resources—New Mexico, North Dakota, West Virginia, Wyoming, Colorado, Nevada, Idaho, Washington and Oregon. Meanwhile, the existence of half of the nation's low-sulphur coal reserves within Montana's borders prompted energy-consuming states to complain that the state was unfairly exploiting its strategic advantage over the other states; *amicus* briefs opposing the tax were filed by Kansas, New Jersey, Michigan, Minnesota, Iowa and Wisconsin. * * *

Local disputes were also the source of state conflicts. A commuter tax pitted Maine and Vermont against New Hampshire, which attracted the *amicus* support of New Jersey. Disagreement over the legal basis for abating a nuisance caused by interstate water pollution resulted in Wisconsin's filing an *amicus* brief against the respondent states of Illinois and Michigan. The issue of whether a state could prohibit the exportation of hydroelectric energy produced within its borders by a federally licensed facility resulted in Massachusetts and Rhode Island challenging New Hampshire. * * *

NATURE AND EXTENT OF PARTICIPATION

State *amicus* activity has steadily increased over the past 25 years. An earlier study of *amicus* participation by state attorneys general in all decisions reaching the merits in the 1960 through 1973 terms of the Supreme Court identified 164 cases (4 per cent of the total cases decided on the merits). State *amicus* activity by attorneys general in this study for three fewer terms of the Court amounted to 234 cases (13 per cent of the total cases argued). * * *

One measure of the importance attached to *amicus* activity is the number of states joining such briefs. Twenty-four cases in this study attracted more than half of the states as *amici*. The states won all five of the criminal cases falling into that category; three of those cases were decided in the 1983 term when the states enjoyed the *amicus* support of the Solicitor General's Office. In one-third of the non-criminal cases, the states joined together as *amici* in important antitrust cases before the Court.

* * *

The states suffered three major setbacks in antitrust enforcement despite the *amicus* support of the Solicitor General.[25] *Illinois Brick Co. v. Illinois* (1977) restricted antitrust actions to direct purchasers, thereby limiting the effectiveness of state attorneys general acting as *parens patriae* on behalf of state consumers because most such suits are indirect purchaser actions. In *Illinois v. Abbott and Associates* (1983), the states also failed in their effort to convince the Court that federal law should be interpreted to permit state attorneys general access to grand jury files pertaining to federal antitrust violations without having to demonstrate a "particularized need." Finally, in a 1984 decision, the Court rejected the states' argument on the standard of proof to find a vertical price-fixing conspiracy.

Unanimous state support was forthcoming for Maryland's position of categorically denying in-state status to domiciled non-immigrant aliens holding G–4 visas. Nevertheless, the state policy was held invalid under the Supremacy Clause of the United States Constitution.[26] Other cases attracting large numbers of state *amici* dealt with the award of attorney's fees for plaintiffs prevailing in civil rights actions (three cases), Indian ownership of land, and the preemption of California's food labeling statute by federal laws.[27]

Noticeably missing from the category of large-scale state *amici* participation were the major decisions of the Burger Court during the period of this study in such controversial areas as race and sex discrimination, abortion, freedom of speech and press, and church-state rela-

25. Illinois Brick Co. v. Ill., 431 U.S. 720 (1977); Ill. v. Abbott and Associates, 460 U.S. 557 (1983); Monsanto Co., v. Spray–Rite Service Corp., 465 U.S. 752 (1984).

26. Toll v. Moreno, 458 U.S. 1 (1982).

27. Hensley v. Eckerhart, 461 U.S. 424 (1983); Patsy v. Board of Regents, 457 U.S. 496 (1982); Blum v. Stenson, 465 U.S. 886 (1984); Wilson v. Omaha Indian Tribe, 442 U.S. 653 (1979); and Jones v. Rath Packing Co., 430 U.S. 519 (1977).

tions. Only two cases of those involving half the states could be classified as civil liberty cases. Thirty-three states filed two *amicus* briefs supporting Florida's challenge to an interpretation of the Rehabilitation Act of 1973 requiring "affirmative conduct" by states in the admission of handicapped persons to clinical training programs. The Court agreed with the states' position even though opposing *amicus* briefs were filed by the Solicitor General and the attorney general of California. Similarly, in 1982, 31 states joined in a brief *amicus curiae* where the petitioner alleged that her state employer had denied her employment opportunities solely on the basis of her race and sex. The Court rejected the states' argument that state administrative remedies must be exhausted as a prerequisite to the petitioner's action under federal law.

Whereas the Solicitor General has generally been active in civil liberty and civil rights cases, states seldom choose in either large or small groups to participate as *amici* in cases litigating First and Fourteenth Amendment issues. * * * A case in which states take a "pro-rights" or "pro-individual" stance as *amici* against another state, as occurred in *Gideon,* is truly exceptional.

Past research has demonstrated that *amicus* activity is significantly less likely to occur in criminal cases. The results of this study largely confirm that research. Prior to the 1983 term, the states participated as *amici* in only 30 criminal cases, representing 16 per cent of the state *amicus* activity, and five of those were the death penalty cases argued by an assistant attorney general of California in 1976. Furthermore, 20 cases consisted of only 1 state submitting an *amicus* brief. The 1983 term, however, provided evidence of increased cooperation among the states in criminal cases. In that term alone, *amicus* briefs were filed by the states in 11 criminal cases. * * *

Not surprisingly, the cases most likely to attract significant state *amici* are those dealing with federalism issues. Twenty-six (38 per cent) of the non-criminal cases involving more than ten states fell into this category. * * * The Solicitor General's Office participated in opposition to the state position in all but three of the cases. The states, not surprisingly, were only half as likely to be in agreement with the Court as was the Solicitor General. In the Section 1983 cases, only one of which attracted federal participation, the states fared better, agreeing with the Court three out of five times. * * *

Practically no federal opposition was encountered in the other non-criminal cases in which more than ten states were involved as *amici.* The Solicitor General did not participate in the seven cases pertaining to state taxation issues or the two cases in which in-state student status was litigated. In seven of the ten antitrust cases, the Solicitor General took similar positions to those assumed by the states. Likewise, the federal office was supportive of the state position in two challenges to municipal zoning ordinances as constituting a taking of private property without just compensation in violation of the Fifth and Fourteenth Amendments.

PATTERNS AND SUCCESS

The California attorney general's office participated in one-third of the cases attracting state *amicus* briefs. It earned the top ranking for the states by filing more separate briefs than any other state and by participating in well over half of the criminal cases in this study. The New York office was also a leader in drafting briefs and was involved in 28 per cent of the state *amicus* cases. After the top two states, the rate of participation did not vary dramatically; three-fourths of the states were involved in from 15 to 25 per cent of the cases, and no state participated in fewer than 10 per cent of the state *amicus* cases.   * * *

The dominant role played by the California and New York offices is not surprising when you consider that each employs more than 450 attorneys while more than half the state legal offices have fewer than 100 lawyers on their staffs. California and New York also lead the states as direct parties in Supreme Court litigation. States with few cases before the high court and small legal staffs can, nevertheless, magnify their impact by choosing to participate as a friend of the court. Interviews by this author with selected attorneys general revealed that they take seriously the decision as to whether to join *amicus* briefs submitted to their offices. They recognize that whether they like it or not, a U.S. Supreme Court decision adverse to the interests of another state may very well apply to their state. Comaraderie among the attorneys general is another factor influencing support of sister states. On the other hand, professional norms and limited personnel require attorneys general to consider carefully both the quality and relevance for their state of *amicus* briefs before agreeing to have their names listed.

* * *

If anything, movement toward greater cooperation among the states has reduced the number of cases in which more than two state briefs are filed. What has changed, in addition to the greater number of cases in which states are participating, is the number of states involved in each case. There are almost as many instances, for example, when more than ten states participated as *amici* during the 1981, 1982, and 1983 terms of the Court as there were in the preceding seven terms.

The range of state *amici* in individual cases from one to 49 states makes it difficult to evaluate the success of state cooperation. The significance of an *amicus* brief filed by one state might be greater than one with unanimous state support, depending on the quality and persuasiveness of the argument. Nevertheless, by examining the record of the one-third of the cases in which more than ten states participated as *amici,* a clearer picture of state cooperation emerges than would be reflected if all cases were considered.

The won/loss record for the state legal officials in non-criminal cases was somewhat higher (56 per cent) than when they participated as direct parties in such cases (49 per cent). A phenomenal record of 11 wins in 12 criminal cases attracting more than 10 states increases the overall success rate for the states to 63 per cent. In 10 of the criminal cases won by the states in this category, they submitted *amicus* briefs in support of the appealing party. Given the Supreme Court's record over the past 30 years of reversing the lower court in two out of three *certiorari* cases, it is generally advantageous to be supporting the appealing party. Another significant variable in determining success before the Court in light of the Solicitor General's record is advocacy of a position consistent with the one advanced by the federal office. Not surprisingly, therefore, the success rate in all cases attracting more than 10 states as *amici* went up when they were supportive of the position taken by either the Solicitor General (75 per cent) or the appealing party (77 per cent).

CONCLUSION

* * *

[T]he record of state *amici* when more than ten states participate is considerably higher than when the states appear as direct parties. Increased coordination of state *amicus* activity as part of an overall effort to improve state advocacy has apparently been successful in increasing state participation. Not all state cases are "winnable," of course, but *amicus* briefs can contribute to narrowing the legal or constitutional basis for a decision in hopes of avoiding a sweeping ruling that might adversely affect all states. After all, an *amicus* brief joined by a good number of states provides the Court with an excellent impact analysis in state litigation.

GLENDON SCHUBERT,* CONSTITUTIONAL POLITICS
69–70, 78–82 (1960)

LOBBYISTS BEFORE THE SUPREME COURT

The lobbying of interest groups with Congress and state legislatures is accepted today as a fundamental and desirable political process in a democratic polity. Administrative lobbying was less well understood, and certainly less generally accepted, a generation ago than it is today; and even now, there are many critics who insist that pressure politics has no legitimate role in relationship to certain kinds of administrative decision-making, such as government contracting or adjudication by regulatory commissions. When it comes to the judiciary, however, the norms of our society engender an attitude of open hostility toward lobbying tactics. * * * Thus, group behaviors that are considered to be the very essence of the politics of democracy, when focused upon the Congress, are castigated as the antithesis of "a government of laws, not men" when the object of group pressures is the Supreme Court.

Nevertheless, lobbying with the Supreme Court has been going on for a long time. As Twiss has shown, the now staid American Bar Association was originally formed, in 1878, as a national organization stemming from the Association of the Bar of the City of New York, which began in 1870. The latter association was organized "chiefly to combat the corruption of the judiciary by the Tweed Ring. At least in its early years it was a good example of how a bar association can be an important political pressure group." During the first three decades of the present century, the National Consumers' League was particularly active in defending labor legislation from attack in the courts. The League enlisted the services of such distinguished counsel as Louis Brandeis and Felix Frankfurter; and although its efforts met with greater success in the state courts than in the Supreme Court, a major change in the technique of persuasion before the Supreme Court resulted from the League's sponsorship of advocacy by means of the sociological or Brandeis brief. The purpose of such briefs, which were in essence compendious compilations of economic and social facts, with a minimum of emphasis upon the citation of legal precedents and doctrines which (then as now) made up the substance of conventional legal briefs, was to educate Supreme Court justices concerning the facts of industrial life in a changing world. Half a century ago, the novel sociological briefs met with just as severe criticism and resistance as has the Court's own reliance, in a more recent period, upon generalizations regarding human behavior based upon the research of social psychologists.

Three Tactics for Lobbying with the Supreme Court

The conventions surrounding judicial decision-making, at least as a formal process, stigmatize as illegal or unethical certain kinds of group-pressure activity. Thus, for instance, the picketing of federal court-houses is defined as a criminal act by congressional legislation; and the sending of mass petitions to the Supreme Court on behalf of condemned criminals has been condemned by the justices. There are, however, a number of pressure tactics which have become increasingly common, including (1) the use of test cases; (2) building up a favorable professional climate of opinion in the law reviews; and (3) presenting the Court with a show of strength, by the temporary alliance of groups to support a formal party to a case through the *amicus curiae* device. * * *

Is the *amicus curiae* brief incompatible with the dispensation of "dispassionate justice" in the Supreme Court? Or is it a desirable device for extending the vision of the justices beyond the blinders imposed by the record of and the immediate interests of the direct parties to a case? The answers to these questions hinge, no doubt, upon the assumption that most appropriately defines the modern role of the Court. If the justices sit as a "Supreme Tribunal of Errors and Appeals" to right every wrong in the lower courts, then the rights of the immediate parties are most important. But if the justices sit as major formulators of national policy, then it would seem desirable to encourage a broad proliferation of interest representation before the Court.

The NAACP as a Supreme Court Lobby

During the modern period, organizations prominent for their attempts to mold policy-making by the Supreme Court have included the American Liberty League of anti-New Deal fame; the Watch Tower Bible and Tract Society (Jehovah's Witnesses), which built up the imposing record of forty-four wins out of fifty-five cases in the Supreme Court, for a batting average of .800; and the National Association for the Advancement of Colored People, which won more than fifty Supreme Court cases in the half-century following its establishment. The victories of the NAACP in the Supreme Court have had a tremendous impact upon our national policy, our political system, and our very way of life, so we shall use the lobbying activities of this group as a concrete example of the three lobbying tactics described above.

NAACP Strategy in the Restrictive Covenant Cases [19]

* * *

Scrutiny of the NAACP's part in the successful litigation which ended the court enforcement of racial restrictive covenants will indicate how the organization went about urging constitutional change. This was a long campaign from 1918, speeded up after 1945 and climaxed in 1948. Then, in *Shelley v. Kraemer,* the Supreme Court ruled that when a state court enjoins Negroes from taking restricted property it is state action in violation of the equal protection guarantee of the Fourteenth Amendment. In two cases from Washington, D.C., it was held contrary to the Civil Rights Act of 1866 and the nation's public policy for federal courts to use their equity powers to enforce racial restrictive covenants. [In 1953], in *Barrows v. Jackson,* the Supreme Court extended the doctrine by holding that a state court could not sanction a racial covenant by awarding damages in a suit at law.

* * *

It takes time for a group to persuade the Court to accept a case as a test. Through the years after 1926 when the judicial enforcement of a covenant was sanctioned by the Supreme Court the NAACP made five applications for writs of certiorari. In 1929 and 1937 these applications were denied outright. In 1940 the Court heard a case from Chicago and held the covenant unenforceable because of fraud so did not reach the constitutional issue. In 1945 the NAACP gained encouragement despite another denial of certiorari. Since only four votes are needed for certiorari to be issued, the dissents of Justices Rutledge and Murphy in 1945 told the Association that its chances were improving.

* * *

19. This selection is taken from "The Impact of Pressure Groups on Constitutional Interpretation," a paper read by Professor Vose at the Annual Convention of the American Political Science Association (Chicago, Illinois: September 8, 1954), pp. 1–4. For an extended development and documentation of these same points, see Vose, *Caucasians Only: The Supreme Court, the NAACP, and the Restrictive Covenant Cases* (Berkeley and Los Angeles: University of California Press, 1959).

By 1945 potential test cases had begun in the trial courts of Los Angeles, Chicago, St. Louis, Columbus, Detroit, New York and Washington, D.C. The controversies grew out of Negro-white rivalry for homes with suits for injunction originating from the white side. Negroes in jeopardy turned naturally to the leading NAACP attorneys in their own city. As the cases progressed these lawyers shared notes at four conferences on racial covenants called by the national leaders of the Association. Careful work was done to establish a sound trial record in order to have the best possible vehicle available for the constitutional test because there was no way of knowing which cases would be accepted for review by the Court. In 1947 new writs of certiorari were applied for and granted in cases from St. Louis, Detroit and Washington, D.C.

Planning test cases is a necessity for any pressure group desiring a hearing before the Supreme Court for it is their primary means of access. The test case represents others which never advance to appellate courts. Quite clearly, the pressure group with continuity, central control and a far-flung network of alert attorneys is well-equipped to produce the necessary number of cases from which the Supreme Court may select a test.

* * * In addition [to] presenting a "case or controversy" to the Supreme Court—the one essential that any person or group must do to test a constitutional rule—other things will be attempted by a resourceful organization like the NAACP. Thus the campaign against racial covenants included an effort to influence legal opinion by publicizing a favorable innovation in constitutional theory. Scholars like Professor Robert Hale of Columbia had long stood for a broad view of state action when, in 1945, in the *California Law Review,* Professor D.O. McGovney offered a carefully prepared argument that the concept of state action should encompass the enforcement of racial restrictive covenants by state courts. This filled a serious gap in Negro legal theory. McGovney's argument was taken up in other law review articles and soon found its way into NAACP briefs.

The accumulated losses of thirty years standing as precedents against the NAACP led to reliance on sociological argument. In order to quote authority, leaders of the Association arranged for publication of social and economic criticism of racial restrictive covenants. A coordinated effort was made to place articles in the law reviews. Spontaneity doubtless played its part to produce an impressive list of publications supporting the Negro position with only a single article in opposition.

Briefs filed with the Supreme Court relied heavily on the law review articles and thereby brought these constitutional and sociological points to the attention of the justices. In this way the NAACP sought again to bring a change in constitutional doctrine. If the bar and the law schools are regarded as part of the justices' professional constituency, then it may not be the election returns but the law reviews that the Supreme Court follows.

* * * In the Shelley case nineteen briefs were filed by friends of the NAACP while five amici curiae briefs were entered by opposing groups. Since the parties permitted all interested groups to present briefs, a record number in a single Supreme Court case was established.

The NAACP had an impossible task of controlling the substance of these briefs as each organization had its own ideas of the best content. Some groups repeated the points of the main briefs without a line of novelty while others wrote briefs to distribute to its membership for propaganda purposes. Of course, each group opposed racial discrimination for its own private reasons. Jews, Indians and Japanese–Americans feared discrimination against themselves. Congregationalists and Unitarians preached the brotherhood of man while briefs of the A.F. of L. and C.I.O. protested that housing discrimination against Negroes nullified their economic gains as trade unionists. Civil liberties groups like the A.C.L.U. contended that restrictive covenants prevent the achievement of constitutional rights. The American Association for the United Nations pointed to the injury of United States prestige abroad. At times the NAACP feared that its friends would bore the Court with duplication of these and other arguments but no serious effort was made to eliminate briefs or fashion their content.

The reading of these briefs, and those filed in opposition by various neighborhood protection associations and the National Association of Real Estate Boards, shows the successful adjustment of numerous pressure groups to the judicial process. These amici curiae briefs provide a fascinating display of the accommodation of constitutional values to self-interest.

An amicus curiae brief by the Department of Justice in the *Shelley* case was another expression of interest group effort to influence the Court. Solicitor General Perlman has explained that he and the Attorney General, Tom Clark, were urged by organized groups to enter the case as a friend of the Negroes. The Department's action thus reflected pressures and added an official group to the Negro alliance. Since the United States appears as a party in controversy in [a majority] of the Court's cases, entering a case as a friend supplie[s] matchless prestige and expertness in preparing cases to the groups it favors.

SUSAN BEHUNIAK–LONG,* FRIENDLY FIRE: AMICI CURIAE AND *WEBSTER* v. *REPRODUCTIVE HEALTH SERVICES***
74 Judicature 261 (1991)

The unprecedented number of amicus curiae briefs filed in *Webster v. Reproductive Health Services* [1] signaled not only the intensity of the

* Susan Behuniak–Long is an associate professor of political science at Le Moyne College in Syracuse, New York.

** Excerpts from Friendly Fire: Amici Curiae and Webster v. Reproductive Health Services, by Susan Behuniak–Long, associate professor of political science, Le Moyne College.

abortion battle, but also the extent of interest group politics before the United States Supreme Court. If the response of 57 amicus briefs to *Regents of the University of California v. Bakke* was unusual, the response to *Webster* was extraordinary. A total of 78 amicus briefs were filed; 46 on behalf of the appellants and 32 on behalf of the appellees. With over 400 organizations signing on as cosponsors, and thousands of individuals joining as signatories, *Webster,* though not a typical case, demonstrates the importance of interest group politics before the Court.

With the 1988 appointment of Justice Anthony Kennedy to fill the vacancy left by Justice Lewis Powell, a reversal of *Roe v. Wade* [3] was possible. Court watchers tallied a 4–1–4 line-up. Expected to support *Roe* were Justices Harry Blackmun, William Brennan, Thurgood Marshall and John Paul Stevens. The original dissenters in *Roe*, Justices William Rehnquist and Byron White were expected to be joined by Justices Antonin Scalia and Kennedy. With Justice Sandra Day O'Connor viewed as the swing vote, *Roe* was now subject to a 5–4 reversal. When the Court agreed to hear *Webster* during its 1988 term, the time was ripe for a major abortion decision. Such anticipation led to the unprecedented number of amicus briefs.

At issue in *Webster* was a Missouri statute which contained: (1) a preamble stating that "the life of each human being begins at conception," (2) sections restricting public facilities and employees from performing or assisting in an abortion (except to save the mother's life), (3) sections prohibiting the use of public funds, employees or hospitals from encouraging or counseling a woman to have an abortion (again, with the maternal life preservation exception), and (4) sections requiring that when a physician believes a woman to be 20 or more weeks pregnant, viability will be tested by performance of "such medical examinations and tests as are necessary to make a finding of the gestational age, weight, and lung maturity of the unborn child."

Because of the number of briefs filed and the fact that all the briefs were spawned by the same constitutional issue, the *Webster* amicus briefs offer a unique opportunity to study this particular form of interest group litigation and to examine how the public debate over abortion is carried out in a legal arena. In focusing on these amicus briefs, several questions will frame the study: who submitted the briefs, what was argued in the briefs, and what impact did the briefs have on the outcome of the case? These questions are asked with two goals in mind. First, what do the amicus briefs demonstrate regarding this type of interest group activity? Second, what do the amicus briefs reveal concerning the nature of the two movements involved in the struggle over abortion rights?

1. 492 U.S. 490, 109 S.Ct. 3040 (1989).   **3.** 410 U.S. 113 (1973).

WHO FILED?

* * *

Eighty-five organizations filed on behalf of appellants, while 335 filed on behalf of appellees. The percentage of briefs with a single sponsor was 76 per cent for the appellants and 44 per cent for the appellees. The number of appellants' sponsors per brief ranged from 1 to 19 (the high being the 19 branches of the Rutherford Institute), while the number of the appellees' filers per brief ranged from 1 to 115 (the high being the brief submitted by the National Council of Negro Women and 114 others). Using rough averages, appellants had 2 sponsors per brief, while appellees had 10 sponsors per brief. What these numbers suggest is that the two sides differed concerning the value of coalition building.

Clearly, the appellees acted as if the number of sponsors was more important than the number of briefs filed, while the appellants favored the strategy of filing the most briefs (46 to 32). This raises the question of which is a more effective strategy, to file as many individual briefs as possible or to gather a larger total number of cosponsoring organizations? Caldeira and Wright have observed that there "is [a] general absence of large coalitions of groups on individual briefs," and that this implies that those who make the decision about filing the amicus believe "it is the number of briefs, not the number of organizations listed on each brief, that impresses the justices." [8]

So why did the appellees appear to reject this general belief? There are several possible explanations: * * *

First, while the amicus brief offers groups that are limited in time and resources the access to influence litigation without assuming the financial and time burdens required of a full-fledged party, there is no question that even the filing of an amicus makes demands upon the organization. In Caldeira and Wright's study of the amicus briefs filed during the Court's 1982 term, the cost of preparing and filing a brief ranged from $500 to $50,000 with a mean slightly above $8,000. For some groups, the cost of filing an amicus is prohibitive. Caldeira and Wright note, "The litigation budgets of most organizations are quite modest, and most do not have sufficient in-house manpower and legal expertise to prepare briefs on their own." Many of the appellees' cosponsoring groups would appear to fit this profile. For them, cosponsorship allowed participation in the *Webster* case without the financial hardship involved in preparing an individual brief.

Second, the appellees seemed to act on the democratic belief that the justices would be swayed by the numbers associated with the abortion rights position. Indeed, several of their briefs resembled petitions as they included lists of individuals as signatories.[12] Collectively, the

8. Caldeira and Wright, *Amici Curiae Before the Supreme Court: Who Participates, When and How Much?*, Forthcoming 18 J.Pol. (1990).

12. *See,* Brief for Women Who Have Had Abortions (2887 signatures and 627 signatures of friends); Brief for 608 State Legislators from 32 States; Brief for Group

appellees' briefs signaled to the Court that their position has the support of the majority of the population and that a reversal of *Roe* would place the Court in the uncomfortable position of fighting against the mainstream. However, reliance on the democratic argument also poses risks. Justices may take offense at being pressured to defer to majority rule.[13] Another risk of assembling petition briefs is that coalition building may work to limit the number of arguments presented to the Court by decreasing the number of amicus briefs.

The appellees, however, seemed to minimize both risks. While the democratic argument was implicit in the number of sponsors and signatories, this claim was not explicitly made by the appellees. Instead, appellees let the numbers speak for themselves, thereby avoiding reliance on the democratic argument while at the same time signaling to the Court in a not-so-subtle way where the majority of the population stood on the issue. The second risk was overcome by the filing of a significant number of briefs. While 14 less than the number submitted by the appellants, 32 briefs is by any measure a considerable number. Therefore, the appellees' coalitions did not come at the price of sacrificing the number of arguments presented. In sum, the appellees' strategy of garnering the support of several hundred cosponsors was intended to add weight to the already numerous briefs.

A third explanation of the appellees' coalition building is that since there is a finite number of legal arguments to be made on any issue, too many briefs lead to repetition and perhaps even work to irritate the justices. In light of charges that amicus briefs are a waste of time, "repetitious at best and emotional explosions at worst," and that a large number would increase the already heavy burden on the justices, the appellees may have opted to limit the number of briefs even though they knew that the appellants would file more.

Fourth, an examination of multi-issue interest groups versus single-issue interest groups may explain the different values appellants and appellees attributed to coalition building. Appellees' base of support was largely multi-issue interest groups while single-issue interest groups were more prevalent among the amici of the appellants. [This fact will be discussed in greater detail below.] Multi-issue interest groups enjoy more of a choice in determining whether or not to file an amicus brief than do single-issue interest groups. "The broader a group's political interests, the less intense its attachment to a particular interest * * *. Focus is crucial to intensity." Single-issue interest groups must react when there is a direct threat to their membership's interests. Within this context, the appellants' pro-life organizations were compelled to file

---

of American Law Professors (885 signatures); 281 American Historians; Brief for 167 Distinguished Scientists and Physicians; Brief for Certain Members of the Congress of the United States; Brief for Catholics for a Free Choice; Brief for Bioethicists for Privacy.

13. In fact, Justice Scalia's *Webster* opinion did object to the belief of interest groups that unelected and life-tenured justices should weigh popular opinion. *See,* Scalia's dissent at 3065–66.

independent briefs. In contrast, the multi-issue interest groups of the appellees could meet internal demands through coalitional activity rather than as independent sponsors.

Finally, the appellees' amici were organized according to a strategy that favored impact over the number of briefs. Kathryn Kolbert, who worked on behalf of the American Civil Liberties Union and Planned Parenthood Federation to coordinate all of the amicus briefs, attempted to discourage duplication among the briefs and to encourage coalition building among amici with similar interests. It was believed that overlapping arguments would work to "dilute the overall impact of the collection," so groups who shared interests were encouraged to form a coalition. Coalitions were organized so that each argued points most appropriate to their interests and expertise. This contrasted with appellants who appeared to strive for a large number of briefs at the expense of repetition. For example, attorney Robert L. Sassone filed six separate briefs on behalf of clients with very similar interests rather than one brief with six sponsors.

* * * An attempt was also made to look closer at the groups who filed in order to determine the level of diversity among the first sponsors of the 78 briefs. Seven of the 14 membership categories developed by Caldeira and Wright were used to distinguish the groups: individuals, citizen-based interest groups, professional organizations (where members share the same occupation), public interest law firms or research groups, government sponsors, peak organizations (an organization consisting of groups), and other. * * *

[B]oth appellants and appellees drew the most support from briefs filed by citizen-based groups, 45.7 per cent and 46.8 per cent, respectively. Of all seven categories employed, the citizen-based groups category contains the most diversity in ideology, membership numbers, prestige, goals, and resources. For instance, The American Civil Liberties Union, Population–Environmental Balance, American Life League, and Agudeth Israel of America are all classified as citizen-based groups.

Next in order of frequency for the appellants were briefs filed by: public interest law firms (15.2 per cent), government sponsors (13 per cent), professional groups and individuals (both with 10.9 per cent), then peak organizations, and other (both with 2.2 per cent). Appellees had no briefs filed by individuals, public interest law firms or other. After the citizen-based groups, the order of frequency were briefs filed by: professional groups (31.3 per cent), peak organizations (12.5 per cent), and government sponsors (9.4 per cent).

One drawback of the seven divisions is that they hide three types of groups relevant to the abortion controversy—the religious groups associated with the pro-life position, the feminist groups aligned with the pro-choice cause, and the single-issue interest groups present in both movements. * * * The appellants drew great support from religiously oriented groups (16 sponsors), but also drew support from one feminist sponsor (Feminists for Life). There were nine feminist sponsors for the appellee side, but also two from religious groups. Altogether, these 28 religious and feminist sponsors account for only about 36 per cent of the amicus briefs filed. Clearly, the abortion issue was of great concern to organizations whose memberships did not fit either description.

Indeed, * * * single-issue interest groups played an important role in this case. In order to study the abortion issue here, a single-issue interest group is defined as an organization that is formed to advocate a position on the abortion rights question. While it is admittedly arguable whether a pro-life group has an agenda that is broader than the abortion issue, or whether NOW is more a single-issue than a multi-issue interest group, an initial appraisal of the groups indicates that about 70 per cent of the first sponsors on behalf of the appellants were single-issue interest groups, while about 40 per cent of the appellees' first sponsors were single-issue interest groups. When these single-issue interest groups are compared, it becomes evident that there was a difference in the nature of the permanency of the groups. Appellants drew support from permanent single-issue organizations, while appellees' single-issue organizations tended to be ad hoc groups of professional individuals or peak organizations.

Some tentative conclusions can be drawn from this information concerning the nature of the two movements. Overall, the appellants' amici appear to be more singular in purpose. The public interest law firms, the individuals, the governmental coalitions, and even the professional groups were united in that most were specifically formed either to oppose abortion rights or already had religious tenets supportive of such a political posture. With the exception of the government coalitions, these were permanent groups. In contrast, the appellees relied heavily on the support of professional groups with multiple interests, five of which were ad hoc organizations formed in order to file a brief. These observations suggest that the appellants had a more single-mindedly committed and more permanent group of amici, while the appellees relied on the support of amici who joined together temporarily and who distributed their resources over a range of issues. The question of whether diversity or homogeneity translated into unity will be examined below.

In sum, the question of who filed these 78 briefs has revealed differences in coalition building and a diversity of interests among the sponsoring groups. It is expected that these organizations employed an assortment of strategies as well as provided the Court with a variety of information. The next question to be examined, therefore, is what was argued in the briefs. Did the diversity among the sponsors translate into a richness of resources for the Court?

WHAT WAS ARGUED?

Both Webster and the Reproductive Health Services had to launch an offensive campaign while maintaining a defensive posture. The appellants had to defend the Missouri statute while attacking the legal doctrines set down in *Roe*. The appellees guarded *Roe* as precedent while they took aim at the restrictive law. The strategies of the sides and the roles left to the amicus briefs are best informed by an examination of the party briefs. The party briefs carry the burden of presenting the legal arguments for the litigants and, therefore, form a good basis for comparison of the two sides as well as the 78 amicus briefs.

The appellants' brief first summarized the case and then opened its argument by attacking *Roe,* criticizing the "viability" dividing point as arbitrary and calling for the Court to overrule *Roe.* This offensive took only four pages. The rest of the party brief, approximately 28 pages, was a point-by-point defense of the Missouri law. In contrast, the appellees' brief, which omitted a reconstruction of the case, began by defending *Roe* as a fundamental constitutional right and supporting the viability concept as both legally and medically sound. This defense occupied 17 pages. The next 32 pages challenged the Missouri law section by section. For both sides, then, *Roe* was of primary concern. It was only once this precedent was either challenged or defended that a discussion of the state law could begin.

Arguments. Turning to the amicus briefs * * * a point and counterpoint pattern emerges. There were six main points of contention concerning *Roe:* (1) fetal vs. women's rights, (2) if a constitutional basis for a right to abortion exists, (3) whether the trimester scheme is of utility, (4) how abortion fits within the context of American history and tradition, (5) the applicability of the doctrine of *stare decisis,* and (6) the consequences of overturning or following *Roe* as precedent. There were also six main disputes regarding the Missouri statute: (1) whether the state had the power to restrict abortion through its democratic process, or whether the Court must act to prevent the violation of constitutional rights, (2) the rational basis test vs. strict scrutiny as the appropriate standard of review, (3) if the statute's preamble was prefatory or of substance, (4) the constitutionality (or mootness) of the ban on funding abortion counseling, (5) the constitutionality of the ban on abortions in public facilities, and (6) the constitutionality of the viability tests requirement.

Amid the noise of these debated issues, silence is also instructive. Some of the arguments presented by the amici were not present in the party briefs. * * * [A]bsent from the appellants' party brief were arguments that: fetuses are constitutionally protected persons; abortion has harmful effects on women and on society; the law would not involve criminal prosecutions; and the states are better suited than the courts to decide such a politically charged issue. On the appellee side, there was a greater overlap between the party and amicus briefs. Only two major points made by amici were not present in the party brief: the freedom of religion argument and an examination of the consequences of a *Roe* reversal. The latter, nonlegal point constituted an important focus for many of the appellee amicus briefs.

Strategies. The differences between party and amicus argumentation suggest that appellants and appellees adopted different strategies.

Once again the 4–1–4 Court configuration must be appreciated. Litigants had to hold together their four-person coalition while vying for O'Connor's vote. The two sides divided the workload in different ways. O'Connor appears to be the main target of the appellants' party brief while appellees seem to make a bid for her vote through the filing of amicus briefs which focus on her central concerns.

The appellants' party brief is striking in its avoidance of any "pro-life" rhetoric or argumentation. It carefully sidesteps any discussion of the rights of the "pre-born," the sacredness of human life, or the uncertain basis for the right to privacy (discussing it in terms of a liberty interest instead). The party brief challenges *Roe* in terms that would most appeal to O'Connor. It questions the textual, historical, and doctrinal basis of *Roe* and challenges the trimester approach by citing O'Connor's dissent in *Akron v. Akron Center for Reproductive Health*.[21] The brief also argues that should the Court uphold *Roe,* then it should apply the "undue burden" test (favored by O'Connor) to uphold the Missouri regulations. This moderate approach, then, appears to be crafted for O'Connor. However, this strategy was not universally applied as some of the amici did include language and claims from the pro-life movement. The more controversial arguments on behalf of fetal rights and a ban on abortion were voiced not by the parties but by the amici. It was the amici who urged Rehnquist, White, Scalia, and Kennedy to go further than the party brief suggested and to make abortions illegal by recognizing constitutionally protected fetal rights.

The division of labor helps to explain why the appellant briefs, sponsored by organizations more homogeneous than those of the appellees, had more conflicts, inconsistencies, and contradictions. One trouble undoubtedly arose from the fact that the party brief appeared willing to "give" on two important points within the abortion debate. First, it did not call for a total ban on abortion, instead arguing that should the Court overturn *Roe,* the law should once again allow the states to determine abortion policy (presumably either way). Second, it did not assert that a fetus is a constitutionally protected person. Since these were concessions that not all the 46 amici could accept, why would the parties risk such conflict? Again, the answer seems to be the effort to capture O'Connor's vote while hoping that the arguments presented by the amici might persuade all five justices to recognize fetal rights.

In contrast, the appellees appeared to assign the amici the task of capturing O'Connor's vote. There were at least two routes to her. One was to challenge O'Connor to use her test of whether the abortion restrictions in question posed an "undue burden" on women exercising their constitutional right. The amicus briefs presented her with technical information regarding the dire impact of a *Roe* reversal. In fact, the brief from the National Council of Negro Women, citing the disproportionate impact on women of color, the poor, and the young, was crafted especially for O'Connor and her test. A second strategy was to challenge

---

21. 462 U.S. 416, 452 (1983).

her statement in *Akron* that *Roe* is "on a collision course with itself." O'Connor had used scientific sources to conclude that the point of "viability" would shift forward as medical technology improved. The Brief by 167 Scientists and Physicians not only refuted her argument, but included the signatures of some of the authors on whom she had relied in *Akron*.

What may seem surprising is that the more diverse appellee side produced the more internally consistent argument. This can be explained in two ways. First, the parties and all the amici were aware of how the Court had already chipped away at the right to abortion. All understood that there was no room for concessions without jeopardizing the right itself. Second, this consistency was yet another payoff of organization and coalition building. Kathryn Kolbert, the coordinator of the briefs, helped groups identify what was at issue in *Webster* and how they could best contribute to the case. What emerged was a collection of evidence startling in its singularity of purpose.

Roles. While it is difficult to accurately assess the roles adopted by each interest group, the amici do appear to serve three general purposes. First, there are the endorsement briefs that either repeat the party's position or offer a variation. These briefs may recount all the party's arguments or may center and expand on one point alone. Second are the technical briefs which offer the Court specialized knowledge which is predominantly nonlegalistic in nature. Third are the risk takers. These briefs range from those who undertake an unconventional legal argument to those who shun the legal elements of the case in favor of an emotional appeal. Among the *Webster* briefs, all three types of briefs were present on each side. Some examples illustrate the different roles and strategies that amici can assume.

The endorsement briefs allow interest groups to throw their prestige behind a party. While these briefs are often repetitive, Barker argues that "this very repetition reflects the 'group combat' flavor of the briefs." [29] This was true with the briefs on behalf of appellants filed by the United States, National Right to Life Association, and the Center for Judicial Studies and on behalf of appellees filed by Members of Congress, NOW, and 77 Organizations Committed to Women's Equality. These briefs presented legal arguments already present in the party briefs, although they usually focused on one element and expanded on it.

The technical briefs concentrated on providing information concerning history and medical science. Many focused on the questions of whether abortion is a part of the American social tradition, how the medical and social sciences contribute to our understanding of fetal life, and what impact legal versus illegal abortion has on women. For the appellants, the Association for Public Justice and Certain American State Legislators argued against abortion being an acceptable part of

29. Barker, *Third Parties in Litigation:*   29 J.Pol. 62, (1967).
A Systemic View of the Judicial Function,

American society. Briefs filed by the American Association of Pro-life Obstetricians and Gynecologists, Doctors for Life, Paul Marx, and Bernard Nathanson argued that the "preborn" are persons. For the appellees, refutations of these arguments were offered by 281 American Historians, the American Medical Association, 167 Distinguished Scientists, and the Association of Reproductive Health Professionals. The National Council of Negro Women (with 114 other groups) offered both statistical and anecdotal information illustrating the disproportionately severe impact that a reversal of *Roe* would have on poor women and women of color.

The risk takers offered the most unusual arguments. On the appellants' side, the Free Speech Advocates took a confrontational approach, arguing that the abortion cases were "shams" and that the Court "has grown to accept fawning over all its errors." James Joseph Lynch, Jr. contradicted the party brief's assurance that preambles are without legal effect by asserting that the fetus is protected by the reference to "posterity" made in the United States Constitution's preamble. Agudeth Israel also challenged the party line by insisting that the Missouri preamble be struck down as a violation of religious freedom. American Collegians adopted an argument sometimes used by abortion rights advocates that the Ninth and Tenth Amendments are substantive in that they reserve rights that are not listed in the Constitution's text to the states and citizens. Birthright admitted that its brief contained "very little legal precedent," and instead relied on "logic, common sense, reasoning, intelligence, and conclusions in accord with what is best for all the people of this nation."

The risk takers on behalf of the appellees argued that there was a right to be free from government imposed harm to health (American Public Health Association), that a denial of abortion rights would violate the equal protection clause (National Coalition against Domestic Violence), and that religious freedom demanded that women be free to choose (Catholics for a Free Choice). An emotional appeal made by Women Who Have Had Abortions took the form of a petition-like brief containing letters of testimony.

This survey of the three types of amici suggests that certain types of groups tend to gravitate to a specific amicus role. The most obvious connection is that between professional organizations and technical briefs. A professional organization has the knowledge and expertise necessary to provide the Court with information outside of the legal realm. There also seems to be a relationship between single-issue interest groups and the role of risk taker. Since these groups enjoy a unified constituency that is devoted to promoting a particular issue, these groups may have more freedom in speaking from a perspective outside the mainstream. They can assume a challenging voice without losing their constituents. The endorsement briefs are sponsored by a variety of groups, but tend to gain the support of multi-issue interest groups. These groups tend to have less of a stake in the interest at issue, and they have to hold together a diversified constituency. Multi-issue interest groups can satisfy organizational demands by merely endorsing the party brief.

This analysis would explain why the appellants had more amici act as risk takers while the appellees had more amici submit technical briefs. Since single-issue interest groups were more prevalent among appellants' amici, it could be expected that appellants would have more amici who assumed the role of risk taker. In contrast, since professional organizations were three-to-one behind the appellees, it was predictable that this side would submit more technical briefs.

Together these three types of briefs offered the Court not only an abundance of information concerning abortion, but a sense of the urgency and complexity of this political issue as well. The Court saw briefs which towed the party line, others which offered specialized information, and still others that challenged the Court to break new legal ground. While many perspectives were present, the next question is how many were heard?

WHAT IMPACT?

While the main purpose of an amicus brief is to persuade the Court to rule on behalf of a particular litigant, * * * [i]nterest groups may also claim success if the Court adopts the language or perspective of the brief, or if the litigant's argument is strengthened by the endorsement of the amicus. In filing an amicus, an interest group may gain publicity, an opportunity to refine and articulate its position, and experience in the judicial system. Such third-party involvement also allows groups to feel as though they have participated in the decisional process. Some of the impact of amici may not be apparent until future cases emerge which reflect the information, argument, or concerns of the earlier amici.

Impact is of course most readily identifiable in terms of the winners and losers of a case. However, such an approach is obviously limited for a case like *Webster* where the Court lineup was 4–1–4 from the start. With this in mind, the discussion here will also include a content analysis of which briefs were cited by the justices in the decision, and a study of how some of the arguments made by the amici seemed to sway certain justices.

In a 5–4 vote with two concurrences and two dissenting opinions, the *Webster* decision upheld the sections restricting public employees and facilities from performing or assisting in abortions, and the sections requiring viability testing. While the Court did not rule on the constitutionality of the statute's preamble, it declared the counseling section moot. In the course of deciding these issues, the Court also began to dismantle the principles of *Roe,* the trimester scheme in particular. Chief Justice William Rehnquist, with Justices Byron White and Anthony Kennedy, attacked the "rigid trimester analysis" as inconsistent with the Constitution. He argued, "We do not see why the State's interest in protecting human life should come into existence only at the point of viability * * *." Justice Antonin Scalia concurred stating that Rehnquist's argument would effectively overrule *Roe,* but that he would do so more explicitly. Justice Sandra Day O'Connor agreed with the constitutionality of the Missouri statute, but not with the need to unravel *Roe*. She relied instead on *Roe* and its progeny to uphold the Missouri law. The four dissenting justices, Harry Blackmun, William Brennan, Thurgood Marshall, and John Paul Stevens, would have used *Roe* to void the Missouri statute.

Therefore, when speaking strictly in terms of win versus lose, the appellants emerged as the victors in this case. The Missouri law was upheld, the Court signaled its willingness to uphold restrictive state abortion policies, and four justices indicated a willingness to overturn *Roe*. Within these terms, appellees could claim only that *Roe* survived—for now. Yet, measuring impact in this way assumes that the win is due to arguments set forth by amici. It also ignores the fact that amici on the losing side have impact as well. Therefore, it is important to consider as well two other indicators: the amici cited by the Court, and evidence that the Court accepted arguments advanced only by the amici.

The counting of citations demonstrates that the justices considered the arguments set forth by the amici. This is not to say, of course, that the only briefs which had impact were the ones cited, but the data are useful as a "blunt indicator" of how the Court used the briefs. * * * References to the appellants' party briefs totaled six while the appellees' party briefs were cited eight times. Excluding party briefs, amicus briefs were cited 29 times. Twelve different amicus briefs, six from each side, were cited at least once. Appellants' amici were cited 12 times while appellees' amici were cited 17 times. The amicus briefs cited tended to be those that contained either religious arguments or which provided technical information on medicine or on the law. Besides the direct references to the amicus briefs, Justices Blackmun and Stevens together cited seven different published articles: three which were largely scientific, two commenting on religious issues, one on the impact of illegal abortions, and one on the law.

Rehnquist, writing for the majority, cited the appellants' brief four times and the appellees' brief five times. The only amicus to which he referred was that of the United States. In O'Connor's concurring opinion, she cited the appellees' brief three times, and referred to the four amicus briefs containing medical and scientific information, again indicating her struggle with the viability issue. Scalia's concurrence made no direct references to briefs or outside sources. The dissents of Justices Blackmun and Stevens did not cite the party briefs of either side. These justices referred instead to the amicus briefs for a total of 29 citations. As with O'Connor, most of Blackmun's references came from the technical medical briefs. In contrast, Stevens cited mostly the religiously oriented briefs.

Yet, briefs can be cited and then rejected. Did the briefs have any real influence on the justices in constructing their decision? It is suggested that the answer is yes. Consider again the role of the amici. The appellants' amici seemed to urge their coalition of four justices to overturn *Roe*. The appellees' amici appeared to focus on convincing O'Connor to cast the fifth vote to protect *Roe*. The amici on both sides enjoyed some success.

The victory enjoyed by the appellants was not of the parties' making alone. The Court went further than the parties had urged, surging ahead on the path marked by the appellants' amici. When the Court accepts an argument that was advanced only by an amicus brief, it is an indication of influence. Again, the party brief had devoted only four pages to challenging *Roe* and the viability point. It was instead the amici who supplied both the technical and legal information which subverted the *Roe* trimester scheme.

There are signs that the appellees' amici had influence as well. Again, their target was O'Connor and the two routes to her were to have her apply her "undue burden" test to strike down the Missouri statute, and to have her retreat from her criticism of *Roe* 's trimester scheme. While the amici were unsuccessful concerning the first point, there are signs that they made some progress concerning the second.

It is not what O'Connor's *Webster* opinion says but what it does not say that is important. Considering her *Akron* dissent in which she argued that the trimester approach was "completely unworkable" and on a "collision course with itself," and that she adhered to this position three years later in *Thornburgh v. American College of Obstetricians and Gynecologists,*[45] it is curious that in *Webster*—a case that brings the viability issue to the forefront and causes four other justices to voice concerns that the trimester framework is indeed unworkable—O'Connor remarks only that she continues to regard the trimester approach as "problematic." [46] She cites her *Akron* dissent not to repudiate the trimester scheme, but to illustrate how to apply the "undue burden" test. If indeed O'Connor is retreating from her *Akron* critique, the appellees' amici may be responsible for planting the seed of doubt in her mind.

CONCLUSION

The 78 *Webster* amici produced an incomparable collection of information on the abortion rights issue. While *Webster* is certainly not a typical case, nor was the response of interest groups usual, it does serve to magnify the amicus curiae role. Interest groups can lobby the Court concerning an issue even as politicized as abortion if they enter the Court through the open door extended to amici. In working to present their arguments before the Court, the pro-life and pro-choice movements also revealed something about themselves. The briefs reflected the composition of their constituencies, their legal strategies, and their core values. The study of amici, then, is not only instructive for court watching but for monitoring interest group politics as well.

45. 476 U.S. 747, at 814 (1986).   **46.** Webster, *supra* n. 1, at 3063.

The writing and organization of 78 briefs was a monumental undertaking, but it was not a wasted effort. It appears that the amici on both sides made in-roads with the Court. The briefs were not only read; they also had impact. Their arguments and information helped to shape the terms of the Court debate. Whether the justices refuted the briefs, modified an argument because of them, or accepted and integrated their points, the amici mattered. Through the presentation of the briefs, the battle over abortion rights was waged before the Court. It is no surprise, then, that in the midst of this friendly fire, some of the justices were struck.

Chapter Six

PROPOSALS FOR REFORMING
THE INSTITUTION

One overriding message of all the materials in this book is that the Supreme Court of the United States is largely free to be the best court it can be. Neither the Constitution nor federal law substantially constrains the way the Court works. The Constitution does limit the Court to adjudicating "cases" or "controversies." [1] Congress can regulate the Court's jurisdiction somewhat and has controlled the extent to which that jurisdiction is discretionary or mandatory. [2] Nevertheless, it remains true that the Court is free to determine what cases it will hear and by what method it will choose them, to hire its own support staff, to choose the adjudicatory and deliberative processes it employs, and to craft the opinions and results it desires. Regardless of what the public thinks of any of these choices, the justices remain constitutionally entitled to retain their jobs and their salaries. [3]

The key factor that substantially affects the nature and quality of the Court's work but remains beyond the justices' control is the selection of the justices themselves. [4] The President and the Senate decide who will be "The Brethren." The law gives the justices no say in these decisions and they exercise little influence in practice. Whether and how the nomination and confirmation processes for Supreme Court

1. See U.S. Constitution art. III, § 2.
2. See Chapter Three, supra. Although Congress has enacted the governing statutes, changes are frequently made at the request of the Supreme Court and the Judicial Conference, chaired by the Chief Justice. See O'Brien, *Storm Center: The Supreme Court in American Politics*, 136–138 (3d ed. 1993).
3. See U.S. Constitution art. III, § 1.
4. Lacking the power to tax, the justices also have little control over the Court's budget. In truth, however, the Court does not need a lot of money to do its work. For at least the Court's first hundred years, the

justices worked out of their homes and wrote their own opinions. During the 1960s, when the Congressional seniority system put Southern Democrats in very powerful positions, particularly throughout the Senate, displeasure with Brown v. Board of Education, 347 U.S. 483, 74 S.Ct. 686, 98 L.Ed. 873 (1954) was often manifested in refusals to grant modest increases in funding for the Court. When Earl Warren retired as Chief Justice in 1969, each justice's chambers had manual typewriters, no photocopying machines, and only two law clerks. Most people can't tell this from looking at the opinions.

justices might be improved is considered throughout Chapter Two, *supra.*

The Court also must take the remainder of the federal court system as it finds it. There are now 94 federal district (trial) courts and 13 federal circuit courts of appeal.[5] In 1992, these were staffed by 161 active circuit judges, 554 active district judges, and 364 retired circuit and district judges.[6] There were also 294 bankruptcy judges and 475 magistrate judges.[7]

The very large size of the federal judicial system and the enormous volume of court judgments it spawns can affect the Court's work in several ways. First, increasing numbers of lower court decisions inevitably mean increasing numbers of petitions for certiorari. Some fear that the growing caseload at the certiorari stage will mean the justices have too little time both to consider adequately each petition and to adjudicate responsibly those cases selected for plenary review. Second, the volume of lower court litigation handicaps the Court insofar as it wishes to perform the functions of assuring uniformity in federal law or correcting errors in individual cases. This is because, all other things being equal, more lower courts and more judges adjudicating more cases will generate more conflicts and more errors. This, in turn, might tend to confine the Court's docket primarily to cases involving apparent conflicts or errors below or would require the Court to leave such cases unattended.

For these reasons, many have proposed the creation of a national court of appeals, an appellate tribunal that would sit below the Supreme Court but above the thirteen circuit courts. Such a court might be designed either to assist the Supreme Court in its case selection or to resolve conflicts among the circuits or simply to expand the capacity of the federal judicial system to render nationally binding declarations of law.

The materials in Section A of this chapter explore these possibilities. The central questions presented are: Would a national court of appeals enable the Supreme Court, and the federal judicial system as a whole, to perform better their various functions? If so, how should such a tribunal be structured and staffed? How should its jurisdiction, relative to the Supreme Court and other federal courts, be defined? Would it help to add more justices to the existing Supreme Court? On the other hand, if no changes are made, will the Court be able to continue indefinitely to fulfill its several roles in the federal judicial system? If not, which will it have to abandon?

Section B of this chapter explores another issue that is frequently raised but is wholly within the Court's control, the secrecy in which the Court operates. The parties' briefs are accessible to everyone, but oral

---

5. See 28 U.S.C. § 44 (circuit courts) and § 133 (district courts).

6. Data compiled by Analysis and Reports Branch, Statistics Division, Administrative Office of the United States Courts

and transmitted to the authors by telefax dated August 16, 1993.

7. *Id.*

arguments are open only to the 300 or so people who can squeeze into the courtroom; several journalists cover the Court regularly, but the Court permits neither radio nor television coverage.[8] The Court's conferences are open to no one except the justices. Only final opinions, not the exchanges that generate them, are published.

To some extent, the Court's veil of secrecy lifts as time goes by. The justices frequently leave many of their papers to libraries, usually for inspection sometime after the donor's death. These papers can provide rich insights into the Court's otherwise hidden deliberative processes.[9] Therefore, we break the secrecy materials down into two broad categories: release of information as the processes unfold and the subsequent handling of the justices' papers.

A. A NATIONAL COURT OF APPEALS?

JAMES A. GAZELL,* THE NATIONAL COURT OF APPEALS CONTROVERSY: AN EMERGING NEGATIVE CONSENSUS**

6 Northern Illinois U.L.Rev. 1 (1986)

I. INTRODUCTION

Now, rather than a permanent intermediate court * * * a National Court of Appeals—I propose [that] we create a temporary and experimental panel—an Intercircuit Panel—made up of judges of the [United States] courts of appeals, including, of course, senior circuit judges. We can experiment with that panel for up to five years by assigning to that panel the task of resolving conflicting holdings of the several circuits.

This comment is an excerpt from Chief Justice Warren Burger's most recent annual speech to the American Bar Association in February, 1985 on the state of the federal judiciary. The proposal contained in this part of his address represents the latest public sign that even the nation's highest judicial officer and foremost advocate of structural alteration of the federal court system has begun to lower his expectation for drastic organizational revision as the most effective approach for reducing the substantial caseload of the Supreme Court of the United States as well as for enhancing the appellate capacity of the national judiciary.

Burger's less audacious proposal suggests the central theme of this article: The intermittent but spirited debate in the legal community over the desirability of a national court of appeals lodged between the

---

8. Written transcripts of oral argument are prepared. They may be inspected at the Court or purchased from the transcriber. Tape recordings of oral arguments are lodged in the National Archives. See Section B of this chapter, below.

9. Much of the material reprinted in Chapters Three and Four, supra, are based on subsequently released internal Court memoranda concerning particular cases.

* Professor of Public Administration and Urban Studies, San Diego State University. B.A., M.A., Roosevelt University; Ph.D., Southern Illinois University.

** Reprinted by permission of Northern Illinois University Law Review.

Supreme Court and the federal courts of appeal has evolved through three stages, each of which involved less drastic recommendations than the preceding periods. As a result, a consensus has begun to emerge, rejecting not only such proposed structural changes as premature, unnecessary, and inefficacious but also other legislative efforts to supply relief to the nation's highest court and the rest of the federal judiciary. Consequently, the Supreme Court is left with no practical choice but to try aiding itself as much as possible (perhaps in collaboration with other national courts) if it continues to feel burdened by the caseload. Such self-help may lie in an overlapping combination of administrative and jurisdictional steps as well as case law further limiting access to the lower federal courts and the Supreme Court.

* * * [T]he controversy over a proposed national court of appeals * * * has evolved [through three stages]: (1) advocacy of a structure to screen the Supreme Court's caseload, (2) pressure for a general tribunal to augment federal judicial appellate capacity by hearing cases referred to it by the nation's highest court or transferred to it from various federal courts of appeal rather than to regulate the docket of the Supreme Court, and (3) espousal of a new specialized court, a panel to hear chiefly intercircuit disputes. * * *

II. BACKGROUND

A. A Growing Supreme Court Caseload

The caseload of the Supreme Court began its sharp ascent during the 1950s, climbing from 1,181 at the start of that decade to 1,862 at the end—an increase of 57.7%. This escalation as well as subsequent ones derived from at least five causes: population increase, national economic expansion, more social and economic legislation, the greater availability of lawyers for indigents, and decisions of the Supreme Court itself.

The rise was sufficient to prompt one member of the nation's highest bench, Justice Felix Frankfurter, to urge strict docket control for the Court—that is, restrictive standards for granting writs of certiorari—as a means of assuring that the growing caseload would not leave the jurists with insufficient time for study, reflection, and discussion among themselves and thus impair the quality of their decisions. * * *

B. Procedural Regulation

Since 1925 the Supreme Court has managed its docket through a passel of devices—such as abstention from other judicial proceedings, class actions, comity, exhaustion of administrative remedies, justiciability, mootness, political questions, standing to sue, ripeness for review, strict certiorari standards, and standing to sue *inter alia*.

* * *

However, this edifice of restrictions, even if rigorously followed by the Supreme Court, had merely slowed the stream of petitions to the nation's tribunal of last resort. Consequently, by the late 1950s, concern about the Court's expanding docket began to extend beyond Justice

Frankfurter and a few of his colleagues to the general legal community. For instance, Henry Hart, Jr., a Harvard law professor, examined the Court's docket for the 1958 term; made cautious assumptions about the time available for the justices to do their work * * * and concluded that "the Court is trying to decide more cases than it can decide well." [9]

* * *

Not everyone on the nation's highest bench and in the wider legal community viewed the burgeoning Supreme Court calendar as a serious problem. Associate Justice William Douglas, for example, scoffed at "the idea that the Court is overworked, that if the Court were only relieved by statute or by voluntary action of some of the cases it would make 'better' decisions." [11] Rejecting this outlook as a myth, he maintained that the justices were hearing fewer oral arguments, writing fewer opinions, experiencing shorter work weeks, and having more time available for individual reflection and collective discussions. He attributed the Supreme Court's rising docket to a steady influx of *in forma pauperis* (indigents') petitions, the overwhelming number of which, in his judgment, were so patently frivolous that the justices needed little time to screen them.

Nevertheless, Douglas joined Frankfurter and Hart in perceiving the Court's expanding docket from a procedural vista. Stated another way, Douglas' view of the Supreme Court's caseload implied that, if this judicial body ever felt overburdened due either to additional filings or fewer but more complex litigation, the remedy for such a development was basically internal, depending, for instance, on changes in the time allotted for oral arguments, opinion writing, the length of the individual justice's workweeks, as well as the use of appropriate cases to alter the scope of its discretionary jurisdiction.

C. Pressures for Structural Change

Pressures for changing the structure of the national judiciary dates from 1944 when legal scholar Erwin Griswold publicly advocated the establishment of separate tribunals to relieve the Supreme Court of some business that would otherwise come before it, especially complicated matters such as tax issues.[13]

Not until 1967 is anyone known to have openly espoused a general structural approach to reverse the lengthening Supreme Court calendar. That year a noted legal analyst, Philip Kurland, urged the creation of an appellate court to be located between the nation's final tribunal and the various courts of appeal. Composed of seven-to-nine members (presumably selected the way federal judges have historically been chosen—that is, by Presidential nomination and Senate confirmation), the new judicial

9. Hart, *Foreword: The Time Chart of the Justices,* 73 Harv.L.Rev. 84, 100 (1959).

11. Douglas, *The Supreme Court & Its Case Load* [*sic*], 45 Cornell L.Q. 401, 402 (1960).

13. Griswold, *The Need for a Court of Tax Appeals,* 57 Harv.L.Rev. 1153 (1944).

body would be authorized to "review, at its discretion, all cases involving the interpretation and application of Federal statutes and common law, whether arising in state or Federal courts."[18] Decisions from this court could be appealed to the Supreme Court only if they embraced a constitutional issue.

One ineluctable aspect of Kurland's proposal was to transform the Supreme Court into an exclusively constitutional tribunal by shifting its statutory jurisdiction to a new institution. Although aware that his plan, if enacted, would create another federal judicial layer and probably delay further the handling of appellate business, he postulated that the new structure would relieve the Supreme Court of numerous cases and leave it free to decide only the most salient controversies. * * *

However, Kurland's suggested remedy drew only a scattered response in the legal community. * * *

III. The First Stage: A Screening Structure

In 1971 Chief Justice Burger named a seven-member panel of legal scholars, headed by Harvard Law School professor Paul Freund, to study the expanding calendar of the Supreme Court and to recommend possible solutions. The official name of this task force was the Study Group on the Caseload of the Supreme Court (more widely known as the Freund Study Group or Freund Committee). In 1972 its report was made public.[24]

This panel endorsed several procedural and jurisdictional remedies: the elimination of direct Supreme Court review of three-judge federal district court decisions, the transfer of inmate petitions to a non-judicial body for resolution, and increased staff (clerks, librarians, and secretaries). However, its chief recommendation was the establishment of a structure to screen the caseload of the Supreme Court. The proposed tribunal, called a national court of appeals, was to occupy a niche between the country's highest judicial body and the echelon of federal courts of appeal. The new structure was to consist of seven judges chosen on a rotating basis from the membership of the federal courts of appeal for staggered three-year-terms. * * *

Although the authority of the proposed National Court of Appeals extended to the resolution of conflicting decisions among federal courts of appeal, its principal function would have been to review the climbing number of petitions for writs of certiorari, which by the time the Freund Committee was formed in 1971, had risen to an unprecedented level of 4,515, more than tripling since 1950. After screening these requests, the new tribunal would be empowered to select about 400-to-450 cases a year and certify them as worthy of further consideration by the Supreme

---

18. Kurland, *The Court Should Decide Less & Explain More,* N.Y. Times, June 9, 1968, § 6 (Magazine), at 126, col. 4 (late city ed.). For the development of his structural proposal, see Kurland, *Jurisdiction of* the United States Supreme Court: Time for a Change?, 59 Cornell L.Rev. 616 (1974).

24. 57 F.R.D. 573 (1972).

Court, which would grant review to whatever portion of those certified cases it desired.

The most prominent public defenders of the committee's report, not surprisingly, were Freund and Burger, albeit on mostly different grounds. The Harvard Law School professor who chaired the committee cited five bases for its decision to embrace a national court of appeals. One reason was the expanding docket of the Supreme Court, which segued into a second justification: a need to improve the Court's increasingly burdensome working conditions. A third explanation was that the first two bases warranted drastic change, hence the structural proposal, but one which would not exacerbate the caseload pressures facing the nation's tribunal of last resort.

Consequently, the Study Group rejected several structural alternatives because of various perceived shortcomings. For instance, it refused to espouse a fifteen-member national court of appeals sitting in divisions and deciding cases on the merits because the Group viewed the proposal as too far reaching and as spawning another layer of appellate review. It declined to endorse a new appellate court whose docket would consist of disputes referred to it by the Supreme Court, for the latter would confront the additional work of deciding which petitions for review merited such references and would also turn the nation's final court into an exclusively constitutional court freed from the discipline of statutory interpretation and more able to indulge its political and social values. It spurned the advocacy of criminal appeals panel because it would deny access for a particular class of appellants to the nation's highest bench and might become politicized with regard to issues of criminal procedure.

The final two reasons were that the Supreme Court, through its rulemaking, would enable the new tribunal to become an effective screening device and that such an appellate body would not amount to a second supreme court because the Supreme Court's appellate jurisdiction has always been less than total and subject to the will of Congress.
* * *

Chief Justice Burger lauded the report of the Freund Study Group without explicitly endorsing its proposed national court of appeals. His praise stressed four points. One centered on the composition of the panel. He said that he deliberately excluded federal judges from it because he wanted an outside perspective on the Supreme Court's workload. * * * His second contention was that the committee's diagnosis of the Supreme Court's caseload problem was universally accepted—an assertion to which Justice Douglas would undoubtedly have taken exception. His third point paralleled Freund's: that the stresses of a rising caseload on the justices would eventually diminish the quality of their work. Finally, Burger expressed his belief that the proposals of the Freund committee (structural and non-organizational) deserved serious consideration by the nation's legal community.

Of all the Freund Study Group recommendations, the one providing for a new judicial body to regulate the flow of business into the nation's highest tribunal engendered the most intense widespread reaction—largely critical. In fact, opposition to this proposal started before the public release of the Study Group's report, for some of its contents had been leaked to the press. For example, retired Chief Justice Earl Warren reportedly wrote to all his former law clerks stating his objections and seeking to mobilize their opposition. He also began to emerge as the most prominent critic of the panel's report. Justice Douglas used a dissent in an unpublicized case to foreshadow his opposition to the anticipated proposal by contending that the screening of cases for review is "in many respects the most important and, I think, the most interesting of all our functions." [39] Furthermore, he restated his contention that, since most cases coming before the Supreme Court had already been reviewed by other judicial organizations, an additional level of consideration was "seldom important." For Douglas the Supreme Court was, "if anything, underworked, not overworked." "Our time," he continued, "is largely spent in the fascinating task of reading petitions for certiorari and jurisdictional statements." Moreover, he noted that the cases accepted by the Court for plenary review had remained about the same for the last three decades.

With the publication of the Freund Committee report, attacks on it, led by the former Chief Justice, came swiftly. Although no critic publicly endorsed Douglas' position that the Court may have lacked enough work, they generally contended that this institution could manage its caseload more effectively not through structural alteration but through a mixture of procedural and jurisdictional changes as well as more stringent internal management. * * *

Criticisms of their report fell under three broad rubrics. The first—and most basic—complaint centered on the subject of institutional preservation: namely, that the proposed National Court of Appeals threatened the Supreme Court's status as the final arbiter of disputes and expositor of the law; for the new tribunal would take over the docket of the country's highest bench and greatly influence what the latter could hear. Some opponents of the recommended structure argued that the Supreme Court's primacy rested, in part, on its right to determine the size and composition of its caseload, even though for much of its history (specifically, until 1925) its appellate jurisdiction was largely mandatory. They contended, furthermore, that the Supreme Court's screening function, because of its inherently subjective nature, could not be soundly delegated to another judicial body and that the proposed appellate court, because of its short-term rotating membership, would not even be able to sense what petitions the Supreme Court might regard as candidates for writs of certiorari. Because the new tribunal would set national constitutional and statutory priorities through its screening functions, the nation, according to critics, would in effect be left with two supreme courts in violation of the Constitution. Ironically, those who saw the

39. Tidewater Oil Co. v. United States, 409 U.S. 151, 175 (1972) (Douglas, J., dissenting).

Supreme Court's screening work as its paramount function did not discern any conflict with the reported tendency of the justices to spend an average of only one day a week on this kind of task.   * * *

A second protest involved the composition of the Freund Study Group.   Some critics intimated that the makeup of this panel was biased because Chief Justice Burger allegedly wanted a new appellate court in order to restrict the access of litigants to the nation's highest bench and selected a committee made up of notable legal scholars who shared his predilection on this subject.   * * *

A third area of discontent concerned methodology.   * * * The essential mistake of the Study Group, they contended, despite its disclaimer, was the equation of a rising caseload with a growing workload. Opponents intimated that the justices might face less work even in the face of spiraling litigation if those cases were typically uncomplicated. However, they might experience a heavier workload despite a maintenance or decline in the number of suits if the percentage of complex cases increased.

* * *

[T]he Freund Study Group's structural recommendations drew only modest support from lawyers and judges.   The prime reason for this aftermath was the weight, intensity, and breadth of the criticisms, particularly those of the former Chief Justice Warren, who was credited with having virtually assured the demise of the proposed screening tribunal.   A second explanation is that Chief Justice Burger never publicly endorsed and campaigned for the Freund Committee's proposed national court of appeals, although he strongly maintained that this recommendation deserved serious consideration as one possible solution to the Supreme Court's expanding docket.   * * * Even though legal interest in this particular measure waned, pressure for some kind of structural alteration in the federal court system continued and led to the advent of a second stage.

IV.   A Second Stage: Transfer and Reference Tribunals

In 1974 the American Bar Association endorsed a national court of appeals in principle without specifying its functions and composition. The ABA believed that a new appellate organization in one form or another was essential to alleviate the Supreme Court's growing docket.[54] Furthermore, that year marked a shift in the kind of new appellate tribunal advocated for the federal judiciary.   Basically, some legal analysis proposed a second type of national court of appeals, one that would perform no screening functions but would instead perform the less drastic function of deciding cases transferred to it from the various federal circuit courts or referred to it by the Supreme Court.   Two notable commissions espoused such a remedy not only to relieve the caseload pressures on the nation's highest bench but also to augment the appellate capacity of the federal judiciary.

54. A.B.A. Ann.Rep. 182–84, 306–11 (1974).

First, the Advisory Council for Appellate Justice (a thirty-three member panel headed by legal scholar Maurice Rosenberg) proposed the establishment of an intercircuit (or nationwide) division of the federal appellate system to exercise jurisdiction in accordance with rules made by the Supreme Court within limits specified by Congress. The new structure would feature its own—rather than a rotating—membership, and its decisions would apply nationally.[55] The Council's recommendation sought to maintain access to the Supreme Court, which the screening structure proposed by the Freund Study Group would have restricted, while lightening its docket. The Council's proposal with its fixed membership was intended to foster predictability in the new court's rulings, an objective that would probably have eluded a judicial body with a rotating panel, although the principal advantage of the latter would be an avoidance of ideological domination. Furthermore, the Council strongly favored supplementing its structural solution with a variety of efforts to limit the flow of cases into the United States district courts, which would eventually result in lower caseloads for the federal courts of appeals and, eventually, the Supreme Court.

However, because the Council's work and proposals were numerous and wide-ranging, its structural recommendation tended to be obscured. Moreover, it was further eclipsed by the wide-spread attention paid to the organizational change proposed by a congressionally established task force: the Commission on the Revision of the Federal Court Appellate System, headed by Nebraska Senator Roman Hruska.[57] This commission consisted of sixteen members, appointed in equal numbers—four apiece—by the House of Representatives, the Senate, the President of the United States, and the Chief Justice. * * *

This commission unanimously urged the creation of a national court of appeals. Although the name of the new tribunal was the same as the panel recommended by the Freund Study Group, the Commission proposal differed in most other respects. The new court was to consist of seven jurists with Article 3 status—that is, nominated by the President and confirmed by the Senate for a term of good behavior.

The proposed tribunal's business was to come from two sources. One was cases referred to it by the Supreme Court, which would possess discretion to select the types and extent of referrals within broad legislative boundaries. If established, such a national court of appeals would decide which of the referrals to accept for adjudication on the merits and which to decline, unless the Supreme Court ordered it to resolve a particular referred dispute.

* * * This commission was especially troubled by an increasing proclivity among the justices to issue opinions, often lengthy ones, protesting denials of certiorari. To Senator Hruska and his colleagues

---

55. The Advisory Council for Appellate Justice, 1 Appellate Justice 1975: Summary & Background 24 (1975).

57. Commission on Revisions of the Federal Court Appellate System, Structure & Internal Procedures: Recommendations for Change, 67 F.R.D. 195–409 (1976) [hereinafter cited as Commission].

the incidence of such complaints, which rose with the Court's caseload, suggested that the appellate capacity of the nation's highest judicial body was becoming increasingly strained. Its members were growing more distressed that it was failing to review many controversies which, in their view, warranted plenary consideration.

A second source of litigation for the Commission's proposed national court of appeals was to consist in filings from the various federal courts of appeal that were transferred to it because the public interest manifestly required a speedy, nationally applicable decision. The Commission offered a pair of illustrations for this avenue of jurisdiction: (1) tax-law suits where two United States courts of appeal had issued conflicting holdings and where a ruling by a third such tribunal would lack national application and (2) complex cases involving environmental questions where a speedy nationwide decision was "in the interest of [the] efficient allocation of national resources * * *." The Hruska panel forecasted that only a minority of the overall caseload would come to the proposed judicial body by this route and that most litigation would flow from the Supreme Court. Moreover, such a tribunal would possess the power to refuse transfer cases because of their nature or its desire for docket control.

This commission summed up its argument for a new judicial institution by declaring:

> The proposed National Court of Appeals would be able to decide at least 150 cases on the merits each year, thus doubling the national appellate capacity. Its work would be important and varied, and the opportunity to serve on it could be expected to attract individuals of the highest quality. The virtues of the existing system would not be compromised. The appellate process would not be unduly prolonged. There would not be, save in the rarest instance, four tiers of courts. There would be no occasion for litigation over jurisdiction. There would be no interference with the powers of the Supreme Court, although the Justices of that Court would be given an added discretion which can be expected to lighten their burdens.
>
> * * * The new court would be empowered to resolve conflicts among the circuits, but its functions would not be limited to conflict resolution alone: It could provide authoritative determinations of recurring issues before a conflict had ever arisen. The cost of litigation, measured in time or money, would be reduced overall as national issues were given expedited resolution and the incidence of purposeless relitigation was lessened. The effect of the new court should be to bring greater clarity and stability to the national law, with less delay than is often possible today.

In addition, the Hruska Commission's report noted that, since the Supreme Court would be empowered to review holdings of this national court of appeals through granting writs of certiorari, the access of litigants to the nation's highest court would remain.

The Commission's structural proposal resulted in a myriad of complaints whose cumulative effect undermined all congressional efforts to turn this recommendation into a reality. Although less intense than the protests raised against the Freund Study Group's proffered national court of appeals, the rejoinders to the Hruska Commission's version belong in five categories, which may be illustrated by using the conclusion of the panel's report.

The first part of the conclusion centered on the extent of national judicial appellate capacity, which this commission, citing increasing published dissents from denials of certification, had found to be inadequate. This facet of the summary presupposed that the Supreme Court would continue to decide annually about the same number of cases—roughly 150—and that this level of output was still feasible and appropriate. * * * Under the Hruska Commission's plan, the Supreme Court might still grant certiorari to 300 cases a year, settling approximately 150 of them itself while referring the remaining 150 to the new tribunal. Such an enhancement of federal judicial appellate capacity would come at the expense of diminishing the Supreme Court's appellate capacity by increasing its work, for it would have to select disputes for referral—potentially time-consuming and divisive for the justices—and later whether to certify appeals from the new judicial body. All accepted petitions would entail the additional duties accompanying plenary review.

The second part of this conclusion argued that a diversified caseload would help make membership on the proposed national court of appeals attractive. A critic might counter that the tax-law and environmental examples suggest routineness rather than variety in the proposed tribunal's docket. The Supreme Court could reinforce this condition by referring only appeals concerning statutory interpretation while saving the litigation involving constitutional issues for itself. Moreover, one might ask whether intercircuit disputes—whether they focus on statutory construction, constitutional problems, or both—are really among the kinds that the Supreme Court ought to adjudicate.

The third aspect of the conclusion to the Commission's report predicted that the proposed national court of appeals would furnish an opportunity for service attractive to outstanding members of the legal profession. This facet deserves summary treatment because it was the only incontrovertible part of the summary.

The fourth—and most extensive—part of this conclusion suggested that the proposed court, if enacted, would not harm the existing federal judiciary. This component is the most important facet because it drew the strongest critics, led by Chief Judge Wilfred Feinberg and all his colleagues on the United State Court of Appeals for the Second Circuit. Their principal contentions were twofold: that the Hruska Commission had failed to establish the need for a reference-and-transfer national court of appeal and that this commission had underestimated the costs of its proposed structural change to the national court system. To these critics another appellate tribunal was not essential for several reasons. One was the absence of numerous intercircuit conflicts that the Supreme Court had declined to settle because of its expanding docket. A second reason was the limited categories (mostly tax and patent cases) into which unresolved circuit disputes fell, suggesting that the appropriate structural remedy should be a specialized court foreshadowing the one established in 1982 (the Court of Appeals for the Federal Circuit). A third consideration was the paucity of conflicting intercircuit rulings spawning intolerable legal uncertainties and thus requiring prompt nationwide resolution.[71]

Such opponents viewed the costs of the Commission's recommended judicial organization as heavier than its proponents admitted. One alleged price would be a reduction in the power and status of the federal courts of appeal, which might make these positions less attractive to potential candidates. Besides, such a national court of appeals might cast a similar shadow over the prestige of the Supreme Court, whose justices would choose the cases for the new tribunal and thus putatively function as if they were super law clerks. This situation would be exactly the opposite of the one envisioned by the Freund Study Group in making its screening-court proposal. A second reputed cost centered on additional delay, expense, and complexity in the federal judicial appellate process. Such alleged problems would be concomitants of another judicial appellate level and inescapable jurisdictional ambiguities over the circumstances under which litigation might be transferred to the new court and appealed from it. A third alleged disadvantage encompassed skepticism over whether the establishment of such a tribunal was the most cost effective way of reducing the Supreme Court's docket and enhancing the appellate capacity of the federal court system. Finally, some opponents feared that a preoccupation with the creation of such a court to make early declarations of national law would divert the legal community's attention from what such critics viewed as the most efficacious route to lighten the Supreme Court's docket: a search for ways of restructuring the entry of cases into the federal judicial system.

A fifth aspect of the Commission's conclusion that drew public criticism focused on the expectation that its proposed national court of appeals, if established, would provide a higher level of clarity and stability in the national law and thus reduce filings and delays in adjudication to a considerable extent. * * * For critics, uncertainties in the law stemmed from sources other than ambiguous Supreme Court decisions resulting from heavy caseload pressures. For instance, Chief Judge Feinberg cited a persistent federal governmental policy of relitigating unfavorable decisions in the various circuits in order to provoke conflicting courts of appeal decisions and increasing the possibility of Supreme Court review.

71. Feinberg, *A National Court of Appeals?*, 42 Brooklyn L.Rev. 611, 614–25 (1976).

* * * In December, 1975, six months after the public release of the Commission's report, Senator Hruska (joined by Senators John McClellan of Arkansas, Quentin Brudick of North Dakota, and Hiram Fong of Hawaii) introduced a measure to establish a national court of appeals with both reference-and-transfer jurisdiction—essentially the Commission's proposal. However, the measure's journey through the legislative process ended in the Senate Subcommittee on Improvement in Judicial Machinery.

* * *

President Ford's Department of Justice opposed these measures for three reasons: (1) its doubt that a new appellate court would really accelerate the disposition of federal litigation; (2) a concern that such a tribunal would lower the prestige of the federal courts of appeal and impair the morale of their members; and (3) an absence of any discernible link between the proposed structure and rectification of what the Administration regarded as the crux of expanding dockets throughout the national court system—namely, excessive federal jurisdiction. * * *

[T]he Supreme Court as well as the rest of the federal judiciary remain divided on the merits of structural renovation. * * * Even though Chief Justice Burger and associate justices Harry Blackmun, Lewis Powell, Jr., William Rehnquist, and Byron White expressed sympathy toward the Commission's structural recommendation, other Supreme Court members (William Brennan, William Douglas, Thurgood Marshall, and Potter Stewart) were either critical or skeptical. The previously mentioned opposition of Chief Judge Feinberg and his colleagues epitomized the views of many jurists in the lower federal benches. Although federal court unity behind a measure affecting the judicial branch of the national government does not guarantee its enactment, the absence of such a consensus virtually assures its defeat.

What is surprising about the proponents of such structural changes is their tactic of appearing to favor an all-or-nothing approach: either the Hruska Commission's proposal in one form or another or nothing at all. They might have first pressed for a gradualist approach, such as seeking the enactment of non-structural remedies proposed by the Freund Study Group and the Hruska Commission and urging the Supreme Court to adopt more stringent procedures to manage its docket more effectively. * * *

The non-structural opportunities were considerable. * * * [T]he Freund committee had urged an end to direct Supreme Court appeals from the rulings of three-judge United State district court panels, a change partially effected in 1976 by legislation narrowing the scope for such challenges. This group also supported the establishment of a non-judicial commission to hear prisoner petitions, a still unfulfilled objective. However, the committee's advocacy of greater Supreme Court staffing has come to fruition. Furthermore, the number of law clerks permitted each Justice increased from three to four despite the Freund Study Group's opposition, which rested on its fears of separating work and responsibility for it, weakening close justice-law clerk working relations, isolating the justices from one another, and necessitating an overhaul of the Supreme Court building to accommodate such additional personnel. * * *

Furthermore, advocates of Hruska's * * * measures might have explored another non-structural proposal reluctantly discarded by the Freund Study Group: an extension of the annual terms for the Supreme Court's official business, which runs from the first Monday in October to late June or early July. The Group clearly perceived the disadvantages of the present duration of official work: pressures on the justices to decide some cases prematurely in order to clear the docket and to be hastily agreeable or recalcitrant due to a lack of time to discuss litigation with colleagues and possibly to reach accommodations. But Professor Freund and his colleagues endorsed a continuation of this status quo, for it disciplined the justices to avoid backlogs while affording them a few months during each year to ruminate on some of the business facing them.

* * * [T]here are other possible non-structural measures that [the Freund Study Group] did not consider. Such proposals included the use of three-justice panels to screen petitions with unanimous votes of denial binding on the Supreme Court, the pooling of law clerks to do this job, the establishment of a senior central staff to perform such screening, a resort to increased filing costs to reduce frivolous paid (as opposed to *in forma pauperis*) requests for review, and a confirmed use of case law to discourage particular kinds of filings.

* * *

Although the mere enumeration of these non-structural steps does not demonstrate their validity, this list still suggests the variety of possibilities short of drastic change open to those who wanted to reduce the Supreme Court's work while enlarging the appellate capacity of the federal judiciary.

V. A Third Stage: An Intercircuit Alternative

In February 1983 Chief Justice Burger used his annual speech to the American Bar Association on the state of the national judiciary to review his quest for a new federal intermediate appellate court.[100] He chose this time to pursue structural renovation because the members of the Supreme Court were becoming increasingly bothered by its growing caseload, which had reached a record level of 5,311 for the 1981–1982 term. Eight of them were upset enough to speak out in public, although they remained disunited on possible remedies. Associate Justice John Paul Stevens even went so far as to advocate a national court of appeals empowered not only to screen petitions, as the Freund Study Group envisioned, but also to grant or deny writs of certiorari.[103] In this

---

100. Burger, *Annual Report on the State of the Judiciary,* 69 A.B.A.J. 442 (1983).

103. Stevens, *Some Thoughts on Judicial Restraint,* 66 Judicature 177, 181–82 (1982).

atmosphere the Chief Justice may have believed that the moment was ripe to try again.

However, Burger's advocacy of structural change manifested two novel features. First, he specifically endorsed a particular kind of structure whereas in the past he had simply given general approval to the idea of a new appellate tribunal without intimating whether he favored a screening, reference, or transfer court or a fusion of the latter two. * * *

Second, the Chief Justice lowered his expectations for appellate change in the federal judicial system by publicly espousing a proposal less far-reaching than the structural recommendations made by the Freund Study Group and the Hruska Commission. Instead of advocating a new judicial tier, as those advisory bodies had done, he urged the establishment of an appendage to an existing federal court:

> I propose that without waiting for any further study, a special, but temporary panel of the new United States Court of Appeals for the Federal Circuit be created. This special temporary panel, which I now propose, could be added to that court for administrative purposes. It should have special and narrow jurisdiction to decide all intercircuit conflicts and a limited five-year existence.

* * *

The Chief Justice envisioned that the proposed intercircuit panel, if enacted, would relieve the Supreme Court of "as many as 35 to 50 cases a year from the argument calendar. * * *" He noted that, between 1980 and 1983, the nation's highest bench had decided an average of forty-two intercircuit conflicts a year—all of which it would have referred to such a panel if it had been in existence. Furthermore, the new tribunal's decisions would be appealable to the Supreme Court, although he speculated that it would seldom consent to hear such challenges. However, he failed to consider the possibility that it would have at least to give cursory attention to such appeals before deciding whether to accord them plenary review, a task that might require more time than handling *in forma pauperis* petitions.

Even though the Chief Justice's plan was less drastic than the structured proposals of the Freund Study Group and the Hruska Commission, it experienced the same result: congressional inaction. Like its structural precursors, it drew largely unfavorable reactions in the legal community and in the general public. Although former Senator Hruska endorsed, Professor Emeritus Freund implicitly discounted it as part of his resistance to any "intermediate court for all statutory construction questions as distinguished from constitutional questions. * * *" He cited a pair of reasons for his stance: a tendency of statutory and constitutional issues to be deeply entwined, if not inextricable, and his fear that the Supreme Court justices with only constitutional issues before them would be even more inclined to be "super-legislators" and to experience fewer restraints on letting their political and social values influence their decisions.

The most comprehensive critique came from Arthur Hellman, a law professor and former deputy director of the Hruska Commission, who leveled a potpourri of allegations against the Chief Justice's proposal.[122] Some of Hellman's charges were reminiscent of those leveled against the Hruska Commission's proposed national court of appeals: added work for the Supreme Court due to its reference responsibilities, the threat to the Court from a docket with only constitutional issues, a paucity of enough genuine intercircuit conflicts to warrant the establishment of another judicial body, no guarantee of caseload relief as long as the certification of litigation depended on the rule of four, and no prospect for achieving a greater degree of certainty in the law. However, other complaints were new: no correlation between smaller Supreme Court dockets and sounder holdings and uncertainty about the mode of choosing intercircuit panelists. In addition, a well-known former federal court of appeals judge, Shirley Hufstedler, reportedly feared that the panel's temporary status as a five year experiment would impair its effectiveness, presumably by keeping it from developing a stable membership and case law.

* * *

The objections raised in the press ran parallel to those expressed in the legal community in two respects—the alleged lack of a compelling case for the proffered structure and the apprehension about putative harmful effects on the nation's highest court. However, there was one salient difference: some of the media criticism held the Supreme Court itself mostly responsible for its expanding caseload. In this view, although the Court lacked control over the number of petitions coming to its doors, it still could control its docket through denying writs of certiorari. If the justices felt burdened, they should first seek to put their own house in order through stringent internal practices before calling for drastic redress, as exemplified by recommendations for a new federal appellate court. Furthermore, some opponents feared that if federal judicial appellate capacity were increased, caseloads would grow to use up this addition.

* * *

In March, 1983, (a month after the Chief Justice's first public advancement of the intercircuit proposal), Senate and House members sponsored bills to effectuate it. * * *

Even though a Department of Justice committee of assistant attorneys general favored an intercircuit tribunal with reference jurisdiction, the White House declined to endorse this committee's position. * * * First, [the Administration] agreed that the Supreme Court had been experiencing a severe workload problem, which it attributed chiefly to a

---

122. Hellman, *How Not to Help the Supreme Court,* 69 A.B.A.J. 750 (1983). *See* also Hellman, *Caseload, Conflicts, and Decisional Capacity,* 67 Judicature 28 (1983).

pair of causes: the growing litigiousness of citizens and alleged judicial activism pervading the federal system, including the Supreme Court. To the Reagan Administration, the latter aggravated the former. Increased judicial activism engendered the filing of additional cases. Furthermore, one Administration representative, Jonathan Rose (the Assistant Attorney General, Office of Legal Policy) also blamed Congress for enacting nebulous laws and economic regulations and previous administrations for encouraging such actions, all of which fueled the caseload problems of the federal bench, including the Supreme Court. However, he denied that federal governmental policy to relitigate questions had contributed to the burdens of the nation's highest court.

Second, the Reagan administration voiced a variety of concerns about the efficacy of the proposed intercircuit tribunal to lighten the Supreme Court's docket. For instance, another Administration spokesperson, William Bradford Reynolds (the Assistant Attorney General, Civil Rights Division), feared that the new tribunal, rather than serving as a temporary expedient, might readily become permanent after the experimental five-year period despite automatic sun-setting. Although he cited "inertial tendencies" for his position, perhaps he really shared Professor Hellman's apprehension that the new court would persist indefinitely as long as it was not an obvious failure. Reynolds also made the familiar charge that the new tribunal might aggravate the workload of the Supreme Court, which would have to determine the suitability of cases for reference as well as handle appeals for the intercircuit court. Furthermore, he speculated that selection of the new tribunal's membership by the Chief Justice or the entire Supreme Court would give either or both excessive power to shape its direction. Finally, he shared Paul Freund's concern that the existence of the new tribunal would foster greater Supreme Court activism, for the latter's docket would consist mainly or exclusively of constitutional issues. Thus, for the Administration structural renovation was a last resort, an option to be exercised only after other approaches had failed.

As a result of divisions in the legal community and the Administration's opposition, it is not surprising that the proposed intercircuit panel failed. However, the inability to enact non-structural changes is astonishing in light of the consensus on their desirability. The reasons probably include other Administration and congressional priorities, the addition of eighty-five new federal judgeships (sixty-one for the district courts and twenty-four for the courts of appeal) as a part of bankruptcy legislation passed in 1984, and an uneven but significant decline in the Supreme Court's caseload over the last three years from a peak of 5,311 during the 1981 term.

VI. CONCLUSION

* * *

The organizational status quo in the national court system will almost certainly persist indefinitely, particularly if the Supreme Court's caseload does not resume its climb. Thus the nation's highest court has been left with no practical choice but to help itself as much as possible (perhaps in collaboration with lower national courts) if it continues to feel overburdened by its docket.

Consequently, to lighten its docket, the Court may have to consider seriously the melange of possible changes in its internal management practices cited earlier in this article. Perhaps their individual and collective drawbacks, with regard to practicality and fairness, may outweigh their benefits. But in light of the dim prospect for any kind of legislative rescue, the nation's highest bench may have to travel this route.

* * *

WILLIAM REHNQUIST,* THE CHANGING ROLE OF THE SUPREME COURT
14 Fla.St.U.L.Rev. 1, 9–14 (1986)

Looking back from the perspective of the present day, we can see that there were several distinct stages in the evolution of the role of the Supreme Court and its Justices in the federal judicial system. During the first stage, in the early decades of our country's existence, there was no full-time federal appellate tribunal; the Justices of the Supreme Court spent most of their official time holding court in their circuits and convened only for a month or so in February of each year to sit as an appellate court reviewing the judgments of lower federal courts and of state courts.

During the latter half of the nineteenth century the appellate business of the Supreme Court picked up so much that it became a full-time job for the Justices of the Court; their circuit-riding duties were secondary at best and often fell into desuetude. The Supreme Court was now a full-time appellate court, reviewing all of the decisions of the lower federal courts which were appealed to it. * * *

But such a mission became impossible for any one court to fulfill by the end of the nineteenth century, and with the Act of 1891, the third stage in the evolution took place: a new level of appellate courts between the trial courts and the Supreme Court was created, and appeal as of right from federal trial courts and cases involving no question of construction of a federal statute or of the United States Constitution lay to these courts with only discretionary review from them to the Supreme Court. The Supreme Court had now abandoned its role of assuring error-free trial in the lower federal courts by use of its reviewing authority, and the cases which it decided on appeal now involved only issues of federal law.

For the next thirty-odd years this system worked reasonably well, but once again the growth in population of the nation and the tremendous addition to the business of the federal courts overtook it. A fourth

* Reprinted by permission of Florida State University Law Review.

stage in the evolution of the Supreme Court occurred when Congress passed the Certiorari Act of 1925. Hereafter, in the great majority of cases decided by the federal courts of appeals, even though they involved constructions of federal statutes or of the United States Constitution, there was no appeal as of right to the Supreme Court. Review is by certiorari only in the exercise of the Court's discretion. Congress agreed with the Supreme Court that, in Chief Justice Taft's familiar phrase, "Insofar as justice between individual litigants is concerned, two courts is enough." The Supreme Court was henceforth expected to confine itself to reviewing cases which involved broader legal questions than merely which of the two parties in the case ought to prevail.

The Supreme Court today does not have the sort of docket congestion that resulted in unacceptable delays in its decision of cases in 1890 and in 1925. Our current problem is a more systemic one. In 1935, ten years after the Certiorari Act, the Court was deciding roughly 150 cases on the merits each year; today we continue to do that and have for the past ten years or so, although there were times during the 1950's when the Court's output was less than 100 cases per year. But the great difference is in the percentage of cases we are able to review as compared to those which we are asked to review. In 1935, for example, there were roughly 800 petitions for certiorari, so that by granting and hearing 150 of them we reviewed somewhere between fifteen and twenty percent of the cases we were asked to review. But for the past ten years the petitions for certiorari have numbered more than 3,500; by granting review and deciding only 150 of those petitions, we grant review in less than five percent of the cases in which it is asked. This is simply not a large enough number of cases to enable us to address the numerous important statutory and constitutional questions which are daily being decided by the courts of appeals and by the fifty high courts of the states.

* * *

If we were talking about laboratory cultures or seedlings, the concept of issues "percolating" in the courts of appeals for many years before they are really ready to be decided by the Supreme Court might make some sense. But it makes very little sense in the legal world in which we live. We are not engaged in a scientific experiment or in an effort to square the circle, with respect to which hoped for dramatic and earth-shaking success at the end of the line may justify many years of cautious preparation and experimentation. But what lawyers and litigants in our country's federal courts are seeking to know may be, for example, the meaning of a particular subsection of the Internal Revenue Code. If we were all members of a monastic order presided over by Plato or by Saint Thomas Aquinas, we might accede to the idea that there need be no rush to judgment on such a question, and that an occasional hypothetical or tentative answer proposed and thought about for a while may help us reach the ultimately "correct" solution. But there is no obviously "correct" solution to many of the problems of statutory construction which confront the federal courts; Congress may have used ambiguous language, the legislative history may shed no great light on it, and prior precedent may be of little help. What we need is not the "correct" answer in the philosophical or mathematical sense, but the "definitive" answer, and the "definitive" answer can be given under our system only by the court of last resort. It is of little solace to the litigant who lost years ago in a court of appeals decision to learn that his case was part of the "percolation" process which ultimately allowed the Supreme Court to vindicate his position.

Two thousand years ago Cicero observed that the law is not "one thing at Rome and another at Athens, one now and another in the future." [28] He was talking, of course, about natural law, and there have been later political philosophers who disagreed with him. But surely it is hard to dispute that, in a country with a national government such as ours, Congress should not be held to have laid down one rule in North Carolina and another rule in North Dakota simply because the Court of Appeals for the Fourth Circuit and the Court of Appeals for the Eighth Circuit disagree with one another on the meaning of a federal statute. In short, we need today more national decision-making capacity than the Supreme Court as presently constituted can furnish.

I venture to predict that, for the reasons I have very roughly summarized, we will in the not-too-far-distant future have another stage in the evolution of the Supreme Court. It will largely relinquish its role in run-of-the-mine statutory construction cases to a new court—whether called a national court of appeals or something else—which will function in effect as a lower chamber of the Supreme Court. The Supreme Court will continue to deal as it has in the past with questions of constitutional law and other federal questions that now come before it. * * * I think the creation of such a court makes eminent good sense. * * * It will have either by practice or by statute the all-but-final say in determining in cases referred to it what an act of Congress means. Thus, it will not really constitute a fourth tier in the system of federal courts, but will be more like a lower chamber of the Supreme Court, a chamber which will take over from the Supreme Court a class of cases which the latter court will have had to give up for the same reason that it has had to give up all the other functions which it has surrendered during the history of its evolution.

Lawyers and judges as a profession are conservatives in the sense that most all of us are: we are familiar with a certain way of doing things and would prefer not to see that system change. But change has been the destiny of our federal court system since it was first brought into existence in 1789. * * *

Two hundred years of history show that evolution has been the destiny of the Supreme Court from the time it was first created by article III of the Constitution. The present proliferation of litigation in

---

28. *See* Wilson v. McNamee, 102 U.S. 572, 574 (1880) (citing Cicero, *Lactantius Inst. Div.*, bk. 7, c. 8).

both state and federal courts throughout the country and the tremendously increased number of undecided federal questions which this litigation raises are presently preventing the Supreme Court from adequately discharging its role as the final arbiter of questions of federal statutory and constitutional law in the United States. No one court can any longer discharge both of those functions, and I think it is the beginning of wisdom to recognize that fact and frankly concede that one or the other of these functions should be in large part transferred to a new court. Certainly, if one is to choose between the Supreme Court's active role in constitutional adjudication and its active role in statutory adjudication, no one would seriously question that it ought to retain the former function while surrendering as much of the latter as is necessary to enable it to perform the former. It is, in my opinion, time for still another in the many evolutionary steps which have marked the history of the Supreme Court of the United States.

ARTHUR D. HELLMAN,* PRESERVING THE ESSENTIAL ROLE OF THE SUPREME COURT: A COMMENT ON JUSTICE REHNQUIST'S PROPOSAL**
14 Fla.St.U.L.Rev. 15, 15–31 (1986)

I.   Introduction

* * *

In arguing for the creation of this new court, Justice Rehnquist relies on a straightforward syllogism. Constitutional adjudication is more important than statutory adjudication; the Supreme Court cannot resolve all of the undecided federal questions that arise in both areas; therefore cases involving only statutory interpretation should be shunted off to a new tribunal that would "function in effect as a lower chamber of the Supreme Court."

Justice Rehnquist deserves full credit for his candor in acknowledging that the proposed Intercircuit Panel does not involve simply a matter of judicial housekeeping, but implicates basic questions about "the proper role of the Supreme Court in our system of government." However, both his diagnosis and his prescription are flawed in fundamental respects. First, the available evidence does not support the proposition that "we need today more national decision-making capacity than the Supreme Court as presently constituted can furnish." Second, Justice Rehnquist relies on a superficial description of the Supreme Court's role in the American system of government. When the full measure of that role is taken into account, it becomes apparent that eliminating statutory cases from the Court's docket could seriously handicap the Court in the performance of its essential responsibilities.

* Copyright © 1986, Arthur D. Hellman. Reprinted by permission of the author, Arthur D. Hellman.

** Professor of Law, University of Pittsburgh. B.A., 1963, Harvard College; J.D., 1966, Yale University. Deputy Executive Director, Commission on Revision of the Federal Court Appellate System, 1973–75.

I shall discuss each of these points in turn, but before doing so it will be useful to touch briefly on an aspect of the controversy that Justice Rehnquist does not mention at all. Totally absent from his analysis is any suggestion that the Supreme Court is overworked. * * *

Justice Rehnquist's failure to say anything about the burdens imposed by the Court's caseload is no oversight. In an earlier speech, * * * Justice Rehnquist explicitly disavowed the "overwork" argument. He stated that the Supreme Court is busy, "but probably no busier than many other courts and private practitioners." And he saw no reason for the Court to cut back from the 150 cases that it now hears even if "fifty or so cases" were being transferred to a new court for decision.

* * *

II. ADEQUACY OF THE NATIONAL DECISIONAL CAPACITY

In arguing that "we need * * * more national decision-making capacity than the Supreme Court as presently constituted can furnish," Justice Rehnquist advances two propositions, one empirical, the other normative. The empirical proposition is implied rather than stated: the Supreme Court cannot resolve all of the intercircuit conflicts presented to it. The normative proposition is put more straightforwardly: definitive resolution of important federal questions should not await the development of a conflict, but should come at an earlier stage. Neither argument is persuasive.

On the empirical side, proving a negative is always difficult, and never more so than when the question is one as elusive as whether the Supreme Court is leaving conflicts unresolved because its docket is too full. The difficulty is twofold. In all but the clearest cases, reasonable people can disagree as to whether two rulings are actually in conflict.[15] Even when the presence of a conflict is indisputable, six or more Justices may vote to deny review for a wide variety of reasons other than the lack of decisional capacity. Nevertheless, I think it is now possible to render something stronger than a "not proven" verdict on the claim that numerous unresolved conflicts can be found in the cases the Court does not hear. The reason is epitomized by one of Justice Rehnquist's favorite literary allusions: the dog that did not bark in the nighttime.[17]

At least since 1974, prominent judges, lawyers, scholars, and legislators have been asserting that unresolved intercircuit conflicts constitute a problem of significant magnitude. Yet in all that time no one has been able to cite more than a handful of conflict cases in which review has been denied.[19] Surely, if the problem were as pervasive as supporters of

---

15. For example, two decisions may be perceived as conflicting with one another if the issue is defined in broad terms, but not if it is defined narrowly.

17. See Harrison v. PPG Indus., 446 U.S. 578, 596 (1980) (Rehnquist, J., dissenting).

19. In the early 1970's, the Commission on Revision of the Federal Court Appellate System (Hruska Commission) sponsored "a major project to determine the extent to which the Supreme Court [was] denying review despite the existence of a conflict." U.S. Comm'n on Revision of the Fed. Court Appellate Sys., *Structure and Internal Pro-*

the proposed new court assert, a lengthy list of cases would have been forthcoming by now.

Within the Court, the most persistent advocate of the view that intercircuit conflicts remain unresolved because the Court cannot make room on its docket has been Justice White. A casual reader of the Court's weekly order lists might get the impression that Justice White has identified a substantial number of cases in which the Court denied review despite the presence of a conflict. But careful counting reveals that in the four Terms 1981 through 1984 Justice White published no more than sixty opinions dissenting from the denial of certiorari on that ground. In some of the cases, other members of the Court filed concurring opinions disputing Justice White's contention that a conflict existed. And several of the issues flagged by Justice White were resolved by the grant of review in subsequent cases.

The upshot is that after more than ten years of debate over various national court proposals, there is almost no evidence to support the claim that the incidence of intercircuit conflicts has outgrown the capacity of the Supreme Court to resolve them. The inference is strong that unresolved conflicts are not a problem of great magnitude.

In this light, it is understandable that Justice Rehnquist places little reliance on the argument that the Court does not have the capacity to resolve all of the intercircuit conflicts that are presented to it. Instead, he puts forth a more interventionist conception of the Court's role as ultimate arbiter of the meaning of the federal Constitution and laws. He rejects the premise that the Court should await the development of a conflict before resolving "an important and undecided federal question." And he denies the value of "percolation," implying that "definitive" answers to recurring issues should be rendered at the earliest possible moment.

* * *

[I]t is true that the Court often will wait for the development of a conflict before resolving a recurring issue. And in some areas of statutory law, the plenary docket is overwhelmingly dominated by con-

cedures: *Recommendations for Change,* 67 F.R.D. 195, 221 (1975). The study concluded that "when duplicate issues, cases resolved at the time review [was] denied, and serious procedural problems [were] taken into account," the number of conflicts denied review would come to about 50 per year. *Id.* at 222. However, the Commission's report gave only a few examples of unresolved conflicts. *See id.* at 307–08, 321–24. Contemporary commentators questioned whether the Commission had adequately supported its conclusion "that the Supreme Court has been denying review of cases that truly present conflicts among the circuits." Alsup, *Reservations on the Proposal of the Hruska Commission* *to Establish a National Court of Appeals,* 7 U.Tol.L.Rev. 431, 441 (1976). More recently, a re-examination of the cases relied on by the Commission's study has cast further doubt on the prevalence of unresolved conflicts in the early 1970's. Note, *Identification, Tolerability, and Resolution of Intercircuit Conflicts: Reexamining Professor Feeney's Study of Conflicts in Federal Law,* 59 N.Y.U.L.Rev. 1007 (1984). And a study of all paid cases that were denied review in the 1982 Term found only 19 intercourt conflicts that the Court failed to resolve. Estreicher & Sexton, *A Managerial Theory of the Supreme Court's Responsibilities: An Empirical Study,* 59 N.Y.U.L.Rev. 681, 778–79 (1984).

flict cases. But when we look at the docket as a whole, we find that a substantial majority of the cases have received plenary consideration for other reasons and in the absence of a conflict. Thus, not only does the evidence refute the contention that the Supreme Court cannot resolve all of the conflicts presented to it; it also negates the proposition that the Court can intervene only to resolve conflicts. The effect is to further undercut the argument that the "national decision-making capacity" is inadequate.

If the argument is to succeed, then, it must be through redefining the lawmaking role of the Supreme Court. Justice Rehnquist essays this task with characteristic zeal, and he does so primarily by denigrating the value of percolation. * * * He argues, in essence, that because problems of statutory interpretation have "no obviously 'correct' solution," there is no value in testing the soundness of the various possible approaches before imposing one of them as the "definitive" answer.

This is a non sequitur. The argument might be persuasive—in practical terms if not as a matter of logic—if we could assume that Congress would generally act quickly to correct an improvident or less-than-optimal interpretation of a statute. But that assumption would fly in the face of reality. And if lawyers, litigants, and people who must act in accordance with federal law will have to live indefinitely with the construction of a statute given by the court of last resort, surely it makes sense for that court to defer a definitive judgment until some "hypothetical and tentative answer[s]" have been tested in the crucible of litigation.

No great effort is required to find cases in which the Supreme Court's task has been made easier by the work of lower courts in analyzing the issues and considering possible solutions. For example, in 1981 leading commentators pointed out that "[t]here has been considerable controversy over the question of the res judicata effect to be accorded a state court decision in a subsequent federal court action under [42 U.S.C.] § 1983." [40] They suggested that the full-faith and credit statute, 28 U.S.C. § 1738, ought to be "[a] starting point for analysis in such cases," but acknowledged that "many of the judicial discussions of the problem" had failed to recognize this fact. Although several cases raising the issue were brought to the Supreme Court, none were heard until the 1983 Term. The Court then resolved the question in a brief opinion, joined by all nine Justices, that relied primarily on section 1738. [43] It is highly unlikely that the controversy would have been dealt with so easily and with such unanimity if the Court had addressed the issue in one of the earlier cases, before the significance of section 1738 had crystallized. [44]

40. P. Bator, P. Mishkin, D. Shapiro & H. Wechsler, Hart and Wechsler's The Federal Courts and the Federal System 243 (1981 Supp.).

43. Migra v. Warren City School Dist. Bd. of Educ., 465 U.S. 75 (1984).

44. For other cases in which much-debated issues proved surprisingly easy when the Court finally addressed them, see Lan-

Apart from rejecting the value of percolation, Justice Rehnquist does not explicitly define what makes a case appropriate for consideration by the Supreme Court. However, he implies that review by a national tribunal should be available whenever the petitioner "raises [an] important federal question[ ] not foreclosed by any decision of [the Supreme] Court." If this standard were applied literally, it would mean that the Court should grant review in many cases where the gain in certainty and predictability from a Supreme Court decision would be minimal. For example, in the 1984 Term the Court denied certiorari to a petition presenting the question whether Title VII of the Civil Rights Act of 1964 prohibits employment discrimination against transsexuals.[46] The question was important, in the sense that it had been litigated in numerous cases, and the result certainly was not foreclosed by any existing Supreme Court decision. But every court of appeals to consider the issue (and most of the district courts) agreed that if transsexuals were to be protected by the civil rights law, "the new definition must come from Congress."[47] How much would a Supreme Court ruling have added to the ability of lawyers and litigants to know what the law is on that subject?[48]

I do not disagree with Justice Rehnquist's premise that uniformity and predictability in federal law are important goals of the judicial system. But * * * decisions by a national court are likely to advance those goals in a substantial way only when the issues they resolve are doubtful, recurring, and discrete. In a common law legal system, issues of that kind are the exception rather than the rule.

Beyond this, it cannot be assumed that a larger number of Supreme Court decisions in any given area of the law will necessarily make for greater certainty and predictability. Over the last decade, no area of

---

dreth Timber Co. v. Landreth, 105 S.Ct. 2297 (1985) (8–1 decision) (validity of "sale of business" doctrine in securities regulation); * * * Wilson v. Garcia, 105 S.Ct. 1938 (1985) (7–1 decision) (selection of appropriate state statute of limitations in actions under 1871 Civil Rights Act); Berkemer v. McCarty, 104 S.Ct. 3138 (1984) (unanimous decision) (applicability of *Miranda* ruling to interrogations involving minor traffic offenses); NLRB v. Transportation Management Corp., 462 U.S. 393 (1983) (unanimous decision) (allocation of burden of proof in unfair labor practice cases).

46. Ulane v. Eastern Air Lines, Inc., 742 F.2d 1081 (7th Cir.1984), *cert. denied,* 105 S.Ct. 2023 (1985).

47. *Id.* at 1087.

48. For additional illustrations of this pattern, see United States v. Appoloney, 761 F.2d 520, 523 (9th Cir.) (joining other circuits that have "uniformly" rejected fifth amendment challenges to the new federal law requiring wagering tax returns), *cert. denied,* 106 S.Ct. 348 (1985); Germantown

Hosp. & Medical Center v. Heckler, 738 F.2d 631, 633 (3d Cir.1984) ("The specific constitutional objections raised by appellants in the cases before us now have been * * * uniformly rejected by" all four circuits that have considered them.), *cert. denied,* 105 S.Ct. 906 (1985); Mid–America Nat'l Bank v. First Sav. & Loan Ass'n, 737 F.2d 638, 640 (7th Cir.1984) (finding no implied private right of action under National Flood Insurance Program; noting that "[p]laintiffs do not cite nor does our research disclose any reported decision not overruled that reaches a contrary result."), *cert. denied,* 105 S.Ct. 911 (1985). *See also* Connolly v. Pension Benefit Guar. Corp., 54 U.S.L.W. 4208, 4211 n. 6 (U.S. Feb. 26, 1986) (unanimous affirmance in appeal from three-judge district court) (upholding constitutionality of federal pension statute amendments; noting that decision below was "consistent with the result reached by every other court to have considered the issue").

legal dispute has received more consistent or more sustained attention from the Supreme Court than the fourth amendment. In the eight Terms 1977 through 1984, the Court handed down sixty-six decisions on the law of search and seizure—more (by one case) than were devoted to any other specific constitutional guarantee, including the free speech clause of the first amendment. Yet the law of search and seizure remains one of the most confused and contradictory areas of constitutional adjudication. Doctrines have proliferated to the point where the legality of almost any warrantless search arguably will be controlled by two, three, or even more lines of precedent.[50]

Perhaps there is some pathology about the fourth amendment that has created this unhealthy state of affairs. But the fact remains that the one area in which there is no shortage of nationally binding precedents is one in which there is tremendous confusion and uncertainty. Unless Justice Rehnquist can explain why this phenomenon is not representative, it would be foolish indeed to create a new structure that would expand the national decisional capacity and thus permit the replication of the fourth amendment quagmire in other areas of the law.

It is possible that I have misunderstood the thrust of Justice Rehnquist's position; regrettably, he provides no examples of important questions of federal law that have remained unresolved because the Court could not make room on its docket. But we need not rely wholly on speculation or read between the lines of his article to identify the kinds of cases he has in mind. To give flesh to Justice Rehnquist's abstract formulations, we can look at his dissents from the denial of certiorari.

During the last eight Terms, Justice Rehnquist has published a dissenting opinion or notation in more than 120 cases in which the Court denied review. By far the largest number of these—more than half the total—consisted of civil rights cases in which the lower court had ruled in favor of the constitutional claimant. This is a class of cases that already enjoys extraordinary favor with the present Court; more than one-fourth of all such petitions are granted, compared with one-twentieth of all petitions that are filed.

---

50. *See, e.g.,* United States v. Owens, 782 F.2d 146 (10th Cir.1986) (rejecting, seriatim, government's arguments that defendant had no reasonable expectation of privacy in his motel room; that search was justified by "consent" of motel manager; that search fell within "protective sweep exception" to warrant requirement; that "good faith" exception to exclusionary rule applied; and that contraband could be admitted into evidence under "inevitable discovery" exception to exclusionary rule); Sharpe v. United States, 660 F.2d 967 (4th Cir.1981), *vacated,* 457 U.S. 1127 (1982) (remand for reconsideration in light of intervening Supreme Court decision), *on re-* mand, 712 F.2d 65 (4th Cir.1983) (disavowing one holding, but readopting prior opinion with modifications), *rev'd,* 105 S.Ct. 1568 (1985); People v. Carney, 668 P.2d 807 (Cal.1983) (holding that motor home should be treated as a home for fourth amendment purposes; rejecting applicability of "automobile exception"), *rev'd,* 105 S.Ct. 2066 (1985) (holding that "automobile exception" applies); Castleberry v. State, 678 P.2d 720 (Okla.Crim.App.1984) (holding search invalid under "container" precedents; rejecting applicability of vehicle search precedents), *aff'd mem.,* 105 S.Ct. 1859 (1985) (equally divided Court).

In short, Justice Rehnquist appears to be arguing that we should make a radical change in the structure of the federal judicial system so that the Supreme Court can consider a larger number of cases in which lower courts have found merit in a civil liberties claim. Even those who are most alarmed by perceived excesses of judicial activism might well question whether such a drastic remedy is necessary.

III. THE SUPREME COURT AND CONSTITUTIONAL ADJUDICATION

Notwithstanding what I have just said, there is a strong intuitive appeal to the proposition that given the vastly expanded role of federal law in the American legal system and the proliferation of litigation in state and federal courts, one Court of nine Justices cannot possibly resolve all of the doubtful recurring federal questions that arise in those courts. And if Justice Rehnquist's proposal for increased decision-making capacity could be implemented with little or no risk to other values, opposition would indeed appear to rest on an unthinking attachment to old ways. In my view, however, remitting statutory issues to a new court would interfere significantly with the Supreme Court's ability to perform its most important functions in the legal system.

Justice Rehnquist starts off on a sound footing by recognizing that the desirability of his proposal will depend ultimately on one's "concept of the proper role of the Supreme Court in our system of government." And few would disagree with his premise that the Court's role in constitutional adjudication is more important to the country than its role in statutory adjudication. Unfortunately, Justice Rehnquist goes no further in defining the Court's role in the decision of constitutional questions.

The cases that invoke the Court's constitutional function are, of course, a varied lot. Most often the Court is called upon to adjudicate claims based on the Bill of Rights, the fourteenth amendment, and other constitutional provisions that protect individual rights against government action. But some of the cases involve the allocation of powers between state and national governments. A distinction can also be drawn between the supremacy function, embracing cases in which an exercise of state power is challenged on the ground of repugnance to federal law, and the checking function, encompassing review of actions by other branches of the national government. Cases from state courts may implicate different aspects of the Court's role than do cases from federal courts, and those implications in turn may depend on whether the court below accepted or rejected the constitutional claim. But the common thread that runs through all of these cases is that the litigant invoking the Constitution is asking the Court to overturn action taken or supported by the executive or legislative branches of government. In other words, "constitutional adjudication" means judicial review; and judicial review, in the phrase made familiar by the late Alexander M. Bickel, is counter-majoritarian. Thus, if Justice Rehnquist's proposal were to be adopted, nearly every case on the plenary docket would require the Court to second-guess decisions by the representative branches of government.

This arrangement would have several consequences for the Court's performance of its constitutional functions.[63] First and most important, the elimination of statutory cases from the Court's docket would pose dangers for the way in which the Court's work is perceived by legislators and other citizens. Judicial review is difficult to defend under the best of circumstances, but supporters of the institution as we know it today can emphasize that the Constitution is, after all, law, and that the Court provides authoritative interpretations of the Constitution just as it does for other kinds of laws. If the Court were to decide only constitutional cases, that analogy would be gone. To the popular eye, the Court would be nullifying decisions by the representative branches of government, not "as a correlative of [its] dual duty to decide those cases over which [it has] jurisdiction and to apply the federal Constitution as one source of the * * * governing legal rules," but as a "superlegislature" very much like the Council of Revision rejected by the Framers.

This perception would be reinforced by the heightened degree of divisiveness that could be expected within the Court. Of the constitutional decisions issued in the last four Terms, nearly half drew at least three dissenting votes, and little more than one-fourth were unanimous in result. In contrast, only one-third of the statutory decisions generated three or four dissenting votes; nearly half were unanimous. Even when the Justices were able to agree on the result in a constitutional case, their harmony often turned to discord when they attempted to articulate a rationale. For example, more than 250 civil rights cases were decided on the merits in the four Terms 1981 through 1984, but there were not even forty in which all participating Justices joined in a single opinion. On the other hand, among the 200 or so statutory decisions, more than seventy fit this description. It is relevant, too, that constitutional issues, including questions of federalism and separation of powers, accounted for all but two of the twenty-four cases that were decided by plurality opinions during this period.

From the standpoint of public perceptions, the effect of removing statutory cases from the Court's docket might be even worse than these figures suggest. The reason is that voting blocs within the Court tend to persist across a wide range of constitutional issues, but often break up when less earth-shaking questions of statutory interpretation are presented.[68] The existence of cases in which the Court finds itself unified—

---

63. Justice Rehnquist does not actually suggest that the Supreme Court give up *all* responsibility for statutory interpretation; rather, he anticipates that the Court would "largely relinquish its role in *run-of-the-mine* statutory construction cases." I surmise that the purpose of this limitation is to exclude most cases arising under statutes like the 1871 Civil Rights Act or the Sherman Antitrust Act—statutes that have the breadth of a constitutional provision and offer almost as much latitude for judicial policymaking.

68. For example, in the four Terms 1981 through 1984 the Court divided 5–4 in more than fifty civil rights cases and about forty cases involving matters of statutory law. Chief Justice Burger and Justice Brennan took opposing positions in all but

or divided along unexpected lines—thus serves to moderate the tensions that are likely to build up in cases involving the Bill of Rights, the fourteenth amendment, and the division of powers between state and national governments. Conversely, the loss of routine statutory issues could be expected to intensify and make more bitter the divisions that do exist among the Justices. * * *

Finally, the Court would lose an important source of self-discipline if it were able to shunt routine statutory cases to a "lower chamber." When the Justices consider a constitutional issue, they are guided only by the broad, even cryptic, language of the constitutional text and by the Court's own precedents. In contrast, when the Court decides cases under statutes like the Clean Air Act, the Truth in Lending Act, or the Internal Revenue Code, it must work within the confines of detailed and specific statutory language, and often other legislative materials as well. These cases serve two important functions within the Court. They assure the continued involvement of the Justices in the traditions of the lawyer's craft, and they remind the members of the Court that the Constitution is not the only source of values, and that the decisions of the representative branches of government are entitled to respect.

Some people think that the Court has been rather "activist" over the last two or three decades. Perhaps it has. But it has at least had the anchor to conventional adjudication that comes from having to consider, in each argument session, a few cases of a more obviously and traditionally "legal" nature. That anchor would be gone if all or most of the routine statutory cases were routed to an auxiliary tribunal. * * *

B.   SECRECY OF SUPREME COURT PROCESSES

In this section, we ask whether the Court has shrouded itself in too much secrecy; is it time to pierce the "red velvet curtain?" The section has three parts. The first gives an historical account of the Court's views on secrecy; the second examines the confidentiality maintained while the decisional process is underway; and the third looks at the materials available for study after the fact.

1.   *Overview*

The following article by Professor Alexandra Wigdor gives an interesting historical overview of the Court's long-standing policy of secrecy. As she notes, there is a continuum of views, ranging from those who support a virtually opaque curtain of secrecy that is maintained forever to those advocates who espouse public disclosure of the entire decision-making process as it unfolds. In between are those who believe that the Court needs to be able to maintain confidentiality while the process is underway, but that, at some point, disclosure is appropriate and desirable.

one of the civil rights cases, see Anderson v. Celebrezze, 460 U.S. 780 (1983), but they found themselves on the same side in eight cases where issues of statutory law were involved.

ALEXANDRA K. WIGDOR,* THE PERSONAL PAPERS OF SUPREME COURT JUSTICES: A DESCRIPTIVE GUIDE
3–27 (1986)

PAST PRACTICE AND CURRENT ATTITUDES TOWARD THE PRESERVATION OF JUDICIAL COLLECTIONS

Justices of the Supreme Court and judges of the lower federal courts have traditionally treated the papers they create for their own use as a species of personal property, protected by and alienable according to the laws of private property. Insofar as the chambers files of judges are preserved in research institutions—and the trend for Supreme Court collections is certainly in that direction—they reside there as the gift or loan of judges, their heirs or executors, or by purchase.

A judge's chambers files often contain two kinds of materials: 1) working papers, by which is meant all the papers generated in the course of rendering decisions, including conference notes, notes exchanged between judges or justices, bench notes, draft opinions, research notes, law clerks' memoranda, docket books, notes of conversations, and certiorari memoranda; and 2) private papers, including correspondence with family, friends, and professional colleagues, files on bar association activities, private financial papers, and personal diaries.

The history of the preservation and disposition of the papers of Justices of the Supreme Court and of lower court judges has been governed by the preferences of individual members of the bench and their families and by the availability of repositories to receive collections. Until the emergence of manuscript repositories in the twentieth century, the principal custodians of such papers were families and private collectors, which made for a high probability of irretrievable dispersal and chance destruction.

It should be emphasized that this pre-twentieth-century system of private custodianship of chambers files developed in the absence of other conventions, arrangements by the government, or, indeed, any practical alternative.

Two factors unique to the judiciary have affected the content and survival of the chambers files of Supreme Court Justices. The first of these is the fact that the Supreme Court is a court of record. According to the practice of common-law courts, certain kinds of materials were retained as the record of the official acts of the Court. Given the paucity of working papers in the late eighteenth- and nineteenth-century collections, the existence of a clearly defined official record seems to have discouraged the preservation of the preliminary working materials. Until recent decades, most Supreme Court Justices have not placed any

---

great value upon such materials. The William Howard Taft Papers, for example, one of the largest and most valuable collections among the holdings of the Library of Congress, contain very little in the way of judicial working papers, but virtually everything concerning the presidency. The great value of the Taft papers for the Court years lies in the voluminous correspondence files, for Taft frequently discussed important cases, his fellow Justices, and the decision-making process with numerous correspondents.

The responses to a questionnaire sent by the Public Documents Commission in August 1976 to all members of the federal judiciary except Justices of the Supreme Court indicate that this attitude is still very prevalent among lower court judges. Almost 80 percent of the 369 respondents reported that they had made no plans to place their personal papers in a research institution. A large number of judges added that they had never considered the matter, while others remarked that they could not believe that any institution would want their papers or that they had any research value.

The second factor affecting the content of judicial collections is the tradition of judicial secrecy, which was firmly established by the Marshall Court. The felt necessity to protect the confidentiality of the Court has been so pervasive that, until recently, judges have tended to destroy their working papers. Herbert A. Johnson, editor of the *Papers of John Marshall*, reports that no substantial amount of material concerning Marshall's actual work on the bench exists, and has offered the opinion that the habit of destroying working papers and conference notes was established early in the Court's history.

Attitudes toward the Supreme Court and toward the appropriate means of ensuring the confidentiality of judicial proceedings have changed dramatically in recent decades, as the existence of the Murphy, Burton, Frankfurter, Brennan, and other collections of working papers and judicial correspondence indicates. Yet the tradition of secrecy with its attendant assumptions has had such an impact on the content and survival of judicial papers as to merit some discussion.

Judicial Secrecy in Historical Perspective

The tradition of judicial secrecy is rooted in the procedures and conventions of the Marshall Court and may, in large part, be attributed to the personal influence and particular political vision of its Chief. When John Marshall took his place on the Supreme Court in 1801, it was by far the least prestigious branch of the federal government. It was indeed of so little consequence that it had to meet in a Senate committee room on the main floor of the Capitol, the architects having forgotten it entirely when designing the Capitol City. It was not unusual for a man to decline appointment to the Supreme Court in favor of service on state courts.

Marshall, it will be remembered, was appointed Chief Justice late in the administration of the Federalist President, John Adams, and remained to carry into the decades of Republican ascendancy the nationalist principles of that otherwise shattered party. Marshall was motivated by three major concerns: the prestige of the Supreme Court; the supremacy of the national government; and the authority of law. These concerns are reflected not only in the famous opinions that went far to establish the bases of our constitutional system, but in the procedure for judicial decision-making that he established immediately upon assuming leadership of the Court.

Marshall convinced his brethren on the bench of the novel proposition that the Court should speak with a single voice, contrary to the traditional practice of delivering opinions *seriatim,* with each judge stating in turn the reasons for his judgment. Whatever differences might exist in conference, Marshall insisted that the Court should face the outside world with a united front in the form of a single opinion, preferably written by the Chief Justice. In fact, in the first five years of Marshall's tenure, he delivered the opinion of the Court in every case except those in which he disqualified himself because he had a personal interest in the litigation. Although Marshall was unable to retain so complete a measure of control throughout his entire career on the bench, and indeed on one occasion entered a dissenting opinion himself, the practice of *seriatim* opinions was not revived as the normal procedure of the Court despite strong arguments in its favor.

Later in the century, John M. Shirley, who did not share the general admiration with which Marshall had come to be viewed, described the changes [Marshall] brought to the Court:

> * * * the judges reheard the causes which they had decided at the circuit; the practice of giving individual opinions was repressed; the practice became general of making one judge "the organ of the court," of virtually assigning causes, and of taking them home for the purpose of writing up opinions in vacation; and of having an opinion read by a single judge as the opinion of the court, when the judgment received the assent of but three, and sometimes two, of the judges, and the reasoning of a less number. This vicious practice occasioned great dissatisfaction.

While there was indeed a good deal of dissatisfaction with the Marshall Court and its methods, very little was felt within the brotherhood itself even when, after 1812, Republicans, appointed to counteract his Federalist views, held a majority of the seats. If, as one scholar has described it, Marshall manipulated his fellow judges "like putty," his seems to have been a pleasant domination, based on camaraderie, force of argument, great energy, and the ability to generate respect in those who worked closely with him.

The Justices of the early Supreme Court lived together in a boarding house during the term and shared meals in a common dining room. They discussed current cases not only in conference, but also in the informal atmosphere of the parlor. Marshall's ability to encourage uniformity of opinion and to ensure for the most part that that opinion would be in the direction of a nationalist explication of the Constitution was greatly enhanced by the physical closeness of the Justices during term. He was very upset at Justice Johnson's decision to live apart from the group in 1831, fearing that separate living quarters would lead to *seriatim* opinions.

Chief Justice Marshall's system ultimately triumphed so completely that his predilections came to be viewed as the necessities of our constitutional system. E.J. Phelps expressed the conventional late nineteenth-century assessment of Marshall in the following manner:

> Federalist as he was, and whatever may be said of his party or their views, we can find no more trace in any line of those great judgments that would indicate the political sentiments or bias of the Chief Justice than if we were to study his opinions upon charter-parties or policies of insurance.

Yet, one cannot escape the conclusion that Marshall's views of the Court and its functions were not the only nor indeed the majority view in his own day. Thomas Jefferson, whose political adherents and descendants controlled the popular branches of government during the period of Marshall's tenure on the Court, was violently opposed to judicial secrecy. It reflected, he complained, an elitist political theory. Marshall and his Federalist colleagues wanted to keep government and law remote from the people, inaccessible to the popular will.

* * *

In 1822, disturbed by a series of Supreme Court decisions that both expanded federal powers and asserted federal judicial review of state laws and judicial decisions (*McCulloch v. Maryland,* the Dartmouth College Case, and *Cohens v. Virginia,* among others), the aged Jefferson struck up a correspondence with Justice William Johnson, whom he had appointed to the Supreme Court in 1804. In this correspondence Jefferson attacked not only the constitutional interpretation of the Marshall Court but its instrumentation through the novel procedures that Marshall had brought to the Court. Jefferson reminded Johnson that, with the exception of Mansfield's Court, English judges had always rendered their opinions *seriatim.* He suspected that Mansfield's novel practice "* * * of making up opinions in secret and delivering them as the Oracles of the Court, in mass," had been introduced into America after the Revolution by Mansfield's great admirer, Edmund Pendleton, of the Court of Appeals in Virginia. Whether inspired by Mansfield, Pendleton, or some other source, Marshall had introduced the single opinion, contrary to the main body of English and American tradition, into the practice of the Supreme Court.

Jefferson opposed judicial secrecy and the single opinion on two grounds: it contradicted the fundamental republican principle of responsible government; and it implied a false simplicity in judicial decision-making.

Since Justices are appointed for life and not subject to popular control through the ballot, Jefferson explained, their sole constraints are the threat of impeachment and concern for their reputation. Secret opinions destroy both constraints, for no one could know who had written an opinion that constituted an impeachable offense, or indeed whether "the lazy or incompetent justice" had bothered to make up an opinion at all.

Jefferson applauded the system of *seriatim* opinion-giving because it threw greater light on difficult subjects, it was more educative, and it showed whether the judges were unanimous or divided, thus giving more or less weight to the decision as a precedent. In Jefferson's view, the Marshall Court, although it had decided cases of tremendous gravity and difficulty, rendering decisions that were offensive to large sectors of the community, deprived the citizenry of the chance to consider other opinions. The authority of law so produced, Jefferson felt, was hollow.

In a later letter to Johnson, Jefferson warned,

The very idea of cooking up opinions in conclave, begets suspicions that something passes which fears the public ear, and this, spreading by degrees, must produce at some time abridgement of tenure, facility of removal, or some other modification which may promise a remedy.

Justice Johnson responded favorably to Jefferson's plea for a return to *seriatim* opinions. He wrote to Jefferson that he had decided to register his opinion in all big cases, and he did so. He described to Jefferson his surprise on first joining the Court at finding the Chief Justice delivering all the opinions, " * * * even in some Instances when contrary to his own Judgement and Vote." His fellow Justices explained that they concurred in the system as a mark of respect to Marshall, but the real reason, he wrote, was that

Cushing was incompetent. Chase could not be got to think or write—Paterson was a slow man and willingly declined the Trouble, and the other two [Marshall and Bushrod Washington] * * * are commonly estimated as one Judge.

When he dared to deliver a dissenting opinion, he

* * * heard nothing but Lectures on the Indecency of Judges cutting at each other, and the Loss of Reputation which the Virginia appellate Court had sustained by pursuing such a Course.

The *seriatim* mode was not reestablished, although the judges on two occasions, in 1805 and 1806, took advantage of Marshall's absence to deliver their opinions *seriatim*. But Justice Johnson did, during his early years on the Court, break the Chief Justice's monopoly on delivering the opinion of the Court, and managed through the years to win grudging acceptance of the practice of dissent.

Johnson, however, did not agree with Jefferson that the whole process of reaching a decision should be open to public scrutiny. The confidentiality of the conference must be maintained, he felt,

* * * for I do verily believe that there is no Body of Men, legislative, judicial or executive, who could preserve the public Respect for a single year, if the public Eye were permitted always to look behind the Curtain * * *. I never met with but one Man who could absolutely leave his Vanity and Weakness at home!

There were, then, in the formative years of our constitutional system, two radically different approaches both to the meaning of the Constitution and the place and procedure of the Supreme Court. John Marshall represented the nationalist position; that is, that the Supreme Court should enjoy a position of parity with the other two branches of government, and that the supreme authority of federal law must be established. Marshall was not concerned with the question of judicial accountability. He shared the Federalist faith in government by "the rich, the wise, and the good," which happy concurrence of traits in the "respectable classes" obviates the need for artificial mechanisms of accountability. Justices were responsible to their consciences, God, and the Constitution. But as to the people, Marshall felt that the Supreme Court must at all costs be shielded from the pressures of public opinion—by training, by permanence of tenure, by secrecy of proceedings, and by uniformity of opinion. Only by enhancing the prestige of the Court and through it establishing the authority of law could the centrifugal tendencies in the new nation and the chaos of popular passions be restrained.

Jefferson called a judiciary independent of the will of the people in a republic a "solecism." He voiced the traditional republican suspicion of unrestrained power and called for specific measures to make judicial power responsive to the people. Jefferson understood judicial accountability to extend to the substance of a judge's opinions as well as a judge's behavior, for he considered the people themselves to be the ultimate interpreters of the Constitution. He sought to reestablish judicial accountability by suggesting at various times the legislative instrument of impeachment; removal by the President on the request of both houses of Congress; institution of a six-year term with the possibility of reappointment by the President with the approval of both houses of Congress; joint remonstrances in Congress against unconstitutional decisions, which would lead the states to block execution within their borders of those decisions; and of course, a return to *seriatim* argument.

Jefferson and those of a similar persuasion—Judge Spencer Roane, James Madison, and John Taylor of Caroline, for example—were the partisans of a lost and now largely forgotten cause. Marshall's interpretations of the status of the Supreme Court and the nature of judicial decision-making emerged triumphant from the Civil War to find their logical extension in "mechanical jurisprudence" and the "Cult of the Robe." By the end of the nineteenth century, the Supreme Court had attained the pinnacle of prestige and power, far removed from popular control, and, some felt, from popular concerns. Marshall's reputation was virtually unassailable.

In a later and more critical age, Justice Felix Frankfurter remembered with some consternation that Oliver Wendell Holmes nearly disqualified himself from a Supreme Court appointment by questioning whether Marshall was an original thinker. "So deeply," wrote Frankfurter, "had uncritical reverence for Marshall's place in our national pantheon lodged itself in the confident judgment of President Theodore Roosevelt."

Since the 1920s, however, there has been significant questioning of robism and the traditions of judicial secrecy, first on a jurisprudential and later on a functional level.

Mechanical jurisprudence, as the dominant nineteenth-century legal philosophy came to be called by its detractors, posited law as a closed system containing fixed principles of certain application. Legal precepts were considered to be the reasoned extrapolation of the accumulated experience of humankind. In effect, the mechanical jurist reduced all legal problems to a series of assumptions and applied those assumptions in accordance with their internal logic. The premise contained the conclusion within itself. As Roscoe Pound, a major early twentieth-century critic defined it, mechanical jurisprudence was "the rigorous logical deduction from predetermined conceptions in disregard of and often in the teeth of the actual facts."

Mechanical jurisprudence was complemented by assumptions about the role and the status of judges that critics have since labeled the "Cult of the Robe." If the law was seen as a set of universals floating far above the mundane battle of competing interests, so the judge was understood to be a disinterested law finder, the living symbol of an abstract impersonal justice. Judicial secrecy was an essential element in sustaining the assumptions of judicial neutrality, decisional certainty, and the rule of law.

In the 1920s and 1930s, the legal realists, drawing upon the insights of pragmatism, sociological jurisprudence, the ideas of Oliver Wendell Holmes, and the example of Louis D. Brandeis, launched a many-sided attack upon mechanical jurisprudence and its attendant assumptions about the status and function of judges. Skepticism lay at the core of legal realism. The realists were suspicious of all quests for first principles. The most commonly shared suspicion among the realists was "rule-skepticism," which Karl Llewellyn defined as the "distrust of the theory that traditional prescriptive rule-formulations are *the* heavily operative factor in producing court decisions." The rules of law, said the realists, are inadequate descriptions of the realities of law, and their prominence in published judicial opinions often obscures more basic determinants of judicial decision-making.

The emerging discipline of sociology led the realists to study law in terms of its environment. Psychology encouraged the reevaluation of legal decision-making. Realists argued that traditional legal thinking began with conclusions rather than premises, and that lawyers undertook the search for relevant principles only as a final ritualistic gesture.

The legal realists wanted to clear away the layers of secrecy and myth surrounding law and lawmakers. They called for functional analysis rather than speculative thinking, and talked much of facts and consequences and the difference between "paper rules" and "real rules." Their examination of the judicial process replaced the analysis of rules with the study of behavior. The realists looked at judges—and asked judges to look at themselves—not as impersonal and impartial vehicles of judgment, but as people like all others with class affiliations, economic interests, and social assumptions. The realists called for judicial introspection and the analysis of unspoken assumptions as a first step in bringing the law and its administrators into tune with the needs of modern society. (One small evidence of the realists' call for judges to descend from the Olympian heights to labor among their fellow citizens was Judge Julian Mack's custom of wearing a business suit in court.) Only a scientific jurisprudence and a self-conscious bench could adapt to the accelerated pace of change which had made an anachronism of John Marshall's concerns and prescriptions.

Legal realism has long since faded as a movement. The present generation is perhaps less sanguine about the prospects of a scientific jurisprudence. Yet the concerns of the realists, in less dramatic fashion, continue to inform scholarly inquiry. The legal realists focused scholarly attention on the judicial process. Realism, as two recent commentators put it, "is an effort to find out how the law in operation, as contrasted to the law on the books, is working." This impulse can be seen along the whole spectrum of current research on the American judiciary, for example: behavioralist studies, with their emphasis on the prediction of decisions; projects like the University of Chicago studies of the operation of the jury system; and the new style of judicial biography ushered in by A.T. Mason's *Harlan Fiske Stone: Pillar of Law* (1956).

It is within this larger framework that the heightened interest in the working papers and correspondence of members of the judiciary must be viewed.

While "piercing the curtain" of judicial secrecy has by no means lost its controversial aspects, the interest of scholars in understanding the process of judicial decision-making has been complemented by the willingness of many Supreme Court Justices and a number of prominent federal judges to make available for research the manuscript evidence of their labors. Justice Frankfurter was very much concerned that the public understand the Supreme Court if it were to retain its respect for law. To understand the Court, he wrote, it is necessary to understand both what manner of men make it up, and to know about the "private rehearsals * * * behind the impenetrable draperies of judicial secrecy," which tell much more about the individual and the group than the public performance remotely reveals. Although Frankfurter objected to certain features of Mason's biography of Stone, his objections did not prevent him from donating his extensive collections of personal and Court papers to the Library of Congress and the Harvard Law School.

Despite ambivalence, and in some cases outright rejection, the trend in recent decades has been for Supreme Court Justices to create, preserve, and ultimately donate to a manuscript library large collections of papers including both correspondence and case files.

Current Views on Balancing the Needs of the Court and the Public Interest

In the course of its study, the Public Documents Commission communicated with a large number of scholars who have used collections of personal papers to supplement the official record of the Court. These scholars were unanimously of the opinion that such collections are of immense value in understanding the judiciary and the law. Some emphasized the importance of personal correspondence and intracourt notes in providing an intimate portrait of a Justice or of the Court in a particular period. Others placed particular value on working papers that reveal the development of a judge's thinking on a particular case or legal issue, reveal the contributions of colleagues to his thoughts or language, or illustrate the collegial functioning of the Court. Several made the point that more than the written opinion is required if one is interested in the judicial process or in the behavioral aspects of judicial decision-making.

There is, however, a certain amount of ambivalence as to the propriety of using these materials and producing the kinds of studies they make possible. If the myths and symbols surrounding the Supreme Court are now recognized as such, still they are justified in some quarters on the grounds of functional legitimacy.

A number of arguments have been advanced for maintaining a cloak of secrecy around the judicial process. These include the need to uphold the authority of law, the need to protect the interplay of ideas preceding collective judgment, and the need to secure judicial independence within the tripartite structure of government and, given the distinctive political tasks of the Supreme Court, in the face of popular pressure.

While readily admitting that the Blackstonian concept has many shortcomings as a description of reality, Paul Mishkin, a well-known legal scholar, defends the "declaratory theory" precisely because it expresses a symbolic concept of the judicial process upon which, he feels, much of our courts' prestige and power, and, therefore, the authority of legal decisions depend. There is, Mishkin has written,

> * * * a strongly held and deeply felt belief that judges are bound by a body of fixed, overriding law, that they apply that law impersonally as well as impartially, that they exercise no individual choice and have no program of their own to advance.

Mishkin emphasizes the central role of symbol and myth in cementing the social bonds. He argues that a tremendous loss would occur if judges could not appeal to "the law" or "the Constitution" to justify their decisions. He recognizes, as nineteenth-century legal thinkers did not, the political element in Supreme Court decision-making, but sees in the Court's political tasks a functional justification of secrecy. Because the Court must decide matters of major public concern, and because its decisions will often be very unpopular with certain sectors of the community, it needs the shield of secrecy and symbol to operate effectively.

Other commentators have stressed the damaging effects of breaching the tradition of confidentiality upon the collegial functioning of the Supreme Court and the United States Courts of Appeals. In his 1957 review of Alpheus T. Mason's biography of Harlan Fiske Stone—the first judicial study to be based primarily upon judicial working papers, correspondence, and intra-court communications—Edmond Cahn expressed a widely held feeling of concern about this "unprecedented" breach of confidentiality. "If the present trend continues," he wrote, "our lecherous curiosity may produce nine bitter adversaries instead of a Supreme Court." This reaction may now seem a bit overheated, but the publication of *The Brethren* a few years ago rekindled such anxieties.

One of the participants in the Buffalo Symposium on Secrecy suggested another possible problem with the current interest in going beyond the printed opinion to study the inner workings of the judicial process.* How can we be sure, he asks, without creating some sort of massive waste retrieval system, that the whole decisional picture has been reconstructed. Even the complete decisional file of one judge will reflect but a partial understanding of how a particular decision was reached. And if the mass of material contained in a judge's working files is made available to outsiders, "who is to decide what is relevant * * *?" A number of responses to the questionnaire the Public Documents Commission sent to federal judges echoed the latter concern.

What might be called the Jeffersonian position in the discussion of myths, symbols, and secrecy was advanced by Professors Arthur S. Miller and D.S. Sastri in the Buffalo Symposium on Secrecy. They argued that democratic theory requires that the citizenry know not only who governs, but how policy decisions are made. In order to effect such openness in the federal court system, the writers suggested a return to open deliberation of cases in court. They expressed the opinion that the secrecy of the Supreme Court's conference cannot be successfully defended on functional grounds. "It came into existence at a time when the Court was a weak, infant institution * * *," which has long since ceased to be the case. Secrecy, Miller and Sastri conclude, is neither a universal nor a necessary practice. Public conference would make possible a fuller understanding of the Supreme Court, and thereby improve the process of judicial policy-making. It would, moreover, advance the ideal of the accountability of public officials in a democratic society.

* [Ed. Note: The spring 1973 edition of the Buffalo Law Review presented a symposium addressed to "Piercing the Red Velour Curtain," and included articles by Eugene Gressman, Arthur S. Miller, D.S. Sastri, and J. Woodford Howard. See 22 Buffalo Law Review 799 (Spring 1973).]

Between the extremes of complete secrecy and immediate disclosure during the decisional process itself is the more frequently held position that the privilege of present confidentiality should be accompanied by the responsibility of eventual disclosure. Professor J. Woodford Howard contributed an articulate exposition of this position to the Buffalo Symposium on Secrecy. The robist contention that secrecy produces a mystique that is the basis of the Court's power, he acknowledged, was a Platonic lie, compatible with neither the republican nor the nationalist traditions of American jurisprudence; but Howard advanced some compelling arguments for the proposition that secret deliberations are functionally necessary both to the effective working of the judicial system and to the just adjudication of causes. "One need only," he wrote, "imagine the financial windfalls of leaks in the Penn Central Merger, not to mention the political uproar surrounding open deliberations in *Brown v. Board of Education*," to grasp the continuing importance of preventing premature disclosure and protecting the independence of judges. (The "Impeach Warren" campaigns of the 1950s might also be adduced in defense of using confidentiality to protect the independence of judges.)

Howard also discussed the importance of secret deliberations in permitting the ripening of judgment. If not forced to take a public stand on an issue under consideration, appellate judges can more readily avail themselves of the benefits of collegial discussion and thoughtful compromise. He pointed out that many of the recent judicial collections—those of Stone, Frankfurter, Murphy, and Burton—reveal vigorous discussions among Justices, the development of ideas, and, on occasion, complete changes of mind. There would, Howard feels, be small opportunity for this process to take place in a system that allowed immediate or premature disclosure.

Howard proposed one final reason for the efficacy of secret deliberations, this one based on the policy-making aspects of appellate judicial decision-making. Confidential deliberations allow judges to test out the implications of their ideas and thereby avoid "cutting too broad a legislative swath."

Against these positive values of judicial secrecy, Howard wrote, must be balanced the risks involved when power is exercised unseen—risks of corruption, impropriety, and irrationality. His opinion is that the balance will be well met if judges accept the responsibility of "ultimate exposure at the bar of history":

> * * * the judicial papers of deceased Justices should be left to the public, preferably in public depositories like the Library of Congress, under reasonable restrictions as to laws of libel, state secrets, and passage of time to prevent intrusion in the Court's current functioning.

Whatever their views on judicial secrecy, many commentators are opposed to any abridgement of the property rights traditionally exercised by judges with respect to their working papers and court-related correspondence. Some of the scholars whose work depends upon such materials take this position and are concerned that any radical changes in the system will dry up what in recent decades have become tremendously valuable sources of information about judges and the judicial process. They stress instead the desirability of strengthening the present voluntaristic system through education and various incentives. At least one federal judge, however, would carry Howard's reasoning to its logical conclusion. The Hon. J. Skelly Wright, of the U.S. Court of Appeals for the District of Columbia, wrote to the Public Documents Commission in 1976:

> It would seem obvious that any papers and other materials which are generated by persons on the public payroll, working in government offices, doing the government's business, should belong to the government and should not be the private property of the head of the office or of the person or persons in the office who contributed to their preparation. It would seem further that any memoranda, tapes, and drafts generated in the production of such documents or other materials for the same reasons should also be the property of the United States. In short, if the government paid the cost of production of the papers or other materials they should belong to the government.

2. Secrecy During the Decisional Process

The Court has consistently been very protective of its privacy and very difficult to scrutinize closely. Even oral arguments, although public, are hard for the average citizen to witness first-hand. Given that the courtroom is small and not mobile, few citizens can actually observe an argument in person; most people get their view of the Court from the media. But, as Professor Elliott Slotnick notes, it is difficult for the media to cover the Supreme Court accurately. Cameras are not permitted. The only visual information the media can transmit is via artists' sketches; the only verbal accounts are reporters' summaries. The article by Todd Piccus argues that the Court should at least allow cameras into the Court during oral argument. (Although everything Piccus says about television seems to apply even more persuasively for radio coverage, few commentators discuss radio separately.) Several federal district courts and courts of appeal have begun experimenting with cameras in the courtroom. The results of the experiment are expected in 1994 and may provoke the Supreme Court into reexamining its current policy of excluding all the electronic media.

Recently, the court has had two occasions to discuss the question of access to its proceedings. At the time of the swearing-in of Justice Thomas, the Court, uncomfortable with the newly-developing tradition of having two swearings-in, one at the White House and one at the Court, considered allowing television coverage of the proceedings in the Court. The hope was that, if there were sufficient "photo-ops" at the Court, there would be less incentive for the President to want a session also at the White House. However, as the article by Tony Mauro reveals, the Court ultimately feared "letting the camel's nose into the tent."

The closest the Court has come to allowing a permanent record of courtroom proceedings to be made is to tape oral arguments and deposit the audiotapes in the National Archives, a process begun in 1955. But, even here, the Court has been very restrictive. Responding to what it believed to be CBS correspondent Fred Graham's inappropriate use of the tapes in a television report on the Pentagon Papers case, the Court adopted the following restrictions on the use of the tapes: All persons seeking to copy a tape of a Supreme Court oral argument must sign an agreement pledging to "use such audiotape for private research and teaching purposes only" and "not to reproduce or allow to be reproduced for any purposes any portion of such audiotape." Mauro, *Supreme Court to Legal Scholar: Keep Oral Arguments to Yourself,* Legal Times, Aug. 16, 1993, p. 1. As this article by Mauro reveals, a law professor's announced plan to market edited tapes and transcripts of several historic oral arguments initially angered the Court and led it to label the proposed sale a breach of the agreement. Ultimately, however, the Court chose not to fight and instead lifted the restrictions on usage. On November 1, 1993, the Court announced that the restrictions "no longer serve the purposes of the Court," and that it would "make the audio-tapes available to the public on a generally unrestricted basis." 114 S.Ct. CXIII (1993). While this about-face certainly was a loosening of restrictions, it would be a stretch to view this modification of the use of audiotapes as a signal that cameras in the courtroom are around the corner.

In reading this section, consider whether the Court is being too protective of its privacy. Should it allow the electronic media at least into the already public but not very accessible courtroom proceedings? Can and should Congress mandate such access? Or would television coverage of the courtroom proceedings only mislead the public into thinking that they are witnessing an important part of a decisional process that, in fact, takes place in the privacy of the justices' chambers and the Court's conference room? [1]

ELLIOT E. SLOTNICK,* MEDIA COVERAGE OF SUPREME COURT DECISION–MAKING: PROBLEMS AND PROSPECTS
75 Judicature 128, 128–136 (1991)

The importance of journalistic coverage of governmental activities in the policy-making arena is difficult to overestimate since the media serve as the primary link between the government and the governed. The

---

1. Chapter Four explains the Court's decisionmaking process in detail.

* Excerpts from *Media Coverage of Supreme Court Decision–Making: Problems and Prospects,* by Elliot E. Slotnick. Copy-right © 1991 by Elliot E. Slotnick. Permission granted by "Judicature, the journal of the American Judicature Society" and the author.

multifaceted nature of the media's role in American politics is well tapped by Paletz and Entman:

> Much of what most adults learn about government—its institutions and members, their activities, decisions, defects, strengths, capabilities—stems from the mass media. The self-same media have the power to decide which issues will be brought before the public, the terms in which they will be presented, and who will participate, under what conditions, in the presentation. By dint of the subjects they cover (and do not cover) and the ways they structure them, the mass media tell Americans what to think about, how to think about it, sometimes even what to think.

* * *

The centrality of the media link between governmental institutions, their policy making, and the policy may be most telling for the judiciary, the branch of government about which most Americans are decidedly uninformed. Indeed, for most Americans, the press may be the sole source of information about the Supreme Court. As noted by Caldeira, "Research on the attitudes of adults reveals that there is only a relatively shallow reservoir of knowledge about * * * the Court in the mass public * * *. Few * * * fulfill the most minimal prerequisites of the role of a knowledgeable and competent citizen vis-a-vis the Court." It is in this context of the importance of media coverage for public information and opinion about the Court that this essay focuses on the inherent problems in and future prospects for media coverage of Supreme Court decision making.

The reasons for the Court's relative invisibility and the fact the public must rely virtually exclusively on the news media for information about the Court lay partly at the doorstep of the institution itself and its members. As noted by Duke, "The justices themselves are among the most anonymous public figures, preferring to stay out of the spotlight * * *. In the face of trends toward more openness in government, the Court still clings to its Delphic ways, perpetuating the remoteness that is part of its character." Indeed, as Justice Antonin Scalia concluded in a recent speech that explored the relationship between the judge's decision-making obligations and press coverage of the Court, "I hope to have explained * * * the wisdom of judge's ancient belief that no news, by and large, is good news." [7]

The Court's shunning of the public eye, low general levels of knowledge about the Court and its work, and the primacy of media coverage for whatever understanding of the Court that does exist all serve to strengthen the media's role in determining the public consequences of judicial decisions. Indeed,

---

7. Scalia, Francis Boyer Lecture delivered at the American Enterprise Institute Policy Conference, December 6, 1989, Washington, D.C. I am indebted to Tim O'Brien of ABC News for providing me with a copy of Justice Scalia's provocative remarks. The text I have quoted from in this article was verbated [sic] from an audio tape of Justice Scalia's unpublished lecture.

press reports have political * * * consequences even for what is often thought of as the least political aspect of the policy-making process. For example, how particular decisions are reported stimulates opposition to some of the Court's actions, thereby quite possibly affecting the justices' behavior and promoting shifts in the direction of public policy. When other decisions are left uncovered or reported only cursorily, the ability of ordinary citizens to judge and their power to respond in their self-interests to political events and power holders is decreased.[8]

THE IMPORTANCE OF TV

The media are not monolithic and, increasingly, an understanding of the role of television news for explicating public policy has taken primacy. Studies have documented for over two decades that television is perceived by the majority of the public as its "main source" of information and the advantage enjoyed by television has, if anything, grown as an increasing proportion of the citizenry has been "raised" in a television-dominated environment. The majority of the public admit to receiving *all* of their news from television, while a plurality cite television as the "most thorough" national news source. Indeed, as Ron Nessen, a former network news correspondent and presidential press secretary has noted, "if it didn't happen on network television, then it didn't happen."

* * *

The problems associated with television news take on added significance with reference to coverage of the judiciary because of the Court's isolation and relative public invisibility. Berkson has characterized two publics that receive Supreme Court messages: a "continuous public" (composed of attorneys, judges, law enforcement officers, and lawmakers) and a less attentive "intermittent public." Continuous publics have, in most instances, the greatest need for accurate information and, arguably, they generally "utilize the most reliable channels." It is the unknowledgeable intermittent publics who are most likely to depend on the media for the information they possess. When they look to television, they are met by a medium that has been portrayed as having a "lack of interest in what the Court does. Even if a citizen desired to learn more about the operation and output of the Court, this information could not be obtained by relying on the coverage in the mass media."

THE "MEDIUM OF CIRCULATION"

In such a setting, the policy consequences in a democratic polity could be substantial. Citizens might be unable to gauge the legal and political ramifications of numerous constitutional rulings that have a dramatic impact on their lives. Yet, "if democratic society is built on a constitutional foundation of rights and liberties, a foundation which is often altered by decisions of the Court, citizens must know the nature and scope of their rights." Justice William Brennan has characterized

8. Paletz and Entman, Media Power
Politics 108–109 (1981).

the press as "the medium of circulation" in American society, "the currency through which the knowledge of recent events is exchanged, the coin by which public discussion may be purchased." This has particular relevance for the Court according to Brennan, "because through the press the Court receives the tacit and accumulated experience of the Nation, and because the judgments of the Court ought also to instruct and to inspire—the Court needs the medium of the press to fulfill this task."

For his part, Justice Scalia has demeaned the press' instructional and inspirational roles as portrayed by Justice Brennan. According to Justice Scalia, the unique nature of the judicial process and the real world operation of the journalistic calling render it impossible for the press to well serve the Court vis-a-vis the public.

> My intent * * * is not to disparage * * * reporting and commentary. It is what it is for very understandable reasons, and cannot be expected to be otherwise. But I do hope to induce some of you to read that reporting and commentary with an appreciation that things are not always as they seem * * *. I am about to appeal to the principle that law is a specialized field, fully comprehensible only to the expert. That is not, I confess, an attractive proposition. The "this is too complicated for you to understand" argument is trotted out to cloak incompetence in many fields. Let me try to explain why it has unique validity in the field of judging. In most areas of human endeavor, no matter how technical or abstruse the process may be, the product can be fairly evaluated by the layman: the bridge does or does not sustain the loads for which it was designed; the weather forecast is or is not usually accurate; the medical treatment does or does not improve the patient's condition. I maintain that judging, or at least judging in a democratic society, is different. There, it is frequently the case that the operation is a success, even though the patient dies. For in judging, process is a value unto itself and not—except in a very remote sense—merely a means to achieving a desirable end. The result is validated by the process, not the process by the result.

Thus, for Justice Scalia, "Like moral rectitude, judicial rectitude is ultimately determined not by result but by reason. Judges must of course give reasons, unlike umpires who can simply call the runners safe without specifying whether that is because the throw arrived too late or because the first baseman's foot was off the bag." In such a setting, being right for wrong reasons "is a disaster." Yet the media focus on results, not reasons, which "is to miss the principal point * * *. [H]ow easy it is for the casual observer to make that mistake."

In Justice Scalia's view, most of what the Court does "is pretty dull stuff," beyond the interest of the public and the media.

> One would not expect the public to be interested in it. Indeed, one would fear for the republic if the public was interested in it. And since the public is not interested in it, one would hardly expect the

press to report it. That is why the University of Chicago Law Review is not sold at 7–Eleven.

When cases *are* covered, the press' result-orientation cannot offer sufficient detail and complexity to serve the educational role that Justice Brennan contemplates.

> Before coming to the bench, I was editor of a magazine * * * that frequently commented upon * * * court decisions. I know from experience how hard it is to describe them accurately to the layman, and also ... how unenthusiastic the layman is to have them accurately and thus boringly described. The magazine is, as you know, no longer in existence.

For Justices Brennan and Scalia the media–Court link appears to offer uniquely different possibilities and prospects. For Brennan, the media can be the vehicle through which a democratic polity is informed and energized and through which the Court learns about the public it serves. For Scalia, the media cannot fulfill effectively an informative function. Consequently, its task need not be facilitated by judges, and media (and public) criticism are treated as generally irrelevant to the pursuit of the judicial function.

THE MEDIA-COURT LINK

Regardless of which view of the media is closest to reality, the media-Court link generates concern from many sources and has important implications. For one, the media help to shape the judiciary's views of the public its decisions affect. Perhaps more importantly the centrality of television news in the public's information network suggests that much of what we know and our attitudes about our perceptions are derived from the media's message. As noted by Judge Irving Kaufman, "The force of judicial decisions * * * depends on a fragile constitutional chemistry, and it flows directly from popular knowledge and acceptance of their decisions. Courts cannot publicize; they cannot broadcast. They must set forth their reasoning in accessible language and logic, and then look to the press to spread the word." If the press "gets it wrong," important consequences can follow. Thus, for example, public misperception of a ruling can have a direct effect on compliance with the ruling as well as on its broader impact. Public perceptions may have importance for the development of further litigation, and its broadcast implications may be felt in the distorted role a misinformed democratic polity may play in ongoing policy formulation and debate.

Commentary has been frequent in criticism of the press for its coverage of the judiciary. Journalist Max Friedman, for example, wrote years ago that, "It seems simply inconceivable * * * that the average American èditor would ever dare to write on a debate in Congress or a decision by the President with the meager preparation which he often manifests in evaluating the judgments of the Supreme Court. * * * I must declare my conviction that the Supreme Court is the worst reported and worst judged institution in the American system of government." Perhaps even more telling is the criticism levelled by First Amendment absolutist Justice William O. Douglas who characterized coverage of the Court as producing "news stories which the author of the court opinion would hardly recognize as descriptive of what he had written." Arguably, such observations may sit well in a journalistic time capsule, but no longer ring true today. Thus, according to ABC News' Supreme Court correspondent Tim O'Brien:

> Max Friedman's observations about the news media and the Court years ago are simply no longer valid; television has changed most dramatically since those days, making the beat more competitive for all. The New York Times and the Washington Post both have experienced veterans at the Court. The wires similarly are staffed with Supreme Court veterans who provide newspapers around the country with competent coverage. Felix Frankfurter lamented that the Supreme Court doesn't get the media attention the World Series does. It does too!

While press coverage of the Court has historically presented an easy target, it is critical to view such coverage in the context of the special problems reporting on the Court entails, the nature of the Supreme Court press corps, and the unique considerations characterizing television reporting of the Court, subjects to which we now turn.

THE COURT AND THE PRESS

Analyses of the media-Court relationship have always been premised, and justifiably so, in the unique circumstances that coverage of the Court entails for the reporter. "Journalists must understand that the Court is different and must remain different. It speaks once and is silent. Its critics seldom cease speaking." [27] Several ingredients have implications for the media-court brew including the nature of the Court's work, its administrative habits and, at times, the press' own lack of capacity for sound Court coverage. From the press' perspective, its difficulties are not simply or solely explained by accusations that reporters are "untrained" although, as developed below, this has been a historically significant problem. Clearly, however, journalistic needs for speed in reporting and brevity in reports are coupled with the demands of pressured editing to exacerbate the troubled relationship of the fourth estate with the least dangerous branch.

Veteran *Washington Post* Supreme Court reporter and current *New York Times* editorial board member John Mackenzie has asserted that, "Between the Court and the press stands perhaps the most primitive arrangement in the entire communications industry for access to an important source of news material and distribution of the information generated by that source." The parameters of that relationship are easily noted with "some of the problems * * * built into the system of both institutions."

---

27. Newland, "Press Coverage of the United States Supreme Court," 17 West. Pol.Q. 15–35 (1964).

The Court begins as a mystery, and the reporter or editor who fails to appreciate the fact that certain things about the Supreme Court will remain unknowable * * * simply does not understand the situation. The Court's decisions are the start of an argument more often than they are the final definitive word on a given subject. * * * Secrecy at several levels both protects and obscures the Court and its work. * * * I would suggest that murky decision-reporting may be the reporting of murky decisions as well as the murky reporting of decisions.[31]

Supreme Court decisional processes are not open to the reporter's view as they are, at least in part, in other governmental settings. Yet, as Anthony Lewis has noted, "The process of decision is often more newsworthy than the end result. And it can certainly be more instructive in the ways of our government. * * * Judges make accommodations just as their political brothers do, but we can only guess at what they were." While critical judicial decisions are made in private, "What reporters see inside the Courtroom—all they see—is designed more to elevate than to display the judicial process."

An inherent danger for those reporting on the Court is the "intimidation factor" and acquiescence that the elevation of process can lead to. Shaw has noted that, "The formal panoply of the courtroom and the stilted language of the lawyers and judges cow some reporters into silence." Larson has similarly observed that, "The mystique that justices are 'above politics' and the secrecy, rituals, and physical setting, which is said to 'awe reporters' * * * might discourage critical coverage of the institution."

If an institutional problem of intimidation does exist among reporters covering the Court, it may stem in part from the lack of knowledge among those who, at least in the past, were assigned to the Court beat. * * * For veteran respected Supreme Court reporters such as Lyle Denniston of *The Baltimore Sun* the results of his colleague's efforts are often frustrating and he does not hold them blameless. "I've been in the business since 1948 * * * and I know of no beat where reporters are lazier and do less to penetrate the process they're supposed to cover than legal reporting." Yet as Newland observed in his pathbreaking study of media coverage of the Court, "The merits of laborious advance preparations by the reporter * * * for final speedy reports may * * * be obscured in stories which stress other factors more than the Court's decisions and opinions."

Clearly, a large part of the problem for the Court reporter stems from the dearth of traditional news sources. The Court's members and functionaries all place a premium on secrecy and, to the extent that the relationship between journalists and their sources are generally based on mutually beneficial exchanges, journalists are perceived to have little to

31. DeVol (ed.), Mass Media and the Supreme Court: The Legacy of the Warren Years, 3rd ed. 139 (1982).

offer to the Court in this regard. Veteran journalist Fred Graham, who covered the Court for many years for the *New York Times* and CBS News, notes that Supreme Court justices could hardly be considered "news sources" in the journalist's lexicon. "There was an understanding in my dealings with them that all conversations were off the record, and confidential Court business was usually not discussed." While justices might assist the journalist in confirming or denying material for a story, "none played the spin-control game that is routine everywhere else in Washington. None of them tried to manage the news by putting their views, or themselves, in a favorable light." Graham offers a vivid description of the task the Court's reporters consequently faced:

> Covering the Supreme Court was like being assigned to report on the Pope. Both the justices and the Pope issue infallible statements, draw their authority from a mystical higher source, conceal their humanity in flowing robes, and because they seek to present a saintly face to the world—are inherently boring. They also both have life tenure, which implies a license to thumb their noses at the news media. * * * [T]he justices were so withdrawn that covering the Court for any news medium was in a journalistic class by itself.

REPORTING DECISIONS

Any consideration of the problems that exist in media coverage of the Court must take full account of the inherent difficulties associated with understanding complex litigation and technical legal arguments and then filing stories on them within a few minutes or a few hours. Case decisions often include numerous concurring and dissenting opinions that may obfuscate the issues even further and, as Dennis has noted, "The opinions of the Court as a source of news are only as informative as the reporter's lay comprehension of them." Indeed, writing an opinion in *Pennekamp v. Florida* (1946) Justice Rutledge took note that legal news is often reported inaccurately. He attributed this, in part, to haste, carelessness and, in isolated instances, "bias or more blameworthy causes." He went on to admit, however, that "a great deal of it must be attributed, in candor, to ignorance which frequently is not at all blameworthy. For newspapers are conducted by men who are laymen to the law. With too rare exceptions their capacity for misunderstanding the significance of legal events and procedures, not to speak of opinions, is great. But this is neither remarkable nor peculiar to newsmen. For the law, as lawyers best know, is full of perplexities."

Supreme Court opinions are not written for a lay or journalistic audience and justices rarely do anything to make them more accessible to such publics. Indeed, some jurists seem to go to great lengths to trump complex legal questions with complexities in their own prose. Justice Frankfurter, for example, has been credited with authoring opinions that are "repositories for some of the most exotic words in the English language." Generalizing the point, Berkson writes, "Although Frankfurter's style was uncharacteristically eloquent, it is not unique in terms of those to whom it was directed. Indeed, this lack of concern for the general audience is perhaps the greatest weakness in Supreme Court messages. It places the responsibility of interpreting decisions squarely on the press * * * and other encoders. As Wasby has observed, when this situation occurs, 'the chances for misinterpretation * * * increase radically.' "

Other facets of media coverage of the Court are dictated by the operating regimens of both institutions and the difficulties of effectuating change, even where such change seems possible. From the media's perspective, the idiosyncrasies of the newsday have much to say about whether and how well a Supreme Court decision is covered. In addition to competing with other news beats, Supreme Court cases are often in competition with each other as the media follow "the practice of highlighting what is felt to be the major decision of the day at the expense of the other decisions that day." This problem would not be a major one if Supreme Court rulings were announced randomly during the news year or, indeed, during the Court's less lengthy nine-month term. Such randomness is, however, patently not the case. Historically, all Supreme Court decisions were announced during a series of "decision-Mondays" with the Court convening at noon. Marginal reforms of judicial procedures moved the Court's starting time to 10 a.m. in 1961, a time that is considerably more conducive to the demands of the newsday. In 1965, the exclusivity of Mondays for the announcing of decisions was abandoned, making newsworthy rulings less likely to pile up on a given newsday. Chief Justice Warren, it appears, initiated such reforms in an explicit effort to facilitate media coverage.

Such reforms have been beneficial but in no way have they sufficiently alleviated the problems they address. For one, decisions are not spread equally across the newsweek despite the formal demise of "decision Monday." More importantly, over a third of the Court's rulings (and the preponderance of its important ones) are generally announced in June reflecting the difficulties of reaching decision closure as well as the demands of opinion writing. As Graham notes, "On Monday, June 12, 1967, the Warren Court handed down enough decisions and new Court rules to fill an entire 991 page volume of the Supreme Court's official case reports. There was no way for us even to read so many pages, much less write coherent stories about them." Graham recognized that, consequently, he may have given short shrift to one case in particular and, "my failure * * * began what proved to be a long and eventually hurtful estrangement between me and a gentle and kindly justice, William J. Brennan." Further commenting on the demands of such late June decision days (and this one in particular) Mackenzie adds, "Many of these decisions have remained under advisement until the end of the term precisely because of their difficulty and complexity, elements that frequently correlate with newsworthiness." Empirical analysis by Wasby underlines further the Court's end of term deluge:

> Changes in Decision Day practices have not been accompanied by changes in the flow of cases throughout the term. Few opinions can be expected in October, November, and December when oral argu-

ment has just begun, but disparities in output between the second three months (January–March) and the last three (April–June) have been considerable. * * * [O]nly a small portion of the Court's output appears by the end of December. Less than half the Court's full opinions have been announced by the end of March. * * * Not only does the Court release most of its output in the last third of the term, but as much as one-third of the Court's entire output for the term is announced in the last six weeks, with more than two-fifths of the opinions appearing in that period in some terms.

In some instances over 40 per cent of the Court's opinions were released during the last three weeks of the term, while nearly one-fifth were released during the final week of the term.

Time Constraints

Unreasonable time constraints remain among the most serious grievances some Supreme Court reporters have with their job. Associated Press Court reporter Richard Carelli often has to report on 20 to 30 cases in a given day. The possible consequences for his performance are understandable.

* * *

Little Assistance

For its part, the Court appears to be relatively unconcerned about journalistic difficulties. Indeed, in the words of Anthony Lewis, "All of official Washington except the Supreme Court is acutely conscious of public relations. The Supreme Court is about as oblivious as it is conceivable to be." There is much truth in Lewis' comment. The Court does have a clerk of the court as well as a press officer, but neither sees their job as a vehicle for fostering the Court's public image. Indeed, the press officer's role is very different from that of a public information officer or press secretary in other institutional settings. According to Grey, the Court's press officer is, in the final analysis, "primarily a feeder of information, not a source. His job is primarily to disseminate materials—not ideas, explanations, or background information on judicial reasoning. * * * The job of Supreme Court press officer is severely restricted in scope. He is in no way a spokesman for the Court."

In an institutional setting where the press officer serves almost exclusively as a conduit for information, Supreme Court reporters find themselves more isolated than journalists acting in other governmental arenas. Interviews with justices remain rare, despite their relative increase during the past decade, and they remain inadequate and inappropriate mechanisms for in-depth coverage of actual cases and controversies. Press briefings and press conferences are not held by justices or other Court personnel. In short, "The newsman has only his background knowledge, notes, typewriter, desk and phone—and whatever resources or contacts they can provide as he hastens * * * to get down * * * what the Court has decided." In some respects, the Court reporter's lot is a uniquely simple one "because, in theory, anyone interested has access to most of the same sources that the news reporter has. In contrast to other areas of newswork, the Supreme Court reporter operates with few special advantages or facilities, few special means of access to personal sources, and few special materials or documents." [55]

As already noted, most judges simply do not see a great deal to be gained in an exchange relationship where the reporter's work is facilitated. The numerous contrasts between the two functionaries begins with their very work ethic. According to Knoche, "The fora for judge and reporters are quite different. A judge may take three pages to discuss a minute point of law, while a reporter may have three sentences to explain the meaning and impact of the entire decision." The judiciary is distinct from the other branches in the "sober second look" that lies behind its formulations, the attempt to develop reasoned, logical arguments. The media and, most particularly, television bow to brevity and simplicity. The judges' perspective on their needs is well summarized by Dreschel, underscoring Justice Scalia's position discussed earlier.

> Judges occupy positions in an institution in which they may perceive relatively little tangible need for publicity and relatively little need for much of the judicial information published or broadcast by the news media. Judges appear not to need the news media as a source of information on which judicial decisions are based, as a communication channel linking one court with another or as a vital channel linking the courts with other branches of government. Nor is there any overt effort by the judiciary to use publicity to mobilize or prepare public opinion for upcoming judicial action. With such needs apparently minimized in the judicial branch, judges inherently would not seem to need journalists and the news media in the same ways as public officials in other branches of government.[57]

This is not to suggest that press relations with the Court have been completely static and that no changes have occurred in them. For one, as we have seen, some reforms have been made with regard to decision Mondays and the Court's traditional starting time. Over time, many other alterations have transpired in the judge/journalist interface. Indeed, until the late 1920s reporters did not have access to copies of opinions at the time that they were announced and they were forced to rely on their understanding of what they had heard. At that time proofs of decisional texts became available, but only after rulings were completely read or announced in the courtroom. In the mid-1930s press aides began to distribute proofs at the start of a decision's announcement rather than at its conclusion. Today, concurrences and dissents are available concurrently with the announcement of the Court's decision, which is accompanied by a summary headnote. Formerly, the headnote was only available with the opinion's eventual publication.

55. Grey, The Supreme Court and the News Media 45 (1968).

57. Dreschel, "Uncertain Dancers: Judges and the News Media," 70 Judicature 264, 271 (1987).

Full opinions are now handed out directly in the pressroom virtually simultaneously with the generally cursory announcement of decisions in the Court and, consequently, reporters no longer have to wait to have opinions dispatched to them by the press officer through antiquated (and now closed) pneumatic tubes.

Curiously, many of these recent reforms transpired during the watch of staunch media critic Warren Burger as Chief Justice. According to Graham,

> Burger never conceded that there was a legitimate public interest in such matters as the justices' health, their finances, their reasons for disqualifying themselves from cases, their votes on deadlocked appeals and their off-the-bench activities. To him, the news media's role was to convey to the public the official actions of the justices, no more. Thus, Burger became an enthusiastic reformer of the mechanics of covering the Supreme Court, perhaps in hopes that by facilitating our efforts to cover the formalities we would be less likely to fritter away our energies on personalities and gossip.

In this sense, the chief justice sought to bring added efficiency to dissemination of the information already distributed by the press officer. In no sense was the scope of distributed information altered. * * *

REFORMS

Proposals for more radical reforms to facilitate the media's job in covering the Court have met with little success. Clearly, the most-often-mentioned desire, at least among the broadcast media's functionaries, is the allowance of cameras in the courtroom. More generally, reporters have sought advance notification that a decision was to be announced and/or advance access to opinions. Some have been willing to study opinions in a locked room until their formal announcement. Indeed, in an interview with Stephen Wasby, Chief Justice Earl Warren noted that the television network heads had met with him and "suggested giving reporters the opinion earlier in the day, keeping them under lock and key until the opinion was announced in Court. Warren said that the Court 'would be laughed out of town' for doing that, and rejected the idea."

Some suggested reforms have, perhaps, received greater attention than the likely impact of their implementation might warrant. Tim O'Brien, for example, has noted that, "Cameras in the courtroom * * * may be less helpful to coverage of the Court's work than the adoption of a system providing for the orderly release of opinions * * * so that major decisions are not announced on the same day or on a day when an important case is being argued." Regarding the suggestion that reporters receive advance word that a specific decision was about to come down, O'Brien adds,

> Reporters regularly assigned to the Court really don't need advance word on what decision is going to be announced. By the time a

major ruling is released by the Justices, the regular correspondents * * * have had three prior opportunities to examine the case and the issues it raised: when certiorari was sought, when certiorari was granted and when the case was argued. Advance word to reporters would only help those poor chaps assigned to the Court on an infrequent or irregular basis.

For its part, the Association of American Law Schools (AALS) has suggested that a scholar be on hand to represent the Court in answering questions when decisions are announced. Of such proposals, Tim O'Brien opines, "considering that the Justices themselves often disagree on what a given decision means, it borders on the absurd to have any official court spokesman assist reporters in understanding the significance of a decision." While the AALS proposal was rejected, the Association did play an important role in developing an alternative nonofficial source that offers guidance to those journalists covering the Court.

The project was first suggested in 1963 by the Association's Committee on Education for Professional Responsibility. A Special Advisory Committee on Supreme Court decisions * * * was subsequently appointed to prepare short memoranda explaining the significance of Supreme Court cases, the issues involved, and possible alternative bases of decision. The memoranda were reproduced and distributed through the Association's Washington office to the 'regulars' who report the work of the Court for newspapers, wire services, radio, and television.[66]

In its second year, the AALS sought the cooperation of the news media and Chief Justice Warren. By 1965, 195 reporters were on the mailing list for the background memos. By 1972, however, the project's funds were exhausted and no memos were distributed for that October's Supreme Court term.

The project was re-instated on a subscription basis in 1973. Now known as *Preview of United States Supreme Court Cases,* the publication includes advance coverage of all cases argued before the Supreme Court. Academic lawyers recruited by an overseeing editor prepare the memos for each case and, in addition to circulation among a mailing list, copies of *Preview* are available at the Public Information Office of the Supreme Court. What began as a mimeographed handout has evolved into a professionally finished photo-composed pamphlet.

* * *

It should be stressed that *Preview* is a totally private initiative and that while some cosmetic reforms have been made around the edges of the Supreme Court/media edifice, the fundamental nature of the Court's media relationships have not been significantly altered during the past

66. Berkson, The Supreme Court and Its Publics 96–97 (1978).

century. In the words of ABC's Tim O'Brien, "Today * * * the justices seem more intent on closing their doors than on opening them. The Supreme Court remains the most secretive and inaccessible of government institutions * * *. Most justices avoid reporters like lepers." In such a setting a more detailed understanding of the Supreme Court's press corps is called for, a subject to which we shall now turn.

THE COURT PRESS CORPS

The Supreme Court beat is a relatively uncluttered one when compared with the number of reporters who routinely cover the White House or the halls of Congress. Except, perhaps, for landmark decision days and crowded oral arguments in prominent, dramatic, and often emotionally laden cases, approximately 50 reporters cover the Court on a routine basis. * * *

In the eyes of many analysts, the Supreme Court beat was not, historically, a prized one for journalists since reporting on the Court "has all the features that most journalists try to avoid."

> Reporters sit in a basement room waiting to be presented a complicated legal document that they quickly have to puzzle out for themselves. They cannot interview the major sources of the story to ask them what they meant. * * * Meanwhile they know that * * * editors do not regard most judicial decisions as very important or very newsworthy. * * * An ambitious reporter, already making a name in bylines, is likely to consider assignment to the Court a dead end.[73]

Today, Tim O'Brien disputes the notion that the Court assignment is not a prized one. "It certainly is for those who work there: it is the most 'stable' beat in Washington; those who cover the Court * * * like the Justices themselves * * * have exceptional staying power."

Clearly, Supreme Court reporters are less "participatory" in the processes that they cover than are their colleagues in other governmental settings and it would be difficult to sustain the argument that journalists have any impact on what the Court actually decides. It is in this sense that the Court's press corps "probably has less power and influence than any other major news group in Washington."[75] Nevertheless, as we have seen, the media have a potentially great role in developing public perceptions of the Court and in providing a baseline of information about what the Court has done.

Because of the unique institutional setting in which the Court's reporters operate, the skills that are required of them may be somewhat different than those that would best lead to success among their colleagues. Indeed, the prototypical model of the aggressive investigative reporter with all of its connotations may give way in this domain to the

---

73. Press and Ver Burg, American Politicians and Journalists 253 (1988).

75. Grey, supra n. 55, at 55.

primacy of one's analytical skills. Supreme Court reporters often spend more time reading than they do on their feet or on the telephone. As noted by Berkman and Kitch, "A good Court journalist is simply one who can read a complex court decision, understand the legal reasoning, and write a short story that can be understood by the general public."

Grey characterizes the Supreme Court reporter's lot as a "role reversal * * * a switch from the searching-out approach of newsgathering to a somewhat sit-back-with-the-feet-up approach." Perhaps Grey's characterization of a "role reversal" is overdrawn and somewhat outdated. As noted by Tim O'Brien:

> This may have been true twenty years ago; it certainly isn't today. Reporters for the Washington Post, the New York Times, and all three networks go all over the country doing background work on the cases that reach the Court. * * * Few Washington correspondents travel as much as the network correspondents at the Supreme Court; and much of their work involves the same investigative techniques required of their colleagues * * * in Washington * * * and beyond.

It remains true, however, that the posture the Court reporter takes towards the institution tends to be more laden with respect and deference than one finds on other governmental beats. Coupled with the vestiges of intimidation discussed earlier and problems of adequate preparation there is a tendency for the Court to get off relatively "easy." While some facets of Supreme Court activity are critiqued by journalists, "Judicial reasoning and the wisdom of decisions are seldom attacked." There is a "generally accepting philosophy of the press" which "is in marked contrast to relationships existing between the news corps and many other news sources in Washington. Policy decisions are constantly under scrutiny in most areas of government, but Court newsmen give little evidence that they see themselves in such a 'watchdog' role." [79]

One of the major problems confronting the Supreme Court reporter is the great tension that often exists between making a story both understandable to a lay audience as well as accurate. There is an ever-present risk of oversimplifying things to the point where important nuances of a critical ruling are lost in translation. * * *

Perhaps the most common inaccuracy to appear in print or over the airwaves is the assertion that the Court "affirmed," "upheld," or "let stand" a lower court ruling when, in fact, its only "decision" may have been an allegedly neutral denial of certiorari. While certiorari denials, of course, may have critical implications for the party denied review, their policy implications are less clear and they are certainly different actions in kind from holdings and affirmations.

* * *

79.   Grey, supra n. 55, at 53–54.

TODD PICCUS, * DEMYSTIFYING THE LEAST UNDER-STOOD BRANCH: OPENING THE SUPREME COURT TO BROADCAST MEDIA
71 Texas L.Rev. 1053 (1993)

* * * An effective and legitimate way to satisfy America's curiosity about the Supreme Court's holdings, Justices, and *modus operandi* is to permit broadcast coverage of oral arguments and decision announcements from the courtroom itself. The media's failed attempts to gain access to Supreme Court proceedings and the dearth of legal literature addressing the policies implicated by these failures suggest that a detailed examination of the issues at stake is warranted.

* * *

I. THE CUMULATIVE COURTROOM BROADCASTING EXPERIENCE

A. *The Media's Concerted Efforts to Gain Broadcast Access*

Soliciting the Court's favor and combating its reticence over broadcasting its proceedings have preoccupied media groups and their attorneys for many years. On two separate occasions during the past ten years, with two different Chief Justices sitting on the High Court, coalitions of media organizations have asked the Court to consider their requests for broadcast access.

In 1982 the National Association of Broadcasters and the Radio and Television News Directors Association asked Chief Justice Burger for permission to set up a demonstration of the use of broadcasting equipment in the Court. Although no demonstration was actually performed, the media representatives did meet with Chief Justice Burger's administrative assistant and the Court's public information officer. After touring the Court's facilities, the media groups concluded that cameras could be placed unobtrusively in the courtroom and still provide a clear picture of the proceedings. Several months later, in response to a memo detailing the media groups' findings, the Court's chief administrative assistant informed the media groups that their request had been denied.

More recently, Washington, D.C. attorney Timothy Dyk, representing a coalition of thirteen media organizations, made a similar request. Although the Supreme Court's doors remain closed, substantial inroads were made during the demonstration that ultimately took place. In November 1988, with Chief Justice Rehnquist and Justices White and Kennedy in attendance, Mr. Dyk supervised a private broadcast simulation in the courtroom and made a fifteen-minute presentation on the technology involved. The simulation used the existing courtroom lighting and audio system and it employed two small cameras—one tucked into an alcove to focus on the Justices and the second placed under the

Justices' bench to focus on the podium from which lawyers argue their cases.

The Justices reportedly asked about lighting, editing, and the anticipated amount of exposure the Court's arguments would receive. In response, they were told that C–SPAN had committed itself to broadcast all 150 oral arguments in full, and that commercial news organizations might cover twelve to fifteen hearings per year.

Late the following year, however, Chief Justice Rehnquist informed Mr. Dyk that the Court declined to change its policy against broadcast coverage. Regrettably, and consistent with Mr. Dyk's comment that "we were not attempting to publicize [what transpired]," both he and Supreme Court Public Information Officer Toni House declined to comment on or release any written or video materials prepared before, during, or after the simulation.

II.   OPENING SUPREME COURT PROCEEDINGS TO BROADCAST MEDIA

A.   *The Unique Nature of Supreme Court Proceedings and the Qualitatively Superior Reproductive Integrity of Broadcast Media*

1. The Mise-en-Scène *of Oral Argument and Decision Announcement.*—Nearly every public policy argument suggesting that state and federal trials should be broadcast is even more compelling with regard to the Supreme Court's proceedings. Perhaps the most convincing argument relates to the participants themselves: only veterans of the Court actively participate in oral argument and decision announcement.

There are no lay jurors whose judgment may be compromised, whose home life may be invaded, or who may have ulterior motives; there are no victims or witnesses who would not otherwise come forward and whose identities need to be protected; there are no defendants whose constitutional rights warrant scrupulous protection; and there are only legal issues, not fact issues, to be resolved—effectively eliminating the concern that incompetent materials might be presented to the tribunal.

Equally important, because attorneys delivering oral argument are officers of the court and because the Justices themselves are public servants appointed for life, it does not seem wholly unreasonable to subject the already public process and its participants to the increased scrutiny of a broader audience. The roles played by the Justices and attorneys are also noteworthy: there are no witnesses or jurors with whom they must interact and no split-second evidentiary and procedural decisions that must be made.

An excellent summary of appellate courtroom dynamics was written in a mock brief presented at an ABA forum over a decade ago. Its authors assessed the appellate courtroom milieu in the following manner:

> The atmosphere of an appellate court is quiet and sombre * * *. Counsel do not interrupt each other because time is allotted at the outset. They have a limited time in which to make their arguments

and then sit down. The rules are plain and clear, they are unyielding, they are strictly enforced, and they are rarely violated. Because of the small number of participants, the judges control the courtroom in a way that can rarely, if ever, be accomplished at the trial level. Whatever drama exists stems from the force of the advocate's presence and the strength of his argument.

If the Supreme Court gave these elements the consideration they deserve, even it would be hard-pressed to maintain the ban, for nearly thirty years ago the Court announced that "where there [is] 'no threat or menace to the integrity of the trial,' we have consistently required that the press have a free hand, even though we sometimes deplored its sensationalism." [89]

If, via its *Chandler* opinion, the Supreme Court can permit vulnerable lay persons—including jurors, witnesses, victims, and defendants—to be placed in front of an unblinking and unforgiving camera lens, then how can the Justices, who "are supposed to be men [and women] of fortitude, able to thrive in a hearty climate," [90] rationalize maintaining the broadcast ban in their own courtroom?

2. *Portraying the Existential Aspects of Court Proceedings.*—The existential elements of Supreme Court proceedings deserve the unassailable reproductive integrity that the broadcast media is uniquely capable of providing. The adversarial nature of the proceedings and the demeanor of the attorneys and Justices form an integral part of the courtroom experience. Yet only the broadcast media—television in particular—can accurately convey every nuance, gesture, and intonation of the participants. The broadcast media's ability to provide qualitatively superior coverage can empower the press corps to substantially improve its reporting of the Supreme Court, which many observers contend is substandard and woefully inadequate, and which some point to as impeding America's understanding of the Court and its holdings.

* * *

[On] attending oral announcement of Supreme Court decisions, legal scholar David Grey commented that "[s]ometimes there will be clashes among specific members of the Court" and "sometimes the unexpected happens and hearing the oral announcement gives a newsman further insights into judicial thinking." These insights, he added, are "often significant for the newsman," for they enable him "to get at exactly what was decided by the Court, how and why." The written word, he explained, simply "cannot convey strong emotion that may be evident."

89. Sheppard v. Maxwell, 384 U.S. 333, 350 (1966) (citations omitted).

90. Chandler v. Florida, 449 U.S. 560 (1981), held that in order to prevail on a claim of denial of due process caused by broadcast coverage, the complaining party must meet a relatively high standard: she must demonstrate that the broadcast coverage either (1) compromised the ability of the jury to judge her fairly, or (2) had an impact on the trial participants sufficient to constitute a denial of due process. Absent such a showing, no finding of undue prejudice or of a constitutional due process violation is warranted.

Likewise, veteran Court reporter Anthony Lewis found attending oral argument instructive "because it discloses better than anything else what the real issues are * * * and what troubles the members of the Court." Lewis added that the "moments of tension and drama and humor, [when the] personalities on the bench are unveiled," augmented his understanding of the Court's members and their decisions.

Though the import of these observations may seem subtle on the surface, beneath them lies a powerful notion, one readily acknowledged by University of California sociologist Todd Gitlin:

> [T]elevision news stories are built around images of particular personages and dramatic conflict. Stories are personified [and they] include visual images that will secure the flickering attention of the mass audience. Other things being equal, the dramatic image—a burning flag, a raging fire, a battle—gets priority * * *.

Gitlin's thesis is easily and convincingly extrapolated to broadcast coverage of the Supreme Court: if broadcast media were permitted to transmit Supreme Court proceedings, the American public would become increasingly familiar with the Justices as the public formed images and impressions of each Justice's physical presence, facial expressions, idiosyncrasies, and demeanor, as well as the nature of the questions they direct at counsel and their responses thereto. By animating and personifying the Court, the American public may increasingly identify with the Justices themselves. Consequently, the public might be more eager and receptive to learn about events surrounding the Court.

Personifying the Court via broadcasts of its proceedings also can effectively facilitate the demystification of the Court, which one author characterized as being "clothed * * * in nearly two centuries of Delphic dignity," and "enigmatic" and "mysterious" even to attorneys arguing before it.[103] Cultural historian Maxwell Bloomfield decries such characterizations, acknowledging that "writers have endowed the judicial role with almost magical properties of character building and intellectual enlightenment. Donning the black robe, especially at the Supreme Court level, is, one gathers, a bit like entering the priesthood."

Deifying and venerating the Justices, however, merely perpetuates the Court's isolation from the polity that supports and is ruled by it. It is important to humanize the judicial system and its active participants, all of whom are public servants to some degree. Maintaining a veil to insulate Supreme Court proceedings from the public's eye effectively impedes that process. Indeed, the American polity might be shocked to learn that, during the four hours for which the Justices sit on oral argument days, "[l]ike other mortals, they shift about in their chairs to ease cramped muscles," and unlike saints, they do have to go to the bathroom.[105]

103. Richard L. Williams, "Supreme Court of the United States: The Staff That Keeps It Operating," Smithsonian, Jan. 1977, at 39.

105. Richard L. Williams, "Justices Run 'Nine Little Law Firms' at Supreme Court," Smithsonian, Feb. 1977, at 84.

In 1898, Justice David Brewer addressed the public's apotheosizing of the Court and its members, as well as its isolation from the public:

> It is a mistake to suppose that the Supreme Court is either honored or helped by being spoken of as beyond criticism. On the contrary, the life and character of its Justices should be the object of constant watchfulness by all, and its judgments subject to the freest criticism. The time is past in the history of the world when any living man or body of men can be set on a pedestal and decorated with a halo. True, many criticisms may be, like their authors, devoid of good taste, but better all sorts of criticism than no criticism at all.

And what better way is there to subject the Court to that "constant watchfulness by all" than through the unblinking eye of the broadcast media?

Admittedly, although the demeanor, composure, and idiosyncrasies of the attorneys and Justices are interesting and informative, they, unlike the demeanor of a witness during a trial, are legally insignificant and contribute nothing to the development of the law. But it is likely that they can be instructive and may facilitate an increased understanding of the Court, the legal issues it resolves, and the judicial process in general.

3. Fostering Greater Accountability.—New York Times Co. v. United States, the *Pentagon Papers Case,* provides a salient and significant example of an oral argument that would have benefited from broadcast media presence. While the *New York Times* organization spent four months reviewing forty-seven volumes of purloined government documents, it insisted on accelerated consideration of the petition for certiorari that it filed seeking to vacate a lower court's prior restraint of publication of material from the documents. The oral argument was scheduled to be heard within seventy-two hours of both the district court's and the appellate court's judgments, and it took place a scant fifteen hours after the Court received the record and only two hours after the briefs were received. Not surprisingly, "counsel on both sides * * * were frequently unable to respond to questions on factual points. * * * [T]hey pointed out that they had been working literally 'around the clock' and simply were unable to review the documents that give rise to these cases and were not familiar with them." Chief Justice Burger conceded that "[t]his Court [was] in no better posture" because it "literally [did] not know what [it was] acting on."

It is quite likely that the Court's decision would have been the same had the attorneys and Justices been given time to prepare soberly for the oral argument. But it is jurisprudentially unwise to precipitously prepare for and schedule an argument, and hastily issue a decision pursuant to it, when the constitutional dimension of the issues at stake is so dramatic and the inherent national security interests are unascertained. That attorneys can advocate a legal position and Justices can render a decision endorsing one without first resolving the "factual points" defies tenets of appellate jurisprudence. Had the attorneys and Justices been haunted by the specter of their unpreparedness being broadcast around the nation, perhaps the attorneys would not have insisted on an accelerated hearing and the Justices would not have permitted it.

* * *

B. Illegitimate Concerns with the Editorial Prerogative

1. *Introduction.*—Broadcast opponents invariably buttress their anti-coverage arguments by disparaging the editorial process and by focusing on its potential for distorting court proceedings. These detractors prefer that the Supreme Court exercise the supreme editorial power—the power to prohibit coverage altogether—rather than create a presumption in favor of broadcast access, coupled with unassailable discretion to prohibit coverage when the circumstances so indicate.

* * *

2. *The Editorial Prerogative.*—Subjecting Supreme Court proceedings to broadcast coverage would unquestioningly empower networks and cable operators to edit the proceedings in a manner that may distort their content. But that this potentiality upsets and preoccupies anti-coverage advocates is immaterial from a public policy perspective. While this concern is genuine and is not unfounded, the broadcast media, as a practical matter, must be able to adapt to commercial use the material they elect to air, and as a legal matter, they must be unfettered in exercising their constitutional prerogative to edit as they see fit.

* * *

[R]ecently, in the specific context of the Supreme Court's oral arguments, Chief Justice Burger insisted that selective coverage of only a few arguments each year and the editorial treatment of those arguments would generate a "distorted conception" of the Court, which would be "bad for the country, bad for the court and bad for the administration of justice." Burger characterized television news as "pure and simple show business," insisting that it would "serve no useful purpose and damage the whole process" to air only "bits and pieces" of the Court's proceedings.

Justice Lewis Powell also disparaged commercial broadcast coverage. He commented that "[i]n fairness, I think you'd have to show little segments of each one's argument, and that would take more time than the nightly news would allow, * * * [s]o I doubt the feasibility of TV in the courtroom being fair." Unfortunately, Justice Powell left an important question unanswered by failing to specify to whom and in what manner such coverage would be "unfair." Would it be "unfair" to the petitioner or respondent, neither of whom participate in the proceeding, and neither of whose rights would be prejudiced? Would it be "unfair" to lay witnesses, alleged crime victims, or unwitting defendants, none of whose testimony is at issue and who would not even be present at the proceeding? Would it be "unfair" to the attorneys, who are officers of the court, and whose performance is deserving of public scrutiny?

Would it be "unfair" to the viewing public, which would otherwise be relegated to a reporter's interpretation of the arguments, and which would otherwise have little or no exposure to the Court in general or to the argument in particular? Or perhaps Justice Powell simply feared that selective coverage and the editorial process would be "unfair" to the Justices themselves—the appointed-for-life public servants, whose official actions are unappealable, and whose actions ultimately and sometimes intimately affect every American citizen.

Some scholars, legal correspondents, and practitioners make the same objections. George Gerbner, the distinguished former dean of the Annenberg School of Communications at the University of Pennsylvania, analyzed and analogized the broadcast portrayal of courtroom proceedings in the following manner:

> The problem is that the opaque reality of the courtroom is less illuminating of the judicial process than is translucent fiction. One must go behind the scenes to see how things really work. Surface appearances are more likely to conceal than to reveal how the judicial system operates. Television will create popular spectacles of great appeal but deceptive authenticity as it selects and interprets trials to fit the existing pattern of law in the world of television.

Gerbner's writing is vivid and colorful, but beneath his imagery lie some disconcerting assertions. His words intimate that any portrayal of court proceedings, even if fully presented and unedited, would still be "less illuminating * * * than is translucent fiction." Even if, in accordance with Chief Justice Burger's concerns, only unedited broadcasting of oral arguments were permitted, in Dean Gerbner's eyes the transmission would constitute a surface appearance of the judicial system and therefore would be an inaccurate, incomplete, and deceptively authentic portrayal of the judicial process. If this were, in fact, true, then the requirement that court proceedings be public would be meaningless, for as Dean Gerbner sees it, the attendees—unable to "go behind the scenes"—would be witness only to a "surface appearance" of the judicial system, and they would be incapable of ascertaining whether or not the proceedings were being executed fairly and equitably.

Broadcast opponents argue that editors tend to focus on sensational cases and cover only short segments that appeal to the prurient interest, and Dean Gerbner is among those who contend that this type of coverage does not add to public understanding. Likewise, Bruce Fein, a lawyer and legal correspondent, complains that "[e]ditors instinctively promote the sensational." Fein, apparently oblivious to the milieu in which *Sheppard v. Maxwell* was tried, inaccurately writes that the "print media, in contrast, raise little danger of distorting public perceptions [because newspaper] [r]eporters enjoy the time and space to place isolated courtroom statements in proper context; they are not relegated to misleading 'sound bites.'" And practitioner Seth Waxman concurs: "[T]he only cases that are covered by cameras are those of great public interest and the only coverage that typically appears is of short sound bites that distort what actually happens in the courtroom."

3. *The Real Issue at Stake.*—The above objections to broadcast coverage miss the point on several fronts. Many cases argued before the Supreme Court deserve thorough, unfettered broadcast and newsprint coverage because, often, cases argued before and decided by the Court involve critical legal issues with potentially far-reaching effects on the entire American polity and on America's social, political, and economic landscape.

Indeed, broadcast media will report on "sensational" cases and those of "great public interest" regardless of whether or not broadcast equipment is allowed into Supreme Court proceedings. But *with* broadcast coverage, viewers need not rely on a journalist's perspective on what transpired during the proceeding. This empowers viewers with an alternative and supplemental source of information and, consequently, the risk that they rely on potentially inaccurate Supreme Court reporting is effectively reduced.

Furthermore, it seems that broadcast critics have lost sight of the public policies at stake. Decades ago the Court wrote that "[f]reedom of discussion should be given the widest range compatible with the essential requirement of the fair play and orderly administration of justice." And years later the Court elaborated:

> This Court has * * * been unwilling to place any direct limitations on the freedom traditionally exercised by the news media "for [w]hat transpires in the courtroom is public property." The "unqualified prohibitions laid down by the framers were intended to give to liberty of the press * * * the broadest scope that could be countenanced in an orderly society." And where there was "no threat or menace to the integrity of the trial," we have consistently required that the press have a free hand, even though we sometimes deplored its sensationalism.[153]

The above excerpt is irreconcilable with the continued prohibition of broadcast coverage of Supreme Court proceedings. Furthermore, the states' unequivocal endorsement of broadcast media in their courts and the Court's own *Chandler* opinion effectively sterilize all justifications of the broadcast ban, and they fully embrace the observation set out above in the Court's *Sheppard* opinion.

But liberty of the press is clearly *not* being accorded "the broadest scope that could be countenanced in an orderly society": the state-court broadcast experiments, sanctioned by the Supreme Court, provide ample evidence that even in state trials, where the risk of prejudice to the litigants is far greater than the risks that exist during Supreme Court proceedings, a properly managed courtroom effectively eliminates threats to the integrity of the trial. This observation, coupled with the Court's recognition of the media's tendency to be sensational, renders indefensi-

153. Sheppard v. Maxwell, 384 U.S. 333, 350 (1966) (citations omitted).

ble the notion that the current broadcast ban is justified on the ground that the editorial process would otherwise distort and sensationalize Supreme Court proceedings.

In reviewing his state's broadcast experiment, Matthew Crosson brilliantly (and, probably, unwittingly) coalesced the *Sheppard* excerpt and the broadcast critics' preoccupation with the editorial prerogative. He opined that

> if gavel-to-gavel coverage is acceptable, but other coverage is not, then it is not the *presence* of cameras in court that is objectionable, it is what the media chooses to broadcast or publish. [But we should] not * * * evaluate the editorial judgments made by television stations and newspapers, however much we might disagree with some of those judgments.

In that same vein, Justice Stewart in his *Estes* dissent extrapolated *Sheppard* and legitimately invoked constitutional principles when he wrote that "the proposition that non-participants in a trial might get the 'wrong impression' from unfettered reporting and commentary contains an invitation to censorship which I cannot accept." [155] And oddly enough, Chief Justice Burger—the most vociferous opponent to Supreme Court broadcast coverage whose concerns stem from the editorial prerogative—authored *Chandler*. Although Chief Justice Burger recognized that "[s]election of which trials, or parts of trials, to be broadcast will inevitably be made not by judges but by the media," [156] and believed that "[t]his concern is far from trivial," [157] he nevertheless condoned state broadcasts of court proceedings. These observations underscore the inescapable conclusion that, in maintaining its broadcast ban on Supreme Court proceedings, the Court's objections must hinge largely on its preoccupation with the *content* of what may be reported rather than the *effect* on the Court's proceedings.

* * *

4. Differential Treatment of Broadcast and Print Media Is Unjustifiable in the Context of Supreme Court Reporting.—Anti-broadcast advocates also position their arguments on another erroneous front: they insist that, with regard to coverage of Supreme Court proceedings, different rules should apply to broadcast and print media. Only if the broadcast coverage added a marginal risk of prejudice either to the parties or to the administration of justice would this notion be tenable; but the state court experience clearly indicates that it does not.

Once again, Chief Justice Burger's *Chandler* opinion is instructive here, for it alludes to what is purported to be the improper differentiation of access rules as applied to print and broadcast media. Chief Justice Burger deemed it "noteworthy" that no evidence suggested that

---

155. Estes v. Texas, 381 U.S. 532, 615 (1965) (Stewart, J., dissenting).

156. Chandler v. Florida, 449 U.S. 560, 580 (1981).

157. *Id.*

"electronic coverage creates a significant adverse effect upon the participants in trials—*at least not one uniquely associated with electronic coverage as opposed to more traditional forms of coverage.*" He noted that an absolute ban on broadcast coverage of state courts is not warranted simply because some risk of prejudice exists, and that the intrinsic interest of the public in a given legal issue and fact pattern may attract a high level of public attention regardless of the enforced broadcast ban. Furthermore, *Sheppard* suggests that, even had broadcast media been barred from the courtroom, adverse effects would not have been wholly eliminated.

* * *

C. Focus on the Audience: The Educating Role of Broadcast Media

One commentator suggested that the legal literature's preoccupation with the educating benefits of televised court proceedings shifts the emphasis of the courtroom camera debate from courtroom concerns to audience benefits. Though this observation undoubtedly has intuitive appeal to anti-broadcast advocates, it is somewhat incomplete and therefore misleading. The "audience" referred to is not, as is implied, a collection of individuals patronizing a commercial establishment; rather, the "audience" consists of the American polity at large—the very individuals who must observe, respect, and defer to the Court's decisions.

Seventy years ago and long before the first court proceeding was broadcast, historian Charles Warren offered a more genuine appraisal of what is at stake: "The reaction of the people to judicially declared law has been an especially important factor in the development of the country; for while the Judges' decision makes the law, it is often the people's view of the decision which makes history." But in a society in which members of the proverbial "audience" ask "where's the jury room?" when visiting the Supreme Court, and when even secondary-school teachers do not command a rudimentary understanding of the Constitution, the true extent to which the American citizenry is uninformed seems quite alarming.

Indeed, in light of the facts that the courtroom camera experience spans nearly sixty years, that forty-seven states currently permit at least one form of camera coverage, and that the Supreme Court condones such experimentation, the recent shift to the "audience" is not wholly unreasonable. Appealing to the anachronistic and reticent broadcast-ban holdouts in this manner seems proper, legitimate, and academically honest, particularly since the most significant and influential holdout, Chief Justice Rehnquist, purports to be so concerned about the American polity's ignorance of the judiciary and judicial issues.

Justice Harlan, in his *Estes* concurrence, which proved so instrumental in *Chandler's* authorization of broadcast coverage, recognized that "television is capable of performing an educational function by acquainting the public with the judicial process in action." Not surprisingly, others concur, often adding that an educated and informed citizenry fosters confidence in the judiciary and the judicial process. Justice Felix Frankfurter, for example, who quipped that he longed for the day when the news media would cover the Supreme Court as thoroughly as it did the World Series, believed that public confidence in the judiciary hinges on the public's perception of it, and that perception necessarily hinges on the media's portrayal of the legal system. Likewise, Judge Irving Kaufman commented that the influence of the judiciary "depends on a fragile constitutional chemistry, and it flows directly from popular knowledge and acceptance of their decisions * * *. Courts cannot publicize; they cannot broadcast. They must * * * look to the press to spread the word."

Anti-coverage advocates frequently suggest that public understanding of and appreciation for the integrity of the judicial processes are not enhanced if the public is only exposed to segmented and edited excerpts of court proceedings. This, they contend, actually distorts the posture and content of the proceedings and the results thereof. However, this argument merely addresses the *content* of the news stories, not the issue of whether or not broadcast media should transmit the proceedings. Crosson rhetorically asked: "Is it better for the public to see *real* images of *actual* testimony? * * * Reality, it seems to me, is more educational than interpretation."

Reliance on ordinary nonbroadcast coverage of the Court relegates the American public to learn only about the *results of the judicial process,* as opposed to learning about the *judicial process itself.* Only by granting broadcast media access to oral arguments can the public observe the demeanor and competency of the Justices and the attorneys, the adversarial nature of the hearings, and the other existential aspects of the proceedings.

In *Richmond Newspapers, Inc. v. Virginia,*[191] the Supreme Court again acknowledged the crucial role of the broadcast media in educating the public. In his opinion of the Court, Chief Justice Burger wrote:

> "It is not unrealistic even in this day to believe that public inclusion affords citizens a form of legal education and hopefully promotes confidence in the fair administration of justice." Instead of acquiring information about trials by firsthand observation or by word of mouth from those who attended, people now acquire it chiefly through the print and electronic media. In a sense, this validates the media claim of functioning as surrogates for the public. *[M]edia representatives* * * * *"contribute[ ] to public understanding of the rule of law and to comprehension of the functioning of the entire * * * justice system."*

The Court's failure to reconcile its recognition of the broadcast media's educational role with its own broadcast ban warrants serious scrutiny by

191.   448 U.S. 555 (1980).

the American public, as well as intellectually honest introspection by the Court itself.

* * *

D. The Public Has a Keen Interest in the Supreme Court and its Affairs

That the broadcast media can educate and enlighten the American public via telecasts and radio transmissions would be immaterial if the public would be either uninterested or unresponsive to them. While the public's dependence on television as a source of information was noted earlier, discussing the public's interest in the Supreme Court in particular is instructive as well.

* * *

Regardless of the social, economic, or political import of a given oral argument, the number of spectators who are permitted to see and hear the arguments unfold is necessarily limited. Approximately 300 seats are available in the courtroom and the number of lay persons able to attend oral arguments or decision announcements varies inversely with their popularity: the more popular arguments attract more media personnel, who, as "surrogates for the public," are invariably allocated space at the expense of the lay public. The Court has acknowledged the keen interest in its proceedings and it has devised what it apparently deems a satisfactory solution: spectators are permitted to attend the Court's proceedings in rotations of three-minute intervals.

Even with the three-minute rule, a total of 200 spectators were turned away from oral arguments in *Regents of the University of California v. Bakke,* and among those denied admission were enthusiasts who had waited in line, huddled under heavy blankets and sleeping bags, since one a.m. on the morning of the hearing. But those who began waiting in line at nine p.m. during the prior evening *were* granted admission and, indeed, they were able to see and hear the arguments—for their allotted three minutes.

* * *

A decade after *Bakke* was decided, *Webster v. Reproductive Health Services* came before the Court, and the public interest that it generated paled *Bakke*—and, in fact, all other Supreme Court cases—by comparison. An unprecedented seventy-eight amicus briefs were filed, with 425 organizations signing as co-sponsors and thousands of individuals joining as signatories, unequivocally demonstrating the keen and broad public interest in the legal issues at stake. Similarly, in advance of the oral argument, the Supreme Court received a record-setting number of letters—up to 46,000 pieces of mail in a single day—a quantum leap from the usual daily flow of 1,000 letters. Furthermore, on the eve of the last Monday of the Term when the Court was expected to issue its long-awaited decision, a Yale undergraduate from New York and another enthusiast from Beverly Hills began waiting in line at 10:30 a.m.—a full twenty-three hours before the Court would convene. Randall Terry, director of the anti-abortion group Operation Rescue, was so bent on gaining admission to the public gallery that he bought the eleventh space in line for $100. Is "scalping" the mechanism that should govern who is able to see and hear Supreme Court proceedings? * * *

Detractors may argue that the mail, spectators, and signatories responding to a particular legal issue simply reflect the nature of a few isolated cases decided by the Supreme Court. But that is irrelevant. At times, the import and impact of the issues resolved by the Court ultimately (and sometimes intimately) affect the lives of all Americans, and the American polity's vested interest in the resolution of those issues understandably arouses curiosity. So long as satisfying the public's interest via broadcasting Court proceedings does not prejudicially affect any participant or the administration of justice, no valid reason justifies the continued broadcast ban.

Justice Scalia sees it differently, however, and his views regarding the public's interest in the Court's goings-on illuminate the rationality of many who support the broadcast ban. Justice Scalia perceives his Court's affairs as "pretty dull stuff" and describes its work in the following manner:

> One would not expect the public to be interested in it. Indeed, one would fear for the republic if the public was interested in it. And since the public is not interested in it, one would hardly expect the press to report it. That is why the University of Chicago Law Review is not sold at a 7–Eleven.

Justice Scalia's possibly facetious argument is counterfactual in light of the anecdotal evidence set out above. He also erroneously relies on a disingenuous conclusion, for the absence of law reviews for sale at convenience stores obviously has no bearing on the magnitude of public interest in legal affairs. Significant to my thesis, however, is the following observation: If Justice Scalia's 7–Eleven consumer is stymied by his inability to acquire a law journal at the local convenience store, he is free to obtain an issue from a law library or from the publisher itself. The stymied Court enthusiast, on the other hand, who, contrary to Justice Scalia's expectations, finds the Court's work compelling and worthy of her attention, has no viable alternative through which to secure a firsthand impression of the proceedings she is unable to attend. Sadly, Justice Scalia prefers to protect the American public from boredom proactively, rather than permit it simply to tune out when Supreme Court broadcast coverage is aired.

In any event, if Justice Scalia's argument had any merit, then the Court's concerns are moot at best because broadcasting is an inelastic medium: if broadcast media were granted access to the Court's proceedings, and if Justice Scalia's predicted public disinterest in his Court's activities actually materialized, then the commercial networks would alter their programming by discontinuing their coverage, and only C–SPAN would be left to air the proceedings, unedited, just as Chief Justice

Burger had hoped. But the public response to the broadcasting of Supreme Court proceedings should fail on its own merits—that is, because the public finds it uninteresting, not because the Court believes that the public finds it uninteresting.

E. Justices Favor Broadcast Access and Increased Understanding of Judicial Processes

Not surprisingly, the pro-coverage issues discussed in this Note have not escaped the notice of all members of the Court. But before exploring the comments of past and current Justices who favor broadcast coverage, it is interesting and instructive to examine the statements of two prior Chief Justices who were well known for their animosity toward the media.

There is a fortuitous irony inherent in the context of Chief Justice Earl Warren's and Chief Justice Warren Burger's public responses to queries about broadcast media in their Courts and the circumstances surrounding their statements. Chief Justice Warren's prediction that "[w]e will have a man on the moon before there will be cameras in this courtroom" was widely circulated by the media during his tenure as Chief Justice. Ironically and conveniently, Apollo 11 made its lunar landing in July 1969—effectively removing the metaphysical barrier Chief Justice Warren erected—during the same summer Chief Justice Warren stepped down from the bench. Yet more than two decades later, the ban continues.

Though Chief Justice Burger believed that a television camera was "the most destructive thing in the world" and insisted that "[t]here will be no cameras in the Supreme Court of the United States while I sit there," he made an overt and substantial ideological retreat only months prior to his retirement. During a meeting of the American Society of Newspaper Editors, he commented that "if there was some way of * * * saying that no one * * * could reproduce any part of [an oral argument] without producing all the rest of it, that conceivably might open things up." Chief Justice Burger's timing was brilliant: he subtly reversed his long-standing support of the ban and offered this lukewarm support for unedited broadcast coverage only months before ending his seventeen-year career on the Court.

The timing and circumstances surrounding Chief Justice Warren's and Chief Justice Burger's comments set the stage for continued acrimonious debate and they subtly suggest that the outgoing Chief Justices were inclined to favor broadcast coverage of the Court, so long as it was not *their* Court that was being broadcast.

In contrast to Chief Justices Warren and Burger, whose comments and the extraneous circumstances surrounding them may have obfuscated their genuine positions, some Justices have openly endorsed broadcast coverage of the Supreme Court while sitting on the bench, even with no apparent plans to retire soon thereafter. During an interview in the midst of William Rehnquist's nomination to replace Chief Justice Burger, Justice Brennan commented: "I feel strongly that we should allow television and radio broadcasts of our proceedings." Justice Brennan couched his favor for live broadcast coverage in the context of eliminating the mystique surrounding the Court and of creating "a better understanding of the court's functioning and the way the court operates." Justice Brennan elaborated with anecdotes from his own experience:

> I don't know how the dickens we can really educate on what the Constitution's all about unless there's some knowledge of the institution and how we work.
>
> * * * Our security officers and those who give tours tell us how abysmally the * * * I don't want to use the word ignorant * * * unknowledgeable people are about the functions of the court. "Where's the jury room?" they ask, and that sort of thing. I wish high schools would do a better job of educating students * * *. When I went to school we had a civics course that taught you something about the local mayor [but] nothing about the Constitution. You had to wait until you went to law school, and that shouldn't be.

Likewise, Justice John Paul Stevens, citing the justification that public understanding of the Supreme Court would be enhanced if proceedings were televised, said that he was saddened by the ban and commented that televising the proceedings is "worth a try." In 1986, Justice Marshall, joined by Justices Brennan and Stevens, also went on record, in response to a specific request from journalists, as favoring coverage.

Justice Lewis Powell, like Justices Brennan and Stevens, also favored broadcast coverage as a means to educate the American polity. But unlike his colleagues, Justice Powell only supported coverage for viewing in law school environments, and conveniently waited until his retirement to publicly express that support. Ironically, Justice Powell would limit broadcast viewers of Supreme Court proceedings to those who already have access, in the law school environment, to some of the human and physical resources necessary to educate themselves about the Court. Justice Powell's caveat necessarily forecloses the lay public—the very people who lack access to legal scholars, librarians, former Supreme Court law clerks, and attorneys who have argued before the Court, and the very people who lack easy access to legal periodicals, law journals, and reporters—from viewing those proceedings. Though Justice Powell's plan would increase the legal community's understanding of the Supreme Court's goings-on, it fails to address the interest and ignorance of the American polity at large. Furthermore, his suggestion that only law schools be given access to the hypothetical tapes is subject to the same constitutional challenge as the one invited by Chief Justice Burger's proposal that broadcast access be granted only to those networks willing to air oral arguments unedited.

* * *

III.   CONCLUSION: TOWARD A BROADER DEFINITION OF "PUBLIC ACCESS"

True public access to the Supreme Court necessarily includes broadcast access.   The Court-acknowledged television viewing habits of the American polity and the Court-acknowledged functions of the press require that a meaningful right of public access to the Court incorporate a permissive right of broadcast access.

Indeed, the Court acknowledges that "most people receive information concerning trials through the media," and the empirical facts demonstrate that Americans watch an average of seven hours of television per day and rely on it as their principal source of news.   The Court also explicitly recognizes that "[w]hat transpires in the courtroom is public property," upon which the media, as "surrogates for the public," should "bring to bear the beneficial effects of public scrutiny."   Furthermore, adding broadcast coverage of Supreme Court proceedings is within both the spirit and the letter of the Court's recognition that "liberty of the press [should be accorded] the broadest scope that could be countenanced in an orderly society."   Absent the argued-for broadcast coverage, the level of publicity required to ensure the integrity of the judicial process is stifled, rendering "all other checks * * * insufficient."

In light of the cogent public policies implicated and impaired by the current broadcast ban and those advanced by a grant of access, it would behoove the Supreme Court to broaden and update its notion of what constitutes true public access in the context of its own proceedings. Failing Supreme Court action in this regard, Congress should exercise its constitutional prerogative to intervene.

TONY MAURO,* A CAUTIOUS VOTE FOR CAMERAS IN HIGH COURT
Legal Times, August 2, 1993, at 10

A 1991 exchange of correspondence contained in the Thurgood Marshall files gives us the latest glimpse of the justices' thinking on the question.

The letters were prompted by a request from Timothy Dyk of the D.C. office of Jones, Day, Reavis & Pogue, acting on behalf of several broadcast organizations, to televise [Clarence] Thomas' investiture at the Court.   Dyk has made numerous similar requests in the past, all of them turned down.

This one, too, would likely have been dismissed without much thought, except for the fact that Dyk's request came at the same time that justices were fuming over President George Bush's plan to have Thomas sworn in at the White House, not at the Court.

"We should do whatever we can to terminate the practice" of White House swearing-in ceremonies, wrote Justice John Paul Stevens in a Sept. 19 memorandum.   "In my opinion a decision on where a Supreme

Court investiture should be held should not be made in the executive branch.''

But apart from that, Stevens said that he would grant the media request to televise the investiture. Count Stevens as a vote for cameras.

Harry Blackmun, in a memorandum the same day, said, "I could be persuaded to join John on this," noting, "There is much to be said * * * in favor of the media's request to televise a ceremonial occasion."

On the question of general camera access, Blackmun said, "I am about where I have been, that is, to defer to any strongly expressed wishes of the chief justice (WEB or WHR)," referring to both Warren Burger and William Rehnquist. Count Blackmun as on the fence, but susceptible to good arguments in favor of cameras in the Court.

The other justices were more negative. Marshall himself, who supported camera coverage until the 1987 Robert Bork hearings scared him off, said no to the Dyk request, as did Justices Byron White, David Souter, Sandra Day O'Connor, and Anthony Kennedy.

Justice Antonin Scalia, who favored cameras before he joined the Court but has since soured on them, had perhaps the oddest position on Dyk's request.

Scalia suggested offering cameras in the Court as a lure to help persuade the Bush administration not to have a showy ceremony for Thomas at the White House.

"The president's men are going to want good theater," wrote Scalia. "As far as I am concerned, an investiture ceremony, unlike an oral argument, is for show and not for go, and awareness of the cameras' presence is no problem."

But if nobody thought his ploy would work, Scalia said that he would oppose camera access. "I believe in the camel's nose, and would not permit cameras for the investiture unless there is some offsetting benefit." Count Scalia as a no vote.

What of Chief Justice William Rehnquist, whose views Blackmun said are the most important?

Rehnquist in a Sept. 19 memo wrote that Scalia's suggestion was interesting, but tricky to pull off. "It is somewhat awkward to invite someone to your house on the condition that he not invite you to his house."

But on the broader question of camera access, Rehnquist took an interesting wait-and-see position, which is far more positive than his predecessor's flat-out no. Rehnquist referred to the ongoing experiment with camera access being conducted in six federal district courts and two federal appeals courts, which has one more year to run.

"I think it would be a mistake for us to change our present practice with regard to televising our regular proceedings until the returns are in from these experiments," Rehnquist wrote. "I doubt that the televising of a ceremonial occasion involving the attendance of the president is the best way to introduce television here.''

3. Secrecy After the Fact

In this section, we examine the current policy, or more accurately lack of policy, regarding the preservation of justices' papers. As Professor Wigdor indicates in the excerpt in Section B.1 of this Chapter, the current understanding is that the justices' papers are their personal property. They are free to do whatever they wish with them—preserve them, burn them, sell them, or make paper airplanes with them. And virtually all these variations have been adopted by the various justices over time. Many, including Justices Roberts and Edward Douglas White, destroyed their papers. Justice Black burned his conference notes. Others have made their papers available but only ten years after their death (Warren); or only a designated number of years after the creation of each individual paper (sixteen years for Frankfurter; ten years for Byron White); or only after the retirement of each of the involved participants (O'Connor). For a complete listing of the various collections and their accessibility, see A. Wigdor, *The Personal Papers of Supreme Court Justices,* Garland Publishing Co., 1986.

Should this policy of individual preferences be maintained or should uniform rules of preservation and public access somehow be mandated? As Wigdor reports, Professor Howard noted that even if there are significant reasons for providing for secret deliberations before the Court's decision, it does not necessarily follow that the process should be forever shrouded from public scrutiny. But who can and should mandate rules and what should those rules be? Can Congress constitutionally prescribe what the justices may and may not do with their papers? It did so with respect to presidential papers in the Presidential Records Act of 1978. Should Congress do the same with the papers of Supreme Court Justices? Or would it be better if the Court itself adopted a uniform rule?

In 1993, provoked by the outcry over what many believed to be a premature release of Justice Thurgood Marshall's papers,[1] the Senate Subcommittee on Regulation and Government Information held hearings addressed to three issues—first, whether justices' papers should ever be made public; second, if their papers are to made public, when this should occur; and third, who should make these decisions. This was not the first time these issues had been considered. Chief Justice Warren Burger had appointed a committee to review these issues twenty years earlier. *See,* Prettyman and Snyder, *Breaching Secrecy at the Supreme Court—An Institutional or Individual Decision,* The Legal Times of Washington, June 12, 1978, p. 6 (describing Chief Justice Burger's appointing a committee soon after he became Chief Justice, noting its recommendation to adopt restrictions on the release of Court-related

---

1. *Compare* Seidman, *A Modest Proposal for Solving the Marshall Mystery,* Legal Times, June 7, 1993 *with* Bloch and Jackson, *Marshall Papers: The Library (and Our Colleague) Got It Wrong,* Legal Times, June 14, 1993.

files, and lamenting the ultimate failure of the Court ever to act on the recommendation). The issues were explored again in 1977 by the National Study Commission on Records and Documents of Federal Officials, a commission established by Congress and chaired by former Attorney General Brownell. As can be seen in the excerpts included herein, this Commission—whose report formed the basis for the Presidential Records Act of 1978—recommended that a justice's working papers be made public property, and that public access be allowed fifteen years after the justice leaves the Court. Notwithstanding Congress' adoption of the Commission's proposals with respect to presidential papers, nothing was done to implement the recommendations concerning Supreme Court documents.

Following the excerpts from the 1977 Commission, we include testimony from the 1993 hearings held by the Senate Subcommittee on Regulation and Government Information. One of the key witnesses whose testimony is included herein, E. Barrett Prettyman, Jr., a private practitioner who clerked for the Court and has been concerned with this issue for years, suggested that justices' papers should be made public but only twenty-five years after the death of the particular justice. As to what institution should make this decision, Prettyman prefers that the judiciary make it but believes, based on past experience, that no such consensus exists on the Court and therefore suggests that Congress should, and constitutionally can, mandate such a rule. After reading Mr. Prettyman's testimony, note the letter by Chief Justice Rehnquist in which he, speaking on behalf of the Court, both declines the Senate's invitation to testify at the hearing and then warns the Senators not to consider legislation in this area. Note, however, that he does not promise any action by the Court itself.

After reading all this, consider what should happen in this area? Who should act and how? Should the Court be able to control access to its proceedings and papers in any manner it chooses? To what extent will new technology and the likely increased use of "e-mail" make these problems easier or harder to solve?

FINAL REPORT OF THE NATIONAL STUDY COMMISSION ON RECORDS AND DOCUMENTS OF FEDERAL OFFICIALS
March 31, 1977

To the President and Congress of the United States:

We, the Commissioners of the National Study Commission on Records and Documents of Federal Officials, in accordance with Section 202 of Public Law 93–526, have the honor of transmitting the final report of the Commission.

* * *

VI. THE JUDICIARY

For the purpose of the following recommendations, documentary materials accumulated in the offices of Justices of the Supreme Court, lower court Judges, and their staffs should be divided into three categories: (A) Federal Records, (B) Public Papers, and (C) Personal papers of Judges.

A. Federal Records

Federal records, which include case files, dockets, minutes, administrative and other materials, are official records of the United States Government. Federal records are now retired to the National Archives, and current practice should be continued, with the following additions:

Recommendation 24:

The definition of Federal agency in 40 USC 472 should be clarified so as to specify that the provisions of Federal law and regulations relating to archival administration and records disposition apply to all records of the judicial branch, including the records of the Supreme Court and the records of committees or other agencies established within the Federal judiciary that act or advise with respect to the exercise of the constitutional authority of the judicial branch.

Comment: Although the U.S. Code definition of "Federal agency" does not specifically exclude the Supreme Court as it does the Senate and the House of Representatives, the National Archives has not attempted to apply the records provisions of the Code to the Supreme Court. It is suggested that the Supreme Court now be brought within the scope of the provisions in order to rationalize and regularize the disposition of Supreme Court records. At present, the records of the Supreme Court are retired to the National Archives at irregular intervals, so that the Archives cannot anticipate the arrival of materials and allocate staff and fiscal resources accordingly.

Since the initial transfer of Supreme Court records to the physical custody of the National Archives in 1956, the Archives has organized, inventoried, preserved, and, above all, made easily accessible to the public, Supreme Court records through the 1970 Term. It is felt that the successful experience of the past 21 years, and the apparent absence of any legal or constitutional impediments, warrants regularizing the system by bringing the official records of the Supreme Court under the records-management provisions of Title 44 of the U.S. Code and the implementing regulations of the Code of Federal Regulations.

The Judicial Conference of the United States is the major policy-making body for the Federal courts. The Judicial Conference publishes an annual *Report of Proceedings.* In addition, the records of the Conference are made available to members of the public who make a legitimate request, at the discretion of the Conference. It is suggested that the records of this very important policy-making body and its advisory committees be brought within the regular system of Federal records management and disposition in the interest of preservation and of greater public awareness of and access to these materials.

* * *

B.   Public Papers

Recommendation 26:

The Public Papers of Justices and Judges should consist of those documentary materials, exclusive of court records, generated or received by Federal Judges in connection with their official duties and retained in their files after final judgment has been entered in a case. These materials should be the property of the United States.

Comment: As is the case with the Public Papers of Presidents and Members of Congress, the Public Papers of Federal Judges are created in the course of doing the public's business, using Government facilities, and at public expense. The Commission can find no distinctions that would modify its conclusion that all such materials should be the property of the United States.

The existing system of private custodianship of Judges' office files has not functioned well in terms of preserving an adequate historical record of the judicial decision-making process, of the individuals who have served on the courts, or of the relationship of the courthouse to the larger society. The inadequacies of the present system are particularly apparent with regard to the working papers of lower court Judges. There are very few collections of District and Appellate Judges to be found in research institutions. Most have been destroyed or remain in family hands to be scattered and lost.

There are more Supreme Court collections available for public use, and in recent decades many Supreme Court Justices have given large and informative collections to research libraries. Yet the record is uneven. Some Justices have destroyed virtually the entire corpus of their working papers; others have destroyed portions of their papers. This inevitably makes more difficult our understanding of the Court and impoverishes the record of the nation's past.

The present system is also burdensome to Judges and their families. While many Judges would not be averse to placing their papers in a repository, they, or, given the tendency of Judges to serve well into old age, their families, are faced with the entire task of removing the files from chambers and sorting through the materials. The Commission's recommendations would remove that burden from Judges, while at the same time reserving to them the benefits of the present system. [See Recommendations 28, 29]

Recommendation 27:

Disposition standards for the Public Papers of Justices and Judges should be developed by the Judicial Conference of the United States in consultation with the Archivist of the United States, and published by the Archivist in the Federal Register. *These standards may be applied to Public Papers by the depository which receives them. However, it is preferable that selection and disposal be carried on during the Justices' and Judges' service.*

Comment: The Commission recognizes that there will be neither sufficient resources nor interest in preserving all of the court-related papers of all Federal Judges. The development of disposition guidelines by the Judicial Conference will provide the basis for selecting the most important elements of judicial office files. There is an obvious need for such guidelines, and every indication that most Federal Judges would welcome them. Of the 371 respondents to the questionnaire sent by the Commission to all lower court Judges, 222 or 60.2 percent, indicated that they would be well disposed toward guidelines to aid them in the organization, control, and disposition of their papers.

However, should the Judge prefer to keep his files intact until transferred to a designated repository, that institution would then be enabled to cull the collection in accordance with the established standards. This will reduce the public expense of housing judicial collections in Federal facilities, and will make the participation of private institutions more likely.

Recommendation 28:

Justices and Judges should be allowed to choose the depository for their Public Papers, except for ongoing files they may choose to leave behind for a successor. A Justice or Judge may begin to deposit his Public Papers that merit permanent retention in a depository at any time, but upon the conclusion of his judicial service, he must deposit his Public Papers in a depository, or, if he has not arranged for the deposit of these materials, the Archivist of the United States shall assume custody of the files. The Archivist should have authority to dispose of material which he finds lacks sufficient value to warrant permanent preservation by the Federal Government. A description of such material shall be published in the Federal Register *and notice provided to Congress at least sixty days in advance of any proposed disposition.*

Comment: The disposition of the chamber files of Federal Judges has until now been left to the discretion of the individual Judge, with mixed results. The intent of the recommendations is to regularize the disposition of Judges' files, while at the same time encouraging the active involvement of the Judges in the process.

The Commission believes that it is desirable to encourage the participation of a variety of institutions, public and private, in the preservation of historical materials. It is also felt that Judges will respond more favorably to the exercise of public ownership in judicial working papers if they may choose a depository which reflects their regional identification, university affiliation, or other interest.

Reserving to Judges the privilege of designating a repository for their Public Papers will, therefore, lessen the possible "chilling effect" of loss of ownership rights and promote a healthy dispersal of such materials.

Since most Federal Judges have indicated that they seldom, if ever, have the need to refer to their files once they have passed final judgment, it seems reasonable to permit them to begin the transfer of their files at any time during their service. These files could be stored under seal, should the Judge think it necessary, or the collection could be processed in anticipation of the time when public access would be allowed.

Should a Judge not care to be involved in the disposition of his Public Papers, the Archivist of the United States will provide the service in accordance with guidelines established by the Judicial Conference of the United States [see Recommendation 29], thus ensuring the preservation of and eventual public access to those portions of the collection deemed worthy of permanent retention.

Recommendation 29:

Justices and Judges should be permitted to place restrictions on the availability of their Public Papers for a period of time not to exceed fifteen years from the time the Justice or Judge leaves Federal office. At the expiration of this period, the Public Papers shall be open to general access, subject only to limitations upon disclosure of materials which would constitute an unwarranted invasion of privacy. The Judicial Conference should establish guidelines for custody of and access to the Public Papers of Justices and Judges who die or become disabled before they set the restrictions that will apply during the fifteen-year closure period.

Comment: Although the Public Papers of Federal Judges are to be declared the property of the United States, the Commission recognizes certain balancing interests which have led it to conclude that, as a matter of policy, Judges should be permitted the privilege of controlling access to these papers for a period not to exceed fifteen years.

The first of these is the need to protect ongoing litigation. A number of respondents to the judicial questionnaire sent by the Commission to all lower court Judges, particularly those who serve on the District Court level, cautioned against premature access to working papers for fear of jeopardizing convictions or the interests of litigants.

There is an equally clear need to protect the constitutional role of the courts as imposers of final judgment and to prevent any impairment of the collegial functioning of the appellate courts.

The Commission feels that the special needs of the judiciary can be most adequately met by allowing each Judge to control access for the specified period of time. The extension of the Freedom of Information and Privacy Acts during or immediately after a Judge's tenure would inject an element of uncertainty into the judicial process. It could result in damage to the collegial functioning of the appellate courts. It could as well encourage litigants to try to upset judgments.

The arrangement recommended by the Commission has the additional merit of allowing a good deal of flexibility, for the Judge is the person most likely to be able to make informed decisions as to which portions of the collection might be opened earlier and which are sensitive enough to require closure for the entire fifteen years.

A further consideration which led the Commission to recommend this period of control of access by the Judge involved or the Judicial Conference is concern about the so-called "chilling effect." If Judges can feel confident that materials they consider sensitive will be protected from premature disclosure, they are far more likely to produce a full and candid record of their judicial activities. Given the fact that official court records, unlike other agency records, come immediately into the public domain, the fifteen-year rule would not unduly infringe upon the public's right to know and would enable the people to obtain in the longer run the fullest reconstruction of the judicial process possible.

A final consideration in allowing Judges a period of control over access to their office files is the hope that it will encourage them to use that time to write legal dissertations and memoirs. There is a tradition in the judiciary that Judges should extrapolate from their experience for the instruction of the next generation, a tradition not unworthy of support.

* * *

C. Personal Papers of Judges
Recommendation 31:

A Justice's or Judge's personal papers, which should at all times be filed separately, should include only those materials of a purely private or non-official character that pertain to the Judge's personal affairs. Personal papers (such as diaries and journals, personal correspondence, speeches, and non-court writing) should be considered the Judge's private property. However, Judges, especially Justices of the Supreme Court, should be encouraged to make such arrangements as will assure the preservation and the eventual availability of their personal papers, especially the deposit of their personal papers in the same depository they select for the Public Papers.

Comment: The Commission recognizes that Judges are quite likely to keep certain kinds of materials in their chambers that do not pertain to the Judges' official functions. While these materials are in no sense public property, they are often of great historical value. The weekly letters of William Howard Taft to his sons, for example, are very informative about the Court, important cases, and the personalities of his colleagues. Judicial biography, one of the most popular vehicles for writing the history of the judiciary, is particularly dependent upon personal papers.

STATEMENT OF E. BARRETT PRETTYMAN, JR. before the
SUBCOMMITTEE ON REGULATION AND GOVERNMENT
INFORMATION of the SENATE COMMITTEE ON
GOVERNMENTAL AFFAIRS June 11, 1993

* * *

Fifteen years ago, in 1978, my partner Allen Snyder and I wrote a piece in *The Legal Times of Washington* (June 12, 1978, p. 6) dealing with the problem of Supreme Court Justices' papers and what should be done with them. * * * The article made the point that if the notes of one Justice were to be preserved, the notes of all should receive the same treatment. The reason can be illustrated by what happened between two Justices who sat on the Court at the same time. Justice Black kept relatively few conference notes and, like a number of other Justices,[1] ordered that those he did keep be burned. Justice Burton, on the other hand, kept detailed conference sheets and diaries which became immediately available, without restriction, upon his death. Thus, someone seeking to discover the views of Justice Black at a given conference could not go to the Justice's own interpretation of what he had said but rather would look to what Justice Burton *thought* Justice Black had said. This is particularly disturbing in light of the fact that Justice Black himself considered the Burton papers to be not wholly reliable.[2]

Justices have traditionally used widely varying methods of preserving and protecting their papers. As of 1986, 23 Justices had left no collections, 28 had left small collections (up to 1,000 items) consisting mostly of correspondence, 12 had left medium-sized collections consisting of up to 5,000 items, and 29—mostly in the Twentieth Century—had left large collections, including working papers. And, of course, restrictions placed on whether and how these papers are to be accessed and used vary even more widely.

Mr. Snyder and I suggested that "the Government—preferably the Court itself, or possibly Congress—should have a stronger hand in formulating a policy applicable to all." I cannot speak for Mr. Snyder, but that is still my view, and the recent release of Justice Marshall's papers has only reinforced it.

There are, it seems to me, three questions relating to the release of Supreme Court papers. The first is whether they should be made public at all—ever. The second, assuming that the answer to the first is that they should become public, is when this should occur. And the third is who should make that decision.

An argument can be made that the Justices' papers relating to their official duties should all be destroyed. It is of the utmost importance, the argument would go, that the deliberations of the Justices and the give and take between them be free, open, candid, frank, critical and spirited. This cannot happen if the Justices are taking notes or keeping copies of on-going debates and discussions and other exchanges, written

1. *See Location of the Personal Papers of Justices of the United States Supreme Court,* Case File, Memorandum, 1956, Library of Congress. Justices who destroyed all or large parts of their papers have included Lurton, McReynolds, Roberts, Edward Douglas White, Cardozo, Minton and Peckham.

2. S.S. Ulmer, "Bricolage and Assorted Thoughts on Working in the Papers of Supreme Court Justices," 35 *The Journal of Politics* 286, 289 (May 1973) (based on letters to the author from Justice Black).

or oral, between them, with the knowledge that these papers will eventually become part of the public record. How can a Justice speak his or her mind with complete candor if the thoughts expressed, no matter how tentative, will be assessed just as surely as the final written product signed off on by the Justice? Only by making the published opinion stand on its own, unadorned by all that led up to it, can the Court be assured the uninhibited debate so essential to its deliberations.

While this argument has intellectual force, the countervailing demands of history weigh heavily in favor of the preservation and ultimate release of Court papers. Without such papers, for example, we would not have before us the important contribution to our understanding of the Court as appears in Richard Kluger's *Simple Justice* and the more recent book by former Attorney General Herbert Brownell, *Advising Ike*—both dealing with the momentous decision in *Brown v. Board of Education*. We in all likelihood would not be able to read biographies like that of Chief Justice Stone by Professor A.T. Mason, or delineations of constitutional crises such as appear in Maeva Marcus' *Truman and the Steel Seizure Case*.

Is it not fair to conclude, as one commentator has argued, that "when a man"—and of course we can thankfully now include, "or woman"—"becomes a member of the Supreme Court of the United States, his [or her] files become 'affected with a public interest'; they belong to the nation, not to the judge"? And as such, they should be preserved for the historical record so that the American people can better understand how one of the three coordinate Branches of Government did its job. I simply do not believe in burning documents of historical value, no matter what the excuse. Moreover, I cannot imagine a Congressionally-mandated order to the effect that all Court papers be destroyed.

Assuming that the Justices' papers should be preserved, when should they become available to the public? My own view is that making them immediately available upon the death of a Justice would be an unfortunate development, causing great mischief. For example, one of the ongoing problems wrestled with by the Supreme Court over the last several years has been the issue of retroactivity in the application of tax rulings. If a State, for example, has collected millions of dollars in taxes through a method that the Supreme Court rules is unconstitutional, is that ruling to be applied retroactively to force the return of the taxes (and, if so, are taxes returned only to the litigants or to all others similarly situated), or is the ruling to be applied prospectively? Such an issue is before the Supreme Court right now. Those culling the Marshall papers have found a March 1991 memo by Justice Souter in which he writes to his colleagues, "I am disposed to preserve the judicial option to rule purely prospectively" if the alternative is a crushing financial blow to government.

Several points should be made. First, this revelation is unfair to Justice Souter, whose views may be developing, and could be misleading to litigants who rely upon it.   Second, even if it accurately reflects his current thinking, the litigant located in Washington with easy access to these papers has an unfair advantage over litigants in other states who do not know of the memo—except, in this particular instance, by reading about it in the *Wall Street Journal*.   Third, even the publication of this information could have an impact—how, we do not know—upon the ongoing deliberations of the Justices about this issue.   In sum, there should not be, as there is now, a race by lawyers to the Library of Congress to gain an advantage over their adversaries in pending or prospective cases.   Surely there is a legitimate distinction between current events and history.

Another example has been identified in a recent letter to the editor of the *Washington Post* by former law clerks to Justices Blackmun and O'Connor, who point out that next Term the Court will determine, in the fifth of a series of related cases on the propriety of the use of peremptory challenges, whether such challenges can be used to strike jurors on the basis of gender.   The parties will be able to rummage through Justice Marshall's files for signs of how the Justices feel about the application of the prior cases on racial challenges to challenges based on gender.

Thus, I would suggest that the release of Court papers upon the death of a particular Justice is not the answer.   The fact is that some Justices die early—even, as was the case with Chief Justice Stone and Justice Robert Jackson, while in office—while others pass away many years after retirement.   What has occurred in connection with Justice Marshall's papers demonstrates that the proviso "upon my death" offers no protection at all.

In fact, I would respectfully suggest that an attempt by Congress to legislate that Court papers be made immediately public upon the death of a Justice, or even within a relatively short time frame thereafter, might not pass constitutional muster.   If the practical effect of such a statute would be to force the disclosure of the deliberations or thinking of the Justices in ongoing matters, such as is now taking place with the papers of Justice Marshall, the courts might well rule on separation-of-powers grounds that Congress has unduly intruded into the judicial process.   In any event, I am sure that Congress has no desire to engage in any such intrusion.

Parenthetically, there may also be a constitutional takings problem as to Justices who are sitting, and those who have retired, at the time any such statute is passed.   As of now, the papers they have collected are theirs, and an attempt to restrict their right to dispose of them as they please might be deemed a taking as to which they could claim just compensation.   In fact, a decision from a Court of Appeals has recently been rendered holding that former President Nixon stated a takings claim when his papers were taken over by the Government prior to the passage of the Presidential Records and Materials Preservation Act of

1974. One way of dealing with this problem would be to make the statute prospective in operation.

My personal view is that Court papers should be released when they are truly history. Historians may not agree on how long that period is—how long it takes for a given document to cease being current and to become truly part of the past, just as there is no magic date by which a piece of furniture becomes an antique. It does seem to me, however, that an appropriate period might be 25 years after the death of the Justice who created or possessed the documents. Such a span would tend to assure that most members of the Court who served with the Justice are no longer sitting, and that most matters dealt with by the Court are no longer current.

I realize that the statute dealing with Presidential papers allows release no more than 12 years after the end of the President's term of office, but I would suggest that that is too short a period for judicial papers. For example, if such a statute were now in effect, it would allow the public to see Court papers generated in 1981, which dealt with such continually-troubling problems as police interrogations, school desegregation, searches incident to arrest, just compensation, punitive damages, sex discrimination, RICO, and the rights of the developmentally disabled. In fact, one lead case from that year, involving the use of school facilities by student religious groups, reached its natural climax only this week in the case of *Lamb's Chapel v. Center Moriches Union Free School District*. A President out of office is not involved in such ongoing case decisions, and there is a method, moreover, for protecting secret Presidential papers by the use of classification procedures not generally applicable to the courts. And there is only one President at a time; with the Court, we are faced with the interrelationships between nine persons.

After 25 years, I would not limit access to scholars but would instead make the papers generally available. I am concerned that the power to restrict access to a chosen few might be misused in favor of those who view the particular Justice kindly, whereas the object here, it seems to me, is to bring the public spotlight to bear on the Court, with all its warts.

If I am right that all Court papers should be treated the same, the final issue is who will make that decision. I had hoped that the Justices themselves would issue a controlling rule, and it is my understanding that on at least one occasion some years ago an effort was made to resolve this matter within the Court. The Justices, however, were unable to agree, and that is how the matter now stands. I do not for a moment purport to be speaking for the Court—I have no inside knowledge—but my hunch is that the Justices themselves might welcome a legislative approach to this problem, so long as it does not intrude on the Court's work, as described above.

Such a solution would be fair, because it would treat everyone the same, and each Justice would know in advance exactly how his or her papers would be treated in relation to every other Justice's papers. It is true that the papers of all Justices on a particular Court would not become available at one and the same time, but so long as a significant period had passed, I would not think this would be troublesome. A statute would relieve the Justices of the burden they now carry of deciding just how to treat their own papers without any assurance as to how others will treat theirs.

I do not think that a statute, in "federalizing" the Court's papers, need designate a federal depository for them. If certain Justices prefer to see their papers rest in particular private institutions, such as their own law schools, they should be allowed to do so, since the proscriptions against premature release can be made to apply wherever the papers are located. A statute might be better received, in fact, if it left to each Justice the option of designating where his or her papers would reside. The statute, however, would have to provide adequate protections to make certain that the contents of papers were not disclosed by third parties.

In sum, the Subcommittee is dealing with a delicate and difficult problem, crossing, as it does, the line between the Branches. I personally believe that a constructive approach, mandating that henceforth the Court papers of all future Justices shall become the property of the United States and shall be released to the public only after a period of, say, 25 years from the Justice's death, would be welcomed by all three Branches and by the public.

———

Supreme Court of the United States Washington, D.C. 20543

CHAMBERS OF
The Chief Justice

June 7, 1993

The Honorable Joseph I. Lieberman
Chairman
Subcommittee on Regulation and Government Information
United States Senate
Washington, D.C. 20510–0703

Dear Mr. Chairman,

My colleagues and I have discussed at Conference your letter of June 1st which was sent to each of us. They have each requested that I respond on their behalf as well as my own. We recognize the importance of the issues into which your Subcommittee will be inquiring, and regret that we are unable to either appear personally on Friday, June 11th, or furnish any detailed response to your questions. We have our usual Friday Conference scheduled for June 11th, and the month of June is traditionally one of our busiest because it is then that we try to wind up the Court's business for the current term.

Even with the limited time available to us, however, we have no hesitancy in expressing the opinion that legislation addressed to the issues discussed in your letter is not necessary and that it could raise difficult concerns respecting the appropriate separation that must be maintained between the legislative branch and this Court.

We appreciate your having advised us of the hearings and of the questions that your Subcommittee wishes to explore.

Sincerely,
William H. Rehnquist

Index

References are to Pages